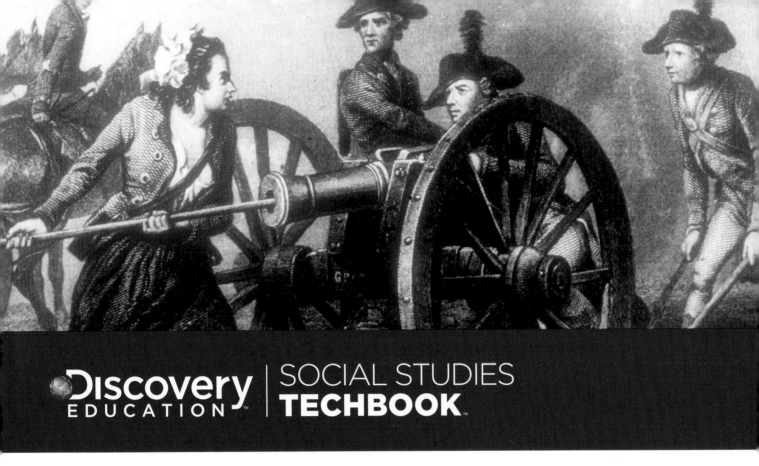

United States History
California Edition
Core Text Companion

**Sign in to Social Studies Techbook
at www.DiscoveryEducation.com**

ISBN 13: 978-1-68220-433-7

2 3 4 5 6 7 8 9 WEB 23 22 21 20 19   A

800-323-9084
One Discovery Place, Silver Spring, Maryland 20910
©2018 Discovery Education. All rights reserved.

Table of Contents

UNIT 2 | Becoming an Independent Nation (1776 to 1800)

Chapter 4 | Establishing a New Government

CONCEPTS

Chapter 5 | Leaders and Challenges of a New Nation

CONCEPTS

UNIT 3 | A Nation Expands (1790 to 1860)

Chapter 6 | Building a New National Identity

CONCEPTS

Dear Student,

You are about to experience social studies like you never have before! In this class, you'll be using Social Studies Techbook™—a comprehensive, digital social studies program developed by the educators and designers at Discovery Education. Social Studies Techbook is full of Explorations, videos, Hands-On Activities, reading passages, animations, and more. These resources will help you experience history, geography, economics, and civics. They will help you develop the ability to apply facts and ideas from the past and present to shape your community, nation, and world in the future. Social Studies Techbook allows you to work at your own pace to investigate meaningful social studies questions. You'll even be able to monitor your progress in real time using the Student Learning Dashboard.

The Core Text Companion is a print resource that accompanies the digital Social Studies Techbook. With this companion, you have access to Social Studies Techbook's core text—the key ideas and details about each social studies concept—even when you do not have access to a device or the Internet. You can use this resource to explore important ideas, make connections to the digital content, and develop your own understanding of social studies topics.

This print resource is organized by concept and includes the following:

- LESSON OVERVIEW: What's it all about? An introduction, Essential Question, Lesson Objectives, and key vocabulary will help you prepare for each social studies concept.

- ENGAGE: What do you already know? Follow a link to uncover your prior knowledge about each concept.

- EXPLORE: What information is contained in the concept? The Explore pages include core text and images to help you address each concept's Essential Question.

- CHECK FOR UNDERSTANDING: What did you learn as you read the concept? How would you respond to the Essential Question?

Throughout this resource, you'll find QR codes that take you to the corresponding online section of Social Studies Techbook for that concept. For instance, the QR code in the Explore section provides a direct link to the Explore tab and its content. Once you are inside Techbook, you'll have access to maps, interactive explorations, and other digital resources to help you investigate each concept's most important ideas.

Enjoy this voyage into the exciting world of social studies!

Sincerely,

The Discovery Education Social Studies Team

Dear Parent/Guardian,

This year, your student will be using Social Studies Techbook™, a comprehensive, digital social studies program developed by the educators and designers at Discovery Education. Social Studies Techbook is an innovative program that brings history, geography, economics, and civics to life. In class, students experience dynamic content, interactive investigations, videos, primary source documents, maps, and other resources that support high-quality social studies instruction.

As a print resource accompanying the digital Social Studies Techbook, *The Core Text Companion* allows students to explore the core Techbook content when the Internet is not available. Students are encouraged to use this resource to read about key concepts, think about the past, understand the present, and shape the future. Each concept online has five tabs: Engage, Explore, Explain, Elaborate, and Evaluate. *The Core Text Companion* includes the following:

- LESSON OVERVIEW: Students preview a concept's Essential Question, Lesson Objectives, and key vocabulary to help them make connections to social studies content.

- ENGAGE: Students activate their prior knowledge of a concept's essential ideas and begin making connections to the Essential Question.

- EXPLORE: Students deepen their understanding of the concept by exploring the Core Text to address an Essential Question.

- CHECK FOR UNDERSTANDING: These links provide students with opportunities to directly address the concept's Essential Question and demonstrate what they have learned.

Within this resource, you'll find QR codes that take you and your student to a corresponding section of Social Studies Techbook. Once in Techbook, students will have access to the Core Interactive Text of each concept, as well as thousands of resources and activities that build deep conceptual scientific understanding. Additionally, tools and features such as the Interactive Glossary and text-to-speech functionality allow Social Studies Techbook to target learning for students of a variety of abilities.

To use the QR codes, you'll need a QR reader. Readers are available for phones, tablets, laptops, desktops, and virtually any device in between. Most use the device's camera, but there are some that scan documents that are on your screen. Download a free QR reader in the App Store or Google Play. To access Social Studies Techbook resources, follow these steps:

1. Open the QR code reader on your device.

2. Hold your device so the QR code is visible within your device's screen. One of two things will happen:

   - The device may automatically scan the code; or,

   - The device will scan the code when you press a button, similar to taking a picture.

3. Once scanned, the QR code will direct you to a page or resource on the Internet.

4. For resources in Social Studies Techbook, you'll need to sign in with your student's username and password the first time you access a QR code. After that, you won't need to sign in again, unless you sign out or remain inactive for too long.

Scan this QR code to access a video that provides a deeper introduction to Social Studies Techbook:

We encourage you to support your student in using the online interactive materials in Social Studies Techbook, as well as the core text and questions in *The Core Text Companion*. Together, may you and your student enjoy a fantastic year of social studies!

Sincerely,

The Discovery Education Social Studies Team

Social Studies Techbook and *Core Text Companion*: Introduction and Guide

How to Use Discovery Education Social Studies Techbook

Discovery Education Social Studies Techbook is a complete digital basal resource designed to engage students in history, geography, economics, and civics. Discovery Education Social Studies Techbook provides teachers with powerful tools for engagement, inquiry, exploration, and evaluation. Unlike a textbook copied into digital format, Discovery Education Social Studies Techbook uses a variety of digital resources, including video, audio, text, and interactive and hands-on experiences, to provide engaging content while meeting the needs of students with different learning styles.

From any browser, navigate to www.DiscoveryEducation.com. Input the username and password that were provided to you.

Course Page

Upon sign in, you will land on the course page. On this page, you'll find links to curriculum standards, the Techbook Atlas, the Interactive Glossary, and Reviewer Materials.

The course page allows you to navigate the content contained within each course and provides quick links to helpful information. From this page, you can access all of a course's units, chapters, and concepts.

Concept Pages: The 5Es

The concept structure is set up to accommodate the 5E Instructional Model, with recommended resources for each of the 5Es: Engage, Explore, Explain, Elaborate, and Evaluate. Both students and

teachers can access the resources for instruction and assessment from the concept page by clicking on each E tab. On any tab, Teacher mode can be turned on or off.

ENGAGE

In Engage, students first encounter and identify an instructional task. They make connections between past and present learning experiences and lay the organizational groundwork for the activities ahead by considering a question, a problem, a surprising event, or an interesting perspective. Engage activities conclude with the introduction of a compelling Essential Question that brings meaning to instruction and can serve as the basis for student inquiry.

EXPLORE

Explore is embedded with resources that support student inquiry. The Core Interactive Text (CIT) provides students with secondary text, video segments, images, maps, infographics, and more—all of which students can analyze to compile evidence that addresses the Essential Question. The teacher acts as a facilitator, providing materials and guiding the students' focus. The students' inquiry process drives the instruction during exploration.

EXPLAIN

In Explain, students begin to assemble the information that they have been gathering into a
more concrete, communicable form. Social Studies Explanations facilitate students' reflections on the Essential Question and also provide students with a means for reporting and evaluating evidence. Students are also encouraged to put these explanations into their own words and demonstrate understanding in various modalities.

ELABORATE

Elaborate includes both interactive and primary-source-based activities that pose investigation questions and include sources for addressing these questions. Elaborate also features a Source Library that includes primary and secondary sources that can form the basis of teacher- or student-created inquiry.

EVALUATE

Evaluate offers flashcards for concept review as well as assessment opportunities. The Evaluate stage should be an ongoing process that occurs throughout the lesson, providing for student practice assessment as well as formal assessment as the learning occurs. Brief and extended constructed response items assess students' ability to analyze a variety of source materials and require students to construct and defend arguments with sound evidence.

Students can review concepts with practice assessments graded in real time. When students answer a question incorrectly, they will have the chance to explore remedial resources on the topic. In the teacher view, teachers can also assign a constructed response item or create their own assessment.

What Is the Discovery Education *Core Text Companion*?

Online, the Core Interactive Text (CIT) serves as a student pathway through each concept. *The Core Text Companion* is designed to work with Techbook and includes the core text, images, and captions from each concept's Explore section. When a device or an Internet connection is not available, students can still access key information, consider Essential Questions, view primary source images, and glean information needed to complete online activities.

LESSON OVERVIEW

For each concept, students will first encounter a Lesson Overview, which briefly introduces the concept's focus, lists key vocabulary terms, and previews the concept's Essential Question and Lesson Objectives. Students can scan the QR code on this page to connect directly to the digital version.

ENGAGE

In Engage, a compelling question encourages students to link their prior knowledge of the topic or related topics. A QR code links to the online Engage activity, and the Essential Question sets the stage for exploration of the concept.

EXPLORE

In Explore, the full Core Interactive Text guides students through key events and ideas in history and highlights visual resources and captions that help them make connections to the text. A QR code at the beginning of each section connects students to the appropriate Explore section online, where they can supplement their reading with multimedia resources and Hands-On Activities. Other QR codes throughout Explore connect students to additional interactive and primary source-based activities

CONSIDER THE ESSENTIAL QUESTION / CHECK FOR UNDERSTANDING

The first box at the end of each concept brings students back to the Essential Question and provides a QR code to the Social Studies Explanation online. The second box at the end of each concept checks students' comprehension by posing a constructed response question. The QR code in this box links to a constructed response item within the digital Techbook.

1.1 Geography of the United States

photo: Getty Images

LESSON OVERVIEW

Introduction

In this concept, you will learn about the different regions of the United States. You will also think about how the landforms, climate, and other geographic characteristics of these regions have shaped human life.

Essential Question

What are the most important geographic characteristics of the United States?

Lesson Objective

By the end of this lesson, you should be able to:

- Analyze and compare contemporary and historical regions of the United States on the basis of physical characteristics, such as landforms, bodies of water, climate, and vegetation, and human characteristics, such as language, religion, economic activities, and political system.

Key Vocabulary
Which terms do you already know?

- [ ] Arctic
- [ ] arid
- [ ] Basin and Ranges
- [ ] biome
- [ ] Canadian Shield
- [ ] Central Plains
- [ ] climate
- [ ] climate region
- [ ] Coastal Range
- [ ] cultural region
- [ ] culture
- [ ] deciduous forest
- [ ] desert
- [ ] ecosystem
- [ ] elevation
- [ ] grasslands
- [ ] Great Lakes
- [ ] Great Plains
- [ ] Gulf and Atlantic Coastal Plains
- [ ] habitat
- [ ] highland
- [ ] humid continental
- [ ] humid subtropical
- [ ] landform
- [ ] Louisiana Territory
- [ ] marine west coast
- [ ] Mediterranean Sea
- [ ] Mexico
- [ ] nomadic
- [ ] Oklahoma (Indian Territory)
- [ ] Oregon Territory
- [ ] Oregon Trail
- [ ] Ozark Plateau
- [ ] plain
- [ ] plateau
- [ ] prairie
- [ ] precipitation
- [ ] region
- [ ] Santa Fe Trail
- [ ] semiarid
- [ ] temperate zone

Discovery | SOCIAL STUDIES
EDUCATION | **TECHBOOK**

What are the most important geographic characteristics of the United States?

ENGAGE

What landmarks define "America the Beautiful"? Visit Engage to learn more.

Essential Question

What are the most important geographic characteristics of the United States?

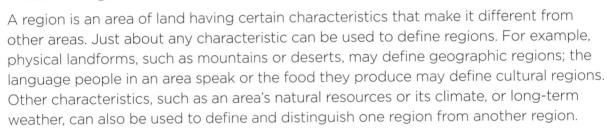

EXPLORE

The Characteristics of Place

What is a region?

A region is an area of land having certain characteristics that make it different from other areas. Just about any characteristic can be used to define regions. For example, physical landforms, such as mountains or deserts, may define geographic regions; the language people in an area speak or the food they produce may define cultural regions. Other characteristics, such as an area's natural resources or its climate, or long-term weather, can also be used to define and distinguish one region from another region.

An area may be divided into many different sets of regions. The Appalachian Mountains, for example, define a geographic region of the eastern United States. This landform region is also characterized by seasonal rainfall and other climate patterns. The area is home to certain animal species, such as deer and owls, but other animals, such as prairie dogs and alligators, do not live there. Certain plants, such as oak trees and blackberry bushes, grow in this region, but other plants, such as the Saguaro cactus, do not. If you live in the Appalachians, people in your town might work as miners, but you probably won't find anyone who works on a deep-sea fishing boat.

Studying the regions of the United States will help you better understand the history of its human inhabitants. When people live in a place, they rely on and adapt to the natural features of that place. They use available materials for food, tools, clothing, housing, and games. They develop habits, customs, and skills that are useful for their livelihood. Just as wildlife adapts to its surroundings, both human behavior and people's daily routines are shaped by the place's characteristics. The physical characteristics of a place directly impact the economic activities of that place.

photo: Library of Congress

A part of the coal mining town in West Virginia.

The physical and human characteristics of a place will also shape the contemporary events that usually occur there. For example, hurricanes and tropical storms are more common for people who live along the Gulf Coast than those who live in the Midwest or New England. Traffic congestion and air pollution are two issues that people living near large, urban cities face, rather than people living in rural areas. In recent decades, states in the nation's "sunbelt" have seen an increase in population as more people have sought warm weather lifestyles. Depending on where you live, you will most likely experience different events than someone living in a different region of the United States.

Think about the climate and physical features of the area where you live. Then, consider how those characteristics along with the area's cultural characteristics help define your way of life. How would you describe the region where you live?

Climate Regions

What climate regions are found in the United States?

What are the winters and summers like where you live? One of the ways regions can be defined is through their weather. A climate region is a region distinguished by the type of long-term weather experienced in the area.

For example, the northern United States typically experiences cooler temperatures than the southern United States. More specifically, the United States is usually divided into seven different climate regions: humid continental, humid subtropical, arid, semiarid, highland, Mediterranean, and marine west coast. Historically, climate has had a lot to do with where and why certain groups settled in different parts of the United States. As a result, climate has strongly influenced the culture of many areas.

Remember, though, that regions are generalizations. When we talk or learn about regions, we look for patterns, comparisons, and trends. Places in the same region are similar to each other in some ways, but they also are different in other ways.

Humid Continental

A humid continental climate is found in the northeastern United States, in places such as Connecticut and New York. Humid continental areas have variable, or changing, weather. Average temperatures differ greatly from summer to winter: summers are hot and humid; winters are cold and rainy or snowy. Temperatures can even change greatly from one day to the next. Humid continental areas are also subject to major storms with thunder, lightning, heavy rains, and high winds.

DISCOVERY EDUCATION | SOCIAL STUDIES TECHBOOK

What are the most important geographic characteristics of the United States?

Humid Subtropical

Humid subtropical areas are found in the southeastern United States, in places such as Florida and South Carolina. Summers are uncomfortably hot and humid, even during the evening. The area is subject to rain throughout the year. Winters are generally mild, but severe winter storms also can occur.

Arid

The word *arid* means "dry." An arid climate is too dry to support most plants, but some plants, such as the cactus, have adapted to the lack of water. Temperatures swing widely from morning to night, with the middle of the day usually being very hot. Nights can become very cold in arid climates because clear skies allow heat to escape into the atmosphere. Hot desert areas in the Southwest have an arid climate, as do the patches of cold desert that can be found in the western United States.

photo: Getty Images

Vegetation is sparse in an arid climate like that of the Mojave Desert in California.

Semiarid

The semiarid region is partially dry, as the name suggests. Do you live in an area of the United States that has dry, hot summers and cool winters? If so, you live in a semiarid region. Semiarid regions in the United States include the states of Nebraska, Oklahoma, and parts of Montana and Colorado.

Highland

The Rocky Mountains stretch from Canada to the southwestern United States and help create a highland climate in which the temperature varies with altitude. The higher up you go, the colder it gets! Parts of Montana, Wyoming, Utah, and Colorado, as well as areas of Canada, are in the highland climate region.

Mediterranean

The Mediterranean climate is found only near a large body of water. California, which borders the Pacific Ocean, has a Mediterranean climate. Summers are hot and dry, and winters are rainy and cool. Further inland, where the sea has less influence, Mediterranean climates change to desert.

Marine West Coast

The marine west coast region includes the Pacific Northwest. This area has mild temperatures and is cloudy and rainy year-round. Winds come from the west, bringing moist ocean air.

Complete this activity to demonstrate your understanding of U.S. regions.

Landform Regions—Eastern and Central United States
What landform regions are in the eastern United States?

Did you know that the United States encompasses more than 3.5 million square miles? It is the world's third-largest country—smaller than Russia or Canada, but larger than China, Brazil, and Australia. There are five major mountain ranges within the United States. There are also 13 major rivers—each more than 1,000 miles long—and four major deserts.

Geographers divide the United States and part of Canada into the following landform regions:

- Gulf and Atlantic Coastal Plains
- Appalachian Mountains
- Central Plains
- Ozark Plateau
- Canadian Shield

- Great Plains
- Rocky Mountains
- Basin and Range
- Coastal Range

However, not all geographers divide the regions in exactly the same way. Geographers use many different methods when defining regions by their physical landforms. That is why you will see several variations if you look at different maps and sources. Let's take a look at these regions from east to west.

What landform region do you live in?

Discovery SOCIAL STUDIES **TECHBOOK**

What are the most important geographic characteristics of the United States?

Gulf and Atlantic Coastal Plains, Appalachian Mountains, Ozark Plateau

The Gulf and Atlantic Coastal Plains are low, flat plains that run along the Gulf of Mexico and partially up the eastern seaboard of the United States. A plain is a wide, flat area of land. The Appalachian Mountain region is west of the Gulf and Atlantic Coastal Plains and stretches from eastern Canada to western Alabama. The Ozark Plateau region is distinguished by a high plain found just west of the Appalachian Mountains. A plateau is an area of land that is flat and raised higher than the adjacent land. The Ozark Plateau region covers parts of Missouri, Oklahoma, Arkansas, and southeastern Kansas.

Canadian Shield

To the north of all these regions is the Canadian Shield, an expanse of hundreds of lakes surrounding Hudson Bay in Canada. This rocky terrain stretches from the Great Lakes into eastern and central Canada and is shaped like a shield around Hudson Bay.

Landform Regions—Western United States

What landform regions are in the western United States?

Great Plains and Rocky Mountains

In the center of the United States, the Great Plains region stretches across the interior of North America. Historically, this region was covered in tall prairie grasses. Today, this area is important farmland. Because of the amount of wheat grown here, the region has been called "the nation's breadbasket." The Great Plains slowly rise in elevation as they spread west to the base of the Rocky Mountains. Because the rise in elevation is so gradual, the Great Plains region is generally considered to be very low and flat.

photo: Denver Public Library

The company town for the Rocky Mountain Fuel Company in Colorado was built near a coal mining mountain.

The Rocky Mountains cut across the entire continent, from Alaska all the way south to Mexico. Part of the Rocky Mountains form a natural division, called the Continental Divide. This division separates the rivers that flow west into the Pacific Ocean from the rivers that flow east into the Gulf of Mexico and the Atlantic Ocean. The Continental Divide is literally a dividing line for continental North America!

Basin and Range

Between the Pacific Ocean to the west and the Rocky Mountains to the east lies a vast area called the Basin and Range region. A basin is a large area of land that is sunken lower than adjacent land. A range is a mountainous area. The Basin and Range region varies from desert in the South to grasslands in the North. The Grand Canyon is one of the amazing physical features found in the Basin and Range region. Another feature of this sparsely populated region is Death Valley. Located in California, Death Valley is the hottest and lowest point in all of North America. The highest temperature ever recorded in the United States—a scorching 134 degrees Fahrenheit in the shade—happened in Death Valley on July 10, 1913!

Coastal Range

Cooling things down a bit to the west, the Coastal Range region follows the high mountain chains that dominate the landscape several hundred miles east of the Pacific Ocean. This region has numerous mountain ranges, including the Sierra Nevada Mountains in the south and the Cascade Mountains in Washington State. Lower mountains in the Coastal Range region lie just inland from the ocean and run all the way up and down the coastline.

Creating Biomes

How do ecosystems help define regions in the United States?

Different plants and animals can be found throughout the United States, and each plant and animal needs a particular kind of environment to survive. An ecosystem is a community of plants and animals and the environment in which they live. Studying the ecosystems of an area is another way to divide a larger place into regions.

Biomes are regional areas defined by their environmental characteristics, including ecosystems. Think about all the different physical features in the United States that you have studied so far, including oceans, rivers, mountains, plains, valleys, and deserts. With all these physical features, the United States is home to many different biomes.

For example, the Great Plains region is home to a prairie ecosystem with a distinctive combination of animals, insects, and plant life. For thousands of years, huge herds of bison roamed the wide expanses of prairie. The flat lands and sturdy grasses formed a habitat well-suited to these bison, as well as to gophers, mice, prairie dogs, and a wide variety of grasshoppers. The birds of the prairie had nest-building habits that were suited to the treeless environment.

Discovery EDUCATION | SOCIAL STUDIES TECHBOOK

What are the most important geographic characteristics of the United States?

Because the Rocky Mountains are a very different landform type from the Great Plains, they are home to a very different ecosystem. For instance, bison do not live in the Rocky Mountains because the steep, slippery slopes are not suitable for huge herds of animals. However, mountain lions, wolverines, and bighorn sheep live comfortably in the Rocky Mountains. Because the Rockies' pine, fir, and aspen trees capture much of the sunlight before it reaches the ground, grasses in the Rockies do not grow tall or thick. In addition, the ground is rocky and the soil is less deep, so plants cannot grow the extremely deep roots that enabled the prairie grasses to survive the cold winters and periodic wildfires in the Great Plains.

photo: Paul Fuqua

Sagebrush characterizes the high desert biome in the Great Basin area of the United States, along with pinyon-juniper woodlands. High deserts experience long, cold winters and short, warm summers.

What are some characteristics of the ecosystem where you live? How do these characteristics affect human life in your biome?

Examples of Biomes

What are some examples of biomes in the United States?

The United States can be divided into different ecosystem regions, or biomes. Each biome has distinctive landforms, climate, and plant and animal life. Think about the area where you live. Is there a forest nearby, or is the area mostly dry and desertlike? How do you think your local biome differs from other parts of the United States?

Rain Forests

The temperate zones surround the tropics. In the Northern Hemisphere, the temperate zone stretches between the Arctic Circle and the Tropic of Cancer. All of the United States is in the temperate zone except for Hawaii. Temperate rain forests are found within the temperate zone. In the United States, temperate rain forests are found along the coast in the Pacific Northwest. Many years ago, rain forests stretched all the way from southern Oregon to Alaska. However, human development, such as logging and population growth, has changed the environment, and the rain forests in the United States are not as widespread anymore.

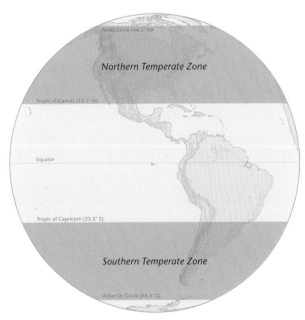

Map showing the temperate zones in the Western Hemisphere.

There are two main seasons in a temperate rain forest: a long, rainy season during which temperatures are low but rarely dip below freezing, and a short, dry summer season in which temperatures can reach the mid-80s. The rain forest in Olympic National Park in Washington State receives as much as 12 to 14 feet of rain a year! This area supports spruce and hemlock trees, Pacific salmon, northern spotted owls, porcupines, deer, elk, and banana slugs, as well as other plant and animal species.

Deciduous Forests

Deciduous forests are found mostly in the eastern United States. Broad-leaved deciduous trees, such as oak, hickory, maple, and other hardwoods, thrive in this ecosystem region. Deciduous forests experience all four seasons—winter, spring, summer, and autumn. To prepare for winter, deciduous trees stop sending nutrients to their leaves so they can store energy in their trunks and branches; as a result, the leaves change color and die in the autumn. In the process, the leaves display fall colors that can be spectacular. The state of Maine draws roughly nine million "leaf peepers" each year! Animals that commonly make their homes in this biome include gray and red squirrels, white-tailed deer, black bears, and many species of birds, such as red-tailed hawks, great horned owls, northern flickers, and chickadees.

Grasslands

Grasslands represent another ecosystem region in the United States. Grasslands are huge fields of grasses, flowers, and herbs, with few trees other than those near rivers and streams. There are two different types of grassland ecosystems—tall grass and short grass. Both are considered prairie ecosystems. Short-grass prairie is more common in a climate that is dry and hot in the summer and cold in the winter. Tall-grass prairie tends to appear where the climate is wet and humid year-round, but not as wet as a forest. The Central Plains region just west of the Mississippi River is an example of a tall-grass prairie. The grasses get shorter as the Great Plains stretch closer to the Rocky Mountains.

Deserts

Deserts are yet another type of ecosystem region found in the United States. There are four major deserts in the United States: the Mojave Desert, the Sonoran Desert, the Chihuahuan Desert, and the Great Basin Desert. Deserts are distinguished by their dry climate. Deserts also generally experience great variations in temperature throughout the day. Deserts are home to certain plants and animals that do not exist anywhere else in the world. For example, Joshua Trees are native to the Mojave Desert and are found nowhere else.

Economic Regions

How can the United States be divided into economic regions?

With a population of more than 313 million people, it is no wonder that the economy of the United States is extremely large and diverse. Manufacturing, mining, and farming are only a few of the many industries that contribute to the wealth of the nation. Although some of the same jobs and industries can be found across the United States, the climate and physical characteristics of different regions make certain activities more important to specific local economies than others. For example, fishing is a major industry on both the Pacific and Atlantic coasts, but it is not as important in the inland Rocky Mountain region.

Economic Regions of the United States

U.S. Economic Region	Resources	Land Uses
A Pacific West	⚒ Coal	▨ Commercial farming
B Rocky Mountains	⚡ Hydroelectric power	▨ Commercial fishing
C Southwest	⚒ Iron	▨ Forestry
D Plains	◉ Natural gas	▨ Little or no activity
E Great Lakes	⚟ Petroleum	▨ Livestock raising
F Southeast	◇ Precious metals (gold, silver, copper)	▨ Trade and manufacturing
G Mideast	✹ Uranium	
H New England		

Pacific West

The Pacific West, or Far West, is the westernmost region of the United States. Pacific West states enjoy a predominantly Mediterranean coastal climate that makes the area ideal for growing crops. Roughly half of the fruits, nuts, and vegetables grown in the United States come from California. The state of Washington's apple industry accounts for approximately 70 percent of the nation's apples. The proximity of the Pacific Ocean also adds to the economy of the region. As of 2010, California ranked fourth in the nation in the amount of pounds of fish caught, Oregon ranked sixth, and Washington eighth. Alaska, which is sometimes considered part of the Far West region, was first. It reported a catch totaling more than 4.3 billion pounds!

The temperate conifer forests found mostly in the northwestern area of the region have historically helped make forestry another important economic activity. The state of Oregon currently leads the nation in plywood and soft wood lumber production. With warm-weather tourism attractions such as Hollywood and San Francisco, as well as several breathtaking National Parks, visitors are also a vital component of the region's economy. California alone brings in nearly $100 billion in direct travel spending per year.

Rocky Mountains

The Rocky Mountain region is found just east of the Far West. The dramatic peaks and mesas of the Rocky Mountains provide rich mineral resources that have long contributed to the mining industry in the United States. Minerals such as copper, gold, silver, lead, and zinc have been mined in Montana, Colorado, Utah, and elsewhere in the Rockies. Known as the Treasure State because of its abundance of numerous gemstones and minerals, Montana is the only place in the world where the unique yogo sapphire is found. Mines in Colorado are some of the world's largest producers of molybdenum, a mineral used in industrial steel production, and contribute some $652 million to Colorado's economy alone. The area in and around northern Idaho is also a productive mining center for silver, zinc, and lead.

In addition to providing mineral resources, the unique landscape of the Rocky Mountains proves a major draw for year-round tourism. Skiers, mountain climbers, white water rafters, and other thrill-seekers generate about $8 billion annually for the state of Colorado, more than $2 billion for Montana, and around $4 billion for Idaho. The large expanses of grazing land in the Rocky Mountain valleys have also made the area ideal for livestock production.

Southwest

Much of the Southwest region is hot and dry, and crops can only be grown with the aid of irrigation. Combined with poor soil quality, this makes the area unsuitable for most large-scale crop production. However, the arid land is useful for grazing, and livestock production has become one of the main economic activities here. Texas ranks as the top cattle-producing state in the nation, with beef cattle generating more than $7 billion annually. Along with the livestock industry, feed crops such as alfalfa are also grown in the Southwest. In New Mexico, for example, alfalfa is the top cash crop. Natural gas and petroleum resources are also a major economic force in the Southwest. More than one million barrels of oil are mined in the Permian Basin in West Texas and Eastern New Mexico per day.

Great Plains

The Great Plains is a region of high plateau, semiarid grasslands. The rich soils, large floodplains, and continental climate provide a beneficial environment for major grain production. As a result, the area once known as the "Great American Desert" has been transformed into "America's Breadbasket." Many of the country's top wheat-producing states are located within this region. Nearly two-thirds of all wheat produced in the United States is grown here. Corn, sorghum, soybeans, and oilseeds are also among the top crops cultivated in the Great Plains. Almost three-quarters of the land area of the Great Plains is used for agricultural purposes.

Great Lakes

The economy of the Great Lakes region is dominated by activities involving the waters of the Great Lakes themselves. Approximately 65 million pounds of fish are harvested from the lakes by the commercial fishing industry each year, generating around $1 billion annually for the regional economy. Sport fishing—which is recreational fishing for fun or competition—brings in another estimated $4 billion. There are more than 110 U.S. shipping ports within the Great Lakes system, and cargo shipping brings in more than $34 billion each year for the United States and Canada. With the growth of industrial production in the region since the beginning of the 1900s, when the Great Lakes region was nicknamed America's "Industrial Heartland" due to the large manufacturing sector, these shipping routes became essential in getting steel, automobiles, and other manufactured items out to the market.

Agricultural production is also important in the Great Lakes, as the region produces around 7 percent of the nation's food. Crops such as corn, soybeans and feed hay are most common, while certain areas are known for specialty fruits or vegetables. One example is the tart (or sour) cherry in northwestern Michigan, which is viewed as an ideal place to grow the fruit due to the more temperate climate created by the Great Lakes and surrounding landscape of rolling hills. Tart cherries are used for pie filling and other processed foods, and Michigan accounts for nearly all tart cherry production in the United States.

Southeast

The humid summers and short winters of the Southeast make the region ideal for growing cash crops such as tobacco, peanuts, and rice. Georgia is the top peanut-producer in the nation, while North Carolina and Kentucky rank number one for tobacco cultivation. Citrus is a $9 billion industry in Florida, and the state produces around 70 percent of all citrus fruits in the United States as well as the most grapefruit in the world. With the Gulf of Mexico and Atlantic Ocean as two borders, the regional economy thrives on fishing, coastal recreation, tourism, and shipping. Altogether, ocean-dependent activities account for approximately $17 billion. The Southeast is also a major producer of both coal and natural gas, which contributes to the energy sector of both the national and regional economy.

Mideast

The Mideast or Mid-Atlantic region is found along the eastern seaboard of the United States between New England and the South. It has a high population density in major urban centers as New York City and the Washington, DC, metropolitan area. The manufacturing and service sectors are both important components of the economy. Banking, insurance, food processing, and high-tech manufacturing are all part of the industrial diversity of this region.

The natural resources and physical features of the Mid-Atlantic states contribute to the economy here, too. Oysters and blue crabs are harvested from the Chesapeake Bay among other seafood. In northeastern Pennsylvania, enough natural gas is being extracted from shale deposits to satisfy the gas needs of about one-eighth the population of the United States. The mountains of Pennsylvania naturally buffer the Mid-Atlantic state of Delaware from cold winter winds and help create a climate beneficial for productive farming. Some 40 percent of the land in Delaware is used for ranching and farming, and the state leads the nation in the production of broiler chickens.

New England

A relatively small region, New England boasts a unique economy closely linked to its climate and natural resources. The dense forests contribute substantially to the economy, both in lumber production and tourism revenue. Most of the maple syrup produced in the nation comes from the maple trees of New England, and Vermont on its own is responsible for more than 40 percent of the nation's supply. Maple sap requires consistent temperatures below 40°F to generate syrup, and the cold winters of New England fit this task perfectly. The natural wetlands marshes, or bogs, that dot Massachusetts make the state an ideal place for cranberry cultivation, and the state is the second-largest producer of the fruit in the nation. In addition, wild blueberries naturally thrive on the acidic soils and cold winters in Maine, and this state produces around 90 percent of the country's entire blueberry crop.

The proximity of the Atlantic Ocean and other waterways has made fishing an important part of the economy in New England. Approximately nine-tenths of the lobster caught and sold in the United States comes from Maine. Groundfishing (the catching of fish that swim close to the bottom) is recognized as one of the earliest industries in the United States and still remains a part of the New England economy. New England's groundfishing industry continues to become more restricted as fish populations dwindle and new government protections are put in place. However, several generations of fishing families still make their living from fishing the region's salt cod, haddock, and redfish.

Discovery EDUCATION | SOCIAL STUDIES TECHBOOK

What are the most important geographic characteristics of the United States?

Cultural Regions

What are some cultural regions in the United States?

In addition to its diverse landscapes and climates, North America also hosts a wide array of cultures. A cultural region is a region in which people share characteristics of the same culture. They can be places where people speak the same language, practice the same religion, or share the same history. They can even be places where people partake in the same traditions or share the same cultural outlets. For example, music is an integral part of the regional culture of the Southeast. The southeastern city of New Orleans is even known as the birthplace of jazz.

Culture in the Southwest

When Europeans first settled in the United States, Native Americans already lived in many geographic regions across North America. Today, many Native American tribes still follow ancient traditions. The Native American reservations in the United States are cultural regions, places where people from the same cultural backgrounds share cultural characteristics. They are also political entities, which means they have their own governments and laws. In the modern Southwest region, a distinctive culture has grown from the blend of Native American and Spanish heritages together with Anglo-American and African American traditions.

photo: Paul Fuqua

Horses pull a wagon loaded with fresh-cut hay on an Amish farm. Traditional Amish farms operate without the use of engine-powered machinery.

Culture in the Northeast

In some areas in the Northeast, particularly in and around Lancaster County, Pennsylvania, you will find cultural regions known as the Pennsylvania Dutch Country. These areas are home to descendants of Germans who immigrated in the 1700s, including many Amish and Mennonites. These are religious sects, or groups, who live much as they did in the 1700s: They practice traditional farming methods and generally avoid modern technology. In addition to speaking English, many Amish and Mennonites also speak a hybrid language known as "Pennsylvania Dutch," a German dialect.

Understanding Cultures

Identifying cultural regions can help you
understand other cultures. When you learn
about characteristics the people in a region
share, you can start to see why
they live as they do. After you learn how
the people of a region are similar, you
can better understand what makes them
unique.

**Complete the activity
to demonstrate your
understanding of the
geography of the
United States.**

Learning about cultural regions also enables you to understand how you are similar to
and different from other people; it enables you to learn more about your own culture
as well.

Consider the Essential Question:

What are the most important
geographic characteristics of
the United States?

Go online to complete
the Social Studies
Explanation.

Check for Understanding:

Which geographic characteristic
do you think most influences
human behavior? Cite evidence
to support your position.

DISCOVERY EDUCATION | SOCIAL STUDIES **TECHBOOK**

In what ways were the cultural traditions of Native Americans, Europeans, and West Africans alike and different?

1.2 Cultures Meet in America

photo: Getty Images

LESSON OVERVIEW

Introduction

In this concept, you will learn how early Native Americans built thriving societies, how European cultural developments lead to encounters with new cultures, and how people lived in West African kingdoms. You also will learn about how trade with Europe and the Americas affected both the lives of West Africans and the course of American history.

Essential Question

In what ways were the cultural traditions of Native Americans, Europeans, and West Africans alike and different?

Key Vocabulary
Which terms do you already know?

- [ ] Adena
- [ ] Algonquian
- [ ] Anasazi
- [ ] Asante
- [ ] Aztec
- [ ] Beringia
- [ ] Calvinism
- [ ] Catholic Church
- [ ] Cherokee
- [ ] Creek
- [ ] Dahomey
- [ ] drought
- [ ] empire
- [ ] Hopewell
- [ ] Hopi
- [ ] hunter-gatherer
- [ ] Inca
- [ ] Inuit
- [ ] Iroquois
- [ ] Iroquois League
- [ ] irrigation
- [ ] Johannes Gutenberg
- [ ] Kwakiutl
- [ ] longhouse

- [ ] maize
- [ ] matrilineal
- [ ] Mayans
- [ ] Michelangelo
- [ ] migration
- [ ] Mohawks
- [ ] natural resource
- [ ] Navajo
- [ ] Oneidas
- [ ] Onondagas
- [ ] Paleo-Indians
- [ ] Protestant Reformation
- [ ] pueblos
- [ ] Renaissance
- [ ] Senecas
- [ ] Spanish Inquisition
- [ ] tepee
- [ ] Tlingit
- [ ] Tomás de Torquemada
- [ ] totem
- [ ] transatlantic slave trade
- [ ] Triangular Trade
- [ ] Yupik

Lesson Objectives

By the end of this lesson, you should be able to:

- Summarize theories regarding the arrival of the first human inhabitants of the Americas.

- Compare and contrast cultural characteristics of civilizations that lived in the Western Hemisphere.

- Explain how various Native American cultures, including the Arctic (Inuit), Plains (Lakota), and Eastern Woodlands (Iroquois), adapted to their surroundings.

- Connect social, political, and technological developments in Europe to the emergence of the Age of Exploration.

- Compare the roles, motivations, and accomplishments of the English, French, Portuguese, and Spanish exploration of North America.

- Describe characteristics of the Dahomey and Asante cultures of West Africa.

- Analyze causes and consequences of trade between West Africa and Europe, including the establishment of the slave trade.

ENGAGE

What do artifacts reveal about the first Americans? Visit Engage to learn more.

Essential Question

In what ways were the cultural traditions of Native Americans, Europeans, and West Africans alike and different?

Discovery SOCIAL STUDIES
EDUCATION **TECHBOOK**

In what ways were the cultural traditions of Native Americans, Europeans, and West Africans alike and different?

EXPLORE

The First Americans

How did human life first arrive in the Americas?

Christopher Columbus is famous for being the first European to "discover" the American continents, but when he arrived, millions of people were already living there. Where did these people come from?

Over the centuries, there have been many theories about how human beings first arrived on the American continents. For years, most scientists believed that these first people simply walked to the Americas—from Asia! This would be impossible today, but about 40,000 years ago, huge portions of the northern oceans froze into glaciers. This freezing caused the water level in the Bering Strait to drop, creating a land bridge called Beringia that connected Asia and North America. Most scientists agree that by about 13,000 years ago, people were crossing this land bridge into the Americas as they hunted and gathered food.

But were these the very first people in the Americas? In recent years, new evidence has changed many scientists' beliefs about the first people to arrive. It now seems probable that people arrived in the Americas as many as 2,000 years before humans crossed the Beringia land bridge. According to this second theory, the first people arrived in the Americas at least 15,000 years ago and may have spread throughout the Americas by traveling by boat along the Pacific Coast.

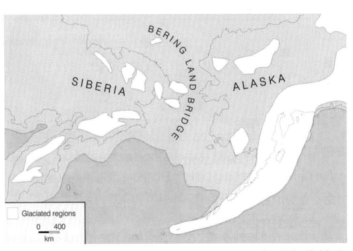

photo: National Park Service
This map shows the Bering Strait land bridge known as Beringia.

However they first arrived, the first Americans, known today as Paleo-Indians, gradually moved south and west across the continent. Over time, they developed hundreds of different cultures. The Americas were their home for thousands of years.

Earth Artists

Who were the earliest people to settle in the Americas?

The Paleo-Indians of North America were nomadic hunter-gatherers. This means that they moved from place to place in search of food. Much of what we know about the Paleo-Indians comes from archaeologists' study of stone remnants of tools and weapons. For example, we know that these early Americans hunted with wooden spears and arrows because archaeologists have found stone points.

These points have markings showing that they were sharpened and then fastened to spears or arrows using cord made from sinew, leather, or plant fibers. Scholars have also concluded that hunting and cooking were group or tribal affairs. Collections of tools and the bones of many animals have been found in what scientists believe were butchering sites.

Between 500 BCE and 500 CE, first the Adena and later the Hopewell cultures settled and lived in the Ohio River Valley. This land includes parts of present-day Ohio, Indiana, Kentucky, and Tennessee. The name Hopewell comes from the location of the first archaeological excavation devoted to learning about these cultures. This excavation took place in 1891 on the Ohio farm of Mordecai Hopewell.

Scientists have determined that people of the Adena and Hopewell cultures lived in cone-shaped homes made of sticks, bark, and willows. They used clay and stones, and later copper, to make ornaments and tools. They used agriculture to provide some, if not most, of their food.

Burial Mounds

The Adena and Hopewell peoples also built mysterious mounds. These mounds were so large and numerous that for many years the people were known as the Mound Builders. From what is known, archaeologists can infer that the people considered the mounds to be very important.

photo: Library of Congress

The Grave Creek burial mound located in Moundsville, West Virginia.

Many of the Adena and Hopewell mounds were tombs, where the dead were buried along with gifts and offerings. Other mounds, known as effigy mounds, were built in the shapes of animals. To a person standing nearby, these mounds look like low bumps that are only a couple of feet high. However, when viewed from the sky, the mounds are clearly seen to be in the shapes of animals, such as birds, buffalo, deer, and bears. The largest and most famous of these mounds is the Great Serpent Mound in southern Ohio. Shaped like a winding snake with an egg-shaped object in its mouth, this mound is three feet high and 1,300 feet long!

While the purpose of the burial mounds is fairly clear, the purpose of the effigy mounds is more mysterious. Some archaeologists believe the mounds were used as defensive walls. Other archaeologists think the mounds may have been used for the construction of temples. Some archaeologists even think that the mound sites were based on observations of the stars.

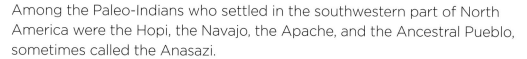

The Southwest

How did the people of the Southwest form the first cities?

Among the Paleo-Indians who settled in the southwestern part of North America were the Hopi, the Navajo, the Apache, and the Ancestral Pueblo, sometimes called the Anasazi.

photo: National Park Service

The Anasazi Gran Quivira Ruins of New Mexico.

The Ancestral Pueblo existed from about 100 to 1600 CE and lived in the areas of what are now the states of Colorado, New Mexico, Arizona, and Utah. When the Ancestral Pueblo first came to this region, they were nomadic hunters and gatherers, often living in caves.

Much of the Ancestral Pueblo land was dry, but the people learned to bring water to the dry areas through irrigation. The Ancestral Pueblo used stones to build dams and reservoirs to direct and hold the water. These advancements allowed the people to farm their food. As the Ancestral Pueblo became more successful at farming for food, their population grew.

The Ancestral Pueblo were expert basket weavers and potters. They used clay found in the ground to mold pots, jars, and pitchers, and then they let the pieces bake and harden in the sun. They used their pottery for cooking and preserving food.

Their homes were built above the ground using stone and adobe bricks. To make the bricks, the Ancestral Pueblo mixed clay with grass or straw and then dried the bricks in the sun. The Ancestral Pueblo built adobe homes in close communities, some with as many as 100 connected rooms.

As the Ancestral Pueblo population continued to grow, they built impressive communities of cliff dwellings into the sides of cliff walls and in canyons. Some of the dwellings could be as tall as four stories and often had terraces on the higher levels. In many ways, these dwellings looked much like today's apartment buildings. You can visit actual Ancestral Pueblo cliff dwellings at various sites in the Southwest, such as Mesa Verde National Park in southwest Colorado and Canyon de Chelly National Monument in northeast Arizona.

Around 1300, the Ancestral Pueblo moved south into what is now southern Arizona. The people most likely moved due to a great drought, or long period without rain. They adapted by farming near hills and mountains that supplied natural irrigation as the water streamed down to their crops.

Three Latin American Empires

How did the powerful empires of Central and South America transform the land?

During the 1300s and 1400s, North American civilizations usually consisted of scattered homes, small villages, or cities. Meanwhile, Central and South America saw the rise of three great empires, each containing hundreds of thousands of people.

The Mayan Empire rose in what are now Mexico and Central America. At its peak, the empire included more than 40 cities, with a total population of about two million people. The Maya cut limestone from huge quarries and built great stone temples, pyramids, and even ball courts. The remains of the great city of Chichén Itzá on the Yucatan Peninsula in Mexico are an example of Mayan architecture and urban planning.

The Maya were excellent farmers, using irrigation to water their crops. However, they also cut down massive amounts of jungle to create farmland. Over time, this may have been one factor that led to their downfall. Without trees, the soil eventually became infertile. By around 900, the great Mayan cities had been abandoned and became overgrown by the returning jungle.

Another great empire, the Aztec Empire, formed in what is now southern Mexico. From the great city of Tenochtitlán, the Aztec Empire covered 80,000 square miles and consisted of almost six million people. Like the Maya, the Aztec were farmers. They made clothes from cotton that they grew and from the feathers of beautiful tropical birds. They also caught fish with nets made from cactus fibers.

photo: Getty Images

Artifacts such as this Aztec obsidian mask, c. 1450, as well as Aztec stone carvings, gold, and featherwork, pay silent homage to the gentle, reflective side of Aztec life.

The Inca Empire first developed in what is now Chile. Although Incan homes were made mostly of stone and adobe mud, evidence of an advanced architecture is visible in the roads, tunnels, and bridges that the Inca built to travel through the Andes Mountains. The Inca also practiced terrace farming, growing maize and other crops, and built elaborate irrigation systems. The Inca raised both dogs and llamas. To make clothes, they blended cotton with wool from the llamas.

Extensive Incan construction is visible in the dwellings of Machu Picchu, near the Incan capital of Cuzco, Peru. Machu Picchu covers 125 square miles and sits nearly 1.5 miles high (7,710 ft.). This ancient city is believed to have been a palace complex built around 1450.

The Mayan, Aztec, and Inca Empires had different beginnings and different ways of life. However, they all faced the same crisis: the arrival of Spanish explorers in the early 1500s.

Discovery EDUCATION | SOCIAL STUDIES TECHBOOK

In what ways were the cultural traditions of Native Americans, Europeans, and West Africans alike and different?

Peoples of the Arctic

How did the environment shape the lives of Paleo-Indians in the Arctic?

Life for Paleo-Indians was not the same everywhere. The regions in which groups of people settled greatly affected their lives, from what they ate to what they wore and how they built their homes.

For example, the Inuit and the Yupik, who lived along the Pacific Ocean in what is now Canada, and the Aleut, who lived on the Aleutian Islands in the Bering Strait, were Arctic peoples. These groups all lived in the far north and faced extreme cold and harsh conditions. They hunted ocean animals, particularly seals and whales, for food, and they burned their blubber for heat. They used seal furs for blankets and clothing. In the summer when the snows melted, they used animal hides to make their homes.

The Yupik relied heavily on whales, seals, and walruses, but they also hunted fur-bearing land animals, such as bears. These people built a variety of boats for fishing as well as for traveling along the coasts. To travel on land, they used sleds pulled by dog teams.

The Aleut built their villages near the sea and hunted sea otters, sea lions, and whales. On land, they hunted caribou and bears. Their multifamily homes were built partially below ground, with wooden beams and struts to support the roof, which would be covered with grass mats and then sod. The women wove baskets out of grass and gathered berries and fish. They made tools and utensils from stone, animal bones, and ivory.

The Inuit lived along the Pacific Ocean in what is now Canada. In winter, they traveled in groups of about 100 people, living in igloos, or temporary dwellings made from blocks of packed snow. Some groups hunted and lived in igloos all winter long; other groups used their regular homes as a base and only used igloos during brief hunting expeditions. In summer, the Inuit hunted in smaller groups of about

An Inuit council house and totem, in Fox Island, Alaska.

photo: Getty Images

a dozen people. They hunted seals and whales for food and used these mammals' skins and fur for clothing.

Forest Peoples

How did the forests shape the lives of people in the Northwest and in the Eastern Woodlands?

Northwest Indians

South of Alaska, along the coast of Canada and into present-day Washington, Oregon, and California, the Tlingit, Haida, and the Kwakiutl cultures developed. Having the Pacific Ocean on one side and dense coastal forests on the other, the Northwest Paleo-Indians took advantage of a variety of resources for food, homes, and clothing.

photo: Getty Images

Reproduction of a wigwam and dugout boat used by Eastern Woodlands Native Americans.

The Northwest people built their homes from wood, such as cedar, and decorated them with beautiful wood carvings representing animals and spirits. Many of their crafts, including totem poles, wooden masks and bowls, and woven baskets, featured animal and spirit symbols. Animal skins and tree bark supplied the materials for clothing. This clothing often established a person's social status. For example, chiefs often wore robes made of otter pelts, which were considered very valuable.

Eastern Woodland Indians

Like the people of the Northwest, the Eastern Woodland people had an abundance of trees and water. The Eastern Woodlands ran from the Great Lakes area to the Atlantic Ocean. Some of the people who lived in this area were the Iroquois, the Creek, the Cherokee, and the Algonquin.

The people of the Eastern Woodlands used trees and animal products in many ways. They used the branches and bark of trees to build longhouses. These large, dome-shaped structures housed entire families. The people carved canoes out of logs and hunted and trapped fish and large and small land animals. They also practiced agriculture, growing crops such as beans, squash, and corn (maize).

Even though the Eastern Woodland peoples took wood and bark from the trees, they did so with great respect for these trees. It was common to offer thanks before harvesting wood or other plants.

Discovery EDUCATION | SOCIAL STUDIES TECHBOOK

In what ways were the cultural traditions of Native Americans, Europeans, and West Africans alike and different?

In the area that is now upper New York State, a group of five nations—the Mohawk, the Oneida, the Onondaga, the Cayuga, and the Seneca—often found themselves fighting for resources and power. Finally, sometime between 1450 and 1600, these five nations joined together to form the Iroquois Confederation. According to legends, they were led by a Mohawk chief named Hiawatha. Together, the five nations pledged to share resources and unite against other nations. Later, leaders in the American colonies, such as Benjamin Franklin, looked to the Iroquois Confederation as a model of unity.

The Great Plains

How did people adapt to life on the open, mostly treeless Plains?

Near the center of North America, the Plains people lived on vast stretches of open land. These people included the Comanche, the Cheyenne, the Lakota, and the Pawnee. They hunted elk, buffalo, and deer. Any part of the animal they didn't eat was used for something else. They made tools from animals, such as rakes from antlers. The Plains people's clothes were mostly made from animal skins.

In areas where some trees could be found, people made homes called lodges from sticks and a mixture of grass and dirt. However, because the plains had very few trees, many people also used animal hides to make homes called tepees.

Perhaps the most important resource for the Plains people was the buffalo, which roamed the plains in huge herds. Hunting buffalo was an important ritual. Some people hunted with spears and arrows, while others drove groups of buffalo

photo: Getty Images

The Lakota recorded their history by using symbolic drawings on animal hides.

off cliffs. When Spanish colonists brought horses to North America, some tribes, such as the Lakota, learned to use horses in their buffalo hunts.

Explore this interactive to learn more about Native American nations.

The Plains people used every part of the buffalo. Buffalo hides were used for blankets, shoes, clothes, and homes. Buffalo bones became tools and utensils. Even dried buffalo droppings were burned for fuel. As with the other peoples of North America, the environment shaped the Plains people's life and the Plains people also shaped their environment.

An Age of Ideas

What changes in art and literature took place in Renaissance Europe?

During the 1400s, across the Atlantic Ocean, several changes were taking place in Europe. These developments would eventually lead to the arrival of the first Europeans in the Americas. During this time period, which is called the Renaissance, people began to explore new ways of looking at the world. Some of this change resulted from the rediscovery of classical culture. Through contact with Southwest Asia, Europeans learned how Muslims had preserved and further developed classical Greek and Roman mathematics, philosophy, science, and art.

photo: Getty Images

Painting of the Sermon on the Mount in the Sistine Chapel.

Architecture was one field influenced by classical Greek and Roman culture. Designers broke away from the ornate, Gothic style of the Middle Ages. They avoided elaborate decorations intended to glorify God's greatness. Instead, Renaissance buildings focused on patterns, proportion, and relations between parts. Architects in Italy visited the classical Roman ruins and, in their works, mimicked features such as the column, the simple round arch, and the dome.

Another aspect of the new thinking was humanism. Generally, humanism refers to the trend of Renaissance artists, scientists, and political leaders studying and glorifying human beings. In contrast, medieval thought was dominated by a concern for social order. Humans were thought of as imperfect, and individuality was not seen as important.

Characters and stories from Greek and Roman mythology inspired the paintings of Sandro Botticelli and others. Renaissance artists such as Leonardo da Vinci and Michelangelo Buonarroti studied the human face and body, striving to portray them as realistically as possible. The revival of the arts also brought new techniques and materials to painting, including linear perspective and oil paints. These gave paintings richness and depth, a departure from the flatness of medieval art.

Renaissance writers also developed their craft by putting a sharp focus on understanding human nature. In the book *Utopia*, Sir Thomas More wrote about how to order society to promote human happiness. Geoffrey Chaucer's narrative poem The *Canterbury Tales* reflects humanism in many ways. Instead of religious themes and heroic adventures, Chaucer's stories feature common people. Servants, criminals, parsons, and homemakers are major characters with interesting personalities.

Discovery EDUCATION | SOCIAL STUDIES TECHBOOK

In what ways were the cultural traditions of Native Americans, Europeans, and West Africans alike and different?

Another humanist aspect of Chaucer's poem is that he wrote it in English, the language of the common people. At the time, most writing was done in Latin, the language of the Church.

In the early 1450s, the German bookmaker Johannes Gutenberg developed a printing press that used the new technique of movable type. Books could now be printed quickly and inexpensively, instead of having to be copied by hand. New ideas could reach more people more easily than ever before. Literacy and education increased dramatically as a result. Renaissance thinking also led to many scientific discoveries in navigation and mapmaking, which helped expand the exploration of distant lands, including the Americas.

The Reformation and the Counter-Reformation

What new challenges did the Catholic Church face?

During the late 1500s and early 1600s, Europe underwent several changes that altered the political landscape. Wars broke out between Spain and the Netherlands, Spain and Portugal, Portugal and the Netherlands, Spain and France, and Spain and England. Countries made alliances, promising to protect each other from common enemies. These alliances often took the form of marriages, with royal families arranging for sons and daughters to marry in order to gain power, or even to merge countries. For example, the marriage between Isabella, crown princess of Castile and Leon, and Ferdinand, crown prince of Aragon and Navarre, eventually led to the unification of Spain.

The Protestant Reformation

The medieval Catholic Church was very powerful, but that power was challenged during the Renaissance. An explosion of new ideas and new approaches to Christianity emerged as people began to challenge the Church's authority.

In 1517, Martin Luther nailed a list of 95 criticisms to a church door. Luther saw the Church as corrupt, focusing on wealth and political power instead of on God. He hoped to encourage the institution to return to what he saw as a purer state. He was excommunicated, or thrown out of the Church, but he quickly gained a large number of followers. This was the beginning of the Protestant Reformation.

photo: Getty Images

One of Martin Luther's main accomplishments was translating the Bible into the language of the common people.

Another early Protestant, John Calvin, believed in predestination. This was the idea that God decided the fate of every human soul before they were born, and no human action could change this fate. This philosophy, known as Calvinism, appealed to some who thought the Church had strayed from biblical teachings.

The Cross and the Sword

In the face of these challenges, the Church responded harshly to heretics, or anyone who disagreed publicly with official Church doctrine. After completing the "reconquest" of Spain from the Muslims in 1492, the Spanish King Ferdinand established the dominance of the Church by strengthening the Spanish Inquisition, an investigation by the Catholic Church that had been enforcing church doctrine for over 10 years. The inquisition investigated, tortured, and punished any dissenters from Catholicism. This included Jews, Muslims, and all varieties of Protestants. The chief inquisitor was Tomás de Torquemada, who ordered the burning of approximately 2,000 people between 1484 and 1498. Many of his victims were "conversos," or Catholics whose ancestors had converted from other faiths. They were accused of not being true Catholics.

In 1545, Catholics met at the Council of Trent. They tried to reform the Church while preserving it as an alternative to Protestantism. Their reforms did not satisfy most critics of the Church. Protestants and other dissenters still felt they needed to escape the Church's control. This need would become a powerful motive for the Age of Exploration.

But Catholics also drove the Age of Exploration. In the early 1500s, Ignatius of Loyola, a Spaniard, founded the Society of Jesus, or Jesuit order. Like the Franciscan monks, Jesuit priests felt a religious duty to spread Catholicism across the globe. Missionaries from both groups traveled to Africa, the Americas, East Asia, and the South Pacific. Their purpose was to convert the people, whom they believed to be primitive savages, to Christianity. The Jesuits also established schools to teach their religion and to prepare people for the priesthood.

Complete this activity to demonstrate your understanding of the Renaissance.

Two African Kingdoms

Who controlled West African trade before the arrival of Europeans?

Exploration and trade did not take place in only the Americas and Europe. West Africa was part of an extensive trade network that crossed the Sahara Desert and the Mediterranean Sea, connecting Africa to Europe and Asia. Over the centuries, numerous empires grew powerful by controlling and profiting from commerce on this network. These included the Empire of Ghana from the 800s to the 1200s, the Songhai Empire from around 1000 to 1592, the Mali Empire from the 1200s to the 1600s, and the Hausa States from the 500s to the 1800s.

Discovery | SOCIAL STUDIES
EDUCATION | TECHBOOK

In what ways were the cultural traditions of Native Americans, Europeans, and West Africans alike and different?

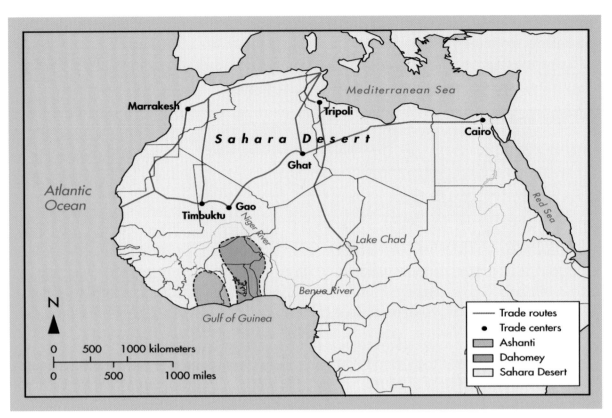

The Asante and Dahomey kingdoms were major traders in West Africa and major sources of the enslaved people who were shipped to the Americas.

For centuries, these kingdoms traded goods such as gold and salt across the Sahara, along the West African coast, and into the interior of the African continent. Their leaders grew wealthy and the kingdoms expanded. In the years from the 1400s through the 1600s, when contact between European, African, and American cultures brought the world closer together, two important kingdoms in West Africa were the Dahomey and the Asante.

In the early 1600s, the Dahomey Kingdom was founded in what is now the southern part of Benin in West Africa. To the west, in what is now southern Ghana, the Asante Empire, also known as Ashanti, reigned. Both peoples practiced agriculture. Unlike the Dahomey, however, the Asante lands were rich in gold. Gold was an important part of Asante's trade with other empires.

Before Europeans arrived in West Africa, many kingdoms enjoyed healthy trade with the outside world, including other nations across the Sahara and nations in Europe. Gold and ivory were two important goods traded throughout West Africa. Because of this, some people in these kingdoms were enslaved and sent to work in the mines. However, when Europeans arrived, the slave trade took on a new importance.

Dahomey Society and Culture
What cultural practices did the Dahomey follow?

The Dahomey people, also called the Fon, were known as both soldiers and farmers. They grew crops, including yams and cassava, for themselves and for trade with other areas. Yams and cassava are root vegetables, as are potatoes. They are still staple foods across Africa today.

Large extended families lived together in villages, and a chief ran each village. The chiefs answered to a king, whose main job was to keep the kingdom ready for war. Dahomey kings sometimes also tried to expand their kingdoms by overthrowing other tribes. Conquered lands were added to Dahomey territory, and their peoples joined Dahomey culture through marriage, shared customs, and laws.

photo: Getty Images

The root vegetable cassava is a staple of the West African diet. It is used to make tapioca flour, also pictured.

photo: Getty Images

This painting of the fierce Mino soldiers decorated a wall of the Dahomey royal palace.

Military culture was very important to the Dahomey. Beginning in the late 1600s, the Dahomey took a regular census, or count, of their population in order to draft soldiers for the army. Dahomey armies often included powerful female soldiers whom the Dahomey called the Mino and Europeans called Amazons. When not in the field, these women also served as royal bodyguards.

Dahomey Art

The Dahomey created artistic pieces with a practical or symbolic purpose. Each king, for example, had a special symbol that was shown on a quilt. This quilt contained the symbols of all of the Dahomey kings. Dahomey men were skilled wood-carvers who made representations of humans and gods, as well as useful pieces such as cups and stools. Scholars believe that the Dahomey connected wood carving with their religious beliefs. The Dahomey were also known for their metalwork, pottery, and basket weaving.

Discovery EDUCATION | SOCIAL STUDIES **TECHBOOK**

In what ways were the cultural traditions of Native Americans, Europeans, and West Africans alike and different?

Kings also influenced Dahomey music. They selected musicians to take part in orchestras. Songs told about kings' qualities and accomplishments. Musicians played for the king as he woke up and often throughout the day. Music was also a part of Dahomey religious practice. Musicians played during ceremonies and festivals. Drums were especially important Dahomey instruments. People danced to drumbeats as part of religious ceremonies, for example.

The Dahomey believed in several gods and goddesses, some more important than others. The Dahomey also believed that the king had religious importance, even though he was not a god himself.

Dahomey religion also contained a series of beliefs known as voodoo, or Vodou. Vodou combines the worship of public gods, the worship of personal gods, respect for one's ancestors, and magic. This "magic" was in fact knowledge about combinations of plants and other natural materials to make ceremonial charms. These charms were thought to carry powers from Dahomey deities. Vodou beliefs are still practiced today in places such as Haiti, a Caribbean island where enslaved West Africans were taken long ago.

Asante Society and Culture

How was Asante society structured? What cultural practices did they follow?

The Asante were farmers who fed themselves using subsistence agriculture, growing the crops they needed for survival and trading any extra for imported goods. Like the Dahomey, the Asante often had large extended families. Unlike the Dahomey, however, the Asante were a matrilineal society. People traced their heritage mostly through their mothers, grandmothers, and other female ancestors. People who shared a common female lineage formed clans.

The Asante also recognized the male line in certain religious activities, and the head of each clan was male. This person had religious duties and was responsible for keeping peace with other clans. Several clans lived together in villages, with the head of one clan acting as the village chief. This chief worked to keep order within the village.

The throne of the Asante leader was the Golden Stool. According to legend, the stool came down from the sky for Osei Tutu, who became the first Asantehene, or king of the Asante. In the late 1670s, Osei Tutu and his descendants began to unite the Akan-speaking groups into a kingdom. The king led a centralized government that ruled over Asante villages and towns through a large bureaucracy, or system of officials with highly specified duties. The Asante also developed a good system of roads and communications to oversee their lands.

The Golden Stool

The Golden Stool was at the heart of Asante politics and religion. The Asante believed that the Golden Stool embodied their national spirit and so must be kept safe from harm to protect the people. It was rarely seen by anyone outside of the Asante Empire.

Asante religion believed in the presence of one supreme creator god who had made all things, including a group of lesser gods. According to the Asante, the spirit of God was in all natural things, so they worshipped the spiritual aspects of nature. A part of the divine spirit was also believed to be present in all human beings. Ancestors were honored as a connection between the past and the present, and special stools were thought to represent their spirits.

photo: Getty Images

This traditional Asante shrine is located in modern-day Ghana.

As with the Dahomey, the Asante were fine metalworkers. Because of the region's rich deposits of gold, the Asante were known for their gold jewelry and other decorative pieces. The Asante were skilled weavers who made a colorful silk fabric known as Kente cloth, which is still popular in West Africa today. The colors of this fabric symbolize various spiritual qualities and human ideals.

Asante music seems to be closely connected with Dahomey music. Chiefs were allowed to play drums and horns. These and other instruments, such as gongs and bells, were played at religious ceremonies. The pattern of the drumbeats

Explore this resource to learn more about West African cultures.

gave specific messages. For example, a drum rhythm could announce the arrival of the king. Today, some people call the Asante drumbeats "talking drums."

Consider the Essential Question:

In what ways were the cultural traditions of Native Americans, Europeans, and West Africans alike and different?

Go online to complete the Social Studies Explanation.

Check for Understanding:

Select one Native American culture. How did this group's ability to adapt to and modify the environment contribute to its growth and development?

Discovery EDUCATION | SOCIAL STUDIES TECHBOOK

How did interaction among European, African, and Native American cultures shape early American history?

yeq̃tla ti tetzavitl yn mal ques.

photo: Getty Images

1.3 Contact and Exchange

LESSON OVERVIEW

Introduction

In this concept, you will learn how trade propelled exploration of the Americas. You will also learn how geography and methods of travel contributed to cultural exchanges among Europeans, Africans, and Native Americans.

Essential Question

How did interaction among European, African, and Native American cultures shape early American history?

Key Vocabulary
Which terms do you already know?

- [ ] Amerigo Vespucci
- [ ] Atahualpa
- [ ] Aztec Empire
- [ ] Bartolomeu Dias
- [ ] Cape of Good Hope
- [ ] caravel
- [ ] Christopher Columbus
- [ ] Columbian Exchange
- [ ] conquistador
- [ ] Dutch West India Company
- [ ] encomienda
- [ ] epidemic
- [ ] Ferdinand Magellan
- [ ] Francisco Pizarro
- [ ] Henry Hudson
- [ ] Hernando de Soto
- [ ] Hernán Cortés
- [ ] Inca Empire
- [ ] indentured servant
- [ ] Jamestown

- [ ] John Cabot
- [ ] Juan Ponce de León
- [ ] line of demarcation
- [ ] Middle Passage
- [ ] mission
- [ ] New Amsterdam
- [ ] New Spain
- [ ] Northwest Passage
- [ ] Prince Henry the Navigator
- [ ] Queen Isabella
- [ ] Roanoke
- [ ] Samuel de Champlain
- [ ] Strait of Magellan
- [ ] Tenochtitlán
- [ ] Treaty of Tordesillas
- [ ] Triangular Trade
- [ ] Vasco da Gama
- [ ] Vasco Núñez de Balboa
- [ ] Virginia Company

Lesson Objectives

By the end of this lesson, you should be able to:

- Identify key figures and exploration routes in the European exploration of North America, such as Prince Henry the Navigator, Vasco da Gama, Bartolomeu Dias, and Christopher Columbus.

- Assess the consequences of cultural exchanges among Europeans, Africans, and early Americans fostered by European exploration and colonization in the Americas.

- Explain factors and events that led to the growth of the slave trade in North America.

- Analyze religious, economic, and cultural factors that led to European colonization in North America.

ENGAGE

How were the explorers like astronauts? Visit Engage to learn more.

Essential Question

How did interaction among European, African, and Native American cultures shape early American history?

EXPLORE

Reaching the Ends of Earth

How did ocean exploration start in the 1400s and 1500s?

One of the origins of ocean exploration among European cultures was a movement known as the Renaissance. The Renaissance began in Italy, where traders brought books, news, and inventions from Asia that helped inspire new thought. The movement spread quickly across Europe. The age marked a "rebirth" of knowledge. It was a time of invention and discovery in all the arts and sciences. People of the Renaissance wanted to discover as much as they could about themselves and the world in which they lived.

Discovery EDUCATION | SOCIAL STUDIES TECHBOOK

How did interaction among European, African, and Native American cultures shape early American history?

Another event added to the Renaissance-era push to explore. The Ottoman Empire, which originated in Turkey, expanded its power by conquering much of Southeast Europe, North Africa, and the Middle East by 1453. These conquests gave the Ottomans control of all the trade routes in and through Southwest Asia and Southeast Europe, closing the routes to Western European countries. Europeans depended on trade with Asia. Asia supplied the spices needed to flavor and preserve meats. Silk was another Asian export, and much of wealthy people's clothing was silk-based. The Europeans needed an alternate route to India and China that did not cross through Ottoman territory. A sea route around Africa would enable Europeans to trade directly with India and China and to avoid sharing their profits with the Ottomans.

Prince Henry of Portugal

Into this situation came Prince Henry of Portugal, known by historians today as Henry the Navigator—even though he never joined the sailors on their voyages! Portugal is a sea-oriented nation—a small country tucked into the corner of the Iberian Peninsula, surrounded on two sides by Spain and on two sides by the Atlantic Ocean. Nearly all of Portugal is less than 80 miles from the sea. As a result, the trading and shipping industries were very important to the Portuguese.

photo: Getty Images

Prince Henry the Navigator of Portugal (1394–1460) sponsored many voyages down the western coast of Africa. Advanced sailing techniques and tools led to better navigation of the oceans.

Prince Henry was the son of the Portuguese king. Henry wanted to spread his Catholic faith and to increase his wealth through trade, but he also had an academic interest in geography. Henry became a patron, or sponsor, of explorations to find a sea route to India. These explorations led to the mapping of Africa's coast and coastal waters. This was important because navigation required sailors to rely on coastal landforms and features. Eventually, European sailors would learn new techniques and develop new tools and instruments, enabling them to sail the open ocean, away from land.

Out into the Deep

After Prince Henry's death, other wealthy leaders continued to sponsor expeditions along the Atlantic coast of Africa. By the late 1480s, the Portuguese were on the verge of a major breakthrough.

In 1487, a wealthy navigator, Bartolomeu Dias, was appointed by King John II of Portugal to find a trade route to India by going around Africa. Dias took three ships down the western coast of Africa, following the paths of Prince Henry's earlier expeditions.

In January 1488, caught in a storm, Dias sailed past the Cape of Good Hope, the southern tip of Africa, without actually seeing it. Legend has it that, due to the rough weather there, Dias originally called it "Cape of Storms." He was the first explorer to find the Indian Ocean from the west.

Ten years later, Dias accompanied Vasco da Gama on his expedition to reach India and break into the Indian Ocean trade. In 1497, their ships sailed around the Cape of Good Hope. Vasco da Gama stopped in Malindi, on the eastern coast of Kenya, to hire an African navigator who could help him reach southern India. He arrived in Calcutta, India, but the local rulers were suspicious of the Portuguese sailor. Although he returned to Portugal in 1499 with ships loaded with spices, da Gama was unable to negotiate a trade contract with India.

Tools of Travel

What technical innovations led to an increase in exploration?

Normally, you can use landmarks to tell how far you have traveled and where you are, but at sea there are no landmarks. Even without landmarks, you can still figure out your location with a map and knowledge of your starting point, speed, direction, and time. Sailors in the Middle Ages could not know these things.

Before the 1700s, the only accurate clocks were pendulum clocks, which do not work if they are moving.

Because both the sun and the water move, sailors at sea could not tell how fast they were traveling, in what direction, or how much time had passed.

Until the oceans had been crossed, how could they be mapped?

Maps

Portolan charts were first developed in the 1200s in Italy and Spain. These were navigational maps based on sea captains' descriptions of their voyages. Early portolan charts focused on coastlines, but later ones included the four cardinal directions—north, south, east, and west. Some portolan charts estimated distances.

Europeans did not learn cartography, the science of mapmaking, until the Renaissance. Mapping had been developed over hundreds of years by Moorish scholars. The Moors built on earlier work from Greece, India, and China.

One of the first effective world maps to put all of this knowledge together was produced in 1527 by Diogo Ribeiro. This was the first map to show the correct size of the Pacific Ocean and the entire Atlantic coastline of North and South America.

Discovery SOCIAL STUDIES
EDUCATION | **TECHBOOK**

How did interaction among European, African, and Native American cultures shape early American history?

Direction

Sailors today still use the compass for navigation. A compass consists of a magnetic needle that always points north and floats over a disc marked with the four cardinal directions. The device allows sailors to see what direction they are going, even in the dark or fog. Europeans and Chinese developed the compass in the 1100s. By the 1400s, people figured out that compasses do not point to true north, but instead to magnetic north.

Latitude

Sailors used the astrolabe to determine a ship's latitude, or north–south position on the globe, by measuring the altitude of the sun or a nighttime star. Used with a map of the sky, sailors could then determine where they were on Earth, even while floating in the ocean. The ideas behind the astrolabe came from ancient Greece, but the actual tool was developed by Muslims in the middle of the 700s. The Moors introduced the astrolabe to Christian monks around the early 1100s. Although the astrolabe was hard to use on choppy water, it was widely used until the 1600s, when it was replaced by the more accurate sextant. Many astrolabes were made of brass and were very intricate and beautiful.

Longitude

The key to navigating the open seas was determining longitude, or east–west position. Without an accurate clock, the key to determining longitude was finding the precise physical distance between your current location and a fixed location. The Greek astronomer Claudius Ptolemy (c. 90–168 CE) imagined an instrument to do this based on star positions. Starting from Ptolemy's idea, Muslim astronomers invented this instrument, the quadrant, before 1200. The quadrant depended on precise data of star positions. Even though Muslims had also improved astronomical measurement, the quadrant could misjudge locations by hundreds of miles. Still, this was accurate enough for an ambitious and courageous adventurer.

Boats

The Portuguese also adopted a new type of ship for expeditions, the caravel. The caravel had a large keel and three masts with triangular lateen sails.

photo: Getty Images

These sailors are shown using an astrolabe, which measures the height above the horizon of the sun, and a cross staff, which determines the height above the horizon of other astronomical objects.

Other sailing ships at the time had large square sails, which were only useful if you wanted to go in the approximate direction the wind was blowing. Due to its shape, the lateen sail can adapt more quickly to changing wind speed and direction. As long as there was wind in any direction, the caravel was faster than other ships at the time. It was also stable in rough water.

Finding the Americas

How did European explorers find the Americas?

While Portugal was one of the leading countries in exploration, other European powers wanted to establish their own routes to India. The Queen of Spain, Isabella I, agreed to sponsor the expedition of Italian explorer Christopher Columbus. Columbus was convinced there was a quicker way to reach India than by sailing all the way around Africa and across the Indian Ocean. Instead, he intended to go southwest across the Atlantic. No one had ever done this before.

photo: Library of Congress

Columbus leaving for his westward voyage to India. Queen Isabella of Spain funded his voyages.

Columbus obtained three Spanish ships and set sail in the summer of 1492. He reached the Bahamas and believed they were the islands of Japan. But Columbus had actually landed in the region that came to be called the New World. Two weeks after originally spotting land, Columbus reached Cuba. However, he did not find the cities of gold he was looking for, only tribes of local people, whom he called "Indians" because he thought he was in or near India. Queen Isabella was very impressed with Columbus, even though he did not return to Spain with ships of gold as he had promised. When he returned to Spain in 1493, Isabella named him Admiral of the Ocean Sea and appointed him governor of the settlements in the West Indies.

Columbus made three more journeys to the West Indies. He sailed to the islands of Hispaniola (today occupied by Haiti and the Dominican Republic) and Trinidad. He also was shipwrecked for a year on Jamaica and even reached Panama. He established Spanish settlements and continued an unsuccessful search for gold by enslaving Native Americans and forcing them to work.

While exploring the Orinoco River in present-day Venezuela, Columbus unknowingly became the first European to set foot in South America. However, he never found his way across the Isthmus of Panama, the narrow strip of land that separates the Atlantic Ocean and the Pacific Ocean. It would not be until 1513 that Vasco Núñez de Balboa crossed the isthmus and reached the Pacific.

Discovery EDUCATION | SOCIAL STUDIES TECHBOOK

How did interaction among European, African, and Native American cultures shape early American history?

The Legend of the Northwest Passage

England also joined the European race to find a trade route through the western sea. Under King Henry VII, a ship captained by explorer John Cabot searched for a northwest passage to India.

John Cabot, or Giovanni Caboto, was an Italian merchant and navigator. He had been a trader in the Mediterranean region and wanted to find a route to India that did not involve competing for business with Arab traders from the Ottoman Empire. After he heard of Columbus's success at reaching the New World, Cabot asked the English monarch to sponsor his proposed exploration. Even though King Henry had previously turned down Columbus, Cabot convinced him there must be a shorter passage across the Atlantic Ocean by a more northern route.

In May 1497, Cabot sailed one ship, the *Matthew*, with a small crew. They headed east across the North Atlantic and landed on the coast of North America near Labrador, about 800 miles from Greenland, in what is modern-day northern Canada. Cabot was the first European since the Vikings to set foot on the mainland of North America. He claimed the land for England.

The Americas and Beyond

What early expeditions explored the Americas?

Columbus and Cabot both thought they had reached India. However, later explorers were convinced it was not India, but a new land.

Amerigo Vespucci

In 1497, the king of Spain gave Amerigo Vespucci, an Italian merchant, permission to explore the western Atlantic. Vespucci sailed south along the eastern coast of South America in 1499 and again in 1502.

On his second voyage, Vespucci realized that the shoreline was not India, but an unexplored land. It was this insight that landed his name—"America," after Amerigo—on a map. Later, a large landmass was found north of the Caribbean, and the two continents were named North and South America. Vespucci never visited the land that became the United States of America.

Ponce de León

Juan Ponce de León explored islands in the Caribbean looking for gold. In 1513, he sailed north and found the mainland of North America, landing on the east coast of Florida, where he named present-day Cape Canaveral. Believing the legends told by the natives of Puerto Rico, Ponce de León searched for a "fountain of youth," a magical spring that would reverse the aging process. He sailed through the Florida Keys and into the Gulf of Mexico, but avoided going inland due to conflicts with the native people of the area.

In 1521, de León attempted to establish a colony on the gulf side of Florida. The colony was soon attacked, and Ponce de León was shot in the leg with an arrow. The colony was abandoned, and the explorer soon died of his wounds.

Hernando de Soto

In 1539, King Charles I of Spain sent Hernando de Soto to colonize, or establish a settlement in, Florida. De Soto made headway into the peninsula's dense forest in search of gold. Unlike de León, de Soto attempted to befriend the natives. He learned that if he found one friendly local, he could use that person as a messenger to the next tribe, and so make his way inland.

De Soto and his men traveled north through present-day Georgia to the Appalachian Mountains in the Carolinas and through Tennessee, Alabama, and Mississippi. In May 1541, they crossed the Mississippi River and moved through Louisiana, eastern Texas, Oklahoma, and Arkansas. However, de Soto found no gold and died of a fever in 1542. His crew then came under heavy attack by native people and only half the expedition survived.

Ferdinand Magellan

While Hernando de Soto searched fruitlessly for gold, the coastal European powers—Portugal, Spain, England, and the Netherlands—were still focused on finding a shortcut to Asia. The Portuguese had reached India by sailing around the Cape of Good Hope of Africa, and they had crossed the Atlantic and established claims in Brazil. The Spanish felt more pressure than ever to find a western route to Asia. King Charles V of Spain supported Ferdinand Magellan's expedition to find a western route to Asia. In November 1520, Magellan reached an inlet at Cabo Virgenes, at the tip of what is now Argentina.

Explorer	Sponsoring Country	Achievement (Year)
Prince Henry of Portugal	Portugal	Sponsored explorations of Atlantic coast of Africa (d. 1460)
Bartolomeu Dias	Portugal	Rounded Cape of Good Hope (1488)
Christopher Columbus	Spain	Crossed Atlantic to reach "New World" (1492)
Amerigo Vespucci	Spain, Portugal	Sailed to South America (1501)
John Cabot	England	Explored the eastern shores of Canada (1497)
Vasco da Gama	Portugal	First to travel to West Indies around Africa (1498)
Vasco Núñez de Balboa	Spanish	Led expedition across Panama to the Pacific Ocean (1513)
Juan Ponce de León	Spanish	Explored Florida (1513)
Ferdinand Magellan	Spain, Portugal	Found southwest passage and circled the globe (1519–1521)
Hernando de Soto	Spain	Explored and mapped American Southeast (1539)
Henry Hudson	England, Netherlands	Explored Hudson Bay, Hudson River, and Hudson Strait (1607–1611)

This chart showcases the explorers, their sponsoring countries, and their achievements.

It took more than a month for Magellan and his crew to travel from that inlet and through the 373-mile channel, now known as the Strait of Magellan, to reach the ocean west of South America. Magellan named the ocean the Pacific because of its calm, peaceful waters.

DISCOVERY | SOCIAL STUDIES
EDUCATION | **TECHBOOK**

How did interaction among European, African, and Native American cultures shape early American history?

Magellan continued west across the vast Pacific Ocean, but he was killed in a battle with native people soon after reaching the Philippines in February 1521. Members of Magellan's crew took over the fleet and continued west through Indonesia, across the Indian Ocean, around the Cape of Good Hope, and north to Spain. The survivors had completed Magellan's voyage, the first complete voyage around the world by sea.

Henry Hudson and the Northwest Passage

How did the English get more involved in exploration of the "New World"?

Nearly 100 years after John Cabot looked for a northern route to Asia, England funded another expedition to continue the search. Because the English did not want conflicts with Spain and Portugal in the southern parts of the North American continent, they focused on exploring northern options. In 1607, Henry Hudson sailed west on behalf of the English, hoping to find the "Northwest Passage." He believed the ice of the northern seas would melt during the summer, allowing

photo: Library of Congress
The arrival of Henry Hudson in the Bay of New York, 1609.

him to cross to the north of the American continent and reach Asia through a northwest passage. Hudson had the experience and maps of previous northern explorers, but ice and winds made him turn around. When a second attempt also failed, the English abandoned the project.

To find a new source of funding, Hudson turned to England's competitors, the Dutch. The Dutch East India Company agreed. On his third voyage, Hudson set a course south along the North American coast. Upon discovering New York Bay, Hudson followed a wide river—we now call it the Hudson River—which he hoped would lead to the Pacific Ocean. However, when the river became narrow and shallow and turned to freshwater, Hudson turned around once more. On the way downstream, he explored the shores and traded with the Algonquin Indians.

Explore this interactive to learn more about explorers and the land they encountered.

Now it was the Dutch who refused to fund another voyage, but Hudson managed to convince England to support one more expedition. His fourth and last voyage led to the discovery of Hudson Bay in 1610. When winter came, his ship became trapped in ice, and the expedition was stranded on the shore of the bay until the spring thaw. When spring came, Hudson wanted to explore further, but his crew were fed up. They set Hudson and some supporters adrift in a boat in the bay and sailed his ship back to England. He was never seen again.

The difficult travels of explorers such as Hudson helped set the stage for European settlement of North and South America. With Hudson's mapping of the eastern and northern reaches of North America, a clear map emerged of the continent. Ten years after Hudson's last voyage, a ship of Dutch and English settlers, the *Mayflower*, landed in New England.

Conquering the American Empires

How did the Spanish take control of land in the Americas?

Spanish conquistadores—Spanish for "conquerors"—followed the explorers across the Atlantic Ocean in search of gold in the New World. Catholic priests accompanied them, hoping to convert Native Americans to Christianity.

Although they were greatly outnumbered by the Native Americans, the Spanish were able to conquer the large Aztec Empire in Mexico and the Inca Empire in South America. There were three main factors that helped the Spanish. First, they had superior weapons—swords made of steel, crossbows, and guns—as well as horses and armor. Second, the Spanish joined forces with local peoples who resented the rule of the Aztec and the Inca Empires. The third factor was something the Spanish could not have predicted: disease.

Because Europeans and Americans had lived in isolation from each other, they had experienced different diseases and developed different natural immunities. However, even people who did not suffer from a disease could carry the germs for it in their bodies. When Europeans and Americans met each other, they exchanged germs. For example, Native Americans had never come across smallpox and had no natural defense against it. After meeting the Europeans who carried the germs, smallpox killed massive numbers of Native Americans and weakened their empires. On the other hand, the Europeans were extremely fortunate that they did not die from American diseases.

Cortés and the Aztec

In 1519, Hernán Cortés came to the land now known as Mexico, following rumors of gold. As Cortés marched up the Mexican Gulf Coast, local people told him of a great empire with large quantities of gold. Cortés claimed the area as New Spain, and he and his conquistadores marched inland to Tenochtitlán, the capital of the Aztec Empire. As they traveled, Cortés received messages from the Aztec king, Montezuma II, both warning him to stay out of Tenochtitlán and offering him payments if he would go away.

photo: Getty Images

A portrait of Hernán Cortés (1484–1547).

DISCOVERY SOCIAL STUDIES
EDUCATION **TECHBOOK**

How did interaction among European, African, and Native American cultures shape early American history?

Cortés ignored the warnings. He spent nearly two years plundering the Aztec Empire while the Aztec resisted his rule. In 1521, Cortés and his conquistadores destroyed Tenochtitlán and built on its ruins a capital for New Spain, which they called Mexico City.

Pizarro and the Inca

Francisco Pizarro had been a part of Balboa's expedition in 1513 that crossed the Isthmus of Panama to the Pacific Ocean. While on this expedition, he heard rumors of an empire to the south that had many riches. In the 1520s, he took two expeditions south that led him closer to the Inca Empire, centered in what is now Peru. These expeditions provided him with proof of the Inca riches, such as turquoise jewelry and sculptures and vases of solid gold.

In 1530, Pizarro set out from Panama to attempt his conquest of the Inca. Taking advantage of chaos caused by a civil war, Pizarro moved closer to the heart of the empire. When the conquistadores met up with the Incan emperor Atahualpa, they opened fire, killing thousands of unarmed men and capturing Atahualpa. The Incan emperor tried to buy his freedom by offering vast amounts of gold and silver, but Pizarro had his conquistadores kill Atahualpa anyway.

While Pizarro's conquistadores clashed with Atahualpa, smallpox took its own victims. Estimates suggest that smallpox killed millions of Inca. Pizarro was able to seize control of the capital and the entire Inca Empire. However, resistance to Spanish rule continued for another 39 years.

Native American and European Interactions

How did the Europeans and the conquered Native Americans treat each other?

The Spanish had two main reasons for enlarging the Spanish Empire: to convert people to their Roman Catholic religion and to gain riches. They pursued these two goals in very different ways.

Missions

Missionaries are people who work to spread their religion to other people. A mission is a building or group of buildings used as a base for missionary work. Catholic priests founded missions throughout what is known today as the Southwest United States.

photo: Library of Congress
The Mission San Juan Capistrano was dedicated in October 1776 by Father Serra.

The Spanish missions generally included a church, living quarters, workrooms, and storerooms, all within a walled enclosure. The first Spanish mission was in present-day Tucson, Arizona. Many missions from the 1500s and 1600s are still standing, including Mission San Juan Capistrano in California. The Alamo in San Antonio, Texas, was also a mission chapel.

The missions became the economic and religious hubs of Spanish activities. Native Americans who had converted to Christianity came to live at the missions, working in exchange for food and shelter. The priests worked hard to replace Native American culture with Spanish culture, forcing converts to speak only Spanish and to abandon their traditional clothing.

Encomiendas

The Spanish intended their colonies to be sources of wealth, and they needed workers to extract that wealth by growing valuable crops and mining gold. They developed a system, known as the encomienda, to organize this labor. An encomienda was a grant by the Spanish monarch of a right to control Native American labor. In return for these grants, the encomendero—the person who controlled the labor—was supposed to care for and protect the Native Americans under his control.

In practice, encomenderos did not protect Native Americans. Instead, the Native Americans often lost their land, became enslaved, and suffered in terrible working conditions. The encomienda system faded as Native Americans died from disease and overwork.

However, some Native American–European relationships were more positive. Native Americans taught Europeans how to grow crops in the Americas and what plants and animals were good sources of food. Europeans brought these new ideas and products back to Europe with them. The early fur trade is another example of a positive relationship between Europeans and Native Americans. The fur trade opened up many channels for trading and gave Native Americans opportunities to gain resources from Europe.

The Columbian Exchange

How did the Columbian Exchange affect life for Europeans, Africans, and Indians?

As Europeans began coming to the Americas, they brought more than just people and ships across the Atlantic Ocean. Before Columbus's voyage, different plants, animals, and diseases had developed independently in the Eastern and Western Hemisphere. After 1492, various plants, animals, and diseases began to cross the Atlantic from one hemisphere to the other. This movement is called the Columbian Exchange.

Without the Colombian Exchange, there would be none of the following:

- Italian spaghetti with tomato sauce—because tomatoes were not known in Europe
- cowboys in Texas—because horses did not exist in the Americas
- Florida oranges—because orange trees were not native to the Americas

The Europeans introduced domesticated animals, such as sheep, horses, and cattle, to the Americas. Farmers in the Americas learned to use oxen and horses to plow fields, increasing farm productivity and the food supply. Horses quickly became a key part of Native American culture and livelihood in the Southwest and Plains of the United States.

Despite the positive aspects of the Columbian Exchange, some of the exchange was disastrous for Native Americans. Diseases such as smallpox from the Old World devastated Native Americans, who had no natural resistance to the illnesses. Often, messengers, lookouts, or animals transferred disease, and a community could be laid to waste before a European settler ever showed up in person.

The Columbian Exchange radically changed the world by mixing together once-sheltered ecosystems, crops, animals, and diseases.

Competing for Land: Spain and Portugal

How did Spain and Portugal divide the "New World" that they found?

Near the end of the 1400s, a great race began among the European countries to explore and claim lands around the world. In the Americas, Portugal and Spain were the first great rivals, but England, France, and Holland were not far behind. Each of these countries hoped to gain power and wealth as a result of its explorations.

Spain and Portugal

Spain and Portugal fought over their claims for several reasons. Neither had good maps of the new lands, which were unexplored by Europeans and uncharted. Explorers would claim large areas of land they had never seen, not knowing how far the land extended, what it was like, or who already lived there. Kings and popes, who also had no maps, granted dominion over lands and did not feel bound by prior decisions.

Spain and Portugal peacefully settled their conflicting claims in 1494 by the Treaty of Tordesillas, although disputes continued for many years. The treaty established a line of demarcation, running from north to south through what is now eastern Brazil and dividing the "New World" into Spanish and Portuguese sections. The Spanish, who had explored farther west than the Portuguese, were granted lands to the west of the treaty line. The only continental land granted to Portugal was a small part of Brazil. Today, Brazil is the only country in South or Central America that speaks Portuguese rather than Spanish.

Competing for Land: Holland and England

*How did Holland and England divide the "New World"
that they found?*

Over time, Spanish power gave way to the increasing importance of England and Holland. In order to fund the expensive and risky exploration of the world, these rising governments partnered with joint stock companies. Wealthy individuals formed joint stock companies to combine their resources and share both the risk and the profits from exploration. Companies such as the Dutch East India Company and the (English) East India Company were examples of these public–private partnerships.

Holland

In the early 1600s, the Dutch were becoming wealthy. They sold fish, wool products, tulips, and manufactured goods, including furniture. Dutch towns and banks became financial centers for world trade.

The Dutch also established colonies. In 1602, the Dutch East India Company began establishing colonies in the islands that are today Indonesia and New Guinea. They profited greatly from trade in spices. In the Americas, the Dutch West India Company began establishing colonies in the Caribbean and Brazil after 1620. As a result of Henry Hudson's explorations, it also established the colony of New Amsterdam on the Island of Manhattan.

England

In England, Queen Elizabeth supported English traders and shippers with subsidies and tariffs and by expanding the navy. A subsidy is a grant or payment offered to make a cost more affordable. A tariff is a tax on goods traded with another country. English manufacturers also aided in economic growth by increasing production and exports of wool and cloth. By 1600, the success of these policies made overseas colonization possible.

photo: Getty Images
Colonists built Jamestown as a fort, protecting it with a large fence.

In 1607, England granted a royal charter to the Virginia Company to establish the English colony of Jamestown in Virginia. The English throne claimed any land explored by the Virginia Company, and the company had to pay taxes on goods it bought from England. However, the Virginia Company was entitled to keep any resources it could extract. Gold was the most sought-after resource that the Virginia Company expected to find in and around Jamestown.

Discovery SOCIAL STUDIES
EDUCATION | **TECHBOOK**.

How did interaction among European, African, and Native American cultures shape early American history?

Most of those who emigrated to colonize Jamestown were farmers, peasants, and middle-class people seeking economic opportunity. The strong European class system limited their economic mobility and their opportunities. In the "New World," colonists had more control over their fates.

Explore this resource to learn more about reasons for European colonization.

Despite their hopes, colonists failed to find gold in Jamestown, but those who worked hard did find economic opportunity. Unlike Roanoke, the first English colony, the Jamestown colony managed to survive. It was the first permanent English settlement in North America. Jamestown colonists established farms and merchant communities that shaped both relations with Native Americans and the subsequent development of British North America.

The Beginning of the Slave Trade

How did European colonists meet the need for labor?

Europeans were amazed by the wealth that they discovered in the Western Hemisphere. However, they needed workers to collect and produce minerals and other goods that could be sent back to Europe. Native Americans were unwilling to give up their lives in order to work for wages. Enslaving the Native Americans had not proved profitable for the Spanish, and the new diseases killed so many Native Americans that there were not sufficient numbers to do the work that the colonists wanted done.

The Portuguese created a solution to the labor shortage. They entered the African slave-trading system and helped expand it. This served as the basis for the transatlantic slave trade, which was the buying and selling of African people and transporting them across the ocean to the Americas.

The Spanish also began to purchase enslaved Africans to ship to plantations in the Americas. As the demand for products from the Americas increased, the number of enslaved individuals taken from Africa also increased. Enslaved Africans were

photo: Getty Images
Enslaved laborers were used on plantations and in mines to extract the riches of the "New World."

sent to work on the sugar cane plantations of the Caribbean and Brazil and in the gold mines of Mexico and the Andes Mountains. The wealth from the labor of enslaved Africans flowed back to Europe in the form of sugar, precious metals, and tobacco.

Slavery in the English Colonies

Slavery developed differently in the English colonies that would become the United States. When the English colonies began, indentured servants were an inexpensive source of labor. Indentured servants were poor laborers from Europe who sought a new life and work in the colonies. In exchange for a boat ticket across the Atlantic Ocean, a servant would agree to work for some number of years, often four to seven, with no pay other than room and board. At the end of some contracts, the master was required to provide land and supplies for the former servant to start his or her own small farm. However, not all masters fulfilled their end of the contract; some masters failed to give servants land and supplies for their own farms.

People were willing to work under these conditions because they could not obtain paid work in Europe, and indentured servitude was a path to a new life. Indenture benefited colonists, too. Because enslaved people in the colonies had high death rates, it did not make sense to buy an enslaved person for life. If an indentured servant did not outlive his or her indenture, there was no payout.

The first Africans to arrive in the English colony of Jamestown in the early 1600s were probably indentured servants. However, as conditions in the colonies improved, death rates dropped, the value of land rose, and it became more expensive to contract indentured servants. Colonial settlers who wanted inexpensive labor began to purchase enslaved Africans to work their plantations for life.

The Slave Trade and Triangular Trade

How did the slave trade function?

At the beginning of the slave trade, most enslaved people were prisoners from wars between neighboring African kingdoms. As the global demand for enslaved laborers grew, coastal African kingdoms began to raid villages in the African interior, with the sole purpose of capturing and enslaving people to sell to the European traders. In exchange for enslaved Africans, the European traders gave the African sellers guns and ammunition. The guns made it easier to capture and enslave more Africans, who would then be sold. Gradually, the economy of West Africa began to revolve around the slave trade.

The transatlantic slave trade was a part of a triangular trade among the Americas, Europe, and Africa. Goods and people flowed among these three regions, with each trade reinforcing the others.

Triangular Trade

Craftspeople in Europe used raw materials from around the world to create manufactured goods, such as clothing, tools, and weapons. Ships carrying these manufactured goods sailed from Europe to the coast of West Africa. The ships docked at the slave castles along the coast, where European traders exchanged these finished goods for enslaved Africans.

Discovery EDUCATION | SOCIAL STUDIES TECHBOOK

How did interaction among European, African, and Native American cultures shape early American history?

Enslaved Africans were kept in European slave castles along the coast of West Africa for weeks or months until the next ship came. Then, the people were chained, shackled, and loaded onto the ships for the journey to the Americas. This journey between Africa and the Americas was called the Middle Passage. More than 10 percent of the enslaved Africans on the Middle Passage died before reaching the Americas. This included people who were so distressed at their

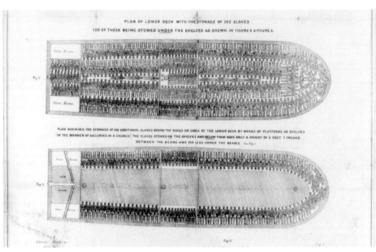

photo: Library of Congress

During the Middle Passage, enslaved people were often arranged on ships "like rows of books on a shelf." This practice resulted in the deaths of many enslaved people.

treatment that, rather than continue to live, they dove into the ocean with their hands and feet chained together. Cramped conditions on the ships meant that illnesses and death could easily sweep through a boat. Below the ship's main deck, food, water, sunlight, fresh air, and sanitation were inadequate. For example, many enslaved Africans found themselves with ceilings only 18 to 24 inches above their heads when lying down.

Most slave ships traveled to the Caribbean or Brazil, where large sugar plantations created a high demand for enslaved laborers. When the ships arrived, the people were sold at auction, like cattle. Then, the ships were loaded with raw goods, such as sugar, rum, tobacco, and furs, for the return trip to Europe.

Although many European and American countries began to ban the slave trade beginning in the early 1800s, the slave trade continued well into the 1850s.

Consider the Essential Question:

How did interaction among European, African, and Native American cultures shape early American history?

Go online to complete the Social Studies Explanation.

Check for Understanding:

Explain why the institution of slavery grew in the Americas during the 1500s and 1600s.

2.1 Three Colonial Regions

LESSON OVERVIEW

Introduction

In this concept, you will learn how each colonial region was settled. You will discover how the geography of each region influenced trade and how the colonists interacted with Native Americans. You also will discover how the cultural and religious values of the colonists influenced government and democracy in the United States.

Essential Question

How did location affect daily life in the New England, Middle, and Southern Colonies?

Key Vocabulary
Which terms do you already know?

☐ Anne Hutchinson
☐ assembly
☐ Bacon's Rebellion
☐ Boston
☐ cash crop
☐ corporate colony
☐ democracy
☐ House of Burgesses
☐ James Oglethorpe
☐ Jamestown
☐ John Winthrop
☐ King Philip's War
☐ Lenni Lenape
☐ Lord Baltimore
☐ Massachusetts Bay Colony
☐ Massasoit
☐ Mayflower Compact
☐ Metacom

☐ Pennsylvania
☐ Pequot War
☐ Peter Stuyvesant
☐ Philadelphia
☐ Pilgrim
☐ plantation
☐ Powhatan Indian Confederacy
☐ Powhatan War
☐ proprietary colony
☐ proprietor
☐ Puritan
☐ Quakers
☐ reservation
☐ Roger Williams
☐ self-government
☐ subsistence farming
☐ Thomas Hooker
☐ town meeting
☐ treaty
☐ William Penn

Discovery EDUCATION | SOCIAL STUDIES TECHBOOK

How did location affect daily life in the New England, Middle, and Southern Colonies?

Lesson Objectives

By the end of this lesson, you should be able to:

- Describe the motives and circumstances of the colonists who settled in each of the three colonial regions.

- Describe how the physical geography of the New England, Middle, and Southern Colonies influenced trade in each region.

- Assess the interactions of European settlers in each colonial region with Native Americans.

- Describe the prominent political and cultural characteristics of the New England, Middle, and Southern Colonies.

ENGAGE

How did where colonists lived affect how they lived? Visit Engage to learn more.

Essential Question

How did location affect daily life in the New England, Middle, and Southern Colonies?

EXPLORE

New England Colonies: Settlement

How were the New England Colonies established?

In the 1600s and 1700s, a new religious group, the Puritans, was developing a large following in England. They called themselves Puritans because they wanted to purify the Church of England, which they thought was corrupted by the practices of the Roman Catholic Church. One group of Puritans was the Pilgrims. The Pilgrims believed they could not fix the problems within England. First, they moved to the Netherlands, but eventually, they looked for a new home on a new continent. In September 1620, they set sail for North America on a ship called the *Mayflower*, hoping to create a new society where they could practice their Puritan beliefs.

After crossing the Atlantic Ocean and getting blown far off course, the Pilgrims sailed around Cape Cod and found a protected inlet. They settled in a place they named Plymouth and established the Plymouth Bay Colony. Many more Puritans followed. In 1630, English colonists established the Massachusetts Bay Colony. The governor of the colony, John Winthrop, declared that the new colony would be a "city upon a hill" that would provide a model of devout Christian life for the rest of the world. Salem and Boston became two of the largest Massachusetts Bay Colony settlements.

Because the settlers were English, they named the area New England. New England includes the areas that eventually became the states of Maine, New Hampshire, Vermont, Massachusetts, Connecticut, and Rhode Island. Plymouth and Massachusetts Bay were the first permanent colonies founded in New England. Although the Puritans came to New England to practice their religion freely, they were not tolerant of different religious practices inside their communities. The Puritan church established strict rules of behavior, and all colonists had to follow them. People who did not were punished. They could be put into the stocks, branded like cattle, banished, or even killed!

Connecticut

The name Connecticut is taken from the Algonquian word *Quinnetukut*, meaning "at the long tidal river." The colony of Connecticut formed around the Connecticut River, which today forms the Vermont–New Hampshire border. In the early 1630s, English colonists began to establish small farms and trading posts near this river and its tributaries. Thomas Hooker was one of many colonists who settled in Connecticut. Like many others, he disagreed with the strict religious policies of Massachusetts. In 1636, Hooker, Reverend Samuel Stone, and several followers moved to the new town of Hartford to escape the rigid rules of the church in Massachusetts.

Rhode Island

Roger Williams, the founder of Rhode Island, had a long history of disagreeing with religious and political authority. Williams was a Puritan chaplain who first came to Boston, Massachusetts, in 1631. He refused to serve as a pastor in Boston because the established church had ties to the Church of England. Furthermore, Williams challenged the Massachusetts colonial charter because he thought it treated Native Americans unfairly and because it established a single faith for the colony. In 1635, Williams was banished from Massachusetts. He fled south to Narragansett Bay, where he befriended Native Americans and purchased land from them. There, he founded the Colony of Rhode Island and Providence Plantations.

Williams saw the new colony as a haven for people who were persecuted for practicing their religions. The other colonies considered them to be heretics, a negative term used to describe people who do not practice the accepted religion. Anne Hutchinson sought shelter in Rhode Island when the Puritans banished her from Massachusetts because of her views on religion and the treatment of women. She believed religious faith was a matter of belief and conscience rather than one of obedience to a minister.

Discovery EDUCATION | SOCIAL STUDIES TECHBOOK

How did location affect daily life in the New England, Middle, and Southern Colonies?

She questioned the Puritan doctrine that people earned salvation by performing good deeds. She continued to teach and lead religious meetings, even though Puritan leaders insisted women must be silent in public. About 70 people followed Hutchinson to Rhode Island, where they founded the community of Portsmouth, Rhode Island.

New Hampshire and Maine

Colonists looking to escape religious persecution settled many of the New England Colonies. However, the colonists who settled New Hampshire and Maine were looking to make a profit. In 1622, the king granted John Mason, former governor of Newfoundland, the land between the Merrimack and Piscataqua Rivers. Mason had spent time hunting pirates in the coastal waters off Newfoundland and Nova Scotia. He was interested in settling a colony to make his fortune. At the mouth of the Piscataqua, Mason founded the town that eventually became Portsmouth, New Hampshire. The first English settler in Mason's New Hampshire colony, a man named David Thompson, arrived in 1623. He worked as a fur trader and fisher.

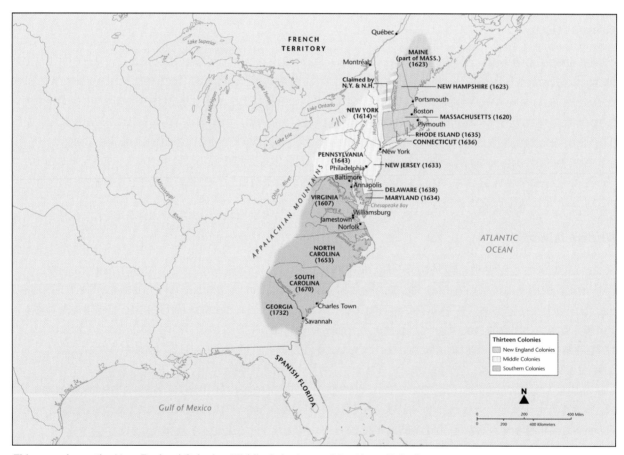

This map shows the New England Colonies, Middle Colonies, and Southern Colonies.

Another immigrant looking for his fortune was Sir Ferdinando Gorges. He was given the land east of the Piscataqua River, extending to the Kennebec River. Gorges was a financier who, like Mason, was interested in operating a colony as a profit-making enterprise. Gorges's colony was incorporated into Massachusetts in 1652—so the colony of New Hampshire was sandwiched between two parts of Massachusetts.

In 1820, the territory east of the Piscataqua River seceded from Massachusetts and became the state of Maine.

New England Colonies: Geography and Trade

How did the geography of the New England Colonies affect how people lived?

New England was not a paradise. The region had long, harsh winters, and the growing season was short. Much of the land was covered with thick forests, which made the land difficult to clear for farming. However, the forests provided fruits and nuts as well as timber for building houses, ships, and tools. Forests also had animals that colonists could hunt and trap.

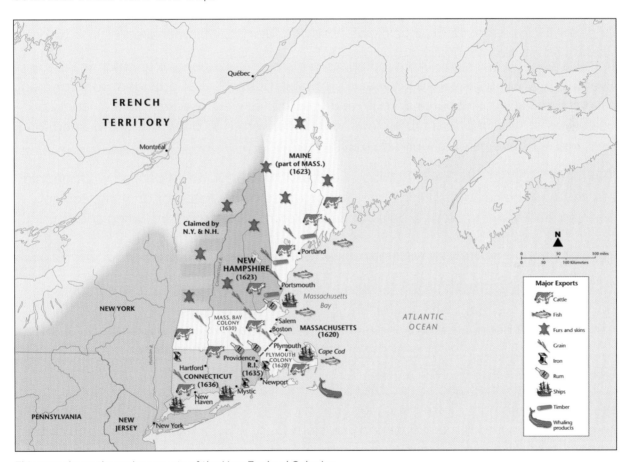

This map shows the major exports of the New England Colonies.

Farming remained difficult after settlers cut down the forests. The soil was thin and rocky. Farmers dug so many stones out of their fields that they could build walls around their property with them. These stone walls can still be found today in rural parts of New England. They are part of what makes New England a unique cultural region, an area that is distinctive because of shared characteristics.

Discovery SOCIAL STUDIES
EDUCATION | TECHBOOK

How did location affect daily life in the New England, Middle, and Southern Colonies?

Large plantations were not practical in New England because of the hills, boulders, and streams. In addition, the climate was not warm and humid enough to sustain a large plantation. Most colonists in New England were subsistence farmers. They farmed to feed themselves and stay alive.

Life by the Sea

The coasts of Massachusetts, New Hampshire, and Maine lie on the Gulf of Maine, an area of the Atlantic Ocean extending north from Cape Cod to Nova Scotia. A gulf is a large bay. East of Cape Cod is Georges Bank, a shallow area that is extremely attractive to fish. Massachusetts has a large, sheltered bay and deepwater harbors. This enabled colonists to develop a thriving ocean-based economy. Fishing, shipbuilding, and whaling made the colony prosperous. A giant wooden codfish has been hanging in the Massachusetts House of Representatives meeting chamber since 1747. This "Sacred Cod" symbolizes the importance of the fishing industry to Massachusetts.

In the late 1600s and early 1700s, colonists in Massachusetts began to catch whales. Eventually, whaling became a large and profitable business that provided work for many sailors. Whales were a source of food, and their bones were used to make a variety of useful items. Most important, their fat could be converted to oil, which was burned for heat and light and used to lubricate machines.

The marshes, inlets, and swift-flowing streams of New England influenced what people ate and how they made a living. The rivers provided clean water for drinking, cooking, washing, and growing crops. Bodies of water also provided food, including shellfish, ocean fish, and freshwater fish. Colonists also could hunt waterfowl, such as ducks and geese. Colonists used reeds from the water to make thatched roofs.

The coast of New England had many bays, or areas where the land curves around a portion of the sea. Bays were important to the colonists because they provided calm harbors for anchoring, loading, and unloading ships. Many of the region's population centers emerged on bays or near the mouths of rivers to support water-based economic activities, such as fishing, shipbuilding, and whaling. New England's rocky soil made much of its land unsuitable for development. As a result, New England settlements commonly were bunched together. They often had higher populations than colonial settlements in the Middle and Southern Colonies. For example, the large colonial city of Boston, established in 1630, is located only 50 miles from the colonial city of Derryfield (now Manchester, New Hampshire), which was established in the early 1700s.

New England Colonies: Native American Interactions
How did the colonists in the New England Colonies interact with Native Americans?

The colonial settlements in New England owed some of their success to the help of Native Americans. Native American groups knew the best regions for hunting and fishing. They also had perfected strategies for cultivating corn and other crops.

At first, Native Americans were friendly with the settlers. They allowed the settlers to establish settlements on their territory and shared their knowledge of farming and of native plants and animals in the region. The settlers in Plymouth quickly allied with Massasoit, leader of the local Wampanoag Native Americans. Trade with Native Americans flourished because it helped both groups. The colonial population grew, and new settlers continued to come from England.

Over time, relations became tense. As the colonial settlements grew, they began claiming more and more land belonging to Native Americans. Native Americans objected, but the colonists had guns. Minor conflicts were common, and as more colonists came, major conflicts arose. Two conflicts that permanently changed relations between colonists and Native Americans were the Pequot War and King Philip's War.

The Pequot War

In the 1630s, English colonists and the Pequot people in western Massachusetts fought what is known as the Pequot War. When Massachusetts colonists began expanding into the Connecticut River Valley, there was already conflict in the area. Several Native American clans and nations were in competition for control of the fur trade. The competition led to violence. In a 1634 conflict, members of the Niantic Pequot nation killed an English colonist named John Stone. The English demanded justice, but the English and Pequot failed to agree on a truce.

photo: Getty Images

Roger Williams's friendship with the Narragansetts of Rhode Island had a powerful impact on the history of New England.

In 1637, English colonists John Mason and John Underhill led an attack on a Pequot village in Mystic, Connecticut. The colonists burned the village to the ground, killing nearly every villager, including women and children. Historians are unsure what motivated the colonists to destroy the village. It may have been greed for land or retaliation for the death of Stone. The Pequots' enemies also may have lied to the colonists to provoke the attack.

The Pequots struck back by attacking English settlements along the Connecticut River. However, the Pequots already were very weak. A terrible smallpox epidemic in the previous year wiped out much of their population, and they suffered losses during a conflict with the Dutch in New York. In addition, the Pequots made enemies with two neighboring Native American nations: the Mohegans and Narragansetts. These groups took the side of the English. In the end, the Pequot War nearly wiped out the Pequot people, eliminating them as a threat to the colonists.

Discovery EDUCATION | SOCIAL STUDIES TECHBOOK

How did location affect daily life in the New England, Middle, and Southern Colonies?

King Philip's War

The Pequot War was small in scale compared with King Philip's War, which took place between 1675 and 1676. As trade between Native Americans and colonists grew, Native Americans became dependent on English goods. Colonists used this dependence to force or trick Native Americans into giving up more land. Over time, negotiations became more tense and hostile. In 1675, a Wampanoag man was killed because he had betrayed his people by helping the English. In retaliation, the English captured and killed three Wampanoag. These events led to King Philip's War, fought between the colonists and the Wampanoag, whose chief, Metacom, also was known as King Philip. Metacom was the son of Massasoit, the Native American leader who had helped the first settlers at Plymouth. Unlike his father, Metacom saw the English settlers as a threat to the Wampanoag and other Native Americans in the region.

The war did not have formal battles between soldiers, but rather was a series of raids by each group on the other group's forts and villages. The raids targeted soldiers as well as civilians. Many colonists and natives were killed working in their fields or sleeping in their beds. One reason the war intensified was that Metacom was able to unite his people with the Narragansett and most of the other neighboring Native American nations in New England. All of these groups had complaints against the English settlers. At first, Native American warriors were so successful that the colonists initiated a military draft to defend themselves. A military draft is a system for selecting and compelling people to serve in the armed forces.

The tide turned in the spring of 1676, when the colonists destroyed Native American corn fields. Because of this destruction, Native Americans not only were killed on the battlefield but also died of disease and starvation. King Philip's War ended after Metacom was shot and killed. Colonists cut off his head, mounted it on a pole, and carried it to Plymouth, where it was put on display for 25 years.

King Philip's War was a disaster for both sides. Overall, about 3,000 Native Americans and 600 Europeans were killed. Native Americans in the area were nearly wiped out. On the colonists' side, more than 50 colonial towns had been attacked, and 13 of those were completely destroyed. Any friendship between colonists and Native Americans was destroyed as well.

New England Colonies: Government and Democracy
What democratic practices were formed in colonial New England?

The New England colonists had to determine how to govern the colonies in a way that promoted peace and prosperity. New England's location affected its politics because it was so far from England. As a result, it was hard for the king to govern the colonies, so New England could create its own institutions. The democratic practices that grew in New England would lay the groundwork for later state and national governments.

photo: Getty Images

The Mayflower Compact was an important first step the Pilgrims took toward self-government.

The colonists began planning their government while still on the *Mayflower*. When the passengers on the *Mayflower* found that they had gone off course and arrived in Massachusetts, they realized they had a problem. Their English charter, or land grant, was for a settlement in Virginia. In Massachusetts, their charter was meaningless. The 41 Puritan adult males on the ship decided to draft a contract of their own. They established a government that was under the rule of the English king. Because they signed the document while still on the ship, it became known as the Mayflower Compact. The term *compact* means "contract or bargain." The signers of the Mayflower Compact promised one another that they would obey whatever laws the community established.

Democratic Practices

Although the people of the New England Colonies were legally bound to obey the king, the king and other leaders in England provided only loose oversight of the colonial governments. The settlers would need to make arrangements to govern

Explore this resource to consider differing viewpoints of colonial New England residents.

themselves. Most New England communities held town meetings. Participants in town meetings made decisions and rules concerning the business of the town. They elected government officials, made local laws, set taxes, and spent money on schools, public improvements, and law enforcement. Anyone at the meeting could speak to bring up problems and propose solutions. However, the only colonists who could vote or have any say in town meeting decisions were white men who owned property and were respected members in good standing of the town church.

Another early example of democratic practices was the writing of a constitution. Britain had no written constitution. Instead, Britain had a large body of treaties, laws, legal decisions, and traditions. Leaders of Connecticut drafted the Fundamental Orders, which some historians consider to be the first constitution written in America. The Framers eventually used the document as a model for the United States Constitution, which is why Connecticut is called the Constitution State. The Fundamental Orders defines the terms and oaths of government office and describes the processes for running town meetings and elections. The settlers of Connecticut rejected a religious requirement for voting. They believed the right to vote should not be limited to Puritan men.

Discovery | SOCIAL STUDIES
EDUCATION | TECHBOOK

How did location affect daily life in the New England, Middle, and Southern Colonies?

South of New England, a more diverse group of colonies had been established. The mix of nationalities and religions in the Middle Colonies would lead to communities and policies much different from the ones Puritans established in New England.

Middle Colonies: Settlement

What were the important politics and religions of the settlers of the Middle Colonies?

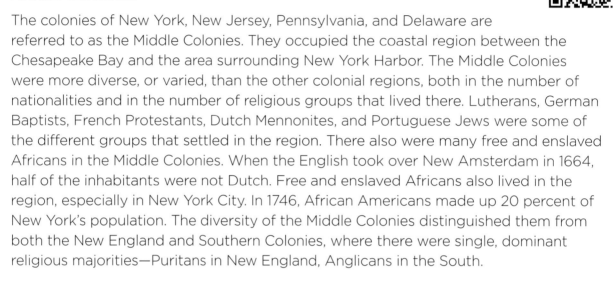

The colonies of New York, New Jersey, Pennsylvania, and Delaware are referred to as the Middle Colonies. They occupied the coastal region between the Chesapeake Bay and the area surrounding New York Harbor. The Middle Colonies were more diverse, or varied, than the other colonial regions, both in the number of nationalities and in the number of religious groups that lived there. Lutherans, German Baptists, French Protestants, Dutch Mennonites, and Portuguese Jews were some of the different groups that settled in the region. There also were many free and enslaved Africans in the Middle Colonies. When the English took over New Amsterdam in 1664, half of the inhabitants were not Dutch. Free and enslaved Africans also lived in the region, especially in New York City. In 1746, African Americans made up 20 percent of New York's population. The diversity of the Middle Colonies distinguished them from both the New England and Southern Colonies, where there were single, dominant religious majorities—Puritans in New England, Anglicans in the South.

Henry Hudson claimed the territory of the Middle Colonies in 1602 on behalf of the Dutch. Although the Dutch soon began trading with Native Americans for beaver and otter pelts, they did not send colonial settlers until 1624. Starting in 1625, the Dutch brought enslaved Africans to work as household servants and in various trades. In 1626, the Dutch West India Company purchased Manhattan Island from local Native Americans and established the colony of New Amsterdam. The Dutch who colonized New Amsterdam were Protestants motivated by economic gain. They sympathized with other Protestants from Europe who faced persecution or discrimination in their home countries. The Dutch welcomed these dissenters to their colonies. During the period of Dutch colonization, people came to the Middle Colonies from Scandinavia, France, Belgium, Germany, and other countries.

In 1638, Swedish settlers established the colony of New Sweden in an area along the Delaware River. New Sweden included parts of present-day New Jersey, Pennsylvania, and Delaware. For many years, the Dutch, Swedish, and English competed to control trade in the area. In 1655, the Dutch gained control of New Sweden. In 1664, the English took over the Dutch colonies and claimed the entire region.

England's Proprietary Colonies

When England claimed the territory, King Charles II of England created several proprietary colonies. These were colonies owned by a single person, called the proprietor.

- Charles gave part of the region to his brother, the Duke of York, who named his colony New York.

- The duke sold part of his grant to two proprietors, John Berkeley and George Carteret. They named their colony New Jersey after Carteret's homeland, the English island of Jersey.

- Charles gave another large chunk of land to William Penn to pay off a debt that he owed to Penn's father. Penn named his colony Pennsylvania, Latin for "Penn's woods."

Because individuals controlled these colonies, the beliefs and goals of their proprietors strongly affected the lives of the people who settled there. For example, the proprietors of New York and New Jersey wanted to attract settlers to their colonies. They sold land rights at relatively low prices and allowed freedom of religion and some political freedom.

photo: Getty Images

Painting of when Penn's treaty was made with the Native Americans.

William Penn also allowed settlers in his Pennsylvania colony many freedoms. Penn was a member of the Religious Society of Friends, a Christian religious group more commonly known as the Quakers. The Quakers rejected priests and religious ceremony and believed that faith was a matter of the individual's inner consciousness. England punished the Quakers because their beliefs differed from those of the Church of England. Between 1660 and 1685, English authorities imprisoned 13,000 Quakers for their beliefs. Penn objected to this religious persecution. He wanted his colony to be a place where all people were free to worship as they pleased. He also wanted to provide a refuge for Quakers who wanted to escape England's strict religious rules. The relative freedom of the Middle Colonies made them attractive to people from many parts of Europe.

Middle Colonies: Geography and Trade

How did the geography of the Middle Colonies affect life in the region?

The region of the Middle Colonies has fertile soil, which means that crops grow well there. There also are rolling hills and valleys. The climate of the region is milder than New England's climate. It includes cold, wet winters and long, hot summers with plenty of rain.

Discovery EDUCATION | SOCIAL STUDIES TECHBOOK

How did location affect daily life in the New England, Middle, and Southern Colonies?

These factors made the Middle Colonies a very good place for agriculture, or farming. Before European colonists arrived, the Lenni Lenape, a group of Native Americans also called the Delaware, farmed maize (corn), beans, and squash. The European colonists raised livestock and grew fruits, vegetables, and grains such as wheat and corn. The land and climate in the Middle Colonies were good for growing wheat, barley, and oats. The Middle Colonies produced so much grain that they have been called the "breadbasket colonies."

Grain farming is not labor-intensive, so landowners relied more on labor from other settlers and indentured servants than on slave labor. In 1700 in Pennsylvania, about 3 percent of the population was enslaved, or 1,000 out of a total population of 30,000.

Rivers and Cities

Another important feature of the Middle Colonies was the region's long, wide rivers, including the Hudson River and the Delaware River. The native Lenni Lenape used rivers in many ways. When hunting, they would surround a group of deer and herd them into the river. They used clay from riverbanks to make pottery. They also made dugout canoes, which they used on the rivers for transportation and fishing. The rivers allowed colonist farmers to ship surplus, or extra, crops to be sold in cities such as Philadelphia and New York. Philadelphia was the main ocean port on the Delaware River, and New York was located where the Hudson River meets the Atlantic Ocean.

The rivers and ports in the Middle Colonies allowed merchants to bring goods in and out of the area. This contributed to the region becoming a center of colonial trade. For example, merchants in the region's cities purchased wheat from local farmers, milled the wheat into flour, and exported the flour to other colonies and to Europe. They also imported manufactured goods, such as tools, porcelain ware, and home furnishings, from England and other European countries.

photo: Brooklyn Museum

This 1868 painting shows the slow, wide Hudson River, which farmers used for shipping their surplus crops to the city of New York.

The physical geography of the Middle Colonies supported the emergence of some of the largest and most important cities in the modern United States. Large cities and towns often developed near bodies of water that provided river access to the interior areas and sea routes to Europe and other colonial regions. These waterways facilitated trade of the region's agricultural products and encouraged population growth. For example, New York City, located near the mouth of the Hudson River, emerged during the 1600s. Philadelphia, located on the Delaware River, grew and expanded throughout the 1700s.

Although most of the people in the Middle Colonies were farmers, the growth of large cities in the region created the need for specialized jobs. By the early 1700s, cities like New York, Newark, and Philadelphia had tailors, blacksmiths, wheelwrights (wheel makers), chandlers (candle makers), coopers (barrel makers), cobblers (shoemakers), printers, and other specialized tradespeople.

Middle Colonies: Native American Interactions

How did settlers in the Middle Colonies interact with Native Americans?

photo: Getty Images

In this black-and-white illustration circa 1865, Delaware Indians gather during the Civil War.

The Lenni Lenape people were a large Native American group in the Middle Colonies when the Europeans arrived. The Lenni Lenape lived in the southern part of the Middle Colonies, mostly near what is now called the Delaware River. When William Penn created his colony, he wanted to treat the Lenni Lenape fairly and show respect for their traditional lands. Penn did not want to fight Native Americans for land. As his colony grew, he and his agents negotiated prices and signed treaties to purchase every piece of land. According to some historians, Penn signed a "Great Treaty" in 1682 that promised a "chain of friendship" between the settlers and the Lenni Lenape. No original copies of the document exist, but there are many reports of what it may have said. Whether or not this document existed, Penn's dealings with Native Americans were peaceful business negotiations.

In a 1737 treaty called the "Walking Purchase," Penn agreed to buy the amount of land that a man could walk in one and a half days. It appears that Penn did not actually walk the distance, but instead took the Lenni Lenapes' word for the measurement. After Penn's death, however, his sons used the terms of the Walking Purchase treaty to gain more land. Penn's sons hired three men to run as fast and as far as they could in the time allotted and claimed much more land than the Lenni Lenape had agreed to.

Settlers in New Jersey and other parts of the Middle Colonies also signed treaties with the Lenni Lenape for more land. In some cases, colonial leaders lied to or improperly informed the Lenni Lenape about the treaties. The Lenni Lenape were forced to give up their lands permanently. They did not have the same concept of land ownership that Europeans did, and the Europeans exploited this difference.

Departure of the Lenni Lenape and Wappinger

Continued losses of land forced most of the Lenni Lenape to move west to get away from the settlers. However, the land west of the colonial settlements already was assigned to the Iroquois. These Lenni Lenape continued drifting and eventually settled in scattered areas of Ohio and Indiana.

Besides taking their lands, the treaties also forced the Lenni Lenape onto reservations, or land set aside for the exclusive use of Native Americans. In exchange for the reservation land, the Lenni Lenape gave up all rights to other lands in the state. In 1704, Delaware forced the Lenni Lenape onto two reservations. In 1758, New Jersey also created a reservation for the Lenni Lenape. By this time, there were few Lenni Lenape left in New Jersey, and only about 200 people moved to the reservation. European colonists, and later Americans, did not respect the treaties and continued to take the reservation lands.

Other Native Americans in the Middle Colonies suffered fates similar to that of the Lenni Lenape. For instance, at the time of the Dutch arrival, the Wappinger people occupied parts of southeastern New York and western Connecticut. Many Wappinger gave in to Dutch pressure, sold their lands, and moved away. Others chose to stay and fight. They warred with the Dutch from 1640 to 1645 but could not keep the newcomers off their lands. Eventually, the remaining Wappinger were forced to move. They joined other displaced Native Americans in the Northeast and the Midwest.

European settlers were attracted to the excellent soil and resources of the Middle Colonies. As the settlers expanded their control in the 1600s and 1700s, they displaced Native Americans who had lived in the region for generations.

Middle Colonies: Government and Democracy

What democratic practices existed in the Middle Colonies?

William Penn called his colony a "holy experiment" because he tried to govern it according to his Quaker beliefs. One of those beliefs was the idea of democracy, or government in which the people have the power to make political decisions.

As part of that idea, Penn created a colonial assembly, or group of representatives, to make laws for the colony. Pennsylvania's assembly was called the Provincial Council. Penn allowed colonists to elect the council's members, one-third of whom were elected every year for three-year terms. This election process prevented an active faction from replacing the entire group at once.

photo: Library of Congress
Painted depiction of the landing of William Penn in 1682.

A faction is a group of people who share a particular political or economic interest. However, the government of Pennsylvania was not a complete democracy: Penn alone chose the colony's governor.

The governments of New York and New Jersey were structured similarly. The proprietors appointed the colonial governors, while the male landowners of the colony elected the legislative, or lawmaking, assemblies. This structure was an early step toward establishing a tradition of self-government in the American colonies.

Religious Tolerance

Another important tradition established in the Middle Colonies was the idea of religious tolerance. Tolerance means accepting and protecting people who are different, in this case, people of different religious faiths. In the Middle Colonies, there were no restrictions on what religion people could practice. Other British colonies, such as Massachusetts and Virginia, had established state religions. In these colonies, only people who were members of the officially approved church were permitted to vote and hold office.

In the Middle Colonies, a tradition of religious tolerance not only attracted a greater variety of settlers, but also set a standard that would become important to American government.

Religious tolerance did not apply to all faiths. For example, Peter Stuyvesant, the governor of New Amsterdam from 1647 to 1664, asked the Dutch West India Company for permission to remove Jewish settlers from his colony. Because some investors in the company were Jewish, Stuyvesant's request was denied. New Amsterdam allowed Jews to own land and establish businesses, although they were prohibited from holding public office or building synagogues.

Explore this resource to learn more about democratic government in Pennsylvania.

Southern Colonies: Settlement

How were the Southern Colonies established?

During the 1600s, England set up a dozen colonies along the East Coast of North America. Georgia, the 13th colony, was established in 1732. These colonies were either corporate colonies or proprietary colonies. A corporate colony was owned by stockholders who were given authority by a charter signed by an English ruler. The charter was a document that outlined the purposes of the land and the specific privileges the stockholders could exercise over the colony. Of the five Southern Colonies, only Virginia was a corporate colony. The other four Southern Colonies—Maryland, North Carolina, South Carolina, and Georgia—were proprietary colonies. A proprietary colony formed when an English ruler gave ownership to an individual or a group of individuals, who became the proprietor or proprietors.

Discovery SOCIAL STUDIES TECHBOOK

How did location affect daily life in the New England, Middle, and Southern Colonies?

Virginia

The first English colony in North America was Virginia, sponsored by the Virginia Company of London. The Virginia Company was a group of stockholders who hoped to profit from a Virginia colony. They sponsored Jamestown, the first permanent English settlement in North America, in 1607. Jamestown was located on the coast of Virginia. Before long, new settlements and farms developed in Virginia.

After enduring years of hardship, including conflict with Native American nations, harsh winters, lack of food, and disease, the Jamestown settlers established a thriving colony. At first, the investors of the Virginia Company hoped they would gain a profit from gold mined by the settlers. When little gold was found, the settlers cultivated tobacco as a cash crop. A cash crop is a plant grown to be sold for profit, as opposed to subsistence crops, which are intended to feed the farmers' families.

photo: Paul Fuqua

Tobacco was an important cash crop in colonial Virginia and Maryland.

Maryland

Cecilius Calvert, the second Lord Baltimore, owned the area around the Chesapeake Bay, northeast of Virginia. Calvert was a Roman Catholic. Like the Puritans, the Catholics' beliefs differed from those of the Church of England. Calvert wanted to set up a colony in which Catholics were free to worship according to their faith. His colony would become Maryland. In 1634, Leonard Calvert, Cecilius's younger brother, formed a settlement along the lower Potomac called Saint Mary's City. It became the capital of Maryland, and Leonard became the first governor of the colony. As in Virginia, the farmers in Maryland developed tobacco as a cash crop.

The Calvert family wanted to ensure that Maryland would remain a safe haven for people who practiced Roman Catholicism. To do this, the General Assembly in Maryland passed the Act of Religious Toleration in 1649. This document allowed religious freedom for all Christians living in the colony, whether Protestant or Catholic. During the second half of the 1600s, the Protestant population in Maryland and the surrounding colonies grew rapidly. In Virginia, the Anglican Church became the official religion. Despite these developments, Maryland remained a haven for people who did not follow the beliefs of the Anglican Church.

The Carolinas

In 1663, the English monarch Charles II granted eight proprietors the land between Virginia and Florida. They called it Carolina. Soon, it attracted many settlers, including newcomers from other American colonies and Britain and many French Protestants, called Huguenots. In 1712, the British government divided the region into three parts: North Carolina, South Carolina, and Georgia. The northernmost part was North Carolina. North Carolina settlers often set up small farms that practiced subsistence agriculture. The middle part was South Carolina. Wealthy South Carolina landowners formed plantations that grew rice and indigo as cash crops that they sold in bulk for profits.

Georgia

Then, in 1732, King George II of England granted a corporate charter for the remaining region. The leader of the corporation was James Oglethorpe. Oglethorpe wanted a colony both as a new start for people in poverty and as a model society that embodied justice and equality. In 1733, Oglethorpe led a group of 120 settlers to what is now the city of Savannah and established the first settlement in the colony of Georgia. During Oglethorpe's nine years as governor, he battled and defeated invading Spanish troops, securing the region for Great Britain.

The original charter for Georgia prohibited the importation of enslaved people. As a result, the colonists established small farms but not plantations. By 1750, the law was changed, and Georgians began importing enslaved laborers and developing plantations.

Southern Colonies: Geography and Trade

Why did plantations form in the Southern Colonies?

The Southern Colonies had a long growing season, flat land, a variety of soils, and a hot, humid climate. Because of these factors, the region proved to be ideal for agriculture. There were also calm rivers leading to many excellent harbors, especially in South Carolina, from which goods could be exported.

The Middle and New England Colonies had shorter growing seasons and rougher land than the Southern Colonies, which made them less suited for large farms. Because of this, the use of enslaved people was not nearly as common. A small New England farm required the work of only a few people and only for half of the year. Even though enslaved persons were not paid, they needed to be housed, fed, clothed, and supervised. Economically, it was not worthwhile for most small New England farms to purchase and manage large numbers of enslaved people.

Plantations

Most Southern farms remained small, and most Southern farmers practiced subsistence agriculture. However, the few farmers who found financial success were able to buy more land and increase their production of cash crops. Wealthy landowners began to establish plantations. A plantation is a large estate built to grow cash crops. At first, the primary cash crops in the Southern Colonies were tobacco and rice.

Discovery EDUCATION | SOCIAL STUDIES TECHBOOK

How did location affect daily life in the New England, Middle, and Southern Colonies?

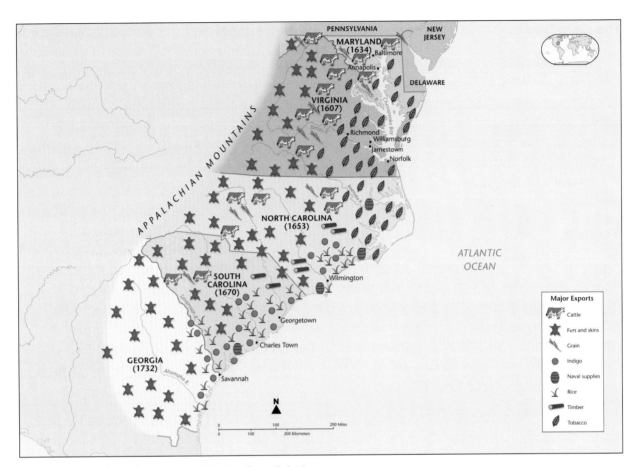

This map shows the major exports of the Southern Colonies.

Many English and Scots-Irish settlers were granted large estates, which allowed them to develop plantations. Tobacco became the primary cash crop on the plantations of Maryland and Virginia. In South Carolina and Georgia, indigo and rice became the main crops. Raising tobacco, rice, and indigo required a lot of human labor.

Because of their size and the labor-intensive crops, plantations required large numbers of workers. Plantation owners preferred to keep the profits for themselves and not to pay these workers. At first, plantation owners used indentured servants to till their land. These people worked for a set amount of time to pay for their passage to North America. They received room and board but no wages. After the time of service was over, the indentured servant could leave the plantation and obtain land to farm. As a result, landowners always needed to look for laborers.

Enslaved people were prisoners forced to work without pay. This condition was permanent unless the owner decided to free the enslaved laborer. The children of enslaved persons also were enslaved and considered property of the slaveholder.

The mansion, or main house, of most plantations was situated on a hill near a bay or river. Gardens and orchards often surrounded the mansion. The owner and his family lived in luxury. Their homes often included furniture imported from England and elegant fabrics. This lifestyle proved to be a stark contrast to the lives of the enslaved people who labored on the estates.

Southern Colonies: Native American Interactions

How did the Southern Colonists and Native Americans interact with each other?

Wherever the British colonists settled in North America, they came into conflict with Native American groups. The colonists wanted permanent ownership of the land that Native Americans had occupied for centuries. But Native Americans did not own and occupy land in the same way that Europeans did. Many Native Americans moved seasonally and did not have permanent residences. Some occupied a location for a few years until the soil was depleted and then resettled elsewhere.

In the last few decades, historians have begun to study the effects of the differences between Native Americans' and English colonists' ideas about land and property. Below is a list of some of their conclusions:

- Before meeting European settlers, Native Americans did not buy or sell land.

- Native Americans did not have a written language before 1800. As a result, English colonists recorded property claims, deeds, and treaties in English. This forced Native Americans to work in the British legal system.

- Colonists usually tried to obtain land rights by means they believed to be legal.

- In less than 200 years, the English colonists completely displaced Native American nations that occupied the Coastal Plains region.

photo: Library of Congress

Chief Powhatan led the Powhatan Confederacy.

Resistance, Force, and Alliances

At the time of the settlement at Jamestown, the Powhatan Confederacy dominated eastern Virginia and southern Maryland. This confederacy consisted of a group of Native American nations led by Chief Powhatan. After Powhatan's death in 1618, his brother led the confederacy.

At first, the Virginia colonists tried to cooperate with the Powhatan. Their survival depended on it. However, when the colonists began to farm tobacco, they wanted more land for this cash crop. They began to take control of land in Powhatan territory.

The Powhatan Confederacy attacked the settlers in retaliation, killing 347 of them in 1622. This incident sparked the Powhatan War, which lasted for more than 20 years.

Discovery SOCIAL STUDIES
EDUCATION | **TECHBOOK**

How did location affect daily life in the New England, Middle, and Southern Colonies?

Then, in 1644, the Powhatan Confederacy killed about 500 settlers. The British struck back with overwhelming force. They crushed the confederacy and ended its power. This pattern of English settlers seizing Native American land, Native Americans resisting, and English settlers subduing them by force was repeated throughout the colonial period.

Several Native American nations lived in southeastern North America, including the Yamacraw, Creek, Choctaw, and Cherokee. After James Oglethorpe and his followers landed in Georgia, he formed a treaty with the Creek that allowed the colonists to settle in the area. During the next 20 years, about 4,000 settlers arrived. In the late 1600s, Native American nations got involved in the struggles between France, England, and Spain for control of the region. Native American nations that made alliances with European powers often found themselves tangled in a web of European conflict.

Southern Colonies: Government and Democracy

How did the Southern Colonies help develop a representative government?

In 1619, Virginia created the first representative legislative body in colonial America. This body was called the House of Burgesses. The first session included two representatives, called burgesses, from each of Virginia's 11 boroughs. The Burgesses were selected in local elections. Only male landowners had the right to vote in these elections.

The House of Burgesses met in Jamestown, the capital of the Virginia colony. The legislature had the authority to write laws for the colony, but the governor had the right to veto these laws. After 1625, the English government became less involved in colonial affairs. As a result, the House of Burgesses began managing all of the political matters of Virginia.

photo: Getty Images

In 1676, a group of Virginians led by Nathaniel Bacon set fire to Jamestown.

In 1676, some of Virginia's colonists, led by Nathaniel Bacon, revolted against the colony's government. Bacon and his followers claimed that Virginia's governor, William Berkeley, refused to help stop Native American raids on western settlements. In addition, the rebels insisted that the governor was corrupt and granted special favors to his friends. Although Bacon died later that year, Bacon's Rebellion led to the removal of Berkeley and to government reforms known as Bacon's Laws. To reform government means to fix weaknesses and make the government run more efficiently. Bacon's Laws included reform measures such as limiting the term of the office of sheriff to one year and making the office of justice of the peace an elected position.

With the establishment of the Southern Colonies, England gained control of the entire East Coast of North America with the exception of Florida. Although many of the colonies in the region put in place democratic traditions, not everyone benefited from these practices. Enslaved people, women, and white men who did not own land had little or no input in the colonial governments. Slavery, which became common in the South, later would become a source of conflict for the people living in the United States.

Complete this activity to demonstrate your understanding of the geography of the 13 colonies.

Each of the three regions that made up colonial America offered different perspectives on colonial life, religion, and government. Together, these colonies would shape the foundation for the country that would become the United States of America.

Consider the Essential Question:

How did location affect daily life in the New England, Middle, and Southern Colonies?

Go online to complete the Social Studies Explanation.

Check for Understanding:

Describe how immigrant groups who settled in the New England, Middle, and Southern Colonies interacted with the environment in different ways. What factors were most responsible for these differences?

Discovery SOCIAL STUDIES
EDUCATION **TECHBOOK**

For various groups, what did it mean to be "American" in 1750?

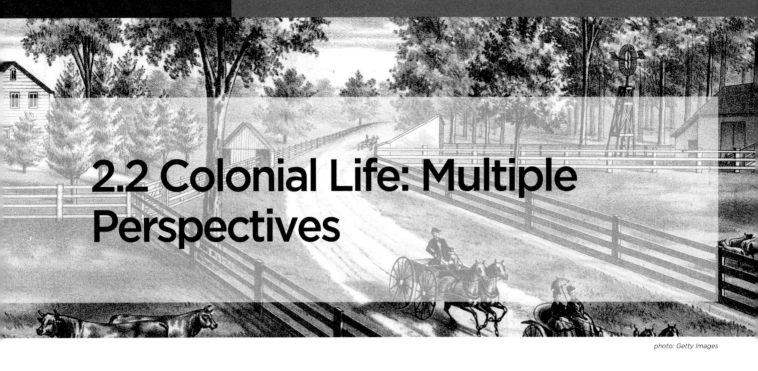

photo: Getty Images

2.2 Colonial Life: Multiple Perspectives

LESSON OVERVIEW

Introduction

In this concept, you will learn about daily life in the colonies as it was experienced by different groups of people.

Essential Question

For various groups, what did it mean to be "American" in 1750?

Lesson Objective

By the end of this lesson, you should be able to:

- Describe and evaluate the quality of life in the colonies from the perspectives of various groups, including city dwellers, farmers, women, children, and different social classes.

Key Vocabulary

Which terms do you already know?

- ☐ Benjamin Banneker
- ☐ Benjamin Franklin
- ☐ Eliza Lucas Pinckney
- ☐ encomienda
- ☐ gentry
- ☐ George Whitefield
- ☐ indentured servant
- ☐ indigo
- ☐ John Peter Zenger
- ☐ Pennsylvania
- ☐ Phillis Wheatley
- ☐ plantation
- ☐ Quakers/ Religious Society of Friends
- ☐ slavery
- ☐ tenant farmer
- ☐ William Paterson

ENGAGE

Why was there no "typical" colonial American? Visit Engage to learn more.

> ## Essential Question
>
> For various groups, what did it mean to be "American" in 1750?

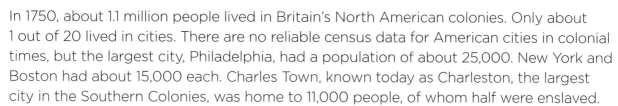

EXPLORE

Urban Islands in a Rural Culture

How did the importance of cities shape life there?

In 1750, about 1.1 million people lived in Britain's North American colonies. Only about 1 out of 20 lived in cities. There are no reliable census data for American cities in colonial times, but the largest city, Philadelphia, had a population of about 25,000. New York and Boston had about 15,000 each. Charles Town, known today as Charleston, the largest city in the Southern Colonies, was home to 11,000 people, of whom half were enslaved.

New England Cities

photo: Library of Congress

Boston in 1764.

Colonial cities may have been small by today's standards, but they were important as centers of industry, trade, and politics. In New England, nearly every town by a river mouth was a small seaport and engaged in shipbuilding. Shipowners and merchants became the wealthiest members of the community.

Shipping and shipbuilding supported a lively economy with a diverse assortment of businesses—in Boston especially, but also in smaller cities such as Newport, Rhode Island; Portsmouth, New Hampshire; and New London, Connecticut. Some industries, such as lumber milling and rope making, grew directly in support of shipping and shipbuilding. Cities needed produce supplied by local farmers.

They also supported shopkeepers who sold goods that merchants imported from England and the West Indies. Boston's economy supported artisans who made luxury goods, such as silversmith Paul Revere, and even artists, such as the portrait painter John Singleton Copley. A number of New England shippers became wealthy by importing and selling enslaved Africans.

Cities of the Middle Colonies

Cities in the Middle Colonies grew as merchants became wealthy by trading with people in other colonies and across the Atlantic. New York developed an economy serving the British soldiers who arrived there in ships from England. Long before it became the nation's leading metropolis, New York was an important port for merchants who traded with the French and Native Americans. Small manufacturers sprang up to supply them with goods, providing jobs for artisans and profit for their owners. New York was the most diverse city in the colonies. Visitors remarked on the number of languages they heard spoken on its streets. New York also had the largest African American population of any large city. About half of New York's African Americans were enslaved and half were free.

Philadelphia in 1750 was not only the biggest colonial city, but also the most literate. It had more bookstores than any English-speaking city except London. And it was in Philadelphia that Benjamin Franklin founded America's first public library, in 1731.

Southern Cities

What was life like in Southern cities? How did cities bring different ideas together?

In 1690, Charleston, South Carolina, was the fifth-largest city in the colonies. It had a population of 1,200. If Philadelphia had the most readers, Charleston may have had the most playgoers. By 1750, this Southern city, with a free population of less than 6,000, boasted two theaters. Charleston also had a tax-supported free library—one of the first in the North American colonies.

photo: Getty Images

The College of William and Mary was an important education center in the colonies.

Williamsburg, Virginia, was founded in 1699 as the new capital of the largest and most populous colony. Williamsburg was a planned city, meaning the city was planned before it was built in an undeveloped area. The city was placed next to the College of William and Mary, established in 1693 as the second college in the colonies. Harvard, in Massachusetts, was the first.

Public Life in the Colonies

In all of the colonies, cities were the focus of politics. Cities were the meeting places of government. They were also home to the coffeehouses and taverns where people of many walks of life read newspapers and discussed politics. The first American newspaper, the *Boston News-Letter*, was established in 1704. By 1750, there were newspapers in all the larger colonial cities and many smaller ones. In 1735, John Peter Zenger, publisher of the *New York Weekly Journal*, won a court case that helped establish the American principle of freedom of the press. A few years later, Americans in all the colonies would be seriously debating this and other freedoms, both publicly and privately.

Farmsteads and Plantations: New England and the Middle Colonies

How did daily responsibilities shape family life on colonial farms?

Only about two of every hundred Americans today live on a farm or in a rural community. For most Americans in the colonies, farming was the only way of life they knew. Farming, however, was not a single way of life; rather, it differed in each region of the colonies.

photo: Library of Congress
Farming on the Appalachian frontier took place on river valleys isolated from one another by mountains.

From New England to as far south as Pennsylvania, most people lived on small family farms, typically 50 to 100 acres in size. Farm families had to be self-sufficient, though there was often community support for large tasks such as raising a barn, or in times of need, such as when a woman had a baby.

Farm families often lived in villages, which were also home to general stores and trade workers such as blacksmiths and wagon makers. On market days, farm families might spend time socializing. On Sundays, they would attend church. Otherwise, farmers worked with their families on their own land. Depending on the season, they were busy plowing, planting, harvesting, keeping their animals fed and healthy, cutting wood for the stove and fireplace, washing laundry, and cleaning the house—all without power machinery. Even Sarah Knight, who had little good to say about the farmers she met, remarked on the cleanliness of their cabins.

Farm families sometimes supplemented their diets by hunting, but for the most part they raised all their food themselves. If they had a surplus, they would sell their goods in markets in nearby towns and cities. The money they earned from this trade allowed them to buy manufactured goods, such as window glass, and perhaps even a few luxuries.

Discovery SOCIAL STUDIES
EDUCATION | TECHBOOK

For various groups, what did it mean to be "American" in 1750?

In Massachusetts, there was little extreme wealth or poverty among farmers. This was not so in New York's Hudson Valley, where tenant farming supported a few large landowners. A tenant farmer is one who lives on someone else's land and farms it for pay. These landowners earned greater profits with the additional labor, while tenant farmers earned a very modest living.

Farmsteads and Plantations: The South and the Backcountry

What was life like on plantations and in the backcountry?

Large Farms in the Middle and Southern Colonies

There were also wealthy landowners in the Chesapeake region, Tidewater Virginia, and the coastal areas of the Carolinas and Georgia. In these regions, plantation agriculture was the general rule. Virginia plantations measured hundreds of acres in size; the larger plantations were 20,000 acres or more. They were typically owned by a single family and worked by indentured servants and enslaved people. Servants who earned their freedom were granted small plots of land to farm, but few were able to profit by growing food for market.

Because plantations were so large, villages were less common in the South. Instead, plantations had to be self-sufficient, and each plantation formed its own economic unit. Plantations grew cash crops for export and raised a variety of food crops to support themselves. In the Chesapeake colonies and North Carolina, the main cash crop was tobacco. Plantations farther south often grew rice or indigo. Except for luxury goods imported from England, enslaved people and indentured servants made what their plantations needed and performed all the farm and household tasks.

photo: Library of Congress

Rice was grown in low-lying marsh areas in the low country of Georgia and South Carolina.

Family Farms in the Backcountry

On the western frontier from Pennsylvania to Georgia, small farming was again the rule. This backcountry, in the foothills of the Appalachian Mountains, had fertile land in river valleys and "hollows" separated by steep, high country. As a result, each valley formed its own community and had little contact with neighboring ones. Typically, members of the same extended family would settle in a valley together. The soil was rich and, as it was said, a community could prosper "if God's willing and the creek don't rise."

If the creek did rise, farm families would simply cut some trees uphill and begin again. There were few towns in the backcountry and no cities; instead, there was a fierce sense of independence and community based on family ties.

In a Man's World

How did women's roles in the colonies differ from men's?

Attitudes Toward Women

Anne Bradstreet was both the first woman and the first poet in colonial America to be a published writer. In 1650, she described the relationship between women and men this way:

"It is but vain unjustly to wage war,
Men can do it best, and women know it well.
Preeminence in each and all is yours--
Yet grant some small acknowledgement of ours."

A hundred years later, gender inequality was still the rule in British North America. In Bradstreet's New England, Puritan religion preached that men and women were spiritually equal; however, women were not allowed to be ministers and were forbidden to preach to men.

Women and Work

Men's work and women's work were strictly defined, but these definitions varied from place to place. On New England farms, women were confined to household tasks and rarely worked in the fields with the men. Among Pennsylvania Germans, however, it was common for women to work in fields and barns alongside their husbands.

photo: Paul Fuqua
This woman, dressed in colonial costume, demonstrates a traditionally female household craft.

Business and trade were regarded as "a man's world," but there were exceptions. Sarah Knight was a trader in real estate and an expert on real estate law. Her famous journey from Boston to New York was a business trip. Mary Katherine Goddard edited and published the first newspapers in Providence, Rhode Island, and Baltimore, Maryland. In South Carolina, Eliza Lucas Pinckney was managing three plantations at the age of 16. Through careful plant breeding, she developed the cultivation of the indigo plant, from which a blue dye was made. Her work made indigo one of South Carolina's most important plantation crops.

Discovery | SOCIAL STUDIES
EDUCATION | **TECHBOOK**

For various groups, what did it mean to be "American" in 1750?

Women in Families

What was family life like for women in the colonies?

Doing "men's work" did not give women equality. A husband was the head of the household; his wife's role was to obey quietly and cheerfully. Girls' training in humility began when they were quite young, as it was not uncommon for them to marry at age 13 or 14.

A woman could inherit property, but English law held that when she married, she forfeited it to her husband. Legally, she did not even own the clothes she wore. In parts of New York where Dutch customs were strong, a wife could write a will that indicated who should inherit the property she had brought into a marriage. The same was true among German communities in Pennsylvania. But English law did not recognize this right.

One example from a wealthy household in Virginia shows the unequal power in colonial marriages. Landowner William Byrd II sold the estate of his wife, Lucy, and kept his own property for himself. He did not even let her borrow his books without asking permission. On at least one occasion, he and his male guests devoured everything on the table, leaving his wife nothing to eat. Lucy, who came from a Virginia family as rich and distinguished as her husband's, made her displeasure known. However, by law, she had no formal way to change her situation.

Complete this activity to demonstrate your understanding of women's roles in colonial America.

Only among the Quakers did women enjoy anything close to equality with men. Quaker women preached in churches and managed their own money. Quakers recognized both men and women as "heads of family." Laws in Quaker communities regularly used the double pronoun "he and she." The men in their communities consulted Quaker women for their wisdom in "difficult matters." Their husbands encouraged them to take leading roles in their communities. Such relations between the sexes were rare in New England and unknown in other regions of the English colonies.

A Short Childhood

What were work, education, and leisure like for colonial children?

Children and Work

If you were growing up in colonial America, chances are you would be done with school by now. Education, like other aspects of colonial life, varied greatly according to geography, gender, and social class. For all but a privileged few, school included little more than reading, writing, and simple math. With few exceptions, childhood ended early. Children were generally regarded as miniature adults.

From an early age, boys were instructed in farm tasks by their fathers, and girls were instructed in domestic tasks by their mothers. They were expected to work alongside their parents as their age and strength allowed. If a family had too many children and not enough land, boys would become apprentices in a town. There, they would live with a craftsman and his family while they learned a trade, such as blacksmithing, sailmaking, or carpentry. Girls would perfect their domestic skills until they were old enough to marry.

Children and Discipline

If you were a child in Puritan New England or Dutch New York, your upbringing would be very strict. A child's stubborn will, it was taught, was "of the devil" and needed to be broken. In Pennsylvania, Quakers rejected the idea that children were "born evil." Quakers raised their children with a great deal of what today is called "permissiveness," relying on their own good example to guide their children's behavior.

In the South, children of wealthy plantation owners were encouraged to express their independence but also to respect customs of social rank. And on the frontier, children, especially boys, were encouraged to show a strong will and stubborn independence. All of these different approaches to parenting were meant to prepare children for the adult world in which they would live.

Schools

There was school in colonial America, and there was fun to be had when learning and chores were done. In New England, literacy was considered important so that children could read and be guided by the Bible. Schools were established quite early in New England, in cities and towns that could afford a teacher. The teacher typically would "board in," living with students' families a month at a time. Most boys, and about half of the girls, learned to read and write. In farm communities, there were few schools, and parents usually taught their children at home.

Schools were usually made up of one poorly heated room, where boys and girls sat on opposite sides and grades were arranged from front to back. Older students were expected to help teach younger students. Boys who showed promise might go on to attend the Boston Latin School. Founded in 1635, Boston Latin is still educating students today. A few exceptional young scholars might then attend Harvard or Yale college to train as church ministers.

In other regions, literacy was far less common. In Virginia, for example, plantation owners took pride in their private libraries. They hired tutors for their children and established good schools. Their sons would go on to the College of William and Mary or to universities in England. But children of other classes were actively discouraged from learning to read. Fewer than half of boys were literate, and the rate was even lower among girls. Only about one in four indentured servants could read or write, and only about one in every hundred African Americans. In some colonies, it was illegal to teach enslaved people to read or write.

Discovery | SOCIAL STUDIES
EDUCATION | **TECHBOOK**

For various groups, what did it mean to be "American" in 1750?

Play

There was little time for leisure and play, except for the children of the very rich. Farm chores took up much of a child's day, but children still found ways to have fun. Some of the games colonial children played, such as hopscotch, cat's cradle, and hide-and-seek, are still familiar today. Children made toys out of spare materials found around the farm. They flew handmade kites and played with handmade dolls. They raced hoops taken from old barrels. There were foot races and swimming in summer, and

photo: Getty Images

Nine Men's Morris was an old English board game that colonial children played. It was similar to checkers.

ice-skating and sledding in winter. In New England towns, older boys played a rough game that was an ancestor of American football. Both boys and girls played bat-and-ball games that would evolve into baseball.

Social Rank

What distinguished colonial social classes?

In the 1740s, a Virginia schoolboy wrote out a list of 110 "rules of civility and decent behavior in company and conversation." This young man was a member of the landowning gentry. His name was George Washington.

Gentry means people of the upper class of society. In all of the colonies, but especially in Virginia, people were well aware of social rank. Young George Washington's "rules of civility" applied only to members of his own class, but members of each class were expected to show proper respect to those of higher rank.

In a culture where 95 percent of the people lived on farms, being a member of the gentry was a matter of owning land. Plantation owners made up perhaps 10 percent of the population, but they owned 50 to 75 percent of the land, and they profited from it. The plantation gentry owned most of the property in Virginia's cities and towns, too.

Middle and Lower Classes

The middle class was made up of small farmers who owned their own land and worked it themselves, some with the help of an indentured servant. The remainder, perhaps two-thirds of Virginians, did not own land. Some were tenant farmers, working land that belonged to others. Others were poor laborers and indentured servants who owned little or nothing. There were indentured servants in all the colonies, but in Virginia and neighboring Maryland, they made up perhaps half to two-thirds of the white settlers.

photo: Library of Congress

An indenture contract obligating a man to a period of servitude.

At the bottom of the social ladder were enslaved people who were considered property. Enslaved people were prisoners of their "owners" and forced to work without pay. They had neither civil rights nor basic human rights. In 1750, the enslaved population of the Southern states ranged from less than 20 percent in Georgia to 60 percent in South Carolina. About 60,000 enslaved persons lived in South Carolina and Georgia, about 150,000 in the Chesapeake region, and 33,000 in the North.

In the cities of the North, the gentry were merchants and lawyers. Independent artisans and shopkeepers made up a robust middle class. Below them was a laboring class made up of free white people, indentured servants, free African Americans, and a small number of enslaved people.

Consequences of Class Distinctions

What were the differences between colonial social classes?

For the most part, the privileges of class resulted from the privileges of wealth. While a landowner or merchant might work as hard at his livelihood as a small farmer at his, the former enjoyed a great deal more leisure and luxury. The fine colonial furniture and silver serving sets in museums today did not belong to people of the middle classes. Hunting on horseback with hounds was a favored sport among the Virginia gentry, but for their tenant farmers, hunting could be a matter of survival.

As for indentured servants, those without skills were set to hard labor. Their living conditions were at their master's pleasure. They could not marry without their master's consent, and many suffered poor food, beatings, and other abuse at their masters' hands.

Enslaved people were worse off. Regarded as property, they could be treated in any way their owners liked, with no protection of the law.

Discovery EDUCATION | SOCIAL STUDIES TECHBOOK

For various groups, what did it mean to be "American" in 1750?

Inequality was greatest in Virginia, although strong distinctions between social classes existed in all the colonies. In Pennsylvania and Delaware, Quaker customs remained strong. William Penn had despised the English system of social rank. He believed instead in an "aristocracy of Christian virtue," in which a person should be judged by what he or she did as an individual. For Quakers, wealth did not bring status. Quakers addressed all members of their church as "friend." But even among Quakers, there was a growing distinction in wealth and a division of society among large landowners, middle-class farmers, and tenants and laborers who owned no land.

Slavery and Servitude

What was colonial life like for indentured servants and for enslaved people in the South?

Slavery and Indentured Servitude

The first African laborers in the colonies were 17 individuals brought to Virginia by a Dutch ship in 1619. These people were not enslaved; they were indentured servants. It was illegal under English law to enslave a Christian. In 1662, however, Virginia passed a law declaring that only white people could be indentured servants. Those of African descent, regardless of religion, were forced into a permanent condition of slavery. The colony of Maryland followed with a similar law. By 1750, enslaved Americans of African descent lived in every one of the 13 colonies. In the five Southern Colonies, they made up more than a third of the population.

Indentured servants had the right to sue abusive masters and to testify against them in court. They had the promise of freedom and a piece of land of their own once the term of their indenture was over. None of this was so for enslaved people. They were legally recognized as property. They could be bought and sold, like a house or a horse. By having children, they increased their owner's property. They were not free to marry without their owner's consent. It was forbidden in some Southern Colonies for an enslaved person to learn to read, and the punishment for writing could include having one's finger cut off.

Slavery in the South

Slavery existed in every colony, but from the beginning, it was more common in the South than in the North. In the South, plantation owners grew crops such as tobacco, rice, indigo, and sugarcane. Plantation owners required a large labor source to plant, tend, and harvest them. A law passed in South Carolina in the 1760s demonstrates how hard enslaved people worked. The law forbade slave owners from forcing their enslaved laborers to work for more than 15 hours a day. The purpose of the law was not to benefit enslaved people but to protect the white population by preventing violent revolts of enslaved people against their masters.

photo: Getty Images

Interior of slave quarters, Magnolia Plantation, South Carolina.

A social ranking existed among enslaved people on the plantations, just as it did among free Americans. At the top were the house servants, who worked in the "big house" where their owner and his family lived. These enslaved house laborers were cooks, kitchen workers, maids, butlers, and valets, such as served in the mansions of the English gentry. Of course, these servants were not free to leave their jobs as they pleased. Below them were artisans who had learned particular skills, such as metalworking, saddle making, or even playing music. Slave owners could hire out or sell the time and talents of enslaved people with special skills; some slave holders allowed these enslaved people to keep some of the price of their hire. In this way, some enslaved people were able to buy their freedom. Lowest in the ranks of the enslaved were the field hands, whose lives were mostly made up of unceasing labor.

Slavery in the North

What was colonial life like for free and enslaved African Americans in the North?

In the North, conditions for enslaved people were usually somewhat better than in the South. There were no large plantations. Few farmers owned enslaved laborers, and those who owned more than one or two were rare. In Pennsylvania, where the Quakers and other religious groups had opposed slavery since the 1690s, slavery became increasingly unpopular. Some enslaved people worked in the shipyards of Boston and New York. Others were skilled craftspeople, while still others worked in the homes of the urban gentry. In New York especially, where there was a large African American population, enslaved people often lived apart from their slave owners in a state of semi-freedom. But frequent slave revolts in New York City (and their ruthless suppression) were constant reminders of the differences between slavery and freedom.

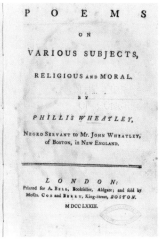

photo: Getty Images

Phillis Wheatley (1753–1784), an American enslaved woman was educated by her owner. She began writing poetry at the age of 13 and is recognized as the country's first notable African American poet.

Discovery | SOCIAL STUDIES
EDUCATION | **TECHBOOK**

For various groups, what did it mean to be "American" in 1750?

Free African Americans

In the New England and Middle Colonies, there were a number of free African Americans. They held many of the same types of jobs as the enslaved people of the North, but they received wages and could come and go as they pleased. They were not equal to whites under the law, and few white people regarded them as equals.

Despite their lack of legal rights, some free African Americans achieved distinction. Benjamin Banneker of Maryland was a self-taught engineer and astronomer—and one of the first scientists in America. Phillis Wheatley was captured in Africa at the age of 7 or 8 and sold to a family in Boston. She became a poet and the first African American woman to publish a book of poems. After being given her freedom, she made her living as a writer.

Explore this resource to learn more about colonial perspectives.

Enslaved and free African Americans had very different experiences of what it meant to be American. So did merchants, tenant farmers, whalers, and domestic servants. Britain's American colonies exhibited diversity arising from geographic, economic, gender, ethnic, and religious differences. Today, we know that the colonists united and created the United States of America, but in the 1750s, it was neither obvious nor inevitable that this would happen. Before the colonists could come together to create a nation, something would have to unite them with a common purpose.

Consider the Essential Question:

For various groups, what did it mean to be "American" in 1750?

Go online to complete the Social Studies Explanation.

Check for Understanding:

Not all children in colonial America had identical experiences. How did social class affect the experiences of children in colonial America?

3.1 The Colonies Come of Age

photo: Getty Images

LESSON OVERVIEW

Introduction

In this concept, you will learn how the American colonists developed their ideas about government and democracy. You will also begin to see how these ideas helped lead the colonists to see themselves as Americans rather than British subjects. Finally, you'll read about the French and Indian War—the conflict that started the colonies on the road toward independence.

Essential Question

In what ways were the American colonies becoming their own nation before 1763? In what ways were they still part of the British Empire?

Lesson Objectives

By the end of this lesson, you should be able to:

- Discuss the relationship between the colonial and British governments, including British democratic influences and the degree of colonial autonomy.

- Trace and explain tensions on the frontier between Great Britain, France, American colonists, and Native Americans.

Key Vocabulary
Which terms do you already know?

- [ ] Albany Plan
- [ ] Appalachian Mountains
- [ ] autonomy
- [ ] Daughters of Liberty
- [ ] democracy
- [ ] English Bill of Rights
- [ ] Enlightenment
- [ ] French and Indian War
- [ ] George Washington
- [ ] House of Burgesses
- [ ] James Otis
- [ ] King George III
- [ ] Magna Carta
- [ ] Mayflower Compact
- [ ] mercantilism
- [ ] monarch
- [ ] Navigation Acts

- [ ] nobility
- [ ] Ohio River Valley
- [ ] parliament
- [ ] Plymouth
- [ ] Pontiac
- [ ] Pontiac's Rebellion
- [ ] Proclamation of 1763
- [ ] propaganda
- [ ] Quartering Act
- [ ] representative assembly
- [ ] representative government
- [ ] royal governor
- [ ] self-government
- [ ] Sons of Liberty
- [ ] town meeting
- [ ] William Pitt

Discovery EDUCATION | SOCIAL STUDIES TECHBOOK

In what ways were the American colonies becoming their own nation before 1763? In what ways were they still part of the British Empire?

ENGAGE

Who said, "a man's home is his castle"? Visit Engage to learn more.

Essential Question

In what ways were the American colonies becoming their own nation before 1763? In what ways were they still part of the British Empire?

EXPLORE

The Democratic Heritage

How did democratic traditions emerge in the American colonies?

By the 1700s, the British had a long-established tradition of representative government. In 1215, King John of England signed the Magna Carta. In this agreement, the king promised to share power with the English nobility, or ruling classes. The Magna Carta was an early example of a law placing limits on the power of a ruler.

The ideas of the Magna Carta would later inspire residents of the American colonies as well as the Founding Fathers. For example, when the founders of the Plymouth Colony wrote the Mayflower Compact to establish rules for their new settlement, they incorporated the principles of the Magna Carta. Both documents were written with the idea that a government's authority to rule is based upon a contract between that government and the people to be ruled. These documents also stated that rulers must obey the law in the same manner that the people they rule do. In 1776, the Declaration of Independence was written with the same principles in mind.

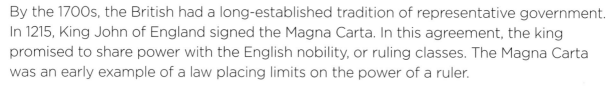

photo: Getty Images

A detail of the Magna Carta, the "Great Charter." The important principle established by the Magna Carta is that legal procedures apply to royalty with the same force that they apply to others.

The Declaration declared the "Right of the People to alter or to abolish" governments that abused their power and therefore failed to fulfill their contract with the citizens they governed.

Representative government continued to evolve in Great Britain during the colonial period. A series of events in the middle of the 1600s resulted in Parliament, the British law-making body, becoming the most powerful branch of the British government. In 1649, for example, Parliament used its authority under the Magna Carta to place the King of England on trial for treason.

In 1689, Parliament passed the English Bill of Rights. This law further limited the powers of the British monarch. It also granted the people of England the right to petition the king and the right to have free elections for members of Parliament.

American colonists—still British subjects—watched these events very closely. They were proud of their political heritage. They valued their rights and expected to have a voice in their government.

Local Governments Rule

How were Britain's American colonies governed?

British Controls

Because the American colonies were owned by Great Britain, they were formally under the control of Parliament and the king. The colonies were not permitted to select representatives to serve their interests in Parliament.

Some of the colonies had royal governors, who were appointed by the king. Royal governors were given the authority to exercise powers over the local governments that were established in each colony. They could veto the decisions of the local governments. Royal governors could even dissolve, or disband, these local governments. They appointed government officials such as tax collectors and judges. The British government also sent troops to protect Britain's land claims and to ensure that the American colonists could successfully supply their home country with valuable raw materials such as wood and furs.

In spite of these controls, Great Britain did not govern its colonies very closely. After all, North America was very far away from Britain. In the days before the Internet and telephones, messages could take weeks or even months to cross the ocean. Because of this, laws that were passed to govern the colonies were difficult to enforce. As long as Britain profited from colonial trade, it mostly left the colonists to make their own decisions. By 1760, only eight royal governors were in place in the American colonies. As a result, the settlers of each of the 13 colonies developed their own systems of government.

Discovery SOCIAL STUDIES
EDUCATION TECHBOOK

In what ways were the American colonies becoming their own nation before 1763? In what ways were they still part of the British Empire?

Democratic Traditions

The farmers, trappers, and merchants in the colonies had needs and problems that government officials on the other side of the Atlantic Ocean could not understand. They were self-sufficient people who valued their freedom. They believed in British democratic traditions as individual rights, representative government, and the rule of law. They also believed in civic virtue, which is the idea that citizens and leaders should be dedicated to the welfare of all above their own individual interests.

As a result of these beliefs, there were elements of democracy present in colonial governments. Some colonies set up representative assemblies. Most notable was the Virginia House of Burgesses. The House of Burgesses was America's first representative governing body. It consisted of 22 elected lawmakers. Not all Virginia residents could vote to select representatives to the House of Burgesses—in most of the colonies, only male landowners could vote. But the representative assemblies were far more attuned to local interests than the British officials were. Over time, many colonists came to believe that their locally elected representatives were more likely to embody civic virtue than officials in London.

Democratic traditions were present in other colonies as well. For example, beginning in the 1600s, many localities in New England conducted town meetings. During these public gatherings, the male residents of a town came together to make decisions about how their community would be governed. They established policies on local matters such as taxation, schools, and maintaining peace. Town meetings are examples of direct democracy. In this type of government, the people, rather than elected representatives, are directly involved in making policy decisions.

Another democratic tradition present in some colonies was religious tolerance. For example, William Penn founded Pennsylvania on the notion that all of its residents would be free to worship according to their own beliefs and religious traditions. Penn wanted to provide refuge for Quakers who hoped to escape religious persecution in England. In Maryland, the Calvert family hoped to ensure that their colony would become a safe haven for Roman Catholics. In 1649, Maryland's General Assembly passed the Act of Religious Toleration. This law granted religious freedom for all Christians living in the colony, whether Protestant or Catholic. Pennsylvania and Maryland contributed to a tradition of religious tolerance that attracted a greater variety of settlers to the New World, and later became a foundation of the government of the United States.

The Great Awakening

From around 1730 to the 1770s, a religious movement spread throughout the colonies. This movement was later called the Great Awakening. Popular preachers such as Jonathan Edwards and George Whitefield spread the ideas of the Great Awakening through the American continent.

photo: Library of Congress

*English-born George Whitefield
(1714–1770) was a leading evangelical
Calvinist preacher of the Great
Awakening.*

Whitefield came to the colonies in 1739 and spent a year preaching up and down the Atlantic coast. His impassioned sermons drew people from across denominations in crowds that were so large that he had to preach in open fields.

Overall, the Great Awakening emphasized individual religious experience rather than established church traditions. It introduced the idea of worship as a voluntary choice rather than a requirement of the state. Some people disagreed with Whitefield's style of preaching. They said he was overly emotional and did not approve of him criticizing existing churches. They were concerned that the Great Awakening was encouraging colonists to question traditional sources of authority such as the Church of England. The spirit of the Great Awakening later contributed to a revolutionary fervor that would lead to the colonists' demand for independence.

The Navigation Acts

How did Britain hope to profit from its colonies?

The economic relationship between the American colonies and Great Britain was based on a system known as mercantilism. This system was centered around three ideas:

- A country earns profits by exporting more goods than it imports.

- A country's wealth is determined by the value of the gold and silver it owns.

- An important purpose of government is to enforce policies that increase a country's ability to acquire wealth and export products abroad.

Under mercantilism, the countries of Europe competed with one another for profits and wealth. As a result, in 1651, Britain enacted a set of laws called the Navigation Acts. These trade laws had two purposes.

First, the Navigation Acts were meant to keep Britain's colonies from trading directly with other European nations. After all, Britain was in a race with these other nations for power and wealth. The colonies' role in the mercantilist system was to help Britain become more powerful than its competitors.

Under the Navigation Acts, all shipments to or from the colonies had to be in British-owned ships staffed by primarily British crews. Additionally, certain specified goods, including sugar, cotton, and tobacco, could only be shipped to or from England.

Discovery EDUCATION | SOCIAL STUDIES TECHBOOK

In what ways were the American colonies becoming their own nation before 1763? In what ways were they still part of the British Empire?

By requiring colonial trade to go directly to or from England, the acts served a second purpose. Every time a shipment of goods was loaded or unloaded in England, the British government collected customs duties, or special taxes on imports and exports. According to the Navigation Acts, shippers and merchants were now required to pay duties on every sale.

photo: Getty Images

Virginia settlers load barrels of tobacco onto a ship for export.

During the colonial period, a profitable triangular trade pattern developed between New England in the American colonies, the West Indies, and Africa. American-made rum was shipped to Africa and traded for enslaved Africans. These enslaved people were then transported to the West Indies and traded for molasses and sugar. Finally, West Indian molasses and sugar were shipped to the American colonies to make rum. Under the Navigation Acts, all the ships involved in this exchange, including the slave ships, had to be British. In addition, West Indian sugar and molasses were required to pass through England before they could be shipped back to America.

Although Great Britain did gain wealth from its colonies, the Navigation Acts were very difficult to enforce. Smuggling, or illegal trade, was common and enabled American merchants to avoid paying import duties. Britain could not control all the ports across all the seas. Thousands of miles away, the colonies were growing and enjoyed a great sense of freedom. Britain's relaxed style of governing the colonies continued.

A European War on American Soil: 1754–1763

What were the causes of the French and Indian War?

European Rivalries

By 1750, France's territorial holdings in North America were even greater than Britain's. France occupied much of the land to the west and north of Britain's 13 colonies. The French had developed a valuable fur trade and enjoyed fairly peaceful relations with the Native Americans who lived throughout the area.

Back in Europe, Britain, France, and Spain had been involved in on-and-off wars with one another for many years. The rivalry between these nations extended to America, where Britain and France competed to extend their colonial holdings to the Ohio River Valley and throughout the Great Lakes. This area was important because the Ohio River opened up a navigable route all the way to the Gulf of Mexico.

Colonel George Washington on his mission to the Ohio Country, May 1754.

photo: Getty Images

To increase their control of the region, the French attacked English settlers and forcibly evicted them from the area. They also began building forts throughout the valley. In 1754, the British sent a young officer named George Washington to warn French colonists to stay clear of British-claimed territory in what is now Western Pennsylvania. The French refused. When Washington returned from his mission with the news, the British sent soldiers to the area.

The conflict erupted into the French and Indian War. For nearly a decade, Britain and its American colonists were locked in a military struggle with France and its colonists. The war was fought by British troops from England and from the colonies. During the war, George Washington emerged as a respected military leader. He commanded one of several colonial armies called to serve in battle.

Native Americans and the French and Indian War

Also drawn into the war were a large number of Native Americans who lived in the disputed territories. Although their loyalties were divided, most Native Americans sided with France. French fur traders had historically cooperated and developed friendly relations with Native Americans. They also were less interested in establishing large, permanent settlements in America than the British and their colonists were.

Some Native American groups sided with the British in the French and Indian War. Two factors pushed most of the Iroquois League, or Six Nations, to fight alongside the British. First of all, the Iroquois had long been enemies of the Algonquian and the Huron, two tribes who were closely allied

Explore this resource to learn why many Native Americans supported the French.

with the French. Second, the Iroquois had a history of poor relations with the French. Back in the 1740s, the French had tried to force British settlers out of the Ohio country. They raided British settlements and ordered the Iroquois not to trade with the British. The Iroquois had good relations with the British and resented these French policies. Those Iroquois who did side with France changed their allegiance to Britain after 1760, when it became clear that the French would not win the war.

Discovery EDUCATION | SOCIAL STUDIES TECHBOOK

In what ways were the American colonies becoming their own nation before 1763? In what ways were they still part of the British Empire?

New Troubles on the Horizon: 1763

What events led to Great Britain's victory in the French and Indian War?

In the early years of the French and Indian War, the British and Americans repeatedly lost major battles. Then, in 1757, William Pitt became the Prime Minister of England. Under Pitt's leadership, the British adopted new strategies, including establishing a naval blockade of the Gulf of St. Lawrence. As a result, the British won a series of important battles in late 1757 and in 1758, in Canada, New York, and the Ohio Valley.

Throughout the summer of 1759, the British laid siege to the walled city of Quebec. In September, the British conducted a sudden sneak attack on the Plains of Abraham outside Quebec. After about 15 minutes of fighting, the British captured Quebec. They were able to hold onto the city through the following year. In September of 1760, the British launched a successful attack on Montreal, securing a complete victory in the war.

photo: Getty Images

The taking of Quebec, September 13, 1759.

In 1763, the Treaty of Paris formally ended the French and Indian War and outlined the terms of peace. France lost much of its land in North America. Britain's American empire more than doubled.

More Land, More Problems

Why was Great Britain's victory a mixed blessing?

The acquisition of new territory presented Britain with several problems, including a much larger frontier to maintain and defend. British American colonists were eager to settle the Ohio River Valley and other lands to the west, but Native Americans already lived on these lands. The British government had made promises to its Iroquois allies to hold back settlement.

Many Native American peoples had enjoyed peaceful trade relations with France—trading furs at French trading posts and hiring themselves out as guides and porters. They fought on France's side during the French and Indian War. When Britain took over French lands, these groups suddenly shared territory with a new European power.

What impact did Pontiac's Rebellion have on British rule?

photo: Getty Images

British troops in the area treated Native Americans harshly. In contrast to the French, they refused to take part in the traditional Native American ceremonial exchange of gifts. They limited the trade in weapons. And they failed to stop American settlers from taking Native lands. Anger spread through the Native American nations, and Native Americans joined together to attack British forts in the area. Pontiac, an Ottawa leader, is generally credited with bringing many Native American nations together and leading the first attack on Fort Detroit. The subsequent war became known as Pontiac's War.

Although the rebellion failed, it did great damage to the colonies and British rule. Eight British forts fell to Native American attack. Hundreds of colonists were forced to flee their homes. Britain wanted to ensure that such a conflict would not happen again.

A King's Proclamation: 1763

How did King George respond to problems on the western frontier?

The Proclamation of 1763

When the French and Indian War ended, King George III was caught in a dilemma. How should he handle the colonists' demands to move westward into Native American territories? Granting the colonists the right to move would make them happy, but it could also stir up conflicts with Native Americans. Providing the colonists with protection was expensive and would require the presence of British soldiers. What would you have done if you were in the king's position?

The British monarch decided that the best way to resolve the conflict was to limit settlement. To this end, he issued the Proclamation of 1763. This order established a line beyond which American colonists could not settle. The lands beyond the line were reserved for Native Americans.

As with the Navigation Acts, enforcement of King George's proclamation was nearly impossible because the American frontier was very far away from London. In addition, the French and Indian War had weakened the British military and left the country badly in debt.

Discovery EDUCATION | SOCIAL STUDIES TECHBOOK

In what ways were the American colonies becoming their own nation before 1763? In what ways were they still part of the British Empire?

Independent Thinking

Back in North America, many colonists resented the King's proclamation. Some simply disobeyed or ignored it. They had fought in the war for Britain, and they felt they had earned the opportunity to settle on the frontier. American colonists continued to push west of the Appalachian Mountains, hunting and trapping, clearing land, and building new homesteads.

Explore this interactive to consider colonial perspectives during the mid-1700s.

American resistance to the Proclamation of 1763 was a sign of change in the colonies' relationship with Great Britain. Over time, the colonies had developed a distinct set of interests and their own American culture. What was good for Great Britain was no longer seen as necessarily good for the colonists. Many colonists even began to see themselves as Americans rather than British subjects.

The Proclamation of 1763 would not be the last act of the British government to anger the American colonists. Over the next several years, the quarrel would intensify.

Consider the Essential Question:

In what ways were the American colonies becoming their own nation before 1763? In what ways were they still part of the British Empire?

Go online to complete the Social Studies Explanation.

Check for Understanding:

Identify and explain reasons for the growth of representative government and institutions during the colonial period.

3.2 Britain vs. the Colonists

photo: Getty Images

LESSON OVERVIEW

Introduction

In this concept, you'll learn the story of how Americans' attitudes changed so dramatically.

Essential Question

Why did the colonists risk their lives to fight for independence from Great Britain?

Lesson Objectives

By the end of this lesson, you should be able to:

- Explain British efforts to tax and increase controls over colonists after the French and Indian War and evaluate American reactions to these policies.

- Trace and explain the significance of events between 1763 and 1775 that led to the outbreak of the Revolutionary War.

Key Vocabulary

Which terms do you already know?

- ☐ Benjamin Franklin
- ☐ Boston Massacre
- ☐ Boston Tea Party
- ☐ Committees of Correspondence
- ☐ Continental Congress
- ☐ Crispus Attucks
- ☐ Daughters of Liberty
- ☐ First Continental Congress
- ☐ French and Indian War
- ☐ import duty
- ☐ Intolerable Acts
- ☐ John Hancock
- ☐ King George III
- ☐ legislature
- ☐ Lexington and Concord

- ☐ Mercy Otis Warren
- ☐ Navigation Acts
- ☐ parliament
- ☐ Paul Revere
- ☐ Pontiac's Rebellion
- ☐ Proclamation of 1763
- ☐ Quartering Act
- ☐ representative government
- ☐ Richard Henry Lee
- ☐ Samuel Adams
- ☐ Second Continental Congress
- ☐ Sons of Liberty
- ☐ Stamp Act
- ☐ Sugar Act
- ☐ Tea Act
- ☐ Townshend Acts
- ☐ Treaty of Paris

 **Discovery** EDUCATION | **SOCIAL STUDIES TECHBOOK**

Why did the colonists risk their lives to fight for independence from Great Britain?

ENGAGE

How important was independence to the Founders? Visit Engage to learn more.

Essential Question

Why did the colonists risk their lives to fight for independence from Great Britain?

EXPLORE

The Cost of Victory

What challenges did victory in the French and Indian War bring for the British?

In 1763, as a result of its victory in the French and Indian War, Great Britain added a large amount of land to its territory in North America. The British now controlled Canada to the north of the original 13 colonies. To the south and west, the British controlled Florida and all land east of the Mississippi River.

But with victory came challenges. The British were now in control of territory inhabited by English colonists, Native Americans, and French-speaking Canadians. A large number of Native Americans had sided with the French in the war. Many were willing to use violence to block English colonists from establishing new settlements and taking over more of their homelands.

Complete this activity to demonstrate your understanding of perspectives on the French and Indian War.

Managing new land and a greater population were not the only challenges the British faced. Like all armed conflicts, the French and Indian War had been expensive. Much of the war effort had been paid for with borrowed money. Now, the British were responsible for repaying a large war debt in addition to governing and protecting their expanding colony.

The British Tighten Control

How did Great Britain tighten control over its North American territory?

You might recall that the economic relationship between the American colonies and Great Britain was based on a system known as mercantilism. Because of this system, Britain's primary economic goals were to accumulate wealth and to export more goods than it imported. The British established and maintained colonies around the world, including in North America, because of their belief in mercantilism. They believed that holding colonies would give their country greater access to raw materials and also more customers to buy goods manufactured in Great Britain. After the French and Indian War, British officials began to believe that they needed to tighten control over the American colonies to preserve this profitable relationship.

Following the war, the British attempted to maintain peace between Native Americans and potential settlers on the western frontier. The British solution was the Proclamation of 1763. This law announced that colonists would not be permitted to establish settlements west of a line drawn through the Appalachian Mountains. But many colonists remained eager to discover new lands. Other colonists wanted to make money by buying land and selling it for profit. The Proclamation of 1763 did not work as expected, and the colonists continued to settle land west of the Appalachian Mountains. The British military would be needed to keep peace between settlers and Native Americans in the West. Would the colonists be willing to pay their fair share of costs for their own security?

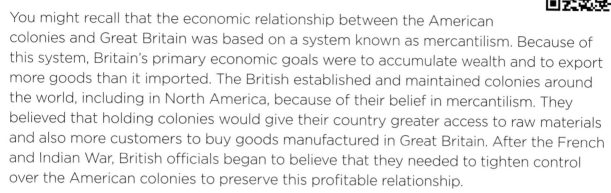

Acts of British Parliament, 1763–1775		
1763	**Proclamation of 1763**	Declared that American colonists would not be permitted to establish new settlements west of a line drawn through the Appalachian Mountains.
1764	**Sugar Act**	Taxed the import of sugar, wine, coffee, molasses, and other goods. Allowed British officers, not colonial judges and juries, to try offenders. Barred colonies from trading lumber and iron to countries other than Britain.
1765	**Stamp Act**	Required colonists to pay a direct tax on all paper used. Colonists had to use stamped paper from London for all printed materials.
1765	**Quartering Act**	Made colonists' house British troops and provide them food, weapons, and supplies.
1766	**Declaratory Act**	Declared Parliament's right to make laws for the colonies.
1767	**Townshend Acts**	Taxed the import of paper, lead, paint, glass, and tea. Cut tea taxes in Britain. Set up British courts in the colonies to enforce acts.
1773	**Tea Act**	Tried to help the British East India Company by shipping its surplus tea to the colonies to sell below the price of colonial merchants.
1774	**Intolerable Acts**	Closed Boston's port to all trade except for food, fuel, and provisions for British troops. Expanded powers of British-appointed governor and appointed a new governing council in Massachusetts. Moved trials of British officials.

The British Parliament imposed many policies on the American colonies from 1763 to 1775.

Between 1764 and 1765, Parliament, the British lawmaking body, passed a series of tax laws. These laws were designed to raise funds for repaying war debts and keeping the colonies secure. First came the Sugar Act. This law actually lowered the tax rates that colonists paid when they purchased items, such as molasses and sugar. But the Sugar Act also improved the British government's ability to collect taxes. For many colonists, the taxes just felt like a new expense.

Discovery SOCIAL STUDIES **TECHBOOK**

Why did the colonists risk their lives to fight for independence from Great Britain?

In 1765, Parliament passed the Stamp Act. This law required many written or printed items, including newspapers, legal documents, and playing cards, to be produced on special paper stamped in Great Britain. In order to purchase this stamped paper, colonists had to pay a tax.

The Stamp Act provided the colonists with unwelcome everyday reminders that their relationship with Great Britain had changed forever.

No Taxation Without Representation

Why did the colonists oppose the new British policies?

By 1763, generations of American colonists had grown accustomed to life without interference from the British government. For most, Great Britain and its government seemed far away. Colonists had avoided British taxes by bribing tax collectors and smuggling goods into the colonies. Suddenly, the British began to enforce tax policies. Additionally, Britain imposed new taxes on items that the colonists bought and sold every day. Many colonists felt an economic pinch.

The colonists also had strong opinions about representative government. For many years, they had elected representatives to make laws for them in colonial legislatures, or lawmaking bodies. As a result, many colonists felt that only representatives whom they had elected had the right to tax them. Because the colonists were not allowed to select representatives to the British Parliament, "no taxation without representation" became the rallying cry against British attempts to raise funds for the empire.

photo: Getty Images

The Stamp Act Stamp, 1765.

The Colonists Respond

How did colonists respond to the new British policies?

Across the colonies, from Boston in the north to Charleston in the Deep South, colonists came up with a variety of ways to protest the new British policies. Many colonists organized boycotts of British goods. Some colonists participated in town hall meetings. A few colonists even tarred and feathered British tax collectors.

photo: Library of Congress

Cartoon of Bostonians abusing a tax collector.

[January, 1770]
(1773 &)

WILLIAM JACKSON,

an IMPORTER; at the

BRAZEN HEAD,

North Side of the TOWN-HOUSE,

and Opposite the Town-Pump, in

Corn-hill, BOSTON.

It is desired that the SONS and
DAUGHTERS of LIBERTY,
would not buy any one. thing of
him, for in so doing they will bring
Disgrace upon *themselves*, and their
Posterity, for *ever* and *ever*, AMEN.

photo: Getty Images

Colonial leaders distributed notices like this, urging colonists to stop purchasing British goods.

In response to the Stamp Act, citizens from different areas of the British colonies began to organize. In October of 1765, representatives from 9 of the 13 colonies met at a special Stamp Act Congress. The Stamp Act Congress published a document known as the Declaration of Rights and Grievances. This document demanded a repeal of the Stamp Act. It also stated that Parliament lacked the authority to tax the colonies. The Stamp Act Congress was the first meeting of elected representatives from across the colonies.

Colonists also formed secret societies. These groups organized protests against the British. They also publicized the concerns of the colonists. In Boston, Samuel Adams led the most famous of these societies, the Sons of Liberty.

The colonists' protests were successful. Sales of British goods fell dramatically. Parliament decided to repeal, or cancel, the Stamp Act. But they also passed the Declaratory Act. This law reminded the colonists that Parliament could still tax them.

The march toward revolution was only beginning.

Tensions Mounting

How did tensions continue to rise after the repeal of the Stamp Act?

Keep in mind that after repealing the Stamp Act, the British still needed funds to keep the colonies safe. In addition, the British still were in debt from the French and Indian War. So, they kept trying to collect revenues, or income, which meant more taxes for the colonists.

Discovery EDUCATION | SOCIAL STUDIES TECHBOOK

Why did the colonists risk their lives to fight for independence from Great Britain?

In 1767, Parliament passed the Townshend Acts. These laws imposed import duties, or special taxes on goods imported into the colonies. Import duties were placed on many everyday items that the colonists purchased from Britain. The Townshend Acts taxed goods such as lead, glass, paper, paint, and tea. The Townshend Acts also took steps to increase British officials' ability to stop smuggling and enforce tax collections.

In response to the Townshend Acts, many colonial merchants signed agreements to stop importing goods from Britain. A group of colonial women supported the effort by forming the Daughters of Liberty. The Daughters of Liberty helped make fabric for clothing and find other alternatives to boycotted items.

Colonial resistance to the Townshend Acts also turned violent. After British officials in Boston tried to seize an American merchant ship that belonged to John Hancock, colonists rioted in protest. British troops were sent to quell the violence.

Things were about to take a turn for the worse.

A "Massacre" in Boston

What was the Boston "Massacre"?

By 1770, American colonists were not on the best terms with members of the British Army, also known as "Redcoats" and "lobsterbacks." In 1765, Parliament had passed the Quartering Act. This hated law required the colonists to provide shelter for British troops, often in their own homes. When protests of British tax policies grew, British officials sent additional troops to colonial cities to maintain order.

The presence of British forces in Boston created particular tensions. Many Boston residents resisted the Quartering Act from the beginning. Merchants in the city were

very angry about the Townshend Acts. During the cold winter of 1770, a quarrel between one colonist and one soldier ignited what came to be called the Boston Massacre.

On March 5, 1770, British Private Hugh White stood guard outside the Boston Custom House, where officials kept track of imports and exports. While on duty, White watched as Captain Lieutenant John Goldfinch made his way back to the barracks where British troops were housed. A young American colonist named Edward Gerrish cried out that Goldfinch had not paid his bill to the wigmaker.

photo: Getty Images

Paul Revere's engraving has a clear anti-British perspective. Locate three examples of Revere's bias in the painting.

Goldfinch, who was in a hurry and had a receipt for the payment in his pocket, ignored Gerrish and went on his way. White, however, engaged the boy, and the two argued. When White struck Gerrish in the head, a crowd began to gather and White called for help. British Captain Thomas Preston responded by bringing seven British soldiers to White's aid. Meanwhile, hundreds of American colonists had gathered, throwing snowballs and other items at the troops.

After British soldiers fired on the crowd, five American colonists lay dead, including Crispus Attucks, a runaway enslaved African American and sailor. To some, Attucks is known as the first man to lose his life in the fight for American independence.

Although the British troops who fired on the crowd were later acquitted of murder, Samuel Adams and the Sons of Liberty used the events of March 5 to rally opposition to British rule. They called the incident "the Boston Massacre." They even

Explore this resource to decide what really happened during the Boston Massacre.

circulated drawings that made the British soldiers look like bloodthirsty attackers of innocent citizens. Later, continued American resistance led to the repeal of the Townshend Acts.

Patriots United

How did the colonies begin to come together?

After the repeal of the Townshend Acts, many colonists feared new British taxes and governmental controls. Some colonists were beginning to see themselves not as British subjects, but as American citizens. These "Patriots" began to realize their common ideas about how the colonies should be governed.

Many years earlier, in 1754, Benjamin Franklin had published a famous cartoon with the warning "Join, or Die." This cartoon was an early call for unity across the colonies.

photo: Library of Congress

This image, first published by Benjamin Franklin, became a symbol of unity in the colonies during the 1760s and 1770s.

Suddenly, nearly 20 years later, Franklin's message meant something to colonists from Massachusetts to Georgia.

Now, groups of prominent citizens in several colonies decided to share ideas. One such citizen was Mercy Otis Warren, the sister of Patriot James Otis and wife of political leader James Warren. When the conflict over British taxation began, Warren began holding protest meetings in her home. Around the same time, she wrote a series of plays that supported the Patriot cause and criticized British officials in Massachusetts.

Discovery SOCIAL STUDIES
EDUCATION **TECHBOOK**.

Why did the colonists risk their lives to fight for independence from Great Britain?

These early protest meetings and gatherings led to the formation of the Committees of Correspondence. These committees promoted the Patriots' cause. They also planned responses to British actions. At first, the committees met separately in their own colonies. In 1773, however, the Committees of Correspondence from each colony decided to come together.

It is important to keep in mind that not everyone agreed on what the colonial interests really were. Some colonists vowed to keep their allegiance to the British throne. These people became known as Loyalists—they were loyal to the king of England, King George III, and placed the interests of Great Britain over those of the colonies. Loyalists weren't just a handful of colonists; probably about 20 percent of colonists held Loyalist opinions. In the course of the revolution, many Loyalists left America. Some went back to Great Britain, while others moved to Canada.

The Tea Party and Its Aftermath

What happened at the Boston Tea Party? How did the British respond?

In 1773, the British passed the Tea Act. This law was intended to help the British East India Tea company, which had been struggling. It also was designed to help the British raise more revenues. The Tea Act sent millions of pounds of British East Indian Tea to the colonies to be sold at low prices. The tea prices included a tax, which had been placed on tea with the Townshend Acts. The British thought that the East Indian tea would be so cheap that colonists would not mind paying the tax.

But colonial merchants were angry about the Tea Act. They did not want to be told whose tea they had to sell. Many colonists came to think of the East Indian Tea as a symbol of the British government abusing its power over the colonists.

Across the colonies, Patriots protested the Tea Act. In Charleston, South Carolina, British tea was left to rot on the docks. In Philadelphia and New York, colonists refused to let British ships dock, so they had to turn back to Britain. And in Boston, the Sons of Liberty staged the famous Boston Tea Party, dumping hundreds of chests of tea into Boston Harbor.

THE DESTRUCTION OF TEA AT BOSTON HARBOR.

photo: Library of Congress

The Boston Tea Party.

British officials were furious at the city of Boston for the Boston Tea Party. To punish the colonists, they passed a set of regulations that the colonists called the Intolerable Acts. These acts created a blockade around Boston's harbor, closing it off to most forms of trade. The acts took authority away from the elected legislature of Massachusetts and gave new powers to British troops in America. For many Patriots, the Intolerable Acts were an act of war.

Colonial leaders began to fear that the British would use force to maintain control over the colonies. The colonial leaders decided that a new organization and response were needed. On September 5, 1774, delegates from 12 of the 13 colonies met in Philadelphia at what came to be called the First Continental Congress. There, they worked on a joint response to the Intolerable Acts.

From Words to Weapons

What were the final steps leading to war?

On October 14, 1774, the First Continental Congress issued a document known as the Declaration and Resolves. This document was a petition to King George III. It called for the repeal of the Intolerable Acts. It also demanded that Parliament and the king respect the colonists' rights as citizens.

Historians do not agree on the purpose of this petition to the king. Some believe the colonists meant to provoke a war with the British. Others believe they meant to appeal to British officials' sense of reason in order to avoid war.

But British officials viewed the colonial leaders assembled in the congress as traitors and revolutionaries.

In Massachusetts, Patriots began preparing for war with the British. They gathered and stored weapons in the small town of Concord, just outside of Boston. On April 18, 1775, the royal governor of Massachusetts, General Thomas Gage, sent a small force to seize these weapons.

What followed was a "shot heard 'round the world."

The Shot Heard 'Round the World

How did the Revolutionary War begin?

On the night of April 18, 1775, a group of colonists learned about General Gage's plan to send troops to Concord. They sent Paul Revere and William Dawes to ride their horses and warn Americans to stop Gage's troops before they could get to Concord.

The British captured Paul Revere before he could reach Concord. But the news of the British advance spread rapidly. When the British reached the nearby town of Lexington, they faced a group of colonists known as minutemen, led by Captain John Parker. Minutemen referred to the men's ability to assemble quickly, "at a minute's notice."

photo: Getty Images

At Lexington and Concord, colonial militia called minutemen overcame British forces. The British retreated to Boston.

Discovery EDUCATION | SOCIAL STUDIES **TECHBOOK**

Why did the colonists risk their lives to fight for independence from Great Britain?

A skirmish broke out on the Lexington Green when someone—historians still cannot identify who—fired a shot. Eight minutemen died and one British soldier was wounded during the exchange.

Minutemen in Lexington were an organized group, but they were not strong enough to stop the British advance. The royal troops continued to Concord. There, the colonists forced the British to turn back and retreat at the North Bridge. The British suffered heavy casualties on their march back from Concord. At the end of the two battles, the British had lost a total of 273 troops, compared with 95 fatalities for the colonists. The Battle of Lexington and Concord convinced many colonists that war with Great Britain was inevitable. The fateful first shot fired at Lexington became known as the "shot heard 'round the world."

The American War of Independence had begun.

Explore this interactive to learn more about events leading to the Revolution.

Consider the Essential Question:

Why did the colonists risk their lives to fight for independence from Great Britain?

Go online to complete the Social Studies Explanation.

Check for Understanding:

Explain the most important issues and events that directly resulted in the battle of Lexington and Concord.

3.3 The Declaration of Independence Explored

photo: Getty Images

LESSON OVERVIEW

Introduction

In this concept, you will learn why the colonists declared independence and why independence was so important to them.

Essential Question

How does the Declaration of Independence reflect the colonists' ideas about government?

Lesson Objectives

By the end of this lesson, you should be able to:

- Trace and summarize key events that resulted in the colonists' decision to declare independence from Great Britain.

- Explain how the Declaration of Independence outlines basic ideas about the purpose and responsibilities of government.

Key Vocabulary

Which terms do you already know?

- ☐ Abigail Adams
- ☐ Baron de Montesquieu
- ☐ Benjamin Franklin
- ☐ *Common Sense*
- ☐ Declaration of Independence
- ☐ Francis Bacon
- ☐ George Mason
- ☐ Indian Removal Act
- ☐ individualism
- ☐ John Adams
- ☐ John Hancock
- ☐ John Jay
- ☐ John Locke
- ☐ John Ross
- ☐ King George III
- ☐ natural right
- ☐ Oklahoma (Indian Territory)
- ☐ Osceola
- ☐ Patrick Henry
- ☐ representative
- ☐ Robert Livingston
- ☐ Roger Sherman
- ☐ social contract
- ☐ Thomas Jefferson
- ☐ Thomas Paine
- ☐ Trail of Tears
- ☐ unalienable right
- ☐ Voltaire

How does the Declaration of Independence reflect the colonists' ideas about government?

ENGAGE

What does it feel like to start a new nation? Visit Engage to learn more.

Essential Question

How does the Declaration of Independence reflect the colonists' ideas about government?

EXPLORE

Americans Choose Independence

What events led to America's declaring independence from Great Britain?

After the fighting at Lexington and Concord in April 1775, the King of England declared Massachusetts to be in a state of rebellion against Great Britain. This action did nothing to stop the insurrection. Militiamen throughout the New England Colonies poured into Boston to join the fight against the Redcoats. By the time of the Battle of Bunker Hill in June, the militia was 15,000 strong.

After the Battle of Bunker Hill, King George III officially declared all the colonies to be in a state of rebellion. This basically was a declaration of war against the colonies. Many Americans could not decide whether to remain loyal to the British Crown or to join the cause of the American Patriots. Then, in January 1776, Thomas Paine released his revolutionary pamphlet *Common Sense*. Paine argued that King George would never accept limits on his actions. In his pamphlet, Paine convinced many Americans that if they wanted a republican government, they would have to rid themselves of British rule.

Common Sense made an argument for a concept known as the rule of law. Under the rule of law, governmental authority is limited to carrying out the laws. People who work for the government have only the powers that the laws give them. As the Magna Carta had asserted in 1215, the rule of law limits even the powers of the king. Paine's writings helped cement in the American public's mind the idea of a country united under the rule of law, free from the king's abuses of power.

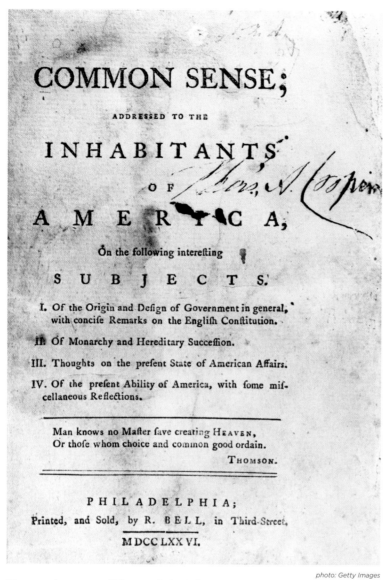

COMMON SENSE;

ADDRESSED TO THE

INHABITANTS

OF

AMERICA,

On the following interesting

SUBJECTS.

I. Of the Origin and Design of Government in general, with concise Remarks on the English Constitution.

II. Of Monarchy and Hereditary Succession.

III. Thoughts on the present State of American Affairs.

IV. Of the present Ability of America, with some miscellaneous Reflections.

Man knows no Master save creating HEAVEN,
Or those whom choice and common good ordain.
THOMSON.

PHILADELPHIA;

Printed, and Sold, by R. BELL, in Third-Street.

MDCCLXXVI.

photo: Getty Images

The opening page of Thomas Paine's Common Sense.

That spring, the colony of Virginia took the ultimate step: It formally declared independence from Great Britain. If the bid for independence was unsuccessful, the leaders of Virginia would be punished as traitors. Knowing this risk, would you have been willing to declare independence?

The Virginia Convention decided to try to win support from the other colonies. They wanted the Continental Congress to approve a unified declaration of independence that would apply to all 13 colonies. Richard Henry Lee, who represented Virginia in Congress, proposed such a resolution on June 7, 1776.

Although the Revolutionary War had been going on for more than a year, there was some debate over Lee's proposal. The individual colonies could not agree on the best time to declare independence. Some representatives wanted to continue to work for reconciliation with the king. But it soon became clear that Lee's resolution would eventually be approved. In response, the Second Continental Congress appointed a committee to write a formal declaration that would announce to the world the colonists' argument for independence. This drafting committee, known as the Committee of Five, included John Adams, Thomas Jefferson, Roger Sherman, Benjamin Franklin, and Robert Livingston. The committee's youngest member, Thomas Jefferson, was appointed to draft this document. The Second Continental Congress adjourned for three weeks and came together again at the beginning of July.

On July 2, 1776, Congress approved Richard Henry Lee's resolution to declare independence from Great Britain. Two days later, the Second Continental Congress adopted the Declaration of Independence. The document was officially entered into the congressional record on July 4, 1776, and signed by the president of the Second Continental Congress, John Hancock.

Discovery EDUCATION | SOCIAL STUDIES **TECHBOOK**

How does the Declaration of Independence reflect the colonists' ideas about government?

Old Ideas for a New Nation

How did the writings of John Locke influence ideas expressed in the Declaration of Independence?

The ideas that Thomas Jefferson expressed in the Declaration of Independence were not new in 1776. John Locke, an English economic and political philosopher from the late 1600s, was one of the chief sources of these ideas. Locke's ideas, like those of Thomas Paine, were influenced by the social contract theory. A contract is an agreement in which people exchange promises. Locke believed that a social contract was a basic agreement by the people to accept the rule of government. Locke believed that a social contract would enable people to live together in peace.

In his social contract theory, Locke stated that every man has the natural right to defend his "life, health, liberty, or possessions." A natural right is a right that people have from birth, simply because they are people. Locke said that natural rights come from God. These natural rights described by Locke influenced the "unalienable rights" Jefferson described in the Declaration of Independence: life, liberty, and the pursuit of happiness.

According to Locke, people form governments to protect their rights. When people form a government, they agree, or consent, to a set of rules that are intended to protect their rights. When entering into a social contract, then, the

photo: Library of Congress

John Locke (1632–1704) wrote his influential essays around the time of the English Civil War—more than 75 years before the American Revolution.

people agree to be ruled by a government. In return, the government agrees to protect the natural rights of the people. For instance, government enacts and enforces laws against assault and theft, and it also raises an army to protect against invasion.

Locke argued that without the consent of the people, government has no right to exist. If government fails to protect people's rights, it violates the agreement. Or if it uses powers that the people have not consented to, it violates the agreement. If government violates the agreement, the contract is broken and the people have the right to abolish the government.

We Hold These Truths

What does the Declaration of Independence say?

The Declaration of Independence is organized into four parts: the introduction, the preamble, the list of grievances, and the resolution.

- **Introduction:** The introduction of the Declaration of Independence announces the document's purpose. It states that it will explain the reasons why the American colonies decided to separate from Great Britain.

- **Preamble:** The preamble sets forth the colonists' beliefs about the purpose of government and outlines the ideals of the new nation.

- **List of grievances:** This section explains in general terms why colonists thought they were justified in declaring independence. Then, it supports these arguments with a list of specific complaints against the king of England.

- **Resolution:** The final section of the Declaration formally dissolves the union between Britain and the colonies and declares independence for the new country, the United States of America. Finally, the signers pledge loyalty to each other.

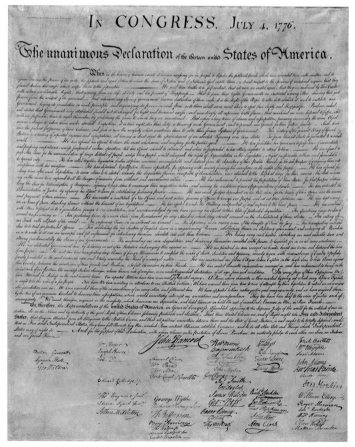

photo: Library of Congress

An original copy of the Declaration of Independence is on display at the National Archives in Washington, DC.

Discovery | SOCIAL STUDIES
EDUCATION | **TECHBOOK**

How does the Declaration of Independence reflect the colonists' ideas about government?

The words of the Declaration of Independence are evidence of John Locke's influence on Jefferson's ideas about government. In the opening, for example, the Declaration states:

"We hold these truths to be self-evident, that all men are created equal, that they are endowed by their Creator with certain unalienable Rights, that among these are Life, Liberty and the pursuit of Happiness. That to secure these rights, Governments are instituted among Men, deriving their just powers from the consent of the governed."

The expression *truths are self-evident* means there are certain facts that are so obvious that they do not need to be proved. According to the Declaration, three facts are self-evident:

- All men are created equal.

- All men have been given rights by their Creator. These rights are unalienable, meaning that they cannot be taken away.

- The purpose of government is to protect individual rights, and governmental authority comes from the people.

What do you think the Declaration says about what should happen when a government fails to protect the rights of its people?

Congress Makes the Break

How did the Declaration of Independence justify rejecting the British government?

The Declaration of Independence argues that when a government abuses its power and ignores or interferes with people's natural rights, it is in effect breaking the social contract. When this happens, citizens have the right to form a new government that protects their rights.

With these words, the Declaration argues that Great Britain's failure to protect the colonists' individual rights justified the colonists' attempt to create a new independent government.

An *usurpation* is the seizure of something that rightfully belongs to someone else. The bulk of the Declaration of Independence lists the ways in which the British government usurped the colonists' natural rights and therefore violated the social contract.

photo: Getty Images

This painting shows the drafting committee presenting its draft of the Declaration of Independence to Congress. The Continental Congress discussed and edited the precise wording for three days.

The charges against King George include the following:

- refusing to make laws to address new problems, prohibiting local governments from making such laws, dissolving local governments, and removing elected officials and refusing to replace them

- removing judges or withholding pay from judges who do not judge according to the king's wishes

- maintaining standing armies in times of peace

- holding fake trials in Britain on falsified charges, imprisoning people without trial by jury, excusing and absolving soldiers who commit violence against civilians

- passing and collecting taxes without the input of colonial representatives, also known as taxation without representation

- capturing colonist sailors at sea and forcing them to serve in the British Navy

- cutting off trade with the rest of the world

The Declaration also says that the colonists had made many appeals for justice and friendship to the king and to the British people. The colonists had tried for years to get Britain to appreciate their point of view. In July 1776, they decided there was nothing left to try. They had done all they could to remain part of Britain and failed. Now, they would go their own way as "free and independent states."

The Declaration ends with the Founders pledging their lives and their "sacred honor" to each other. They knew that their attempt to split from Britain required them to work together, to protect each other, and to trust each other. They knew that Britain would not let them go without a fight; the fighting had already started.

The Legacy of the Declaration of Independence
Why is the Declaration of Independence an important historical document?

Congress had several goals in issuing the Declaration of Independence. One was to send a message of unity to American citizens from Massachusetts to Georgia. After all, the former colonies needed each other. No single colony by itself would have been able to resist British control. Even reluctant colonists were needed to support the revolutionary cause.

The young nation also sought to gain international support for its decision to declare independence. It desperately needed help in fighting a war against Great Britain, one of the wealthiest and most powerful nations on Earth. To gain this support, Congress needed to make a convincing argument to the world that the colonies had no choice but to break their long-standing bonds with the British.

Finally, Congress sought to prove to its own citizens, to the king of England, and to the rest of the world that the United States was a credible part of the international community. Therefore, the Declaration claimed for the young nation the authority "to levy War, conclude Peace, contract Alliances, establish Commerce, and to do all other Acts and Things which Independent States may of right do."

Explore this interactive to take a closer look at the Declaration of Independence.

The words of the Declaration of Independence had an impact far beyond the borders of the United States. The document's statement that people could create their own "free and independent" states later inspired other colonies and countries to overthrow what they thought were oppressive governments. The ideas of Jefferson's Declaration of Independence were borrowed by many: in Europe by the Flemish as they declared independence from the Austrian Empire in the 1790s, in South America by Venezuelans as they declared independence from the Spanish Empire in the early 1800s, and even in Asia by Vietnamese rebels who asserted independence from France in 1945. Today, more than half of the world's independent nations have founding documents that are declarations of independence.

In July 1776, the Declaration's statement that "all men are created equal" did not apply to many groups of Americans. Throughout the United States, for example, voting rights were reserved for white male property owners. Native Americans faced the loss of their homelands to western settlers. Finally, many of the document's signers continued to support the institution of slavery. During the many decades following Congress's approval of the Declaration of Independence, much of American history has been defined by the struggles of African Americans, women, Native Americans, and other groups, to realize the full meaning of Jefferson's words.

Consider the Essential Question:

How does the Declaration of Independence reflect the colonists' ideas about government?

Go online to complete the Social Studies Explanation.

Check for Understanding:

Define and give examples of unalienable rights. How does the Declaration's statement about unalienable rights connect with the colonists' desire to declare independence?

3.4 Fighting for Independence

photo: The New York Public Library

LESSON OVERVIEW

Introduction

In this concept, you will learn how a band of novice soldiers with inadequate supplies fought and defeated the most powerful military force in the world. In doing so, they helped create a new country.

Essential Question

How did the United States manage to win the Revolutionary War?

Lesson Objectives

By the end of this lesson, you should be able to:

- Summarize key battles and events that affected the outcome of the Revolutionary War.

- Describe the accomplishments of key historical figures from the American Revolution.

- Draw conclusions about how the colonists defeated Great Britain in the Revolutionary War.

- Summarize the provisions of the Treaty of Paris and describe its impact on the United States.

Key Vocabulary

Which terms do you already know?

- [ ] Bunker Hill
- [ ] Benedict Arnold
- [ ] Benjamin Franklin
- [ ] Bernardo de Gálvez
- [ ] Charles Cornwallis
- [ ] Continental army
- [ ] Deborah Sampson
- [ ] emancipation
- [ ] Ethan Allen
- [ ] Francis Marion
- [ ] Friedrich von Steuben
- [ ] Henry Knox
- [ ] Hessian
- [ ] Horatio Gates
- [ ] Hudson River
- [ ] James Armistead
- [ ] John Burgoyne
- [ ] John Paul Jones

- [ ] Loyalist
- [ ] Marquis de Lafayette
- [ ] Mary Ludwig Hays
- [ ] Massachusetts
- [ ] militia
- [ ] minutemen
- [ ] Nathanael Greene
- [ ] Nathan Hale
- [ ] Patrick Henry
- [ ] Patriot
- [ ] Peter Salem
- [ ] Phillis Wheatley
- [ ] Samuel Prescott
- [ ] Saratoga
- [ ] Thaddeus Kosciusko
- [ ] Thomas Gage
- [ ] Treaty of Paris
- [ ] Trenton
- [ ] Valley Forge
- [ ] William Dawes
- [ ] William Howe
- [ ] Yorktown

Discovery | SOCIAL STUDIES
EDUCATION | TECHBOOK

How did the United States manage to win the Revolutionary War?

ENGAGE

How did the colonists win? Visit Engage to learn more.

> ## Essential Question
>
> How did the United States manage to win the Revolutionary War?

EXPLORE

War Begins at Bunker Hill

What was the fighting like at the first major battle of the Revolutionary War?

In the spring of 1775, the British viewed Boston as the head and heart of the rebellion. They brought in ships and troops to occupy the city and control the surrounding waters of Boston Harbor. Soon after this, they sent troops to Concord to try to take control of colonial armaments.

The city of Boston is on a peninsula attached by a thin neck to the mainland. Where the neck joined the mainland, the British set up defenses to protect their land access to and from the city. After the fighting at Lexington and Concord, the colonial militia—regular citizens organized for military service—had positioned troops surrounding these British posts. The militia threatened to cut off the British posts from the mainland.

Just across the water from Boston was Charlestown, at the base of Breed's Hill and Bunker Hill, which overlooked the harbor. In June, the British generals decided to improve their control of the harbor by capturing Bunker and Breed's Hills. The generals included General Thomas Gage, who was not only a British general, but also the royal governor for Massachusetts.

Spies enabled the American colonists to get early news of Gage's plan. On June 13, 1775, the colonist soldiers snuck up Breed's Hill in the middle of the summer night. While it was dark, they dug and built an entrenchment—a trench to protect them from enemy fire. In the morning, the British woke up to find a large redoubt, or defensive wall, on top of the hill. This made Gage and British General William Howe doubly determined to capture the hill.

photo: Getty Images

The battle of Bunker Hill actually took place on Breed's Hill, the lower of the two heights above Charlestown, Massachusetts. Here, British ships fire on Charlestown during battle.

The British plan was to land at Charlestown Point and march up the hill, directly into the face of the American forces. In the ensuing Battle of Bunker Hill, the British sent three assaults up Breed's Hill.

It was in this battle that American rebel leader Colonel William Prescott told his troops to hold their fire until the British were close enough that they could see the color of their eyes. It is a popular misconception that Prescott said ". . . whites of their eyes"; the whites are visible from much farther away. Prescott knew that his untrained troops could fire much more accurately at close range. Also, they needed to preserve their powder and ammunition.

The Americans withstood the first two charges, but the third attack was too much for them. Out of ammunition, they were forced to retreat. By the end, some soldiers used broken glass and rocks as bullets. The British took the hill. In doing so, the British suffered 1,054 casualties to the Americans' 411. Even though the Americans lost the hill, they cost the British Army far more casualties than they themselves suffered. The colonists' efforts at the Battle of Bunker Hill proved that the Americans would not be easy to defeat.

Complete this activity to show what you know about places of importance in the Revolution.

New Battlefields of America

What tactics did the Americans use to fight the British?

War in Europe during the 1700s was orderly and structured. Armies marched in blocks or lines, advancing on the opposing forces. Closer and closer they would march until they were face-to-face in firing range. Often, the winning army was the one that did not simply run away in terror. Imagine how untrained colonists felt facing large armies of professional warriors!

During the first battles of the war, Americans were underprepared. The colonists were regular workers: farmers, merchants, tradespeople, and sailors. They had not been trained in military methods like the soldiers of the British Army. At Bunker Hill, the colonists managed to fortify a hill, but they did not have the supplies needed to hold it. The battle lasted only a few hours before the Americans ran out of ammunition.

Discovery SOCIAL STUDIES
EDUCATION | TECHBOOK

How did the United States manage to win the Revolutionary War?

To survive the British attacks, colonists worked at two things. First, they trained heavily in traditional warfare techniques, such as following orders, marching in straight lines, and taking turns loading and firing.

More important, they started using the war tactics of their neighbors, the Native Americans. Instead of marching in lines toward the larger British Army, the colonists began to ambush the British. Their knowledge of the geographical features of the area gave the Americans an advantage. Colonial soldiers knew shortcuts and ideal places for ambushes. They also knew where to find local people they could trust.

photo: Getty Images

An American painting from the 1800s of Washington crossing the Delaware in preparation for the Battle of Trenton.

During the Battle of Bunker Hill, the colonists hid snipers behind a rock wall by the river and in the town of Charlestown and surprised the English as they began up Breed's Hill. Sometimes, they even hid up in trees.

Another method of surprise was to attack in the middle of the night. On Christmas night, 1776, George Washington, commander of the Continental army, led his troops across the icy Delaware River in the middle of the night. Washington knew that many of the enemy soldiers were not British citizens, but Hessian mercenaries. A mercenary is a professional soldier for hire. During the Revolutionary War, Great Britain hired Hessians, or mercenaries from an area in Germany known as Hesse. Washington guessed that these paid soldiers would be enjoying their holiday off rather than standing watch in the freezing cold night. His army took the British completely by surprise and won the Battle of Trenton.

Foreign Influences

How did other countries impact the outcome of the Revolutionary War?

England had many enemies in Europe. From the beginning, the revolutionaries received aid from some of these countries, including from France and Holland. These countries wanted to keep their aid secret. France, which for hundreds of years had been in and out of war with England, did not want to enrage the British.

But the colonists needed more than aid. They wanted actual forces to add numbers to the struggling colonial army. Benjamin Franklin went to France and waged a diplomatic campaign to bring the French into the war. At first, France did not believe that the American rebels had any chance of victory. The French did not want to invest lives, money, and their own reputation in a hopeless cause.

Only after the Battle of Saratoga in 1777 did the French begin to see the American cause as one that could be won. The battle came about in this way: The British already held control of New York City and the lower Hudson River. The British General John Burgoyne planned to march south from Canada to capture Albany, New York, on the upper Hudson River. British control of the Hudson would isolate New England from the rest of the colonies.

photo: Getty Images

The surrender of Burgoyne at Saratoga, New York, October 17, 1777.

Burgoyne's march south through Vermont's mountainous wilderness was slowed by the lack of roads. His army had to clear brush and trees to enable supply wagons and artillery, or large, heavy weapons such as cannons, to travel. The army also hauled a huge amount of the general's fine furniture and his extensive wardrobe. The delay gave the Americans time to build fortifications, such as trenches and protective barriers. Meanwhile, the British began to run low on supplies. To top it off, the English General Howe, who had been ordered to provide reinforcements for Burgoyne, never showed up. Instead, Howe decided to lead an attack on Philadelphia. After a month of fighting near Saratoga, Burgoyne formally surrendered on October 17.

Impressed with this major American victory, the French agreed to finance the Americans and to send troops and ships to support the cause.

Although the French forces remained separate from the American, there were also Frenchmen who joined the Continental army. One was the Marquis de Lafayette. Lafayette was wealthy, young, idealistic, and untrained, but he learned quickly: Eventually, the Marquis was named a major general, and served as a division commander at the Battle of Yorktown.

Spanish forces were also involved in the Revolutionary War, particularly along the coast of the Gulf of Mexico. For example, the Viceroy of New Spain, Bernardo de Gálvez, aided the American war effort by smuggling supplies to American troops and capturing four British forts along the Gulf Coast. After the British surrendered, de Gálvez retained right to the lands he conquered during the war as a thank you from the King of Spain. He was also made a Lieutenant General and governor over Louisiana and West Florida. The city of Galveston, Texas, is named in his honor.

Other Europeans in the Revolutionary War included Tadeusz Kościuszko (TA de oosh kosh CHOOSH ko), an experienced Polish general, and Friederich von Steuben, a leading German general, who helped train the Continentals in conventional fighting. Today, there are many streets, parks, and monuments across the country dedicated to Lafayette, Kościuszko, and von Steuben.

After the war, ideas from the American Revolution crossed the Atlantic and affected events in Europe, particularly in France. Lafayette and other French nobles who fought alongside American patriots favored making democratic reforms to France's absolute monarchy. They were encouraged by prominent American Founders who lived in France as diplomats, including Benjamin Franklin and Thomas Jefferson. In 1789, at the beginning of the French Revolution, France's National Assembly drafted the Declaration of the Rights of Man and of the Citizen. Influenced by the American Declaration of Independence, this document listed a series of rights that would be guaranteed to all French citizens. It also stated that all men were created equal.

Civilians Pitch In

How did civilian colonists support the Revolution?

Americans' faith in their cause wavered after early British victories and the capture of major cities such as Boston, Philadelphia, and New York. Supplies were tough to obtain, and the soldiers had to endure grueling conditions. In response, just as Thomas Paine's *Common Sense* had spurred Americans to declare independence, Paine's pamphlet series *The American Crisis* energized the Patriot cause throughout the Revolution.

The winter of 1777–1778 was a particularly rough time for Washington's troops, who were quartered at Valley Forge, about 20 miles west of Philadelphia, in Pennsylvania. Not only were food supplies inadequate, but there was insufficient fuel for fires to keep the barracks warm. There was also a shortage of boots, and some soldiers had only rags for clothes. George Washington's success in keeping this army together—and persuading soldiers not to desert—contributed to his reputation as a great leader.

The soldiers in the militias and the Continental army were all men except for a handful of women who disguised themselves and kept their gender secret. But these were not the only women contributing to the Revolutionary cause. Women did essential work to supply the troops. They made clothing, including winter coats. They ran family farms and businesses while husbands and sons were away fighting. They collected and communicated information about troop movements.

Women also worked and lived under fire. Molly Pitcher was a nickname for women who assisted on the battlefield. Molly Pitchers traveled with the troops, serving as cooks, seamstresses, and nurses. They also distributed gunpowder and brought water to troops on the battlefield.

Probably the most famous Molly Pitcher was Mary Ludwig Hays. Hays followed her husband's regiment to help cook and take care of wounded soldiers. During the Battle of Monmouth, Mary took over her husband's cannon after he was injured. She fought throughout the entire battle, which the Americans won. Afterward, she was appointed sergeant and put on the regular army payroll.

photo: Library of Congress

"Molly Pitcher" took over the cannon after her husband was injured at the Battle of Monmouth.

Phillis Wheatley was enslaved at the age of seven or eight and lived in the North. Unlike nearly all other slaves, Phillis was taught by her masters to read and write. And unlike many other writers, Wheatley was successful enough during her lifetime to earn a living as a writer. She wrote poetry in praise of George Washington and the Revolution. Washington called her poetry "a striking proof of your great poetical Talents."

Civilians also provided financial assistance to the often cash-strapped American government. Haym Salomon, a Polish-born Jewish immigrant, negotiated with the French to secure financial aid for the American war effort. Solomon also personally gave interest-free loans to individual American leaders such as James Madison, as well as to the American military. Many of these loans were never repaid.

Divided Loyalties

What roles did African Americans play in the Revolutionary War?

The British actively recruited Loyalists and enslaved people to serve in their armies. The royal governor of Virginia even issued a proclamation promising freedom to any enslaved people who fought for the British. Many had escaped from American farms when their owners fled from the British Army. They chose to fight for the British because they believed—or at least hoped—that Britain would protect their freedom better than the American colonists had. Others were enslaved people who were forcibly enlisted by their Loyalist "owners."

On the colonists' side, African American soldiers had been fighting in the state militias since the start of the war. After 1776, when, in desperate need of soldiers, General Washington lifted the ban on black enlistment, at least 5,000 African American soldiers also served in the Continental army.

Peter Salem was an African American soldier from Massachusetts. Salem played a vital role in the Battle of Bunker Hill when he shot Major John Pitcairn. When Pitcairn was lost, the British were sent into chaos, allowing the Americans time to retreat. Salem continued to fight in the war until it was over.

One man, James Armistead, was recognizable on both sides. An enslaved man, Armistead received permission from his owner to join the regiment of Marquis de Lafayette. He asked to join as Lafayette's servant, but the Marquis believed Armistead would be more useful as a spy. Armistead infiltrated the camp of British General Lord Charles Cornwallis, who then hired Armistead to spy for the British—making him a colonial double agent. Armistead allowed the Americans to find out about the fortifications at Yorktown, leading to the final battle of the war.

While many enslaved people on both sides were promised freedom for their roles, only a few were granted full emancipation. James Armistead had a letter written by Lafayette declaring him a brave hero who deserved freedom. It still took two years for him to be freed from slavery.

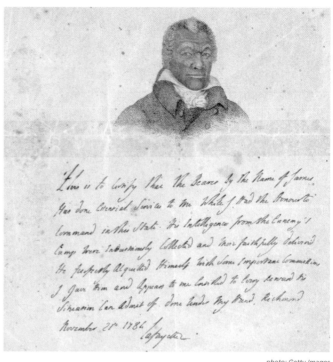

photo: Getty Images

Marquis de Lafayette's original certificate commending James Armistead for his Revolutionary War service, 1784.

Native Americans Choose Sides

How did Native Americans participate in the Revolutionary War?

Because the Revolutionary War took place on the Native Americans' homeland, it directly affected their lives. Yet, there was much division between different Native American communities over which side to support in the conflict.

A few Native American nations, mainly in the northeastern parts of the country, were on friendly terms with colonists. But the majority of Native Americans did not want to encourage colonial expansion westward. Because England had sought to protect Native American lands from settlers, many Native Americans found it easier to back the British. They used their knowledge of the land to help the English armies. Many who had fought against the British in the French and Indian War remained hostile to Britain and chose to help the Americans.

photo: Getty Images

Mohawk chief Joseph Brant fought for the British.

About 1,500 Iroquois fought for the British throughout the war. One was Joseph Brant, whose native name was Thayendanegea. Brant was a Mohawk warrior who led four of the six nations of the Iroquois Confederacy into the war. He was educated at an Anglican missionary school in Connecticut and was the brother-in-law of the British superintendent of Indian Affairs. He had built a reputation as a skilled warrior. Colonists feared him after his raid on Cherry Valley, New York, in 1778, known as the Cherry Valley Massacre.

Fruits of Victory

How did the Revolutionary War come to an end?

With the French supporting the colonists, the British increased their efforts to seek support from Loyalists in America. By 1779, British forces were focused on the Southern Colonies. There were more Loyalists in the agriculture-based South, where the British taxes did not hit as hard. In the South, the British could also more easily obtain supplies from their territories in the Caribbean.

The southern campaign began with the British capture of the important port cities of Savannah, Georgia, and Charleston, South Carolina. From there, the British campaign in the South did not go well. Repeatedly, the Americans managed to lure the British into useless battles. The British claimed several victories but gained no territory. After many months in the Carolinas, British General Cornwallis led his troops north to Virginia to regroup. He planned to gather reinforcements and launch a massive campaign to overwhelm the South. Cornwallis settled on Yorktown as the place to wait for the troop ships to arrive. Yorktown was the port that served for Virginia's capital city of Williamsburg, which the Americans held.

photo: Library of Congress

The signing of the Preliminary Treaty of Peace at Paris, November 30, 1782, by the joint commissioners of the United States and England. Jay and Franklin are standing at the left.

General Washington saw his chance. With the British isolated on a small peninsula, the Americans marched out of Williamsburg and cut off Cornwallis from the mainland, setting the stage for the Battle of Yorktown. Using redoubts, or fortifications, that the English had left unguarded, the Americans were able to set up their artillery very close to the British camps. A French fleet sat off the coast, blocking the inlet to the Chesapeake Bay and preventing a British escape by sea. On September 30, 1781, the Americans began shelling.

British supplies held out until October 19. General Cornwallis surrendered, and the war was over.

Discovery SOCIAL STUDIES
EDUCATION | **TECHBOOK**

How did the United States manage to win the Revolutionary War?

Complete this activity to learn more about key events in the Revolutionary War.

A peace treaty between the Americans and British was signed in 1783. The Treaty of Paris embodied many specific agreements, but the first was the most important to the colonists.

This recognized the independence of the former American colonies—now the American states—from the British Crown. The United States had become its own country.

The Treaty of Paris

What were the provisions of the Treaty of Paris, and what was its impact?

On November 30, 1782, a preliminary peace treaty between Britain and the United States was signed. The definitive Treaty of Paris officially ending the war was signed on September 3, 1783. (Separate treaties were also made between Britain and France, Spain, and the Netherlands.)

The United States-Britain treaty recognized the United States as independent and sovereign. It set the United States' boundaries at British Canada, Florida, and the Mississippi River, which was guaranteed to remain open to international travel.

Americans won rights to fisheries in the Grand Banks off of Newfoundland, and creditors from both countries were to be allowed to collect on their debts. Congress also agreed to recommend to the states that they treat Loyalists fairly and restore confiscated property. But some of these provisions caused difficulties and disputes later, and large numbers of Loyalists fled America for Canada, the West Indies, or England.

Free from British control, the Americans now needed to govern themselves. The plans were already in place. The Articles of Confederation had been written following America's declaration of independence. At that time, the Continental Congress instructed each state to create its own constitution and charged one group to write a national constitution. The Articles of Confederation were ratified by all the states by March 1, 1781. This agreement was the first U.S. Constitution.

Under the Articles of Confederation, the states remained independent and sovereign. The Confederation Congress had the right to do only the following:

- regulate foreign affairs
- wage war
- operate the postal service
- appoint military officers

- control Native American affairs
- borrow money
- determine the value of coin
- issue bills of credit

Read the list carefully, and you will see that the Articles gave Congress little power to enforce its decisions. Congress could wage war, but it could not demand that states provide armies. It could borrow money, but had no power to collect taxes to repay its debts.

The colonies had freed themselves of British rule and established their own independent government, but they also faced a number of new challenges. They could no longer rely on a mother country for financial support and supplies. The new government would have to compete economically with the major world powers such as Great Britain, France, and Spain. To win the revolution, the colonies had accumulated a significant war debt, and paying this debt would become a major concern during the early years of the republic.

Consider the Essential Question:

How did the United States manage to win the Revolutionary War?

Go online to complete the Social Studies Explanation.

Check for Understanding:

Describe the immediate effects of the United States' victory in the Revolutionary War. In what ways did independence bring both challenges and opportunities to the young nation?

DISCOVERY EDUCATION | SOCIAL STUDIES TECHBOOK.

What roles did different groups of Americans play in the Revolutionary War?

3.5 The Revolution in American Society

photo: Library of Congress

LESSON OVERVIEW

Introduction

In this concept, you'll learn about how different groups of people throughout American society participated in the war and how their lives were affected by it.

Essential Question

What roles did different groups of Americans play in the Revolutionary War?

Lesson Objectives

By the end of this lesson, you should be able to:

- Describe the roles of various groups of Americans during the Revolutionary War, including women, Native Americans, and African Americans.

- Discuss political, social, and economic outcomes of the Revolutionary War.

Key Vocabulary
Which terms do you already know?

- [ ] Abigail Adams
- [ ] abolition
- [ ] American Revolution
- [ ] Battle of Trenton
- [ ] Battle of Yorktown
- [ ] Battles of Lexington and Concord
- [ ] civil war
- [ ] democracy
- [ ] indentured servant
- [ ] Iroquois League
- [ ] James Armistead
- [ ] John Adams
- [ ] Loyalist
- [ ] national debt
- [ ] Patriot
- [ ] revolution
- [ ] siege

ENGAGE

How did the colonists answer the call to fight? Visit Engage to learn more.

> ## Essential Question
>
> What roles did different groups of Americans play in the Revolutionary War?

EXPLORE

African Americans—Patriots and Loyalists

Did the war change conditions for enslaved African Americans?

Before the end of slavery, free African Americans made up about one-tenth of the African American population. The free African American population consisted mostly of former indentured servants and their descendants. Indentured servants were people who had borrowed the fare for their journey to North America and agreed to pay back the loan by working without pay for a specified number of years. Free black immigrants from the West Indies and former enslaved people who had been freed by slave owners added to the numbers.

The British were concerned that they did not have enough troops to overwhelm the colonists. To encourage enlistments, Lord Dunmore, the royal governor of Virginia, issued his Dunmore Proclamation in 1775. The Dunmore Proclamation promised freedom for enslaved laborers and indentured servants who would fight on the side of the British. Dunmore hoped not only to add to the numbers of British troops, but also to weaken the Patriots and possibly incite the enslaved laborers to attack their owners. Although many African Americans left to fight for their freedom, they did not attack their former owners or cause the turmoil Dunmore had hoped for.

Many enslaved laborers continued to support their Patriot owners. Some helped defend their homes. Others took their owners' places as soldiers. An African American enslaved woman planned and carried out her owner Stephen Heard's escape from a British prison. Heard escaped execution and later became governor of Georgia.

Discovery | SOCIAL STUDIES
EDUCATION | **TECHBOOK**

What roles did different groups of Americans play in the Revolutionary War?

Another African American who supported the Patriots was Wentworth Cheswell, a well-respected church and community leader from Newmarket, New Hampshire. Cheswell, as town messenger on the Committee of Safety, rode north from Boston to warn New Hampshire residents of British troop movements at the beginning of the war. In 1777, Cheswell enlisted and served in the Continental army.

photo: Getty Images

Peter Salem shooting British Major Pitcairn at Bunker Hill, 1770.

James Armistead also played an important role for the Patriots during the American Revolution. Born a slave, Armistead volunteered for the U.S. Army in 1781. He was soon enlisted as a spy. Armistead earned the trust of British generals by posing as a runaway slave, and he gathered critical information about British troops' plans. He brought this information back to the Patriots, allowing them to surprise the British and win the Battle of Yorktown. Armistead was later granted freedom from slavery for his heroics during the war.

Perhaps 5,000 African Americans fought on the side of the Patriots. It is hard to know for sure because, surprisingly, the muster rolls did not indicate soldiers' races. After the war, some African American veterans in the North were freed in return for their military service. But these people still did not receive political equality. In the South, most African Americans had fought against their owners, on the British side, hoping to win their freedom. The British could not fulfill the promise to grant them freedom. Instead, the victorious Americans recaptured many African Americans and forced them back into slavery.

Explore this resource to discover a famous poet's perspective on the Revolution.

In general, then, the war did not change the conditions faced by free or enslaved African Americans. However, it did add some strength to the abolition movement and the ideal that America could eventually become a land where all people were free.

Native Americans—Taking Sides

Did the war change conditions for Native Americans?

For Native Americans concerned with preserving their lands and ways of life, neither the British nor the Americans seemed deserving of support in the Revolutionary War. The British promised that they would prevent colonists from moving west and settling on Native American lands. However, the British had already made this promise, before 1763, and had failed to keep it. On the other hand, Native Americans had seen the colonists' land grabs and knew they could expect more of the same from them. No truly good option was available. Thus, Native Americans took a variety of positions in the Revolutionary War.

Many chose to stay out of the fight. They knew that for them, nothing good could come of the war.

Some New England Native Americans supported their colonist neighbors. They had remained on friendly terms, probably because the New England colonists were less aggressive about settling lands to the west. Native Americans near Stockbridge, Massachusetts, officially served in the Continental army.

The Battle of Oriskany, New York, 1777.

photo: Library of Congress

West of the Appalachians, a majority of those who fought either collaborated with the British or took action against the colonists independently. For instance, early in the war, Cherokee warriors attacked many American frontier settlements in the South.

The six nations of the Iroquois League were split. Some of the Iroquois nations, such as the Mohawks—led by Chief Joseph Brant, or Thayendanegea—fought on the British side. They were joined by most Cayugas, Onondagas, and Senecas.

However, two of the Iroquois nations, the Oneidas and the Tuscaroras, sided with the Americans. For the Iroquois, the Revolution became a civil war, or war between groups of citizens of the same country. At the Battle of Oriskany in 1777, two Iroquois groups, the Oneidas and the Senecas, found themselves battling each other.

After the war was over, Britain gave up control of western lands to the new U.S. government. Observers noted that the lands belonged to the Native Americans, and that the British did not have the right to give them to anyone. Eventually, Native Americans lost their lands, whether they had sided with the British or not. Even Native Americans who had supported the Americans lost their land.

Discovery | SOCIAL STUDIES
EDUCATION | **TECHBOOK**

What roles did different groups of Americans play in the
Revolutionary War?

Female Patriots in the War Effort

How did women participate in the Patriot cause?

Women were actively involved in many aspects of the war for independence.
Many men went off to war, leaving wives and daughters at home to do their
former work, such as managing farms and shops. During the war, Abigail Adams, whose
husband John spent time away from home as a delegate to the Continental Congress,
managed the Adams' farm, ran the family business, and raised the children. Because
supplies were needed for the army, women on the "home front" learned to adjust to
shortages of everyday goods. For instance, when salt was scarce, women learned to use
walnut ash to preserve meat.

When their survival at home was threatened by dwindling supplies or enemy advances,
women had no choice but to follow the army. Gathering up children, pets, and valuables,
they traveled on foot to winter encampments. Women at Valley Forge gathered wood,
cooked, washed clothes, and nursed sick and wounded soldiers. Some were there for
pay, but the majority were ordinary women who came for survival and protection.

Other women raised money for
Washington's army. Sarah Bache, Benjamin
Franklin's daughter, and Esther DeBerdt
Reed organized Philadelphia women into
teams to divide the city into wards and
solicit donations door-to-door. They raised
more than $300,000.

Many young women and girls were spies
and messengers for American generals.
They risked being caught and executed as
they traveled through enemy lines to bring
reports of British troop movements and
other important messages. Lydia Darragh,
a Quaker woman from Philadelphia, saved
Washington's men from an ambush in
1776. When Sybil Luddington's father was

photo: Library of Congress

*Deborah Sampson (1760–1826) enlisted in the army under
the name of Robert Shurtleff.*

unable to muster his militia, the teenager took over for him. She galloped through New
York rousing the troops to gather to defend Connecticut.

Women were an important part of the Continental army, and many wives were
carried "on the rations." They served as cooks, seamstresses, nurses, and scavengers
of battlefield equipment. They also helped to bury the dead. During battles, women
nicknamed "Molly Pitcher" would bring water to swab out the guns and hand powder or
shot to the men as they loaded and fired. Women such as Molly Ludwig Hays even filled
in for soldiers who were wounded or killed.

Some prominent women hoped the Revolution would improve women's status in American society. In a letter to her husband, written in March 1776, Abigail Adams encouraged the Continental Congress "remember the ladies and be more generous and favorable to them than your ancestors." Although women's contributions to the war effort led to few changes in their legal or political status, leaders such as John Adams and Benjamin Rush declared it women's duty to educate the next generation in patriotism and civic virtue. This caused an increase in academies for the education of women in the 1780s and 1790s. While the purpose of these schools was to enable women to educate their sons, the result was the beginning of a revolution for women in the field of education.

The New Nation

What were some political, social, and economic outcomes of the Revolutionary War?

Politically, the major effect of the American Revolution was independence. Independence meant there would be no more protection from the British. The new country would deal directly with other nations, such as France and Spain and the Iroquois, on its own. During the war, representatives from the 13 colonies, or states, had gotten together to create a United States government.

The United States in 1763.

photo: Library of Congress

Discovery EDUCATION | SOCIAL STUDIES TECHBOOK

What roles did different groups of Americans play in the Revolutionary War?

Socially, the Revolutionary War was in many ways like a civil war. The land war was mostly fought on American soil. Between one-quarter and one-third of the colonists stayed loyal to Britain and the king. Loyalists worked against the Patriots by spying, by selling supplies to the British Army, and by performing direct military service. They also used propaganda to create dissension within the population as a whole. Thus, Loyalists were widely considered traitors; they could be arrested and their property could be confiscated.

For this reason, the end of the war led to exile, or forced absence, for many Loyalists. Many found they could no longer live alongside their neighbors. They saw no option but to leave the United States for British Canada or England, giving up their homes, businesses, and land.

Explore this interactive to learn more about how the American Revolution changed the United States.

The American Revolution made it obvious that the new country needed a national economic system. Wars are expensive. The new country had not had the money to pay for all the weapons and supplies it needed to wage the war, so it had borrowed the money. Now, the United States had to repay its debts, but how? One way to repay debts would be to print money. However, because the country was brand new, no one would trust the newly printed money to retain its value. The new country would have to create a trustworthy financial system and find a reliable way to raise money.

Economic stability would be a major goal of the nation in the coming years. The Revolution had decided the issue of American sovereignty: The United States was its own country, not ruled by anyone else. As for economics, governance, and social justice, however, the new country still had many decisions to make and many problems to address.

Consider the Essential Question:

What roles did different groups of Americans play in the Revolutionary War?

Go online to complete the Social Studies Explanation.

Check for Understanding:

What were the terms of Dunmore's Proclamation? How did it affect African American life in the United States during and after the war?

4.1 The Articles of Confederation

photo: Getty Images

LESSON OVERVIEW

Introduction

In this concept, you will learn how the Founders created the first government of the United States. You will also evaluate the government's effectiveness.

Essential Question

How well did the Articles of Confederation address the needs of the new nation?

Lesson Objectives

By the end of this lesson, you should be able to:

- Evaluate the confederate form of government created by the Articles of Confederation.

- Connect key events and trends leading to the Constitutional Convention with weaknesses in the Articles of Confederation.

Key Vocabulary
Which terms do you already know?

- ☐ alliance
- ☐ arsenal
- ☐ Articles of Confederation
- ☐ Bill of Rights
- ☐ commerce
- ☐ confederation
- ☐ Constitution
- ☐ Constitutional Convention
- ☐ currency
- ☐ Daniel Shays
- ☐ depression
- ☐ executive
- ☐ independence
- ☐ inflation
- ☐ John Adams
- ☐ judicial

- ☐ Land Ordinance of 1785
- ☐ legislative
- ☐ Northwest Ordinance of 1787
- ☐ Northwest Territory
- ☐ Richard Henry Lee
- ☐ Second Continental Congress
- ☐ Shays's Rebellion
- ☐ tariff
- ☐ territory

Discovery EDUCATION | SOCIAL STUDIES TECHBOOK

How well did the Articles of Confederation address the needs of the new nation?

ENGAGE

How would you design a new government? Visit Engage to learn more.

Essential Question

How well did the Articles of Confederation address the needs of the new nation?

EXPLORE

Governing a New Nation

How did a new nation begin to govern itself?

Most people living in the United States today identify themselves as Americans, but this was not always the case. Colonists were not united under a central government. They felt much more connected to their separate colonies. Likewise, the states in 1776 thought of themselves as independent political units. Each had its own laws and its own militia. Each also had its own independent representative governing body. The only central government was the British one, and even that seemed very foreign. Although the colonies had sometimes cooperated with each other, that cooperation was purely voluntary. The Committees of Correspondence, for instance, shared information with each other and made plans together, but they had no power over the states.

In the first step toward replacing the British government, the Continental Congress, a convention of delegates from the states, instructed each state to create its own constitution. A constitution is a written document that organizes and outlines the operations of a government.

The new state constitutions were alike in many ways. For example, they established governments based on popular sovereignty. This is the idea that the people are the highest authority in the political system. In addition, they limited the power of elected officials and protected the natural rights of citizens, including free speech, freedom of religion, and a free press. Finally, the new state constitutions embraced representative government. They created strong, bicameral legislative branches whose members were selected in popular elections.

Actions taken by the 13 state governments during the Revolution eventually influenced the Framers' work on the U.S. Constitution. For example, in 1777, Thomas Jefferson drafted the Virginia Statute for Religious Freedom. This proposal stated that no persons in that state could be forced by the government to support "any religious worship, place, or ministry," or suffer because of "religious opinions or belief." When Virginia's General Assembly passed the statute into law in 1786, that state was the first to establish separation of church and state. The law became a model for the First Amendment to the Constitution.

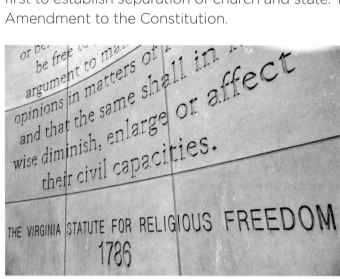

photo: Getty Images

Virginia Statute for Religious Freedom Monument, Richmond, Virginia.

Under the new constitutions, most states restricted voting to white men who owned specified amounts of property. However, most constitutions expanded voting rights to greater numbers of property owners than before. Although it required voters to pay taxes, Pennsylvania's state constitution ended all property restrictions on voting.

The new state constitutions created 13 separate governments. The young United States still needed a central government, one that could act on matters affecting all the states. The states would have to give up some of their power to this outside body.

Accepting a Central Government

How did the Founders limit the power of the country's first government?

The Second Continental Congress continued meeting until 1781, when it was replaced by the Confederation Congress. The word *confederation* means "alliance." Congress appointed a committee headed by John Dickinson of Delaware to write the plan. The result was the Articles of Confederation, or *The Articles of Confederation and Perpetual Union*, presented to Congress in July 1776.

The Articles of Confederation would not take effect until all the states had ratified, or agreed to, them. By 1779, 12 states—all but Maryland—had ratified the Articles. Maryland refused to ratify the Articles unless Virginia renounced its claims to western lands. Virginia eventually did so, and Maryland accepted the Articles of Confederation on March 1, 1781. The United States now had its first constitutional government.

Discovery | SOCIAL STUDIES
EDUCATION | **TECHBOOK**

How well did the Articles of Confederation address the needs of the new nation?

The first government of the United States was designed as a confederation because it was intended to be weak. The former British colonists did not want a strong central government that would infringe on their rights, as the British government had done. The former colonists also did not want their government far away from them. They believed that a local government would be more responsive to the people's needs.

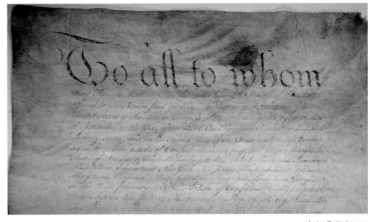

photo: Getty Images

The Articles of Confederation, 1777.

The Articles of Confederation organized the U.S. government around a weak legislative body known as the Confederation Congress. Under the Articles, the individual states remained sovereign, or self-governing and not subject to a superior authority. States gave up most of their claims to western lands. The Confederation Congress was given no authority over the individual states.

Additional provisions demonstrate the weakness of the national government:

- The western territories became the property of the national government.

- Each state received an equal vote in the Confederation Congress. Approval of 9 states was needed to pass a law. Approval of all 13 states was needed to amend the articles.

- The states, rather than Congress, had the right to tax. Congress could raise money only by asking states for it, borrowing money, or selling western lands.

- Congress had the right to manage foreign and Native American affairs. It could declare war as well as peace, and it could make alliances, or partnerships, with other countries.

- Congress had no power to raise an army, govern trade, or enforce international agreements.

- There were no federal courts and no president. Disputes between states were heard by Congress.

Although ratification took years and the central government was very weak, the Articles were effective enough to steer the young nation through the final two years of the Revolutionary War.

A Blueprint for Expansion

What important laws were made under the Articles of Confederation?

While the Founders deliberately limited the powers of the U.S. government, under the Articles the new government achieved some important accomplishments. One great success was the government's plan for the future of the Northwest Territory, the western lands north of the Ohio River. Congress's actions created a simple process by which the nation would expand into western lands.

In 1785, Congress passed the Land Ordinance. The word *ordinance* means "a law or legal decree." The Land Ordinance provided for a complete survey of the entire Northwest Territory—more than 265,000 square miles. The survey divided the land into 36-square-mile townships and divided each township into rectangular plots that people could buy. This plan allowed the country to collect revenue, or income, and individuals and families to own and operate their own farms. The Land Ordinance also set aside one plot of land in each township to be used for a school.

photo: Getty Images

This drawing shows Thomas Jefferson's proposed division of the Northwest Territory.

The Northwest Ordinance of 1787 outlined a process for creating new states. This process for a territory to become a state was based on democratic principles, including outlawing slavery, establishing public education, respecting Native Americans, and implementing a bill of rights. To accomplish this, the Northwest Territory was divided into districts. Each district was governed by officers appointed by Congress. When the population in a district reached 5,000 adult males, the people were to draft a state constitution. A district whose population grew to include 60,000 free males could request statehood if it also had a bill of rights, or list of guaranteed individual rights and liberties. In addition, slavery was prohibited throughout the Northwest Territory. The Northwest Ordinance guaranteed citizens of new states the same civil rights as people in other states, while also stating that Native American "lands and property shall never be taken from them without their consent."

Discovery EDUCATION | SOCIAL STUDIES TECHBOOK

How well did the Articles of Confederation address the needs of the new nation?

Problems with the Articles of Confederation at Home

What were the major weaknesses of the Articles of Confederation in resolving problems among the states?

In spite of its successes, the government under the Articles of Confederation had many problems. The Articles gave Congress the power to coin money and borrow from other nations. However, each state also could issue its own currency, or paper money. What would you think if you needed different currency to buy things in New York, Virginia, and Massachusetts? States often disagreed with other states about the value of their currency.

photo: Library of Congress

Paper currency issued in Rhode Island, 1786.

Congress also did not have the power to regulate trade, or commerce, between the states. Without a central authority, each state had to rely on its own trade laws. States imposed their own import tariffs, or taxes on goods brought in for sale. Some states also had rules that restricted imported goods so they could be unloaded only in certain ports. Plus, the states were in competition not only with foreign countries but also with each other. A merchant who wanted to travel along the coast buying and selling in a chain of several ports would face a complex tangle of rules and taxes.

Additionally, there were more basic problems with the confederation:

- The government did not have the power to impose or collect taxes. The nation owed money to France and Holland and could not pay. Congress sent bills to the states, but the states ignored them and Congress could do nothing about it.

- A vote of a two-thirds majority, or nine states, was required to pass laws. Unless nine states agreed on a solution, Congress could not solve any problems.

- A unanimous vote of 13 states was required to change the Articles of Confederation. Congress could not fix itself.

These basic problems reinforced each other. The United States faced crises in its dealings with Britain and Spain, as well as internal conflicts that threatened to lead to disaster.

Problems Competing with British Commerce

How did the nation's dealings with Great Britain reveal weaknesses in the Articles of Confederation?

With the states focused on their own concerns, several foreign relations problems developed. In the Treaty of Paris, Britain had agreed to vacate its military outposts in the Northwest Territory, but now it refused to do so. The United States was powerless to force them out, so the British continued to occupy its western forts.

As colonists, Americans had been forced to pay taxes to support the British Empire. In partial exchange, they enjoyed the empire's protection of U.S. business interests around the world. For instance, U.S. merchants were confident that their ships traveling to Europe would be protected by the British navy. After the Revolutionary War, Britain no longer protected U.S. businesses and consumers. It now saw the young nation as a competitor rather than a colony.

After the Revolutionary War, the U.S. economy was wrecked. U.S. exports, or sales of goods to other countries, declined. Britain restricted imports, or goods brought in to the country, from the United States and forbade its Caribbean sugar colonies from trading with the United States. Also, the British flooded the market with manufactured goods that were cheaper and better than U.S. products. These factors combined to create an economic depression, a period of widespread business difficulty, lower sales, and higher unemployment. The depression of the 1780s threatened the future of the United States.

John Adams was appointed to represent the United States in negotiating a trade treaty with Britain. No treaty came about because Adams had nothing to offer. His government had no actual power, and he could not promise that the states would accept any agreement he made.

Problems with Spanish Land Claims

How did the nation's dealings with Spain reveal weaknesses in the Articles of Confederation?

In the Treaty of Paris, Britain acknowledged U.S. claims to the lands between the Ohio River and Florida. However, Spain was not involved in the Treaty of Paris. The Spanish still held Florida and New Spain, which included all the lands west of the Mississippi River. Spain would not recognize U.S. claims. Spain also cut off U.S. merchants and farmers from using the Mississippi River for commerce. That meant farmers west of the Appalachian Mountains would have to send their crops across the mountains to get them to eastern markets.

Congress did not have the power to address these issues. Northerners were willing to make a deal with Spain; they would give up access to the Mississippi River if the United States could get something in return. But Westerners and Southerners insisted they needed the Mississippi River. The Confederation Congress could hardly begin to negotiate. It could not call on military force either. The Congress could create and maintain an army, but doing so required 9 of the 13 states to agree, and they could not agree. Each individual state retained control of its own militia, which it used to protect itself.

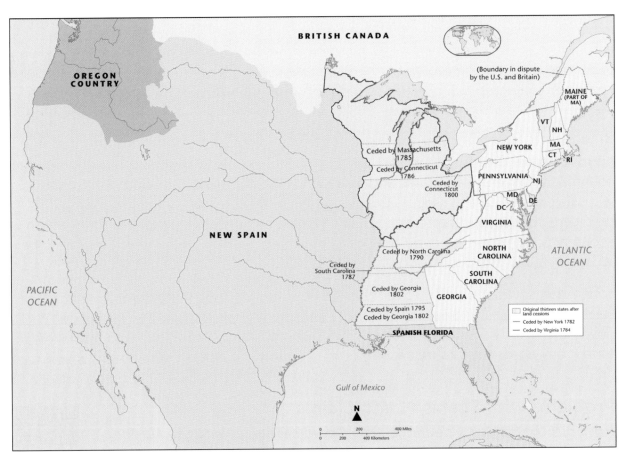

This map shows the land holdings in North America in 1783.

In the 1780s, the young United States faced challenges to its sovereignty from other countries and squabbles among its own member states. Those who had wanted a weak national government had succeeded.

Rebellion in a New Nation

What did Shays's Rebellion indicate about the United States in the 1780s?

Massachusetts had large debts from the Revolutionary War and wanted to pay them off quickly. To do this, the state increased land taxes by 60 percent. This tax hike led many farmers in the western part of the state to go deeply into debt. Banks began to foreclose on farmers who could not pay their loans. The word *foreclosure* means "taking possession of a borrower's property when the borrower is unable to make debt payments." Soon, demonstrations and riots against the foreclosures broke out.

Daniel Shays, a Revolutionary War veteran, raised a militia to fight the foreclosure courts. Historians cannot agree on the size of Shays's militia. Some put it at 700 men; other historians put it at 1,200 men; and still others put it at 2,000 men. One thing was certain; Shays's "rebel" militia overwhelmed Massachusetts's courts and shut them down. Then, Shays's militia marched toward Springfield, Massachusetts, the largest city in the area.

The rebel militia intended to capture the federal arsenal, or storage facility for weapons. The Massachusetts state militia was called to stop the rebels. The state militia killed 4 rebels during the battle and captured 150. Shays escaped to Vermont.

photo: Getty Images

What did Shays's Rebellion reveal about the Articles of Confederation?

Shays's Rebellion brought to light a common problem. Shays's followers were not the only ones who were desperate. Many people were suffering from high debt after the war. There was a currency shortage that made the value of money high. People were going bankrupt, losing their farms, their homes, and their livelihoods. The government could not pay its own debts. The people needed effective solutions to the economic issues and political conflicts they faced.

The Articles of Confederation had been made weak to prevent the abuse of central power. The rebellion drew attention to what many people already knew: The U.S. government was failing its people. The country had no money and no power. The weak government that the Articles created now seemed too weak to survive.

Discovery EDUCATION | SOCIAL STUDIES **TECHBOOK**

How well did the Articles of Confederation address the needs of the new nation?

Shortly after the unrest in Massachusetts began, representatives from five states met in Annapolis, Maryland, to discuss common concerns related to trade and commerce. The Annapolis delegates agreed that their problems could not be addressed without revising the Articles of Confederation. They decided to call for a larger convention that would feature representatives from each of the United States.

Explore this interactive to learn more about different perspectives on the Articles of Confederation.

This meeting, later known as the Constitutional Convention, took place in Philadelphia, Pennsylvania, in 1787. The decisions made in Philadelphia would change the course of U.S. history. They also created a new system of government that would later be emulated by countries around the world.

Consider the Essential Question:

How well did the Articles of Confederation address the needs of the new nation?

Go online to complete the Social Studies Explanation.

Check for Understanding:

In what ways did the Articles of Confederation reflect the Founders' desire to avoid problems similar to what they had experienced under the government of Great Britain?

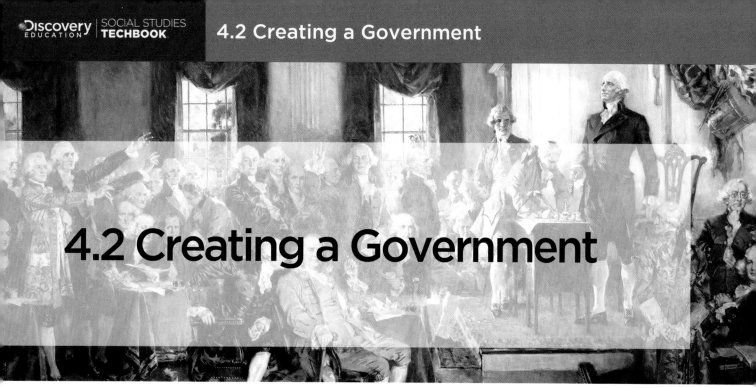

4.2 Creating a Government

photo: Getty Images

LESSON OVERVIEW

Introduction

In this concept, you will learn how the people at these meetings, the Framers of the Constitution, worked together to make a new plan for the government of the United States.

Essential Question

How did decisions made at the Constitutional Convention affect the balance of power in the new nation?

Lesson Objectives

By the end of this lesson, you should be able to:

- Identify and analyze key issues addressed by the Framers at the outset of the Constitutional Convention.

- Describe major areas of disagreement among delegates to the Constitutional Convention and explain compromises intended to resolve these issues.

Key Vocabulary
Which terms do you already know?

- [ ] amendment
- [ ] Anti-Federalists
- [ ] Bill of Rights
- [ ] checks and balances
- [ ] Confederacy
- [ ] Constitutional Convention
- [ ] Declaration of Independence
- [ ] Edmund Randolph
- [ ] enumerated power
- [ ] executive branch
- [ ] federal
- [ ] Federalist Papers
- [ ] Federalists
- [ ] Framers
- [ ] George Mason
- [ ] Great Compromise
- [ ] habeas corpus
- [ ] House of Representatives
- [ ] implied power
- [ ] interstate commerce
- [ ] James Madison
- [ ] judicial branch
- [ ] legislative branch
- [ ] New Jersey Plan
- [ ] nominating conventions
- [ ] Pierre L'Enfant
- [ ] precedent
- [ ] ratification
- [ ] republic
- [ ] reserved powers
- [ ] Roger Sherman
- [ ] Senate
- [ ] separation of powers
- [ ] Three-Fifths Compromise
- [ ] usurp
- [ ] veto
- [ ] Virginia Plan
- [ ] William Paterson

Discovery | SOCIAL STUDIES
EDUCATION | **TECHBOOK**

How did decisions made at the Constitutional Convention affect the balance of power in the new nation?

ENGAGE

How did the Framers manage to finish their work? Visit Engage to learn more.

Essential Question

How did decisions made at the Constitutional Convention affect the balance of power in the new nation?

EXPLORE

A More Perfect Union?

How did the Philadelphia Convention begin?

In 1786, representatives from five states met at a convention in Annapolis, Maryland, to discuss amending, or improving, the Articles of Confederation. They soon realized that the changes they were discussing were too significant for such a small group; a meeting of all the states was necessary. That meeting occurred in May 1787 in Philadelphia, Pennsylvania.

One state decided not to attend. Rhode Island, the smallest state, was satisfied with the Articles of Confederation and refused to participate. The legislatures of the other states elected representatives, or delegates, to attend the meeting. States sent varying numbers of delegates, but each state's delegation received only one vote. All together, there were 55 delegates.

photo: Library of Congress
The State House in Philadelphia, where the Constitutional Convention was held.

Some of the country's leading political figures were absent from the convention. Patrick Henry of Virginia refused to attend because he opposed the creation of a stronger central government. Thomas Jefferson and John Adams were in Europe on foreign missions. However, many distinguished and well-known leaders participated. Pennsylvania's Ben Franklin, 81 years old at the time, was the oldest of the delegates.

Gouverneur Morris and James Wilson, also from Pennsylvania, were among the most vocal. Morris alone delivered 173 speeches, and Wilson eventually served on a Committee of Detail that drafted the new Constitution. James Madison attended every session and compiled detailed notes on the proceedings.

When the meetings began, the delegates elected George Washington to serve as president and lead the discussions. At first, the delegates discussed ways to revise the Articles of Confederation to make the nation's government stronger. Soon, however, most of the delegates agreed that the Articles of Confederation were completely insufficient and that what the country needed was to start over with an entirely new constitution. The meetings became known as the Constitutional Convention. The delegates to the Constitutional Convention are now referred to as Framers because they are the men who designed, or framed, the structure of the U.S. Constitution.

The Framers voted to keep all their discussions secret. Secrecy enabled them to wonder aloud and to say whatever they thought without worrying about how someone could misinterpret it. Throughout the hot summer of 1787, they even kept all the windows in the State House shut so that no one could overhear their discussions. As the Framers left their meetings at the end of the day, people pestered them for news about what they had decided. The Framers kept their secrets and made no announcements until their work was completed. For decades after the convention had ended, the Framers kept their private notes about the discussions secret.

Great Compromise

How did a major disagreement lead to one of the key features of the U.S. government?

As the Framers began to agree that what was needed was an entirely new constitution, they put forward many new ideas.

Small States Versus Large States

One idea, developed by James Madison and called the Virginia Plan, called for a federal system of government. A federal system of government is one in which power that comes from the people is divided and shared between a central government and the several governments of the states. The central government is called the federal government. Madison's plan called for a federal government composed of three parts, or branches. The legislative branch would make laws. The executive branch would enforce, or carry out, laws. The judicial branch would explain the meaning of, or interpret, the laws.

The Virginia Plan called for representation in the legislative branch to be based on each state's population. Under this plan, larger states would elect more representatives to the legislative branch, so larger states would have more power than smaller states. Virginia was the most populous state. Edmund Randolph, the lead delegate from Virginia, presented this proposal to the Constitutional Convention.

Discovery SOCIAL STUDIES
EDUCATION TECHBOOK

How did decisions made at the Constitutional Convention affect the balance of power in the new nation?

How do you think Framers who represented smaller states reacted to the idea of having less power than the larger states?

In response to the Virginia Plan, a delegate named William Paterson proposed the New Jersey Plan. Paterson's plan had some similarities to the Virginia Plan. However, one major difference was that, like the Articles of Confederation, it called for the creation of a single national legislature in which each state would have the same number of representatives. Paterson's plan was designed to protect the political power of smaller states, such as his home state of New Jersey.

The Great Compromise

Roger Sherman of Connecticut proposed a compromise. He proposed that the legislative branch be made up of a Congress that had two parts, or houses. In one house, known as the Senate, each state would have the same number of representatives, just as under the Articles of Confederation. In the other house, known as the House of Representatives, each state's population would determine its number of representatives. Each state would have equal power in the Senate, but larger states would have more power in the House of Representatives. To enact a law, both houses would have to agree.

Mayor Roger Sherman

photo: Library of Congress

Connecticut's Roger Sherman (1721–1793) attended the First and Second Continental Congresses and was a member of the committee assigned to draw up the Declaration of Independence.

The Framers debated this issue for a month. Finally, on July 16, the delegates at the Constitutional Convention agreed to the compromise. Because Sherman's plan resolved the deep division between the large states and the small states, it became known as the Great Compromise.

One major concern was settled. But many more would have to be dealt with before the Constitutional Convention was finished.

The Question of Slavery

How did the question of slavery shape the new government?

The words *slavery* and *slave* do not appear in the Constitution. The Framers avoided using these terms because they believed the terms would discredit the document. However, more than 20 convention delegates owned slaves, and the issue of slavery threatened to destroy unity at the convention. Many Northern delegates opposed slavery, while Southerners would not consider outlawing or limiting it.

Some Southern delegates threatened to leave the convention if anyone attempted to undermine slavery. There could be no compromise on this issue. If Northern states wanted to have a United States, they would need to preserve slavery and make concessions to those who benefited from it.

At the convention, the Framers debated a proposal from South Carolina to limit the new federal government's role in regulating the transatlantic slave trade. They settled on a compromise. Importing enslaved Africans would be allowed until 1808; after that, Congress could restrict or prohibit international trade of enslaved persons.

On the same day the Framers reached the slave trade compromise, they also agreed on a fugitive slave clause. Placed in Article IV, this policy required that enslaved persons who escaped to other states be returned to their owners. This policy in effect blocked citizens who morally opposed slavery from protecting enslaved persons attempting to find freedom.

The issue of slavery also affected debates about congressional representation. Because a state's population determined its representation in the proposed House of Representatives, Southern states wanted enslaved people counted in the

Complete this activity to create an "interview" with a key player at the convention.

census. Northern states objected. On the other hand, a state's population could also determine how much it was taxed. For purposes of taxation, Southern states did not want enslaved people counted. Northern states objected again.

The issue was settled with the Three-Fifths Compromise, which said that states would count a portion of their enslaved population both for representation and for taxes. A state's population would include "the whole number of free persons," no "Indians," and three-fifths of "all other persons," meaning enslaved people. For example, if an area had 100 free white residents and 500 enslaved residents, its representation in Congress would be based on a population count of 400. The 100 free residents would count as 100, and the 500 enslaved residents would count as 300.

The Framers' compromises on the issue of slavery made possible the completion and eventual ratification of the Constitution. However, scholars to this day debate whether the Constitution is a proslavery document. They also question the morality of concessions delegates made to keep the convention together. The Framers' compromises also put off conflicts the nation would confront later in its history.

Discovery SOCIAL STUDIES | EDUCATION **TECHBOOK**

How did decisions made at the Constitutional Convention affect the balance of power in the new nation?

States' Powers

In what ways does the Constitution limit the powers of the national government?

Even though the Convention was making progress, one issue still worried many people: Was this new government going to weaken the states? Was it going to turn into the kind of government they had just fought a revolution to escape from? Would the president—the planned head of the executive branch—gain too much power and become a king?

Recall that in the Declaration of Independence, the American colonists listed many grievances against King George III of Great Britain. For example, the Declaration accuses the king of preventing the colonists from passing laws he disapproved of, and of replacing judges whose rulings he disagreed with. The Declaration also accuses the king of forcing the colonists to support British soldiers, even during times of peacetime. Sometimes, British soldiers were not punished for crimes they committed against American colonists. Meanwhile, colonists accused of crimes were sometimes tried without juries in British courts. To keep the United States government from engaging in similar abuses of power, the Framers designed the Constitution to include three important components: enumerated and reserved powers, separation of powers, and checks and balances.

Enumerated and Reserved Powers

To address concerns about state powers, the Framers agreed to list the specific powers that would rest with the national government. These are known as the enumerated powers. To enumerate is to list. If a power was not listed, it was denied to the federal government and reserved for the states. These reserved powers included such powers as managing elections and education.

Separation of Powers

To avoid putting too much power in the hands of a few people, the Framers adopted Madison's plan for a three-branch government with a separation of powers. For instance, the legislature would make laws but could not enforce them; the executive enforced the laws but could not change them. No one branch of government would control the others or act without their approval. By limiting its power, the Framers intended to prevent the federal government from usurping, or taking over, the power of the state governments.

photo: Library of Congress
Baron de Montesquieu (1689–1755) is best known for his Spirit of the Laws, *1748.*

Checks and Balances

In addition to separating powers, the Framers built in checks and balances on the powers of each branch. This means each branch was empowered to stop the others from exercising too much power. For instance, the president can appoint assistants, advisers, and federal judges, but only with the approval of Congress. Supporters of the new Constitution argued that these provisions would stop any part of the federal government from becoming too powerful.

The compromises on representation, slavery, big states versus small states, and states' rights resulted in a document that the Constitutional Convention could support. On September 17, 1787, 39 delegates, representing all 12 states present, signed the new U.S. Constitution.

The Question Goes to the People

How did debate over the Constitution lead to the creation of the Bill of Rights?

At the beginning of the Constitutional Convention, the Framers were divided between those who wanted to change the Articles of Confederation and those who wanted a new constitution. Now, at the end of the convention, some who had wanted to discard the Confederation were having second thoughts. They had agreed to increase the power of the national government. But now, they feared they may have gone too far and taken too much power from the individual states.

Likewise, as the new Constitution became public, people all over the country disagreed as to whether the new government would be too powerful. Because the word federal refers to the national government, people who supported the Constitution became known as Federalists. Those who did not support the Constitution became known as Anti-Federalists.

Anti-Federalist Arguments

Anti-Federalists, such as Patrick Henry, John Hancock, and Samuel Adams, argued that no federal government could pass laws that would be suitable for all states. They also believed that the proposed federal government took too much power away from the states.

Discovery Education | SOCIAL STUDIES TECHBOOK

How did decisions made at the Constitutional Convention affect the balance of power in the new nation?

Another Anti-Federalist argument was the one that people found most powerful. George Mason argued that any constitution was unacceptable if it did not protect Americans' basic rights, such as freedom of speech, freedom of religion, and trial by jury. These were the rights that had justified independence from Britain. These were the rights people had died for in the Revolutionary War. Even the Federalist Thomas Jefferson said, "A bill of rights is what the people are entitled to against every government on earth."

Federalist Arguments

Federalists realized they had to educate the people about why they should support the Constitution. James Madison, Alexander Hamilton, and John Jay began to publish essays designed to show the weaknesses of the Anti-Federalist ideas. These essays were first published anonymously in newspapers, signed under the pen name *Publius*. The word *publius* means "public" in Latin and was a common name in ancient Rome. Hamilton, Jay, and Madison chose the name to emphasize that they were motivated by the public interest. The essays were later collected in a book we know as *The Federalist Papers*.

The Federalist Papers explained the branches of the new government. They explained the reasons the Framers had made the decisions they did. They described how each of the checks and balances would work to make the government effective and, at the same time, prevent it from gaining too much power.

In one of the most famous Federalist papers, No. 10, James Madison argues that a strong federal government is more effective than a confederacy of local governments at controlling factions. A faction is a group of people who pursue a common interest. According to Madison, once in power, factions tend to advance their own interests at the expense of the community's. In No. 10, Madison argued that at the state and local levels, it is easier for factions to gain power because fewer people oppose them. In contrast, a national government representing a large and diverse population is less threatened by factions because it is composed of more people with differing interests. As Madison writes, "The influence of factious leaders may kindle a flame within their particular States, but will be unable to spread a general conflagration through the other States."

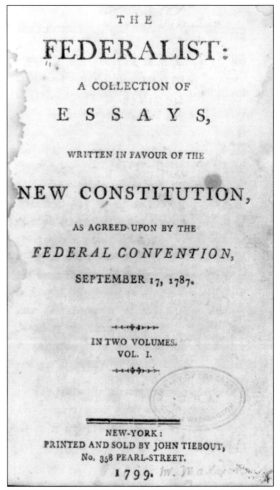

THE
FEDERALIST:
A COLLECTION OF
ESSAYS,
WRITTEN IN FAVOUR OF THE
NEW CONSTITUTION,
AS AGREED UPON BY THE
FEDERAL CONVENTION,
SEPTEMBER 17, 1787.

IN TWO VOLUMES.
VOL. I.

NEW-YORK:
PRINTED AND SOLD BY JOHN TIEBOUT,
No. 358 PEARL-STREET.
1799.

photo: Library on Congress

Title page of 1799 book containing The Federalist Papers.

In response to the Anti-Federalists' call for a bill of rights, the Federalists argued that naming individual rights would only serve to limit those very same rights. As Alexander Hamilton wrote in No. 84: "Why declare that things shall not be done which there is no power to do? Why for instance, should it be said, that the liberty of the press shall not be restrained, when no power is given by which restrictions may be imposed?"

Explore the sources in the activity and decide which side you would have joined.

Hamilton also wrote that, while bills of rights are useful for claiming rights against a king, they serve no purpose once it is agreed that all of a government's power comes from the people.

Ratification

How was the Constitution finally agreed upon?

The Struggle over Ratification

For the new Constitution to become the law of the land, nine states needed to ratify, or approve it. The Confederation Congress directed each state to hold a ratification convention. The Constitution had been produced in complete secrecy, without public input or debate. The conventions would allow the people to have a say in how they would be governed.

On December 7, 1787, Delaware became the first state to ratify the Constitution. By January 9, 1788, just a month later, Pennsylvania, New Jersey, Georgia, and Connecticut had also ratified the Constitution.

But the lack of a list of basic rights remained a serious problem for many people. After Massachusetts initially voted against ratifying the Constitution, the Federalists realized that a list of individual rights would be needed for the document to be approved by nine states. The Federalists pledged that if Massachusetts voted for ratification, Congress would add a list of rights as amendments, or changes, to the Constitution. With this promise, Massachusetts voted to ratify the Constitution.

In June 1788, New Hampshire became the ninth state to ratify the Constitution, making the new Constitution official. March 4, 1789, was chosen as the date when the Constitution would take effect.

Discovery | SOCIAL STUDIES
EDUCATION | **TECHBOOK**

How did decisions made at the Constitutional Convention affect the balance of power in the new nation?

But strong Anti-Federalist challenges developed in New York and Virginia. If Virginia, the most populous state, and New York, the fourth most populous state, did not join the Union, they would be foreign countries. Interstate trade would have to go through these foreign countries. The military would need special permission whenever it needed to move troops and supplies. The new country needed these states. Eventually, New Yorkers and Virginians decided they

photo: Library of Congress

On September 17, 1787, 39 of the 55 delegates to the Constitutional Convention signed the Constitution of the United States. Only Rhode Island refused to send delegates.

also needed the United States. The Federalist papers and the Federalists' promise to add a list of rights convinced enough people, and ratification succeeded in both New York and Virginia.

In 1790, Rhode Island decided not to become a foreign country surrounded by the United States. By a margin of only two votes, Rhode Island became the 13th state to ratify the Constitution.

The Bill of Rights

On September 25, 1789, just a few months after the Constitution took effect, the first Congress officially proposed the list of individual rights that had been promised to Massachusetts. The rights were proposed as amendments, or changes, to the Constitution. We now know these amendments as the Bill of Rights. The Bill of Rights was added to the Constitution on March 1, 1792.

Did the inclusion of the Bill of Rights alter the balance of power among the federal government, the states, and the people? Most people believed that it did. They believed that having Britain's Bill of Rights of 1689 in writing had served as an important check on the British government. The people wanted the same protections from their new government.

By limiting the powers of the federal government, the U.S. Bill of Rights protects the people and preserves the authority of the states. For instance, the First Amendment says that "Congress shall make no law . . . abridging [or limiting] the freedom of speech." This amendment limits the power of the federal government by preventing it from making laws that punish people for expressing unpopular views. The Tenth Amendment declares that powers not assigned to the federal government are reserved to the states.

This amendment is intended to prevent the federal government from claiming powers that it was not intended to have, such as the power to establish public schools.

Adding the Bill of Rights to the Constitution demonstrated that the document could be amended to meet the needs and ideals of future generations. The Bill of Rights is a promise of rights from the government to its people and serves as a reminder to the people that they must always protect these rights.

Consider the Essential Question:

How did decisions made at the Constitutional Convention affect the balance of power in the new nation?

Go online to complete the Social Studies Explanation.

Check for Understanding:

Were the Framers of the Constitution more fearful of a central government that was too strong or one that was too weak? Cite evidence to support your position.

DISCOVERY EDUCATION | SOCIAL STUDIES **TECHBOOK**.

How does the Constitution reflect major principles of American democracy?

4.3 A More Perfect Union

photo: National Archives

LESSON OVERVIEW

Introduction

In this concept, you will learn about the structure of the government that was created by the Constitution. You will also learn how the Constitution limits the power of each part of the government, protects the rights of U.S. citizens, and reflects important democratic ideals.

Essential Question

How does the Constitution reflect major principles of American democracy?

Key Vocabulary
Which terms do you already know?

- [ ] amendment
- [ ] Articles of Confederation
- [ ] Baron de Montesquieu
- [ ] bicameral
- [ ] Bill of Rights
- [ ] bond
- [ ] cabinet
- [ ] checks and balances
- [ ] confederation
- [ ] Congress
- [ ] Constitution
- [ ] Elastic Clause
- [ ] electoral vote
- [ ] executive branch
- [ ] federal
- [ ] full faith and credit
- [ ] impeach
- [ ] judicial branch
- [ ] judicial review
- [ ] legislative branch
- [ ] limited government
- [ ] Magna Carta
- [ ] majority rule
- [ ] popular sovereignty
- [ ] preamble
- [ ] privileges and immunities
- [ ] separation of powers
- [ ] Supremacy Clause
- [ ] Supreme Court
- [ ] treaty
- [ ] unicameral
- [ ] veto

Lesson Objectives

By the end of this lesson, you should be able to:

- Explain the organization of the Constitution and describe its important features.

- Explain how the Constitution reflects American democratic principles, including separation of powers, checks and balances, judicial review, individual rights, limited government, and consent of the governed.

- Compare the most important features of the government created by the Articles of Confederation with the most important features of the federal form of government created by the Constitution.

ENGAGE

What principles bind Americans together? Visit Engage to learn more.

Essential Question

How does the Constitution reflect major principles of American democracy?

EXPLORE

Features of the Constitution

How is the Constitution organized?

A constitution creates and organizes a country's government and outlines how it operates. The U.S. Constitution is the oldest national constitution in use today throughout the world. It is also one of the shortest. The Constitution can be organized into the following parts:

1. Preamble

2. The Parts of the Government (Articles I–III)

3. How the Government Works (Articles IV–VII)

4. Amendments

1. Preamble

A preamble is an introduction. The Preamble to the Constitution is a single sentence that explains the purposes of the Constitution. The Preamble begins with the phrase "We the People," which reflects the important idea that the power of the government comes from the people. That idea, known as popular sovereignty, is the heart of the U.S. government. The rest of the Preamble lists six different goals of the Constitution.

photo: National Archives

The United States Constitution is on display at the National Archives building in Washington, DC.

2. The Parts of the Government (Articles I–III)

The main body of the Constitution is made up of seven articles, or parts. The first three articles describe the three branches of the federal government. A *federal* government is the central authority in a system formed by the union of bodies or groups—the states.

- Article I describes the legislative branch. The legislative branch has legislative power, the power to make laws.

- Article II describes the executive branch. The executive branch has executive power, the power to carry out and enforce laws.

- Article III describes the judicial branch. The judicial branch has judicial power, the power to apply and interpret the laws.

- Articles I–III describe the powers of each branch. They also provide details about how each branch carries out its duties and how people are chosen for each branch. They are the three longest articles in the Constitution.

3. How the Government Works (Articles IV–VII)

The next four articles of the Constitution describe other aspects of how the federal government works, such as how the federal government relates to the state governments:

- Article IV describes relations among the states and steps for creating new states.

- Article V describes the process of amending, or changing, the Constitution, because the Framers of the Constitution knew that the country's needs would change over time.

- Article VI explains how public debts will be paid and also establishes the important principle that the Constitution and other federal laws are the "supreme law of the land." This is known as the Supremacy Clause.

- Article VII describes the process for ratifying, or approving, the Constitution. At the time the Constitution was to be ratified, Article VII called for only 9 of the 13 original states to ratify the document. However, by May 1790, all 13 of them approved the new constitution.

4. Amendments (Article V)

The Framers recognized the need to establish a system of government designed to last far into the future and to deal with events that they themselves could not anticipate. As a result, they created a process in which the Constitution could be changed, or amended, if necessary. The Constitution has been amended 27 times in its history.

Outlined in Article V of the Constitution, the amendment process has two different steps: proposing an amendment and ratifying the amendment. Amendments can be formally proposed by Congress with two-thirds of the votes in both the House of Representatives and the Senate. They also can be proposed by a national convention called for by two-thirds of all state legislatures (currently 34 states). All 27 amendments to the Constitution have been proposed by Congress. Once amendments have been proposed, they are ratified, or accepted, if they are approved either by three-fourths of the legislatures of states (currently 38 states), or by conventions held in three-fourths of the states. Of the 27 amendments to the Constitution, 26 have been ratified by the state legislatures. Only the Twenty-First Amendment was ratified by a convention.

The Constitution has been amended for a variety of purposes. The first ten amendments, known as the Bill of Rights, were proposed and ratified to address concerns that the federal government might exercise unlimited power if the Constitution did not list rights that should be retained by the people and the states. After the Civil War, the Thirteenth, Fourteenth, and Fifteenth Amendments were added to protect the rights of African Americans who had recently been freed from slavery. Ratified in 1920, the Nineteenth Amendment guarantees voting rights to women. Other amendments, such as the Twentieth, Twenty-Second, and Twenty-Fifth, have clarified matters such as the length of the president's term in office and the procedures for replacing a president who resigns or dies in office. Only a single amendment, the Eighteenth, which prohibited alcoholic beverages, has been repealed. That amendment was overturned by another— the Twenty-First Amendment.

Discovery SOCIAL STUDIES
EDUCATION **TECHBOOK**

How does the Constitution reflect major principles of American democracy?

The Legislative Branch (Article I)

What are the powers of the legislature?

The legislative branch, also called Congress, is a group of lawmakers representing the people of the United States. Congress is split into two main bodies. The Senate includes two senators from each state. Representation in the House of Representatives is proportional to each state's population. This means that the states with the greatest population send the most representatives to Congress. For example, because a lot of people live in New York, it has more power in the House than Wyoming, which has many fewer residents. Congress is responsible for making laws and for controlling money for the federal government. To pass a law, both the House of Representatives and the Senate must agree.

Members of the House of Representatives are directly elected by the people of their states. When the Constitution was written, senators were chosen by the state legislatures. The Seventeenth Amendment, passed in 1913, established that senators would also be directly elected by the people of their states.

Article I, which organizes and outlines the functions of Congress, is the longest article of the Constitution. It lists Congress's expressed, also called enumerated, powers. Congress's enumerated powers include passing

photo: Library of Congress
The Capitol building in Washington, DC, is home to the U.S. Congress.

laws for borrowing money, regulating commerce, and imposing and collecting taxes. Other enumerated powers of Congress include declaring war, approving treaties, and approving the national budget. Article I also lists several powers that are specifically denied to Congress.

Article I also states that Congress may make laws that are "necessary and proper" for carrying out the enumerated powers. This "necessary and proper clause," more commonly known as the elastic clause, allows Congress to take actions that the Framers did not specifically list. For this reason, powers taken using the necessary and proper clause are often called the implied powers. For instance, in 1870, Congress created the National Weather Service. The Constitution says nothing about such an agency, but Congress decided a weather service was needed to provide important information for the military. The elastic clause has led to some controversies because officials often disagree on which government actions are necessary and proper and which are not.

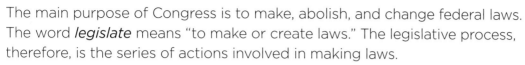

The Legislative Process

What is the basic law-making process in the federal government?

The main purpose of Congress is to make, abolish, and change federal laws. The word *legislate* means "to make or create laws." The legislative process, therefore, is the series of actions involved in making laws.

For a proposed law, also called a *bill*, to be enacted, it must receive a majority vote in both the House and Senate and then be signed by the president. Because a law must pass both chambers and receive the president's signature, the structure of legislative process, as established by the Constitution, makes lawmaking difficult.

Because both the House and Senate are organized along political party lines, there always is a majority party and a minority party in each chamber. For example, if more than half of the House's membership belongs to the Democratic Party, the Democrats are the majority party and the Republicans are the minority party. The majority and minority parties have different elected officers within the House and the Senate. Congressional elections have an important impact on policies made and enforced by the federal government because the party in the majority of each chamber of Congress sets the legislative agenda. It also has the voting power to block the goals of the minority.

Barriers to Passage

The structure and organization of Congress make it difficult for a bill to become law. It can take months or even longer! Many things can happen along the way to prevent a bill from becoming a law. More than 90 percent of bills and resolutions introduced in Congress each session are never passed.

In 1954, President Eisenhower signed legislation that created the federal Interstate Highway System.
photo: Getty Images

One barrier is the congressional committee. Committees review and often revise bills before they are considered by the full chambers. There are instances in which members of a committee either object to the bill or decide it is not ready to be discussed with the entire chamber. In many such cases, they simply will ignore the bill. In this case, the bill never moves beyond the committee stage. This is known as getting "stuck in committee," or *pigeonholing*. Committees also can defeat legislation by voting to reject it. It is often difficult for members of the minority party to have their bills considered by the full chamber because the majority party will simply ignore the bills in committee.

Another obstacle is the filibuster. In the early years of the republic, no rules governed how long a debate on a bill could last in either house of Congress. However, the full chambers could not vote on bills until their debate officially was over. Because of this, opponents of a bill attempted what became known as "filibusters."

DISCOVERY EDUCATION | SOCIAL STUDIES TECHBOOK

How does the Constitution reflect major principles of American democracy?

Filibustering is a strategy used to stall a bill's progress by preventing formal debate on that bill from coming to an end. At first, members of both the House and the Senate used this technique to block legislation from passing. As the House grew larger, it began to set limits on debate. In the Senate, unlimited debate was preserved, and filibusters continue there to this day. Members of the minority party frequently use filibusters to block or stall legislation before it can be approved by a simple majority of senators.

After a bill passes in both chambers, it can still be vetoed. Even if both chambers have passed a bill, if the president does not want to sign it into law, he or she may block, or veto, it. After a veto, the bill can go back to the House and start the process again. A lesser-used type of veto is called a *pocket veto*. Usually, if the president does not sign a bill and Congress is in session, the bill automatically becomes law after 10 days. A pocket veto, described in Article I, Section 7 of the Constitution, says that if Congress is not in session, after 10 days, the bill will *not* become law.

Influencing Legislation

How does the Constitution provide opportunities for citizens to participate in the political process?

The actions of Congress impact all people in the United States. For example, new laws can add environmental rules that affect the ways businesses make products. They can alter tax rates and even provide benefits to groups of citizens. Because laws impact so many citizens and communities, many people work to influence how representatives and senators write bills and then vote on them.

Lobbying is the activity undertaken by individuals and interest groups to influence the policymaking process. Professional lobbyists are people who are paid to represent the interests of individuals and groups as legislation is written and considered. In addition to attempting to have an impact on the lawmaking process, lobbyists will try to influence public policy after a bill becomes law. They do so by suggesting alternate ways that laws can be interpreted or enforced.

Interest Groups and Lobbyists at Work

Interest groups are organizations that have a stake in the outcome of bills. For example, oil companies have a stake in bills that require cars to be more fuel-efficient. If those bills pass, the oil companies might make less money because people would not be buying fuel as often. Interest groups employ lobbyists to work in Washington, DC, and in state capitals. Lobbyists usually are experts on the political process. Often, they are former senators or representatives. They use their expertise to try to convince government officials to write bills and then vote in a way that benefits their interest.

Lobbyists use a variety of techniques to persuade legislators. They can activate grassroots support. This means they use strategies to motivate average citizens to pressure elected officials. For example, lobbyists might begin campaigns to encourage citizens to make telephone calls and send letters and e-mails that apply pressure on public officials. Lobbyists also can provide important information to policymakers, such as in-depth research into legislative proposals and testimony before committees. In addition, lobbyists make campaign contributions and provide other forms of assistance to legislators, including positive media coverage. Lobbyists even can write drafts of bills, with the hope that the drafts will make it easier for the policies they support to be introduced.

Criticism of Lobbying

Some politicians and citizens want to see reforms in the lobbying process. These reform advocates say that special interest groups have too much influence on the political process. Reformers fear that lobbyists convince politicians to act in ways that benefit their interests rather than the common good. How would this happen?

Interest groups can impact a candidate's election campaigns significantly. For example, they can organize people to support or oppose candidates. They also can donate large sums of money to a political campaign. Many candidates view such support as necessary for winning elections. To get this support, candidates may push for programs and policies for which an interest group advocates. These programs and policies might not be for the common good.

Over the years, policies have been enacted to ensure transparency and prevent unethical activities by lobbyists and public officials. *Transparency* is a term used to indicate that the actions of political officials are known by the public. A lack of transparency can lead to unethical actions. For instance, voters sometimes are not aware of how much lobbyists are influencing legislators to support issues that the lobbyists favor. For example, lobbying groups might be providing officials with expensive meals, tickets to sporting events, or luxurious vacations.

The Slow March of Congress

The Founders realized that it is part of human nature to respond swiftly when events arise. These early American politicians wanted a congressional system that would not sway and change every time an issue seized the country's attention. This is why they created a long process for bills to become laws. In your opinion, is the process too difficult, or does it reflect the principle of balancing power?

Discovery SOCIAL STUDIES
EDUCATION | TECHBOOK

How does the Constitution reflect major principles of American democracy?

The Executive Branch (Article II)

What are the powers of the president?

The executive branch is headed by the president of the United States. It is responsible for executing, or carrying out, the laws passed by Congress. For instance, in 1792, Congress passed the Coinage Act, a law that established the U.S. Mint and instructed it to make coins. The president has the responsibility to follow Congress's instructions and make coins; the president appoints the director of the Mint, who hires and supervises the Mint staff.

Article II describes an elaborate process for electing the president. The Framers believed the public could not get adequate information about candidates. On Election Day, people do not actually vote for a presidential candidate. Instead, the voters choose between groups of electors to represent the state in the presidential election. These electors, who are chosen by political parties in their states, cast their electoral votes in favor of one of the presidential candidates.

Each state is permitted the same number of electoral votes as it has representatives in both houses of Congress. The candidate who receives the majority of the electoral votes wins the presidency. This process was also intended to balance power between large and small states.

The Constitution created only two positions in the executive branch, the president and vice president. The nation's first president, George Washington, asked Congress to create four executive departments to help him carry out his duties. These first four departments were the Justice Department, the War Department, the Treasury Department, and the State Department, which dealt with foreign affairs.

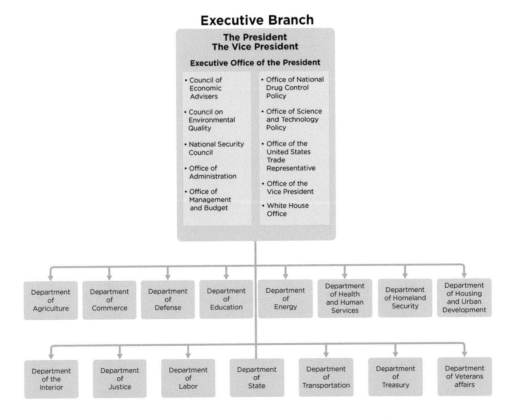

Executive Branch

The President
The Vice President

Executive Office of the President

- Council of Economic Advisers
- Council on Environmental Quality
- National Security Council
- Office of Administration
- Office of Management and Budget

- Office of National Drug Control Policy
- Office of Science and Technology Policy
- Office of the United States Trade Representative
- Office of the Vice President
- White House Office

Department of Agriculture | Department of Commerce | Department of Defense | Department of Education | Department of Energy | Department of Health and Human Services | Department of Homeland Security | Department of Housing and Urban Development

Department of the Interior | Department of Justice | Department of Labor | Department of State | Department of Transportation | Department of Treasury | Department of Veterans affairs

Over the years, more executive departments were added to do the work of the government. Today, the executive branch includes 15 departments. Each department head is chosen by the president and also serves in the president's cabinet, a board of advisers and deputies. The executive branch also includes numerous boards, agencies, commissions, and committees, such as the Central Intelligence Agency (CIA), National Aeronautics and Space Administration (NASA), and the United States Postal Service (USPS).

The Constitution establishes the president as commander in chief of the military and gives the president the power to make treaties, or international agreements, with other nations and to appoint people to government offices. It also describes how the president is elected and how the president can be impeached, or tried and removed from office, for committing serious crimes.

The Judicial Branch (Article III)
What are the powers of the judiciary?

The judicial branch is made up of the U.S. Supreme Court and other federal courts. This branch is responsible for interpreting federal laws, determining whether people have broken those laws, and using federal laws to settle disputes.

photo: Library of Congress

The Supreme Court building in Washington, DC.

The Constitution created the Supreme Court as the most important part of the judicial branch. Then, the first Congress passed the Judiciary Act of 1789, which created other federal courts. The first level of federal courts is made up of the U.S. district courts, which hear cases involving federal laws. Each state has between one and four district courts. At the next level are the U.S. courts of appeals, also called circuit courts. An appeal is a legal challenge to a court's ruling. There are only 12 circuit courts in the United States.

The Supreme Court, the highest level of the judicial branch, is mainly an appeals court. A large number of cases are brought to the Supreme Court's attention, so the justices must choose which cases they will hear. The judgments of the Supreme Court are final; the Supreme Court's interpretation of the law cannot be challenged or appealed.

If Congress disagrees with a Supreme Court decision, its only remedy is a constitutional amendment. However, a Supreme Court ruling can be overturned by the ruling of a later Supreme Court. For example, the decision in *Brown v. Board of Education of Topeka, Kansas*, in 1954, made segregated schools illegal. This decision overturned the 1896 *Plessy v. Ferguson* decision that upheld the legality of segregation as long as facilities such as schools were "separate but equal."

Discovery EDUCATION | SOCIAL STUDIES TECHBOOK

How does the Constitution reflect major principles of American democracy?

Democratic Principles

What democratic principles are reflected in the Constitution?

The Framers of the Constitution believed that a representative government could only survive if its citizens and leaders possess civic virtue, or civic

Complete this activity to show your understanding of how the Constitution supports democratic principles.

republicanism. This means that they place the common good above their own individual interests. The Founders believed that citizens who possess civic virtue fulfill basic responsibilities, such as taking responsibility for their actions, taking care of their families, keeping informed on public issues, voting, and serving on juries.

As a result of their belief in civic virtue and civic republicanism, the Framers believed in certain ideals that became the basis for the U.S. government.

Popular Sovereignty

One of these important ideals is the idea of popular sovereignty, or consent of the governed. This means that the government's power comes from its citizens. Thomas Jefferson described this idea in the introduction to the Declaration of Independence in 1776, when American colonists decided to change their government from the one in Great Britain to a new one they created themselves. Eleven years later, in 1787, the Constitutional Convention again proposed to the people that they change their government. People elected representatives to attend the ratifying conventions, and these representatives freely decided to approve the Constitution.

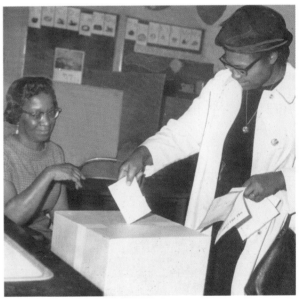

photo: Getty Images

African American citizens voting during an election, Washington, DC, May 11, 1968.

The idea of popular sovereignty is reflected in many different places in the Constitution. For example, Article I requires that members of the House of Representatives be elected directly by the people. Article V provides the means to amend the Constitution through the elected representatives of the people. The "We the People" opening of the Preamble also establishes the idea that the people of the United States are the source of the government's authority.

Closely tied to popular sovereignty is the principle of majority rule. This is the idea that democratic government cannot exist unless the people agree to accept decisions made by the greatest number of voters in free elections.

Americans' strong belief in majority rule helps ensure that the country's frequent transfers of power from one political party to another are peaceful and legitimate. The principle of majority rule is balanced by the country's commitment to protecting the rights of individuals in the minority. Members of groups or parties who are defeated in elections retain their rights to have their voices heard in the democratic process.

Individual Rights

The Constitution also upholds the principle of individual rights. A *right* is a claim or privilege to which people are entitled. The Framers strongly believed that people had certain rights the government could not take away. They were influenced by the philosophy of classical liberalism, which emerged during the Enlightenment. One of the most important beliefs of classical liberalism is the idea that government exists to protect individual rights.

The Bill of Rights was added to the Constitution to address Anti-Federalist objections. Anti-Federalists thought the Constitution gave the central government too much power. The Bill of Rights lists specific rights to be protected, such as freedom of speech and religion. It also lists many rights of people who are accused of crimes. In addition, the Ninth Amendment states that people have more rights than those listed in the Constitution. Over the course of U.S. history, people's rights have been expanded by constitutional amendments and federal laws and policies.

Limited Government

The purpose of establishing a political system based on limited government is to protect both individual rights and popular sovereignty. The principle of limited government can be traced back to the Magna Carta of 1215, which was an agreement between British nobles and the king. The Magna Carta established limits on the king's powers that were designed to keep him from abusing his power. It also promoted the idea that government should be based on a contract between the rulers of a society and the people to be ruled. Following the example of the Magna Carta, the Framers of the U.S. Constitution designed a political system that established many different limits on the power of the federal government. For example, the Constitution grants to the people of the United States the authority to elect and reject representatives to Congress at regular time intervals. The frequent words "Congress shall make no law" in the Constitution also reveal how the Framers limited the government's ability to restrict certain freedoms.

Discovery EDUCATION | SOCIAL STUDIES TECHBOOK

How does the Constitution reflect major principles of American democracy?

In addition, the Bill of Rights established several freedoms for citizens, further limiting the power of the government. For example, the Tenth Amendment states that powers not granted to the federal government are reserved to the states and to the people.

Republicanism, or Representative Democracy

The Constitution also reflects the principle of republicanism, or representative democracy. Instead of all citizens being involved in the government like a direct democracy, U.S. citizens elect leaders to represent their interests. The Framers' design of the American republic was strongly influenced by English parliamentary traditions that dated back to the 1200s, when counties began sending representatives to work with the King to make policies. These traditions include the formation of a bicameral legislative branch consisting of two separate houses.

In the United States, people choose whom to elect as their state representatives and senators in Congress, which is established in the Constitution as the legislative branch of the government. They also vote to select the president, the leader of the executive branch. Such a republican system is designed around the idea that supreme political power of the government rests with the people.

How Much Is Too Much?

How does the Constitution limit the powers of the government?

The Constitution limits the powers of government in several ways.

Separation of Powers

In an essay written in 1750, French philosopher Baron de Montesquieu described a government with a separation of powers. Montesquieu said a government should have different parts, or branches, and that the branches should have different powers. For example, one branch would write laws and a separate branch would carry them out. The purpose of separating powers was to prevent any part of the government from having too much power.

The U.S. Constitution created a government with three branches. No other national government had used this exact structure before the United States put it in place. However, several individual states within the United States did already have this structure for their state governments.

Checks and Balances

The Framers also created a system of checks and balances. They gave each branch a way to check, or limit, the power of the others. For example, Congress can pass laws, but the president can veto, or formally reject, a law Congress has passed. Another example of a check is that the president nominates ambassadors and Supreme Court justices, but the Senate has to approve those nominations.

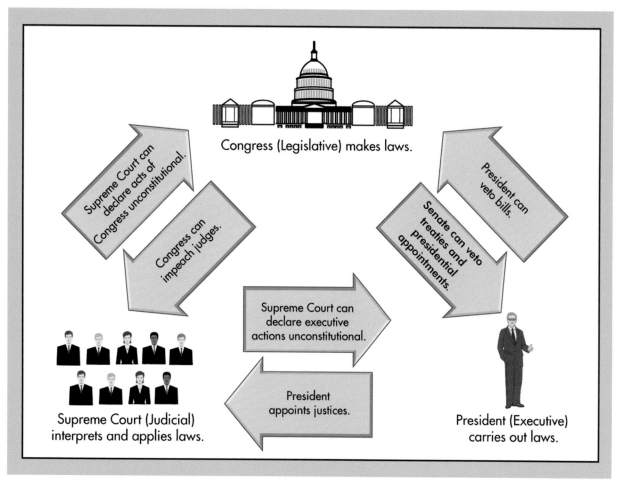

A diagram showing the federal government's system of checks and balances.

One important check that the Supreme Court has on the other two branches is the power of judicial review. This means the Supreme Court justices can declare a federal or state law invalid if they find it disobeys the Constitution. The court can also declare executive actions unconstitutional. This prevents Congress and the president from using powers the Constitution did not give them.

The power of judicial review is not described in the Constitution. Instead, it was established in an 1803 case called *Marbury v. Madison*. In this case, the Supreme Court declared that a law passed by Congress was not valid because it conflicted with the Constitution. John Marshall, the chief justice at the time, wrote that the Constitution was the nation's highest law, even supreme over laws passed by Congress. Because the Court's duty was to uphold the law of the land, the Court had the authority to say that any act by Congress that violated the Constitution was invalid.

A More Perfect Union?

What is federalism?

Federalism

Another way in which the government's power is limited is through federalism. *Federalism* is the division of power between the national, or federal, government and the several governments of the states. The Framers of the Constitution assigned to the federal government certain powers, such as making international treaties and regulating interstate commerce. However, they did not give the federal government direct authority over matters concerning education, land use, local elections, or building safety. These powers are reserved for the states. Some powers, such as the power to tax, are allotted to both the federal and state governments.

The Constitution denied certain powers to the states, such as making international treaties. It also required the state courts to uphold federal laws. Without these provisions, the federal government could not act effectively.

The Tenth Amendment to the Constitution says that any powers that are not specifically granted to the federal government are reserved, or set aside, for the states. Through this federal structure, the framers limited how strong the federal government could become.

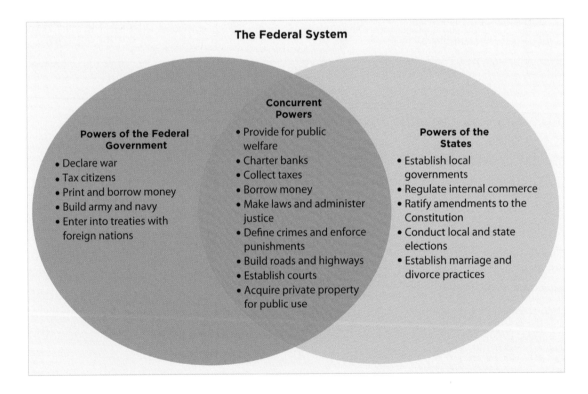

The Federal System

Powers of the Federal Government
- Declare war
- Tax citizens
- Print and borrow money
- Build army and navy
- Enter into treaties with foreign nations

Concurrent Powers
- Provide for public welfare
- Charter banks
- Collect taxes
- Borrow money
- Make laws and administer justice
- Define crimes and enforce punishments
- Build roads and highways
- Establish courts
- Acquire private property for public use

Powers of the States
- Establish local governments
- Regulate internal commerce
- Ratify amendments to the Constitution
- Conduct local and state elections
- Establish marriage and divorce practices

Relations Between the States

Recall that the Articles of Confederation gave the national government little power to regulate economic and political relationships between individual states. This permitted states to act almost as separate independent countries and to tax goods flowing through them to other states. As a result, disputes between states interrupted commerce and harmed the overall U.S. economy. Framers such as Alexander Hamilton believed that establishing a common market among the states would benefit not only the country as a whole, but individual states as well. As a result, the Constitution established guidelines for interstate relations.

Article IV, Section 1 contains the full faith and credit clause. This clause requires every state to recognize and respect the laws, records, and court decisions of all other states. If a person gets a driver's license in California, this person is allowed to drive across the country to New York. Every state must recognize the California driver's license as valid.

Article IV, Section 2 addresses two important matters regarding how states may treat residents of other states. The privileges and immunities clause forbids any state from discriminating against residents of another state. This gives residents of another state the right to travel, purchase property, and conduct business within that state.

The principle of extradition necessitated cooperation between two states. *Extradition* is the act of returning an individual accused of a crime to the state where the crime was committed. In other words, if a suspected criminal commits a crime in one state and crosses the border into another state, it is that state's duty to return the suspect to the state where the crime was committed.

Limits on Interstate Compacts

Article I, Section 10 of the Constitution declares that "No state shall, without the Consent of Congress . . . enter into any Agreement or Compact with another state." The Framers feared the potential threat of states forming alliances with one another. This clause prohibited states from acting as sovereign nations, an idea that many states desired after the Revolutionary War.

For example, imagine that two states disagree with the federal government's policies on interstate trade. They decide to form an alliance to prevent other states from trading with them. Without the interstate compacts clause, the federal government would not be able to stop the states from forming this alliance. This means the states could act as independent nations and undermine the unity of the United States.

Confederation Versus Federal Union

The Articles of Confederation created a confederation, or loose union of states without a strong central power. The Confederation Congress was a decision-making body that had no enforcement powers. The state governments remained sovereign.

Discovery SOCIAL STUDIES
EDUCATION | **TECHBOOK**

How does the Constitution reflect major principles of American democracy?

In contrast, the Constitution created a federal structure. The central government and the states share power. Unlike the Confederation Congress, the new central government was given not only legislative powers, but also executive and judicial powers. The federal government uses executive powers to conduct its business, exercise its powers, and enforce its laws. The federal government uses judicial powers to ensure that federal laws are interpreted and applied uniformly throughout the country.

Adding executive and judicial branches strengthened the central government. A government with three branches instead of one was also more complex. The Constitution needed to describe how the branches would relate and share power. It created the system of checks and balances that prevents any one part of the government from gaining too much power.

Federal Supremacy

How does the Constitution balance power between the federal government and the states?

To balance power between the federal government and the states, Article VI included the Supremacy Clause, which specifically says that the Constitution and the federal government are "the supreme law of the land." If a state law and a federal law conflicted, the federal law would rule. The Supremacy Clause was vital if the federal government was to be able to enforce its laws.

The new Congress had the power to control relations among the states. States were also denied powers that would interfere with the functions of the federal government. States were prohibited from taxing imports and from making international treaties. States were required to respect the laws and contracts of the other states.

In 1819, the power of the federal government grew even stronger with the Supreme Court decision in *McCulloch v. Maryland*. The case concerned the federal government's bank, the Second Bank of the United States. Maryland passed a law imposing a special tax on the national bank, but the bank refused to pay the tax. The Supreme Court ruled that no state had the power to tax the federal government. It ruled that Maryland's state law violated the federal Constitution and was therefore null and void. This confirmed the Supremacy Clause and set a precedent that would influence court cases in the future.

The Articles of Confederation was written during the American Revolutionary War, and the authors had relied on the individual states to govern in a way that would uphold important principles and values. Unfortunately, the government they created did not meet the needs of the new nation. The authors of the Constitution understood the problems of the Articles of Confederation and worked to create a government with more centralized power. Still, they took care to build democratic values and principles, including limited government, into the structure of the new government.

The history of the United States from 1789 until today is partly the story of how well this system of government has worked. Has the government upheld the values of the Constitution? Has it protected individual rights? Has the government reflected popular consent? These questions are not simple to answer, but they are important to think about as you learn more about U.S. history.

Complete this activity to rule on controversies involving the Constitution.

Consider the Essential Question:

How does the Constitution reflect major principles of American democracy?

Go online to complete the Social Studies Explanation.

Check for Understanding:

Describe the most important effects of the ratification of the U.S. Constitution in 1787. How did ratification change the U.S. political system?

Discovery EDUCATION | SOCIAL STUDIES TECHBOOK.

How does the Bill of Rights help government balance rights and order in the U.S. political system?

4.4 The Bill of Rights

photo: Getty Images

LESSON OVERVIEW

Introduction

In this concept, you will learn how the U.S. Constitution protects the people from government abuse of power.

Essential Question

How does the Bill of Rights help government balance rights and order in the U.S. political system?

Lesson Objectives

By the end of this lesson, you should be able to:

- Explain the political and historical significance of the Bill of Rights.

- Explain the importance of specific rights and freedoms guaranteed by the Bill of Rights.

Key Vocabulary

Which terms do you already know?

- [ ] Appalachian Mountains
- [ ] Bill of Rights
- [ ] defendant
- [ ] double jeopardy
- [ ] due process
- [ ] Eighth Amendment
- [ ] English Bill of Rights
- [ ] establishment clause
- [ ] Federalist Papers
- [ ] Fifth Amendment
- [ ] First Amendment
- [ ] Fourth Amendment
- [ ] free exercise clause
- [ ] George Mason
- [ ] grand jury
- [ ] indictment
- [ ] James Madison

- [ ] John Hancock
- [ ] John Peter Zenger
- [ ] jury
- [ ] majority rule
- [ ] Ninth Amendment
- [ ] Patrick Henry
- [ ] probable cause
- [ ] prosecution
- [ ] Samuel Adams
- [ ] Second Amendment
- [ ] seizure
- [ ] self-incrimination
- [ ] Seventh Amendment
- [ ] Sixth Amendment
- [ ] Tenth Amendment
- [ ] Third Amendment
- [ ] warrant

ENGAGE

What's more important: liberty or security? Visit Engage to learn more.

Essential Question

How does the Bill of Rights help government balance rights and order in the U.S. political system?

EXPLORE

Rights Before the Revolution

Why were Americans fearful of a strong central government?

As a result of their experiences as British subjects, many Americans during and immediately after the Revolution feared that a political system with a strong central government would threaten their individual rights. For example, Americans were aware that many of their ancestors had settled in the colonies as a result of Great Britain's establishment of a state church.

photo: Getty Images

James Otis was a Massachusetts lawyer who objected to the British writs of assistance.

Before the Revolutionary War, the British government not only ignored Americans' opinions about laws such as the Stamp and Tea Acts, but it also censored newspapers and even jailed some colonists who complained. They also had passed the Quartering Act, which authorized the British Army to use private homes and other buildings to house troops. The law even required colonists to provide these troops with food and drink.

Discovery | SOCIAL STUDIES EDUCATION | TECHBOOK.

How does the Bill of Rights help government balance rights and order in the U.S. political system?

The Founders also remembered the British writs of assistance. These were search warrants that had no limits: They were not required to name specific places to be searched; they could be issued based on suspicion, without evidence that a crime had been committed; and they did not expire. In effect, the writs of assistance gave British officials the power to search any place at any time.

Finally, the Founders remembered how the Revolutionary War began: The British governor of Massachusetts sent the army to seize colonial armaments stored in the town of Concord. Without their weapons, the colonial militias would not have been able to resist what they saw as British abuses of power.

Explore this interactive to examine the tension between providing security and protecting individual rights.

As a result of these experiences, preserving individual rights has become an important reflection of the American identity. The Founders were determined to create a system of government whose purpose was to protect the rights of the people. The Declaration of Independence not only stated this purpose, but it also listed British actions that violated the colonists' "unalienable rights."

Protecting the People

How did the Bill of Rights calm peoples' fears about a strong central government?

Given the experiences they had as British colonists, the Founders wanted to place clear limits on government power. When the U.S. Constitution was proposed in 1787, it spelled out the structure and powers of the new government, but no article specifically described the powers or privileges of the people.

The Constitution had no bill of rights because participants in the Constitutional Convention believed the government had only the powers it was given. If a power was not listed as belonging to the government, it was not a power of the government. According to this argument, there was no need for a bill of rights because the Constitution did not give government the power to violate people's rights. For instance, the right to travel freely was not mentioned in the Constitution. Did Americans in 1789 have the right to travel from one state to another? Of course they did. This was not written down—nobody thought it needed to be.

Opponents of the Constitution, including Anti-Federalists such as George Mason, worried that the central government would be oppressive and that it would threaten individual rights. Even though the British government did not have a Constitution, it had the English Bill of Rights. This document, from 1689, specified many limits on the king's power and named rights of individuals against the government. Many Americans wanted a similar guarantee that key rights would be specifically protected. Thomas Jefferson, though he was not an Anti-Federalist, believed the people were entitled to a list of rights. Many state constitutions already included bills of rights limiting the power of state governments.

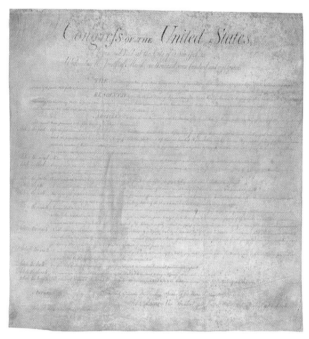

photo: Our Documents Gov

Congress's original joint resolution that was the basis for the Bill of Rights.

Recall that James Madison, Alexander Hamilton, and John Jay wrote a series of essays, *The Federalist Papers*, in which they argued for ratifying the U.S. Constitution. Prominent Anti-Federalists wrote a similar series of letters and essays arguing against ratification. (Historians are less certain of the identities of the Anti-Federalist writers.) Orators also joined the Anti-Federalist cause. In a 1788 speech, the Virginia statesman Patrick Henry criticized his fellow citizens for not demanding stronger protections from their national government.

In Massachusetts, Anti-Federalists led by John Hancock and Samuel Adams demanded that a bill of rights be added before they could support ratification. Federalists promised that the first Congress would add a bill of rights. This promise turned out to be enough: Massachusetts voted to join the Union in February 1788.

James Madison drafted the proposed amendments to identify specific rights of the people against the government. To amend something means to change and improve it. In several states, the proposed amendments helped convince state legislatures to accept the Constitution. By 1791, the states ratified 10 amendments known as the Bill of Rights.

In the years since the Bill of Rights was ratified, 17 more amendments have been added to the Constitution. Nine of these also protect individual rights, for example, the Thirteenth Amendment, which outlawed slavery, and the Nineteenth Amendment, which gave women the right to vote.

Discovery | SOCIAL STUDIES
EDUCATION | **TECHBOOK**

How does the Bill of Rights help government balance rights and order in the U.S. political system?

Personal Liberty

How does the Bill of Rights protect personal freedom?

Our Personal Liberties

American colonists such as Patrick Henry were prepared to die to preserve their liberty. Personal liberty enables us to live our lives the way we want and is protected by the first three amendments.

Freedom of Expression

The First Amendment secures the rights of the people to meet together, to engage in political activity, and to share ideas. It protects citizens' rights to free speech and a free press. This means that the government may not prevent individuals or groups from speaking or publishing their opinions and it may not punish them for what they say or write. The speech and press freedoms guaranteed by the First Amendment are essential to a properly functioning constitutional republic. Citizens who are not free to attempt to influence their government by expressing their ideas about the issues of the day cannot be considered the source of the government's authority. In addition, a society that lacks a free press is unable to keep citizens informed about issues, events, and government policies. As a result, such societies cannot hope to use the democratic process to hold government officials accountable for their conduct in office.

photo: Getty Images

Students protesting segregation during the civil rights movement.

The protections of the First Amendment contrast with undemocratic, or authoritarian, governments that do not allow free expression. In authoritarian systems, leaders maintain power by controlling what the people and the press can publish and say publicly. In democratic systems, the people are permitted to criticize the government and express their concerns. For example, satire, or criticism through humor, is a popular form of expression in democratic systems, often on late-night television programs. Satire often attempts to make leaders look ridiculous. As a result, authoritarian leaders tend to forbid it as a form of expression.

Because the First Amendment protects free expression, American citizens often encounter speech they may disagree with or find offensive. Courts have often permitted groups such as the Ku Klux Klan to express freely their hateful opinions. The amendment also includes symbolic actions that express opinions, such as students wearing arm bands to protest the country's involvement in foreign wars.

The First Amendment also protects freedoms of assembly and association. This means the government may not prevent people from joining and peacefully gathering in groups, in public or in private. Freedom of assembly gives citizens a chance to discuss their thoughts, opinions, and common interests with others. It also can raise individuals' awareness of issues.

Setting Limits

At various times in the nation's history, the U.S. government has placed limits on free expression. Free expression has been restricted during wars, times of national crisis, and times of perceived crisis. In 1919, the Supreme Court ruled that speech that might be permitted during peacetime can be restricted if it presents a "clear and present danger" to the nation. In addition, courts have ruled that the government may place limits on written or spoken words that purposefully defame one's character or reputation. It also may restrict speech that stirs up violence or creates chaos, such as shouting "fire!" in a crowded theater.

Protecting Religious Freedom

The First Amendment also includes two provisions that protect Americans' freedom of religion. The establishment clause prohibits Congress from passing laws "respecting an establishment of religion." This means that the government cannot create a state church or promote one religion over others. It also includes the free exercise clause, which prohibits the government from interfering with individuals' and groups' religious rituals and practices. The dual religious freedom protections of the First Amendment reflect Virginia's Statue for Religious Freedom, which Thomas Jefferson wrote back in 1777. Adopted by the Virginia General Assembly in 1786, this document provided the Framers with a model for creating a separation between church and state in the United States.

The Second and Third Amendments

The Second Amendment asserts a right to own firearms. This right has long been at the center of a debate in the United States. Is the right to bear firearms a right of every individual, or does the amendment protect only the rights of militias? In a 5-4 decision announced in 2008, the Supreme Court ruled that the Second Amendment protects an individual's right to possess firearms unconnected with service in a militia. However, Americans have continued to debate whether or not the amendment permits governments to pass some restrictions on gun ownership.

The Third Amendment, which prohibits the quartering of soldiers in people's homes, might not seem important today, but it was of crucial importance to Americans in the 1700s, who remembered when occupying British troops were quartered in inns, businesses, and civilian homes.

Discovery SOCIAL STUDIES
EDUCATION | **TECHBOOK**

How does the Bill of Rights help government balance rights and order in the U.S. political system?

Rights of the Accused

How does the Bill of Rights protect against abuse of the justice system?

One of the government's most basic duties is to enforce the laws and protect people from criminal acts. To accomplish this, the government needs to be able to accuse people of crimes, to jail them, to search them, to seize items for use as evidence, and so on. Without these powers, the government cannot be effective. But these powers are also dangerous, and if they are misused, the government can ruin people's lives. The purpose of many of the Bill of Rights amendments was to create a balance between respecting individual rights and protecting people from crime.

Accusing People of Crimes

Much of the Bill of Rights prevents abuse of government power by protecting the rights of persons accused of crimes. Remember that some people accused of crimes are guilty and some are innocent; the Bill of Rights protects the rights of both the innocent and the guilty.

The Fourth Amendment limits the government's powers of search and seizure. Police may not conduct a search without a *warrant*, which is written permission to search for evidence. A warrant may not be issued without a good reason to suspect that a crime has taken place.

A Fair Trial

The Fifth Amendment and the Sixth Amendment guarantee due process, meaning fair and reasonable treatment. Persons accused of a crime have rights to be told what crime they are charged with and what evidence the charge is based on. They have the right to the protection of an attorney and to be tried by a jury of regular citizens. Government witnesses must testify in open court, and the accused person has the right to question them. The accused also has a right to bring witnesses. In addition, the government may not keep people in prison without a trial.

Rights in Civil Trials

The Seventh Amendment ensures the right to a trial by jury in civil cases. Legal matters are either civil or criminal. In a criminal case, the government tries to prove that a citizen committed a crime and should be punished. In a civil case, one citizen tries to prove that another person acted unfairly and should pay compensation. The Seventh Amendment provides the right to a jury trial for civil cases in which the disputed asset value exceeds twenty dollars.

photo: Getty Images
A female attorney speaks to a jury in a courtroom.

Appropriate Punishments

The words of the Eighth Amendment, barring cruel and unusual punishments, come directly from the English Bill of Rights and reflect the basic idea that the punishment should fit the crime. Corrupt governments have been known to use extraordinary fines to punish critics and prevent disagreement.

Prohibiting cruel and unusual punishments also prevents horrors such as torture. The Constitution was not intended to establish a government that forced people to live in fear. Cruel and unusual punishments cannot be imposed by a government that rests on the consent of the governed.

Limited Government

How does the Bill of Rights limit the power of the central government?

Restraining the Government

One argument against including a bill of rights in the Constitution was the fear of leaving something out. All of the amendments limit the power of government, but people feared that a list of specific rights would suggest that the government could violate any rights they had forgotten or had not thought of.

photo: Getty Images
The Tenth Ammendment gives states the power to run public schools.

The Ninth and Tenth Amendments were meant to address both these issues and to ensure that federal power was limited. The Ninth Amendment says that people have rights other than those listed in the Constitution. For example, the Ninth Amendment has been used to establish the right to privacy, the right to travel, and the right to be presumed innocent until proven guilty. The Tenth Amendment confirms the Ninth Amendment and adds that states have powers other than those expressly reserved in the Constitution.

Discovery EDUCATION | SOCIAL STUDIES **TECHBOOK**

How does the Bill of Rights help government balance rights and order in the U.S. political system?

With the addition of the Bill of Rights, the vast majority of U.S. citizens felt more comfortable about the structure of the new government and its ability to protect citizens' rights. The addition of the Bill of Rights proved that the Constitution's amendment process worked and that the Constitution could be adapted over time to meet the country's needs.

Complete this activity to learn more about the Founders' debate over the Bill of Rights.

Consider the Essential Question:

How does the Bill of Rights help government balance rights and order in the U.S. political system?

Go online to complete the Social Studies Explanation.

Check for Understanding:

How did events from the colonial era and the American Revolution contribute to the Founders' determination to protect individual rights?

5.1 Washington's Presidency

photo: Library of Congress

LESSON OVERVIEW

Introduction

In this concept, you will learn how George Washington dealt with the problems facing a young United States. You will see how political parties developed. You will also explore the recommendations Washington gave at the end of his presidency.

Essential Question

In what ways did George Washington's presidency influence the future of the U.S. political system?

Lesson Objectives

By the end of this lesson, you should be able to:

- Identify economic and governmental challenges of the new nation and analyze conflicting solutions to these problems proposed by the nation's leaders.

- Describe and explain the significance of precedents established during the presidency of George Washington and evaluate the significance of Washington's Farewell Address.

Key Vocabulary
Which terms do you already know?

- [ ] Appalachian Mountains
- [ ] Alexander Hamilton
- [ ] Benjamin Banneker
- [ ] cabinet
- [ ] Democratic-Republican Party
- [ ] Edmund Randolph
- [ ] Federalists
- [ ] French Revolution
- [ ] George Washington
- [ ] Henry Knox
- [ ] Pierre L'Enfant
- [ ] precedent
- [ ] Thomas Jefferson
- [ ] Washington's Farewell Address
- [ ] Washington, DC

Discovery | SOCIAL STUDIES
EDUCATION | **TECHBOOK**

In what ways did George Washington's presidency influence the future of the U.S. political system?

ENGAGE

What were George Washington's hopes and fears? Visit Engage to learn more.

Essential Question

In what ways did George Washington's presidency influence the future of the U.S. political system?

EXPLORE

Washington Sets Some "Firsts"

What examples did George Washington establish that others would follow?

Although it named the powers and duties of the president of the United States, the U.S. Constitution was only a framework. As the first person to accept the duties of the office, George Washington himself would define what it meant to be the nation's chief executive. Washington's actions and decisions as president established examples that would be followed by future U.S. heads of state.

As an experienced leader, Washington realized he would need help to govern effectively. He asked Congress to create the Department of State, the Department of War, and the Department of the Treasury, as well as positions to head each of these departments. This group of department heads became known as the president's cabinet, a term that had been used for the advisers to the British crown. Every president since Washington has had a cabinet to advise him and to carry out his decisions.

photo: Library of Congress

George Washington delivering his inaugural address, April 1789.

Washington chose Thomas Jefferson as secretary of state, his chief adviser on matters dealing with other nations. Henry Knox, a Revolutionary War veteran, was named secretary of war. Alexander Hamilton was chosen as secretary of the treasury, the president's chief adviser on financial and economic issues. Washington also named Edmund Randolph as attorney general, the president's chief adviser on the law. Randolph did not head an official executive branch department; the Department of Justice was officially created in 1870, with the attorney general as its head.

Washington set other precedents, or examples, that later presidents would follow. For instance, he had to decide what people would call him. Congress considered calling him "His Highness the President of the United States of America and Protector of their Liberties." Washington preferred a title that showed respect for the office but clearly rejected any hint of nobility. He chose to be called "Mr. President."

George Washington was elected to a second term as president in 1792. Following Washington, most U.S. presidents have run for a second term, and 19 standing presidents have been reelected. However, Washington set another important precedent when he refused to run for a third term in 1796.

Complete this activity to show your understanding of the most important events from Washington's presidency.

Washington was very popular and probably could have been elected again, but he had good reasons for stepping down after two terms. He believed the presidency should change. After all, the public had not elected a king to rule forever. New ideas and new enthusiasm were needed. Washington had grown tired from dealing with quarreling in his cabinet and in Congress. In a letter to a friend in January 1795, he wrote, "I can religiously aver [swear], that no man was ever more tired of public life."

A New Nation, Conceived in Debt

How did the United States deal with its debt problems after the Revolutionary War?

State Debts

The young United States faced economic challenges following the Revolutionary War. The country owed millions of dollars to foreign governments and private citizens, both of which had helped finance the war. The federal government owed most of the debt—about $54 million. But the state governments owed another $25 million. The federal government had given bonds to soldiers who had served during the war. The bonds were promises that the government would pay the soldiers back what they owed, plus some interest.

Discovery SOCIAL STUDIES
EDUCATION TECHBOOK

In what ways did George Washington's presidency influence the future of the U.S. political system?

Hamilton thought the federal government should take on the states' debts from the Revolutionary War. His main reason was how it would affect creditors, the people who were owed money by the states. If the federal government took on the states' debts, this would give creditors a strong reason to want the federal government to succeed. If the federal government failed, creditors would not be repaid.

A New Capital City

Many people thought Hamilton's proposal was unfair. States that had already repaid some of their debts would be forced to finance the other states' debts. In particular, the Northern states owed much more than most of those in the South. They were opposed to being taxed by the federal government to pay the other states' debts. Debate over assuming the states' debts continued for months.

photo: Library of Congress

An early city plan for Washington, DC.

Eventually, the two sides made a deal. In exchange for Southern support for Hamilton's plan, Hamilton would support a relocation of the nation's capital. Instead of its then-location in New York, the new capital would be built on the banks of the Potomac River, on land given by Maryland and Virginia. Southerners hoped that having the new capital in the South would make the federal government more responsive to their needs.

Playing Politics

How did political parties emerge?

As the young American government worked to define itself, an important question emerged: How strong should the central government be? Some people thought the government should only be able to do what was clearly stated in the Constitution. Others thought the Constitution also gave the government powers that were not specifically declared.

A national debate began over the extent to which the government could exercise its powers. Two members of Washington's cabinet emerged on opposite sides of the issues. Alexander Hamilton favored a strong central government that acted to improve the economy and support private businesses. Hamilton's views were shared by the upper class and those with ties to manufacturing and commerce. Many members of those groups lived in New England and the Middle Colonies.

Thomas Jefferson believed the people should have a say in their government and that power should be in the hands of the states. He thought the states were more likely to protect people's rights than a federal government would be. Many of Jefferson's supporters lived in the South and West.

photo: Getty Images

Thomas Jefferson believed state and local governments should exercise most of the political power.

Hamilton and Jefferson's disagreement played out in real issues that faced the nation. For instance, Hamilton wanted the federal government to assume the states' war debts, that is, to take responsibility for repaying money the states had borrowed to fund the military during the Revolutionary War. Jefferson believed the individual states should remain responsible for their own debts. Additionally, Hamilton wanted the government to invest in a national bank to help support the economy. Jefferson disagreed; he thought establishing a bank would exceed the powers given Congress by the Constitution.

Newspapers reporting on these issues linked Hamilton's positions with those of the Federalists, those who had supported ratifying the Constitution. They linked Jefferson's positions with those of the Anti-Federalists, who had opposed the Constitution on the grounds that it gave the central government too much power. These labels stuck, so when Hamilton, Vice President John Adams, and other like-minded leaders officially formed a political party in 1791, they called it the Federalist Party.

Soon the Federalists' opponents, led by Jefferson and James Madison, formed the Republican Party. The party later became known as the Democratic-Republican Party, but its members continued to call themselves Republicans. These early Republicans did not have much in common with today's Republican Party.

President Washington did not want to see political parties emerge and never aligned himself with a party or a political viewpoint. He thought people should base their decisions on the needs of the country as a whole. But Hamilton and Jefferson's disagreement mirrored what was going on across the nation, and in the election of 1796, the two contenders for the presidency were Adams, a Federalist, and Jefferson, a Democratic-Republican.

Discovery Education | SOCIAL STUDIES TECHBOOK

In what ways did George Washington's presidency influence the future of the U.S. political system?

Washington Bids Farewell

What advice did George Washington give to the country as he left office?

After two terms as president, George Washington decided he would not run for a third term. He preferred to retire to Mount Vernon, the home he loved, and enjoy farm life again. After making this decision, Washington wrote a letter to the nation. This letter, which became known as George Washington's Farewell Address, was published in a newspaper called the *American Daily Advertiser* in September 1796. In his Farewell Address, Washington discussed the nation's accomplishments and gave advice to the country on how to move on without him:

"The name of American, which belongs to you in your national capacity, must always exalt the just pride of patriotism more than any appellation derived from local discriminations. With slight shades of difference, you have the same religion, manners, habits, and political principles. You have in a common cause fought and triumphed together; the independence and liberty you possess are the work of joint counsels, and joint efforts of common dangers, sufferings, and successes."

photo: Library of Congress

A draft of Washington's Farewell Address.

As he was leaving office, Washington urged all Americans to reject party allegiances and pursue the national interest. He warned against making permanent alliances with foreign powers. He reminded his fellow citizens that "honesty is always the best policy."

For many U.S. citizens, Washington's Farewell Address is an important statement of their country's political beliefs and ideals. They will often point to Washington's words in support of their belief that public officials with conflicting interests should place country first, seek compromise, and work together to solve the nation's problems. But in spite of Washington's advice, political parties have become one of the most important features of the U.S. political process. The systems for electing public officials and passing new laws are controlled by the Democratic and Republican parties.

In the course of history, as the nations of the world have become more interconnected, U.S. presidents have also ignored Washington's warning against foreign entanglements. Over the years, the United States has entered into numerous military and economic

Explore this investigation to learn more about Washington's final speech as president.

agreements and conflicts with other countries. For example, when the United States joined the North Atlantic Treaty Organization (NATO) in 1949, it agreed to treat an attack against any NATO country as an attack on all NATO countries. But much of the public continues to believe that the United States should minimize its dealings with foreign countries. Washington's words are often used to support this position.

Consider the Essential Question:

In what ways did George Washington's presidency influence the future of the U.S. political system?

Go online to complete the Social Studies Explanation.

Check for Understanding:

Describe the precedent established during Washington's presidency that you think had the greatest influence on the U.S. political system.

Discovery SOCIAL STUDIES
EDUCATION **TECHBOOK**

How did the nation's early problems reveal different philosophies about government?

5.2 Hamilton vs. Jefferson

photo: Library of Congress

LESSON OVERVIEW

Introduction

In this concept, you will find out how political differences impacted Washington's and Adams's presidency and drove a wedge between some of the nation's leading statesmen.

Essential Question

How did the nation's early problems reveal different philosophies about government?

Lesson Objectives

By the end of this lesson, you should be able to:

- Analyze the development of early political parties and ideologies, particularly those supported by Thomas Jefferson and Alexander Hamilton.

- Describe conflicts at home and abroad during the presidencies of George Washington and John Adams.

Key Vocabulary
Which terms do you already know?

- ☐ Alexander Hamilton
- ☐ Alien and Sedition Acts
- ☐ Bank of the United States
- ☐ cabinet
- ☐ Democratic-Republican Party
- ☐ elitist
- ☐ Federalist Party
- ☐ implied power
- ☐ Jay's Treaty
- ☐ John Adams
- ☐ Kentucky and Virginia Resolutions
- ☐ *McCulloch v. Maryland*
- ☐ national debt
- ☐ neutrality
- ☐ Neutrality Proclamation
- ☐ "Necessary and Proper" Clause
- ☐ political party
- ☐ speculator
- ☐ Thomas Jefferson
- ☐ Whiskey Rebellion
- ☐ XYZ Affair

ENGAGE

Why did Washington warn about "the spirit of party"? Visit Engage to learn more.

> ## Essential Question
>
> How did the nation's early problems reveal different philosophies about government?

EXPLORE

The First U.S. Political Parties

Why did the first U.S. political parties form?

Conflicts in the Cabinet

When President George Washington first took office in 1789, political parties as we know them did not exist. Washington chose people with varying points of view to serve in his cabinet, his group of close advisors. Strong disagreements soon began to surface about the purpose and role of the federal government.

Alexander Hamilton was appointed to act as secretary of the Treasury. As the president's chief advisor on economic policy, Hamilton was responsible for helping the United States develop a strong economy. He believed that the federal government needed to use its powers to build a solid financial system of banks and a strong currency. He argued for strengthening the government's role in the nation's economy. To avoid the economic problems the country had faced under the Articles of Confederation, the young nation needed a single, national economic system. From Hamilton's perspective, power in the hands of the separate states was dangerous.

photo: Library of Congress

Alexander Hamilton was an early proponent of a strong federal government.

photo: Library of Congress

Because Thomas Jefferson fundamentally disagreed with Hamilton's views, he worked with James Madison to organize opposition to Hamilton's Federalists.

Thomas Jefferson was Washington's secretary of state, Washington's chief diplomat and chief adviser on foreign affairs, or dealings with other countries. Jefferson disagreed with Hamilton on the need for centralized economic power. In his view, centralized economic power was the cause of the British tyranny that had forced the colonists to revolt. According to Jefferson, increasing federal power over the economy was taking a step toward tyranny. He feared that the aristocracy, people of wealth and privilege, would control power and place their interests above those of the nation as a whole. He feared that increased federal power would inevitably trample individual liberties.

Explore this interactive to learn more about two different visions for the country.

Because of these fundamental differences in their thinking, Hamilton and Jefferson often gave Washington conflicting advice on all sorts of issues. Washington valued both of their viewpoints and remained neutral, but he more frequently shared Hamilton's pro-government views. First Hamilton and then Jefferson formed active political parties.

Differing Views About Democracy

How democratic was the new government?

Democracy and the Constitution

Democracy means government by the people. Is the United States a democracy? The government's power comes from the people, and the people can change the government, but it is the government that makes and enforces the laws. What is the people's role?

A direct democracy is a government in which the people make the decisions and there are no representatives. The United States is not a direct democracy. The Framers decided that the people should elect representatives to the state legislatures and the House of Representatives. The state legislatures would elect the members of the Senate. Why did the Constitution create this elaborate arrangement? Why not simply have the people vote on everything? During the debate over ratification of the Constitution, one of the primary points of disagreement concerned this issue.

Competing Views on Democracy

People like Alexander Hamilton believed that ordinary people had little interest in or understanding of government. He wrote that the average citizen was generally self-interested and would vote according to private concerns rather than what was best for the country. He feared that common people would not vote intelligently. He trusted the wealthier, better-educated citizens to preserve an ordered society.

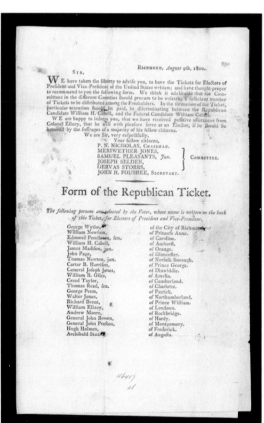

photo: Library of Congress

This broadside provided Virginia voters with a list of Republican electors for the presidential election of 1800.

Hamilton's viewpoints were shared by the Federalists. The Federalists supported the property requirement for voting because they believed that only property owners had a real stake in the government. Jefferson accused Hamilton and the Federalists of being "royalists" who wanted to create a class society, one in which some groups are more powerful and privileged than others, and to use the government for personal gain.

Thomas Jefferson was for extending voting rights "to all who had a permanent intention of living in the country. . . . Whoever intends to live in a country must wish the country well, and has a natural right of assisting in the preservation of it." This included landowners but also those who had lived in the country for a certain amount of time or had established a family or a business.

DISCOVERY | SOCIAL STUDIES
EDUCATION | **TECHBOOK**

How did the nation's early problems reveal different philosophies about government?

Jefferson belonged to a group that opposed the Federalists on many issues. He thought that it was within the people's rights to make decisions about their nation and their leaders. He believed on principle that the will of the people should prevail, even if the majority sometimes made poor choices. Jefferson also did not trust the wealthy to preserve liberty as much as he trusted the entire people, and he believed in making education more available to help people make better decisions.

Dealing with Debt

How did Hamilton address the nation's debt problem?

The National Debt

Hamilton believed that the key to a strong union was a strong economy. As secretary of the Treasury, Hamilton made managing the nation's debts and improving its credit his first priority. The United States had credit problems because, during the Revolutionary War, the American government had borrowed money by issuing bonds. A bond is a promise to pay a specified amount at a specified date. Bonds were sold to people who wanted to invest in the United States and support independence. Purchasers of bonds included other countries, wealthy private lenders, and ordinary American citizens. Bonds were also used instead of cash to pay soldiers.

After the war, many Americans sold their bonds at a discount because they needed quick cash to rebuild their lives. Hoping to make big profits later, wealthy investors called speculators bought many of these bonds. A speculator is someone who attempts to make large amounts of money from risky investments. During the late 1700s, buying U.S. government bonds was considered risky because the federal government was not yet able to repay them.

Some officials argued that the nation should not reimburse speculators for the full value of the bonds they held. In the first place, these officials argued, the government simply could not afford to pay full price for the bonds. In addition, because speculators had purchased the bonds at a discount, it was not necessary for the government to redeem, or pay them back, at full price. Finally, these officials thought it would be wrong for the Treasury to collect taxes from the general public for the purpose of providing speculators with additional wealth.

But Hamilton disagreed. He argued that the federal government should redeem all bonds at full value, whether or not they belonged to speculators. Hamilton also thought that the federal government should pay off the states' debts from the Revolutionary War. He believed these steps were needed to earn the new federal government greater trust, both within the country and worldwide. In Hamilton's mind, earning financial trust would help the economy grow and make it easier for the government to borrow money if needed in the future.

The Business of America

What other economic measures did Hamilton offer?

Supporting Business

Hamilton and the Federalists wanted the federal government to aid manufacturing and banking throughout the country. Part of his plan was to construct roads, bridges, and canals to develop the transportation of people, raw materials, and manufactured goods.

Democratic-Republicans opposed federal spending on transportation because they thought it would not benefit the majority of people. Jefferson and the Democratic-Republicans wanted the government to support independent farmers rather than urban manufacturers. They accused the Federalists of being elitists, or people who believe that they are superior to others and therefore entitled to special powers and privileges. They said the Federalists wanted to re-create a monarchy based on an aristocratic system of bankers and businesspeople.

Raising Money

How was the federal government going to raise the money to pay off the national debt and the state debts and fund transportation projects? Hamilton convinced the legislature to enact an import tariff in 1789, to increase the tariff in 1790, and to increase it again in 1792. An import tariff is a tax on goods brought into a country for sale. You may recall that import tariffs were supported by the mercantilist theory, which held that economic success depended on maintaining a favorable balance of exports over imports. A high tariff on imports not only brought in funds, but because it resulted in higher prices for imported goods, it made American-made goods more affordable in comparison.

photo: Getty Images

Washington reviews the troops in 1794 as he prepares for action against the Whiskey Rebellion.

The increased tariffs still did not bring in enough money to fund the government, so Hamilton looked for a new source of income. He chose to tax whiskey. Farmers earned much more money selling whiskey made from their grain crops than they did selling the grain itself. Grain was bulky and thus expensive to transport. It could also be risky for farmers to transport grain long distances. For farmers living west of the Appalachian and Allegheny Mountains, grain could easily spoil on the long trip east. In some western parts of the United States, whiskey was even used as currency instead of money.

Discovery EDUCATION | SOCIAL STUDIES **TECHBOOK**

How did the nation's early problems reveal different philosophies about government?

Farmers in western Pennsylvania who depended on whiskey sales found the new tax unacceptable. They objected to a clause in the tax that charged small whiskey producers more per gallon than large producers. Many whiskey producers refused to pay the taxes. Others formed groups of rebels who threatened tax collectors. In 1792, President Washington issued a statement criticizing the rebels, but tensions only increased. In July 1794, standoffs between tax collectors and rebels escalated. In one county, a shootout between rebels and a tax collector left one rebel dead. The next day, 500 local militiamen attacked the tax collector and a small group of federal soldiers who had come to guard his property. Rebels in other counties burned the homes of tax collectors and stole mail. At the end of July, several thousand armed rebels met near Pittsburgh, Pennsylvania, to show their opposition to the tax.

Fearing that the farmers were challenging the authority of the new government, in 1794 Washington sent in troops to stop the Whiskey Rebellion. The protesters fled before any shots were fired. Unlike Shays's Rebellion, which showed the central government was too weak to solve its problems, the Whiskey Rebellion seemed to demonstrate that the new federal government could take care of the nation's needs and maintain order.

The National Bank

How did the national bank become a source of debate?

Another part of Hamilton's plan was to establish a national bank. According to the Federalists, a national bank would help businesses, state governments, and the federal government transfer funds. In exchange for their deposits, agencies or businesses would receive paper notes, issued and backed by the bank. Bank notes would then be used as money. This means that the notes could be exchanged for their equal value in gold, or they could be exchanged with merchants or tradespeople for goods and services.

Thomas Jefferson and James Madison strongly opposed Hamilton's plan for the bank. They argued that the Constitution did not authorize the government to create a national bank. Hamilton responded by saying that incorporating a bank was an implied power. This means that Congress had powers that were not explicitly stated in the Constitution. Hamilton was referring to the "necessary and proper" clause in Article I, Section 8. This clause empowers Congress "to make all laws which shall be necessary and proper" for carrying out its powers.

photo: Library of Congress

This image shows the Bank of the United States in Philadelphia in 1800.

Jefferson and Hamilton argued about the word *necessary*. Jefferson said something was necessary only if there were no other alternative. Hamilton argued that something was necessary if it was "needful, requisite, incidental, useful, or conducive to" carrying out a legitimate action.

President Washington asked Hamilton and Jefferson to write statements justifying their positions about a national bank. Ultimately, Hamilton's views won. President Washington and Congress approved his plan to create the Bank of the United States. In 1791, Congress passed a 20-year charter for the country's new national bank.

Because the bank was backed by the government, as well as a great deal of private funds, people had faith in the value of the bank's notes. Very quickly, the Bank of the United States notes served as money that was accepted all over the country.

With John Marshall, a strong Federalist, as Chief Justice, the U.S. Supreme Court later upheld the bank in the case *McCulloch v. Maryland* (1819). In doing so, Marshall approved Hamilton's interpretation of the "necessary and proper" clause. The concept of implied powers later became a rationale for many of Congress's legislative powers not mentioned in the Constitution.

France Versus Britain

How did political differences affect foreign policy?

In February 1793, war broke out between Great Britain and France. Washington's cabinet was again divided in its response. Hamilton thought the United States should support Great Britain because it was an important trade partner.

photo: Getty Images

War broke out between France and Great Britain in 1793. Leaders in the new American government took opposing sides in the conflict.

Jefferson thought the United States should support France in return for French support of the colonies during the Revolutionary War. Further, France had undergone a revolution in 1789 that overthrew the monarchy and established a republican government. Like the Patriots in the American Revolution, the French had fought against a tyrannical monarch to win respect for their rights. Now, they were being threatened by European monarchs, who did not want similar revolutions in their own countries. Jefferson wanted to give support to these revolutionaries.

Discovery | SOCIAL STUDIES
EDUCATION | TECHBOOK

How did the nation's early problems reveal different philosophies about government?

Washington Declares Neutrality

President Washington agreed with Hamilton and favored Britain. However, he also believed that the United States should remain neutral in the conflict. He issued the Neutrality Proclamation on April 22, 1793. It said:

"The duty and interest of the United States require that they should with sincerity and good faith adopt and pursue a conduct friendly and impartial toward the belligerent powers."

Not everyone agreed with Washington's Neutrality Proclamation. Some, including James Madison, thought that only Congress had the constitutional authority to make this kind of decision.

Jefferson was frustrated that Washington had not sided with the French. Much to his dismay, Hamilton continued to influence Washington's foreign policy. Jefferson's disagreements with Hamilton over policy grew so deep that in 1793 he resigned from the cabinet.

In addition to the problems with Britain and France, Washington's administration had to address border disputes with Spain. Spain threatened to cut off American shipping on the Mississippi River. The president commissioned Thomas Pinckney to negotiate with Spain. When conflicts with Native Americans broke out in the Northwest Territory, the president sent out troops to fight in a frontier war. In both cases, President Washington's strong stance led to a successful outcome and seemed to support Hamilton's understanding of the proper uses of federal power.

U.S. Neutrality Violated

Why did Great Britain and the United States sign Jay's Treaty?

Jay's Treaty

Late in 1793, Great Britain violated U.S. neutrality by seizing or forcibly taking possession of U.S. ships bound for French colonies in the West Indies. Many Americans were outraged and thought the United States should declare war on Britain. Hamilton was worried because his economic plans depended on trade with Britain. He asked Washington to send Supreme Court Chief Justice John Jay to represent the United States in negotiations in London.

Jay's Treaty, 1794	
Great Britain agreed to: • give up Northwest Territory • reimburse Americans for damages to shipping • give the United States a better trading status with Great Britain	**United States agreed to:** • prevent French privateers (private ships) fighting the British from gaining supplies in U.S. ports • keep the Mississippi River open to shipping of both countries • pay pre-Revolutionary War debts owed by Americans to British businesses

The treaty was extremely unpopular with many Americans, who thought it did not punish Britain enough for its actions. It was also very unpopular with the French, who began attacking American ships in protest.

In November 1794, the two sides negotiated what became known as Jay's Treaty. The details of the treaty are shown in this chart.

John Adams Takes Office

How did disagreements between the parties continue during John Adams's presidency?

The Washington Era Ends

In 1796, Washington decided not to run for a third term in office. As you read previously, Washington warned in his Farewell Address against the dangers the United States was facing, particularly those that were dividing Americans along political lines. But politicians did not listen to Washington's advice.

The divisions between the Federalists and the Democratic-Republicans were fully cemented by the time of the 1796 presidential election. Thomas Jefferson ran as the candidate for the Democratic-Republicans, and John Adams ran as a Federalist. You may recall that the president of the United States is selected by winning a majority of electoral votes in the electoral college system. Back in 1796, the Constitution called for the person who received the second-most electoral votes to become the vice president. Adams won the most votes and became president, defeating Jefferson, who became the vice president.

The XYZ Affair

Upon assuming the presidency, Adams took on the job of solving the problems with France. He wanted to end the French practice of seizing American ships that they suspected were involved in trade with Britain. In 1797, Adams sent a group of diplomats to meet with the French foreign minister, Charles Maurice de Talleyrand.

When the U.S. representatives arrived, Talleyrand refused to meet with them. Instead, a group of three French agents met them and proposed that the Americans pay bribes in order to gain a meeting with Talleyrand. They asked for $250,000 for Talleyrand, plus a loan to France of $10 million. The diplomats refused to pay the bribes and sent word about the meeting to Adams. Outraged, Adams reported the news to Congress. When discussing the situation, diplomats and Adams referred to the agents as Agents X, Y, and Z. For this reason, the incident became known as the XYZ Affair.

The XYZ Affair enraged Federalists in Congress, who had never been sympathetic to France. They wanted war. Adams continued to pursue peace, and in 1800, the United States and France signed a peace treaty that confirmed the two countries as trading partners.

Discovery | SOCIAL STUDIES
EDUCATION | **TECHBOOK**

How did the nation's early problems reveal different philosophies about government?

The Alien and Sedition Acts

Democratic-Republicans still believed that the United States should ally itself with France, in spite of past conflicts and the XYZ Affair. Federalists in Congress attacked this viewpoint and tried to paint the Democratic-Republicans as traitors. To reinforce their idea, the Federalist-controlled Congress passed the Alien and Sedition Acts. These acts limited the rights of immigrants and forbade public criticism of the government. Federalists said that the acts were meant to protect the United States. In reality, they were designed to prevent the Democratic-Republicans from expressing their opposition to Federalist policies.

Many Democratic-Republicans, including Thomas Jefferson and James Madison, believed the acts violated the rights to free speech and a free press protected by the Constitution. Aiming to eliminate the Alien and Sedition Acts, they wrote a series of resolutions to be proposed in state legislatures. The Kentucky and Virginia Resolutions declared the Alien and Sedition Acts unconstitutional. They also raised the idea that the states could challenge the constitutionality of a federal act. The Kentucky and Virginia Resolutions asserted that states had the right to nullify, or cancel, and block the enforcement of federal laws they judge unconstitutional.

photo: Library of Congress

In February 1798, a brawl between Federalists and Democratic-Republicans erupted on the floor of the House of Representatives.

Create an ad for either the Federalists or the Democratic-Republicans.

Congress took no action after the resolutions were passed. Eventually, the Alien and Sedition Acts expired. This would not be the last time that the states would challenge a federal law.

Consider the Essential Question:

How did the nation's early problems reveal different philosophies about government?

Go online to complete the Social Studies Explanation.

Check for Understanding:

In what ways did the emergence of political parties reveal differences over both foreign and domestic affairs?

6.1 The Age of Jefferson

photo: Library of Congress

LESSON OVERVIEW

Introduction

In this concept, you will learn about how Thomas Jefferson brought a new atmosphere to the presidency and how America changed under his leadership.

Essential Question

To what extent did Jefferson's actions as president reflect his principles?

Lesson Objectives

By the end of this lesson, you should be able to:

- Summarize and assess the significance of key events that took place during the presidency of Thomas Jefferson.

- Describe provisions of the Louisiana Purchase and analyze its impact on the United States.

Key Vocabulary
Which terms do you already know?

- ☐ Aaron Burr
- ☐ agrarian
- ☐ Barbary Wars
- ☐ Charles Maurice de Talleyrand
- ☐ Chief Black Buffalo
- ☐ Corps of Discovery
- ☐ Dolley Madison
- ☐ James Madison
- ☐ James Monroe
- ☐ John Marshall
- ☐ judicial review
- ☐ Judiciary Act of 1789
- ☐ Judiciary Act of 1801
- ☐ Lewis and Clark Expedition
- ☐ Louisiana Purchase
- ☐ Louisiana Territory
- ☐ Meriwether Lewis
- ☐ national debt
- ☐ Robert Livingston
- ☐ Sacagawea
- ☐ Shoshone
- ☐ states' rights
- ☐ states' rights doctrine
- ☐ Thomas Jefferson
- ☐ unconstitutional
- ☐ West Point
- ☐ William Clark
- ☐ William Marbury
- ☐ York

ENGAGE

> **How does it feel to meet a new president? Visit Engage to learn more.**

Essential Question

To what extent did Jefferson's actions as president reflect his principles?

EXPLORE

Marbury v. Madison and Judicial Review

What events led to the case of Marbury v. Madison, *and how was it important?*

Adams's "Midnight Judges"

Just before leaving the presidency, John Adams tried to ensure that the Federalist Party would continue to have influence by appointing a large number of judges. These judges are known as the Midnight Judges because some of them were appointed on the night before Jefferson's inauguration. The term of a federal judge is for life, so Adams's appointments meant the Federalists would retain power long after the change of presidential administration. They would be able to continue policies that expanded the power of the federal government.

Jefferson was not happy with the appointments. He had intended to appoint judges who agreed with his principles. He instructed his Secretary of State, James Madison, not to deliver the commissions, or legal papers that made the appointments official. Jefferson and Madison decided that the commissions had expired when Adams left office.

William Marbury was one of the appointed judges who did not receive his commission. After finding out what had happened, Marbury brought a lawsuit against Madison. He asked the U.S. Supreme Court to enforce a law known as the Judiciary Act, which Congress had passed in 1789. The Judiciary Act gave the Supreme Court the authority to require government officials to fulfill their duties. Marbury thought this law could be used to force Madison to deliver his commission.

The *Marbury* Decision

The Supreme Court decided the case of *Marbury v. Madison* in 1803. Chief Justice John Marshall wrote the court's unanimous opinion. On one hand, the Supreme Court ruled that Marbury's commission was valid. More important, however, the court refused to

use powers granted by the Judiciary Act to force Madison to deliver this commission. According to the chief justice, there was a big problem with the Judiciary Act. In passing this law, Congress had given the Supreme Court the power to issue orders requiring government officials to fulfill their duties. But only the Constitution, which Marshall declared to be "the supreme law of the land," could assign powers to the branches of government. Therefore, the Judiciary Act was unconstitutional and void. This was the first time the Supreme Court had determined that a law passed by Congress was unconstitutional.

The *Marbury* decision expanded the role of the judicial branch by establishing the principle of judicial review. Judicial review is the power of the courts to decide whether or not laws passed by Congress and state legislatures are constitutional. Marshall's ruling said that the courts had the last

photo: Getty Images

Chief Justice John Marshall.

say in interpreting the meaning of the Constitution. Since the Marbury decision, the Supreme Court has used the power of judicial review to overturn more than 150 acts of Congress and more than 1,000 state laws. Some of the most important decisions in the court's history have involved the use of this power.

Even though Marbury's commission would not be delivered, Jefferson disagreed with Marshall's decision. Jefferson maintained that only the people—not a branch of government—had the authority to determine the meaning of the Constitution. According to Jefferson, if a congressional representative or a president violates the Constitution, the best solution is to remove him or her from office:

Complete this mind map activity to demonstrate your understanding of the Marbury case.

"I know no safe depository of the ultimate powers of the society but the people themselves; and if we think them not enlightened enough to exercise their control with a wholesome discretion, the remedy is not to take it from them, but to inform their discretion by education."

Eyes on the West

How did trouble with Napoleon lead to a huge land deal?

Early in Jefferson's presidency, a shift occurred in the western region of the country when Spain returned the Louisiana Territory to France. The French Louisiana Territory included the port city of New Orleans and roughly the entire Great Plains region from the western shore of the Mississippi River to the base of the Rocky Mountains. Though largely unknown at the time, the area was rich in minerals, forests, and lands that could be used for farming. It also for centuries had been home to thousands of Native Americans in diverse societies. France's leader, Napoleon Bonaparte, hoped to establish a western empire that included both Louisiana and the profitable sugar-producing Caribbean island of Saint-Domingue.

You may recall that the United States faced difficulty in the 1780s when the Spanish placed restrictions on travel on the Mississippi and on American shipping to and from New Orleans. With Louisiana under the control of Napoleon Bonaparte's France, many in the United States

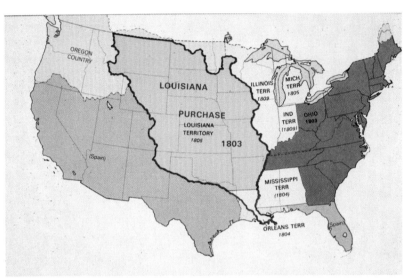

photo: Getty Images

The Louisiana Purchase more than doubled the size of the United States.

feared new restrictions or worse. This was of particular concern to farmers west of the Appalachians, who could not sell their produce if they could not ship it on the Mississippi and Ohio Rivers. Manufacturers in the east also depended on shipping through New Orleans and up the Mississippi River for delivering their goods to people in the west, as did merchants who imported goods from Europe, Africa, and Asia. Some Federalists called for the territories along the Mississippi to secede, or withdraw, from the Union so that trade would not be interrupted.

President Jefferson was concerned about the possible consequences of France occupying Louisiana. In April 1802, he sent a letter to U.S. Minister to France Robert Livingston. In this letter, Jefferson encouraged Livingston, who had served with Jefferson on the drafting committee of the Declaration of Independence, to resolve the situation. Jefferson suggested that France wanted to give up control of New Orleans and the Floridas to the United States. Over the next several months, Jefferson's concern intensified. In January 1803, the president decided to strengthen U.S. negotiations with France. He sent James Monroe of Virginia to join Livingston in France. Previously, Monroe had been a leader in demanding that the Bill of Rights be added to the Constitution. Jefferson presented Monroe with written instructions to offer $10 million for the purchase of the Port of New Orleans and the Floridas.

Monroe arrived in Paris on April 12, 1803. But by this time, things had changed. Formerly enslaved revolutionaries in Saint-Domingue had defeated Napoleon's forces there and prepared to establish a new country they called Haiti. Napoleon decided that without Saint-Domingue under French control, Louisiana was far less valuable. He decided to sell the entire Louisiana Territory to the United States. On April 11, 1803, one day before Monroe arrived, French foreign minister Charles Maurice de Talleyrand made the formal offer to Livingston. Napoleon needed money to strengthen his army in Europe. If he sold the territory, besides receiving the price paid for the land, he would avoid the expense of maintaining military forces in the Mississippi River Valley.

Closing the Deal

How did the Louisiana Purchase become official?

Despite not having the authority to negotiate such a deal, Monroe and Livingston recognized the importance of the offer and immediately entered into negotiations. On April 30, 1803, the negotiation team agreed to the Louisiana Purchase, offering to pay $15 million for 827,000 square miles of North America. The purchase more than doubled the size of the United States. It included the city of New Orleans and gave the United States complete control of the Mississippi River and the entire Mississippi River Valley. While many rumors circulated at the time, the official announcement of the offer in the United States did not occur until July 4, 1803.

photo: Library of Congress

On March 10, 1804, the U.S. flag was raised for the first time over the city of St. Louis.

With the purchase under review by Congress, Jefferson found that the Constitution did not provide for the addition of new land to the Union. He accepted that a loose interpretation of the Constitution would allow the government to purchase the land with a treaty rather than an amendment. Stretching the executive power in this way was not consistent with Jefferson's stated principles, but he decided to change his mind in the interests of the nation's future.

Not all Americans supported the Louisiana Purchase. Some thought Jefferson and his diplomats had been tricked into purchasing millions of acres of useless land. Many Federalists were concerned that the growth of the country and the addition of more states to the Union would provide the Jeffersonian Republicans with additional votes and weaken the federal government. In 1804, a group of Federalists from New England even discussed leaving the Union.

Discovery EDUCATION | SOCIAL STUDIES TECHBOOK

To what extent did Jefferson's actions as president reflect his principles?

On October 20, 1803, by a vote of 24 to 7, the Senate ratified, or formally approved, the treaty finalizing the Louisiana Purchase. France officially transferred the Louisiana territory on December 30, 1803. However, although France had bought Louisiana from Spain, it had left the Spanish to manage the territory. Before the French could hand over actual control to the United States, they had to gain possession of the territory from Spain. Eventually, in a ceremony held in St. Louis in March 1804, the Spanish flag was symbolically lowered and replaced with the French flag. Twenty-four hours later, the French flag was lowered and the United States flag was raised west of the Mississippi for the first time.

The Roots of Exploration

How did the famous Lewis and Clark Expedition begin?

Even before the Louisiana Purchase, Thomas Jefferson was curious about the American West. In January 1803, the president asked Congress for $2,500 to fund an exploration to find a northwest passage to Asia. Congress approved the money.

Jefferson picked Meriwether Lewis to conduct the expedition across the Louisiana Territory. Lewis was an army captain who had served Jefferson as his personal secretary. Lewis chose William Clark as his coleader. Clark had been one of Lewis's army commanders. Jefferson gave Lewis and Clark detailed written instructions for their journey. Their primary goals were to explore and map the Missouri River and to find a navigable water route to the Pacific Ocean.

photo: Library of Congress

Meriwether Lewis (1774–1809) was a friend of Thomas Jefferson. He and William Clark sought a route to the Pacific Ocean and recorded observations of the plant and animal life of North America.

photo: Library of Congress

William Clark (1770–1838), coleader of the 1804–1806 Corps of Discovery. Clark was later superintendent of Indian affairs and governor of the Missouri Territory.

True to his agrarian nature, Jefferson also asked the men to document the soil conditions, plant life, and animals along the way. The explorers were expected to maintain communications with the French and Spanish outposts on the frontier and take detailed notes to send back. In addition to instructions, Jefferson supplied them with items to trade and gifts to present to any unknown Native American tribes they met.

The president instructed Lewis to investigate ports from which to engage in sea trade with Asia and to return as soon as possible if any such areas were discovered. Jefferson was confident that the expedition would reach the Pacific, and in this he was correct. The explorers did reach the Pacific Ocean, but they had to cross the Rocky Mountains to do so. Jefferson's dream of an all-water route from St. Louis west to Asia was not to be realized. Nevertheless, the Louisiana Purchase and Lewis and Clark's experiences would generate hope for Americans who were ready for more open space.

The Journey West

How did Americans learn about the Louisiana Territory?

Lewis and Clark began preparing for their journey even before the Louisiana Purchase was announced to the public. In the summer of 1803, Lewis had a boat constructed in Pittsburgh and began traveling down the Ohio River. He picked up Clark along the way. In the fall, they established headquarters at Camp Wood, just a few miles from where the Missouri and Mississippi Rivers meet. Both men gathered the supplies they would need for the expedition and put together a team known as the Corps of Discovery. On May 14, 1804, they began their journey up the Missouri River.

By fall of 1804, the Corps had entered the Great Plains. They captured a prairie dog to return to Jefferson, who had never seen one before. They encountered several Native American groups, including Yankton Sioux, Teton Sioux, Mandan, and Hidatsa. The first encounters with the Sioux were tense but friendly. At first, the Teton Sioux demanded a boat from the Corps as a toll to travel through their lands up the river, but the two groups made peace and the expedition stayed with the Teton Sioux for three days.

In November 1804, the Corps built Fort Mandan on the Missouri River in what is now central North Dakota and prepared for the winter. At the fort, they met a French-Canadian fur trader, Toussaint Charbonneau, and his Shoshone wife, Sacagawea. Sacagawea had been captured by the Hidatsa and later sold to Charbonneau. Sacagawea said her people lived at the source of the Missouri River. Lewis and Clark hired Charbonneau as an interpreter to help them on their trip up the river. Because Charbonneau spoke little Shoshone, they agreed to bring Sacagawea along as well. Over the winter, Sacagawea gave birth to her son Jean-Baptiste at the fort, and brought him along on the expedition in the spring. Her skills collecting edible plants and making clothes were valuable to the expedition, and the presence of a young woman and her child with the group of men was a signal to many of the local Native American groups that the expedition was peaceful.

In the early spring of 1805, Sacagawea led the men up the Missouri. As they made their way up the river, the expedition came upon many plants and animals previously undocumented by Europeans in North America, including grizzly bears, bull snakes, and birds that would later be known as Lewis's woodpeckers. Lewis and Clark collected samples and also recorded detailed notes and drawings in their journals. Following Jefferson's orders, Lewis and Clark sent a boat with scientific specimens, maps, and journals back toward St. Louis.

The Corps arrived in the Shoshone camp in western Montana in August 1805, where Sacagawea was briefly reunited with her family. Lewis and Clark called the camp "Camp Fortunate" and stayed there for about two weeks. By late October, the expedition reached the Columbia River. Clark thought he saw the Pacific Ocean, but they were still more than 20 miles and a month away. By late November, the expedition finally stood on the shore of the Pacific. They prepared a winter camp at Fort Clatsop in northern Oregon. It would be their second winter away from their family and friends back east.

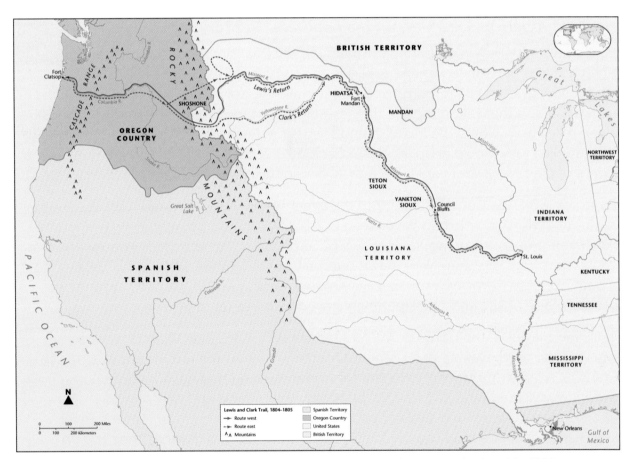

Lewis and Clark's journey from St. Louis to the Pacific and back lasted more than 28 months: from May 1804 to September 1806.

Accomplished Explorers

What did the Corps of Discovery accomplish?

The return journey to St. Louis took much less time than the trip out to the Pacific Ocean. The Corps had completed the work required by Jefferson. They were anxious to get home and were heading downstream with the current. Once they recrossed the Rocky Mountains, the two leaders split up so they could take different routes and cover more territory. On September 23, 1806, their expedition ended in St. Louis.

photo: Library of Congress

William Clark carried this compass on a chain during the expedition.

Honored as national heroes, Lewis and Clark were each given 1,600 acres of land as a reward for their service. Clark was given the post of Indian Agent for the West, and Lewis was named governor of the Louisiana Territory.

Maps of the areas explored by Lewis and Clark bear the names of many of their adventures. Independence Creek in present-day Kansas was where the Corps spent July 4, 1804. It was the first time Independence Day was celebrated west of the Mississippi. In Sioux City, Iowa, Floyd's River and Floyd's Bluff are markers of the only American to die on the expedition, Sgt. Charles Floyd. He died of appendicitis.

Traveling more than 8,000 miles over two years, Lewis and Clark collected information on animals, plants, terrain, and local peoples. Their journals and the journals of the other men in the Corps captured Americans' imaginations and sparked further exploration and growth.

While the addition of the Louisiana Territory may have been the biggest change to the United States during Jefferson's presidency, it was not something he had planned beforehand. Did buying Louisiana promote Jefferson's main goals of limiting federal power and promoting agriculture? Jefferson probably wrestled with that question, but he could not have predicted the full impact of his decision.

Explore this interactive to trace Louis and Clark's expedition to the Pacific.

DISCOVERY | SOCIAL STUDIES
EDUCATION | **TECHBOOK**

To what extent did Jefferson's actions as president reflect his principles?

Changing Direction of the Country

What ideals did Thomas Jefferson bring to the presidency?

Thomas Jefferson came to the presidency after a long and bitter presidential campaign. But he had a plan for policy changes in the government. The election that placed Jefferson in office had been a divided one. He would now have to work to unite the country again.

Jefferson was the first president to hold office in the District of Columbia. He and Vice President Aaron Burr were the first executive officers to be sworn in on Capitol Hill. But even as the new city rose around him, Jefferson longed for a rural life. Jefferson wanted the United States to remain a primarily agrarian, or agriculture-based society. He believed a person who owned a farm and worked the land would be economically independent, and that independence would develop and preserve wisdom, self-control, courage, and fortitude. He thought commerce was a corrupter of morals that made people greedy and dependent on others.

President Jefferson pressured Congress to abolish, or end, measures imposed during John Adams's presidency, including the direct tax of 1798 and the Alien and Sedition Acts. Jefferson pardoned the 10 individuals who had been imprisoned under the Alien and Sedition Acts.

THOMAS JEFFERSON
President of the United States

photo: Library of Congress

Thomas Jefferson served as President Washington's secretary of state before becoming the third president of the United States.

Jefferson also was concerned about the national debt. He believed that increased federal spending was a sign the government was growing and accumulating power—power that Jefferson thought should be reserved for the states. During his presidency, he lowered the national debt by $23 million. He cut the navy and army to two regiments, although he did not disband the standing army. In 1802, Jefferson signed the Military Peace Establishment Act that established an officer training school for a professional army. The U.S. Military Academy at West Point, in New York, was created to ensure that officer candidates were chosen on merit rather than on wealth or family connections.

Life in the Early Republic

How did American daily life and culture change during the early 1800s?

The decades after the Revolutionary War saw more than just the beginnings of a new and stable government in the United States. They also saw the emergence of a unique, American way of life. The ideals of the revolution, such as equality and a government of the people, shaped every aspect of American life, including jobs, art, and even the roles of specific groups within society. Sometimes, these values brought about radical changes. Other times, reality fell far short of the ideals.

Employment

Following the war, a small class of professionals provided services for those living in towns or cities. This class included shop owners, doctors, lawyers, and blacksmiths. In the years after the war, however, the vast majority of Americans lived and worked on small farms. These farms were mostly self-sustaining. Families grew enough crops to support themselves and also produced occasional surpluses to sell to others. The exception to this subsistence style of farming was the South. While the majority of Southerners were small-scale farmers, most land in the South was owned by wealthy plantation owners. Unlike the small, neighboring farms, plantations used the labor of enslaved people to grow crops for export rather than simply to feed their own families.

While life in the United States seemed very similar to that of colonial times, the nation's economy was beginning to change. A small industrial sector began to grow during the war. Then, in 1791, Samuel Slater engineered the first machine for spinning cotton. In 1793, Eli Whitney introduced the cotton gin, which significantly increased the amount of cotton that could be processed from the field. Innovations and industrialization would soon expand the country's cities, begin a wave of immigration, and connect regions of the country to one another.

Women's Roles

During the revolution, women were inspired by the rhetoric of equality just as men were. Although there was no public talk of a change in women's rights, some women privately pushed for greater equality under the law. In most states, women were not allowed to vote. They also were restricted from holding public office and had limited property rights. Most famously, Abigail Adams, wife of Founder and future president John Adams, wrote to her husband shortly after the signing of the Declaration of Independence. She asked him to "remember the ladies" and to "be more generous and favorable to them than your ancestors." Despite Adams's plea, women's rights remained unchanged for many years to come.

However, the roles women played in society did shift somewhat. Among the middle class, two separate spheres of influence emerged: public and private. Men acted in the public sphere through work and political involvement. Women worked in the private sphere of the home, tending to the education and upbringing of the nation's youth.

Discovery | SOCIAL STUDIES
EDUCATION | **TECHBOOK**

To what extent did Jefferson's actions as president reflect his principles?

Unexpectedly, this new division became a gateway to the public sphere for women. To properly educate their children, more women were encouraged to attend college. In addition, women gradually took on the task of morally improving the public sphere, partly because women were considered purer than men. Beginning in the 1830s, women established schools, created asylums for the mentally ill, worked to abolish slavery, and promoted temperance in both public and private life.

Free and Enslaved Africans

After the revolution, many freed Africans settled in cities like Philadelphia, New York, Washington, DC, and Charleston. They were formerly enslaved people who had escaped during the revolution or been freed by the abolition of slavery in their state. These communities of freedmen still faced many restrictions during this time. Immediately after the revolution, freedmen were able to vote in several Northern states. However, by the 1830s, voting rights had expanded for white men but had disappeared for freed Africans. As a result, freedmen developed their own social institutions, and the black church was at the center.

While some enslaved Africans were freed after the revolution, most were not. The first census was held in 1790. It showed that one-quarter of the population was African American, 90 percent of which were enslaved. Slavery had seemed to be fading at the time when the Constitution was adopted. However, Eli Whitney's cotton gin and the growing Northern textile industry revitalized the practice. While the population of freed Africans grew from 60,000 in 1790 to 185,000 in 1810, the enslaved population grew from 720,000 to 1,200,000 in 1810. The cotton gin also expanded the institution of slavery into the Deep South, triggering a widespread sale of enslaved people from the Upper South to the Deep South. This was a kind of second Middle Passage that tore apart many families.

The Arts

In the years after the revolution, American artists continued to follow the lead of their British counterparts. Many traveled across the Atlantic for both training and work. The great American literary works were primarily political in nature. Some of the early painters, such as Gilbert Stuart, did attempt to convey an American point of view by focusing on patriotic imagery. These artists produced portraits of George Washington and the other Founders. However, after the War of 1812, a rise in nationalism led to a renewed commitment to American ideals and the birth of a truly American artistic movement.

photo: Library of Congress
The production of cotton textiles dramatically changed labor—both free and enslaved—in the United States.

In literature, Washington Irving became the first internationally recognized American author. He combined English, Dutch, and American themes in his short stories, including his most famous story, "The Legend of Sleepy Hollow." Meanwhile, James Fenimore Cooper became the first celebrated American novelist. He did so by writing solely on American themes. The majority of his books were about the Navy, but his most famous was the *Leatherstocking Tales*, which romanticized both the frontier and characters who lived in nature, uncorrupted by the modern world. Narratives about enslaved people also gained popularity, particularly in Northern abolitionist circles. In 1789, a former enslaved person named Olaudah Equiano published the first of these narratives in Britain, igniting tensions over slavery in the United States.

Foreign Affairs

How did Jefferson deal with foreign affairs?

The Barbary Pirates

As the United States matured as a nation, opportunities for worldwide trade increased and contributed to the country's growing prosperity. But expanded commerce also had unintended consequences.

The Barbary Coast of North Africa was home to several small states, including Morocco, Algiers, Tunis, and Tripoli. For many decades before Jefferson became president, the leaders of these Barbary states had sent pirates into the Mediterranean Sea to capture European and American ships, cargo, and sailors. They then held their crews for ransom and demanded cash payments called tribute in exchange for the ships' safe passage. The United States and European countries alike routinely gave in to these demands because they decided tribute was less expensive than war.

photo: Library of Congress

When the U.S Navy could not rescue the USS Philadelphia *from the pirates, Lieutenant Stephan Decatur commanded a raid that destroyed the captured ship.*

As President George Washington's secretary of state, and earlier as a U.S. foreign minister, Jefferson had experience dealing with the Barbary states. He opposed making ransom payments and providing tribute, believing these actions would only lead to more demands. In 1801, after Jefferson became president, the ruler of Tripoli demanded that the United States provide $250,000 in tribute, plus an additional annual payment. After Jefferson refused, Tripoli declared war on the United States.

Discovery Education | SOCIAL STUDIES TECHBOOK

To what extent did Jefferson's actions as president reflect his principles?

Before his presidency, Jefferson had opposed the creation of a large American navy. But he responded to Tripoli's call for war by sending a permanent naval force to the Mediterranean to protect U.S. shipping interests. A four-year struggle ensued. In 1805, during Jefferson's second term, U.S. Marines landed on what is now the coast of Libya and threatened to control the city of Tripoli. This resulted in a peace treaty that eased tensions between the United States and Tripoli. The other Barbary states continued to demand payments from the United States. After Jefferson left office, additional U.S. naval victories helped put an end to the United States' tribute payments to the Barbary states once and for all.

Great Britain and France

As president, Jefferson was also forced to confront troubles with Great Britain and France. When the two European powers once again went to war in 1803, each attempted to block the other's commerce with the United States and the rest of the world. Both the British and the French issued naval orders requiring the seizure of ships from neutral countries that traded with the enemy. The British also began capturing U.S. ships and forcing American sailors to serve in the Royal Navy. This crisis would soon lead to a second war with Great Britain.

Consider the Essential Question:

To what extent did Jefferson's actions as president reflect his principles?

Go online to complete the Social Studies Explanation.

Check for Understanding:

Did the Louisiana Purchase support or contradict Thomas Jefferson's core beliefs?

6.2 The War of 1812

photo: Library of Congress

LESSON OVERVIEW

Introduction

In this concept, you will learn about the issues and events that led to a second war with Britain and about important battles and events in the conflict. You will also explore the impact of the War of 1812 on the United States.

Essential Question

What was the impact of the War of 1812 on the early history of the United States?

Lesson Objectives

By the end of this lesson, you should be able to:

- Explain underlying issues and trace events that led to the War of 1812.

- Identify and describe key battles and important events from the War of 1812.

- Assess the impact of the War of 1812 on the United States.

Key Vocabulary

Which terms do you already know?

- [ ] Andrew Jackson
- [ ] Battle of New Orleans
- [ ] Battle of Plattsburgh
- [ ] Battle of Tippecanoe
- [ ] Battle of York
- [ ] Confederacy/ Confederate States
- [ ] Dolley Madison
- [ ] embargo
- [ ] Embargo Act
- [ ] Fort McHenry
- [ ] Francis Scott Key
- [ ] impressment
- [ ] James Madison
- [ ] Non-Intercourse Act
- [ ] Northwest Ordinance of 1787
- [ ] Oliver Hazard Perry
- [ ] "The Star-Spangled Banner"
- [ ] Tecumseh
- [ ] Tenskwatawa
- [ ] Treaty of Ghent
- [ ] war hawk
- [ ] War of 1812
- [ ] William Henry Harrison
- [ ] Winfield Scott

Discovery | SOCIAL STUDIES
EDUCATION | **TECHBOOK**

What was the impact of the War of 1812 on the early history of the United States?

ENGAGE

Why did the United States return to war? Visit Engage to learn more.

Essential Question

What was the impact of the War of 1812 on the early history of the United States?

EXPLORE

Great Britain Angers the United States

What caused tensions between the United States and Great Britain?

During Thomas Jefferson's second term as president, a problem emerged. France and Great Britain were at war again. Their fight threatened American shipping. Both countries began to seize American ships that were trying to deliver goods to Europe.

The British took things further. They began a policy of impressment, which involved capturing American sailors off their ships and forcing them to serve in the British navy. The British claimed the impressed sailors were deserters. In 1807, the British even fired on the American ship *Chesapeake* when its captain refused to let them search the ship for deserters. By 1811, around 10,000 American sailors had been forced into service in the British navy.

photo: Library of Congress

The English angered Americans by seizing merchant seamen from the vessels that they stopped and searched, claiming that these men were really Englishmen and impressing them into the British navy.

A Shifting Trade Embargo

Congress responded to Britain's actions by placing an embargo, or a prohibition on trade, on imported goods from Britain. Jefferson asked Congress to go further. He recommended a total ban on American ships leaving for foreign ports. He believed this harsh economic sanction would harm both Britain's and France's economies and force them to honor American neutrality.

The Embargo Act of 1807 stopped both exports to and imports from Europe, but the country it hurt most was the United States.

American exports, valued at $108 million in 1807, dropped in value to $22 million in 1808. Merchants and manufacturers suffered from the lost sales. Sailors whose ships were idle lost their jobs. Perhaps the worst result was that it made the U.S. government appear ineffective. Without any European competition, American manufactures grew, but only slightly. Rather than do without, many Americans bought goods smuggled in from Canada.

In 1808, Jefferson followed George Washington's precedent by choosing not to run for a third term in office. In the election of 1808, Virginian James Madison won the presidency. Madison had served as Jefferson's secretary of state and was, like Jefferson, a member of the Democratic-Republican party. You may recall that the Democratic-Republicans tended to favor the French over the British in foreign affairs.

Before Madison took office, Congress repealed the Embargo Act and replaced it with the Non-Intercourse Act of 1809. This act resumed trade with all European nations except France and Britain. It also authorized the president to resume trading with either or both of these countries if they dropped their trade restrictions.

In 1810, Congress acted again on the embargo. It passed Macon's Bill Number Two, which allowed trade with both Britain and France, but authorized the president to ban trade with either country if the other agreed to respect U.S. neutrality. Napoleon, emperor of France, quickly agreed, although he did nothing to stop French seizures of American ships. But Madison trusted Napoleon's promise and ordered an embargo on trade with Britain.

Tecumseh and His Confederacy

What caused tensions between the U.S. government and Native Americans?

George Washington's administration negotiated treaties with Native American nations living in territory the country gained when it achieved its independence. These agreements reveal that the federal government initially viewed Native American nations as independent countries. In fact, the government required non-tribal citizens traveling through Native American lands to have passports. The treaties resembled those the United States signed with other foreign nations, such as the Treaty of Paris, the agreement with Great Britain that ended the Revolutionary War. The purpose of these treaties was twofold: to establish borders between the United States and Native American nations and to set rules for interaction between the parties.

Discovery | SOCIAL STUDIES
EDUCATION | TECHBOOK.

What was the impact of the War of 1812 on the early history of the United States?

Signed in 1790, the Muscogee Treaty was the first formal agreement between the early U.S. government and Native American nations. It established guidelines for interaction between the United States and the Creek and Seminole Nations living in the Southeast. For example, it began trade between the federal government and the Creek Nation and reduced Spanish and British presence in the region. Four years later, the Canandaigua Treaty established peace between the United States and the Six Nations of the Iroquois Confederacy, which was located along the border between the United States and Canada in northern New York State.

As white settlers began to move west during the early 1800s, events on the frontier increased tensions between United States, Native Americans, and Great Britain. In the Northwest Territory, settlers clashed with Native Americans, including the Shawnee leader, Tecumseh. In 1809, William Henry Harrison, the governor of Indiana, held a meeting with Native American leaders. He convinced those present to turn over three million acres of tribal land to the U.S. government. But not all tribal leaders agreed.

Tecumseh made no agreement with Harrison. He did not want to surrender the Shawnee's tribal lands. Tecumseh also declared the treaties invalid because they had not been signed by true tribal leaders.

He decided that the best way to protect native land from American settlers was to form a large confederacy of Indian tribes from Florida to Canada. A *confederacy* is a group with loose ties that joins together to achieve a common purpose. Tecumseh and his brother Tenskwatawa began a movement to put an end to land deals with the U.S. government and cast the white settlers out of Native American territory.

Tecumseh.

The Shawnee leader Tecumseh worked to organize Native American resistance against white settlers.

Tenskwatawa, who was also known as "the Prophet," told his people of a vision he experienced. In this vision, the Shawnee's main god, the Master of Life, was unhappy with the Shawnee people for turning away from their traditions. Native Americans had to unite to repel the white invaders. Tenskwatawa promised the warriors that bullets from the whites would not harm them. Still, it was difficult for Tecumseh to build his confederacy because many tribes had already given up their lands. Others did not want to give up political control to a leader outside their own tribe.

Tecumseh negotiated with Harrison to get settlers out of his territory. Harrison promised to explain Tecumseh's complaints to President Madison. Tecumseh promised that if Harrison would annul treaties and give up claims to native lands, he would join Harrison and lead his confederacy in a war with the British. In November 1811, Tenskwatawa led a Shawnee attack on Harrison and his troops. Harrison saw this attack as a betrayal and was furious. At the Battle of Tippecanoe, he burned down the Shawnee capital of Prophetstown. Harrison became a national hero.

A "Second War for Independence" Begins
What finally started the War of 1812?

The Battle of Tippecanoe and its aftermath increased ill feelings against the British. At the time before Tenskwatawa's attack, Americans were already angry with the British. Congress had responded to British impressment of U.S. sailors and seizure of U.S. ships with the Non-Intercourse Act and then Macon's Bill Number Two, which imposed an embargo on trade with Britain. After the Battle of Tippecanoe, U.S. soldiers found that some Shawnee had been using British-made rifles. Furthermore, Tecumseh and other Shawnee had fled to British Canada, presumably because they felt they would be safe there. Many American settlers concluded that the British were providing arms to the Native Americans and encouraging them to attack settlers and raid settlements.

Based on these beliefs, a group of congresspeople, nicknamed the War Hawks by their opponents, aggressively lobbied for war. The War Hawks were led by Kentucky's Henry Clay, the new Speaker of the House, and John C. Calhoun of South Carolina. The War Hawks urged the president to invade British Canada. They hoped to capture the territory from Britain and add it to the United States.

Many New England merchants opposed the War Hawks out of concern that war would interfere with commerce. These merchants were less concerned about westward expansion than their fellow citizens from the south and west. They could reap large profits by buying cheap agricultural products and charging high rates to ship goods to European countries, including Great Britain.

Explore this resource to understand different perspectives on the War of 1812.

Antiwar sentiments were so strong that once the war began, Massachusetts and Connecticut refused to contribute militia to the federal government. Later, at a conference known as the Hartford Convention, war opponents from New England even discussed seceding from the Union.

Discovery | SOCIAL STUDIES
EDUCATION | **TECHBOOK**

What was the impact of the War of 1812 on the early history of the United States?

In June 1812, the War Hawks got their way. President Madison called for war, and Congress agreed to declare war on Great Britain. The War of 1812 had begun.

The War of 1812 would also be known to many as "Mr. Madison's War" or "The Second American Revolution." Why do you think these became popular nicknames for the conflict?

War on Land and Sea

What were the major battles of the War of 1812?

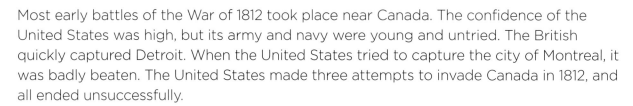

Fighting in the Northwest

Most early battles of the War of 1812 took place near Canada. The confidence of the United States was high, but its army and navy were young and untried. The British quickly captured Detroit. When the United States tried to capture the city of Montreal, it was badly beaten. The United States made three attempts to invade Canada in 1812, and all ended unsuccessfully.

In the Great Lakes, the shared border between the United States and British Canada, it was a different story. In 1813, at the Battle of York, the Americans took control of the capital of Upper Canada. They set fire to the governor's mansion and the city's legislative buildings. In the Battle of Lake Erie, in 1813, Commodore Oliver Perry lost most of his men but continued to fight and defeated a British fleet. In the Battle of Plattsburgh in 1814, U.S. troops led by Captain Thomas McDonough fought the British on Lake Champlain and forced them to retreat to Canada. Thirty years after the Treaty of Paris, in which Britain agreed to abandon forts in U.S. territory, the United States gained control of Lake Champlain, and its northern border was finally secure.

Fighting in the Mid-Atlantic Coast

Battles at sea between British and U.S. ships had been common before war was declared. Both British and U.S. naval warships and privateers were successful in capturing the enemy's merchant ships. The USS *Constitution* became famous for capturing merchant ships and fighting British warships. A victory in August 1812 earned the ship the nickname "Old Ironsides." Old Ironsides won five naval battles during the War of 1812.

photo: Getty Images

This scene above Baltimore Harbor led Francis Scott Key to pen "The Star-Spangled Banner," which was sung to the tune of a popular ballad of the time.

The superior British navy began a blockade of the U.S. East Coast. It blocked all ships attempting to leave the Chesapeake and Delaware Bays. As 1814 began, the U.S. Navy found itself bottled up in port, unable to fight.

The British began to attack towns up and down the East Coast. As the British approached Washington, U.S. government officials and other residents evacuated the city. The president's wife, Dolley Madison, remained in the White House until just hours before the British troops arrived. The first lady supervised her servants in saving important papers and historic treasures. When the British reached the capital city, they sought retribution for the Battle of York. They burned the U.S. Capitol, the White House, and other important buildings. Only a sudden rainstorm saved the rest of the city.

Soon after, the Americans turned back a British attempt to attack nearby Baltimore. Francis Scott Key was an attorney who had boarded a British ship to negotiate the release of a prisoner. As the British bombardment of Fort McHenry began, Key was detained on the ship. The next morning, as dawn broke, he saw the flag of the United States still flying above the fort. He was compelled to write a song that would come to symbolize America: "The Star-Spangled Banner."

Explore this resource to interpret and translate the verses that became our national anthem.

The Creek War

Fighting also took place further south. Tecumseh had persuaded many Creek in Alabama and southern Georgia to join his fight against American expansion into Native Americans' lands. However, the Creek were sharply divided. Some Creek wanted to try to live in peace with the United States as their neighbors. The Creek War was both a civil war between a divided Creek nation and a part of the War of 1812. Most Creek fought on the side of the British, while a large faction fought on the side of the United States alongside troops led by Colonel Andrew Jackson. U.S. troops were also joined by a large group of Cherokees. The Creek and Cherokees had long been enemies.

Jackson and his Creek and Cherokee allies were victorious. Jackson was soon promoted to general. Years later, when Jackson was president of the United States, he led the cause of expelling his former Creek and Cherokee allies and other Native Americans from their homelands in the Southeast.

Discovery EDUCATION | SOCIAL STUDIES TECHBOOK

What was the impact of the War of 1812 on the early history of the United States?

An Era of Pride and Good Feelings
What were the results of the War of 1812?

The War Comes to an End

The last major battle of the War of 1812 was a huge victory for the United States. At the Battle of New Orleans on January 8, 1815, U.S. troops led by Andrew Jackson—now a major general—crushed the British troops. In the end, three British generals and eight colonels were among the 291 British killed. More than a thousand British were wounded. A little over a dozen Americans lost their lives.

The Battle of New Orleans was the final battle of the war; in fact, the battle occurred after the war was technically over. Britain and the United States had signed the Treaty of Ghent two weeks before, agreeing to an armistice, or cessation of fighting. One important effect of Jackson's victory was silencing opponents of the war. After the Battle of New Orleans, the activities of the Hartford Convention quickly ended.

photo: Library of Congress

The Battle of New Orleans was a success for Andrew Jackson and the U.S. Army.

Results of the War

In almost every sense, the War of 1812 was a draw: Neither side could claim victory. No territory changed hands, and no agreements were made about impressment or arming Tecumseh's confederacy. But the War of 1812 did wonders for the country's national pride. In the eyes of other countries, the United States gained status as a world power. Americans were proud they had stood up to a strong European nation such as Great Britain.

In the Treaty of Ghent, the British gave up land claims in the Northwest Territory. The United States and Britain also agreed to stop fighting with Native Americans and to enforce existing prohibitions on the international slave trade. In the years to come, Britain and the United States arrived at additional agreements. They reopened trade, agreed to limit the number of warships on the Great Lakes, and agreed to a joint occupation of the Oregon territory in the Pacific Northwest.

The War of 1812 also contributed to changes in the American economy. Because of disruption in Atlantic trade during the war, American manufacturers began producing goods that the country had previously imported from Great Britain and other European countries. These manufacturers did not want to lose business when cheap European goods once again began flowing into American marketplace after hostilities ended. As a result, many government officials began supporting special taxes on imports known as tariffs. These taxes were designed to raise prices on imported goods and make American-made goods more attractive to domestic consumers as a result. Financial problems created by the war also led to the creation of the Second Bank of the United States in 1816.

In the glow of "success," bickering between political parties eased, and Americans demonstrated unity and an increased pride in their country. The United States' attention turned to domestic issues. Because of this patriotic and nationalistic mood, the period following the War of 1812 is often called the Era of Good Feelings.

Consider the Essential Question:

What was the impact of the War of 1812 on the early history of the United States?

Go online to complete the Social Studies Explanation.

Check for Understanding:

Was the War of 1812 a war of necessity or choice? Use evidence to defend your position.

6.3 Foreign Affairs

photo: Getty Images

LESSON OVERVIEW

Introduction

In this concept, you will learn about the relationships the United States had with other countries in the years after the War of 1812.

Essential Question

How did American foreign affairs after the War of 1812 reveal changing attitudes about the United States?

Lesson Objectives

By the end of this lesson, you should be able to:

- Trace and explain the significance of events after the War of 1812 that led to the announcement of the Monroe Doctrine.

- Explain major provisions of the Monroe Doctrine and assess its immediate and long-term impact on U.S. foreign relations.

Key Vocabulary
Which terms do you already know?

- ☐ Adams-Onís Treaty
- ☐ Andrew Jackson
- ☐ Convention of 1818
- ☐ Democratic-Republican Party
- ☐ First Seminole War
- ☐ France
- ☐ James Monroe
- ☐ John Jay
- ☐ John Quincy Adams
- ☐ Kentucky and Virginia Resolutions
- ☐ Monroe Doctrine
- ☐ nationalism
- ☐ Oregon Country
- ☐ Rush-Bagot Agreement
- ☐ Spain
- ☐ XYZ Affair

ENGAGE

How does a young nation earn respect? Visit Engage to learn more.

Essential Question

How did American foreign affairs after the War of 1812 reveal changing attitudes about the United States?

EXPLORE

Creating a Continental Nation

How did the United States settle its boundary with British Canada?

To end the War of 1812, the United States and Britain signed the Treaty of Ghent in December 1814. Although the treaty ended the war, it did not resolve the disagreements between the two countries. Over the next several years, the two countries continued negotiations and made more agreements.

The responsibility for these negotiations changed when James Monroe, an experienced diplomat, won the presidential election of 1816. Like James Madison and Thomas Jefferson before him, Monroe was a Democratic-Republican from Virginia. Under President Jefferson, Monroe had been one of two special negotiators responsible for the Louisiana Purchase. Under President Madison, Monroe had served as secretary of state and as secretary of war during the War of 1812. Monroe would be the last of the Founders to serve as president.

Soon after taking office, President Monroe signed the Rush-Bagot Agreement, which created a peaceful border in the West between the United States and Canada that still exists today. In this treaty, the United States and Britain each pledged to post no more than two warships on any of the Great Lakes.

The U.S. negotiator of the Rush-Bagot Pact was Richard Rush, the outgoing attorney general. Monroe's appointment to secretary of state was John Quincy Adams, an experienced diplomat and a son of the former president. Adams was unable to begin work right away because he was still involved in his work as ambassador to Britain. Monroe had requested Rush to fill in as secretary of state until Adams returned.

The following year, Secretary Adams negotiated the Convention of 1818 with Great Britain. A convention is a formal agreement. Until this time, the exact boundary between the United States and Canada had been unclear. The 1818 agreement stated that the border would be at the 49th parallel, or 49° north latitude, from the Lake of the Woods, which is partially in Canada and partially in Minnesota, to the edge of the Oregon Country, the land that today is the states of Washington and Oregon and the Canadian province of British Columbia. The Oregon Country was a rich source of valuable beaver furs. In the Convention of 1818, Great Britain and the United States agreed to jointly own the Oregon Country. This treaty helped the United States avoid further conflicts with Great Britain over this region.

photo: Library of Congress

As Secretary of State, John Quincy Adams negotiated the Convention of 1818 with Great Britain.

Agreements with Spain

How did the United States gain territory from Spain?

In 1819, Secretary of State John Quincy Adams became involved in territory negotiations with Spain as well. Spain and the United States each owned part of Florida, but the boundary between the two parts was unclear, and the United States was troubled by Seminole attacks on Georgia, Mississippi, and Alabama that it blamed on the Spanish.

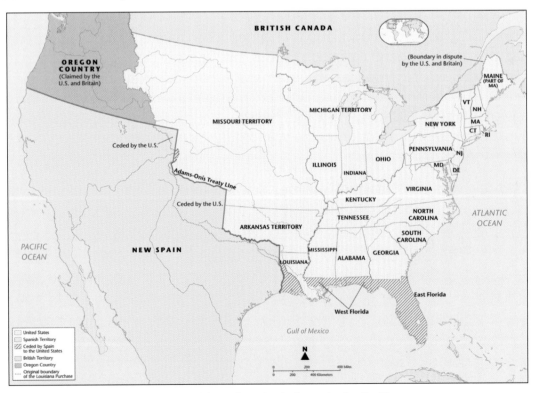

By 1819, the United States claimed land from the Atlantic Ocean to the Pacific.

Two years earlier, in 1817, General Andrew Jackson had led U.S. troops into Spanish Florida. During this raid, which became known as the First Seminole War, Jackson captured most of the Florida panhandle. Jackson's raid had not been ordered or approved by President Monroe. Now that Jackson was in possession of much of Florida, Secretary of State Adams began negotiating with the Spanish official Luis de Onís. At their meeting in 1819, Onís agreed to cede Spanish Florida to the United States.

The Adams-Onís Treaty, also called the Transcontinental Treaty, not only dealt with Florida but also said that Spain would give up any claims it had to the Oregon Country. In addition, the treaty established a clear boundary between the United States and Spanish territory at the 42nd parallel, or 42° north latitude. In exchange, the United States gave up any claims to Texas. The United States also agreed to be responsible for $5 million in Spanish debt claimed by American citizens. By signing this treaty and the others with Great Britain, the United States now claimed territory from the Atlantic Ocean to the Pacific Ocean. It had become a continental nation.

The Monroe Doctrine

Why did the United States issue the Monroe Doctrine? What was its impact?

Issuing the Monroe Doctrine

When James Monroe became president, most of South and Central America was still claimed by Spain and Portugal. However, during the course of Monroe's first and second terms in office (he won reelection in 1821), power shifted in South and Central America. In the years between 1817 and 1823, a number of countries, including Mexico, Brazil, Colombia, and Peru, all gained their independence. The U.S. government felt a kinship with these newly independent countries and worried that European nations might try to reconquer them. In addition, Russia at this time seemed interested in gaining territory in the Northwest, because it had already claimed Alaska. In response to these concerns about European powers, Secretary of State Adams authored a new international policy. This policy came to be known as the Monroe Doctrine. A doctrine is a firm principle or policy.

Adams wrote the policy, but Monroe approved it and presented it in a speech to Congress in December 1823. The speech had two main points. The first was that the United States would not interfere with the affairs of European countries or with any existing European colonies in the Western Hemisphere.

photo: Getty Images

This image depicts Secretary of State John Adams discussing the Monroe Doctrine with other cabinet members.

The second was that the United States would not accept European nations interfering with the newly independent countries in the Western Hemisphere. Monroe warned that any European military action in North or South America would be seen as a threat to the United States.

Impact of the Monroe Doctrine

Before the United States had issued this doctrine, Great Britain's foreign minister suggested that the two countries issue a similar statement together. The British wanted to show unity with the United States because together the two countries would appear much stronger, and the British thought a display of strength would discourage Spain from trying to regain its lost territories. The fact that the United States chose not to work with Britain but instead issued the statement alone reflects the growing nationalism, or strong national pride, that existed in the United States at this time.

Explore this resource to learn more about the doctrine that changed American foreign policy.

In spite of the bold announcement of the Monroe Doctrine, it is not clear that the United States could have stopped European interference in the Americas without Great Britain's help. However, because no European powers tried to recolonize in the Western Hemisphere, the doctrine was not challenged for nearly 30 years. The Europeans were more involved in their own affairs on the other side of the Atlantic. Historians have concluded that the policy was not seen as especially significant at the time; it was not even called the "Monroe Doctrine" until around 1850—more than 25 years after Monroe's now-famous speech.

The Monroe Doctrine does have important historical significance. It established the basis on which the United States would intervene in the Western Hemisphere in later years. It also gave later U.S. leaders goals to pursue and principles to follow as they asserted power in the region in the decades to come.

Consider the Essential Question:

How did American foreign affairs after the War of 1812 reveal changing attitudes about the United States?

Go online to complete the Social Studies Explanation.

Check for Understanding:

Describe the major provisions of the Monroe Docrtine. In what ways did the Monroe Doctrine have a long-term impact on U.S. foreign relations?

6.4 Challenges of Expansion

LESSON OVERVIEW

Introduction

In this concept, you will learn about the new states that joined the first 13. You will see how the Northwest Ordinance provided guidance for the settlement of the American frontier. You will find out how Native Americans resisted this expansion. You will explore the changes the United States made to unite an increasingly diverse land. As you read the text and explore the resources, think about the costs and benefits that westward expansion brought to the United States.

Key Vocabulary
Which terms do you already know?

- ☐ Adams-Onís Treaty
- ☐ American System
- ☐ Andrew Jackson
- ☐ Articles of Confederation
- ☐ Battle of Horseshoe Bend
- ☐ Daniel Boone
- ☐ Erie Canal
- ☐ *Gibbons v. Ogden*
- ☐ Henry Clay
- ☐ James Monroe
- ☐ John Quincy Adams
- ☐ Land Ordinance of 1785
- ☐ Louisiana Purchase
- ☐ market revolution
- ☐ *McCulloch v. Maryland*
- ☐ meridian
- ☐ National Road
- ☐ Northwest Ordinance of 1787
- ☐ pioneer
- ☐ Seminole
- ☐ Tariff of 1816
- ☐ Treaty of Ghent

Essential Question

Did the benefits of American expansion outweigh the costs?

Lesson Objectives

By the end of this lesson, you should be able to:

- Locate and describe the expansion of U.S. territory that followed the War of 1812.

- Analyze consequences of territorial and westward expansion that followed the War of 1812.

ENGAGE

Did westward expansion go as planned? Visit Engage to learn more.

Essential Question

Did the benefits of American expansion outweigh the costs?

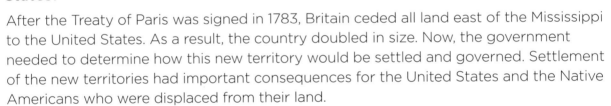

EXPLORE

Settling the Northwest

How did the Northwest Ordinance aid the expansion of the United States?

After the Treaty of Paris was signed in 1783, Britain ceded all land east of the Mississippi to the United States. As a result, the country doubled in size. Now, the government needed to determine how this new territory would be settled and governed. Settlement of the new territories had important consequences for the United States and the Native Americans who were displaced from their land.

Under the Articles of Confederation, Congress made plans for the settlement of the new territory by passing the Land Ordinance of 1785 and the Northwest Ordinance of 1787. An *ordinance* is a law or legal decree. These two laws established the process by which territories could be settled and eventually become states.

The Land Ordinance provided for a complete survey of the Northwest Territory—more than 265,000 square miles, encompassing the present states of Ohio, Indiana, Michigan, Illinois, and Wisconsin. The survey divided the land into 36-square-mile townships. The townships were divided into parcels that were small enough to be affordable but large enough to support a family.

The Northwest Ordinance of 1787 accomplished two distinct but related goals. First, it outlined a process for creating new states. For example, when the population in a district reached 5,000 adult males, the people could write a state constitution. When a district's population reached 60,000 free males, it could request statehood. Second, the Northwest Ordinance codified certain democratic principles in the territory. It outlawed slavery and established trial by jury, habeas corpus, and due process.

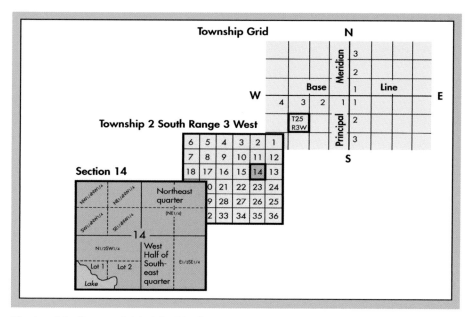

The Land Ordinance divided the Northwest Territory into 36-square-mile townships.

It also identified specific property rights for both settlers and Native Americans, ensured religious liberty, and even encouraged the establishment of schools, which played an important role in preserving liberty. The first goal of creating a path to statehood was based on the fulfillment of the second. This means that if these rights were not upheld, statehood could not be achieved. As you may recall, the Northwest Ordinance is considered one of the most important accomplishments of the U.S. government under the Articles of Confederation.

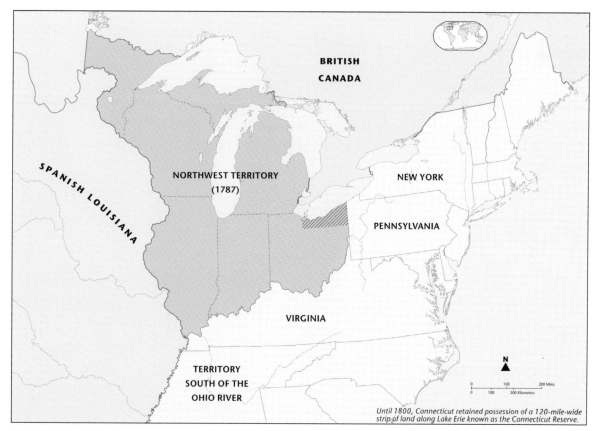

Map of the Northwest Territory of the United States.

The Union Grows

Which Northern states were added to the Union at the beginning of the 1800s?

The early 1800s were a time of increased mobility for Americans. Many people moved from the original 13 states to territories in the South and West. Settlers migrated for new economic and social opportunities. Land was fertile, cheap, and plentiful. Settlers usually traveled with their families, following the course of the rivers. They often traveled with others who came from the same area in the East.

Vermont Becomes the 14th State

The first state that was not one of the original 13 colonies was not in the South or in the Northwest. Vermonters had petitioned for statehood earlier, but their request was denied because New York also claimed the land. Outraged Vermonters declared independence from everyone and established the Vermont Republic in 1777. In 1790, New York gave up its claims, and Vermont was admitted to the Union the following year.

New States in the Midwest

The beginning of the 1800s saw much of the Northwest Territory become states. Ohio joined the Union in 1803. The French had begun exploring Ohio in the 1660s and developed the fur trade there. In the French and Indian War, the British and the Americans expelled the French in Ohio and killed and displaced many Native Americans, clearing the way for white settlers from the East. Ohio's constitution allowed all white men, not just those with property, to vote in elections.

In the War of 1812, the United States increased its hold on the backcountry and the Midwest by finally ejecting the British. After overcoming violent Native American opposition to white expansion, in 1816, Indiana became the 19th state to join the Union. When Illinois became the 21st state in 1818, most of its population was in the southern portion of the state. But lead mines in northwestern Illinois and the emergence of Chicago as a port city on the Great Lakes soon swelled the population in the northern part of the state.

States Admitted to the Union, 1790-1819

State	Year of Admission	Territorial Origin
14. Vermont	1791	Claim by state of New York dropped in 1790
15. Kentucky	1792	Released from state of Virginia in 1792
16. Tennessee	1796	Released from state of North Carolina in 1790
17. Ohio	1803	Northwest Territory
18. Louisiana	1812	Louisiana Territory
19. Indiana	1816	Northwest Territory
20. Mississippi	1817	Mississippi Territory
21. Illinois	1818	Northwest Territory
22. Alabama	1819	Released from Mississippi Territory in 1817

New States in the Southeast

Which Southern states were added to the Union at the beginning of the 1800s?

Louisiana

The Louisiana Territory, purchased from France in 1803, was divided into two parts. The largest part of the territory, the portion north of the 33rd parallel, was called the District of Louisiana. The portion considered to be the most valuable was below this line. It was called the Territory of Orleans. This land included the port city of New Orleans at the mouth of the Mississippi River. The state of Louisiana, formed out of the Territory of Orleans and a small section of West Florida, was admitted to the Union in 1812. Even though West Florida was claimed by the United States as part of this new state, Spain would not give up its claim to West Florida until the signing of the Adams-Onís Treaty in 1819.

Mississippi and Alabama

During the early years of the United States, most of the land that today makes up Mississippi and Alabama was claimed by a variety of entities, including the states of Georgia and South Carolina, the U.S. federal government, Great Britain, Spain, and several Native American tribes, including the Chickamauga, Creek, Cherokee, and Yazoo. In 1798, the U.S. government established the Mississippi Territory and opened the area for settlement. In 1817, the Mississippi Territory was divided into two, so Mississippi could enter the Union. Alabama became a state in 1819.

Florida

Between 1810 and 1812, the United States annexed, or added, West Florida, which included the Gulf Coast portions of what are now Mississippi, Alabama, and Louisiana. As you read, a portion of this land was added to the new state of Louisiana.

Although Spain was not at first willing to give up either West or East Florida, its control over these areas was weak. The United States was concerned that British spies were operating there. In addition, the Seminole, a Native American people living in East Florida, often conducted raids from their homes into Georgia, Alabama, and Mississippi. The United States suspected that the Spanish were supporting these raids. Finally, the lack of government in the Floridas made it a potential refuge for runaway enslaved people.

Andrew Jackson, now an army general, was ordered to find British spies and runaway slaves and to put a stop to the Seminole raids. But Jackson had more ambitious plans,

Explore this interactive to learn more about the impacts of territorial expansion.

which he acted on without permission from the president. He marched his troops deep into Spanish Florida, capturing two Spanish forts.

With Florida now controlled by the U.S. military, President James Monroe and Secretary of State John Quincy Adams convinced Spain to sell the Floridas to the United States. In 1819, under the Adams-Onís Treaty, Spain gave up its claims to East Florida, southern Mississippi and Alabama, and the Oregon Country.

Native American Resistance

How did Native Americans react to America's early expansion?

American settlers who migrated to the West considered themselves pioneers because they established homesteads in unmapped, wild areas away from white settlements. However, the lands they explored and settled were already home to Native Americans. The Louisiana Purchase, in 1803, and the Treaty of Ghent, which ended the War of 1812, had unfortunate consequences for Native American tribes living in the West. Once European influence was removed from the territory, Americans felt not only free but also obliged to spread out over the continent and claim it as theirs.

By the 1800s, most Native Americans recognized that the arrival of American settlers meant they would soon be pushed off their land. When peaceful resistance failed, some tribes reluctantly but peacefully ceded their lands to the federal government. Then, they left for sparsely populated areas in the West. Others decided to fight to protect their homelands, their families, and their way of life. On August 30, 1813, the Red Stick Creek attacked Fort Mims in the Mississippi Territory, killing around 145 militia and perhaps 400 civilians. In response, Colonel Andrew Jackson's troops destroyed the Creeks in the Battle of Horseshoe Bend in March 1814.

photo: Getty Images

An aerial view of Horseshoe Bend National Military Park in Daviston, Alabama.

In the Treaty of Fort Jackson, the surviving Creek surrendered more than 20 million acres of land to the U.S. government when they left for Indian Territory in what is now Oklahoma.

Victory in the War of 1812 removed key obstacles to westward settlement. As settlers moved into new parts of the country, the national infrastructure of roads, canals, and railroads arrived with them. These developments changed the nature of the relationship between the federal government and Native American Nations.

Recall that in the early years of the republic, the government viewed the nations as independent countries. After the War of 1812, many American leaders began to view Native Americans from a position of dominance. They favored policies of Indian removal and rejected peace agreements as unnecessary. During this time, the federal government signed more than 200 treaties in which Native Americans ceded land to the United States. These agreements also led to the creation of Indian reservations west of the Mississippi River.

A System to Unify America

What was the American System?

To address the travel and communication problems presented by westward expansion, Speaker of the House Henry Clay of Kentucky, South Carolina Senator John C. Calhoun, and Massachusetts Senator John Quincy Adams proposed a plan that became known as the American System. The American System was created during the period of national unity that followed the War of 1812. Its purpose was to unite various regions of the country and establish economic independence from Europe. The plan had three components:

- "internal improvements," projects that would create a better transportation system for moving people and goods more quickly and safely around the country,

- a protective tariff that would encourage people to buy American-made products by placing a tax on European goods, and

- a new national bank to increase confidence in the U.S. economy.

Supporters of the American System argued that it would benefit all Americans by making different regions of the country dependent on one another and independent of Europe. They were responding to the market revolution, a trend in which the world's economic systems were transformed from subsistence economies to market-oriented societies. This means that instead of communities producing and consuming most of their own products, people were beginning to specialize and purchase goods from other communities and regions. The market revolution was marked by increased regional interdependence, as individuals and businesses began to rely on one another for goods and services.

The American System was designed to support the North's manufacture of items that farmers in the West and South were not suited to make themselves. Industrialization of the North would increase demand for agricultural products and other raw materials that were available in the South and the West. An improved transportation system would connect sellers and buyers—to the benefit of all regions. A national bank would provide a sound currency, or system of money.

photo: Library of Congress

Henry Clay persuaded Americans to forego their sectional interests and back the American System for the good of the nation.

Opposition to the American System came from regions of the country that received little advantage from high tariffs and industrial subsidies. The mostly agricultural, cotton-producing South, which had economic ties to transatlantic trade, saw the tariffs as an unfair burden. Additionally, southern planters saw no good reason to financially support industry in northern and midwestern states. These southern states seized on the notion of states' rights as the crucial factor. They argued that the federal government was overstepping its bounds and limiting the power of individual states. These disputes over the American System would ultimately make their way to the Supreme Court.

A National Transportation System

How does transportation improve?

Highways

The National Road was constructed to address this problem. The National Road was the nation's first federally funded interstate turnpike, or toll road. It was an important component of Congress's plan to support the economy by improving transportation.

The National Road started in the town of Cumberland, in western Maryland, and then headed west. The first section, completed in 1818, spanned about 140 miles to Wheeling, Virginia (now West Virginia), and made for easier travel between the Potomac and the Ohio Rivers.

Constructing the National Road was a monumental task. A 66-foot right-of-way was cleared of trees. The paved road was 20 feet wide, made of gravel 18 inches deep, with an additional 6-foot strip of dirt road on either side. By 1838, the National Road extended all the way from Cumberland to Vandalia, Illinois. However, because many Americans were opposed to federal funding of internal improvements, the National Road turned out to be the only interstate turnpike created as part of the American System.

Canals and Steamboats

Canals are human-constructed waterways that provide boats and ships with "shortcuts" and smooth transport from one major natural waterway to another. The Erie Canal, completed in 1825, was the first canal in the United States to connect western waterways such as the Great Lakes with the Atlantic Ocean. The Erie Canal stretched some 363 miles—all the way across the state of New York from Lake Erie to the Hudson River. Constructing this waterway was a major engineering feat at the time. Mountain rock had to be blasted away, and forests had to be cleared for the 40-foot-wide canal.

Lockport, New York, on the Erie Canal.

photo: Getty Images

More important, a system of movable locks, special chambers where operators could control the water level, had to be developed to help boats navigate over the changes in elevation. Canal engineers even designed special locks to move vessels on the canal over the 650-mile long unbroken ridge known as the Niagara Escarpment. Once finished, the canal enabled ships to travel from the Northwest Territories to New York City and then on to Europe. A canal construction boom resulted from the success of the Erie Canal. By 1837, the United States had more than 3,000 miles of canals.

Water transport in the United States was further enhanced by the invention of the steamboat. Steamboats, which featured light, powerful engines that burned wood, allowed for upstream transportation. As they were improved, they also permitted shippers to travel in shallow water.

The American System

What economic measures supported the American System?

Tariffs

Supporters of the American System proposed tariffs to help pay for internal improvements to the nation's transportation network. As you may recall, tariffs are taxes placed on goods purchased from other countries. Proponents of the tariff argued that it would have the added benefit of promoting American manufacturing. This became especially apparent following the War of 1812 when British manufacturers began unloading their manufactured goods on the U.S. market at prices far below cost in an effort to disrupt American industries that had emerged during the war. It seemed as though British manufacturers were intentionally trying to hurt American manufacturers that were just getting off the ground in the early 1800s. The tariffs, especially the 1816 tariff, were designed to drive up prices consumers paid for European goods and, therefore, make U.S. products more competitive.

Many Southerners in particular were used to exchanging their agricultural products for European manufactured goods. Because of this, some Americans were opposed to tariffs. But there was enough support in Congress for passage of Tariff of 1816. Although this component of the American System passed, the tariff would become a divisive issue during the 1830s.

The Second National Bank

You may recall that Alexander Hamilton proposed the first national bank during George Washington's presidency. That bank's charter had expired in 1811. Many Americans thought a Second Bank of the United States would create a stable currency and make it easier for people in different parts of the United States to conduct business. Additionally, the War of 1812 revealed serious weaknesses with the American financial system that many hoped a new national bank could help to resolve. So, in 1816, a second national bank was chartered for 20 years.

The establishment of a second national bank was controversial for two reasons. First, some saw it as a violation of the principles of federalism. States, especially southern states, saw the increasing power of the federal government as an attack on the power of states and a possible route to the emancipation of slavery. Second, many blamed the bank for the prolonged economic recession at the time. When some Maryland banks began to fail, the state of Maryland responded by placing a large tax on the national bank. However, the cashier of the Baltimore branch, James McCulloch, refused to pay, and the state sued him.

photo: Library of Congress

The Second Bank of the United States was an important, yet controversial, part of the American System. It was intended to provide a stable national currency to promote trade.

The case, known as *McCulloch v. Maryland*, was argued before the Supreme Court in 1819. Maryland argued that because the Constitution did not explicitly state that the federal government had the power to authorize the bank in the first place, the national bank was unconstitutional. The court, however, disagreed, stating that Congress was empowered to create the bank and that a state could not tax a tool of the national government. The court pointed to lines at the end of Article I, Section 8 of the Constitution to justify its decision. This section lists specific powers given to Congress, then concludes by giving Congress the power to "make all Laws which shall be necessary and proper for carrying into Execution the foregoing Powers, and all other Powers vested by this Constitution in the Government of the United States or in any Department or Officer thereof." This ruling effectively strengthened the federal government's enumerated, or listed, powers by broadening what was considered "necessary and proper" for the execution of those powers. Additionally, the ruling strengthened the federal supremacy cause of the constitution by declaring it a violation of that clause for a state to tax a tool of the federal government.

This would not, however, be the last time states challenged the power of the federal government. Just a few years after the *McCulloch v. Maryland* case, a dispute arose in New York State between two competing steamboat operators. One operator, Aaron Ogden, claimed New York had given him exclusive rights to run a route between New Jersey and New York City. Another operator, Thomas Gibbons, said the state had no authority to give this exclusive right to routes between two states because Article I, Section 8 of the Constitution gave Congress the power to "regulate Commerce with foreign Nations, among the several States, and with the Indian Tribes." The court, in *Ogden v. Gibbons*, agreed with Gibbons. In the first interpretation of the Constitution's commerce clause, the chief justice said this clause gave the federal government exclusive authority to regulate not only trade, but also navigation between states.

Complete this activity to create an ad for Henry Clay's plan to expand the country.

The opinions in both *McCulloch v. Maryland* and *Ogden v. Gibbons* have strengthened the power of the federal government. However, as the power of the federal government grew, so too did the regional differences between the North and South. As these differences became more pronounced, the threat to national unity became more apparent.

Consider the Essential Question:

Did the benefits of American expansion outweigh the costs?

Go online to complete the Social Studies Explanation.

Check for Understanding:

Describe one challenge presented by the early westward expansion of the United States. Was the federal government's response to this challenge effective?

7.1 Jacksonian Democracy

photo: Getty Images

LESSON OVERVIEW

Introduction

In this concept, you will learn how Andrew Jackson helped shape modern politics, banking, states' rights, and the power of the executive branch.

Essential Question

Was Andrew Jackson a champion of democracy?

Lesson Objective

By the end of this lesson, you should be able to:

- Identify and describe philosophies and policies associated with Jacksonian Democracy.

Key Vocabulary

Which terms do you already know?

- ☐ Andrew Jackson
- ☐ corrupt bargain
- ☐ Democratic Party
- ☐ Democratic-Republican Party
- ☐ Henry Clay
- ☐ Indian Removal Act
- ☐ John C. Calhoun
- ☐ John Quincy Adams
- ☐ Kitchen Cabinet
- ☐ nullification
- ☐ Panic of 1837
- ☐ spoils system
- ☐ suffrage
- ☐ veto
- ☐ Whig Party

ENGAGE

Was Andrew Jackson a tyrant or a champion? Visit Engage to learn more.

> ## Essential Question
>
> Was Andrew Jackson a champion of democracy?

EXPLORE

A Self-Made Man

Who was Andrew Jackson?

Jackson's Youth

Andrew Jackson was born on the border of North Carolina and South Carolina in 1767 to Scottish-Irish immigrant farmers. Jackson's parents were subsistence farmers, which meant that they grew just enough to live. His father died right before he was born. Andrew, his mother, and two older brothers lived with his mother's extended family in North Carolina.

As a teenager, Andrew Jackson fought in the Revolutionary War. During the war, he was held as a prisoner and was slashed by

photo: Getty Images
Andrew Jackson statue in Jackson Square in New Orleans, Louisiana.

a British officer's sword, leaving him scarred on the head and left hand. His mother and brothers died during that war, making him an orphan at 14. Jackson developed a deep-seated hatred for the British as a result of his experiences during the war.

Businessperson and War Hero

After the war, Jackson studied law and taught school in North Carolina. In 1787, he passed the bar, became a lawyer, and moved to Tennessee. It was here that Jackson began to make a name for himself as a frontier lawyer and businessperson. He became a prosecutor, bought property and slaves, owned a general store, and served in the state legislature.

Jackson took time away from his businesses for a successful military career. As a U.S. Army colonel, he won national fame for his victory over Native Americans in the Creek War (1813–1814). He was promoted to general and won a major victory over the British in the Battle of New Orleans (1815) during the War of 1812. In 1818, his forces won the First Seminole War, which led to the United States' acquisition of Florida. While serving in the military, Jackson became known as "Old Hickory" because he seemed to be unbreakable in battle.

Jackson Enters Politics

What inspired Jackson to enter politics?

As Andrew Jackson gained fortune and prestige, the United States was changing. Industrialization and urbanization created and grew a new group of Americans: the working class. At the same time, the country was expanding. Pioneers and settlers crossing the Appalachian Mountains faced hardships similar to those that the original colonists faced. Many were immigrants who came to find a new life. Few of the settlers had much formal education or wealth, but they were prepared for hard work.

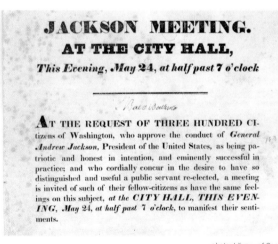

photo: Library of Congress

1832 notice for a meeting in support of Jackson's reelection as president.

Many workers, pioneers, and immigrants—common people—felt that the federal government favored wealthy aristocratic landowners and did not consider their needs. Jackson was determined to protect the interests of these common people. He was elected Tennessee's first representative in Congress in 1796, served two partial terms as U.S. senator, and ran for president in 1824.

Jackson as President

On March 4, 1829, Andrew Jackson was inaugurated as the seventh president of the United States. His experiences would affect his actions as president. But because his background was unlike that of previous presidents, people like Daniel Webster, U.S. senator from Massachusetts, did not know just what to expect.

Whether or not Jackson brought "a breeze with him" to the White House is unclear. As president, Jackson used his aggressive nature to repeatedly challenge Washington's rules and traditions. His determination to remove power from the hands of the wealthy created lasting changes for political parties, electoral campaigns, the banking system, and the relationship between the states and the federal government.

Jackson's battles with the wealthy and well connected in Washington were fought in the name of the "common man." But it is also clear that, for Jackson, the term "common man" excluded not only women, but also many other people who called the United States home.

For example, Jackson's Native American policies, in particular his support for the Indian Removal Act of 1830, led to the forced relocation of thousands of Native Americans from their traditional homelands. The tragic march of the Cherokee from the Southeastern United States to Oklahoma is now known as the "Trail of Tears."

A Corrupt Bargain?

How could Andrew Jackson win the popular vote yet lose the election?

Suffrage, or the right to vote, in the United States was at first granted only to white men who owned property. In the European tradition, it was accepted that only men with property had the interest, education, and skill to make decisions about governing their state and country. Over time, this attitude changed, and by 1824, all adult white men were allowed to vote in most states, whether they owned property or not. Women and African Americans were still discriminated against and denied many citizenship rights, including the right to vote.

At this time, candidates for president were chosen by a congressional caucus, a meeting of all party members in the House of Representatives and the Senate. In 1824, the congressional caucus was bitterly divided on who should become the next president. Four candidates emerged: John Quincy Adams of Massachusetts, Andrew Jackson of Tennessee, Henry Clay of Kentucky, and William C. Crawford of Georgia. Jackson won 41 percent of the popular vote. Jackson's closest rival was John Quincy Adams, an experienced diplomat and the son of former president John Adams. John Quincy Adams received 31 percent of the popular vote.

Because none of the candidates received enough electoral votes to win the presidency, the House of Representatives would determine the winner. Henry Clay was the speaker of the House and, like Adams, was an experienced politician. Clay felt that if Andrew Jackson became president, it would be "the greatest misfortune that could befall the country."

Candidate	Popular Vote	Percentage	States Won	Electoral Vote
Jackson (D-R)	151,363	41	11	99
Adams (D-R)	113,142	31	7	84
Clay (D-R)	47,545	13	3	37
Crawford (D-R)	41,032	11	3	41

Table showing popularity breakdown between candidates in the election of 1824.

Two weeks before the House vote, a newspaper published an anonymous letter stating that Clay had made a deal to support Adams for president in exchange for Clay being named secretary of state. Clay denounced this letter and its author, claiming that no such deal had been made.

On February 9, 1825, the House of Representatives met to select the new president. Clay persuaded his supporters to vote for Adams, who became the sixth president of the United States. Adams then offered the position of secretary of state to Clay, just as the letter in the newspaper had predicted. Clay accepted. Jackson and his supporters accused Adams and Clay of making a corrupt bargain. Clay said he had done nothing wrong: He followed constitutional procedures, and he supported the candidate whose politics were closest to his own.

A Hotly Contested Election

How did the Democratic Party win the 1828 presidential election?

In many ways, the 1828 presidential campaign was a forerunner of modern elections. The race marked the return of the two-party system. The newly formed Democratic Party nominated Andrew Jackson, and incumbent John Quincy Adams represented the National Republicans. After losing the presidency in 1824 due to what he called a Corrupt Bargain, Jackson and his supporters were determined to prevail. They decided that if they were to win the presidency in 1828, they needed a strong political party and a message that would earn the support of a diverse group of American men.

Jackson's New Democratic Party

Jackson and his supporters had abandoned the old Democratic-Republican Party. They formed a new Democratic Party that appealed to men from every part of the country, from many walks of life, and from many economic stations. The Democratic Party presented Jackson as a self-made success story. They emphasized his appeal to the "common man" and convinced voters that he would protect ordinary citizens from the corruption of the upper class.

Jackson's new Democratic Party included men from urban labor unions who wanted better working conditions and the right to share company profits with factory owners. The party also recruited small farmers who wanted land reform and a banking system that was more responsive to small businesses. The Democrats also appealed to Southern planters who wanted to protect states' rights and to lower or remove tariffs on agricultural products. Each of these groups complained that the federal government was favoring wealthy, Northern manufacturers and financiers and was not looking out for the interests of the common people.

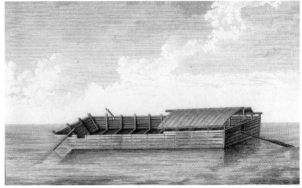

photo: Library of Congress

Flatboats carried freight on the Ohio–Mississippi River system. Andrew Jackson and other Democrats were popular with those who worked on them.

Jackson's Democratic Party also changed campaigning. Martin Van Buren managed Jackson's campaign and used a variety of new strategies to generate excitement about his candidate. Van Buren created a network of local and state Democratic committees that organized election rallies and barbeques. These events brought together voters who had been divided in the prior election to support a single candidate. They held massive fund-raisers and had newspapers all across the country publishing articles in favor of Jackson. For the first time, voters throughout the country followed developments in the presidential race closely.

Jackson's Rivals

Who challenged Jackson in 1828—and why?

John Quincy Adams's National Republican Party (not related to the modern Republican Party, which was created in 1854) was made up of landed gentry who wanted educated, wealthy men to run the government. The party also included business leaders who wanted to run the government like a corporation. Adams's party supported high tariffs, government-sponsored roads and canals, and the Second Bank of the United States as the banker for the U.S. government.

photo: Library of Congress

This broadside encouraged voters to select pro-Jackson candidates for legislative office in an unidentified state.

The National Republican Party ran Adams's campaign as previous campaigns had been run, relying on voters to trust their leaders and to vote as they were instructed. Adams was certain that his continued attention to his duties as president, rather than campaigning, would win him a majority of votes.

In 1828, Jackson and the Democrats were in favorable position compared with their opponents. Many states had recently granted poor and non-property-owning white men the right to vote. More than one million white men voted in the presidential election of 1828. This was four times more than had voted just four years before. The Jacksonian Democrats enjoyed a built-in advantage in the national popular vote.

Jackson went on to win the 1828 election with 56 percent of the popular vote and 68 percent of the electoral vote. He became the seventh president of the United States, with John C. Calhoun, from South Carolina, as his vice president.

After Adams's defeat in 1828, Henry Clay became the leader of the National Republican Party. Clay ran for president against Jackson in 1832 and lost by an overwhelming margin. In 1833, the National Republican Party dissolved and became the Whig Party.

"Old Hickory" Becomes "King Andrew"

How did Jackson's policies change American politics and government?

When running for the presidency, Andrew Jackson appealed to voters by attacking the wealthy and powerful in Washington. Once in office, Jackson made dramatic changes to the way the nation was governed. Because of his aggressive approach to governing the nation, Jackson earned a new nickname from his opponents: "King Andrew."

photo: Library of Congress

This 1877 cartoon reveals criticisms of the system Andrew Jackson created.

The Spoils System

Cabinet members, who head the federal executive departments and report directly to the president, customarily resign their positions when a new chief executive takes office. However, before Jackson became president, it was common for other high-ranking government officials to retain their positions for several years and to serve under more than one president. These positions included bureau chiefs and supervisors, federal marshals, U.S. attorneys and judges, and customs officers. They were filled by educated men whose job was to carry out the law and the instructions of the president, regardless of their political views.

Jackson believed that, over time, people in positions of power became indifferent to the needs of ordinary citizens. He believed long-time government officials were corrupt, meaning that they used their offices as a means to promote their own personal interests. Fixing the system of executive department employment became one of Jackson's first priorities as president.

After an audit of the Treasury Department revealed corruption, Jackson instituted the *rotation-in-office* policy. Upon taking office, Jackson's administration asked government officials for their resignations and placed new people in their positions. Jackson's rotation-in-office policy became known as the "spoils system." The policy received this name after William Marcy, a defender of the president, quipped in Congress, "To the victor belong the spoils of the enemy." Employing the spoils system, Jackson replaced 9 percent of the federal workforce during his first year in office.

The "spoils system" was common in state governments but had not previously been used by the federal government. The system allowed the Democratic Party to distribute government jobs in a manner that rewarded those in the party who helped it achieve its goals. But Jackson's practice of rewarding his supporters with government positions reminded his critics of the Corrupt Bargain that Jackson himself had alleged when John Quincy Adams appointed his own supporter Henry Clay to his cabinet. In addition, a few of Jackson's appointees turned out to be as corrupt as the officials they replaced. For example, Samuel Swartwout, whom Jackson appointed to direct the Port of New York, embezzled more than $1 million.

Explore this resource and come up with your own idea for staffing the government.

Rotation in office was intended to keep corruption of federal officials to a minimum and to support politically reliable men. The spoils system became one of Jackson's far-reaching policy changes. The practice continued with every successive administration until 1883. In that year, the Pendleton Act created the Civil Service Commission, which established a competitive merit system for federal jobs.

Jackson Resists Nullification

What did the Nullification Crisis show about Andrew Jackson?

You may recall that in 1816 Congress passed special taxes called tariffs to help support American industry and to pay for internal improvements. By the time Andrew Jackson became president, such policies were becoming more and more unpopular in the South.

photo: Library of Congress

South Carolina Senator John C. Calhoun.

In 1828, Congress had passed a tariff that opponents called the "Tariff of Abominations." In July 1832, Jackson signed a tariff bill that was intended to replace the 1828 law with a more reasonable tax on imported goods. But Southerners were outraged. Led by John C. Calhoun, the sitting vice president, the state of South Carolina enacted a procedure for nullifying, or overturning, federal laws such as the Tariff of 1832. The Nullification Crisis would be a major test of Jackson's authority as the country's chief executive.

Jackson would not tolerate nullification. In his view, the Constitution was a binding agreement. The people of South Carolina had entered into a contract with the people of the rest of the United States. In exchange for receiving the benefits of being part of the Union, they had given up some of their authority to make decisions on their own. According to Jackson, under the U.S. Constitution, South Carolina did not have the authority to nullify laws passed by Congress.

Jackson also believed that in taking the presidential oath of office, he had accepted a "solemn obligation" to preserve the Union. Accordingly, he prepared to send troops to South Carolina to enforce the federal government's collection of the tariff. South Carolina responded by declaring it would leave the Union if the federal government used force to impose the tariff. Vice President Calhoun resigned from office.

Congress addressed the Nullification Crisis in March 1833. It first passed the Force Bill. This law authorized the president to use military force to collect the tariff. But on the same day, Congress also passed a compromise bill lowering the tariff. Even though South Carolina voted to nullify the Force Bill, it also agreed to accept the lower tariff. The Nullification Crisis had come to an end.

By gaining passage of a lower tariff, South Carolina benefited from the Nullification Crisis. At the same time, the idea that states could refuse to abide by federal laws had at least temporarily been defeated.

Andrew Jackson's Bank War

Why did Americans disagree about the National Bank?

You may recall that the Second Bank of the United States was created in 1816 as a component of Henry Clay's American System. The Philadelphia-based organization was a private business that held millions of dollars in deposits from the federal government. The bank charged the government no banking fees and was exempt from paying any state taxes. In exchange for this special status, the bank paid the federal government $1.5 million.

In 1823, Nicholas Biddle became the president of the Second National Bank. During his tenure, Biddle helped build a reliable national banking system. Federal currency was stable during his time at the bank. Biddle's primary purpose as bank president was to earn money for the bank's stockholders, including the federal government. He was determined not to let anyone, including the president of the United States, interfere with the bank's well-being. In 1824, Biddle wrote, "no officer of the Government, from the President downwards, has the least right, the least authority . . . for interference in the concerns of the bank."

photo: Library of Congress

An 1832 cartoon depicts Jackson as a cat clearing "Uncle Sam's Barn" of "Bank Rats."

President Jackson was suspicious of the bank. He believed it was unconstitutional, resented the special privileges it had over state and local banks, and referred to it as "the Monster."

The End of the Bank

What steps did Andrew Jackson take to destroy the bank?

The bank's first 20-year charter was set to expire in 1836. To keep the bank going, Congress would need to pass, and President Jackson to sign, a law renewing the charter.

The Second Bank of the United States in the Election of 1832

National Republicans, led by Henry Clay, believed the bank was popular with the American public. In 1832, they decided to make renewing the bank an issue in Jackson's campaign for reelection. Clay pushed for early renewal of the bank's charter on the belief that a Jackson veto would cost him a second term in office. When the recharter measure passed Congress in July 1832, Biddle was in Washington and held a party to celebrate. But Biddle's celebration was premature and short-lived. Jackson had vetoed the bill.

The House of Representatives tried to override the veto, but the bill did not receive a two-thirds majority in the Senate, and the veto held.

BORN TO COMMAND.

OF VETO MEMORY.

HAD I BEEN CONSULTED.

KING ANDREW THE FIRST.

photo: Library of Congress

How can you tell this cartoon was critical of Andrew Jackson?

Clay's plan to use the bank as an election year issue did not work. Despite his failure to support the bank, Jackson was reelected. Afterward, Jackson claimed that the government's funds were not secure in the national bank. Congress conducted an inquiry, and its pro-bank Republican majority found the bank was secure. Without the support of Congress, Jackson decided to dismantle the bank on his own. He ordered his secretary of the treasury, William Duane, to quickly withdraw the nation's money and place it in other banks. Duane refused, so Jackson discharged him.

Jackson Destroys the Bank

Jackson replaced Duane with one of his most loyal supporters, Maryland's Roger Taney. Many in Congress were outraged when Taney began moving federal deposits to private banks, which detractors called "pet banks." For this action, Jackson was censured, or officially reprimanded, by the Senate. But the Senate's censure had no real impact. Without any federal deposits, the Second Bank of the United States was doomed. In 1841, what was left of the bank dissolved.

Known for his military victories, Jackson also won this economic Bank War. In doing so, he demonstrated and increased the power of the presidency. But the downfall of the bank contributed to a financial crisis that struck the nation in 1837, after Jackson left office.

Explore this interactive to learn more about criticisms of Andrew Jackson.

Consider the Essential Question:

Was Andrew Jackson a champion of democracy?

Go online to complete the Social Studies Explanation.

Check for Understanding:

Did the development of political parties during Andrew Jackson's term in office make the American political process more democratic? Cite evidence to support your position.

7.2 The Native American Experience

photo: Getty Images

LESSON OVERVIEW

Introduction

In this concept, you will learn about why white settlers discriminated against their Native American neighbors. You will discover why some tribes adopted European practices, while others resisted removal.

Essential Question

What were the causes and effects of Indian removal policies during the 1830s?

Lesson Objective

By the end of this lesson, you should be able to:

- Evaluate American Indian relocation policies implemented during the presidency of Andrew Jackson.

Key Vocabulary

Which terms do you already know?

- ☐ Andrew Jackson
- ☐ Cherokee
- ☐ *Cherokee Nation v. Georgia*
- ☐ Five "Civilized" Tribes
- ☐ Indian Removal Act
- ☐ Indian Territory
- ☐ John Marshall
- ☐ John Ross
- ☐ *Johnson v. M'Intosh*
- ☐ Oklahoma Territory
- ☐ Osceola
- ☐ Trail of Tears
- ☐ *Worcester v. Georgia*

Discovery EDUCATION | SOCIAL STUDIES TECHBOOK

ENGAGE

How did the nation's growth affect Native Americans? Visit Engage to learn more.

Essential Question

What were the causes and effects of Indian removal policies during the 1830s?

EXPLORE

Involuntary Exchange of Lands

What was the Indian Removal Act?

The Cherokee were Native Americans who, long before the English colonists arrived, occupied part of what became Georgia. The U.S. government had acknowledged Cherokee land rights in treaties. However, as the U.S. economy and population continued to expand, white settlers demanded more Cherokee land.

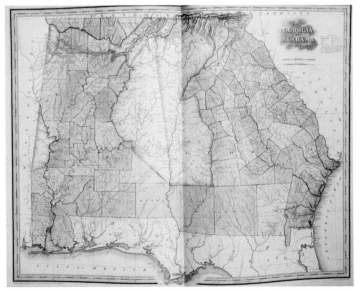

photo: Getty Images

A map of Alabama and Georgia prior to the removal of Native Americans.

The year Andrew Jackson was inaugurated president, 1829, gold was discovered in Georgia. Whites already wanted the Cherokee lands in Georgia. Now a gold rush began, bringing even more white settlers to the state and putting more pressure on the Native American population.

In 1830, Jackson signed into law Congress's Indian Removal Act. This law instructed the president to make treaties with all Native American tribes and nations living east of the Mississippi River. Native American land in the East was to be exchanged for land in the West—land that at the time was considered less valuable.

Discovery | SOCIAL STUDIES
EDUCATION | TECHBOOK.

What were the causes and effects of Indian removal policies during the 1830s?

The treaties would authorize the government to evacuate all Native Americans from their tribal homes. Doing so would free up millions of acres of land for white settlers.

In 1834, Congress established Indian country, originally defined as land west of the Mississippi River that was not already part of the states of Missouri or Louisiana or part of the territory of Arkansas. The land set aside as Indian Territory was later restricted to a portion of present-day Oklahoma, the rest of which was open to settlers as the Territory of Oklahoma. Native Americans were granted control of their land and were forced to move there.

Explore this interactive to learn more about the history of Native American–European relations in the Southeast.

Some tribes in the Southeast and farther north relocated peacefully because they were too weak to resist. However, some resisted being forced from traditional homelands where generations of their ancestors had lived.

Native Americans and the Supreme Court

How did the Supreme Court influence government policies toward Native Americans?

The federal judiciary also weighed in on the issue of Indian removal. Between 1823 and 1832, Native Americans, potential white settlers, and the state government of Georgia went to court to settle issues of Native American landownership and sovereignty, or self-rule. As a result, the U.S. Supreme Court, led by Chief Justice John Marshall, made several rulings that influenced the government's policies regarding Native Americans.

In *Johnson v. M'Intosh* (1823), the Supreme Court ruled that while Native Americans had a basic right to live on their tribal lands, these lands were really the property of the U.S. government. Because of this, the court ruled, white Americans could not buy land directly from Native Americans. Decisions about the land could only be made by the federal government. This decision seemingly protected Native Americans from individual and state efforts to encourage white settlement on tribal lands.

photo: Getty Images

The Marshall Court handed down three decisions that influenced the federal government's dealings with Native Americans.

But it also established the policy that Native Americans did not own the land on which they had lived for many generations.

In *Cherokee Nation v. Georgia* (1831), the Supreme Court refused to hear the Cherokees' case against a Georgia state law that abolished their tribal government. The Cherokees claimed they had the right to sue the state in federal court because they were a sovereign foreign nation with the same rights as Great Britain, France, or Spain. The justices rejected this argument. Instead, the court ruled that Native Americans were "domestic dependent nations" whose relationship with the federal government "resembles [that of] a ward to his guardian." This ruling was evidence of the common viewpoint that Native Americans were not capable of taking care of themselves.

The following year, in *Worcester v. Georgia* (1832), the Supreme Court declared that the states did not have any legal authority over Native American territory. This decision made it clear that Native American policy was a federal issue and also further defined the status of Native American nations.

These Supreme Court decisions made it clear that the Native Americans' future was now in the hands of the federal government. The court ruled that Native Americans had some rights and the federal government had an obligation to protect these rights from individual and state actions. But the decisions also authorized the federal government to remove Native Americans from their lands. In addition, rather than recognizing Native American rights, federal officials such as President Jackson often sided with the interests of white settlers and the states.

For example, the state of Georgia refused to obey the court's decision in *Worcester v. Georgia* and continued to enforce state laws within the Cherokee territory. The federal government under Andrew Jackson refused to enforce the court's ruling or to take seriously its role of protecting the Native Americans. White settlers continued to take over Native American land. Meanwhile, Georgia pressured the federal government to enforce the Indian Removal Act.

An Attempt at Assimilation

Why did the "Five Civilized Tribes" adopt European customs?

White settlers called the Cherokee, Choctaw, Chickasaw, Creek, and Seminole the "Five Civilized Tribes" in the Southeast. These groups were thought to be "civilized" because they adopted some European-American customs in an attempt to assimilate. The groups believed that living in the style of the settlers would help persuade the settlers to agree to peaceful coexistence.

The five tribes established representative governments. In 1827, three years before Congress passed the Indian Removal Act, the Cherokee established the Cherokee Nation. They created a constitutional government to show they were not under U.S. control and could not legally be removed from their land. The Cherokee Nation created its own laws, its own courts, and a mounted police force.

Principal Chief John Ross headed the new government. Ross petitioned Congress and the secretary of the War Department to protect Cherokee land rights.

The five tribes also changed their lifestyles. They adopted European family structures and gender roles. Communities reorganized to show individual, rather than communal, land ownership. Men gave up their reliance on hunting and gathering and turned to farming, which had traditionally been the role of women. Traditionally, many Native American

photo: Getty Images

Native Americans attempted to assimilate to white culture by building homes that mimicked those of the Europeans.

nations had diverse gender roles that did not fit into the strict male and female divisions of European Christians. For example, the Cherokee referred to some people as *taliqwodidantvn*, or people with two hearts, because they had mixed male and female roles. To assimilate, many Native American groups stopped recognizing these "two-spirit" roles.

The plan of the five tribes did not work. In *Cherokee Nation v. Georgia*, the U.S. Supreme Court refused to acknowledge the Cherokee Nation's legal status to sue a state. White Americans continued to desire valuable farmland. They looted and burned Native American villagers' homes, settled on property without permission, and stole horses and cattle. And after the discovery of gold on Cherokee land, white prospectors flooded the region. Prejudice against Native Americans grew, and many white settlers came to believe that conflicts with Native Americans would never end if they continued to live side by side. These settlers had the support of President Jackson, who was committed to Native American removal.

Two Illegal Treaties

How did the attempts to gain Native American land end?

Most members of the "Five Civilized Tribes" did not want to leave their homes. They resisted the U.S. government's efforts to drive them out of the Southeast. But neither the states nor the federal government would act against white settlers. After many years of frustration, Native Americans gradually decided that the settlers were unstoppable. Reluctantly, they signed away their land. First to leave were the Choctaw, in Mississippi, who signed a removal treaty in 1830. The Chickasaw gave up their territory in Mississippi and Alabama in 1832.

Not all the treaties went so smoothly. The United States signed land exchange treaties with small groups of Seminoles and Cherokees who did not officially represent their tribes.

ATTACK OF THE SEMINOLES ON THE BLOCK HOUSE

photo: Library of Congress
Seminoles attack Fort Brooke in Florida, 1835.

Because the treaty signers were not authorized to sign, the treaties were not legally valid. Nevertheless, the federal government held the treaties to be binding on the tribes. Those who had signed the treaties did leave and collected cash payments from the U.S. government. When the rest of the tribes did not leave voluntarily, the U.S. Army forced them out.

According to one of the treaties, the Seminole were required to leave Florida by 1835. In that year, the U.S. military began to force them out. Under the leadership of four chiefs, including Osceola, the Seminole stayed and fought. During the war, the United States promised to discuss a truce. When Osceola showed up to negotiate, he was instead captured and imprisoned. Osceola died in prison in 1838. The Seminole lost the war and were forced west in 1842.

Like the Seminole, the Cherokee refused to abide by a false treaty. Chief Ross worked within the U.S. legal system to fight removal. Ross started a petition demanding that Congress cancel the invalid Treaty of New Echota. He gathered nearly 16,000 Cherokee signatures. He believed their rights would be respected, but they were not.

Betrayal and a Forced March

What happened during the Trail of Tears?

The 1835 Treaty of New Echota with the Cherokee required them to evacuate their Georgia homeland, but the Cherokee refused to go because the treaty was unlawful. In 1838, General Winfield Scott was sent to enforce the treaty. By April, Scott and his force of 7,000 troops began rounding up the approximately 16,000 remaining Cherokee. As military squads went about raiding villages and capturing Cherokee people, white rioters followed, robbing and setting fire to Cherokee homes.

The Cherokee captives were kept in wooden stockades. Once all the people had been captured, they would be forced west. The food provided to the prisoners was inadequate. More than 2,000 Cherokee died in the camps from starvation and disease.

The roundup of the Cherokee continued until October, when the trek west began. Throughout 1838 and 1839, 17 Cherokee detachments traveled different paths by foot, horse and wagon, and steamboat. They traveled more than 1,000 miles. The people were ill equipped for their wintertime march westward. Along the way, they battled disease, starvation, harsh winter conditions, and racist violence.

The Cherokee called their forced journey "The Place Where They Cried." It became known as the Trail of Tears. Including the deaths in camp, approximately 4,000 Cherokee died on the Trail of Tears—nearly one-quarter of the Cherokee people.

Discovery SOCIAL STUDIES
EDUCATION | **TECHBOOK**

What were the causes and effects of Indian removal policies during the 1830s?

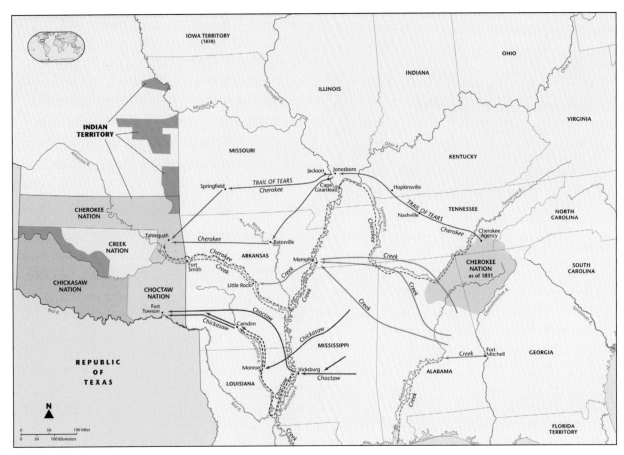

Map showing where Native American groups were forced to relocate.

Consider the Essential Question:

What were the causes and effects of Indian removal policies during the 1830s?

Go online to complete the Social Studies Explanation.

Check for Understanding:

Describe important events and circumstances that led to the westward migration of Native Americans known as the Trail of Tears.

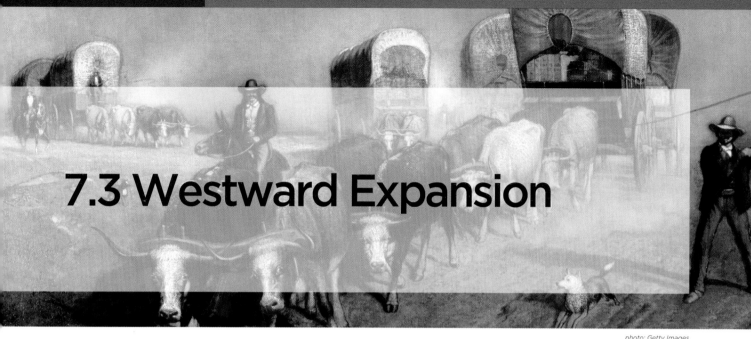

7.3 Westward Expansion

photo: Getty Images

LESSON OVERVIEW

Introduction

In this concept, you will learn how a belief that came to be known as Manifest Destiny led to the territorial growth of the United States during the 1840s.

Essential Question

What impact did Manifest Destiny have on the growth and development of the United States?

Lesson Objectives

By the end of this lesson, you should be able to:

- Explain the concept of Manifest Destiny and describe its effect on the territorial growth of the United States.

- Locate and identify areas acquired by the United States between 1836 and 1853.

- Discuss the causes, key events, and consequences of the Mexican-American War.

Key Vocabulary
Which terms do you already know?

- ☐ 49th parallel
- ☐ Alamo
- ☐ Antonio López de Santa Anna
- ☐ Brigham Young
- ☐ Californios
- ☐ Donner Party
- ☐ empresario
- ☐ forty-niners
- ☐ Franklin Pierce
- ☐ Gadsden Purchase
- ☐ gold rush
- ☐ James K. Polk
- ☐ James Marshall
- ☐ John Sutter
- ☐ Juan Seguin
- ☐ Junipero Serra
- ☐ Levi Strauss
- ☐ Luzena Stanley Wilson
- ☐ Manifest Destiny
- ☐ Marcus Whitman

- ☐ Mexican Cession
- ☐ Mexican War
- ☐ Miguel Hidalgo y Costilla
- ☐ Narcissa Whitman
- ☐ Oregon Trail
- ☐ prospect
- ☐ Republic of Texas
- ☐ Sam Houston
- ☐ Santa Fe Trail
- ☐ Stephen Austin
- ☐ Texas Annexation
- ☐ Texas Revolution
- ☐ Treaty of Guadalupe Hidalgo
- ☐ Wilmot Proviso
- ☐ Zachary Taylor

Discovery EDUCATION | SOCIAL STUDIES **TECHBOOK**

What impact did Manifest Destiny have on the growth and development of the United States?

ENGAGE

Was westward expansion a sign of progress? Visit Engage to learn more.

Essential Question

What impact did Manifest Destiny have on the growth and development of the United States?

EXPLORE

Manifest Destiny

What was Manifest Destiny, and what impact did it have on the United States in the mid-1800s?

In the 1840s, many Americans were proud of their country and saw benefits to the acquisition of new territories. The Louisiana Territory, which the United States had purchased from France in 1803 during Thomas Jefferson's presidency, had doubled the size of the nation and created opportunities for Americans who wanted more land. An early supporter of expanding the country's borders was John Quincy Adams, who believed that the whole continent of North America was destined to be controlled by the United States. President Jackson also supported this idea

photo: Getty Images

How can you tell that John Gast's painting American Progress *is promoting westward expansion?*

through the Indian Removal Act in 1830, which relocated Native Americans to west of the Mississippi River, opening new opportunities for expansion into the southeast. Many American voters and members of Congress thought that the United States should try to gain more land and continue to expand all the way to the Pacific Ocean.

In 1845, a magazine editor named John O'Sullivan first used the phrase Manifest Destiny to describe the belief that the United States was going to control and settle land across the continent, from the Atlantic Ocean to the Pacific. The word manifest means "obvious." The word *destiny* means "fate, future, or conclusion." Many people thought it was God's will that the United States grow to fulfill its manifest destiny. O'Sullivan's phrase captured the views of many Americans, including James K. Polk, who was elected president in 1844. Artist John Gast later expressed this view in his 1872 painting *American Progress*.

Social and economic factors combined with the spirit of Manifest Destiny to motivate westward expansion. The emergence of rail transportation, gold rushes in the West, and the availability of cheap land after the relocation of Native Americans made migration to the new territories attractive and simpler for settlers. The settlers who left their homes in the East hoped to find new economic opportunities and to make a living on their own in the frontier. New immigrants to the country also sought these expanded opportunities by traveling to the West instead of settling in the cities where they arrived. In addition, some settlers had religious motivations for moving West. For example, Mormons who moved to Utah hoped to establish a new society for their believers, away from persecution in the cities where they had once settled.

Polk's belief in Manifest Destiny contributed to actions he took as president that resulted in the United States gaining territory in the West. These actions included annexing territory, fighting a war, and signing treaties. Most Americans supported Polk's policies and were pleased with the results. As the United States added territory, Americans moved west to occupy the land. By 1853, the United States had achieved its "destiny" by claiming an enormous swath of land that stretched from the Atlantic Ocean to the Pacific coast.

The Oregon Country

How did the United States acquire the Oregon Country?

In 1818, the United States and Great Britain signed a treaty saying that both nations would share control of the Oregon Country. Canada was a British colony at this time, and the Oregon Country included areas that today are part of western Canada, as well as areas of the states of Washington and Oregon and parts of Idaho and Montana.

From the 1820s to the 1840s, many Americans moved to the Oregon Country. At first, fur traders and trappers had settled the territory, but in the 1830s, missionaries began moving there. They hoped to introduce Christianity to the region's Native Americans. The missionaries sent back glowing reports about Oregon's fertile Willamette Valley, which made others want to move to the region. In the 1840s, thousands of settlers from the East followed the Oregon Trail to the region.

Discovery | SOCIAL STUDIES
EDUCATION | **TECHBOOK**

What impact did Manifest Destiny have on the growth and development of the United States?

By the mid-1840s, many Americans wanted the United States to own the Oregon Country instead of sharing it with Great Britain. The northern boundary of the region was at 54 degrees, 40 minutes north latitude. People who wanted the United States to take over the entire territory used the slogan "Fifty-four forty or fight." Having just finished a war with Great Britain 30 years before, the federal government was not looking for another one. Instead, they signed a treaty with Great Britain in 1846. The treaty divided the Oregon

THE ROCKY MOUNTAINS.

photo: Getty Images

Emigrants crossing the Rocky Mountains.

Country into two parts by extending the 1818 treaty line along the 49th parallel. Britain received the part north of the 49th parallel, and the United States received the part south of that line. With this territory, the United States now spanned from the Atlantic Ocean to the Pacific Ocean. But the United States was not finished adding territory.

The Republic of Texas

How did the United States acquire Texas?

Texas Independence

After the first Europeans arrived in North America, violent resistance by native Apache, Comanche, and Karankawa discouraged British, French, and Spanish colonists from settling in Texas. When Mexico won independence from Spain in 1821, the Mexican state of Coahuila y Texas remained sparsely settled. Then, Mexico attempted to populate the area. It offered large tracts of land to 24 *empresarios*, businesspeople who received land grants to recruit new settlers to the area. Among the first to arrive was Virginia-born Stephen F. Austin, who in 1821 received a grant to settle 300 families along the Brazos and Colorado Rivers. Most of the new settlers to Texas were from the United States. Many were Southerners who brought with them their enslaved persons.

By the 1830s, more than 30,000 immigrants from the United States had settled in Texas. Although they had been invited by Mexico to establish colonies there, these former Americans became unhappy with actions taken by the Mexican government and its president, Antonio López de Santa Anna. Santa Anna's government imposed higher taxes, attempted to outlaw slavery, and disarmed local militia groups. On March 2, 1836, the Texans declared their independence from Mexico and formally established the Republic of Texas. Santa Anna sent troops to enforce his laws and put down unrest.

Mexico in 1847.

photo: Library of Congress

Only a few days after declaring independence, 183 Texas rebels were killed in the Battle of the Alamo by an overwhelming force of 2,400 Mexican soldiers. But a few weeks later, in April 1836, Texans inspired by the rallying cry "Remember the Alamo" won a major victory at the Battle of San Jacinto. There, forces led by Sam Houston captured Santa Anna and forced him to sign a treaty acknowledging Texas's independence. By October, the government of the Republic of Texas was in place, with Sam Houston as its president.

Texas Annexation

Immediately after Texas gained independence, its leaders asked to join the United States. The request was initially denied. President Van Buren and many in Congress feared that taking on Texas would lead to war with Mexico. Many Northerners also objected to the addition of more slave states to the Union.

By the mid-1840s, however, American sentiment for adding Texas had grown. James Polk had campaigned for and won the presidency in 1844 as a strong advocate of westward expansion. In 1845, Congress voted to annex, or add, Texas to the Union. The Texas Annexation made Texas the 28th state and the 15th state where slavery was legal.

The Mexican-American War

What were the causes and main events of the Mexican-American War?

Tensions Between the United States and Mexico

Events in Texas increased tensions between the United States and Mexico. In the first place, Mexicans accused the United States of supporting the Texas independence movement in order to add Texas to its territory. The United States' actual annexation of Texas reinforced those suspicions. To make matters worse, many American settlers in another large Mexican territory, California, also wanted to become part of the United States.

The United States and Mexico also could not agree on the location of Texas's border. The historic border was the Nueces River, but at the end of the Texas War for Independence, Texan revolutionaries tried to change this. They captured Mexican General Santa Anna and forced him to sign a treaty moving the border to the Rio Grande, also called the Rio Bravo, which was about 100 miles west of the Nueces.

Discovery SOCIAL STUDIES
EDUCATION **TECHBOOK**

What impact did Manifest Destiny have on the growth and development of the United States?

The Mexican government renounced this treaty. Santa Anna remained in exile for a year in the United States and was eventually allowed to return to his home in Veracruz.

Soon after taking office in 1845, President Polk sent troops under General Zachary Taylor across the Nueces, into the disputed territory. According to Mexico, Taylor's forces were an army of occupation that had openly violated Mexican sovereignty. When Polk also sent a representative to the Mexican capital at Mexico City to negotiate the border, Mexican officials refused to meet with him. After fighting broke out between Taylor's troops and the Mexican army, Polk blamed Mexico for starting the fighting. He asked Congress to declare war. Congress agreed, and the Mexican-American War officially began in May of 1846.

The Mexican-American War

People in the Southern and Western states supported the war and were happy to continue the nation's quest for more land. But many in the Northeast felt that going to war to gain more territory was morally wrong. In addition, abolitionists, people who wanted to end or abolish slavery, opposed the war because they knew that Southerners would want to expand slavery into the new territory.

One spokesperson for peace was Henry David Thoreau, a writer from Massachusetts. Thoreau refused to pay taxes that would support the war. To explain his views, Thoreau authored the essay "Civil Disobedience." This essay discussed whether people have a moral duty to break laws that they believe are wrong. The term civil disobedience means that a person actively refuses to obey certain laws or commands of a government.

photo: Library of Congress

General Zachary Taylor at the Battle of Buena Vista, 1847.

It is also sometimes, but not always, defined as "nonviolent civil resistance" against these laws. The essay was influential in many eras of U.S. history, such as when citizens in the North refused to obey the Fugitive Slave Laws because they believed that slavery should be abolished. The essay was also influential in modern events throughout U.S. history, including protests during the Civil Rights Movement of the 1950s and 1960s as well as opposition to the Vietnam War.

In spite of opposition, the Mexican-American War was a huge military success. It was fought in several different locations across the Southwest and Mexico. In the summer of 1846, U.S. General Stephen Kearny captured Santa Fe, New Mexico. Kearny established a new government for the new U.S. territory of New Mexico and then marched to California, where another American leader, John C. Frémont, was leading a revolt against Mexican leaders. The Americans quickly gained control of California.

Explore this resource to analyze propaganda from the Mexican-American War.

The final campaigns came in 1847. First, Zachary Taylor captured Buena Vista, a city in northern Mexico. A month later, American General Winfield Scott landed with troops at Veracruz, Mexico. They fought their way inland and soon captured Mexico City. After this battle, Mexican officials agreed to end the war and signed a peace treaty.

The Southwest

How did the United States gain control of the Southwest?

In 1848, the United States and Mexico signed the Treaty of Guadalupe Hidalgo, which officially ended the Mexican-American War. In this treaty, Mexico recognized the Rio Grande as the northern border of Mexico. Mexico also agreed to cede, or give up, a huge area of land to the United States. This area of land, which became known as the Mexican Cession, includes the modern-day states of California, Nevada, Utah, and parts of Arizona, New Mexico, Wyoming, and Colorado. In exchange for this land, the United States agreed to pay Mexico $15 million and also promised that Mexicans who lived in this region could become U.S. citizens.

photo: Getty Images

Surveyors map territory that will be transferred to the United States in the Gadsden Purchase.

Five years later, the United States gained one last piece of territory from Mexico in a deal now known as the Gadsden Purchase. It involved a strip of low, flat desert in what is today southern New Mexico and Arizona. The United States wanted to build a transcontinental railroad there. President Pierce appointed railroad executive James Gadsden as a minister to negotiate a treaty. In 1853, Gadsden arranged for the United States to pay Mexico $10 million for the land. The deal added the final piece of the contiguous United States. Within a period of only about 10 years, the United States had achieved its Manifest Destiny.

Discovery SOCIAL STUDIES
EDUCATION | TECHBOOK

What impact did Manifest Destiny have on the growth and development
of the United States?

Mexican Settlements: Before and After

The new U.S. territories in the Southwest included Mexican settlements. These
settlements were located across the modern states of Texas, New Mexico, Arizona,
and California. At first, the Treaty of Guadalupe Hidalgo required that the land once
belonging to Mexico would be treated as if it were still governed by Mexican law.
This should have meant that the land grants issued by the Mexican government
protected the current residents' land ownership. However, President Polk and the U.S.
Senate removed this requirement. They ensured that American laws would govern the
newly acquired territories.

The lives of former Mexican citizens changed in different ways, often depending on
who they were and where they lived. For example, Native Americans who lived in the
ceded territories were Mexican citizens prior to the signing of the treaty. However,
they were not considered American citizens after the United States acquired the land.
Mexicans who lived in areas that were not quickly settled by Americans were often able
to retain their economic status and political power. Santa Fe, New Mexico, was one such
community. In California, however, which was settled rapidly as a result of the gold rush,
the flood of immigrants from the East viewed Mexican residents as foreigners. They
treated them as second-class citizens and denied them their property rights, political
power, and language rights.

Meanwhile, the question of whether slavery would be permitted in the formerly Mexican
territories intensified sectional tensions between the North and the South. The inability
of the two sides to reach a lasting compromise would soon tear the Union apart.

Trailblazers

*Who were some of the most famous explorers of the western
United States?*

As the country's territorial holdings began to expand, a group of trailblazing
explorers embarked on dangerous adventures to explore the western United States.
Pioneers and settlers would later follow in their footsteps.

A Mountain Man in California

Jedediah Smith (1798–1831) was born in New York, but his explorations took him all the
way to the other side of the continent. Smith was a mountain man—a fur trapper, trader,
and explorer. When he was 22 years old, Smith joined General William Ashley on an
expedition to trap beavers in Missouri. Smith would later take part in expeditions that
explored pathways into Wyoming and California. His party became the first group to
reach California from the east by crossing the Mojave Desert and to return over land.

In 1827, Smith made the California journey again. Most of his group was killed in a Mojave warrior attack. Smith and the other survivors went on to California and then traveled up the West Coast to Oregon. In 1831, Smith settled in Santa Fe, New Mexico, as a trader. He was killed that year by Comanche warriors. A California state park was named in Smith's honor.

Pike and the Peak

Not all trailblazers were mountain men. Zebulon Pike (1779–1813) was a soldier who joined the army at age 15. In 1805, the army sent him with a party of explorers to what would become Missouri. Pike's party was sent to find the source of the Mississippi River. The next year, the army sent Pike to explore the southwest. While traveling through what would become Colorado, Pike discovered a mountain and tried to climb it. He failed, but the mountain would later be named Pike's Peak after him.

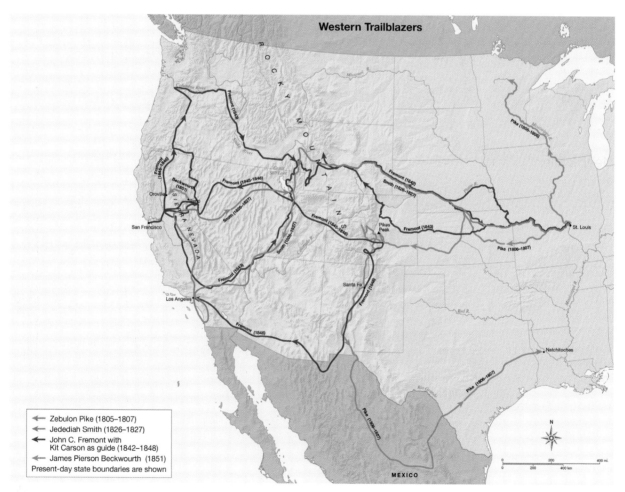

Western Trailblazers

Zebulon Pike (1805–1807)
Jedediah Smith (1826–1827)
John C. Fremont with
Kit Carson as guide (1842–1848)
James Pierson Beckwourth (1851)
Present-day state boundaries are shown

This map shows famous western trails established by Jedediah Smith, Zebulon Pike, Kit Carson, James Pierson Beckwourth, and John C. Fremont.

What impact did Manifest Destiny have on the growth and development of the United States?

Legends of the West

Many of the western trailblazers had stories that sounded more like fiction than history. Some of them actually did become the subjects of books and tall tales. For example, in 1842, frontiersman Kit Carson (1809–1868) became a guide for John C. Fremont (1813–1890), an explorer and military officer. Carson guided Fremont, and in return Fremont wrote about Carson in his expedition reports, making Carson a popular figure in the West. In 1862, Carson helped organize New Mexican forces during the New Mexican Civil War.

Carson had lived with Native Americans, and even married two of them, but toward the end of his life he turned against them. In 1863 and 1864, Carson fought against the Navajo of Arizona, destroying their crops and livestock, and finally forcing them to leave.

Jim Beckwourth (1798–1867) also lived among Native Americans for many years. Beckwourth's father was white but his mother was enslaved, which meant he was legally enslaved at birth. He was freed from slavery as a child and later became a fur trader in the West. He lived with the Crow people for around six years. Then, he left to blaze a trail through the Sierra Mountains into California at the beginning of the gold rush in 1848. A journalist named Thomas D. Bonner wrote a book about Beckwourth that made him famous.

Water in the West

Once the trailblazers had opened paths, more work needed to be done to make the western United States livable. Unlike other parts of the North American continent, the West had very little water. The land was dry, brown, and very difficult to farm. Many pioneers who traveled west in search of a better life were not aware of this. The Native Americans, Spanish settlers, and Mormons who lived in these regions understood how to irrigate the land and share water cooperatively. The pioneers did not have this knowledge.

In 1868, a former soldier named John Wesley Powell began to explore the western United States and the Native Americans living there. Powell believed that to survive in the West, people needed to find a way to distribute water without fighting over it. In 1878, he published a water strategy called *Report on the Lands of the Arid Region*. This strategy involved small communities that shared nearby water resources. However, Powell's strategy did not allow for the growth of large cities, and his advice was ignored.

Western settlements tried to use private irrigation companies to solve their water problem, but they all failed. In 1902, Congress passed the Reclamation Act, which involved building dams in major rivers and taking the water from there. This strategy allowed the western United States to grow rapidly and become the populous place it is today.

Explore this interactive to learn more about how the United States expanded from coast to coast.

Consider the Essential Question:

What impact did Manifest Destiny have on the growth and development of the United States?

Go online to complete the Social Studies Explanation.

Check for Understanding:

Explain the idea of Manifest Destiny. What role did Manifest Destiny play in the expansion of the United States?

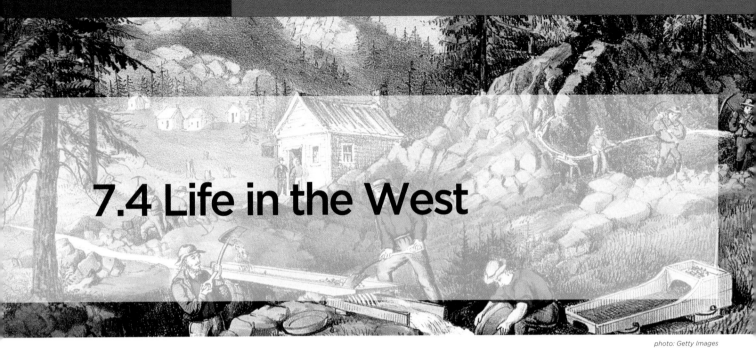

Discovery | SOCIAL STUDIES
EDUCATION | **TECHBOOK**

For various groups, what was life like in newly settled areas of the West?

7.4 Life in the West

photo: Getty Images

LESSON OVERVIEW

Introduction

In this concept, you will discover how moving west transformed the lives of Americans during the 1800s.

Essential Question

For various groups, what was life like in newly settled areas of the West?

Lesson Objectives

By the end of this lesson, you should be able to:

- Describe dynamics of daily life in the West from a variety of perspectives.

- Explain political, geographic, economic, and cultural factors that affected the population of the West during the first half of the 1800s.

Key Vocabulary

Which terms do you already know?

- ☐ Andrew Johnson
- ☐ Brigham Young
- ☐ California
- ☐ California gold rush
- ☐ forty-niners
- ☐ Fugitive Slave Laws
- ☐ missionary
- ☐ Mormons
- ☐ Oregon Trail
- ☐ reservation
- ☐ Santa Fe Trail
- ☐ vaquero

ENGAGE

What risks come with chasing a dream? Visit Engage to learn more.

> ### Essential Question
> For various groups, what was life like in newly settled areas of the West?

EXPLORE

Lure of the West

Why did the western frontier beckon to settlers?

Most Americans lived and worked on farms during the first half of the 1800s. But the eastern United States had become increasingly crowded, and land was becoming expensive. Settlers in search of farmland, often called pioneers, migrated to the West, the part of the United States west of the Mississippi River. The West included the Louisiana Purchase, which in 1803 had added 828,000 square miles to the United States. Between 1803 and 1848, the United States also acquired the Oregon Country, Texas, and the Mexican Cession, an additional 1.2 million square miles.

photo: Library of Congress

Settlers headed west in wagon trains along the 2,000-mile California Trail—a difficult journey that took around five months.

Most pioneers were young and adventurous, but all had to be strong and healthy enough to survive the arduous, or long and difficult, journey. They also had to be prosperous enough to afford it. Less affluent settlers joined them as ranchhands, farmhands, or domestic servants.

Discovery EDUCATION | SOCIAL STUDIES TECHBOOK.

For various groups, what was life like in newly settled areas of the West?

In the early 1800s, pioneers migrated west of the Mississippi River to stake out settlements where they could seek more favorable circumstances. Before departing on the frontier experience, pioneers weighed the advantages and disadvantages involved in relocating into unsettled territories. On one hand, the Western frontier promised boundless opportunities with an abundance of fertile farmland that was affordable or even free. On the other hand, the road westward was paved with difficulties. Travel was expensive, dangerous, and time consuming, taking months to travel across the country. Some travelers journeyed by water, taking steamboats, canal boats, and riverboats to their destinations. Others used overland routes, braving rough roads in covered wagon trains.

Travelers faced hardships caused by severe weather, natural disasters including floods and landslides, diseases such as cholera epidemics, and starvation. In one severe case, heavy snows trapped the Donner Party when they attempted a shortcut through the Sierra Nevada Mountains in 1846. As the 87 pioneers began to starve and freeze to death, some of the survivors resorted to cannibalism.

In the 1830s, missionaries went west too, following the pioneers in wagon trains and joining caravans of fur traders to make the 2,000-mile journey on the Oregon Trail. These missionaries represented various churches: Catholic, Congregational, Episcopal, Methodist, and Presbyterian. The American Board of Commissioners for Foreign Missions sent them to spread their faith and do medical and social work. They established missions where they attempted to convert Native Americans to Christianity and to minister to fur traders who trapped beavers along the Columbia River. The first missionaries wrote letters back home describing Oregon's fertile Columbia River basin. The descriptions attracted new settlers, including farmers, ranchers, traders, and their families, who ventured west seeking economic opportunity.

Explore this interactive to learn more about settlement trends during westward expansion.

Over time, this pattern of western settlement changed the population distribution of the United States. Since colonial times, most of the nation's population had been concentrated in the northeast along the East Coast and other major bodies of water. However, continual migration to the West meant that the population became more concentrated in this direction. For example, consider the mean center of the U.S. population, which is defined by the United States Census Bureau as "the point at which an imaginary, flat, weightless, and rigid map of the United States would balance perfectly if weights of identical value were placed on it so that each weight represented the location of one person [on the date of the census]."

In simplest terms, this point represents the geographic center of the U.S. population. It is a way to measure the spatial distribution of people across the United States. Gradually, this point moved northwest and then southwest as people first moved into the Northwest Territory and then into the other new territories toward the South.

The physical geography of the West influenced this trend in a number ways, such as the large jump of nearly 50 miles in 1870 after the completion of the transcontinental railroad.

Endless Labor on the Farm

What was life like for a farmer in the West?

Farming families heading to the American West could acquire land from speculators, land traders who organized western expeditions for people eager to resettle after the War of 1812. Speculators, or people who try to make large amounts of money from risky investments, purchased large chunks of unsettled territory and sold smaller parcels to individual farmers, often at highly inflated prices. However, after 1841, government land grants were not permitted to go to land speculators. As a result, more farmers could purchase land at a fair price directly from the government.

On western land, President Andrew Johnson's "industrious settlers" raised cattle and grew crops. Every member of a farm family worked, and farmwork was not easy. After a

photo: Library of Congress

Life on the plains prepping supper, 1866.

hearty breakfast that might include flapjacks and sausages washed down with coffee, men labored in the fields. They cleared and plowed with oxen, tended cattle, planted and gathered crops, and built and repaired fences. Some farmers exchanged labor with each other. For example, neighbors who each needed a barn built would work together to build two barns.

Because they frequently came during childbearing years, family decisions to move west were disruptive for many women. On both the long journey west and after settlement, most women performed traditional but essential roles in often difficult circumstances. They were expected to maintain order and stability in a frontier life that presented many challenges. They also raised children and cared for the sick.

In often trying conditions such as extreme weather, women had much to do gathering and preparing food. Farm women frequently baked; preserved fruits, vegetables, and meats; and cooked meals—usually four per day. They gathered eggs, milked cows and goats, churned butter, and made cheese. When they could, they sold these goods to general stores in the nearest city and used the income to purchase goods they could not make themselves, such as flour, cornmeal, and coffee.

Children as young as four labored on the farm. Their daily tasks included fetching water from wells and rain barrels, hauling in wood for the fireplace and cookstove, and filling lamps with kerosene.

Traders and Fortune Seekers

What events attracted settlers to New Mexico and California?

Santa Fe

In 1821, after a successful revolution, Mexico won independence from Spain. This opened up new territories and trade opportunities for merchants from the East. American traders traveled along the Santa Fe Trail, a roadway that linked Independence, Missouri, with Santa Fe, an important settlement on the Mexican frontier. Native Americans established Santa Fe as early as 900 CE, and Spain made it the capital of the colonial province of New Mexico—*Nuevo México*—in 1610.

MARCH OF THE CARAVAN.

photo: Getty Images

Merchants followed the Santa Fe Trail to trade goods at the New Mexico settlement.

New Mexicans were eager for manufactured goods. They welcomed William Becknell, the first trader to bring manufactured goods to sell in New Mexico in 1822. His trip was so successful, earning Becknell a 2,000 percent profit, that other traders quickly followed. Their wagons and pack animals hauled pots and pans, knives, nails, saws, hoes, glass, shoes, and cloth. Santa Fe citizens traded beaver pelts and blankets for merchandise.

The Gold Rush

Farther west, in California, another event ushered in a new surge of trailblazers from across the United States, and eventually around the world. In January 1848, James Wilson Marshall, a worker at John Sutter's sawmill, discovered a golden nugget in the American River near Sacramento.

As word of the discovery leaked out, a trickle of gold seekers arrived from San Francisco in spring of 1848. These early miners were the most likely to strike it rich. They dug with pocketknives or sluiced water in gold pans to discover "easy" surface gold. A surge of prospectors arrived by the end of that year, traveling to the gold fields. In 1849, nearly 100,000 fortune seekers flooded in from every corner of the globe—places as far as Oregon, Hawaii, Chile, and Peru. Forty-niners from the East spent up to nine months on their journey, traveling across mountains by foot or mule.

The gold rush, this sudden wave of migration to new territory after gold had been discovered, helped expand the United States from the Atlantic to the Pacific. In 1850, California was admitted as the 31st state of the Union. Gold-mining production crested to a high of $81 million in 1852. While the annual take steadily declined, California's population continued to grow, reaching 380,000 by the end of the 1850s.

Rushing Toward Riches

What was life like for a miner in the West?

Most of the forty-niners were men, and many of them had left behind their families for this opportunity. Some believed that gold carpeted the ground, flooded the rivers, and was there for the grabbing.

photo: Getty Images

This picture illustrates the crude "placer" mining techniques that the surface deposits in California made possible.

They quickly discovered the harsh reality that mining for gold requires hard work. Prospectors who arrived in the early stages of the gold rush had the greatest likelihood of striking it rich. A miner could pry gold nuggets from rocks using a knife or a pickax. He could also swirl river sediment in a pan of water to see whether any of the heavy gold settled at the bottom.

The fortunate few could unearth $2,000 of gold in a day. Most, however, were lucky to dig or pan $10 worth of gold in a day. Mining became more demanding as more prospectors poured into the region, making surface gold more and more difficult to find.

Before taking up mining, forty-niners had previously practiced other trades, such as farming, teaching, cooking, and keeping shop. Most were not accustomed to hard labor and rough conditions. Miners pitched tents in camps. Many had trouble adjusting to sleeping on the cold ground. They cooked beans over open campfires and, because of their poor diet, suffered from scurvy, an illness caused by a lack of vitamin C. Camps frequently burned down. Accidents and drowning were also common.

Those miners who survived found that supplies quickly became unaffordable. As the competition for gold became greater, mining supplies and even food became scarce. Businesspeople found they could raise their prices higher and higher and the miners would still buy. Flour soared to $40 a barrel; beef cost 75 cents per pound; a single egg cost $1. The going rate for boots was $25. A wagon could cost $80 and a mule $150.

Some enterprising businesspeople earned fortunes providing goods and services to successful miners. Along with selling overpriced goods, they set up boardinghouses, cooked meals, and washed clothes.

Claiming Native Tribal Lands

Why were Native Americans of the West confined to reservations?

As you will recall, the United States expanded by adding Western lands to its territory, including the Louisiana Purchase in 1803 and the Mexican Cession in 1848. These lands encompassed the ancestral homelands of hundreds of Native American tribes. They called this region home long before the United States came into existence. In the push westward, settlers demanded increasing amounts of land—land on which people already lived.

Reservations and Indian Territory

The United States resolved this issue by establishing reservations—specific areas set aside for exclusive use by Native American tribes. The first formal reservation was established for the Choctaw in Mississippi in 1786, but as the population in the East grew, Native American reservations were moved across the Appalachians. The U.S. government continued the policy of forcing Native Americans out of lands that settlers wanted and relocating them on reservations in the West.

For instance, in 1838, the United States relocated several tribes of Iroquois to Kansas from their homes in New York State. Most of the reservation land was undesirable to settlers, who did not know how to deal with the prairie's extreme climate and the grassland ecosystem.

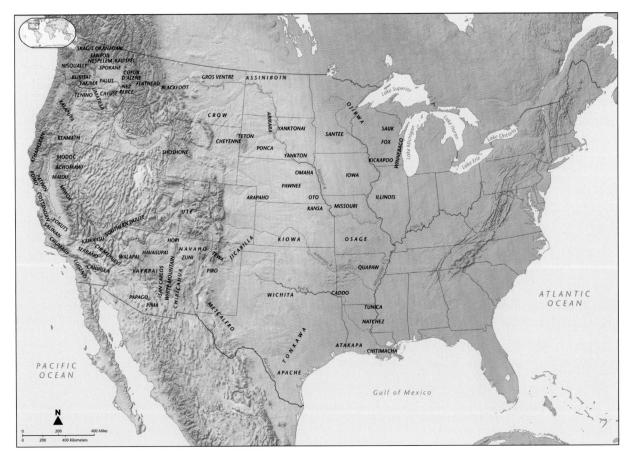

Illustrated map of Native American tribal regions.

This policy continued when the United States annexed lands in the West. In the process of forming new states out of territories, Native Americans were pushed out of areas of California, Oregon, and the Great Plains to make room for settlers. The Indian Appropriations Act in 1851 formally established the Indian Territory, in present-day Oklahoma. Native Americans throughout the country were forced to sign treaties giving up any rights to their homelands in exchange for a parcel of land in Indian Territory. Most Native Americans in the West were *seminomadic*, which means they relocated their villages seasonally, so a year-round home in Oklahoma was not very suitable.

Native American Resistance

Under pressure from the U.S. government, some Native American nations faced the inevitable and agreed to move to reservations. Others put up a fight, attacking settlers who invaded their hunting grounds.

The period between the mid-1830s and 1890 was marked by frequent battles small and large between Plains Indians and settlers. The U.S. Army constructed forts as outposts to house troops and provide protection to settlers from Native American attacks. The settlers, supported by the army, and the natives raided each other's settlements; destroyed each other's livestock, food supplies, and homes; and ruthlessly attacked both civilians and warriors. The battles with the Comanche in Texas in 1836, the Apache in New Mexico in 1849, the Yuma in Arizona and the Ute in Utah in 1850, the Sioux in 1854, the Yakima in Washington in 1855, and the Navajo in New Mexico in 1858 are just a few examples of these encounters.

A New Wave of Immigrants

Why did Asians immigrate to California?

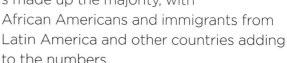

Immigrants from around the world came to the United States after 1849, lured by the prospect of gold. American miners made up the majority, with African Americans and immigrants from Latin America and other countries adding to the numbers.

Chinese Americans made up one-fifth of the population in California's gold-mining region by the end of the 1850s. But not all of them worked as miners. Some worked at jobs providing miners with goods and services. Chinese immigrants opened shops to sell goods to miners and provided services such as cooking meals and washing laundry. These immigrants lived together in neighborhoods known as Chinatowns, including one that continues to thrive in San Francisco.

photo: California State Library
Chinese immigrants arrived in California hoping to make a fortune and then return home to China.

Discovery | SOCIAL STUDIES
EDUCATION | TECHBOOK

For various groups, what was life like in newly settled areas of the West?

While Chinese immigrants played a significant role in the California economy, they faced frequent discrimination. Miners resented the Chinese. Laws prohibited Chinese Americans from filing new mining claims, so Chinese miners were forced to work older, exhausted claims. These immigrants were also forced to pay a Foreign Miners Tax in 1852 on top of an earlier 1850 tax imposed on non-Americans. Low pay combined with these taxes and racial discrimination made financial success largely unreachable.

Explore this activity to learn more about the experiences of Chinese immigrants in the West.

The Mormon Trail to Salt Lake City

Why did Mormons relocate to Utah?

Members of the Church of Jesus Christ of Latter-day Saints are usually known as Mormons. Mormonism was founded in 1830 by Joseph Smith. In the early days of this church, Mormons were persecuted and often driven from their communities because of their religious beliefs, such as *polygamy*, or the custom of having more than one wife at the same time. People also feared that Mormon leaders wanted to provide leadership for both church and state. Mormons sought a safe spot where they could practice their faith peacefully. In 1846, Mormons left their home base in Nauvoo, Illinois, and traveled to a temporary community in Winter Quarters, Nebraska. From there, they moved on to Salt Lake City, Utah.

Brigham Young, second president of the Church of Jesus Christ of Latter-day Saints, led the migration westward to Utah, which was then a part of Mexico. He headed a wagon train of 143 men, three women, and two boys along a route that became known as the Mormon Trail. Previous pioneers, including explorers, missionaries, and fur traders, had roughly blazed this 1,300-mile course. Young and his followers improved the trail by building bridges, setting up campsites, and launching ferries.

photo: Getty Images

A Mormon frontier settlement in the far west.

Approximately 70,000 Mormons would eventually follow the Mormon Trail, migrating in wagons, pushing handcarts, or walking.

In 1847, the first wave of Mormons settled Salt Lake City near the Great Salt Lake in what is now Utah. They irrigated and cultivated the arid soil, planting crops such as potatoes and turnips. The Mormon pioneers built a fort to protect their new settlement. Their city thrived, and Mormons spread out across the area.

Some Mormons relocated to California during the gold rush. They set up an early mining camp known as Mormon Island. Mormon prospectors tithed, or paid one-tenth of their earnings, to the Church of Jesus Christ of Latter-day Saints, which grew wealthy.

Expanding into the Southwest

Who were America's first cowboys?

When the Mexican-American War ended in 1848, Mexico lost almost half of its territory to the United States. In the Treaty of Guadalupe Hidalgo, the United States paid $15 million in exchange for Mexico's northern lands, including much of present-day California, Nevada, Arizona, New Mexico, Colorado, and Utah.

This Mexican Cession, the land ceded by Mexico in the 1848 treaty that followed the Mexican-American War, expanded the United States by more than 500,000 square miles and added approximately 80,000 people of Mexican and Spanish descent to the

photo: Library of Congress
Californio vaqueros (cowboys) roping a steer near San Francisco, 1849.

United States. Most chose to become U.S. citizens. Although these Mexican Americans were guaranteed citizenship and property rights, some settlers who moved into the Southwest treated them as foreigners and pushed them off their land.

A number of these new Mexican Americans were *vaqueros*, or cow herders, in the cattle industry. Vaqueros were the Americas' first cowboys, riding the open range back when Mexico was still a territory of the Spanish Empire. It took skill and courage to control herds of cattle while riding on horseback. The vaqueros invented the lasso to rope livestock that roamed through the valleys and plains. Vaqueros taught new, inexperienced Southwestern settlers how to round up cattle and move them onto ranches. They also showed settlers how to catch and tame mustangs, horses that roamed free throughout western North America.

The Struggle for Freedom in the West

Why did African Americans migrate West?

After the United States won the war with Mexico in 1848 and expanded westward, Congress debated whether to allow or prohibit slavery in the new territory. In 1849, California requested permission to enter the Union as a free state. It received permission in one of the bills that made up the Compromise of 1850. In this compromise, the Southwestern territories of Arizona, Nevada, New Mexico, and Utah were organized. Their inhabitants would decide the issue of slavery later when they applied for statehood.

Discovery | SOCIAL STUDIES
EDUCATION | TECHBOOK

For various groups, what was life like in newly settled areas of the West?

Even though California was supposedly a slave-free zone, slavery still thrived in some regions. Also, the state's 1852 Fugitive Slave Law allowed slaveholders to recapture runaway slaves within its borders. Because African Americans were not allowed to vote or testify in court, they could not defend themselves against the charge of being a runaway slave, regardless of the truth.

When the gold rush began, some slave owners brought enslaved people to do the hard work of mining for gold. A main reason slavery was banned in California was that other miners thought owning enslaved persons provided an unfair advantage. Some slave owners even sent enslaved laborers on their own to California to mine for gold. In some cases, these enslaved laborers were able to make unusual agreements with their owners and earned their freedom by laboring for a few years in the mines or by striking gold and turning the wealth over to their masters in exchange for their freedom.

photo: Getty Images

Enslaved African Americans mined for gold during the gold rush, seeking to buy their freedom from their Southern owners once California was declared a free state.

Despite the racist discrimination, free African Americans continued to arrive in the West after hearing reports of prosperous miners. During the gold rush years, many African Americans mined alongside workers from different backgrounds. Others earned money by providing services and supplies to miners. These African American entrepreneurs cooked meals, cut hair, sold mining supplies and clothing, opened horse stables, and operated hotels and restaurants. By 1852, African Americans were 1 percent of California's population.

Opportunities, Challenges, and Gender in the West

How did life in the West create opportunities for women?

More men than women went west to seek their fortunes in the late 1800s. Traders on the plains and miners in California often married Native American women in the early years of western settlement. Though white men outnumbered white women on the frontier, it was not just men who made the journey to Oregon, California, and other places in the West. Women who went out west often found opportunities that weren't available back east.

Because life in the West was difficult and unpredictable, many states began to provide extra legal rights allowing widows and other women to own and purchase land. Western states were the first to allow women to vote and hold political office, though these rights were usually reserved for only white women.

In the cities and farming communities of the established United States, women were expected to get married, raise children, and focus on domestic work. In the West, single women could become teachers, farm their own land, or even become ranchers. Middle-class white women said that they were helping to "civilize" the West. At the time, women were seen as naturally more moral and religious than men.

Famous Women in the West

Married women were also able to take on larger roles in western society. Annie Bidwell lived with her husband, John, in Chico, California, in the late 1800s. She became famous for attempting to "Christianize" and "Americanize" the Native Americans who worked on her family's ranch. Though people at the time saw her efforts as proof that white women needed to help settle the West, they ignored the impact on Native Americans themselves. She also was active in many of the reform movements of the age, including the movements to outlaw alcohol and allow women to vote. Annie helped secure women's right to vote in the West, and, in 1869, Wyoming Territory was the first western settlement to allow women to vote.

Camp 100 ~ Humboldt ~ River

photo: Library of Congress

Camp 100 on the Humboldt River in Nevada.

Working-class women supported themselves as laundresses, waitresses, and dancers. Still other women were drawn to rougher jobs, like stagecoach driver or ranch hand. Women like Martha "Calamity Jane" Cannary became famous because of their unusual exploits alongside men. Calamity Jane lost both of her parents at a young age and worked as a scout to support her siblings. She became a legend in the West for her rugged personality, horsemanship, and shooting ability. Stories about her adventures—many of them untrue—became very popular. Her legend shows how women were able to chart new lives out west.

Discovery SOCIAL STUDIES
EDUCATION **TECHBOOK**

For various groups, what was life like in newly settled areas of the West?

Forging New Gender Identities in the West

The West's most famous stagecoach driver, Charley Parkhurst, was born a woman. Charley lived as a man, and his gender at birth was only discovered upon his death. Stagecoach drivers had to be tough and quick because there were so many robberies on the frontier. Charley earned a reputation for being especially skilled at defending his passengers and cargo. His life is an example of the ways people could define their own lives on the western frontier, outside the traditional expectations for men and women that were common in the East.

Consider the Essential Question:

For various groups, what was life like in newly settled areas of the West?

Go online to complete the Social Studies Explanation.

Check for Understanding:

Analyze geographic, economic, and cultural factors that influenced the westward shift of the nation's population distribution and settlement patterns. Which factor was most significant?

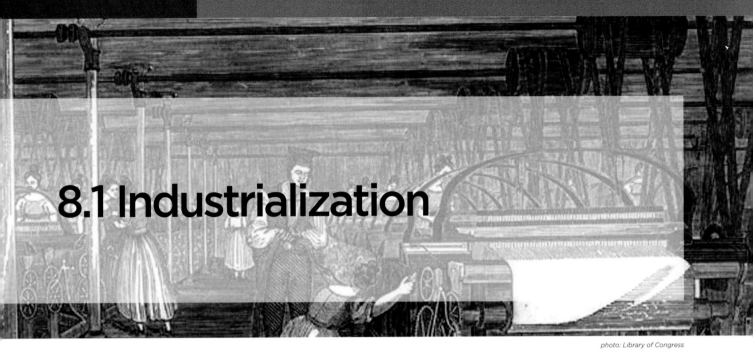

8.1 Industrialization

photo: Library of Congress

LESSON OVERVIEW

Introduction

In this concept, you will learn about the role New England mills played in the Industrial Revolution. This was a time of significant changes in the daily lives of many Americans due to the rise of the factory system and a shift from reliance on human labor to machine labor. You will examine inventions and changes that took place in manufacturing, agriculture, transportation, communication, and daily life. You will see how these changes created a "revolution" in people's lives.

Key Vocabulary

Which terms do you already know?

- ☐ automate
- ☐ cotton gin
- ☐ Cyrus McCormick
- ☐ economy
- ☐ Eli Whitney
- ☐ Elias Howe
- ☐ Erie Canal
- ☐ Francis Cabot Lowell
- ☐ Industrial Revolution
- ☐ industrialization
- ☐ interchangeable parts
- ☐ Isaac M. Singer
- ☐ John Deere
- ☐ Lowell
- ☐ Lowell System

- ☐ market revolution
- ☐ mass production
- ☐ Massachusetts
- ☐ mercantilism
- ☐ Rhode Island System
- ☐ Richard Arkwright
- ☐ Robert Fulton
- ☐ Samuel Morse
- ☐ Samuel Slater
- ☐ socialism
- ☐ steam locomotive
- ☐ technology
- ☐ telegraph
- ☐ textile

Essential Question

Did the benefits of technological advances made during the Industrial Revolution outweigh the costs?

Lesson Objectives

By the end of this lesson, you should be able to:

- Explain the Industrial Revolution and discuss its impact on the production of goods and the workplace in the United States.

- Describe key inventions of the Industrial Revolution, such as the cotton gin, reaper, steamboat, and steam locomotive, and analyze their impact on life in the United States.

Discovery | SOCIAL STUDIES
EDUCATION | **TECHBOOK**

Did the benefits of technological advances made during the Industrial Revolution outweigh the costs?

ENGAGE

Why did factory workers write about the beauties of nature? Visit Engage to learn more.

Essential Question

Did the benefits of technological advances made during the Industrial Revolution outweigh the costs?

EXPLORE

The Rise of Free Enterprise in the United States

How did the free enterprise economic system develop in the United States?

The American Revolution resulted in part from colonists' desire to throw off Britain's economic chains. Evolving political and social ideas about individual liberties combined with innovative economic theories to spur demands for independence. In *The Wealth of Nations*, British thinker Adam Smith proposed a laissez faire economic system. *Laissez faire* is French for "free to do." Known as free market, free enterprise, or capitalist economic system, laissez faire proposes that economies operate best when directed by private individuals and businesses with minimal government intervention. Smith suggested that when they are free to operate, private forces would direct economic choices for the benefit of all.

photo: Library of Congress

Adam Smith proposed a free enterprise, or market, system that emphasized individual self-interest. Such a laissez-faire economy, he said, would be self-regulating.

He believed that citizens should pay taxes to support government functions, such as defense, but that most wealth and property should remain in private hands. The people, not the government, knew best how to produce goods, perform services, and purchase products. Competition between businesses would keep prices of goods low and the quality of goods high. Well-run businesses would do well and poorly run businesses would be pushed out of the market.

During the 1800s, the United States became a nation in which many of its citizens, but not all, enjoyed far more freedoms and opportunities than ever before. Many people in the young nation agreed with Smith's free enterprise ideas and started new businesses, conducted trade, and advanced their economic interests. Entrepreneurs are people who take risks to start businesses, or enterprises. Many entrepreneurs fail, but some succeed and earn large profits. The possibility of financial success, sometimes called the profit motive, provides a strong incentive for entrepreneurs and businesses in a free enterprise system to innovate and grow.

Government's Role in Free Enterprise

In its early years, the United States struggled with financial issues. The revolution had left the nation in debt, and the first Congress lacked the power to require states to contribute. The Constitution granted the federal government powers to regulate interstate and international commerce. It also authorized the federal government to raise taxes to support government services, such as paying national debts. However, many people remained wary of too much government power and too many taxes.

The nation's first government officials struggled to balance public and private interests. Some wanted no government interference in economic affairs. Others argued for limited roles for government to collect taxes and regulate trade. As secretary of the Treasury, Alexander Hamilton believed that the nation needed a national bank and a national currency in order to engage in international trade and get out of debt. However, he also believed that private individuals and businesses needed more of their own money to start enterprises and grow the economy. Hamilton supported passage of copyright and patent laws. These laws protected the rights of authors, artists, and inventors to their creative works, or intellectual property. Individuals were more willing to take risks when they believed that they would "own" the product of their risks and be able to earn money. These intellectual property rights reflected property rights already stated in the Fourth Amendment and the Fifth Amendment to the U.S. Constitution.

Businesspeople also needed money to build machines and factories and to transport their new products to markets. New forms of transportation, too, were on the rise, and needed funding. In 1791, Philadelphia organized the first stock exchange. There, people came to buy, sell, and trade stocks, or monetary investments, in companies. A stockholder could own a share, or a portion, of the company and receive a portion of the company's profits. Businesses used the investments from stockholders to grow.

Discovery SOCIAL STUDIES
EDUCATION TECHBOOK

Did the benefits of technological advances made during the
Industrial Revolution outweigh the costs?

On March 8, 1817, the New York Stock Exchange opened its doors on Wall Street in Manhattan. Banks, too, became big businesses as they began lending more money to entrepreneurs and businesses. Today, entrepreneurs still often start their businesses with a bank loan.

Across Two Centuries

In the 1700s, agriculture and trade were the biggest businesses in the United States. Cash crops such as tobacco and rice grown in the Southern United States were in high demand around the world. Merchants from New England could make a fortune transporting goods between North American ports, Europe, and the Caribbean. Under British rule, however, much of this trade was restricted and taxed. There were limits on which goods could be produced in North America and which countries North American merchants could trade with. The Revolutionary War lifted many of these restrictions, opening new markets for American products.

By the early 1800s, inventors developed new technologies for farming, transportation, and even clothing. These inventors and entrepreneurs took advantage of the free enterprise system to build businesses to develop, promote, and sell their new products. These new inventions would change the way Americans worked and lived.

The Industrial Revolution Begins

How did the Industrial Revolution begin?

In the 1700s, most people in the United States were farmers, and most goods were made by hand, either in homes or in small shops. However, toward the end of the century people in Great Britain began inventing machines to make more goods faster and more efficiently.

The change from hand production to machine production and the development of factories that paid workers daily wages were both part of the movement known as the Industrial Revolution. In a relatively short time, people's home and work lives completely changed because of new inventions and ways of working. The Industrial Revolution spurred another economic development, the market revolution. During the market revolution, capitalism began to become a part of the everyday lives of more Americans. Instead of producing their own food and clothing, for example, more individuals and families began buying mass-produced items in the marketplace.

photo: Library of Congress

Women work in the central office of the Isaac M. Singer Company in New York City.

The first industry to use machines was the textile, or cloth, industry. In the 1700s, the first textile factories appeared in Great Britain. By automating production—using machines instead of people to spin thread and weave cloth—the new textile factories were able to produce huge amounts of cloth quickly and at little cost.

These early factories were built along England's rivers, as they needed water power to run the machines. The British attempted to keep the plans for their factories and machinery secret. They passed laws prohibiting textile machine plans from being sent out of the country and forbade anyone working with those machines to leave the country. The British tried to protect the new industry and the global demand for British textiles, but keeping this technology secret proved difficult.

The Industrial Revolution Comes to New England
How were the first factories in the United States built?

In 1789, a British mechanic named Samuel Slater secretly left Great Britain and went to the United States. Slater had memorized the plans for textile plant machinery and was able to reproduce them. In 1793, Slater and others built the first cotton-spinning mill in the United States in Pawtucket, Rhode Island. Within about 15 years, Slater helped run 12 different mills in New England.

photo: Library of Congress

As this painting shows, numerous mills were built in Lowell, as well as boardinghouses and other buildings for the factory workers.

The textile industry underwent a series of major changes. First came machines that could spin raw cotton into yarn. Soon afterward, people developed power looms, which wove that yarn into cloth. A wealthy entrepreneur named Francis Cabot Lowell built the first factory that combined these different aspects of making textiles all under one roof. He then built a whole complex of factories along the Merrimack River in Massachusetts, in a town later renamed Lowell. Lowell's factories were built along the river because they used water power to run their machines.

At first, the workers in the Lowell mills were mostly girls and young women from nearby farms. They wanted an opportunity to earn money and live on their own. With the country's growing population, there were limited opportunities for farm wives in the East, and women were not expected to pursue education or careers.

Discovery EDUCATION | SOCIAL STUDIES TECHBOOK

Did the benefits of technological advances made during the Industrial Revolution outweigh the costs?

While New England's land was not ideal for farming, it had many rivers to provide the water power the early mills needed. In addition, some New Englanders, such as Francis Cabot Lowell, previously made their fortunes in trade and shipping, so they had money to invest in new factories. These factories went on to manufacture goods other than textiles, including power looms and locomotives, which were shipped to other regions and European countries. The region's economy grew throughout the 1800s as New England became the center of trading between the Southern states and Europe. Many towns and states fostered this economic growth with construction projects for new roads, bridges, and other transportation routes for the manufactured goods. A growing banking industry in New England provided loans to start and grow businesses. In addition, the labor force expanded greatly as more and more people moved to towns to work for wages in factories, rather than working on farms or in small shops where they had made goods by hand.

Explore this resource to learn more about women who worked in Lowell's mills.

However, working conditions in the mills were difficult and dangerous. Aside from the dangers of the machinery, machine noise was oppressive, the air was filled with particles of thread and cloth, and windows were kept closed during the summer. Workers worked long hours for little money—73 hours per week was standard. Workers frequently protested working conditions. Over time, immigrants from Europe replaced women workers.

Eli Whitney

What role did Eli Whitney play in the Industrial Revolution?

Whitney's Cotton Gin

Because factories could create cloth from cotton more quickly than before, they increased the demand for clean, raw cotton from the South. Southern farmers had a hard time keeping up with this demand because the process of cleaning the seeds out of cotton plants was very time consuming.

In 1793, Eli Whitney, a mechanic from Massachusetts, solved this problem by inventing the cotton engine, or cotton gin. This machine used wire teeth to pull the seeds out of the cotton and sped up the cleaning process tremendously. The invention of the cotton gin created economic prosperity in the South by causing massive growth in the production of cotton. For example, the number of cotton bales produced rose from about 750,000 in 1830 to 2.85 million in 1850. Many Southern farmers decided to focus on the growth of cotton instead of other crops, and so the Southern economy began to depend heavily on cotton. Cotton production was tremendously profitable business, in part due to its reliance on slave labor, and cities such as New Orleans in Louisiana, Mobile in Alabama, and Charleston in South Carolina became major ports for shipping cotton to be processed into textile in the North. Because of the large cotton supply, the price of cotton-based products, such as textiles for clothes, decreased for consumers.

However, the number of enslaved people also increased to meet the needs of the South's cotton production, rising to more than 3.2 million in 1850.

photo: Getty Images

Eli Whitney invented the cotton gin and used interchangeable parts in his gun factory—two important developments in the Industrial Revolution.

Whitney's Factory

After Whitney invented the cotton gin, he was hired by the U.S. government to build 10,000 muskets, a type of firearm. The United States worried it might need to go to war soon, so it wanted the guns quickly. At this time, most guns were made by hand and every part of every musket was unique. If one part broke, a new one had to be made specifically to fit that very same weapon.

Whitney came up with the idea of using interchangeable parts to manufacture guns. Whitney designed tools that made parts identical so that they were interchangeable, which means a part from one gun would fit into any of the other guns. No longer did a worker make an entire gun. Instead, each worker or team specialized in making a specific part.

Using interchangeable parts allowed factories to mass-produce parts, meaning they made many identical products at the same time. This process decreased the overall time and effort required to create a single good, which meant more profits for business owners and lower costs for buyers in the market. The development of identical, machine-made parts for assembly into finished products became known as the American System of manufacturing. By the 1860s, clocks and sewing machines had begun to incorporate interchangeable parts as well. A new industry, called machine tooling, began to emerge, specializing in machines that made interchangeable pieces for other machines in various industries. As manufacturing became more profitable and transportation improved, new factories sprang up in towns and cities, providing jobs with cash wages for workers and lower-priced goods for consumers. This transition away from a farm-driven agricultural economy toward a machine-driven manufacturing economy is called *industrialization*.

Discovery EDUCATION | SOCIAL STUDIES TECHBOOK

Did the benefits of technological advances made during the Industrial Revolution outweigh the costs?

Changes in Transportation

How did transportation change during the Industrial Revolution?

In the early 1800s, roads in the United States were typically narrow dirt paths. Moving people on roads was difficult, and moving large amounts of goods over land was almost impossible. However, settlers found other options, such as moving goods by rivers and canals, which were usually easier and faster than moving them by land.

Steamboats

In 1807, an inventor named Robert Fulton changed river travel. He attempted to design a steamboat that worked based on improving the flaws of other design models, and launched his boat, the *Clermont*. His boat could not only travel down the river with the river's natural flow, but it could also travel upriver, against the current of the water. Traveling upriver was done more easily and quickly than other boats could at the time. Soon, his boat made regular trips on the Hudson River between New York City and Albany. While Fulton did not invent the steamboat, he found a way to make steamboats practical and commercially successful in the United States.

Canals

Canals were another important method of transportation in the first half of the 1800s. Canals are artificial waterways that connect natural bodies of water, enabling ships to move goods and people faster and less expensively. The Erie Canal, completed in 1825, was especially important because it connected the Hudson River, which emptied into the Atlantic Ocean, to Lake Erie and the rest of the Great Lakes. This made it much easier to transport goods from the Midwest to the East Coast. The Erie Canal also opened the possibility of new markets in the Midwest for goods manufactured on the East Coast because manufacturers were able to ship new goods to this region.

photo: Library of Congress

Locks on the Champlain Canal were built in the 1820s to link the Erie Canal with New York's Lake Champlain.

At the beginning of the 19th century, the United States had only about 100 miles of canals. At the end of the century, more than 4,000 miles of canals crossed the country.

Railroads

The form of transportation that had the most impact in the 1800s was the steam locomotive, a self-propelled, steam-powered engine for pulling trains. The first steam engines used to pull railroad cars were built in Europe in the early 1800s, not too long before they spread to the United States. The early railroads were built around cities in the East, such as Boston, New York, Baltimore, and Charleston. Railroad tracks were slowly added in the West, and by 1850 cities such as Chicago, St. Louis, and Memphis connected to the East. By 1869, the first transcontinental railroad was completed.

Railroads and canals moved people and goods more quickly, less expensively, and over greater distances than any other form of transportation available at the time. They connected people nationwide and allowed farmers and factory owners to ship their products all over the country. In short, transportation innovations accelerated the market revolution. It gave people access to affordable goods they no longer needed to provide for themselves.

Transportation innovations also changed the way in which goods were designed and marketed. In colonial times, local markets only required certain goods, which were produced nearby. Now, manufacturers could consider the needs of people living in distant parts of the country and how to market their products to these people effectively. For instance, a business that produced textiles might design one type of shirt for a person who worked on a shipyard on the East Coast and a different shirt for a person living on a farm in the Midwest. Similarly, clothes makers in western cities could advertise fashionable whalebone corsets or imported silk cravats to their wealthy customers, even though their shops were hundreds of miles from the ocean.

Opposition and Consequences

Political leaders did not universally support large transportation improvement projects. Canals and railroads were expensive to build, and many officials thought they were too ambitious. Fearing construction costs would bankrupt government treasuries, some officials opposed using public funds to pay for them. Thomas Jefferson was reported to have called the Erie Canal project "little short of madness." Others referred to it as "Clinton's Ditch," after New York governor and canal champion DeWitt Clinton. Opposition to railroads was also vocal. Landowners feared that trains would frighten their livestock and spoil the appeal of their property. Road and canal operators, as well as tavern owners and innkeepers, feared trains would cut in to their business.

Discovery | SOCIAL STUDIES
EDUCATION | TECHBOOK

Did the benefits of technological advances made during the
Industrial Revolution outweigh the costs?

Transportation innovations also had environmental costs. Building the nation's transportation networks first required modifying the physical environment, such as clearing trees, damming rivers, and blasting away rock. These modifications inevitably destroyed much of the natural habitat for native plants and animals. The steam engines on trains required the burning of coal, which created smoke and air pollution. Increased levels of air pollution, especially near major centers of railroad transportation, created health hazards and difficult living conditions for the people there. In addition, the overall shift toward more manufacturing led to the contamination of rivers and other bodies of water due to the chemical waste from the manufacturing industries.

The Telegraph

How did the telegraph change communication in the early 1800s?

In the early 1800s, people who wanted to communicate over long distances wrote letters and waited weeks or months for their letters to be delivered. In 1844, Samuel F. B. Morse invented the telegraph, which was a much faster way to communicate. The telegraph sent electrical signals over wires. The signals could travel almost immediately to any location also possessing wires.

Morse and his partner, Alfred Vail, developed a code in which different combinations of short and long signals—"dots" and "dashes"—stood for different letters. A message in this code, known as Morse Code, could be typed into a telegraph machine in one location, sent along electrical wires, and quickly received in another location.

Morse's invention quickly spread throughout the United States and Europe. Companies such as The Western Union Telegraph Company strung telegraph wires all around the country, and the first transcontinental telegraph line was completed in 1861. Telegraph messages would be sent to the telegraph offices in a distant town. At the office, a telegraph officer would transcribe the message and hand it to a messenger who would race off to deliver it.

photo: Getty Images

This device is a replica of Samuel Morse's first telegraph.

As the United States grew and developed, the telegraph helped keep people and businesses connected. Settlers moving to new towns in the West could stay in touch with their families in the East. News could travel across great distances instantly. Businesses also took advantage of this new technology. Businesses with branches in several cities could communicate orders and report business developments quickly. By the end of the 1800s, telegraph technology could be used to transfer money between people and banks around the country. The increased speed and ease of communication played a significant role in helping the United States both grow and develop.

Changes in Farming

How did new inventions change life for farmers?

As a result of industrialization, many people left farms to work in factories. However, in the 1800s, most Americans still made their living by farming. New inventions helped to make farmers more productive.

The Reaper

One invention that helped farmers was the mechanical reaper, a harvesting machine produced by Cyrus McCormick in 1831. McCormick's reaper was pulled by horses and chopped down grain automatically. Before this invention, people cut grain with scythes, long blades with handles that farmers held in their hands and swung back and forth. McCormick's reaper could cut about as much grain in a few hours as two or three men could cut by hand in a day.

photo: National Archives

This re-creation of a mechanical reaper shows the sharp blades that moved back and forth to cut grain.

The Steel Plow

A few years after the reaper came on the market, in 1837, a blacksmith named John Deere invented another new tool, the steel plow. Iron and wooden plows had been used up to this point, and they worked well enough in the soft soil of the East. However, they could not cut through the heavy, sticky soil of the Midwestern prairie. The steel plow made it much easier for farmers on the prairies and plains to plow their soil, and Deere became very successful selling his plows.

Tools such as the reaper and the steel plow allowed farmers to plant and harvest their crops more quickly. Because of this, individual farmers could farm more land, and people in the mid-1800s began buying larger farms.

Discovery EDUCATION | SOCIAL STUDIES TECHBOOK

Did the benefits of technological advances made during the Industrial Revolution outweigh the costs?

Changes in Daily Life

How did new inventions change the way people lived at home?

As the 1800s progressed, more inventions changed the way people lived. In 1846, Elias Howe, a machinist, invented a sewing machine, which other inventors copied and improved upon. One of those others, Isaac M. Singer, became very successful by manufacturing and selling large numbers of his improved sewing machines.

Sewing machines changed the way people made clothes at home. However, sewing machines also moved the process of making clothes from inside the home into factories. Before the sewing machine, tailors and their apprentices commercially made custom clothing in small shops, with prices usually too expensive for most people. After the sewing machine appeared, clothing factories hired large numbers of workers to mass-produce clothing to be sold in stores. Some of the workers in these factories even owned their own sewing machines and brought them along if they took a job in a different factory.

photo: Library of Congress

This large icebox has separate spaces for the food and the ice.

In homes across the United States, other inventions made life easier for ordinary people. In the early 1800s, people began using iceboxes in their homes to store food. These boxes were made of wood or metal on the outside, and the inside was lined with slate or an insulating metal. Large blocks of ice were put into the box, as well as food that a family wanted to keep cold. The large blocks of ice would last for a couple of days in the summer and longer in colder weather. Iceboxes allowed people to store food they grew themselves, and as more people began buying food in stores, they were able to keep store-bought food fresh as well.

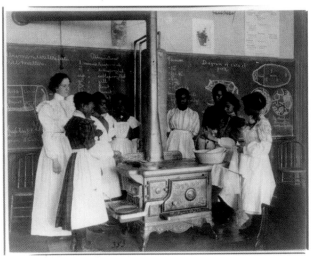

photo: Library of Congress

In the 1890s, these girls were learning to cook on a cookstove in their school.

Another change that affected people's food was the cookstove. However, stoves did not change much after 1744, when Benjamin Franklin invented an improved iron stove that was used for heating homes and for cooking. The main development in cookstoves was the step stove, a stove with two or three cooking surfaces that a cook could, with care and skill, keep at different temperatures.

Explore this resource to consider whether the benefits of industry outweighed the costs.

Consider the Essential Question:

Did the benefits of technological advances made during the Industrial Revolution outweigh the costs?

Go online to complete the Social Studies Explanation.

Check for Understanding:

Explain the most important causes for the emergence of factories in the United States during the early 1800s. In what ways did the increase in factories change life for ordinary citizens?

Discovery EDUCATION | SOCIAL STUDIES TECHBOOK

8.2 Urbanization and Immigration

photo: Library of Congress

LESSON OVERVIEW

Introduction

In this concept, you will learn about two groups of European immigrants who arrived in the United States in the 1800s and why they came here. You will also see how urbanization and immigration changed the American landscape and helped make the United States a more culturally diverse country.

Key Vocabulary

Which terms do you already know?

- ☐ Erie Canal
- ☐ ethnic group
- ☐ factory
- ☐ immigrant
- ☐ Industrial Revolution
- ☐ Irish Potato Famine
- ☐ Know-Nothing Party
- ☐ mass production
- ☐ nativism
- ☐ nativist
- ☐ naturalized citizen
- ☐ peasant
- ☐ population
- ☐ race
- ☐ rural
- ☐ social class
- ☐ suburb
- ☐ tenement
- ☐ unemployment
- ☐ urban
- ☐ urbanization

Essential Question

How did urbanization and immigration change the nature of city life in America?

Lesson Objectives

By the end of this lesson, you should be able to:

- Explain push and pull factors that motivated immigrants to move to the United States in the mid-1800s.

- Discuss key political, cultural, and social dynamics of city life in the mid-1800s.

ENGAGE

How did the rise of industry change the American landscape?
Visit Engage to learn more.

Essential Question

How did urbanization and immigration change the nature of city life in America?

EXPLORE

Industrial Rise and Growth of Cities

Why did industrialization cause cities to grow?

In 1800, there were 5.3 million people in the United States, and most did not live in cities. The four largest cities in the United States—New York City, Philadelphia, Baltimore, and Boston—had a combined population of only about 180,000. By 1850, the combined population of these four cities had reached nearly 1 million, and other cities were continuing to grow, too. The major reason for this change was industrialization.

photo: The New York Public Library

By the 1820s, Boston, Massachusetts, had a population of more than 50,000 people.

The Industrial Revolution began in the late 1700s, continued through the 1800s, and brought tremendous change to the United States. By 1830, industrial manufacturing was an important part of the American economy. Machines and new technologies made it easier for businesses to produce more goods. New industries needed an efficient way to bring in raw materials to factories and transport the goods they produced to market, and they needed workers to do the work.

Discovery EDUCATION | SOCIAL STUDIES TECHBOOK

How did urbanization and immigration change the nature of city life in America?

Business owners began to build factories in cities that were connected by new and more efficient methods of transportation. Constructed waterways such as the Erie Canal made it easier to transport large volumes of goods over long distances. Steamships were already in use on the Delaware and Potomac Rivers, and they provided transportation to and from locations such as Philadelphia and Alexandria, Virginia. The first local railroads were used for industrial purposes, and by the 1830s they provided transportation to cities, including Baltimore, Philadelphia, Boston, and Quincy, Massachusetts. However, the construction of these new water and land routes also required making modifications to the physical environment, including digging, clearing trees, and extracting raw materials. In addition, steam engines produced a large amount of air pollution from burning coal, and the effects of this pollution created difficult living conditions and health hazards in urbanizing areas.

Innovations in communication also affected the trends of industrialization and urbanization during the middle of the 1800s. The telegraph provided an instant way for people to share messages, which greatly improved the transaction of business. In 1851, the company Western Union was established with the goal of creating a unified and efficient telegraph system. As a result, railway operators were now able to exchange updates along the telegraph, and the stock exchange was able to provide minute-by-minute reports through the ticker tape machine. With all these messages being shared, more switchboard operators, engineers, and other technicians were hired to service the expanding telegraph system, which further contributed to the growth of cities.

The relatively large populations of cities provided labor to work in factories. When more factories were built, more workers were needed. Factories provided new jobs that attracted more people to cities. This caused cities to grow. The overall population of the United States grew by more than 30 percent each decade between 1800 and 1830. But the urban areas, where factories were located, grew at twice that rate as farmworkers, immigrants, and free African Americans arrived in search of economic opportunities.

Finding a Place to Call Home

Why did Germans migrate to U.S. farms and cities?

If you were hungry and poor and there were no jobs where you lived, would you move thousands of miles on the promise of a better life? In the mid-1800s alone, the United States took in more than 7.5 million *immigrants*, or people who move from one country or region to another. That was more than the population of the entire country in 1810. The majority of the immigrants were from Europe; about two-thirds were from Germany and Ireland.

German Immigration

During the mid-1800s, a large number of Europeans immigrated to the United States in search of opportunities. Most of these people came in through port cities on the East Coast, including New York and Boston.

photo: The University of Texas at Austin

New Braunfels, Texas, gained a large German American community.

German immigrants came to the United States in the 1830s through the 1850s to escape poor harvests, crowded cities, dangerous and difficult work conditions, low wages, and political unrest. Another reason was that a large number of German Americans had come before them. There were Germans in the first groups of colonists at both Jamestown and New Amsterdam, and William Penn recruited Germans to live in his then-new colony of Pennsylvania.

Many German Americans were successful in their new country. They wrote home to tell friends and relatives, and the news spread. Nearly one million Germans came to the United States in the 1850s. Around 215,000 Germans arrived in 1854 alone.

German Americans

German immigrants usually had more money than the Irish and other immigrant groups. Because of this, they had many more options available to them. Although some remained on the East Coast, many German immigrants moved to the Midwest. There was a lot of land available there, and the climate was suitable for growing familiar crops.

Some German immigrants settled in growing Midwestern cities such as Chicago and Milwaukee and set up communities with German-speaking churches, schools, and businesses. They also organized music and educational groups to keep their traditional culture alive. Instead of looking for unskilled factory work, many Germans became involved with traditional German crafts, such as baking, brewing beer, and carpentry.

By the late 1800s, the largest settlements of German immigrants to the United States were found in the cities of New York, Baltimore, Cincinnati, Saint Louis, and Milwaukee. States with small populations such as Wisconsin wanted to grow their populations and economies. They placed ads in newspapers and sent pamphlets written in German to port cities to entice immigrants to move there. They offered land at a good price and jobs for anyone who arrived in their state.

Rural Americans

Why did people move from rural areas to the cities?

Young men and women from rural areas and small villages moved to cities for new opportunities. Most of the country's early factories were built in the Northeast along rapidly moving waterways that provided power. For example, the Waltham mill was built on the banks of the Charles River, about 10 miles outside Boston. The first factory workers migrated, or moved, from rural areas to factory towns in hopes of finding better work and more money.

Early New England textile mills recruited teenage women from farms. These women worked for low wages and were required to live in company boarding houses and follow strict rules. But they also experienced the freedom of making their own money for the first time. By the mid-1800s, these mills were more often run by immigrant laborers. Outside New England, most early factory workers were men from poor rural families.

Migration of African Americans

Free African American men and women faced discrimination and danger in the American South during the early 1800s. Most Southern states had laws discriminating against free African Americans. By 1859, Arkansas had gone so far as to pass a law requiring the removal of free African Americans from within its borders. In states such as Virginia, African Americans faced whipping for even minor crimes, while other people would receive a small fine for the same offense. In most slave states, African Americans could also be severely punished for learning to read or write.

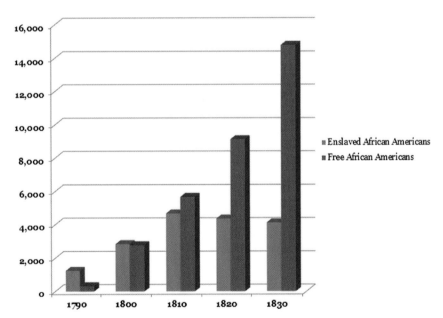

This graph shows the free and enslaved African American population of Baltimore, Maryland, from 1790 until 1830.

It was difficult for African Americans in the South to find work. Many states passed laws to keep them out of certain professions, including working as printers, publishers, and gunsmiths, out of fear they could help lead a slave rebellion. The lives of African Americans were always at risk if there were rumors of a slave rebellion or of an escaped enslaved person.

Faced with these hardships and more, a small number of African Americans were able to move to Northern cities in search of work and a better life. In 1820, African Americans comprised about 10 percent of the population of both Philadelphia and New York City. Urban centers like Cincinnati and Chicago had African American populations as well. By 1860, about one-third of the African Americans living in Boston and two-thirds of those living in Detroit were migrants from the South.

African Americans still faced discrimination in Northern cities. They often were the last hired, were paid lower wages than white Americans, and lived in segregated communities.

A Wave of Immigration

Why did Irish people migrate to U.S. cities?

Irish Immigration

Large numbers of Irish people left their homes to emigrate to the United States during the mid-1800s because of starvation, poverty, and oppressive British rule. Many Irish peasants made a living working as tenants on tiny plots of land. Approximately half of everyone in Ireland depended on potatoes for both food and money for food. Potatoes needed far less land than grains and other crops did. A potato harvest from a single planted acre could support a family for an entire year, so people depended on potatoes all year long.

photo: Getty Images

Irish immigrants sail for the United States during the potato famine, 1850.

Beginning in 1845, a fungus spread through Ireland's potato crop, turning the potatoes into a black, inedible mush. Food became scarce for Irish peasants. Between 1845 and 1852, more than a million Irish peasants died of starvation and disease. This famine, or severe food shortage, is known as the Great Irish Famine. While the Irish poor were starving, wealthy British landlords who owned highly fertile land in Ireland were still able to grow cash crops and export them for profit.

During the late 1840s and early 1850s, about 2 million survivors of the Great Famine fled to the United States, Great Britain, and Canada in the hopes of finding work and food. About 1.5 million Irish immigrants eventually settled in the United States. Most of them were drawn to Eastern cities, where they could find work as unskilled laborers in the factories or building new transportation systems.

Irish Americans

For the most part, Irish immigrants were extremely poor and settled in whatever East Coast city they arrived in, even if they heard of good jobs or opportunities in other cities. By 1850, Irish immigrants represented about one-quarter of the population of Boston, New York City, Philadelphia, and Baltimore.

Have you ever visited a Chinatown or another neighborhood where people who share a cultural and national background, or ethnic group, have established a community? Living in an area where there are people who share your own culture can make you feel more at home. This was true for the immigrants of the 1800s, too. Also, English-speaking Anglo Americans pressured immigrants and African Americans to live in segregated neighborhoods. A section of a city in which people of a minority ethnic group are segregated or isolated is called a ghetto.

The Limerick district in Louisville, Kentucky, is an example of such a place. Early Irish immigrants had settled in Louisville after the War of 1812. They set up businesses and established a community. When the Great Famine occurred and the new wave of Irish immigrants arrived, many headed to Louisville and settled in the Limerick district. The neighborhood had its own grocery stores, churches, and eventually even an Irish American newspaper. These newcomers helped make Louisville the 10th largest U.S. city by 1850.

Explore this interactive to learn more about perspectives on urbanization and immigration.

The Irish who came to America during this time were usually poor and had few skills. Many men took jobs building new forms of transportation, such as canals and railroads. Many Irish women worked as servants in the homes of the wealthy and middle class. Although they had to take the lowest paying and most dangerous jobs, many felt they were better off than if they were in Ireland, where they might starve.

Leaving Home and Family

What was life like for people who moved to the cities?

Urban areas provided jobs for men, women, and even children who could not find work on farms and for immigrants escaping hardships in their native countries. There were hardships in city life, but there were benefits as well.

Men who moved to the cities and worked in unskilled jobs typically did not make enough money to support a family. Women and children in working-class families often had to work to help pay rent and put food on the table. In many working-class families, children under the age of 15 contributed as much as one-fifth of the household income. Starving children begged for money in the streets.

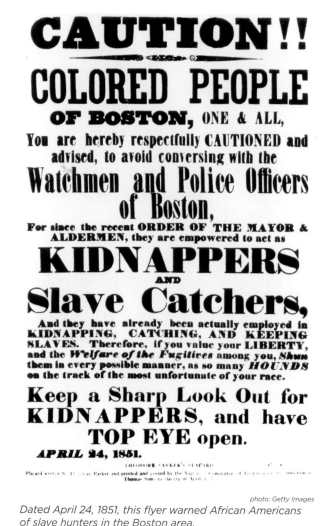

CAUTION!!

COLORED PEOPLE

OF BOSTON, ONE & ALL,

You are hereby respectfully CAUTIONED and advised, to avoid conversing with the

Watchmen and Police Officers of Boston,

For since the recent ORDER OF THE MAYOR & ALDERMEN, they are empowered to act as

KIDNAPPERS

AND

Slave Catchers,

And they have already been actually employed in KIDNAPPING, CATCHING, AND KEEPING SLAVES. Therefore, if you value your LIBERTY, and the *Welfare of the Fugitives* among you, Shun them in every possible manner, as so many *HOUNDS* on the track of the most unfortunate of your race.

Keep a Sharp Look Out for KIDNAPPERS, and have TOP EYE open.

APRIL 24, 1851.

photo: Getty Images

Dated April 24, 1851, this flyer warned African Americans of slave hunters in the Boston area.

The poorest of the working class lived in slums, crowded into musty, unlit cellar dwellings that housed anywhere from 6 to 20 people in a single room. They used outdoor toilets, and their garbage and kitchen waste was thrown into piles in the streets. City officials, who could not keep up with sanitation measures, allowed pigs, goats, and packs of dogs to roam the streets and scavenge through the garbage. Finding clean drinking water was also a problem; the outdoor bathrooms often emptied into cesspools and containers that would leak and contaminate water supplies.

Despite these issues, cities also provided social benefits. Although workdays were long, leisure time took on new importance in the cities. People attended theaters and took their minds off of their day. Horse racing became a very popular spectator sport, with from about 70,000 to 100,000 people from all walks of life showing up to cheer on their pick at the famous North/South race in Long Island, New York, in 1845. The city of Boston outlawed live shows because of the fear of riots and disorderly behavior, but dancing and live music shows were popular in other cities, such as New York, Charleston, and Philadelphia.

Racism and Black Communities

Although Northern cities provided more opportunity for African Americans, urban racism was common. Free African Americans competed with European immigrants for jobs, and in many areas there were rules against hiring African Americans as skilled laborers. There were also obstacles to getting permits and licenses to operate pushcarts to sell food and other goods or to create other small, independent businesses. African Americans also lived in fear of being kidnapped and sold into slavery, even if they were born free.

Race riots, in which mobs of people attacked African American neighborhoods and churches, occurred in many major cities after 1820. African Americans were stoned, beaten, and sometimes killed during these riots. During one incident in October 1834, 45 houses were destroyed in an African American neighborhood of Philadelphia.

Discovery EDUCATION | SOCIAL STUDIES TECHBOOK

How did urbanization and immigration change the nature of city life in America?

Philadelphia officials in general refused assistance to the African American community, blaming the victims for bringing the violence upon themselves.

To avoid discrimination, African Americans joined together to form their own churches, schools, and other organizations. In 1794, Richard Allen, a former slave, founded the first African Methodist Episcopal (AME) Church in Philadelphia. Allen and other free African Americans had previously been denied full rights to participate in white Methodist churches. Allen organized a meeting of black Methodists from around the Northeast that resulted in the formation of the AME denomination. By the 1850s, AME churches appeared in nearly every major city outside of the South, including New York, Boston, Washington, DC, Chicago, and even San Francisco. AME churches were also established in a handful of cities in slave states.

Gaps Between Rich and Poor

How did urban life differ for the wealthy and the working class?

As it is today, life in the city was very different for the wealthy and the poor. As industrialization took hold in the mid-1800s, the gap between the rich and the poor widened. From the outside, the United States might have seemed like a place where anything was possible, but in reality, making dreams come true often depended on a person's social class: Was he or she among the rich and influential, the growing middle class, or the lowly poor?

By 1860, the top 10 percent of the population controlled 70 percent of the wealth in the North. The very wealthy elite and the emerging middle class took advantage of their industrialized world by buying the latest ready-made fashions, dishes, and furniture. Before industrialization, wealthy people lived in the centers of the cities. When more factories were built in the cities, the streets grew crowded and dirty, and city centers became less desirable places to live. Those who could afford to moved their families to large homes or estates away from the center of town. They created wealthy communities away from the factories and pushed for the development of open spaces where they could enjoy nature. Partially in response to pressure from wealthy New Yorkers, for $5 million New York City commissioners purchased over 800 acres of land that would become Central Park.

Industrialization created new jobs for a growing middle class in Northern cities and towns. These jobs included store clerks, salespeople, managers, and retailers. In middle-class homes, the father went to work while the mother took care of the home. It was considered a status symbol to hire servants, who were usually low-paid African American and immigrant women.

Factory workers worked long hours and made very low wages. The jobs did not require skills, so any worker could easily be replaced by another. Competition for jobs kept wages low. While the middle class grew wealthier and abandoned the dirty, smoke-filled streets in the hearts of the cities, the working class and poor moved in.

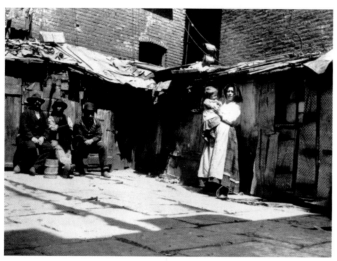

photo: Library of Congress

Many immigrants worked in factories and lived in poverty in cities such as New York City.

Immigrants and people from rural areas provided cheap factory labor in the cities and wanted to live near their jobs. With such a large, low-paid labor force, there was high demand for cheap housing.

Owners of large homes near city factories met this need by dividing their homes into apartments, becoming landlords. By the 1850s, real estate developers and investors were building rows of low-rent apartment buildings, which in 1867 became legally known as tenements. These overcrowded buildings were often unsanitary and poorly maintained. With the population booming, city governments could not keep up with sanitary services. Garbage and sewage became never-ending problems in the poorest areas, bringing illnesses and vermin such as rats.

Anti-Immigrant Sentiments

How did people in the United States react to immigrants?

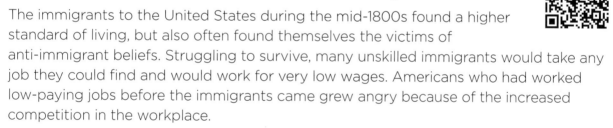

The immigrants to the United States during the mid-1800s found a higher standard of living, but also often found themselves the victims of anti-immigrant beliefs. Struggling to survive, many unskilled immigrants would take any job they could find and would work for very low wages. Americans who had worked low-paying jobs before the immigrants came grew angry because of the increased competition in the workplace.

The Irish in particular faced prejudice and violence in their new homeland. In 1831 in New York City, Protestant Americans burned down St. Mary's Catholic Church. In 1844, anti-Irish riots resulted in the deaths of 13 people in Philadelphia. Dozens of people were hurt, and more than 40 buildings were destroyed. New organizations and political parties developed with nativist beliefs. Nativists believed that U.S. citizens were "native" and should have more rights than new immigrants.

Urbanization and Politics

Various perspectives on immigration and urbanization contributed to political differences among the political party coalitions in America. During this period, Democratic voters tended to be small farmers or unskilled laborers living in rural areas, mostly of Irish Catholic descent. The Democratic Party often used class resentments between the rich and poor to mobilize its membership and elect representatives.

Discovery EDUCATION | SOCIAL STUDIES TECHBOOK

How did urbanization and immigration change the nature of city life in America?

In contrast, the Whig Party of 1830s was composed of British or German Protestant immigrants. The members were mostly skilled laborers and industrialists, who emphasized the unity of labor of capital. As a result of increased urbanization, these two parties often came into conflict about the powers of the federal government with regard to the interests of businesses.

Another group was the American Party, a political party also known as the Know-Nothing Party. This party began as a secret, anti-Catholic, anti-immigrant organization. It earned its name because members were trained to say "I know nothing" when asked about their organization. The party wanted to stop foreign-born people from holding public office and to extend the time it took for immigrants to become naturalized citizens.

photo: Getty Images

In November 1855, the American Party in New York held a "mass meeting" in opposition to "the efforts of fanatical fusionists to destroy the union of the States."

Explore this resource and write a letter objecting to Know-Nothing propaganda.

The American Party peaked when it won 21 percent of the vote in 1856, yet it created enough political divisions to indirectly help Abraham Lincoln win the presidential election in 1860. By the time of this election, about 16 percent of the U.S. population lived in urban areas, and manufacturing generated around one-third of the United States' national income. Urbanization and industrialization had become part of the American way of life.

Consider the Essential Question:

How did urbanization and immigration change the nature of city life in America?

Go online to complete the Social Studies Explanation.

Check for Understanding:

How did urbanization during the middle of the 1800s contribute to conflicts over religion, social class, and politics?

photo: Library of Congress

8.3 Reform Movements

LESSON OVERVIEW

Introduction

In this concept, you will examine the social reform movements of the early 1800s. You will learn about the problems and issues that Americans in the 1800s faced and how they addressed them.

Essential Question

How did the reform movements of the 1840s change American society?

Lesson Objectives

By the end of this lesson, you should be able to:

- Connect the emergence of mid-1800s reform movements to changes in American life caused by industrialization.

- Trace the rise of the abolitionist and women's suffrage movements.

- Describe key cultural advancements (arts and sciences) and political ideas that emerged before the Civil War.

Key Vocabulary
Which terms do you already know?

- ☐ Abigail Adams
- ☐ abolition
- ☐ Andrew Jackson
- ☐ Angelina Grimké
- ☐ citizen
- ☐ Elizabeth Cady Stanton
- ☐ Frederick Douglass
- ☐ George Whitefield
- ☐ Harriet Tubman
- ☐ industrialization
- ☐ Irish Potato Famine
- ☐ Know-Nothing Party
- ☐ Lucretia Mott
- ☐ mestizo
- ☐ New York
- ☐ Olaudah Equiano
- ☐ Prince Hall
- ☐ Puritan

- ☐ reform/social reform
- ☐ republicanism
- ☐ Sarah Grimké
- ☐ Saratoga
- ☐ Second Great Awakening
- ☐ Seneca Falls
- ☐ Seneca Falls Convention
- ☐ slave codes
- ☐ Sojourner Truth
- ☐ suffrage
- ☐ Susan B. Anthony
- ☐ temperance
- ☐ Thomas Jefferson
- ☐ transcendentalism
- ☐ Underground Railroad
- ☐ utopia
- ☐ William Lloyd Garrison

Discovery | SOCIAL STUDIES
EDUCATION | **TECHBOOK**

How did the reform movements of the 1840s change American society?

ENGAGE

What inspires people to stand up for change? Visit Engage to learn more.

Essential Question

How did the reform movements of the 1840s change American society?

EXPLORE

The Need for Social Reform

Why did people see a need for social reform in the 1800s?

The industrialization that took place in the early 1800s brought big changes to the United States. The urban population of the nation increased as young men and women from the countryside moved to the cities to work in factories. There, immigrants primarily from northern and western Europe looking for jobs and a better life in America joined them.

In 1800, the population of New York City, the largest urban center in the United States at the time, was just over 60,000. By 1830, that number had leaped to more than 300,000. New York was not the only place that was expanding. From 1800 to 1840, the total population of the country increased from 2 million to 17 million people.

Urban growth led to overcrowded, dangerous, and unsanitary living conditions for the working class. Factory work required long days in unhealthy and dangerous conditions. As a result, several earlier labor movements called for improving such working conditions. One movement called for limiting the working day. In some cases, workers might spend up to 12 hours on the job. In 1835, workers went on strike in Philadelphia, Pennsylvania, to demand a 10-hour workday. In 1847, New Hampshire enacted the first state law for the 10-hour day.

Men and women workers alike also started to demand higher wages, and as a result, many labor unions started to emerge. In Lynn, Massachusetts, for example, female shoe-binders formed an alliance in 1833 and demanded higher pay. Drawing on the Declaration of Independence and Constitution, these women proclaimed that "Women as well as men have certain inalienable rights, among which is the right at all times of peaceably assembling to consult upon the common good." As industrialization progressed during the middle of the 1800s, working conditions somewhat improved and, in some instances, wages increased. However, there were still many new challenges due to technological innovations and continually changing patterns of migration and urban growth.

photo: Getty Images

Originally a Presbyterian minister, Charles Grandson Finney became one of the most influential leaders in the Second Great Awakening.

Around the turn of the century, a religious movement called the Second Great Awakening helped shift attention to the social problems associated with urbanization and industrialization. Because of low attendance at church services and declining religious convictions, many religious faiths held revivals to reemphasize people's dependence on God. During the Second Great Awakening, these revivals expanded across the nation, serving as an opportunity to hear the word of God. They also were social gatherings in which concerned citizens discussed faith-based solutions to problems in their communities. Charles Finney, a Presbyterian theologian and president of Oberlin College, organized many of the revivals. Finney encouraged women to participate and hoped his revivals would spark reform efforts around the country.

Many problems associated with industrialization primarily affected the North, which was much more industrialized and urban than other regions of the country. But Americans from all walks of life—women and men, North and South, African American and white alike—got involved with social reform, the effort to improve social institutions. These reformers wanted changes that would raise the quality of life for other members of society.

Explore this interactive to learn more about reform movements of the mid-1800s.

Discovery EDUCATION | SOCIAL STUDIES TECHBOOK

How did the reform movements of the 1840s change American society?

A Movement to End Alcohol Abuse

What was the temperance movement?

One of the earliest and most influential social reform movements of the 1800s was the temperance movement, the battle against alcoholic drinks. Many social reformers associated drinking alcohol with poverty, domestic abuse, crime, unemployment, and homelessness. Liquor was cheap and easy to get, and even though it was unhealthy, some people used it to help them forget their troubles.

The temperance movement began in the early 1800s. Churches asked their members to make promises to stay away from hard liquor. By 1808, the first known temperance organization had formed in Saratoga, New York. Over the next 25 years, approximately 6,000 local organizations arose across the country.

During the 1840s and 1850s, the temperance movement found a new population to target. In these two decades, a potato plant disease wiped out Ireland's major food supply. As a result, about 1.5 million Irish immigrants came to the United States, fleeing famine and poverty. Irish immigrants settled in cities where they hoped to find work. Many urban Irish were poor or unemployed, and all struggled with the difficulties of urban living. Some also drank alcohol, and temperance advocates blamed alcohol consumption for Irish troubles. Temperance took on new life.

TREE of TEMPERANCE

BY A.D. FILLMORE.

photo: Library of Congress

This cartoon from 1855 proclaims the benefits of temperance.

Temperance advocates in the 1840s wanted total purity, demanding that people pledge to stay away from alcohol altogether. A new approach called the Washingtonian movement gained steam among the working class. Started in May 1840 by six men in Baltimore, the Washingtonian Temperance Society was made up of reformed alcoholics. These people attempted to convince drinkers to give up alcohol by sharing their real-life tales of alcoholism and its consequences. By 1842, the Washingtonians claimed that over one million people had taken their pledge to stop drinking.

While the Washingtonians used persuasion, other temperance reformers campaigned for coercive laws—laws that threatened punishment if people did not behave as they were told. In 1851, Maine became the first state in the union to pass a statewide ban on the manufacture and sale of alcohol. Between 1851 and 1855, 11 more states followed suit.

Educating the Public
How did education change during the mid-1800s?

The Common School Movement

Today, government funds pay for public schooling, and attendance is mandatory in every state. However, getting an education was not always a legal requirement, and it was not always free. Before the social reforms of the 1800s, education was a luxury.

In the 1600s and 1700s, there was no such thing as free schooling for all. Early Puritans initially required that every town in New England have its own public school, paid for by local fees. However, this notion did not spread, and it did not last.

photo: Library of Congress

Horace Mann served as secretary of the Massachusetts state board of education, as well as a U.S. Representative from 1849 to 1853 and president of Antioch College from 1853 until his death in 1859. He believed that education was key to social reform.

Schooling varied from place to place. In most areas, girls either were not allowed to attend school or could only attend up to a certain age. In the late 1700s, schools were private, and families had to pay for at least part of their children's education. Most families lived and worked on farms, and children were taught and supervised during the day by parents or other elders. In the 1800s, when families moved to cities and parents worked all day in factories, children were often left unsupervised. Some social reformers worried that these children were not being educated, while others focused on the crime and mischief children caused.

In the late 1700s, Thomas Jefferson spread the idea that a democratic society could not survive without an educated public. Many social reformers in the 1800s agreed that education was needed to help people become better citizens. Reformers such as Horace Mann and Henry Barnard believed that providing free, public education would keep young people away from a life of crime and help them develop their potential. These reformers led a movement to create free schooling for all, the Common School Movement.

By 1853, every state in the North had created common schools, publicly run and funded schools to provide general and civic education for all. Subjects taught generally included "the three Rs": reading, writing, and arithmetic. "History" was memorizing names and dates. "Geography" was memorizing place names and capitals as well as data such as principal economic products. Most subjects were taught through repetitive drill. Science, visual art, music, foreign language, algebra, geometry, and trade skills were not taught.

While the South did not introduce common schools until after the Civil War ended in 1865, the seeds for a nationwide public school system had been sown. In 1852, Massachusetts passed the first state law in the nation requiring children to attend school. It only called for students to attend school for 12 weeks out of the year, but the system of public schooling that we know today was putting down its roots.

photo: Getty Images

Prudence Crandell was an American educator. She championed the education of African Americans and women. She twice went to jail for attempting to allow African American children to attend her private all-girls school in Connecticut.

A Perfect World

What social ideals emerged in the mid-1800s?

Crime and violence, unequal rights for women and people of color, alcoholism, long work hours, dangerous working conditions, and unhealthy tenements were just some of the issues plaguing society in the mid-1800s. For some, the problems seemed so bad that all they wanted to do was start over, from scratch.

Out of this, the idea of a utopian society was born. *Utopia* means "an ideal place, a place of true perfection." Utopian societies were communities where people came together to live in their version of an ideal, perfect world.

One group to form these societies was the United Society of Believers in Christ's Second Coming, or the Shakers. They got this name because of the way they would shake and move about during their religious rituals. The first Shakers came to the English colonies in 1774 to live out their beliefs in equality for men and women, celibacy, shared or communal ownership of all property, and leading a simple life. They felt it was time to shed the sins of humanity.

At their peak, the Shakers had some 6,000 members and approximately 20 different settlements. Each Shaker community typically had separate dormitories for men and women, shops where they made wooden furniture and handicrafts, a meeting hall, and barns. Hancock Village, established in 1787, and the Enfield Shakers Historic District, which peaked between 1830 and 1860, are two examples of Shaker communities.

Founded in 1825, New Harmony, Indiana, was one of the first utopian societies not based in religious ideals. British mill owner and social reformer Robert Owen founded this cooperative community based on the idea that humans are shaped by the environment in which they live. At New Harmony, Owen looked to create a system of communal ownership and tried to do away with religion of any kind. The community of about 2,000 people lasted only three years.

photo: Getty Images

Taking over a settlement in Harmonie, Indiana, British mill owner Robert Owen established the cooperative society of New Harmony in 1825.

Some of the utopian societies found inspiration in European ideals. Brook Farm in West Roxbury, Massachusetts, was one such community. Founded in 1841, the philosophy behind the Brook Farm Institute of Agriculture and Education was based on the teachings of a German philosopher, Immanuel Kant, and his ideas of transcendentalism. Transcendentalism stemmed from the belief that God exists in every aspect of nature and that there is an ideal spiritual reality that is found through intuition and not through science.

Brook Farm is perhaps one of the most famous utopian societies because of the well-known literary figures who spent time there. Nathaniel Hawthorne, Ralph Waldo Emerson, and William Henry Channing were among those associated with Brook Farm. The community lasted until 1847, when financial troubles and infighting brought it down. During the six years it existed, the farm provided an experience of "plain living" for its inhabitants, who shared equally in the farm's work and its proceeds. The number of people at Brook Farm never exceeded about 120.

Discovery EDUCATION | SOCIAL STUDIES TECHBOOK

How did the reform movements of the 1840s change American society?

Crime and Punishment

What did social reformers do for convicts and people with mental illness?

Caring for Convicts

In the early 1800s, American prisons overflowed with criminals of all levels, and all prisoners were treated pretty much the same. Adults and children, murderers and debtors, anyone who had been convicted of any crime—all were kept together in large but overcrowded spaces. Prisoners were often charged money for their food and lodging, and at times jailed prisoners starved. Whippings, beatings, and death sentences were not uncommon.

As the spirit of social reform spread throughout the country in the 1820s, many people for the first time began to look at crime as a social problem rather than as an issue of sin or wickedness. Social reformers imagined they could end crime if they could find ways to solve the problems that led people to commit crimes. They lobbied to outlaw the death penalty and to do away with debtors' prisons, where a person who owed money could be jailed until he or she earned enough to repay the debt.

Because criminals were seen as victims of social problems, reformers thought that prisons should be used to retrain and reform convicts, rather than merely to punish them. Primarily, they wanted to change the conditions inside prison walls. They also worked to create juvenile detention centers where minors who committed crimes could be educated and reformed for society.

Thanks to their efforts, in 1847 Massachusetts became the first state to stop sentencing convicts to death (although it would later reinstate the death penalty, only to repeal it once again in 1984). Rhode Island followed Massachusetts's lead to become the second state to outlaw the death penalty in 1852, seven years after the last criminal was killed there.

New prisons like Auburn Prison, built in New York State in 1816, and Eastern State Penitentiary, built in Pennsylvania in 1829, reflected a new model of punishment. In these large, new institutions, convicts

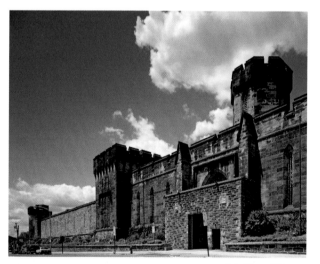

photo: Library of Congress

The exterior of Eastern State Penitentiary, Philadelphia, Pennsylvania.

were kept in small cells in total or partial isolation, rather than in large communal rooms packed with people. As reformers believed that hard work could help the prisoners become more disciplined, everyone was forced to work at manual labor during the day.

photo: Library of Congress

Dorothea Dix was a champion for the mentally ill.

photo: Library of Congress

Social reforms during the 1800s led to reform schools to rehabilitate juvenile offenders.

Treating Persons with Mental Illness

Like convicts, people who suffered from mental illness or mental retardation were treated horribly in the early 1800s. They were sometimes locked in closets or cages, kept in chains, and even beaten until they behaved. They had nowhere to turn and nobody who was looking out for them.

Although many Americans were upset with or even outraged at these practices, little was done to change things until Reverend Louis Dwight, a Congregationalist minister, founded the Boston Prison Discipline Society in 1825. Dwight's actions spurred an investigation by the state legislature and eventually led to reform legislation.

The person largely credited for improving conditions for people with mental illness is Dorothea Lynde Dix. Abused and neglected as a child, Dix grew up to become a nurse. As the story goes, after overhearing two men discussing the horrible conditions at the Middlesex County jail, Dix went to see it for herself and found several mentally ill prisoners being kept in horrific conditions. With that, in 1838, she set out on a crusade to publicize the inhumane conditions in such places.

From 1838 until around the start of the Civil War in 1861, Dix toured the country gathering and spreading information and evidence about how the mentally ill were treated. Through her efforts and leadership, Massachusetts established a new system of state-supported care. It was because of Dix and her work that between 1865 and 1880, more than 24 hospitals and insane asylums were built in 15 states and Canada.

Discovery Education | SOCIAL STUDIES TECHBOOK

How did the reform movements of the 1840s change American society?

Challenging Slavery

What were the goals of the abolition movement?

What Was Abolition?

While antislavery movements had existed in the United States since the latter part of the 1700s, the abolitionist movement, or movement to end slavery, was different. Instead of calling for a gradual end to slavery and raising money to free individuals from enslavement a few at a time, these new abolitionists wanted something more. They called for an end to slavery with the immediate emancipation, or *manumission*, of all enslaved people, and they did not believe that the enslaved people's owners should be reimbursed for the loss of their "property."

The new wave of abolitionists saw slavery as wrong on many different levels. Slavery was illegal because it went against the rights for all men set forth in the Declaration of Independence. They also believed it was sinful for man to act as God above other people, which is how they saw the slave owners' treatment of enslaved people. In addition, they felt that slavery encouraged immoral behavior in owners of enslaved people and destroyed the institutions of marriage and family because enslaved children and wives and husbands were bought and sold as separate properties.

In their campaign to end slavery, abolitionists petitioned Congress and state legislatures to end slavery, ran for government offices themselves, and wrote inflammatory articles against slavery to distribute in both the North and South.

Notable White Abolitionists

The abolitionists in this movement came from many different backgrounds. Some, such as William Lloyd Garrison, were white Northerners. Garrison founded the antislavery newspaper *The Liberator* in 1831. Based in Boston, the paper was one of the country's most influential voices for abolitionism.

White women were also part of the abolitionist movement. Sisters Sarah and Angelina Grimké moved from Charleston, South Carolina, to the Northern city of Philadelphia to help fight slavery. They lectured and wrote articles about putting an end to the institution of slavery.

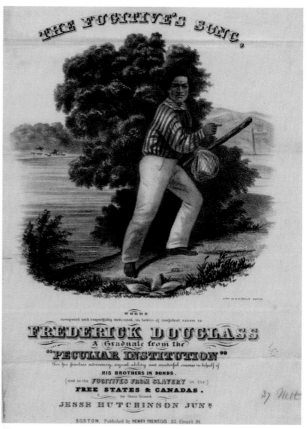

photo: Library of Congress

Sheet music often included lyrics about important issues of the day. This sheet music cover illustrates "The Fugitive's Song," written in honor of Frederick Douglass and published in 1845.

They felt so strongly about their position that in 1838 they were able to convince their mother to gift them any enslaved people they would otherwise have inherited upon her death so that they could set these people free. Fanny Kemble was a prominent British actress who married a Georgia slave owner. Kemble and her husband disagreed over slavery and eventually divorced. In 1838 and 1839, Kemble kept a journal of her observations of plantation life. Published in 1863, Kemble's *Journal of a Residence on a Georgian Plantation* provided one of the most important and detailed accounts of slavery and life in the antebellum South.

African American Abolitionists

White men and women were not the only Americans working in the abolitionist movement. Frederick Douglass had escaped from slavery in 1838 when he was just 20. As a free black, he was deeply involved with the fight to free others. He spent several years reading William Lloyd Garrison's *The Liberator* newspaper before he himself started publishing the antislavery newspaper *North Star* in 1848. In addition to writing the paper, Douglass gave speeches about his life in slavery and in 1845 published his autobiography, *Narrative of the Life of Frederick Douglass, an American Slave, Written By Himself*. As an educated and well-spoken formerly enslaved person, Douglass also became an important face for the abolitionist movement.

Another important abolitionist, Isabella Baumfree, began life in slavery in New York in the late 1700s. She escaped to freedom in 1826 by literally walking away from her home. She wandered around until she fortunately found a white household that would help her. Once free, she devoted herself to singing, preaching, and spreading the word of God's "goodness" and of the plight of enslaved people.

A few years later, she took a new name, Sojourner Truth. Even though she never learned to read and write, Truth's speech was so eloquent and she had so much passion that she developed a large following. Believing in equal rights for all, Truth fought not just to end slavery, but also to provide rights to African Americans and women.

Other prominent African American abolitionists included Charles Lenox Remond, Harriet Jacobs, and Robert Purvis. Remond delivered antislavery speeches around the country and as far away as London. He was the first African American to deliver an address to the Massachusetts legislature. During the Civil War, Remond recruited black troops to serve in the Union army. In 1861, Jacobs published *Incidents in the Life of a Slave Girl*. This book is considered one of the most important slave narratives authored by a woman. Purvis sheltered runaway slaves in his Philadelphia home. As a prominent member of William Lloyd Garrison's American Anti-slavery Society, Purvis also lobbied political leaders from the United States and Europe to oppose slavery.

A Secret Escape

What was the Underground Railroad? How were free blacks treated in the North?

Abolitionists used many strategies to try to put an end to slavery in the United States. They wrote articles in newspapers, they gave speeches to the public, and they lobbied government officials to change the laws about slavery. David Walker, an abolitionist who lived in Boston, authored a pamphlet titled "Appeal." This document urged enslaved persons to rebel against their owners. Walker arranged for copies of his pamphlet to be smuggled into the South on cargo ships.

Activists throughout the country also worked to help enslaved people escape from bondage, or slavery, as part of a secret escape network known as the Underground Railroad. The Underground Railroad was not an actual railroad. Instead, it was a series of escape routes and safe hiding places that were used to bring enslaved people out of the South and into freedom in the North.

Although a system of helping enslaved people escape probably began as early as the late 1700s, it grew much larger and more organized in the 1800s. By the 1830s, this system became known as the Underground Railroad because it was secret (hence "underground") and because those involved with it used railroad terms as code language. Routes were called "lines," the safe stopping places along the way were called "stations," and were guarded by "station masters." "Conductors" were the guides who helped move enslaved people from station to station, and the escaping people themselves were called "freight" or "packages." The entire network extended through 14 Northern states and into Canada, beyond the reaches of people looking to capture and return the escapees to slavery.

Many Northern abolitionists, philanthropists, and church leaders were involved with the Underground Railroad. However, the free black community arguably played the largest role in the network. Free blacks posing as enslaved people would enter plantations to help guide the fugitives to safety. They would generally travel at night, moving about 10 to 20 miles at a time and stopping at "stations" to eat and rest. Between around 1810 and 1850, the Underground Railroad helped move hundreds of people to freedom every year, perhaps as many as 100,000 in total.

Harriet Tubman became one of the most famous conductors on the Underground Railroad. Tubman had escaped slavery herself in 1849. Just one year later, she returned to Maryland and freed her sister and two children. That was the first of many trips she took as a conductor.

photo: Getty Images

The Underground Railroad *is a painting by Charles Webber.*

All told, Tubman returned to slave states about 19 times, leading some 300 people to freedom. Tubman developed such a reputation for her work that a $40,000 bounty was offered for her capture. During the Civil War, she worked as a nurse and spy for the Union army during the Civil War. Tubman accomplished all she did while living with a neurological disability. She suffered from unexpected sleeping spells and seizures that may have been the result of a brutal head injury she sustained while enslaved. In 2016, the U.S. Treasury Department announced that Tubman would become the new face of the American $20 bill.

Although the Underground Railroad helped enslaved people to freedom, even free blacks faced hurdles and discrimination in the North. Many places, such as Philadelphia, were highly segregated, which meant that African Americans and whites were kept separate. In many Northern states, African Americans could not vote, and some states, such as Illinois, did not even allow free blacks to enter or settle in the state at all. African Americans' path to freedom was much longer than the trip to the North.

Rights for Women

What prompted women to begin fighting for their own rights in the mid-1800s?

At the beginning of the 1800s, women had a great many duties at home and in the church, but they had very little political or economic power. They were not allowed to vote, they had no access to colleges and universities, they could not hold any form of government office, and they had few professional opportunities for work. Married women were seen as dependent on and under the control of their husbands. They were unable to own property or make any sort of legal contracts, and in the case of a separation or divorce, the father retained custody of the children. As the 1800s progressed, however, more women became empowered.

As women joined the ranks of the social reformers, working for the benefit of others, they began to see the need for reform and equality for themselves as well. The fight for women's rights began mainly with the abolitionist movement. In the 1830s, many women were involved with the fight against slavery. More than 100 all-female antislavery organizations had been formed by the mid-1830s, and women were working hard behind the scenes to circulate petitions, edit antislavery articles, and help organize conventions. Women remained in the background, however, seen as dependents, not as independent thinkers and leaders.

During the early and mid-1800s, educational opportunities for women began to improve. Some schools for women were "finishing schools" whose purpose was to teach women social graces to prepare them for entry into upper-class society. At other schools, however, education pioneers worked to provide women with rigorous academic programs that offered a variety of courses and four-year programs. Founded by Emma Willard in 1821, New York's Troy Female Seminary was the first school in the United States to provide women with an academic program similar to men.

Discovery EDUCATION | SOCIAL STUDIES **TECHBOOK**

How did the reform movements of the 1840s change American society?

Catharine Beecher's Hartford Female Seminary also offered women students a broad range of academic subjects. In the 1830s, Beecher opened Western Female Institute in Cincinnati.

After it opened in 1837, Mount Holyoke Female Seminary (now College) in Massachusetts became a model for women's colleges in the United States. Its founder, chemist Mary Lyons, emphasized the importance of making education affordable and required Mount Holyoke's students to take many mathematics and science courses.

In 1837, at a national women's antislavery convention, it was decided that women should be allowed to give speeches to mixed gender audiences; their voices should be heard by men and women alike. The abolition movement was split on this idea: Could women really be entrusted with the power to tell men how to think? People such as Sarah and Angelina Grimké, powerful abolitionists in their own right, believed so. When church leaders expressed shock and outrage over Angelina's lecture to a mixed audience, her sister Sarah spoke up and published a pamphlet touting the idea that men and women should not be treated differently and that women deserved equal rights.

photo: Library of Congress

Founded by Mary Lyon in 1836, Mount Holyoke was the first true women's college in the nation and remains a prestigious all-women's college today.

In 1840, still split on the issue, the American Anti-Slavery Society designated three women to represent them at the World Anti-Slavery Convention in London, England, that year. However, when they got there, they were not able to participate because the conventioneers thought that having women speak would offend the British public. This indignation set these women on the path toward championing their own rights. One of them, Lucretia Mott, would go on to organize the nation's first women's rights convention.

The First National Convention of Women

Who led the national women's movement? What happened at the Women's Rights Convention in Seneca Falls?

Today, women work as heads of companies. They are government leaders and can attend almost any college or university in the world right alongside men. But in the early 1800s, women were not allowed to do any of these things. A feminist is a person who supports or fights for equal rights for women. It took some very strong feminists to change the way that women are viewed in the United States.

Discovery EDUCATION | SOCIAL STUDIES TECHBOOK

Born in 1793 in Massachusetts, Lucretia Mott was one of these early feminists. An abolitionist, she helped found the American Anti-Slavery Society with her husband in 1833. However, when she was appointed to represent the organization at a world convention on slavery in London in 1840, the convention organizers decided that Mott and the two other women with her would not be allowed to participate because they were women.

This experience helped convince Mott to begin spending her time fighting for the rights of women.

photo: Library of Congress
Susan B. Anthony (standing) and Elizabeth Cady Stanton.

Eight years after the antislavery convention, in 1848, Mott came together with another feminist, Elizabeth Cady Stanton, to organize the first-ever national women's rights convention in the United States. The convention was held in Seneca Falls, New York, in July 1848. Although the organizers were unsure of how the convention would be received, about 350 men and women attended—a remarkable amount of support for the first-ever convention of its kind.

At Seneca Falls, convention attendees drew up a document that would form the basis of their grievances and lay the groundwork for the fight for women's rights.

Entitled the "Declaration of Sentiments," the document was modeled after the Declaration of Independence. After beginning with the statement that "All men and women are created equal," it went on to name 15 major social injustices that women faced. The convention also came up with a list of demands, including the right to earn wages equal to men's and suffrage, or the right to vote.

Three years after Seneca Falls, in 1851, Elizabeth Cady Stanton joined forces with Susan B. Anthony, another feminist fighting for women's rights. Stanton was a wordsmith with great ideas; she often came up with the speeches that Anthony delivered to audiences. Together, the two also put out a weekly newspaper called *Revolution* and founded the National Woman Suffrage Association in 1869.

Explore this resource to consider arguments made for women's rights.

Discovery EDUCATION | SOCIAL STUDIES TECHBOOK

How did the reform movements of the 1840s change American society?

Stanton and Anthony both believed women would not truly be able to attain all their rights without first earning the right to vote. That did not happen at the national level until 1920.

A New Appreciation for America

How did writers and artists cultivate a new American culture in the 1800s?

Even though the United States broke free politically from British rule by 1783, developing artistic and cultural freedom from Europe took more time. Most art and architecture found in the United States was based on antiquated Roman or European styles. At the country's beginnings, the young nation had only one art museum and very few professional authors or well-known artists of its own.

American English Arrives

Starting in the early 1800s, American authors and intellectuals began to build a culture that was independent of Britain and the ancient European masters.

Language is a key part of any culture, but while Americans had begun to develop a language distinct from that of England, it was not until 1828 that these differences were documented by Noah Webster's *American Dictionary of the English Language.* A scholar, a lawyer, and a founder of Amherst College, Webster spent more than 40 years studying the English language before publishing his monumental dictionary. This massive book contained about 12,000 more words and 40,000 more definitions than any other English dictionary at the time. It also supported an "Americanized" language. In just a few short years, more than 60 million copies had been sold.

Transcendentalist Writers

Participants in the transcendentalist movement were thinkers who wanted to see how people could live simply in connection with nature and who described or shared their process in paintings, essays, poems, and other works. Several were New Englanders, including essayist Ralph Waldo Emerson and writer and naturalist Henry David Thoreau. Some of the transcendentalists experimented with communal living at the utopian society of Brook Farm.

The more popular writers were not transcendentalists, but they also celebrated the American wilderness and the heroic individual. Washington Irving, a native New Yorker, was among the first American authors to win international fame for his work. His story of Rip Van Winkle, published in 1818, and his short story of the headless horseman "The Legend of Sleepy Hollow," published in the 1820s, combined fact and fantasy and European and American culture to thrill audiences to this day. Viewed as the "leader of American literature," Irving also wrote historic works and spent time researching and studying in Europe. His home near Tarrytown, New York, is now a historic museum.

Another popular American writer was James Fenimore Cooper. Originally from New Jersey, Cooper was a novelist and a social critic. His series of popular novels, including the classic work *The Last of the Mohicans* (1826), told the story of fictional frontiersman Natty Bumppo and painted a romantic, idealized version of the American wilderness.

New Styles of Painting

photo: National Gallery of Art

Thomas Moran, a painter living in Philadelphia, Pennsylvania, was enchanted by the West even before he took his first trip to Wyoming in 1871.

Writers were not the only ones to capture and romanticize the natural beauty of the United States. The Hudson River School was a group of landscape painters who mostly lived and painted in upstate New York, near the Hudson River, between 1820 and 1880. Thomas Cole, Frederic Church, and other artists captured the ruggedness of the Catskill Mountains and the awe-inspiring nature in this part of the United States. Another school of artists painted romanticized landscape portraits of the American Southwest and the new Western frontier. Like the transcendentalist writers, these artists sought to capture the natural beauty in the world.

Together, all of these writers, artists, and nature-enthusiasts painted a vision of America that was unlike any other place in the world. There was another component of American culture that developed during the early 1800s, as well: the idea of a distinctly American citizen.

The Values of the Republic
What was Republicanism?

Republicanism, or civic republicanism, was the system of political values that motivated the social reform movements of the 1800s. Although republicanism inspired reformers to seek change, it also represented historical continuity with the nation's beginnings. Republicanism combines the ideas of liberty, justice, and natural rights for mankind, which were promoted in the Declaration of Independence.

Reformers of the 1800s carried with them the republican belief that people should live moral lives free of greed and corruption and that their government also should reflect these values.

Republicanism began as early as the late 1700s, with the notion that the country would survive only if its citizens were both virtuous and educated. In theory, it promoted the idea of government that depended on citizens to put the public good above their private needs. The early fight for women's rights was in some ways closely tied to this idea. As the primary caretakers of the youth, women were responsible for promoting virtue. Thus, the idea of republicanism also helped create a group of women seeking education and other rights for the nation's caretakers, the "Republican Motherhood."

Although everyone who embraced the idea of republicanism was in agreement on the need for a virtuous society, not everyone agreed on how that should come about. Republicanism was open to interpretation. This meant that the idea of republicanism seemed to continue with each president, no matter his political party or background.

When Thomas Jefferson took office in 1801, he wanted to restore civil liberties and get rid of the wealth and privilege that he saw becoming problems for the young country. He made people shake hands instead of bow to one another and had dinner parties at a round table so that nobody sat in a position of highest honor. In 1828, Andrew Jackson rose to the presidency with a dire warning that the nation had again been corrupted by special privileges for the wealthy, and he touted himself as a "champion for the common man" in his effort to restore the ideals of republicanism.

Consider the Essential Question:

How did the reform movements of the 1840s change American society?

Go online to complete the Social Studies Explanation.

Check for Understanding:

Were the reform movements of the mid-1800s solely a response to industrialization? Cite evidence to defend your position.

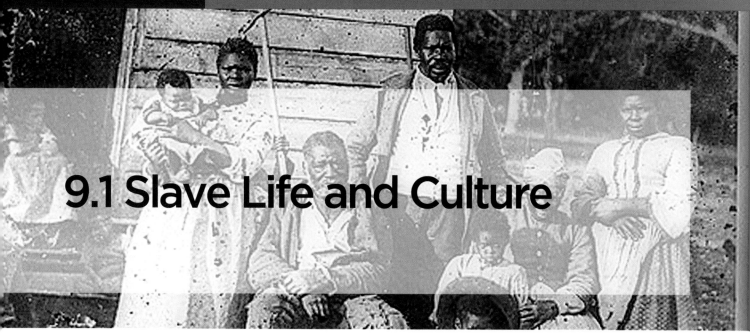

photo: Library of Congress

9.1 Slave Life and Culture

LESSON OVERVIEW

Introduction

In this concept, you will learn about the lives of enslaved people in the South before the Civil War. You will also explore what life was like for free African Americans in both the North and the South.

Essential Question

In antebellum America, what did it mean to be an enslaved African American? A free African American?

Lesson Objective

By the end of this lesson, you should be able to:

- Analyze the experiences of enslaved and free African Americans in antebellum America.

Key Vocabulary
Which terms do you already know?

- ☐ abolition
- ☐ Denmark Vesey
- ☐ discrimination
- ☐ Frederick Douglass
- ☐ fugitive
- ☐ Nat Turner
- ☐ oral tradition
- ☐ overseer
- ☐ plantation
- ☐ segregation
- ☐ slave codes

Discovery EDUCATION | SOCIAL STUDIES TECHBOOK

In antebellum America, what did it mean to be an enslaved
African American? A free African American?

ENGAGE

What was Frederick Douglass's pathway from slavery to freedom?
Visit Engage to learn more.

Essential Question

In antebellum America, what did it mean to be an enslaved African American? A free
African American?

EXPLORE

Life in Slavery

*What was everyday life like for enslaved African Americans in the
South?*

In the rural South, the main staple crop grown was cotton. Northern shippers depended
on the profits from the cotton trade with Europe, and the cotton industry greatly
expanded during the early 1800s. By 1840, cotton accounted for nearly half of all U.S.
exports, and the South produced more than half of the world's supply of cotton. As a
result, the men who owned the land where cotton was grown held a powerful influence
over the U.S. economy.

The intensive work of growing cotton relied on the labor of enslaved African Americans.
They cleared the land, planted the seeds, picked the cotton, and cleaned the cotton
fibers by removing the seeds, all by hand. As landowners in the South gained more
profits from the cotton industry, they bought more enslaved people to work the land.
Because these men and women brought wealth to landowners, not only for the work
they did, but also their value in the slave market, they were treated as investments
in property. Enslaved people were bought and sold at auctions, and families were
separated for economic reasons, such as when the landowner's property was divided
among his heirs or if he went bankrupt. Because the businesspeople involved in the
cotton industry viewed enslaved people as assets, or valuable things that could be
owned, they were not granted the democratic freedoms of citizens. Instead, the majority
of enslaved people spent their lives on farms, performing manual labor that contributed
to the economic success of the landowner and his family.

Slavery on Plantations

The majority of enslaved people in the South worked on large farms called plantations, which were dependent on slave labor to function. Field hands worked from dawn to dusk, six days a week, doing all the hard labor, including clearing land, planting, and weeding. During harvest season, enslaved people might work 18-hour days. No one was exempt from working, even pregnant women or children. Children as young as three or four years of age weeded gardens, carried drinking water, and helped care for animals. Enslaved people who were elderly or disabled were nonetheless required to work unceasingly, doing whatever tasks they were capable of. For example, people who were unable to walk or stand might be forced to weave cloth or sew or mend clothes.

Fieldwork was not just brute labor. Skill and effort were also needed to grow cotton, rice, and tobacco, as well as to care for horses and other livestock. Other enslaved people became skilled bricklayers, carpenters, coopers, or smiths.

Fieldworkers were under the watchful eye of the overseer, a white man whose job was to get the most work possible out of the enslaved laborers. Sometimes, the overseers were cruel and used harsh treatment. However, enslaved people were considered valuable property. If they complained of cruel treatment, an owner would sometimes replace the overseer. Enslaved people who disobeyed or tried to escape, however, were treated harshly. Whipping was a common form of punishment. Sometimes, those who rebelled would be sold to new owners who resided far away, separating them from their families.

photo: Getty Images

Most enslaved persons in the South were fieldworkers on large plantations.

On plantations, enslaved people lived in separate quarters from plantation owners. Usually, enslaved people resided in simple shacks with dirt floors. They were poorly fed. Infants and children in particular did not receive proper nutrition. Many suffered from diseases caused by malnutrition; these included rickets, a vitamin D or mineral deficiency that causes pain and weak bones, and scurvy, a vitamin C deficiency that causes muscle weakness. As a result of malnutrition and other health issues, perhaps a third of all babies born into enslavement died before they were a year old, and hardly more than half lived to their 10th birthday. Malnutrition of enslaved persons was largely due to ignorance; slave owners wanted slave babies to grow strong and healthy so they could be good workers.

Discovery SOCIAL STUDIES EDUCATION | **TECHBOOK**

In antebellum America, what did it mean to be an enslaved African American? A free African American?

Not all enslaved people worked outdoors in the fields. Some enslaved laborers worked in the plantation owner's house. They cooked, cleaned, served as maids or waiters, did the laundry, and cared for the plantation owner's children. Living conditions for enslaved people in the house was better than that of field hands, and they usually received better food.

Slave Codes and Fugitive Slave Laws

Most states had laws, called slave codes, which explained the rights of slave owners. The codes varied from state to state, but there were many similarities. Under these codes, it was forbidden to teach an enslaved person to read and write. Enslaved people could not meet in groups without a white person present. An enslaved person could not keep a gun. Enslaved people could not give testimony against white people in court. For the most part, enslaved people were treated as possessions. They could be sold, passed on to heirs, or given as gifts. Many enslaved people were sexually abused by their owners or overseers and were often forced to bear their owner's children. Some slave codes restricted harsh beatings and made it illegal to kill an enslaved person, but these legal protections were almost never enforced.

The federal government also enforced laws that protected slavery. Recall that Article IV of the Constitution included a fugitive slave clause that guaranteed to slave owners the right to reclaim enslaved persons who escaped to other states. In 1793, Congress passed a Fugitive Slave Act to enforce this constitutional provision. The Fugitive Slave Act permitted slave owners to employ agents to arrest enslaved persons who had escaped from them and then to present escaped slaves before a local judge. Judges were authorized to send fugitives back to their owners. Congress passed an additional Fugitive Slave Law in 1850. The Fugitive Slave laws created slave-catching industries in the United States. Professional bounty hunters traveled around the country searching for fugitive slaves.

Southern White Society

The increase in the worldwide demand for cotton helped plantation families become among the wealthiest in the United States. Plantation owners owned the majority of enslaved persons in the South. They often lived in mansion-sized homes stocked with expensive furnishings imported from Europe. They enjoyed leisure time for travel, the arts, and sports. Most whites living in the South were not as wealthy. Many were self-sufficient yeoman, or small, farmers who produced food for their own use and often bartered with their neighbors to meet other needs. Some owned a small number of enslaved persons who generally assisted with family tasks, such as clearing land, harvesting, raising children, cleaning, and preparing meals. Many Southern whites also belonged to a poorer class that owned no land or slaves. Most hired themselves out to work on plantations or small farms. Others worked in a variety of other jobs, such as mining or on the railroad.

Members of all three white social classes supported a Southern social and legal structure based upon white supremacy. This structure placed all whites in a position favorable to all African Americans, free and enslaved alike.

Family Life

What was family life like for enslaved people?

Enslaved people could not marry without their owners' permission, and slave marriages were not recognized by law. Despite this, many enslaved people formed marriage-like partnerships, and some were able to live with the same spouse for their whole lives. However, owners could sell wives or husbands at any time, and it was not uncommon for a wife and husband to be forced to live apart. Owners used breaking up families as a threat and a punishment.

photo: Getty Images
Enslaved mothers might have their children sold from them.

If an enslaved husband and wife or an enslaved parent and child were lucky enough to live within a few miles of each other, they might be able to obtain special permission from their owners to visit one another. In general, plantation owners accepted slave marriages because they thought married enslaved people were less likely to try to run away.

Despite these restrictions, many enslaved families developed strong bonds and formed alternative family structures within their communities. Parents often named children for family members and kept in touch with kin on neighboring plantations. When parents were absent, aunts, uncles, or cousins cared for children.

Children were frequently sold off from their parents. If a child was sold to a neighboring plantation, relatives on the plantation would often take on the role of parent. If a blood relative was not present, another family would often try to substitute for the parents. Many children were taught to refer to all enslaved adults other than their parents as "aunt" or "uncle" and to call other enslaved children their brothers and sisters. In this way, a strong sense of community developed among enslaved African Americans.

Explore this interactive to learn more about how abolitionists depicted slavery in art.

Discovery EDUCATION | SOCIAL STUDIES TECHBOOK.

In antebellum America, what did it mean to be an enslaved African American? A free African American?

African American Culture

What kind of culture did enslaved African Americans develop?

Religion

You might wonder how human beings could survive living in such conditions. For enslaved African Americans, religious and cultural traditions played a large part in helping them cope with the harshness of their lives. Slave owners encouraged religion as a means of control. They commonly forced enslaved people to attend services where white ministers preached the values of obedience and of accepting one's lot in life. However, many enslaved African Americans also developed their own religious practices. These often blended traditional African and Christian rituals. Prayers, hymns, and sermons often focused on an eventual release from bondage and escape to the "promised land."

Song

Music also served as an important part of the culture of enslaved African Americans. The most important instrument was the voice, often accompanied by clapping or foot stomping. Enslaved people also made drums, rattles, and stringed instruments such as the banjo. Work songs helped make group tasks go more smoothly. American jazz, gospel, and blues music developed as spirited responses to the drudgery and suffering that characterized the daily lives of enslaved African Americans.

SCENE ON A SOUTHERN PLANTATION.—Sketched by A. W. Thompson.—[See Page 94.]

photo: Getty Images

For enslaved African Americans, music offered temporary relief from the hardship of daily life.

Stories

Enslaved people also entertained each other with storytelling. Very few enslaved people learned to read because it was illegal to teach them. Traditions, stories, and songs were passed along orally, that is, by word of mouth. Folktales such as the Brer Rabbit stories bred the value of cleverness. These stories, based on African trickster tales, taught African American children and adults how to survive with dignity in a dangerous world.

Explore this resource to learn more about African American spirituals.

Resistance

How did enslaved African Americans react to slavery?

Because enslaved people outnumbered white people in the South, generations of whites lived in constant fear of slave uprisings. Organized revolts against slavery, although rare, made a strong impression. These incidents dated back to colonial times. In 1739, for example, a large uprising in South Carolina called the Stono Rebellion resulted in 60 deaths. Afterward, colonial officials enforced strict restrictions on African Americans. Nearly a century later, Denmark Vesey was enslaved to a Charleston, South Carolina, slave trader and planter. Vesey purchased his freedom and became a preacher. He began organizing a revolt and was thought to have as many as 9,000 African Americans ready for an uprising. Before the revolt could begin, he was caught, and in 1822, he and 35 of his followers were hanged.

NAT TURNER

photo: Getty Images

Some who escaped, such as Harriet Tubman, returned and helped others escape to freedom on the Underground Railroad, a system of escape routes and safehouses secretly operated by free people. Frederick Douglass escaped slavery and later worked hard for abolition through his writing and speeches.

In 1831, Nat Turner led a revolt in Virginia that killed more than 60 people, including Turner's owner and family. In retaliation, slave owners attempting to put down the revolt killed more than 100 enslaved people, many of whom were not involved in the uprising. Following Turner's revolt, Virginia and other states passed restrictive laws to further limit what enslaved people could do. Nat Turner's rebellion also frightened many white people into believing that slavery was the only effective way to control the African American population.

Discovery EDUCATION | SOCIAL STUDIES TECHBOOK

In antebellum America, what did it mean to be an enslaved African American? A free African American?

Free African Americans

What was life like for free African Americans?

Not all African Americans were enslaved. Many free African Americans lived in both the North and the South. Some had bought their freedom, some had been freed by their owners, and some were descendants of free African Americans. Despite being free, they were not citizens and were considered to be at the lowest rank of the social order. In Charleston, South Carolina, in 1849, free African Americans were employed in 50 different types of work, including such jobs as carpenters, tailors, shoemakers, butchers, barbers, grocers, and cooks.

In the North, free African Americans actively participated in the U.S. economy. The expansion of industry created job opportunities in New England and the Midwest, and families were free to move where they had the best chance to make a living together. Because they were able to keep the profits from their labor, some were able to own land, homes, and businesses, and they also paid taxes.

In some New England cities, African American property owners were able to vote for brief periods of time. A very small number of free African Americans in the South even owned enslaved people, but they were usually relatives whom they later freed. Overall, the freedom to live and work as they pleased made it easier for free African Americans to organize communities and to conduct their daily activities without the fear of an overseer.

Religious life was vital for African Americans, and African American preachers and ministers were important community leaders. Richard Allen founded the African Methodist Episcopal (AME) Church in Philadelphia in 1816; today, it has more than 2.5 million members worldwide.

Free African Americans also were active in the abolition movement. African Americans such as "conductors" William Still and David Ruggles played key roles in the Underground Railroad. Ruggles was prominent in the New York Vigilance Committee, a volunteer organization that protected fugitive enslaved people from recapture and free African Americans from being kidnapped and sold into slavery.

In the late 1820s, John B. Russwurm and Samuel Cornish began publishing *Freedom's Journal*, "devoted to the improvement of the colored population."

But how free were they actually? Public places, such as theaters and restaurants, and most public transportation were segregated, meaning that African Americans and white people were assigned separate areas and facilities. In many places, including in the North and the Midwest, African Americans could not attend schools with white people, and the few schools for African Americans were ill equipped. It would take until the mid-1900s before this began to change.

Discrimination against African Americans, or negative or hostile treatment because of their race, took many forms. Other than in a few locations in New England, free African Americans could not vote, give testimony in court, file lawsuits, sit on juries, meet freely in groups, or intermarry with white people. If they were convicted of any crime, no matter how serious, they might be sold into slavery. Washington, DC, the nation's capital, subjected free African Americans to a curfew. Virginia law required that African Americans leave the state within one year of their emancipation, and North Carolina did not allow free African Americans to enter the state.

Consider the Essential Question:

In antebellum America, what did it mean to be an enslaved African American? A free African American?

Go online to complete the Social Studies Explanation.

Check for Understanding:

In what ways did enslaved persons respond to difficult living conditions?

SOCIAL STUDIES TECHBOOK

Discovery EDUCATION

How did geographical differences between the North and the South lead to conflict?

9.2 Regional Differences

photo: Library of Congress

LESSON OVERVIEW

Introduction

In this concept, you will read about how the geography of the United States created economic differences between the North and South in the first half of the 1800s. You will examine how those differences created bitter policy disagreements on issues such as tariffs and the expansion of slavery. Finally, you will consider why these disagreements led to disunion and the Civil War.

Key Vocabulary

Which terms do you already know?

- ☐ abolition
- ☐ agriculture
- ☐ Angelina Grimké
- ☐ cotton gin
- ☐ Eli Whitney
- ☐ export
- ☐ Frederick Douglass
- ☐ Industrial Revolution
- ☐ plantation
- ☐ Sarah Grimké
- ☐ sectionalism
- ☐ tariff
- ☐ William Lloyd Garrison

Essential Question

How did geographical differences between the North and the South lead to conflict?

Lesson Objectives

By the end of this lesson, you should be able to:

- Explain economic, social, and cultural differences between the North and the South.

- Explain how economic, social, and cultural differences between the North and South resulted in disagreements over public policy.

ENGAGE

In what ways were the North and the South the same country, but different worlds? Visit Engage to learn more.

Essential Question

How did geographical differences between the North and the South lead to conflict?

EXPLORE

The Northern Economy

What was the economy of the North like in the first half of the 1800s?

Between 1800 and 1850, the United States went through many changes. The most obvious change was the growth of the country with the addition of new land in the West. Other changes resulted from the Industrial Revolution, which brought on the rise of factories and the shift from human labor to reliance on machines. The Industrial Revolution changed almost every aspect of daily life in some parts of the United States. As business owners built the nation's earliest factories, increasing numbers of Americans began to earn a living using machines rather than working the land.

Factories

Although the land and climate of the Northern states made them difficult to farm, swift-moving rivers in these states created ideal locations for factories powered by water. Business owners in the North quickly built factories and mills along the rivers to take advantage of their power. Northern *entrepreneurs*, or people who invest in starting new businesses, invested money in these new factories.

Cities

The rapid growth of factories led to an expansion of Northern cities. For example, New York City had about 60,000 residents in 1800, but by 1850, its population was more than 515,000. In New York and other Northern cities, many new residents had moved away from farms to find work in the factories. In addition, new immigrants were arriving from Europe. Some immigrants had enough money to travel to the Midwest and buy farmland. More desperate immigrants, including many from Ireland, had little money and remained in the cities where they first arrived, such as Boston and New York.

Railroads

Along with the growth of factories and cities during the first half of the 1800s, the North saw growth in railroads. The first U.S. railroads were built to connect Eastern cities with each other and with markets in the Midwest. Factory owners in the Northeast needed railroads to ship their manufactured goods to territories in the Midwest, so building railroads in these regions was very profitable. Because the Northeast had more factories and cities than the South, it also had more railroads. By 1850, the Northern states had more than 5,000 miles of railroad track compared with 2,000 miles in the South.

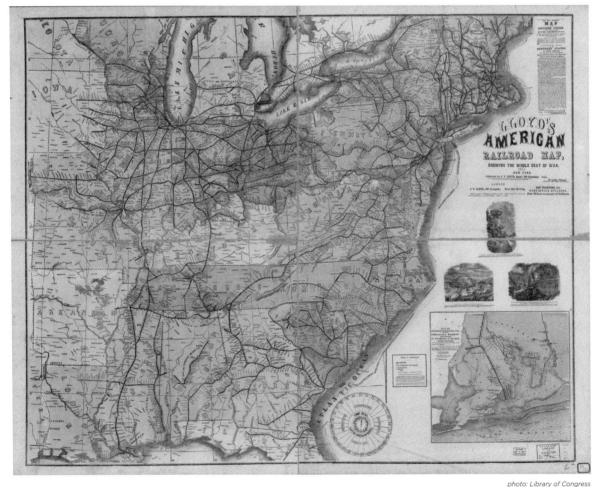

photo: Library of Congress

What does this railroad map reveal about differences between the North and South?

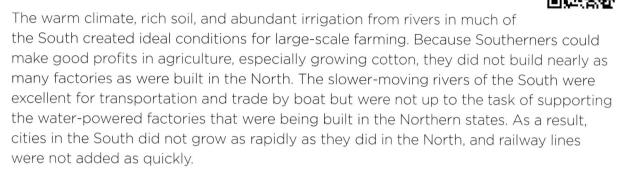

The Southern Economy

What was the economy of the South like in the first half of the 1800s?

The warm climate, rich soil, and abundant irrigation from rivers in much of the South created ideal conditions for large-scale farming. Because Southerners could make good profits in agriculture, especially growing cotton, they did not build nearly as many factories as were built in the North. The slower-moving rivers of the South were excellent for transportation and trade by boat but were not up to the task of supporting the water-powered factories that were being built in the Northern states. As a result, cities in the South did not grow as rapidly as they did in the North, and railway lines were not added as quickly.

King Cotton

Although the Southern economy was based primarily on agriculture, it was also affected by the Industrial Revolution. In the 1700s, cotton was not a very profitable crop because it took many hours of hand labor to prepare cotton for sale. Cotton grows in seed pods called "bolls." The cotton fibers have to be separated from the bolls, which have hard, sharp points that prick a cotton picker's fingers. Numerous tiny seeds are tangled in each boll. Removing the seeds by hand is a long and tedious task.

In 1793, Eli Whitney invented the cotton gin (short for "engine"), a machine that could remove cotton seeds very quickly. A single cotton gin could replace many laborers, so these machines made cotton production more profitable. At the same time, the emergence of new textile mills in the North increased demand for Southern cotton. Together, the rise in demand for cotton and the increased profit from producing it caused Southern plantation owners to devote more land to planting cotton instead of other crops.

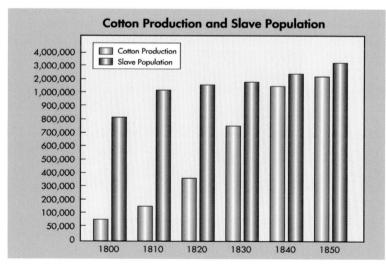

Cotton production increased dramatically between 1800 and 1850.

Slavery

Even though the cotton gin lessened the need for human labor per acre of cotton, the amount of acreage where cotton was planted skyrocketed. Because of this, Southerners needed more labor to work on cotton plantations. During the first several decades of the 1800s, slavery became more important to the South's economy than ever before.

The U.S. Constitution prevented Congress from ending the importation of enslaved people until 1808. As the end of this limitation approached in 1807, Congress passed a ban on the importation of enslaved persons to take effect the following year. Children born to enslaved people were also considered to be enslaved, so the number of enslaved people in the United States continued to grow long after 1808.

Southerners thought their economy depended on slavery, and so they strongly defended it. Even people who did not themselves own enslaved people, such as bankers and small farmers, thought slavery was necessary for the Southern economy and to maintain the region's way of life.

Sectionalism

How did the differences between the North and the South lead to disagreements?

The differences in the North and the South in the first half of the 1800s led to increasing sectionalism. *Sectionalism* means strong loyalty to one region. For many people, sectional loyalty was far stronger than loyalty to the nation as a whole. During these years, Northerners and Southerners had very different priorities for the country, which led to disagreements about public policies.

Northerners, for example, wanted laws and policies that would help the manufacturing industry grow. They wanted the federal government to pay for improvements in roads and other means of transportation that would help them ship goods around the country. Southerners used rivers to transport goods and had no need for additional roads to take goods to market. Northerners also tended to support tariffs, which were taxes on imported goods. The effect of tariffs was to make imported goods cost more, so that consumers would be more likely to buy goods manufactured domestically. Because manufacturing was such a large part of the Northern economy, people living in the North supported higher tariffs.

Explore this interactive to learn more about stark differences between the North and South.

MISSISSIPPI RIVER BOAT WITH COTTON, BATON ROUGE, LA.

photo: Getty Images

Southerners wanted to export bales of cotton like the ones shown here. They did not want the federal government to pass tariffs on manufactured goods.

While Northern manufacturers benefited from higher prices on manufactured goods, Southerners were consumers of manufactured goods and did not benefit from the higher prices that tariffs would create. Southerners generally opposed tariffs. Southerners also worried that if the United States placed tariffs on manufactured goods from Great Britain, for example, Great Britain might retaliate by placing tariffs on Southern cotton, making Southern cotton harder to sell. Southern growers would suffer on both ends, paying more for manufactured goods and struggling in competition with cotton overseas.

The Abolition Movement Grows

How did the abolition movement affect relations between the North and the South?

Transportation and tariffs were two points of disagreement between the two regions of the country, but the issue of slavery created even more serious conflicts. At the same time slavery was becoming even more important to the Southern cotton economy, the people who opposed slavery decided they needed to work more actively for their cause. In 1777, Vermont's new state constitution included a partial ban on slavery. During the late 1700s, all of the New England states outlawed most slavery, and both Pennsylvania and New York had begun to gradually outlaw it as well. During the first half of the 1800s, the national abolition movement—the movement to end slavery—gathered strength.

Many abolitionists opposed slavery for human-rights reasons. Citing Thomas Jefferson's claim in the Declaration of Independence that "all men are created equal," these opponents of slavery argued that the "peculiar institution" could not exist in a truly democratic society.

A large group of abolitionists also opposed slavery for religious reasons. American Quakers had denounced slavery since the 1600s. Their belief system held that all violence is morally wrong, including holding people in captivity. They also believed that all people were equally worthy in God's eyes and equally capable of communing with God. Because of this, all people were entitled to equal treatment by others. Many Quakers added maple syrup to their coffee instead of sugar because they objected to using items produced with slave labor. Quakers were driven out of many Southern towns because of their opposition to slavery. In 1815, Indiana abolitionist Levi Coffin, a Quaker, began operating the Underground Railroad, taking practical steps to improve life for slaves.

In 1831, William Lloyd Garrison began publishing the *Liberator*, an antislavery newspaper that called for the immediate end of slavery in the United States. A few years later, Garrison founded the American Anti-Slavery Society, which took the same position.

While some Southerners, such as sisters Angelina and Sarah Grimké, joined the abolition movement, most abolitionists were Northerners. Some, such as Frederick Douglass, were also formerly enslaved. Douglass, who had escaped from slavery, traveled around the country and spoke out about his experiences. He helped people see slavery from a different perspective.

Many Southerners saw the abolition movement as an attack on their way of life. Some Southerners said abolitionists were trying to take away their ability to earn a living. They argued that their treatment of enslaved African Americans was no worse—or was even better—than Northern factory owners' treatment of immigrants and other workers. Southerners defended slavery and some said that it benefited enslaved African Americans because they would not be able to work for wages in the United States.

photo: Library of Congress

Frederick Douglass was a prominent abolitionist who gave lectures about his experiences under slavery.

The violence and anger that Southerners felt toward abolitionists reflected the growing tensions between the North and the South. During the 1850s, when the federal government had to decide how to handle the issue of slavery in new territory gained during the Mexican-American War, these tensions would grow even stronger. By 1860, some people would begin wondering whether the two regions of the country should even remain parts of the same country.

Consider the Essential Question:

How did geographical differences between the North and the South lead to conflict?

Go online to complete the Social Studies Explanation.

Check for Understanding:

Describe the emergence, growth, and development of the abolitionist movement during the first half of the 1800s. How did this movement contribute to sectional tensions?

photo: Getty Images

9.3 Road to Disunion

LESSON OVERVIEW

Introduction

In this concept, you will learn how Americans reached the point where they were willing to divide the United States and fight a war over its future.

Essential Question

By 1860, why were the nation's leaders unable to keep the Union together?

Lesson Objectives

By the end of this lesson, you should be able to:

- Connect divergent positions on slavery and states' rights with failed attempts at congressional compromise.

- Trace and explain the significance of key events between 1850 and 1860 that deepened the crisis between the North and the South.

Key Vocabulary
Which terms do you already know?

- [ ] Abraham Lincoln
- [ ] Battle of Harpers Ferry
- [ ] Bleeding Kansas
- [ ] Compromise of 1850
- [ ] Daniel Webster
- [ ] Dred Scott
- [ ] fire-eaters
- [ ] free soiler
- [ ] free state
- [ ] Fugitive Slave Laws
- [ ] gag rule
- [ ] Harpers Ferry
- [ ] Harriet Beecher Stowe
- [ ] Henry Clay
- [ ] John Brown
- [ ] John Brown's Raid
- [ ] John C. Calhoun
- [ ] John Quincy Adams
- [ ] Kansas
- [ ] Kansas-Nebraska Act
- [ ] Lincoln-Douglas Debates
- [ ] mandate
- [ ] Missouri
- [ ] Missouri Compromise
- [ ] Nebraska
- [ ] nullification
- [ ] popular sovereignty
- [ ] Pottawatomie Massacre
- [ ] Republican Party
- [ ] Roger Taney
- [ ] sectionalism
- [ ] slave state
- [ ] Stephen Douglas
- [ ] Tariff of Abominations
- [ ] *Uncle Tom's Cabin*
- [ ] Union
- [ ] Virginia

Discovery | SOCIAL STUDIES
EDUCATION | **TECHBOOK**

By 1860, why were the nation's leaders unable to keep the Union together?

ENGAGE

What book "made this great war"? Visit Engage to learn more.

Essential Question

By 1860, why were the nation's leaders unable to keep the Union together?

EXPLORE

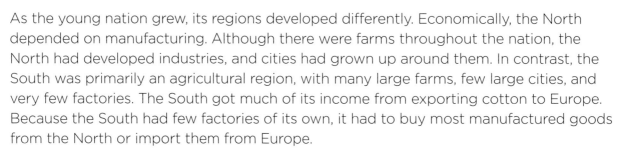

Disagreements Divide

How did economics divide the nation?

As the young nation grew, its regions developed differently. Economically, the North depended on manufacturing. Although there were farms throughout the nation, the North had developed industries, and cities had grown up around them. In contrast, the South was primarily an agricultural region, with many large farms, few large cities, and very few factories. The South got much of its income from exporting cotton to Europe. Because the South had few factories of its own, it had to buy most manufactured goods from the North or import them from Europe.

You may recall that one component of the American System was a tariff on imported goods. The purpose of the tariff was to increase sales of U.S.-made products by making foreign products more expensive. Because the South was a consumer of manufactured goods, the tariff was a tax that benefited Northern manufacturers at the Southerners' expense. This was part of the compromise that was the American System.

photo: Getty Images

The Custom House at Salem, Massachusetts.

However, the Tariff of 1828 raised prices by up to 100 percent. This went beyond making Northern goods competitive; it allowed Northern manufacturers to raise their prices and earn huge profits. On top of that, when foreign countries sold less of their products in the United States, they had less income with which to buy Southern cotton. Hence, the Southern nickname for the Tariff of 1828 was the Tariff of Abominations. An *abomination* is something disgusting and hateful.

Explore this interactive to learn about perspectives on the sectional crisis.

The Nullification Crisis

How did the country almost go to war in 1833?

The South Carolina House of Representatives created a special committee to propose a response to the 1828 tariff. In December, the committee presented its report—which was secretly written by Vice President John C. Calhoun. The South Carolina House then published the report under the title "Exposition and Protest." In this document, Calhoun argued that a tax that supported one industry at the expense of other sections of the country was an unconstitutional abuse of power: "[T]he power of imposing a duty on imports for revenue . . . is abused by being converted into an instrument of rearing up the industry of one section of the country on the ruins of another." Calhoun further argued that individual states had the right to *nullify*, or invalidate and cancel, a federal law if the states decided the law was unconstitutional.

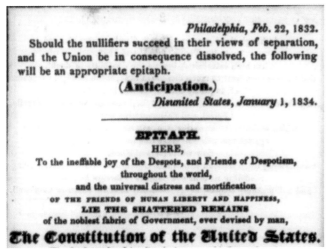

Excerpt from 1832 broadside opposing nullification.

photo: Library of Congress

In 1830, pro-Southern senators tried to use the nullification issue to forge a political alliance with senators from the West. The attempt began when a senator from Connecticut proposed to limit the sale of federal lands in western states. Knowing this idea angered western senators, South Carolina Senator Robert Hayne rose in opposition. Hayne argued that the states rather than the federal government should have authority to control lands within their borders. He also claimed that the United States was a compact, or agreement, of the individual states. Therefore, the states had the authority to ignore federal laws if they wished to do so.

Discovery SOCIAL STUDIES EDUCATION TECHBOOK.

By 1860, why were the nation's leaders unable to keep the Union together?

Massachusetts Senator Daniel Webster was considered the leading orator in the chamber. For two days in January 1830, Webster held the floor and delivered a forceful response to Hayne's position. Instead of being a mere agreement between states, Webster asserted that the United States was "a popular government, erected by the people." For many, Webster's words made nullification seem like treason, or disloyalty to the country.

Members of Congress from South Carolina and other Southern states failed to convince Northerners that the tariff was unconstitutional. In 1832, a compromise was reached and Congress reduced the tariff, but many in the South wanted it reduced more or even eliminated.

Still dissatisfied with the tariff, South Carolina passed a law claiming to nullify the tariff and prohibiting its enforcement. You may recall that years earlier, in response to the Alien and Sedition Acts, Thomas Jefferson and James Madison had argued in the Kentucky and Virginia Resolutions that the states had the right to nullify and block the enforcement of federal laws they judged unconstitutional. South Carolina's nullification law was different. Jefferson and Madison thought a majority of states needed to agree to nullify, whereas South Carolina had nullified on its own.

The main difference, though, was that South Carolina had actually gone ahead and declared a federal law invalid. Nullification supporters once again maintained that the federal government had been created by the states. Therefore, they claimed, its authority to act in the "general welfare" was limited. As President Jackson prepared to send the U.S. Army to South Carolina to enforce the tariff, South Carolina readied its militia to repel an "invasion." The nullification crisis had brought the country to the verge of war.

The South Carolina nullification law went into effect in February 1833. After a few weeks of great tension, the crisis ended in March. Kentucky Senator Henry Clay, also known as "The Great Compromiser," helped broker a second compromise. Congress agreed to reduce the tariff further, and South Carolina repealed its nullification law. But the tariff compromise did not resolve the disagreement about states' rights. South Carolina did not agree that it had no right to nullify federal laws; it merely agreed not to nullify this particular law.

Aside from the tariff, there was another issue lurking behind the states' rights controversy: slavery. Most people agreed the Constitution protected slavery where it already existed; the issue was whether to allow slavery to extend into the territories. If the nation continued to add more free states without adding more slave states, the free states would have a majority in the Senate and the South could no longer block legislation that was against their interests.

SOCIAL STUDIES
TECHBOOK

Division over Slavery

How were arguments over slavery dividing the nation?

The North and South had argued over slavery ever since writing the Declaration of Independence. At the Constitutional Convention in 1787, many of the Framers had wanted to end slavery then and there, but the Southern states had refused to remain in the Union if slavery was forbidden. So the "peculiar institution" had remained, protected by portions of the Constitution that required states to return enslaved persons who ran away.

Even though slavery was protected by the Constitution, by the 1820s public opinion in much of the world had turned against it. Most countries, including the United States, had banned the importation of enslaved persons, and slavery itself was on the way out in the Northern states. The exception was the South. As cotton production became more profitable, due in large part to the invention of the cotton gin, the American South became more and more economically dependent on slave labor.

Positions on Slavery

As the United States' population grew and as new territories were settled, conflict arose over the extension of slavery into these territories. There were several positions on extending slavery:

- Americans who wanted to abolish, or end, slavery were known as abolitionists.

- Free soilers accepted slavery where it existed, but were against its expansion into new territories and states.

- Many people thought the people of each new territory or state should decide the issue for themselves. This position was known as popular sovereignty.

- Those who wanted to break away from the United States and form a separate country in which the right to slave property could be guaranteed were called fire-eaters. Northerners used this term because they believed these Southern extremists used false propaganda to inflame sectional tensions.

The Gag Rule

In 1834, the abolitionist American Anti-Slavery Society began bombarding Congress with petitions to abolish slavery in Washington, DC. Many Northern representatives were either indifferent to abolishing slavery in the District or wished to avoid the topic in the interest of harmony, so as each petition was presented, it was denied. But as petitions continued to come in, Southern legislators became more and more rigid in their defense of slavery. Finally, in 1836, the House voted to adopt a gag rule, which automatically tabled any legislation dealing with the slavery issue. It was called a gag rule because, like a gag tied around a person's mouth, the rule prevented any discussion. The gag rule meant that action on the petitions was postponed indefinitely.

Discovery EDUCATION | SOCIAL STUDIES TECHBOOK

By 1860, why were the nation's leaders unable to keep the Union together?

A gag rule did not prevent the American Anti-Slavery Society from continuing to voice opinions about slavery. In the 1837–1838 congressional session alone, they sent 130,000 petitions to end slavery in addition to 32,000 petitions to abolish the gag rule; 23,000 petitions to prohibit interstate trade of enslaved persons; 22,000 petitions to bar the admission of any more slave states; and 21,000 petitions to abolish slavery in the western territories. Each of these petitions had hundreds of signatures.

The American Anti-Slavery Society was not the only group that was against the gag rule. A small group of congressmen, led by former president John Quincy Adams of Massachusetts, opposed the gag rule, arguing that it interfered with the constitutional right of citizens "to petition the government for a redress of grievances." The gag rule was a House rule that had to be renewed each year; each year, Adams argued to cancel the rule and each year he was defeated. However, as tensions between the North and the South grew during the 1830s, Adams was able to gain more support. He argued that because the U.S. Constitution forbade Congress from obstructing the right of petition, Congress's continual refusal to consider petitions was unconstitutional. The gag rule gradually lost the support of Northern legislators, who felt that this unconstitutional action was wrong, no matter what their views on slavery were. Adams's argument was finally successful in 1844, and the gag rule was overturned.

photo: Library of Congress
John Quincy Adams (1767–1848), the son of John Adams and a brilliant diplomat, won the election of 1824.

Keeping the Balance

How did settling the western territories cause further tension?

In 1819, there were an equal number of free states that outlawed slavery, and slave states that permitted slavery. As long as there were equal numbers of free states and slave states, there was a balance of power in the Senate. But the country was expanding, and the new territories that had been carved out of the Louisiana Purchase were being settled quickly. Southerners who moved into these new territories had taken their enslaved laborers with them. Northerners who moved to the new territories often resented having to compete with cheap slave labor.

The Missouri Compromise

The situation reached a crisis when Maine asked to be admitted to the United States. Because Maine was a free territory, its admission as a state would tip the balance in the Senate. Congress argued about the issue for months. in 1820, the speaker of the House, Henry Clay of Kentucky, came up with a plan for compromise. To earn support for his proposal, Clay argued that a compromise was not simply the product of negotiators saying, "If you do this, I will give you that." Instead, Clay favored a solution in which each

photo: Library of Congress

Henry Clay became known as the "Great Compromiser."

side of the argument would feel that they received what they wanted. He knew that Northerners wanted to rid the nation of slavery, while Southerners wanted to protect this institution. He came up with a plan known as the Missouri Compromise.

According to the terms of the Missouri Compromise, Missouri, which had also requested statehood, would be admitted to the Union as a slave state. At the same time, Maine would be admitted as a free state. This would keep the balance on Congress between 11 free and 11 slave states. In addition, the compromise would draw a line across the Louisiana Purchase at 36°30'N. Slavery would be protected in new states located south of the line, but banned north of the line.

For the time being, the crisis was resolved, but no one knew how long the calm would last. In fact, the Compromise held for 30 years. During that time, six more territories became states, and the balance between slave states and free states was maintained.

Another crisis emerged following the Mexican-American War. The Treaty of Guadalupe Hidalgo, which ended the war, arranged for the United States to purchase California and territory that makes up most of the Southwest. During the debate in the House of Representatives to fund the land purchase, Pennsylvania Congressman David Wilmot proposed that slavery be banned in the entire area. This proposal, called the Wilmot Proviso, passed the House, which was then controlled by representatives from heavily populated free states in the North. It failed to pass the Senate, where an equal number of slave and free states had balanced representation. The debate over the Wilmot Proviso demonstrated the challenges Congress would face attempting to settle disagreements over slavery.

Discovery EDUCATION | SOCIAL STUDIES TECHBOOK

By 1860, why were the nation's leaders unable to keep the Union together?

Following the huge increase in population due to the gold rush of 1849, California asked for admission to enter the Union as a free state. Lawmakers from the South believed that slavery should be legal throughout the country. The Missouri Compromise had only applied to land obtained in the Louisiana Purchase but not further west. Leaders in Congress could not agree on how to resolve this issue. The old arguments exploded once more.

The Compromise of 1850

Henry Clay, now a U.S. senator, negotiated another compromise. He proposed a favorable "arrangement of all questions in controversy between the free and slave States." For six months, Clay led the debate in Congress, until he introduced a bill that would address all disputes, which he proclaimed to be "neither southern nor northern. It is equal; it is fair; it is a compromise."

On March 7, 1850, Massachusetts Senator Daniel Webster delivered a famous address known as the "The Seventh of March Speech" on the floor of the Senate. Webster hoped his words would unite both sides of the slavery issue in support of Clay's compromise bill. He spoke for three hours of the importance of preserving the Union. Webster described what he thought was the pointlessness of eliminating slavery where it existed or worrying about the expansion of slavery into the lands of the Southwest, where plantation agriculture would not work. But Webster also urged the expansion of fugitive slave laws. For this, he was roundly criticized in the North.

In July 1850, the Senate rejected Clay's proposal to reach a grand compromise on slavery by passing a single law. But his ideas survived. With the help of Senator Stephen Douglas of Illinois, who repackaged Clay's proposals into five separate bills, each part of the compromise was enacted. Under the Compromise of 1850, California would enter the Union as a free state. The rest of the Mexican Cession was divided into two territories, Utah Territory and New Mexico Territory. These territories would be governed by the principle of popular sovereignty: Residents in each area would decide slavery's fate at the ballot box.

As part of the Compromise, Congress passed the second Fugitive Slave Act. This law said that any person who knew of an escaped enslaved person and did not assist in their capture could be sent to prison. States that had passed personal liberty laws to prevent the return of runaway enslaved persons were now required to enforce the South's repressive system of slavery. The law also increased government support for slave-catchers, people who earned their living pursuing and recovering enslaved persons who escaped. The Fugitive Slave Act eliminated jury trials for people accused of escaping from slavery. Instead, individual specially appointed commissioners would decide whether a slave-catcher's claim was valid. The commissioners were paid $5 if they released the person and $10 if they declared the person a fugitive and sent him or her back into slavery. The law also banned the slave trade from Washington, DC.

The Compromise of 1850 brought another temporary truce to Congress, but the country was not at peace. The Fugitive Slave Act outraged abolitionists. Many refused to enforce the law and committed acts of civil disobedience in protest. They also continued to support the Underground Railroad. On July 4, 1854, at the annual picnic of the New England Anti-Slavery Society, William Lloyd Garrison publicly burned copies of the Fugitive Slave Law and the Constitution and proclaimed, "So perish all compromises with tyranny."

Bleeding Kansas

What were the effects of the Kansas-Nebraska Act?

When the Compromise of 1850 was passed, the land west of Iowa and Missouri was supposed to be Indian territory—land set aside for Native Americans who had been displaced from their traditional homelands by white settlers. But soon, there was pressure to allow white settlement there, too, both from farmers who wanted the land and from railroad developers.

photo: Getty Images
Proslavery and antislavery battalions formed.

THE MARAIS DES CYGNES MASSACRE, KANSAS, MAY 19, 1858. Page 117.
photo: Getty Images
In May 1858, a proslavery group executed five free soldiers at Marais Des Cygnes, Kansas.

In 1854, led by Senator Stephen Douglas of Illinois, Congress passed the Kansas-Nebraska Act, creating two new territories and opening the land to settlement. According to the Missouri Compromise, slavery should have been banned from Kansas and Nebraska. Instead, the Kansas-Nebraska Act voided the Missouri Compromise and said the question of slavery would be decided by popular sovereignty. Almost overnight, proslavery and antislavery activists streamed into Kansas, hoping to influence the outcome of the vote. It did not take long for violence to break out. A proslavery posse attacked antislavery forces in Lawrence, Kansas, burning a hotel, destroying printing presses, and killing a man.

Discovery | SOCIAL STUDIES
EDUCATION | **TECHBOOK**

By 1860, why were the nation's leaders unable to keep the Union together?

In revenge, John Brown led an attack on proslavery men in Pottawatomie Creek, Kansas, murdering five men and boys. Brown was an extreme abolitionist who felt he had a personal mission to eliminate slavery. A guerrilla war of revenge erupted as proslavery forces fought antislavery forces. The newspapers referred to Kansas as Bleeding Kansas. Before the violence was over, 200 people were dead. When the dust settled, Kansas joined the Union as a free state, but only after the outbreak of the Civil War in 1861.

Divisive Politics

How did the nation's political parties reorganize in the 1850s?

Midterm Elections: 1854

Another result of the Kansas-Nebraska Act was the change in political parties as the parties split along sectional lines. The old Whig Party had fallen apart as members disagreed on the slavery issue. The Democratic Party split into Southern Democrats and Northern Democrats. Northern "free soil" Democrats were angry at representatives who had voted for the Kansas-Nebraska Act. In the election of 1854, most of those Northerners who had voted for the act were not reelected.

These "free soil" Democrats, those who wanted to stop the spread of slavery to western lands, joined forces in 1854 with abolitionists and former antislavery Whigs to form the Republican Party. Republicans said no person should own another and were committed to keeping slavery out of the western territories. One of the party's members was a young lawyer from Illinois named Abraham Lincoln.

Southern Hopes to Acquire Cuba

Southerners hoping to alter the balance of power in Congress in favor of slavery also coveted Spanish-controlled Cuba. Just 90 miles south of the continental United States, this Caribbean island was home to profitable sugar plantations worked by hundreds of thousands of enslaved persons. In 1848, the Spanish rejected an American offer to purchase the island. Between 1849 and 1851, Southerners supported two failed efforts to stage a revolt. In 1853, Spain rejected a second purchase offer.

In 1854, Pierre Soulé, the U.S. foreign minister in Spain, persuaded the American ministers to the United Kingdom and France to sign a declaration called the Ostend Manifesto. This document stated that the United States would be justified in seizing Cuba if Spain continued to refuse to sell it. Although President Franklin Pierce rejected the Ostend Manifesto, angry Republicans condemned it as the Democratic administration's attempt to appeal to voters in the South. Democrats continued to support acquiring the island.

Electing a President: 1856

The presidential election of 1856 was one of the nation's most bitter. Voting was rigidly sectional. The anti-immigration, anti-Catholic "Know-Nothing" Party ran Millard Fillmore. The party concentrated on being against immigration and ignored the slavery issue. Fillmore did poorly and only carried one state.

Democrats selected James Buchanan as their candidate. They supported popular sovereignty, painted Republicans as radicals, and called the Republican candidate, John C. Frémont, a "black abolitionist" who would destroy the Union. Frémont was against the expansion of slavery into the territories. Buchanan won the election. Although Frémont received only 600 votes in the entire South, the election was close nationwide. Frémont was only two states short of winning the election. The Republicans had made a strong showing.

A Lawsuit and a Decision

How did a Supreme Court decision inflame passions?

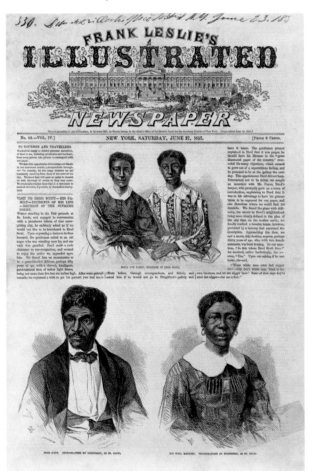

photo: Getty Images

Dred Scott was declared ineligible for citizenship because of his race. Frank Leslie's Illustrated *introduced the country to Scott and his family.*

While many Northerners wanted to stop the spread of slavery to new territories, many proslavery Southerners were now arguing that prohibiting slavery anywhere was unconstitutional. Although often in favor of strong states' rights, in the case of slavery, they wanted a strong federal government to support it. They looked to the Supreme Court to endorse this view and got their wish with the Dred Scott decision.

Dred Scott was a Missouri man who was enslaved to an army officer. The officer had moved several times, taking Scott with him. For a while, the two had lived in Illinois and in Wisconsin Territory, both free soil. Based on the fact that he had lived in free territory, Scott decided to sue in court for his freedom. After several years, Scott's case *Dred Scott v. Sandford* reached the Supreme Court, and in 1857, the Court made its decision.

Slaves are not citizens, Chief Justice Roger Taney wrote, but property. The Constitution protects property, so Congress had no right to make a law that restricted what a person could do with property.

Discovery EDUCATION | SOCIAL STUDIES TECHBOOK

By 1860, why were the nation's leaders unable to keep the Union together?

This decision meant Congress could not restrict the spread of slavery, and, therefore, the Missouri Compromise was unconstitutional. What's more, Taney wrote, African Americans, even free African Americans, were not citizens at all. Therefore, Scott was not entitled to the rights and privileges of a citizen and he could not bring a lawsuit in the first place.

The Supreme Court's ruling in *Dred Scott v. Sandford* is viewed by many as one of the worst decisions ever made by the Court. The ruling had momentous consequences and increased the bitter feelings between the North and South. It meant that even free states would be forced to accept slavery if slaves were brought into their state. It meant, too, that the Republican Party's platform of preventing the expansion of slavery into new territories was unconstitutional. Even Stephen Douglas's "popular sovereignty," the idea that each state should decide the issue for itself, was made unconstitutional.

The Supreme Court had hoped to end the argument over slavery. Instead, the decision divided the country even more, made compromise impossible, and moved the nation closer to disunion and war.

The Lincoln-Douglas Debates

Why was a senatorial election significant?

In 1858, Stephen Douglas, the Democratic senator who wrote the Kansas-Nebraska Act, was running for reelection. This time, his opponent was a relative unknown named Abraham Lincoln. Lincoln had served Illinois in the state legislature and as a representative in Congress. Now, he had won the Republican nomination to run against Douglas for the U.S. Senate. Lincoln challenged Douglas to a series of debates, and one of the topics they debated was slavery.

Douglas supported states' rights and popular sovereignty, despite the Supreme Court's ruling in *Dred Scott.* He thought slavery was one of the issues that each state should decide for itself. Lincoln thought that slavery was morally wrong and opposed its spread to the new territories. Lincoln also expressed that he was opposed to interfering with slavery in the South.

The two traveled by train around Illinois, and huge crowds came out to hear them. Newspapers covered the debates and reprinted what each candidate said, and people everywhere read the arguments. Lincoln lost the election for senator, but the newspaper coverage had made him famous and respected all across the North. Two years later, Lincoln would run for president of the United States.

photo: The New York Public Library
On October 7, 1858, Lincoln and Douglas had the fifth of what would be seven debates.

John Brown Leads an Uprising

What happened at Harpers Ferry, Virginia?

Remember John Brown, who staged antislavery raids in Bleeding Kansas? He had not disappeared. Instead, he had been quietly planning to lead a slave uprising. He had originally wanted to stage a guerrilla war, to help enslaved persons escape, and protect them in the Appalachian Mountains. He was ready in 1858, but when a blackmailer threatened to reveal the plan, Brown postponed his war. He went into hiding for a year and changed his plan. Still, Brown's plan was poorly designed, and his men were hardly trained. Even abolitionists who advocated violence thought it was a bad idea. Frederick Douglass had warned Brown that attacking a federal building was a mistake and would get him killed.

On the evening of October 16, 1859, Brown and his 21 followers overpowered a watchman and seized the arsenal, the armory, and a rifle works at Harpers Ferry, Virginia (now West Virginia). He planned to distribute the weapons to enslaved African Americans who he thought would join his rebellion. Brown's men cut telegraph wires and captured some 60 citizens of the town to hold them hostage. Brown then sent out men to liberate the enslaved persons.

photo: Getty Images

Marines brought a ladder to use in storming the engine house at Harper's Ferry.

But Brown had not spread the word ahead of time, and no enslaved persons joined him. Instead, someone in town managed to ring a church bell to sound an alarm, and the local militia responded. They cut off escape routes, and Brown and his men were soon trapped in the armory. Brown tried to negotiate, sending out his son under a white flag, but the son was shot and killed. By the evening of the next day, a unit of Marines arrived, led by Colonel Robert E. Lee. Brown was arrested, tried for treason, and hanged on December 2.

As Brown was led to his execution, he handed his jailer a note that read "I John Brown am now quite certain that the crimes of this guilty land will never be purged away but with blood."

Many prominent Northerners, including Abraham Lincoln and Stephen Douglas, spoke out against John Brown's raid, condemning the violence. But some abolitionists saw Brown as a saint and a martyr and were inspired by his dedication to the antislavery cause. At his execution, church bells tolled in the North, and flags flew at half-mast. This reaction by Northerners outraged Southerners and convinced many that the North wished to free all enslaved persons and start a race war. More and more, they saw leaving the Union and creating their own slaveholding nation as the only option.

Discovery SOCIAL STUDIES EDUCATION | TECHBOOK

By 1860, why were the nation's leaders unable to keep the Union together?

The Last Straw

What were the outcome and impact of the election of 1860?

By 1860, the differences that divided the North from the South were so severe that the nation was ready to split apart.

The Democratic Party was deeply divided. Southern Democrats wanted the party to guarantee the right to expand slavery into the territories. When the party's convention refused to do this, delegates from the South walked out. They chose their own candidate, John C. Breckinridge of Kentucky. The remaining Democrats nominated Stephen Douglas, who continued to support popular sovereignty.

Another party, the Constitutional Union Party, had formed, consisting of former Whigs, Know-Nothings, and Southern Democrats who supported the Union. The Constitutional Union Party had a simple platform of support for the Union and the Constitution and tried to simply avoid the issue of slavery. It nominated John Bell of Tennessee.

The Republican Party's nominee was Abraham Lincoln. Lincoln was the only candidate who was clearly and solidly against slavery, although he said he did not intend to end slavery in the South. Lincoln maintained that he only wanted to stop the further expansion of slavery into the territories.

The race showed how deeply divided the nation was along regional lines. There were actually two different simultaneous campaigns. In the North, the election was between Douglas and Lincoln. In the South, it was between Breckinridge and Bell. The Republicans did not campaign in the South at all, and Lincoln's name was not even on the ballot in 10 states. Only Douglas ran a national campaign.

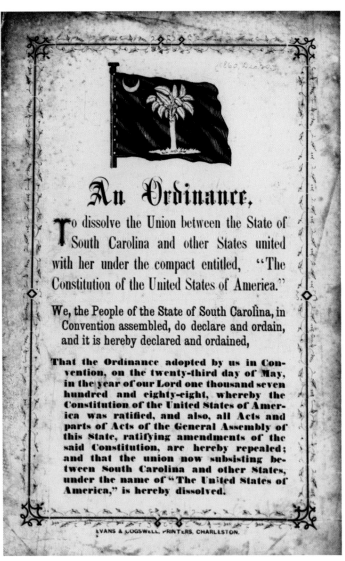

photo: Getty Images

On December 22, 1860, 170 delegates to the special Convention of the People of the State of South Carolina declared South Carolina independent from the United States.

The results were firmly divided by region. Lincoln's Republican Party won the North and the two free states on the West Coast. Bell's Constitutional Union Party won in the non-cotton-growing Southern states: Virginia, Kentucky, and Tennessee. Breckinridge won the South. The only exception was Maryland, a non-cotton-growing slave state that went for Breckinridge. Douglas won nearly 30 percent of the popular vote, but his support was spread thinly over a wide area, and he only carried Missouri. Lincoln won only about 40 percent of the popular vote and did not win a single Southern state, but the 17 states he won gave him 59 percent of the electoral votes and thus victory in the election.

Before the election, some Southern leaders had threatened that their states would secede, or leave the Union, if Lincoln were elected. Even before Lincoln's inauguration, seven states seceded from the Union. South Carolina was first, in December 1860. The Civil War was about to begin.

Complete this activity to show what you know about events leading to secession.

Consider the Essential Question:

By 1860, why were the nation's leaders unable to keep the Union together?

Go online to complete the Social Studies Explanation.

Check for Understanding:

What events between 1820 and 1860 were most responsible for secession and Civil War?

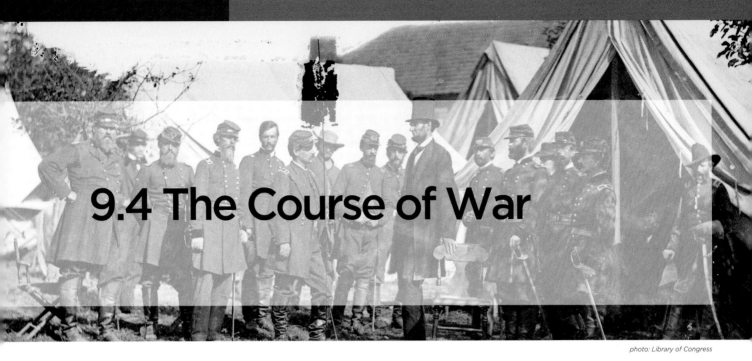

9.4 The Course of War

photo: Library of Congress

LESSON OVERVIEW

Introduction

In this concept, you will learn the tragic and dramatic events of the Civil War.

Essential Question

How did the Union win the Civil War?

Lesson Objectives

By the end of this lesson, you should be able to:

- Compare and contrast the characteristics of the Union and Confederate armies (size, access to resources).

- Describe the outbreak, major battles, turning points (Emancipation Proclamation/Gettysburg Address), and conclusion of the Civil War.

Key Vocabulary
Which terms do you already know?

- [ ] 90-day men
- [ ] Abraham Lincoln
- [ ] Anaconda Plan
- [ ] Antietam
- [ ] Appomattox Court House
- [ ] Belle Boyd
- [ ] blockade
- [ ] border state
- [ ] Bull Run
- [ ] Civil War
- [ ] Confederacy
- [ ] conscription
- [ ] cotton diplomacy
- [ ] Emancipation Proclamation
- [ ] Fort Sumter
- [ ] George McClellan
- [ ] Gettysburg
- [ ] Gettysburg Address
- [ ] greenback
- [ ] habeas corpus
- [ ] Harpers Ferry
- [ ] Jefferson Davis
- [ ] Juneteenth
- [ ] martial law
- [ ] Mathew Brady
- [ ] Mississippi
- [ ] Robert E. Lee
- [ ] secession
- [ ] Seven Days' Battle
- [ ] Shiloh
- [ ] "Stonewall" Jackson
- [ ] total war
- [ ] Ulysses S. Grant
- [ ] Vicksburg
- [ ] Virginia
- [ ] William Tecumseh Sherman
- [ ] Winfield Scott

ENGAGE

What made the Civil War so terrible? Visit Engage to learn more.

Essential Question

How did the Union win the Civil War?

EXPLORE

Secession Leads to War

How did the Civil War begin?

Secession and the Confederate States of America

Abraham Lincoln was elected president in November 1860. In the months before Lincoln's March 1861 inauguration, talk of Southern secession became more common. The theory of secession argued that states that had ratified the Constitution had not given up their fundamental sovereignty, or authority to govern themselves. As a result, they were permitted to leave the Union and retain their full sovereignty. Just as nullification supporters had argued during the 1830s, secessionists saw the Union as a compact of states rather than as a creation of the people. In his annual address to Congress at the end of 1860, President James Buchanan announced that he would not act against rebellious states. Although he rejected the theory of secession, Buchanan believed the federal government had no power to prevent states from leaving the Union.

Most Northerners considered secession to be unconstitutional and treasonous. If states could leave the Union at their pleasure, they argued, it would be impossible to keep the government together. Lincoln argued that individual states had never possessed individual sovereignty, even at the time they had ratified the Constitution. Instead, they were former colonies that had agreed to give up their fundamental sovereignty for the purpose of creating the United States of America.

On December 20, 1860, South Carolina was the first state to secede from the United States. In January 1861, five more states—Georgia, Florida, Alabama, Mississippi, and Louisiana—followed. Two months later, these states, now joined by Texas, ratified the constitution of the newly formed Confederate States of America.

Jefferson Davis, a U.S. Senator from Mississippi and former secretary of war, was inaugurated as the president on February 18, 1861. Davis's inaugural address reflected a common belief among Southerners that the Confederacy was created to preserve ideas expressed by the Founders of the United States. For example, Davis emphasized the principle of consent of the governed. In doing so, he expressed many Southerners' fears that they would lose their way of life if they remained part of a country dominated by Northerners. He also echoed the Declaration of Independence by stating that people have the right to alter or abolish governments that became "destructive of the ends for which they were established." By implication, Davis used these words to defend what he and other supporters of the Confederacy felt were the property rights of slave owners.

Two weeks after Davis began his term, Lincoln was inaugurated as the 16th president of the United States. You might recall that Lincoln had been elected because the majority of voters wanted to keep the United States together and to keep slavery from spreading to newly admitted states. In this inaugural address, Lincoln focused on his support in the North without condemning the seceding states in the South. His address avoided mentioning the Republican Party platform, such as closing the slave trade, preventing slavery in new territories, or interfering with slavery in states where it existed. Instead, he drew inspiration from the Constitution and its overall goal to establish "a more perfect union." He emphasized that liberty does not require destroying the government, to which Lincoln has sworn to "preserve, protect, and defend" as president.

	Date Seceded	Date Joined CSA
South Carolina	Dec. 20, 1860	Feb. 8, 1861
Mississippi	Jan. 9, 1861	Feb. 8, 1861
Florida	Jan. 10, 1861	Feb. 8, 1861
Alabama	Jan. 11, 1861	Feb. 8, 1861
Georgia	Jan. 19, 1861	Feb. 8, 1861
Louisiana	Jan. 26, 1861	Feb. 8, 1861
Texas	Feb. 1, 1861	Mar. 2, 1861
Virginia	Apr. 17, 1861	May 7, 1861
Arkansas	May 6, 1861	May 18, 1861
Tennessee	May 7, 1861	July 2, 1861
North Carolina	May 20, 1861	May 21, 1861

Chart naming the states of the Confederacy.

Lincoln's first drafts of his inaugural address had ended with a question for the South: "Shall it be peace or sword?" However, following the suggestions of a trusted adviser, Lincoln modified his tone dramatically. In the final concluding paragraph, Lincoln ended on a note of conciliation.

The War Begins

Fort Sumter, which was guarded by Union troops, is located on an island in the mouth of Charleston Harbor. Confederate forces protested against the Union's presence so close to Charleston. Major Robert Anderson, the Union leader at Fort Sumter, informed President Lincoln that the fort had only six weeks of supplies remaining. A ship was sent to resupply the fort but was forced by the Confederates to turn away.

photo: Paul Fuqua
This view, from a sandbar in Charleston Bay, South Carolina, shows the damage Fort Sumter suffered during the Civil War.

On April 11, Confederate Brigadier General P. G. T. Beauregard demanded the fort's surrender. Major Anderson refused. At 4:30 a.m. on April 12, Confederates began firing on Fort Sumter. Their assault continued for 34 hours. Abner Doubleday, the man erroneously credited with inventing baseball, was second in command of the Union forces at Fort Sumter. Doubleday ordered the first Union gunfire of the Civil War. Despite the exchange of fire, no one was killed in the battle. Anderson surrendered the fort on April 14. The first battle of the Civil War was a Confederate victory.

Shortly after the attack on Fort Sumter, Virginia, Arkansas, Tennessee, and North Carolina seceded from the Union and joined the Confederate States of America. U.S. Army General Robert E. Lee resigned his commission and returned to his home state of Virginia, where he became the leader of Confederate Virginia's military forces.

President Lincoln Responds

What continued efforts did President Lincoln make to preserve the Union?

The Struggle for the Border States

President Lincoln was desperate to prevent slave states located near the border between the Union and the Confederacy from leaving the United States. These border states of Delaware, Kentucky, Maryland, and Missouri were strongly divided over the issues of secession and slavery.

Kentucky Senator John J. Crittenden was a personal example of the division in the border states. Crittenden was a founder of the Constitutional Union Party, formed in 1860 in hopes of bridging the divide between the North and the South. Crittenden forcefully defended slavery, but he was also determined that Kentucky should stay in the Union. Crittenden's eldest son, Thomas L. Crittenden, became a Union general. His second son, George B. Crittenden, became a Confederate general.

The creation of West Virginia also illustrates the division between the North and the South. When the state of Virginia voted to secede from the United States in April 1861, many of its citizens did not support the move. Thirty-nine counties in the western part of the state decided to separate from Virginia and remain in the Union. In 1863, the state of West Virginia was born—but it permitted slavery and was considered the fifth border state.

Lincoln Acts

Following the Confederate attack at Fort Sumter, President Lincoln decided to cautiously prepare the nation for a war to save the Union. A week after the attack on the South Carolina fort, federal troops from Massachusetts were sent to protect the nation's capital, which was perilously located between Maryland and Virginia. As the regiment passed through Baltimore, angry secessionists rioted. It seemed as though Maryland might leave the Union, placing Washington, DC, in enemy

photo: Library of Congress

The Baltimore Riot of April 1861 led to deaths of 12 civilians and 4 Union soldiers—the first deaths of the Civil War.

territory. They suspended local laws and civilian government and put the city under control of the U.S. Army. The president also ended habeas corpus, the right of citizens under arrest to demand that authorities justify their imprisonment. The president's suspension of habeas corpus would later be extended throughout the country.

Lincoln's struggle to preserve the Union by maintaining the loyalty of the border states often required him to continue to work for compromise even while he was conducting a war. In the border states, the greatest cause of discontent was Lincoln's use of the army against the states that seceded. Support for states' rights was strong in the border states. This put Lincoln in a bind. If he did not use military force to stop secession, he would not be able to preserve the Union. But if he did use military force, he could drive the border states to secede on their own.

Economic Strength

How did the Union's and the Confederacy's economies compare?

As the war began, the North had more money and a thriving economy focused on manufacturing. Almost 90 percent of American factories were located in the North. More than 25 percent of the Northern population lived in cities; many worked in manufacturing, staffing Northern factories.

Agriculture was also mechanized in the North, requiring fewer people to produce food. In 1860, the North produced half of the corn, most of the wheat, and almost all of the oats for the entire nation. It accomplished this even though only 40 percent of the population in the North was involved in farming.

Thus, the Union states were able to outproduce the Confederate states in almost every area—from weapons manufacturing to oats. Northern manufacturers of consumer goods were happy to convert their factories to produce weapons instead because they knew the federal government would be a good customer. Before and during the Civil War, the Union was able to manufacture weapons and provide military supplies to its soldiers at a much faster pace than the Confederacy.

Southern Resources

The economy of the Southern states developed in a different direction from that of the Northern states. The Southern economy was based on agriculture. Only 10 percent of the Southern population lived in cities. Eighty-four percent of the population was involved in agriculture, but the chosen crops were cotton and tobacco, not food. The South had vast amounts of land that were ideal for growing cotton and tobacco, but they relied on manual labor, usually done by enslaved people, rather than farm machinery.

Cotton was so profitable that, wherever possible, farmland was devoted to it. Although the Southern economy depended overwhelmingly on agriculture, the South was a net importer of food. Once the war began, food imports from the Midwest ended. To feed the civilian population as well as the troops, land used for cotton and tobacco farming had to be converted to growing food crops. However, plantation owners resisted because grains and vegetables were much less profitable crops.

The Confederacy thought that the importance of cotton in the international market would bring military assistance from other nations. It was wrong. Although cotton was valued, it wasn't important enough to cause other nations to join the Southern cause. For instance, Britain, the largest importer of U.S. cotton, easily found other sources for cotton—its colonies in Egypt and India. Cotton and tobacco were not weapons and they were not edible, so they did not help the South arm or feed its soldiers.

Transportation

In transportation, the Union also had the advantage. It had 20,000 miles of railroad, which was 69 percent of the U.S. total. During the Civil War, the railroad continued to grow rapidly in the North. Railroads were important in commercial shipping and helped the military. New recruits, replacement troops, and active military units were able to travel quickly, without tiring, to destinations served by railroads. Weapons and supplies could also be easily shipped to military units by rail.

The Union also had numerous ports that enabled the Northern states to ship supplies to other Northern ports and continue its trade with other nations. Northern shipyards continued to build ships during the war.

The Confederacy had few ports, and the Union navy was able to blockade them. Blockades hindered the Confederacy in its attempts to sell cotton to other nations, reducing the Confederacy's trade income dramatically. The lack of resources, money, and labor prevented the Confederacy from expanding its railroads during the war.

Natural Resources

The Union had an abundance of natural resources. Metals could be mined for use in manufacturing. Lumber was used for building. The soil was rich enough for farming, and farm machinery increased the yield.

The South did not have numerous mines or large forests. Instead, the states of the Confederacy had developed by selling cotton and tobacco to buy the resources they needed. When the ports were closed by blockades, resources became scarce. They destroyed railroads to melt the iron needed to produce weapons and ammunition. In some locations, churches melted

photo: Library of Congress

Northern women were able to use technology on the farm to do tasks formerly done by males. They also became the principal workforce of offices and factories.

adornments and bells to make cannonballs and other ammunition. The Southern forces did have a resource advantage, however. Because the war was largely fought in the South, Southern generals often had the advantage in choosing the terrain for battles and the army did not have to ship supplies across enemy terrain.

Soldiers and Weapons

Who fought in the Civil War? What weapons were used?

More than three million soldiers fought in the Civil War. They came from every state. The average Union soldier was 25 years old and 5 feet 8 ¼ inches tall, and weighed 143 ½ pounds.

photo: Library of Congress
Union soldiers from Pennsylvania in a parade formation.

In addition to weapons and gear, many soldiers brought pets. Dogs commonly accompanied soldiers or became mascots for a military unit. Confederate General Lee was rumored to have a pet chicken that laid an egg every day.

Initially, it was thought that the Civil War would be short, and many soldiers were volunteers. The Confederacy began drafting soldiers in 1862, and the Union instituted a draft in 1863. However, both governments allowed ways for draftees to avoid fighting. For example, Union draftees could buy an exemption for $300 or send a substitute to take their place. The Confederate draft law exempted from service wealthy plantation owners who held 20 or more enslaved people. Those who served as Union privates were paid $13 per month, and Confederate privates were paid $11 per month.

photo: Library of Congress
During the Civil War, over 214,000 Confederates were taken prisoner. More than 30,000 of them died while being held in federal prisons.

Weapons

The most common weapon carried by soldiers was a rifle musket. Both Union and Confederate soldiers used rifle muskets to fire the new Minié balls. These were small bullets that were easy to load quickly and could be fired accurately over long distances. A well-trained soldier could load his rifle musket and fire about three shots per minute. Minié balls caused horrible wounds to human flesh and bones. Three-fourths of medical operations on soldiers were amputations. Sixty thousand arms and legs were lost to amputations.

Another Civil War innovation was the steam-powered, ironclad battleship. France had attached armor plates to one of its ships in 1859, but the first battle between two ironclad warships occurred between the USS *Monitor* and the CSS *Virginia* on March 9, 1862, at Hampton Roads, Virginia.

Military Leadership

In the Civil War era, military leaders were not always chosen for their military expertise. Instead, many military appointments were made as rewards for political favors. Early in the war, the North had several military leaders who were not experienced or well trained. As the war proceeded and leaders on both sides realized the combat would be longer than anticipated, both the Union and the Confederacy sought more experienced men to lead their military.

Military academies existed in the North and the South, and both sides had graduates within their armies. The U.S. Military Academy at West Point, for example, is located in New York. Both Ulysses S. Grant, who led the Union forces, and Robert E. Lee, who led the Confederate forces, graduated from West Point. Stonewall Jackson, a notable Confederate general, was also a West Point graduate.

Regardless of which military academy from which they graduated or its location, most graduates fought for their home states in the Civil War, and many graduates came from Confederate states. The Confederacy had highly motivated, well-trained leaders who fought with their heads and their hearts.

War Strategies and Results
How did the Union win the Civil War?

Union Strategy

When the Civil War began, President Lincoln approved a military strategy suggested by Union General Winfield Scott. The strategy became known as the Anaconda Plan because a map of the battle plans resembled an anaconda, a type of snake that surrounds and strangles its prey. The strategy aimed to cut off the Confederacy from commerce and supplies. The Union imposed a naval blockade of Southern ports and tried to control the Mississippi River.

Confederate Strategy

The Confederate strategy had three parts. One was to break the Union's blockade of Southern waterways. Breaking the blockade would allow the Confederates to sell their cotton and to import weapons and other goods they could no longer obtain from the North. A second Confederate aim was to acquire allies. A foreign alliance would help convince the world that the Confederate cause was legitimate.

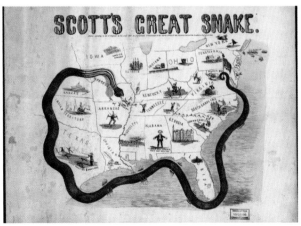

photo: Library of Congress
The Anaconda Plan intended to strangle the South by blocking the transport and import of troops and supplies.

The Confederates hoped European countries that bought Southern cotton would support them in the war. Finally, the Confederates desired to capture the Union capital of Washington, DC. Conquering the capital would force the U.S. government to recognize the Confederacy as a separate country.

The Confederates tried to lure the border states into joining them because their location, manpower, and resources were strategically important. The Confederacy needed allies if it was going to break the blockade. It hoped for help from foreign countries whose economies depended on Southern cotton—particularly Great Britain.

The Course of the War

The first two years of the war saw many deadly battles that did not gain either side much advantage. However, the longer the war lasted, the more the Confederate army weakened. The Union blockade prevented the South from carrying on normal commerce and receiving help via ship at any Southern port. Even if the South had been able to acquire allies, the blockade would have prevented much aid from arriving to help the South.

Investigate this interactive to learn more about key events from the war.

In 1863, Confederate General Lee's unsuccessful invasion of Pennsylvania, which marked the Confederacy's highest point, turned the tide of the war in favor of the Union. That same year, Union General Grant led a campaign to capture the Mississippi River, including the strategic fort at Vicksburg, Mississippi. At this point, the Anaconda Plan was in place; the Confederacy was surrounded and isolated.

In 1864, Union General Sherman led a devastating campaign across Georgia, convincing many observers that the Confederacy had little chance of winning the war. From the end of 1864 to early 1865, Lee's tired and starving troops desperately retreated through Virginia, with Grant in pursuit. In April, Lee finally surrendered.

The Real Fighting Begins

What happened in the first major Civil War battles?

Bull Run

The first major battle of the Civil War occurred on July 21, 1861, near Manassas, Virginia, and a creek named Bull Run. The fighting was about 25 miles from Washington—so close that hundreds of people packed picnic lunches and went to the battlefield to watch. It was a battle between two inexperienced armies that shattered the expectation of a brief, bloodless war. The Civil War was neither. The First Battle of Bull Run was a physically and mentally exhausting bloody combat that lasted all day, leaving 847 men dead and many more wounded.

Manassas was a valuable location because it was a railroad junction. Union General Irvin McDowell planned an attack using 30,000 Union soldiers against 24,000 Confederate soldiers commanded by General P. G. T. Beauregard. Both of the leaders were inexperienced in battle, but the Union general made the more serious mistakes.

McDowell's plan was overly complicated, and it was doomed because the maps on which he based it were inaccurate. Union commanders sent smaller groups into the combat instead of using entire regiments. This eliminated the Union's initial numerical advantage. During the day Confederate reinforcements arrived by rail, fresh for battle, demonstrating the advantage provided by the railroads and the value of using resources wisely. The battle ended when the Union army and its leaders ran back to Washington in a disorganized retreat. The Confederates had won the first major Civil War battle.

General Thomas "Stonewall" Jackson made a name for himself in this battle. A former professor at Virginia Military Institute, Jackson displayed his courage by facing the repeated enemy charges "like a stone wall." Jackson continued to earn recognition in important battles and became a hero throughout the Confederacy.

Shiloh

The Union army began the western part of the Anaconda Plan in Tennessee. Forces led by Union General Ulysses S. Grant planned to proceed through west Tennessee to begin to take control of the Mississippi River. On the morning of April 6, 1862, the Confederates attacked an unprepared Union camp at Shiloh, in southwestern Tennessee. The two days of the bloody Battle of Shiloh resulted in more than 23,000 casualties, the most casualties caused in any battle in American history at that time.

Although the Confederates surprised the Union and won the first day of fighting, the Union recovered on the second day and was able to avoid being pushed out of its position.

photo: Library of Congress

On April 6, 1862, Confederate General A. S. Johnston surprised Union troops at Shiloh.

Turning Point

How did Antietam and the Emancipation Proclamation change the war?

Once the Civil War began, President Lincoln privately became convinced that he should act to abolish slavery, particularly in the Confederacy. Although he personally opposed the "peculiar institution," Lincoln also thought declaring emancipation was a valuable military tactic. Emancipation would weaken the South and give the Union the moral high ground in the Civil War. After consulting with trusted advisers, the president decided to wait to act on the slavery issue until after a Union victory on the battlefield. A military success would demonstrate to American citizens and the world that the Union could win the Civil War and that emancipation could be enforced.

photo: Getty Images

This cartoon was published in Harper's Weekly *in January 1863.*

Antietam

Despite the Union's advantages, in 1862 the Civil War was not going well for the Union. The results on the battlefield were often unclear and in some cases disastrous. To many observers, the Union's military and political leaders seemed ineffective. Hoping to further demoralize residents of the Northern states and force the Union's acceptance of the Confederacy, in the late summer of 1862, Confederate General Robert E. Lee invaded the Union through Maryland.

On September 17, Union General George McClellan attacked Lee's forces near the western Maryland town of Sharpsburg. At the resulting Battle of Antietam, McClellan's armies managed to repel Lee's invasion. But instead of pursuing Lee and earning a more decisive victory, McClellan did nothing, even though his army was twice as large as Lee's. President Lincoln was not happy with McClellan's performance and accused him of having "the slows." Later in the year, the president removed General McClellan from command. But the Union had achieved the victory on the battlefield the president had been waiting for.

The Emancipation Proclamation

In response to the battle of Antietam, on September 22, 1862, President Lincoln issued a preliminary Proclamation of Emancipation.

As promised, Lincoln later issued a final Emancipation Proclamation on January 1, 1863. It is important to note that the Emancipation Proclamation did not end slavery in the United States or in any areas where the federal government could enforce its terms.

Because Lincoln wanted to avoid hostility in the border states, the proclamation did not apply to the slave states that remained in the Union. Emancipation applied only to the states that had seceded, who were already ignoring U.S. laws. Emancipation also did not apply in Confederate territory that the Union Army already controlled. As a result, Tennessee and parts of Louisiana and Virginia were exempted. Secretary of State William Seward said, "We show our sympathy with slavery by emancipating slaves where we cannot reach them and holding them in bondage where we can set them free."

But the Emancipation Proclamation was an important step in adding the abolition of slavery to the Union's original wartime objective of preserving the Union. Though imperfect, it was the federal government's most decisive statement against slavery in the nation's history. It encouraged African Americans to support the Union and authorized them to serve in the Union's army and navy.

After the Emancipation Proclamation took effect, as Union forces moved into Confederate territory, many enslaved African Americans freed themselves by seeking the protection of the Union army and traveling with it. In 1863 and 1864, thousands of emancipated slaves volunteered to serve in the Union army. By the end of the Civil War, about 179,000 African American men fought for the Union army, and about 19,000 served in the navy. One example of African American heroism was William Harvey Carney, who was awarded the Medal of Honor for his heroic actions of protecting the U.S. flag, despite multiple wounds, during the Battle of Fort Wagner in 1863. When he returned to Union lines, Carney modestly stated, "Boys, I only did my duty. The old flag never touched the ground."

Other enslaved African Americans demanded pay for their work. In this, they were obeying the president, whose Emancipation Proclamation said, "And I hereby enjoin upon the people so declared to be free to abstain from all violence, unless in necessary self-defence; and I recommend to them that, in all cases when allowed, they labor faithfully for reasonable wages."

The Emancipation Proclamation gave the Union war effort a moral clarity. It helped convince European countries not to support the Confederate States of America, it motivated the Union, and it demoralized Confederates. It made clear that the war was not just about politics, nor was it about defending the Southern homeland. Confederate soldiers were fighting for the right to keep enslaved people, even though many of them were not wealthy enough to own any.

Gettysburg

What happened at Gettysburg?

The Battle

Several battles and skirmishes occurred in the months after Antietam. Confederate General Stonewall Jackson was wounded at the Battle of Chancellorsville, in Virginia, in May 1863. Confederate General Lee said, "He has lost his left arm; but I have lost my right arm." Jackson died a few days later of pneumonia. Lee wrote, "It is a terrible loss. I do not know how to replace him." But a Confederate victory at Chancellorsville convinced Lee to attempt a second invasion of Union territory.

photo: Paul Fuqua

Painted by the noted Civil War artist Edwin Forbes, this scene shows Federal troops pursuing Lee's army after the Battle of Gettysburg.

photo: Library of Congress

Lincoln's handwritten copy of the Gettysburg Address.

In June, Confederate General Lee led his army of almost 72,000 men into Pennsylvania. Lee invaded the North to gather supplies for his army and because he hoped a major victory in Union territory would make the Union lose the will to fight. This invasion led to the Battle of Gettysburg, a three-day battle from July 1 to July 3, 1863. The Battle of Gettysburg was critical because it would determine whether Lee's invasion of the North would be successful.

Union forces led by General George Meade occupied Cemetery Ridge, the high ground. On the first day of the battle, Colonel Joshua Chamberlain successfully led a charge down Little Round Top, a nearby hill, to capture nearly 100 Confederate soldiers and prevent their advances on the left flank, or side.

On the third day, Confederate General Lee ordered Officer George Edward Pickett and two other generals to lead their divisions up the hill, directly into enemy fire. Pickett's Charge was a disaster for the Confederates. In the end, the three-day Battle of Gettysburg caused more than 51,000 casualties, including close to 8,000 killed. Confederate General Lee's army was seriously weakened, and his second, and final, attempt to invade the North was a failure. The Union had a clear victory. The tide of the war would continue to flow in the Union's favor.

The Memorial

Several months later, on November 19, 1863, a cemetery was dedicated at the site of the Battle of Gettysburg. President Lincoln was the second speaker that day, following a two-hour speech. His simple address lasted only two minutes. He spoke with a serious and solemn tone about the soldiers who had fallen. He invoked the Declaration of Independence and its principles of liberty and equality in the proposition that "all men are created equal." He linked the Civil War to the American Revolution, reinforcing the purpose of the Civil War as a "new birth of freedom" and equality for the nation. Instead of just focusing on preserving the union of government, Lincoln suggested that the real goals of the war were the preservation of both unity and freedom. Lincoln's Gettysburg Address has often been described as one of the most eloquent speeches in history.

Explore this resource and discuss the meaning of the Gettysburg Address.

Turning Point: Siege of Vicksburg

How was the Siege of Vicksburg important?

Vicksburg, Mississippi, lay atop a bluff, or cliff, along the Mississippi River where it is joined by the Yazoo River. Overlooking the continent's largest river, Vicksburg's position gave it control of the major thoroughfare, or transportation route, of the Confederacy.

By spring 1863, Vicksburg had been a Union target for months, but attempts to capture it were unsuccessful until General Ulysses S. Grant took over. Grant's strategy was to circle behind Vicksburg and cut the rail line that provided supplies to the town. Grant's forces moved into position from the east, forcing the Confederates to back up to the cliffs. Union forces spread out until they surrounded the city. The Confederate position was fortified, so Union forces could not overrun it. But the Confederates were trapped.

photo: Library of Congress

Vicksburg before Grant began his operations in January 1863. Grant put the town under siege on May 19; on July 4, he accepted the surrender of Pemberton's defending army of 30,000 Confederates.

The Union army laid siege to Vicksburg on May 19, 1863. Over the following weeks, the city's supplies ran out, and civilians and soldiers began to starve. They ate mules, rats, and tree bark to survive. On July 4, the city finally surrendered. It was only one day after the Union victory at Gettysburg.

With the capture of Vicksburg, the Union now surrounded the South: it controlled the Mississippi River on the west, it controlled the North, and it had blockaded Confederate ports on the Atlantic and the Gulf of Mexico. The Confederate states west of the Mississippi were isolated from those in the east. Control of ports and rivers put a stranglehold on Confederate supplies; the Anaconda Plan was finally being implemented successfully.

Sherman's March to the Sea

What events convinced many Confederates that the time to surrender had come?

Combat continued after the Battles of Gettysburg and Vicksburg. Most of these battles were Union victories, but the Confederacy refused to surrender even though the death toll continued to rise. A key turning point arrived when President Lincoln appointed Ulysses S. Grant general-in-chief in March 1864.

photo: Library of Congress

Destruction of a railroad bridge, North Ana River, Virginia, May 26, 1864.

On September 1, 1864, Union General William Tecumseh Sherman captured Atlanta, Georgia. He held Atlanta until November. Before leaving, Sherman commanded his forces to burn down munitions factories, railroad facilities, and other resources that could be useful to the Confederate war effort. This event was the backdrop for *Gone with the Wind*, a famous novel by Margaret Mitchell.

President Lincoln was reelected on November 8. A few days later, on November 16, Union General Sherman began a military campaign known as the March to the Sea. With 60,000 troops, he marched from Atlanta to Savannah, Georgia. On the way, Sherman's army took food and burned property, destroying everything that could be used by the Confederates.

This policy of total war terrified and demoralized the Confederates—both civilians and soldiers. Sherman stated that the Union was fighting hostile people who supported the Confederacy, as well as hostile armies. He believed that it was important to stop civilians from supporting the war by making "old and young, rich and poor, feel the hard hand of war." On December 21, he captured the city of Savannah.

Surrender

How did the Civil War end?

As Union General Sherman moved through the Confederacy from west to east, the Union's top general, Ulysses S. Grant, began a push toward the Confederate capital in Richmond, Virginia. In the spring of 1864, Union soldiers attacked Robert E. Lee's Confederate troops in several costly battles in Virginia, including the Battles of the Wilderness and Spotsylvania Court House. In each battle, the Union army tried to push past the Confederates to gain a clear path to Richmond. In each battle, the Confederates fought, then fell back, preventing the Union from advancing too quickly. Both armies lost many soldiers.

After a bloody battle at Cold Harbor, Virginia, Grant realized that he would not be able to attack Richmond directly, and moved his army toward Petersburg, an important transportation hub 25 miles away from the capital. In June 1864, the Union army began its attack on Petersburg. The siege on the city lasted over 10 months. Through the fall and winter, the Union army focused its efforts on capturing railroads in an attempt to cut off supplies to Confederate troops. It succeeded in capturing the final supply line, the South Side Railroad, on April 2, 1865.

photo: Library of Congress

The Wilmer McLean House, where General Robert E. Lee agreed to the terms of surrender for the Army of Northern Virginia with General U. S. Grant on April 9, 1865.

Lee and his hungry troops were forced to flee Petersburg. This left Richmond unguarded. Lee attempted to join forces with Confederate General Joseph Johnston, but Grant was positioned to block this meeting. After several brief skirmishes, on April 7, Grant offered Lee the opportunity to surrender.

Investigate the question: Why did it take so long for the Union to win?

After exchanging several letters, the two generals agreed to meet on April 9, 1865, at the town of Appomattox Court House, Virginia. After General Lee surrendered to General Grant and Grant accepted, Union troops provided food rations for Lee's men.

Technically, General Lee's surrender did not end the Civil War. Lee commanded only the Army of Northern Virginia, one of several Confederate armies. But Lee's army was the largest of all the Confederate forces, and Virginia was the key state of the Confederacy, both politically and economically. Over the next few weeks, the other Confederate armies surrendered as well. The bloodiest chapter in U.S. history was over. The reunited states now needed time to heal and recover.

Assassination

How was Abraham Lincoln assassinated?

Second Inaugural Address

On March 4, 1865, President Abraham Lincoln delivered his second inaugural address. One of the most famous speeches in American history, Lincoln's second inaugural delivered a unifying message and explained to fellow citizens his ideas about the meaning of the Civil War.

The president first declared that "all knew" slavery to be the "cause of the war." Then, using strongly religious language, Lincoln suggested that the human suffering brought on by the Civil War was God's will, a cost delivered to both the North and the South for maintaining slavery. "If God wills that" the war continue, Lincoln stated, "until every drop of blood drawn with the lash, shall be paid by another drawn with the sword. . . the judgements of the Lord are true and righteous altogether."

Lincoln hoped Americans on both sides might be united by this higher purpose for the Civil War. He closed his address by calling for "malice toward none" and "charity for all," and expressed hope that the American people would work to "bind up the nation's wounds" and "achieve and cherish a just, and a lasting peace, among ourselves, and with all nations."

THE ASSASSINATION OF PRESIDENT LINCOLN.
AT FORD'S THEATRE WASHINGTON D.C. APRIL 14TH 1865.

photo: Library of Congress

An assassin sneaked up behind the president as the Lincolns and their guests sat in a balcony box.

Assassination

On the evening of April 14, 1865, less than one week after General Lee's forces surrendered at Appomattox Court House, President Lincoln and the First Lady attended a play at Ford's Theater in Washington, DC. When the Lincolns and their guests arrived at Ford's Theatre, the play had already begun. Seeing the president arrive, the actors on stage stopped the performance. The orchestra played "Hail to the Chief," and the audience rose to give the president a standing ovation for the Union victory in the war.

Soon after the president had settled into his balcony seat, someone quietly entered the box. This man was John Wilkes Booth, a well-known and popular actor who was also a passionate supporter of the Confederacy. As the crowd burst into laughter watching the play, Booth *assassinated*, or murdered, Lincoln by shooting him with a pistol. Major Rathbone, one of the president's guests, tried to catch Booth, but Booth slashed at Rathbone with a knife and then leaped 12 feet to the stage below.

Witnesses differed in their recollection of the events because they happened so quickly, but for several minutes, no one realized the president was hurt. Some thought Booth's leap was part of the play. However, when Mary Lincoln screamed, the audience realized what happened. Two doctors soon carried the president to a house across the street for medical treatment. Despite their efforts, President Abraham Lincoln died in the morning of April 15, 1865.

Booth had planned his attack, and there was a horse waiting for his escape. Federal agents tracked Booth to Virginia, near the Rappahannock River. Hiding in a barn, he refused to surrender and was killed on April 26.

photo: Library of Congress

A reward poster calls for the capture of John Wilkes Booth, assassin of President Lincoln.

After Lincoln's death, Vice President Andrew Johnson became the 17th president of the United States. He inherited an unstable country and the staggering task of trying to bring it together.

Consider the Essential Question:

How did the Union win the Civil War?

Go online to complete the Social Studies Explanation.

Check for Understanding:

Why did the Union win the war? Pick and defend your top five reasons.

Discovery EDUCATION | SOCIAL STUDIES **TECHBOOK**

To what extent was the Civil War America's second revolution?

9.5 Impact of the War

photo: Library of Congress

LESSON OVERVIEW

Introduction

In this concept, you will learn about how the Civil War changed the United States, North and South, and how it affected individuals across the country.

Essential Question

To what extent was the Civil War America's second revolution?

Lesson Objectives

By the end of this lesson, you should be able to:

- Analyze key immediate outcomes of the Civil War on various groups and regions in the United States.

- Analyze the political, economic, and social effects of the Civil War.

Key Vocabulary
Which terms do you already know?

- ☐ Abraham Lincoln
- ☐ Appomattox Court House
- ☐ Civil War
- ☐ Clara Barton
- ☐ Compromise of 1877
- ☐ emancipation
- ☐ Emancipation Proclamation
- ☐ greenback
- ☐ inflation
- ☐ infrastructure
- ☐ nationalism
- ☐ Robert E. Lee
- ☐ Thirteenth Amendment
- ☐ Ulysses S. Grant

ENGAGE

How do Americans look back on the Civil War? Visit Engage to learn more.

Essential Question

To what extent was the Civil War America's second revolution?

EXPLORE

Free at Last

What happened to the institution of slavery during the Civil War?

General Robert E. Lee's surrender to Ulysses S. Grant at Appomattox Court House, Virginia, in April 1865 was the beginning of the end to a great conflict that had divided the United States in two. But what would happen now? The end of the war marked many changes for the United States, and there would be many long-term and short-term political, economic, and social problems to face.

During the Civil War, the institution of slavery began to fall apart in the United States. African Americans who volunteered to serve in the Union army immediately earned their freedom upon enlistment, as did their families. Some Union army leaders declared enslaved persons free wherever they won a battle or took control of an area, even though in some cases they were not granted authority to do so. The chaos created by the war provided many enslaved persons with the opportunity to free themselves. With so many men off to war, some slave owners were no longer able to prevent their enslaved persons from escaping.

Many Southern enslaved persons did not get to celebrate emancipation, or freedom, until June 1865, when the last of the Confederate troops laid down their arms. This period in mid-June came to be known "Juneteenth" and is now celebrated on June 19.

In December 1865, the United States ratified the Thirteenth Amendment to the Constitution. This amendment permanently outlawed slavery in all areas of the United States.

DISCOVERY | SOCIAL STUDIES
EDUCATION | **TECHBOOK**

To what extent was the Civil War America's second revolution?

Responses to Emancipation

Initial reactions to freedom varied. In Richmond, Virginia, about 1,500 formerly enslaved persons met at their church to sing together. In Charleston, South Carolina, about 10,000 people attended a parade featuring a coffin covered with the slogan "Slavery is Dead." In Choctaw County, Mississippi, a group of emancipated persons whipped their former owner, Nat Best, to teach him how it felt to be treated cruelly.

photo: Getty Images

Enslaved persons became free after the Civil War. The photograph shows a group of free African Americans in the south shortly after the end of the Civil War.

After the war, there were approximately four million newly free African Americans in the United States. These people needed jobs and they needed places to live. Some emancipated people left their plantations in search of work in the cities. Others went searching for family members who had been sold to different slave owners over the years. Freedom was welcome, but after a life of being told what to do and where to go at all times, it could be a little scary, too. Many formerly enslaved people were uncertain about their rights and their status in American society. Former slave owners shared this confusion. Some formerly enslaved people continued to work as laborers for their former owners.

Despite the end of slavery, African Americans would continue to face discrimination in the United States.

Explore this investigation to consider Lincoln's role in ending slavery.

Devastation in the South

What did the South look like at the end of the Civil War?

For four years, the Union and Confederacy engaged in battle after battle, with nearly all of the fighting taking place in the South. When the war was over, much of the infrastructure in the South lay in ruins.

During the final years of the Civil War, the Union engaged in what later became known as "hard war" tactics or "total war." Instead of merely trying to win conflicts on the traditional fields of battle, Union troops began systematically destroying everything— not only railroads and armories, but also food supplies, streets, businesses, and private homes and farms. The Union army burned crops, barns, railroad buildings, and grain mills throughout Virginia's Shenandoah Valley. It also left a 60-mile-wide trail of destruction in its wake as the army marched through Georgia toward South Carolina in late 1864. Troops robbed houses, stole or killed farm animals, and destroyed all useful farming equipment.

Image showing destruction in the South due to war.

photo: Library of Congress

In South Carolina and Georgia, "Sherman bowties," named after General William Tecumseh Sherman, became frequent sights. Thousands of miles of railroad tracks were torn up, heated, and twisted into unusable shapes, and bent around trees into the shape of a bowtie. Sherman's army also created "Sherman sentinels" by burning down homes and other buildings, leaving only the stone chimney, standing guard like a sentinel.

The Purpose of Total War

The Union's total war tactics served several purposes. One was to disable the Confederate war effort by eliminating anything that could be used in any way to help the rebel army. Another was to demoralize the Confederacy. Union officials hoped Confederate soldiers would adopt the mind-set that if they gave up the fight they would be able to go home to their families and their work. Finally, the Union's total war tactics punished Confederates for being disloyal to the United States.

It is important to remember that the massive devastation the Union inflicted on the South meant that much of the region would need to be rebuilt from the ground up.

Women and the Civil War

How did the role of women change during and after the Civil War?

As American men fought on the battlefields, American women took on new roles. With their men off at war, many women were left on their own to take care of their homes, farms, and families as best they could. In both the North and the South, wives, mothers, sisters, and daughters took on the main responsibilities of running farms and plantations as well as small businesses. They also took jobs in local industries.

In the North, women joined ladies' aid leagues from the time the war started in 1861. They performed such tasks as canning and baking food to send to the troops, sewing uniforms, knitting socks, and raising money.

In addition, about 20,000 women from the North worked directly with the Union army. The army hired working-class white women, free African American women, and, in the earliest years of the war, enslaved people, to work as cooks, launderers, and domestic workers. At the same time, around 3,000 middle-class white women took jobs as volunteer nurses.

Confederate women also engaged in similar activities for their troops. They planned raffles and dances to raise money and set up hospitals in private homes, churches, and town buildings. In the early years of the war, working-class women in the Confederate states took work in ammunition factories or were hired to sew uniforms and tents for troops for money.

Women On and Near the Battlefield

Both Northern and Southern women volunteered as nurses at home and on the battlefield. Many women who served were forced to overcome gender-based discrimination and stereotypes. New York's Mary Edwards Walker, who earned her medical degree in 1855, was first rejected for an appointment as an army surgeon because of her sex. She earned the confidence of army officials by serving as an unpaid volunteer in a military hospital and organizing the Women's Relief Organization to aid relatives of wounded soldiers. After receiving an appointment as an "Acting Assistant Surgeon," Walker was captured and spent four months in a Confederate prisoner-of-war camp. After the war, Walker became the only woman to be awarded the Medal of Honor.

While nursing eventually became viewed as a woman's profession, when the war ended, most women were expected to return to the lives they had led before the war. Many wives looked forward to their husband's return to the home or farm so that they could resume their family life. However, the experiences women had in the absence of their husbands and fathers led many of them to begin fighting political battles for greater equality between men and women.

Women on both sides also worked as spies. Although spying was initially seen as a disreputable thing to do, both armies were desperately in need of information about the other side. Belle Boyd, Harriet Tubman, and Elizabeth Van Lew were some of the women who passed on messages and scouted out the numbers and positions of the enemy before battle. Boyd was even captured and arrested for her work with the Confederates. Luckily for her, a Union soldier fell in love with her and helped her escape.

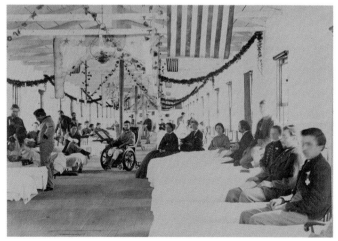

photo: Library of Congress
Some 3,000 women served as nurses during the Civil War.

Some women hid their identities and signed up to fight as male soldiers. Because they were hiding who they were, and it was not legal for women to fight, there is no concrete data about how many female soldiers fought in the Civil War. Some have estimated that around 250 women joined the Confederate army; others say that more than 400 women combined fought in the war.

"This Mighty Scourge of War"

What were the human costs of the Civil War?

The Civil War resulted in more American casualties than any other war in U.S. history. About three million Americans fought in the war, and at least 600,000 were killed. Recent scholars have argued that as many as 750,000 Americans lost their lives. To put these statistics in perspective, the United States lost about two percent of its population in the Civil War. Two percent of the country's current population is approximately six million people. In addition, approximately 277,000 Union soldiers and 195,000 Confederate soldiers were wounded.

photo: Library of Congress

Dead Confederate soldiers at Antietam.

Because it led to President Lincoln's announcement of the Emancipation Proclamation, the Union's victory in the Battle of Antietam is often considered a major turning point in the Civil War. But the battle has another distinction. September 17, 1862, remains the bloodiest day in American military history. In just 12 hours, some 23,000 soldiers fighting at Antietam lost their lives. More Americans were killed in a single day at Antietam than in the entire Revolutionary War.

Although more than 200,000 Union and Confederate soldiers perished on the battlefield, the leading causes of death in the Civil War were disease and sickness caused by infection, bad drinking water, spoiled food, and unsanitary hospital practices and conditions. Approximately 400,000 soldiers died of such causes.

Civilians were also casualties of the Civil War. It is difficult to estimate how many ordinary citizens died due to the war because careful records of civilian deaths were not kept at the time. One expert has put the number at around 50,000 people. Among the innocent victims of war were nonparticipants killed by weapons, people who fell ill from diseases brought by traveling soldiers, and those who died in the South from starvation because of food shortages.

Discovery | **SOCIAL STUDIES TECHBOOK** EDUCATION

To what extent was the Civil War America's second revolution?

Identifying as an "American"

How did the role of the federal government change during and after the war?

You may recall that in the decades before the Civil War, government officials from the South championed the cause of states' rights. Not only did they claim that states had the authority to secede from the Union, but they also asserted states' power to nullify federal laws and preserve the institution of slavery. The Union's victory in the Civil War did not end the rallying cry of "states' rights." But it did establish the supremacy of the federal government over the states. It also affirmed the status of the U.S. Constitution as the "supreme law of the land." In the years during and following the war, the federal government began to play a greater role in the lives of individual Americans.

The war increased not only the power of the federal government, but also its size, its functions, and its budget. When the Civil War began in 1861, the federal government exercised little real power over day-to-day life. Most government functions were handled at the state and local level. Outside of postal workers, the federal government had fewer than 6,000 employees in 1861; in contrast, today's federal government employs roughly two million people.

The main factor causing the government to expand was the war itself. Congress needed to pay soldiers and provide food and weapons for them. The Legal Tender Act of 1862 authorized the Treasury to print $450 million in greenbacks. These were notes, or paper money, that represented debts of the government but were not redeemable in gold or silver.

Some of these notes went to the newly created Bureau of Pensions. Congress created this office to manage payments to wounded

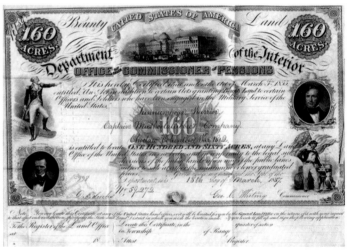

photo: National Archives

As part of the new Bureau of Pensions programs, the federal government gave free land to war veterans after the Civil War.

soldiers and to the wives and families of the dead. During the war, Congress also created the Department of Agriculture to ensure the nation's and the army's food supply. After the war, this office was given responsibility for helping Southern farmers restore their productivity. During the Civil War years, the federal government also spent money building universities, creating infrastructure in western territories, and laying the foundation for a railroad system that would eventually stretch across the United States.

Nationalism

Accompanying the growth of the federal government was the emergence of nationalism, or a sense of loyalty and connection to the nation as a whole. During the Civil War, Americans from outside the South began to see and identify themselves as citizens of the United States more than as citizens of their home states. The song "The Battle Hymn of the Republic" became famous in the Union army. By singing this patriotic song together, the soldiers felt united under a common cause. Following the leadership of President Abraham Lincoln, people from different states had joined together to save the Union and end slavery. As a result, people from different regions of the country felt more connected to one another and to the nation as a whole. In addition, because the federal government was beginning to play an increased role in their lives, Americans began looking to the president as their leader.

Postwar Economies

What were the economic effects of the Civil War?

War is a very expensive endeavor. It requires soldiers and uniforms, weapons and ammunition, food and medical care. Wherever battles are fought, buildings and land are usually destroyed at great monetary and human cost.

According to some historians, the Civil War cost the nation about $6.6 billion. This was almost twice as much as the total value of goods and services produced in the United States at the beginning of the war. While both the North and South lost many soldiers and endured great human suffering, most of the war's economic devastation was centered in the South.

photo: Library of Congress

The Confederate states issued paper money that became worthless after the Civil War.

Before the Civil War, the South had a very strong agricultural economy with very little industry. Southern states sold much of their cotton and other crops to Northern industrialists who produced clothing and other goods in their factories. When war began in 1861, the Confederates had very few factories that could produce the weapons and other supplies soldiers needed to defeat the Union. Everything had to be imported, and this required money. But because the states of the North no longer purchased Southern cotton, where would this money come from?

Like the U.S. federal government, the Confederacy printed its own paper money during the Civil War. However, the U.S. government was able to sell bonds and raise taxes to support its new currency. The Confederates had few banks that could sell bonds, and the Confederate government was unable to collect taxes from its states.

As the Confederacy printed more money to fight the war, Confederate dollars became worth less over time. This created inflation, a condition in which prices increase as the purchasing value of money goes down. By the time the war ended in 1865, inflation in the South was at 9,000 percent. Even before the war was lost, the Confederate dollar had no value. Many Southerners had their savings wiped out, and the only way to do business was to barter.

Inflation wasn't the only economic problem in the South after the war. The South had also lost valuable property and resources—not only land and buildings but also about one-third of its farm animals and about half of its farm equipment and machinery. Many of the factories and railroads the South had before the Civil War were destroyed by the Union army. Major cities such as Charleston and Atlanta were almost completely burned to the ground. Before the war, the net value of all property held by residents of South Carolina was $400 million. By 1865, this figure dropped to $50 million.

Another huge economic loss for the South was enslaved people. This loss of human "property" was valued at about $2.5 billion. Total wealth in the South fell by an estimated 40 percent between 1861 and 1865.

After the Civil War, it was clear that the North was the nation's dominant economic center. While the South lay in economic and physical shambles, many Northern industrialists had actually made money off of the war. Northern factories had profited by supplying the Union army with weapons and other goods. Northern farming had also grown during the war because the Union was not purchasing crops from the South and needed to feed its great army. Because so much of the war had been fought in the South, the North did not have to face the expensive task of rebuilding.

A Social Shift

How was society in the North and South changed by the war?

Once the Civil War ended, immigration and industrialization of the North resumed and accelerated. United States industrial production dropped sharply between 1862 and 1865, but following the war, it returned to its prewar rate of growth. The federal government invested in interregional transportation to support industry. Northern industrialists and bankers increased their wealth and their investments in new factories and growing industries. Lower-class workers labored in dreary jobs, and life in city slums remained dirty and sometimes dangerous.

Southerners had more changes to adapt to. Many blamed and resented Northerners for the wartime destruction of their homes, farms, and cities. Many Southern landowners were broke, and the region's labor system had collapsed. A plantation could not earn wealth for its owners if there was no one to plant, tend to, and harvest crops. Many Southern plantation owners blamed Northerners for the loss of their enslaved people; when the Confederacy lost the war, people throughout the South feared the end of their way of life.

Drawing of former slaves migrating after the Emancipation Proclamation.

photo: HarpWeek

Former enslaved people also had big changes to face. Now, they faced the responsibilities of freedom and self-sufficiency. Yet, they had no homes, jobs, or possessions, and few could read and write. Whites owned all the land and businesses and so were the only employers, yet few whites were eager to treat African Americans with respect.

After the war, life for most Americans would never be the same. Slavery was over, and African Americans were citizens. An expanded federal government was now expected to protect the rights of all its citizens.

Complete this activity to share your understanding of how the war changed the South.

Discovery SOCIAL STUDIES
EDUCATION TECHBOOK

To what extent was the Civil War America's second revolution?

The war may have ended in 1865, but the changes and issues it brought would be felt for many years to come:

- How would the South be rebuilt?

- Would former Confederate leaders be welcomed back into the United States?

- How would emancipated African Americans be integrated into society?

- How would the United States repay its debts?

- After years of hostilities, could Northerners and Southerners work together?

Consider the Essential Question:

To what extent was the Civil War America's second revolution?

Go online to complete the Social Studies Explanation.

Check for Understanding:

The Civil War has been called America's second revolution. Is this an appropriate title?

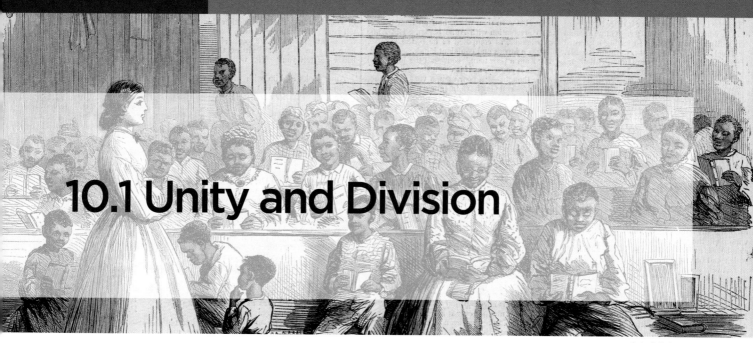

photo: Getty Images

10.1 Unity and Division

LESSON OVERVIEW

Introduction

In this concept, you will learn about the various solutions that were proposed to address the problems the country faced after the Civil War and examine the results of these solutions.

Essential Question

What problems did Reconstruction resolve? What problems did it fail to resolve?

Key Vocabulary

Which terms do you already know?

- ☐ Abraham Lincoln
- ☐ Andrew Johnson
- ☐ black codes
- ☐ Civil Rights Act of 1866
- ☐ Fifteenth Amendment
- ☐ Fourteenth Amendment
- ☐ Frederick Douglass
- ☐ Freedmen's Bureau

- ☐ Hiram Revels
- ☐ impeach
- ☐ infrastructure
- ☐ Ku Klux Klan
- ☐ Military Reconstruction Act
- ☐ Reconstruction
- ☐ Ten Percent Plan
- ☐ Thirteenth Amendment
- ☐ Ulysses S. Grant
- ☐ Wade-Davis Bill

Discovery EDUCATION | SOCIAL STUDIES **TECHBOOK**

What problems did Reconstruction resolve? What problems did it fail to resolve?

Lesson Objectives

By the end of this lesson, you should be able to:

- Explain social and economic problems faced by the nation following the Civil War.
- Analyze and compare Reconstruction plans proposed by Abraham Lincoln and moderate Republicans, the Radical Republicans, and Andrew Johnson.
- Evaluate the effectiveness of key components of Congressional Reconstruction, including the Freedmen's Bureau and the establishment of military control of the South.
- Describe and evaluate the impact of the Fourteenth and Fifteenth Amendments to the Constitution.

ENGAGE

What made Reconstruction a troubled era? Visit Engage to learn more.

Essential Question

What problems did Reconstruction resolve? What problems did it fail to resolve?

EXPLORE

Radical Changes

What was life like for Southerners after the war?

A New and Uncertain Way of Life

Southern plantations had been based on slave labor. Without workers, the huge, sprawling farms could no longer function, and without slavery, there was no longer a source of unpaid labor. Most of the war had been fought on Southern soil, and thousands of homes, businesses, and farms had been burned and looted by Union troops, as well as common criminals taking advantage of chaos. General Sherman's march through Georgia was particularly destructive.

The plantations were not the only major loss. Over 200,000 Confederate soldiers died in the war. Many were killed in battle, but most died from disease and poorly treated wounds. Many of those who survived did not have homes to which they could return.

Many soldiers returned from the war with injuries that made earning a living much more difficult. In sum, the South had lost its main source of income and a great deal of its resources. During the war, the Confederate government printed and distributed its own money; when the Confederates lost the war, money that Southerners had earned and saved was worthless. The Confederacy and individual Confederate states had also issued bonds to raise money to support the war. People who had bought these bonds lost their investments, too.

photo: Library of Congress

Many Southerners lost their fortunes in the war.

Learning to Be Free

The nearly four million newly freed African Americans had problems of their own. The Thirteenth Amendment meant they were no longer enslaved and could no longer be owned as property. They could reunite with their separated families and legally marry for the first time in many states.

Explore this resource and then propose your own plan for rebuilding and unifying the nation.

However, most African Americans had no land, very little money, and few possessions because they had not been allowed them as enslaved persons. Most had little or no education; it had been illegal to teach an enslaved person how to read. They needed jobs, but did not know how to do any work other than the farm labor they had done when enslaved. Many formerly enslaved people found themselves working for their former owners under a system known as sharecropping, which often left the laborers, or sharecroppers, in deep debt.

Lincoln's Plan

What was Lincoln's plan for Reconstruction?

Officials in both Congress and the executive branch and from both political parties agreed that something needed to be done to heal the wounds of war and bring the United States back together. They did not agree on exactly what to do.

President Abraham Lincoln wanted to bring the former Confederate states back into the Union quickly. He supported amnesty, or forgiveness, for rebel soldiers. Moderate Republicans in Congress supported Lincoln's plan. A *moderate* is someone who avoids extremes and makes limited demands. Moderate Republicans were willing to make compromises to bring the seceded states back into the Union.

Radical Republicans thought that Lincoln's plan did not go far enough. A radical is someone who favors extreme change. Radical Republicans insisted that the federal government protect the civil and social rights of newly freed African Americans. The Radical Republicans also favored harsh treatment for traitorous Confederate soldiers and officeholders.

Lincoln's Plan

Lincoln's plans for reconstruction began before the Civil War was even over. They included amnesty for Confederate soldiers and a plan for readmission to the Union of the Southern states. Lincoln's 1863 Proclamation of Amnesty was known as the Ten Percent Plan. A state could be readmitted if 10 percent of its voters swore a loyalty oath to the Union and agreed to the end of slavery. A *loyalty oath* is a pledge of allegiance.

photo: Library of Congress

Do you think Lincoln's amnesty plan was just?

During the war, Lincoln hoped that his plan would further weaken the Confederacy by luring Confederate states back to the Union. The plan was put into action in Union-occupied parts of the Confederacy, but lacked support in other parts of the Confederate South. Lincoln appointed military governors to police the South as states reformed their governments and worked toward readmission. One of these governors, Andrew Johnson, would become Lincoln's vice president in the 1864 election. The governors commanded federal troops, whose job was to keep order as desperate people tried to return to their lives. Under Lincoln's plan, Louisiana, Arkansas, and Tennessee formed new governments and asked to return to the Union.

The Freedmen's Bureau

One piece of early Reconstruction legislation was effective in helping formerly enslaved persons. The Bureau of Refugees, Freedmen, and Abandoned Lands, or Freedmen's Bureau, was established in March 1865 as a welfare agency to help formerly enslaved people become full citizens. Some of the services it provided included handing out food and clothing, building schools and hospitals, and helping find missing family members.

The Radical Republican Plan

How was the Radical Republican plan different from Lincoln's plan?

Congressional reaction to Lincoln's Reconstruction plans deepened the division among Republicans in Congress. While the Moderate Republicans in Congress supported Lincoln's plan for Reconstruction, the Radical Republicans in Congress opposed it. They felt it was too easy on the former rebels and did not do enough to help people freed from slavery. Radical Republicans were also concerned that Lincoln's plan would leave too much political power in the hands of the former Confederate leadership.

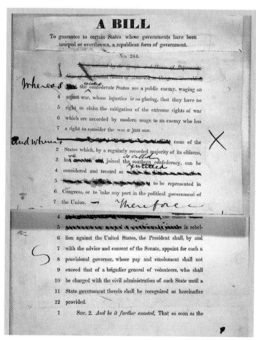

photo: Archives of Congress

The draft of the Wade–Davis Bill, the Radical Republicans' plan for bringing the Southern states back into the Union.

Radical Republicans proposed their own plan, outlined in the Wade–Davis Bill of 1864. This bill required the states to accept the end of slavery and to grant all African American men the right to vote. It called for more than half of a state's voters to sign a loyalty oath before that state could be readmitted. This oath was stricter than Lincoln's loyalty oath; a person had to swear not only that he or she would be loyal to the United States but also that he or she had never supported a rebellion. Requiring this oath would have disenfranchised tens of thousands of Southerners for life.

Lincoln vetoed the Wade–Davis Bill, saying it was too harsh. In return, the Radical Republicans tried to replace Lincoln in the 1864 election. Prior to the Republican National Convention, the Radical Republicans formed the Radical Democracy Party, held a separate convention, and selected John C. Frémont as their candidate.

The move to replace Lincoln did not succeed. Lincoln's leadership in the war had greatly increased his popularity, and Frémont's campaign never attracted much support. Lincoln was reelected in 1864 by a wide margin. Still, the Radical Republicans continued to resist Lincoln's treatment of the former Confederate states as being too lenient.

Discovery EDUCATION | SOCIAL STUDIES TECHBOOK.

What problems did Reconstruction resolve? What problems did it fail to resolve?

Another Tragedy

On the evening of April 14, 1865, one week after the end of the Civil War, President Lincoln and the First Lady attended a play at Ford's Theater in the capital. He was assassinated, or murdered, by John Wilkes Booth, an actor and passionate Confederate supporter. Booth ran off and was killed in a barn in Virginia 12 days later. Lincoln died the morning after the shooting.

After Lincoln's death, Vice President Andrew Johnson became the 17th president of the United States. He inherited an unstable country and the staggering task of trying to bring it together.

The End of Presidential Reconstruction

How did Lincoln's assassination change the course of Reconstruction?

Most people of the South were very unhappy with the changes Reconstruction brought. They resented being forced to live as legal and political equals with the people they had once regarded as private property. They feared the end of their traditional social structure. They also resented the Northerners, known as carpetbaggers, who moved to the South to enforce Reconstruction. This resentment caused many Southerners to feel less willing to rejoin the Union or to give fair treatment to African Americans.

Many Southern whites acted out their resentment with violence. African Americans were commonly beaten or murdered for walking on the sidewalk as an equal, or for a social slight such as failing to tip one's hat to a white man.

Reconstruction Under Andrew Johnson

Andrew Johnson was a very different politician and person from Lincoln. A Southerner and a Democrat, Johnson was chosen by Lincoln to balance the ticket in the 1864 election. He was a less-skilled communicator and politician than Lincoln. He was also a former slave holder. Johnson's goal was to bring the Democratic Party back into power.

Many former Confederates assumed political office as soon as Johnson had readmitted their states back into the Union. Southern legislatures then enacted black codes. These were laws that made African Americans second-class citizens. Black codes included laws that denied African Americans the right to vote. Some states prohibited intermarrying among African Americans and whites and denied African Americans the right to serve on juries. Others required segregation in public places and imposed more severe punishments for African American criminals than for white ones.

photo: Getty Images

Black codes imposed fines on freedmen who violated labor contracts. They allowed the freedman to be auctioned to pay the fine.

Most Southern states also passed laws preventing African Americans from owning land. Vagrancy laws in Mississippi and South Carolina authorized police officers to arrest unemployed African American men and then force them to work off their jail sentences by laboring for a planter. Other codes required African Americans to have special licenses for most occupations.

While Southern states passed and enforced the black codes, President Johnson questioned the need for the Freedmen's Bureau. Johnson thought that the bureau created a protected class of people and unnecessarily extended the power of the federal government. In December 1865, Congress rejected Johnson's plan to close the Freedmen's Bureau, which remained in place until 1872.

Meanwhile, Northern citizens were unhappy with the speed with which the rich and powerful among the Confederate Southerners were allowed to return to positions of leadership. Passage of the black codes? added fuel to their anger.

The Civil Rights Act and the Fourteenth Amendment
How did Congress respond to the black codes?

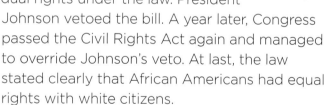

In 1865, Congress passed a Civil Rights Act to declare African Americans citizens and to provide them basic individual rights under the law. President

MENDING THE FAMILY KETTLE.
photo: Library of Congress

How can you tell this cartoonist was critical of Andrew Johnson's approach to Reconstruction?

Johnson vetoed the bill. A year later, Congress passed the Civil Rights Act again and managed to override Johnson's veto. At last, the law stated clearly that African Americans had equal rights with white citizens.

But opponents of the Civil Rights Act thought that it was beyond the reach of Congress's delegated powers and therefore unconstitutional. To remove any doubt, in 1866, Congress also proposed the Fourteenth Amendment to the Constitution. The purpose of the Fourteenth Amendment was to undo legal concessions that had been made to slavery since the writing of the Constitution.

Discovery SOCIAL STUDIES
EDUCATION **TECHBOOK**

What problems did Reconstruction resolve? What problems did it fail to resolve?

You may recall that many Northerners were outraged at the U.S. Supreme Court's 1857 decision in *Dred Scott v. Sandford*. The Dred Scott ruling held that African Americans, enslaved or free, had no legal rights and could never be citizens of the United States. The Fourteenth Amendment overturned the Dred Scott decision. It granted equal citizenship to all persons born in the United States, and prohibited states from passing any laws that would deny the rights of U.S. citizens, including recently emancipated African Americans.

The Fourteenth Amendment also explicitly erased the three-fifths compromise from the Constitution. African Americans would now be counted as full persons in determining congressional representation. But any states that denied African Americans voting rights would be punished by having their representation in Congress reduced.

The Fourteenth Amendment also took a hard line toward former high-ranking government officials who had been involved in the rebellion. The amendment declared that individuals who had once held federal office but then supported secession or the Confederacy had violated the oath of loyalty they had taken to the United States. These individuals were declared ineligible to hold state or federal office again. The amendment also invalidated all debts owed by any Confederate state. These states were illegal, so they had no right to borrow money, and anyone who loaned them money was supporting the rebellion.

Many scholars believe the Fourteenth Amendment was the largest change to the U.S. Constitution since the Bill of Rights. Although it was originally intended to protect recently emancipated African Americans, over the last century the amendment has also been interpreted as extending civil rights to other minority groups. Both Congress and the courts have used the Fourteenth Amendment to affirm important rights for African Americans, women, disabled persons, immigrants, persons accused of crimes, young people, and other groups.

Congressional Reconstruction

How did Congress restore unity?

Many Northerners were outraged by the black codes and with acts of violence used to intimidate African Americans attempting to exercise their rights as citizens. They were particularly angry with President Johnson, who seemed to be doing nothing to stop them. Crowds of people who supported equal rights harassed the president as he gave speeches. People also expressed their opinions about Congress in the voting booth.

The midterm elections of 1866 increased the power of the Radical Republicans in Congress. These included Thaddeus Stevens of Pennsylvania, Charles Sumner of Massachusetts, and Benjamin Wade of Ohio. The Radical Republicans in Congress believed that Johnson's leniency toward former rebels was endangering Reconstruction.

They also believed that Johnson's policies encouraged Southern states to resist accepting African Americans as full citizens. The radicals began to vocally oppose Johnson's policies. They vowed to protect African Americans from violence and to control Southern resistance to political and social change. Gradually, Congress took charge of Reconstruction. This period, beginning in 1867, is known as Congressional Reconstruction.

Radical Reconstruction

In March 1867, the Republican majority in Congress passed the first Reconstruction Act, also known as the Military Reconstruction Act. This law divided the South into five military districts, each governed by a general of the Union army and controlled by federal troops. The military governor was given authority over every government officer in the district, from local police to mayors to state legislators. Three requirements were imposed on states before they could be readmitted to the Union:

- enact a new constitution to be approved by Congress

- guarantee African American men the right to vote

- ratify the Fourteenth Amendment

The Reconstruction Acts also required former Confederates to take oaths of loyalty to the United States before they could vote. Many refused to do so, and were therefore

ineligible to vote. Furthermore, in many areas of the South, African Americans were in the majority. For instance, in 1870, 59 percent of the population of South Carolina was African American. By September 1867 more African Americans than whites were registered to vote in five southern states— Alabama, Florida, Louisiana, Mississippi, and South Carolina.

photo: Library of Congress

Schools like the one in this photograph were opened by the Freedmen's Bureau for former enslaved persons.

Then, Congress went a step further to ensure that all states, including those in the North, granted African American men suffrage. It passed the Fifteenth Amendment to the U.S. Constitution.

The Fifteenth Amendment was ratified in 1870.

Discovery SOCIAL STUDIES TECHBOOK

What problems did Reconstruction resolve? What problems did it fail to resolve?

The Impeachment of President Johnson

How did Congress try to defeat Andrew Johnson?

In 1867, Congress tried to limit President Johnson's power by passing the Tenure of Office Act. This law prohibited a president from removing any executive department officer who had been appointed by a previous president. Johnson vetoed the Tenure of Office Act, but Congress overrode his veto.

Later that year, President Johnson tried to stop military Reconstruction by firing Edwin M. Stanton, the secretary of war and a Radical Republican. Johnson planned to replace Stanton with someone who would not enforce the law. This action brought about a crisis of government.

In response to Stanton's firing, the House of Representatives impeached Johnson in 1867—that is, it tried to remove him from office by accusing him of a crime, using a process described in Article I of the Constitution. The Congressional impeachment bill accused Johnson of violating the Tenure of Office Act.

photo: Getty Images

Facsimile of a ticket of admission to the impeachment trial of President Andrew Johnson, 1868.

Once the House impeaches the president, the Senate conducts a trial. The Senate acquitted, or found Johnson not guilty, by a single vote. A later Supreme Court ruling declared the Tenure of Office Act an unconstitutional limit on the president's constitutional powers.

Following his impeachment, Andrew Johnson was more cooperative about allowing radical Reconstruction reforms. However, he had become very unpopular. In the 1868 presidential campaign, Johnson failed to win the Democratic nomination, and the Republican Ulysses S. Grant, the Northern hero of the Civil War, won the election. Grant would follow a more moderate path for Reconstruction. In 1871, President Grant called for the withdrawal of Union troops from the South. The Freedmen's Bureau also shut down that year.

Granting Freedmen the Right to Vote

How did the Fifteenth Amendment affect Reconstruction?

The Fifteenth Amendment protected voting rights by prohibiting states from denying voting rights because of race. In response to this change, after Reconstruction many states devised a variety of systems and tests to ensure that newly freed African Americans would not be able to vote. For instance, some states passed poll taxes, or fees citizens were required to pay to vote. To maintain the voting rights of white citizens, "grandfather clauses" exempted individuals whose grandfather had voted prior to a certain date.

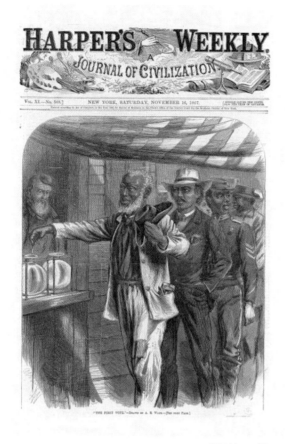

"THE FIRST VOTE."—Drawn by A. R. Waud.—[See next Page.]

photo: Library of Congress

First vote for African Americans.

Another common method of keeping African Americans from voting was the so-called literacy test, in which potential voters would be given passages to read and explain. Under these laws, African Americans were often given complicated passages to read and interpret, or they might be failed on technicalities, while whites easily received automatic passing grades. In spite of the ratification of the Fifteenth Amendment, in some parts of the United States, African Americans continued to be denied the right to vote until the passage of the Voting Rights Act of 1965.

Explore this interactive to learn more about key events that shaped the Reconstruction era.

Consider the Essential Question:

What problems did Reconstruction resolve? What problems did it fail to resolve?

Go online to complete the Social Studies Explanation.

Check for Understanding:

Describe the most important problems that the United States confronted during Reconstruction. Did public officials agree on the best way to handle these problems?

photo: Library of Congress

10.2 Postwar Society

LESSON OVERVIEW

Introduction

In this concept, you will learn about the United States' struggles to recover from the Civil War and from slavery and explore how Reconstruction changed life for both African Americans and white Americans.

Key Vocabulary
Which terms do you already know?

- [ ] amendment
- [ ] black codes
- [ ] Blanche K. Bruce
- [ ] carpetbaggers
- [ ] Civil Rights Act of 1866
- [ ] Compromise of 1877
- [ ] disenfranchise
- [ ] Fifteenth Amendment
- [ ] Fourteenth Amendment
- [ ] Ku Klux Klan
- [ ] *Plessy v. Ferguson*
- [ ] Reconstruction Acts
- [ ] Robert E. Lee
- [ ] scalawags
- [ ] sharecropping
- [ ] tenant farmer
- [ ] William T. Sherman

Essential Question

In what ways did Reconstruction change Southern society?

Lesson Objectives

By the end of this lesson, you should be able to:

- Assess the long-term social and cultural impacts of Reconstruction on various groups.

- Account for Southern distrust of federal governments and Northern interests.

ENGAGE

What were William T. Sherman's views on Reconstruction? Visit Engage to learn more.

Essential Question

In what ways did Reconstruction change Southern society?

EXPLORE

Congressional Reconstruction Brings Violent Reactions

How did Southerners react to Congressional Reconstruction?

During Presidential Reconstruction, 1865–1867, President Abraham Lincoln and President Andrew Johnson focused Reconstruction efforts on readmitting the seceded states. The time period when Congress took over Reconstruction from the president, 1867–1877, is known as both Congressional Reconstruction and Radical Reconstruction. The so-called Radical Republicans who controlled Congress during much of this time were less willing to compromise African American rights and to appease former Confederates.

As Congress and the president argued about how and how much to protect African Americans' rights, former Confederates acted increasingly hostile to their African American fellow citizens. Many white Southerners were frustrated with losing their political power. They resented the new role African Americans were playing in local and state offices and thought that Republicans were capitalizing on the fact that African Americans could vote.

When the collapse of several businesses and banks sent the economy into a downward spiral known as the Panic of 1873, Northern attention was taken away from the plight of African Americans. As economic conditions worsened, living as a free African American became even more difficult.

Postwar Violence

Some Southern whites used force and intimidation to prevent African Americans from exercising their rights. In 1866, a riot began in Memphis, Tennessee, after an argument between a group of African American former Union soldiers and a group of white city police. Mobs assaulted African American neighborhoods, wrecking businesses and burning homes, churches, and schools. Forty-six African Americans were killed. No one was tried for these crimes.

Riots also broke out in New Orleans in 1866—a series of events that have come to be known as the New Orleans Massacre. The violence began as a group of 130 African American citizens marched in support of the Louisiana Constitutional Convention. The mayor of the city organized a mob of ex-Confederate soldiers to block the marchers from reaching the convention. The march continued, but when it reached the convention site, the mob and the police attacked the marchers. Unarmed African American citizens were shot and killed as they attempted to run for safety. The mob also entered the convention hall and fired at the delegates. The violence spread. At least 200 African American veterans of the Union army were killed.

In response to this terrorism, the federal government reinstated military rule in Louisiana and removed the mayor from office. Northern anger over the New Orleans Massacre was an important factor in the Republican success in the Congressional elections of 1866.

The Klan Gains Power

During Reconstruction, secret organizations developed to harass, intimidate, and physically harm African Americans. In 1866, former Confederates created the Ku Klux Klan in Pulaski, Tennessee. Originally formed as a social club, the Klan grew in strength and made its sole purpose to reestablish white supremacy in the South. Dressed in white sheets and robes, Klan members launched nighttime raids against African Americans as well as whites from the Northern states. They attacked, whipped, and frequently killed their victims.

photo: Getty Images

Members of the Ku Klux Klan, which formed in Pulaski, Tennessee, in 1866.

The Klan grew, reaching its peak in the South from 1868 to 1870. In several states, Klan members succeeded in their goal of restoring white supremacy by frightening opposition away from the polls. Beginning in 1870, the federal government launched efforts to suppress the Klan's activities and even sent federal troops to parts of South Carolina. But bringing Klan members to justice was a challenge. Federal prosecutors often faced a lack of funds, as well as juries that were sympathetic to the Klan's goals.

Radical Reconstruction Brings Change

How did Reconstruction affect African American voting rights?

African American Voters Gain Power

Despite the violence and the threats, enforcement of the Civil Rights Act of 1866 and the Fourteenth Amendment protected African American voting rights. In the late 1860s and the 1870s, African Americans in the North and South voted in large numbers for Republican candidates of both races. With their newfound political power, hundreds of thousands of African Americans helped elect the Republican and former general Ulysses S. Grant to the presidency in 1868. Aside from Lincoln, few men were more hated by Southern rebels than Grant.

photo: Library of Congress

Some of the first African American members of the U.S. Congress.

By 1870, politics in most Southern states were controlled by the Republican Party. Across the South, hundreds of African Americans were elected to state and local offices, and 16 African Americans were elected to the U.S. Congress.

The first African American elected to the U.S. Senate was Hiram Revels, who was born free in North Carolina and served as senator from Mississippi. He filled the seat of former Confederacy president Jefferson Davis. Another African American senator was Blanche K. Bruce, who had formerly been enslaved, elected in 1874.

In spite of these temporary political gains, daily life for many African Americans in the South remained difficult, and promises of Reconstruction unfulfilled. As a result of an economic system known as sharecropping, many freedmen remained dependent upon their former owners.

African Americans Want Land for Farming

How did sharecropping affect freed African Americans?

Freed African Americans wanted land for farming so that they could establish independence from their former owners. In the late stages of the war, the federal government had sold or leased confiscated Southern lands to many former enslaved people for farming. By 1865, about 20 percent of confiscated land was being farmed by freed African Americans. In one example in Mississippi, African American farmers leased plantation land owned by Confederate president Jefferson Davis and his brother. Some of these farmers included formerly enslaved people once owned by Davis. Their cotton crop yielded $159,000 in 1865.

In January 1865, General Sherman issued a field order distributing some of the confiscated lands in South Carolina and Georgia to freed African Americans. However, that summer President Johnson declared that the land held by the federal government would be returned to its original owners.

After the war, many Southern states passed laws that made it difficult for African Americans to buy or lease land. As a result, freedmen were often forced to work for wages, sometimes for the very plantation owners who had held them captive. Some landowners could not afford to pay wages due to the short supply of money following the war. To "pay" those working the land, they created a system of sharecropping, in which a landowner rents a piece of land to a farmer in exchange for a share of the crop

photo: Library of Congress

In what ways did sharecropping create a "cycle of reenslavement"?

the farmer grows. The landowner also provides seed and sometimes tools on credit. The sharecropper repays the debt after harvesting and selling his or her crop.

Sharecropping frequently drove both landowner and farmer into debt, because both had to borrow against the sale of the crop to afford to live. More often than not, sharecropping became a cycle of reenslavement for formerly enslaved African Americans. Landowners took advantage of poor and illiterate formerly enslaved African Americans, who were uneducated in the areas of calculating interest payments and auditing account records. A sharecropper who did not produce enough crops to repay his debt would be forced to borrow again and hope that the following year's crop would be more profitable.

Despite its obvious inequities, sharecropping persisted in parts of the South until the 1930s.

Reconstruction Governments Enact Change
How did Reconstruction aim to improve African Americans' lives?

Reconstruction governments worked to improve living conditions by restoring and improving programs, organizations, and businesses as well as roads, railroads, and bridges that had been destroyed during the war. Some of the funds helped establish the first state-funded public school systems. These schools allowed African Americans the opportunity for a free education.

The movement to build schools for African Americans in the South had actually begun before the war was over. As the advancing Union army captured territory in Southern states and enforced the Thirteenth Amendment, abolitionist societies followed close behind. They began to set up schools to teach the newly freed African Americans.

More than 1,000 teachers, most of them white women from Northern states, moved to the South during the war. Another 2,000 teachers followed them during the early years of Reconstruction. African Americans also supported and taught in the new schools.

PRIMARY SCHOOL FOR FREEDMEN, IN CHARGE OF Mrs. GREEN, AT VICKSBURG, MISSISSIPPI.—[See Page 396.]

photo: Getty Images

By 1870, more than 200,000 African American students were enrolled in the 4,000 new schools created by the Freedmen's Bureau and abolitionist societies.

Congress created the Freedmen's Bureau in 1865 to help African Americans transition to freedom. One of its functions was to provide food, clothing, and shelter to tens of thousands of people of both races made homeless and unemployed by the war. It also worked to reunite families by locating people who had been separated by being sold under slavery. The bureau provided legal services to formerly enslaved people, too, including documenting marriages that had begun under slavery and helping African American veterans and their heirs apply for pensions and back pay. Because of this work, the records kept by the Freedmen's Bureau provide valuable insight into African Americans' experiences during Reconstruction.

The Freedmen's Bureau also built and operated hospitals and partnered with abolitionist societies to increase the number of schools in operation. The bureau spent around one-third of its budget during the period from 1865 to 1870 building more than 1,000 schools for African Americans. These included teacher training schools that became today's historically black colleges, such as Howard, Morehouse, Fisk, and Southern universities. Hundreds of thousands of African Americans received an education as a result of these efforts. At the end of the war, only 1 of 10 African Americans was literate; by the end of the 1800s, that number increased to more than 1 in 2.

Explore this investigation and take a position on the effectiveness of the Freedmen's Bureau.

As with other efforts to improve the lives of African Americans, many Southern whites opposed the Freedmen's Bureau and its programs. They opposed efforts to educate African Americans because they wanted to maintain their supremacy. They did not want Northerners teaching racial equality, and they did not want African Americans to be literate.

Carpetbaggers Head South

How did Southern politics reflect social divisions?

While a few African Americans could buy Southern land after the war, most did not have the money to buy land. Northern investors who had earned big profits during the war bought plots of land in the South. Some of these investors also moved to the South, hoping to find financial opportunities. For example, John Hay, President Lincoln's secretary and assistant, invested in orange groves in Florida. Some of these Northerners also desired political power and ran for office after establishing themselves in a Southern community. Former Union general Willard Warner, a native of Ohio, bought plantations in Alabama and later served as one of that state's U.S. senators.

Many Southerners called these Northerners who came South "carpetbaggers," after the bags made of carpet that some used to carry their belongings. Many Southerners hated the carpetbaggers. They claimed carpetbaggers were attempting to profit from the South's misfortune. Though some carpetbaggers hoped to get rich quickly, others came because they truly wanted to help rebuild the South and provide aid to freed people.

Equally despised by former Confederates were the "scalawags," Southerners of European descent who sympathized with Radical Reconstruction, carpetbaggers, and freed people. As many as one-fifth of whites in the South supported Republican policies.

THE "STRONG" GOVERNMENT 1869—1877.

photo: Library of Congress

Many Southerners believed that Northerners were trying to profit from the South's defeat in the war. How does this political cartoon illustrate this belief?

Some scalawags had been Union sympathizers during the war. Others were former business owners and professionals who opposed the plantation class that had controlled the Southern states before the war. Many scalawags ran as Republicans and were voted into office.

Consider the Essential Question:

In what ways did Reconstruction change Southern society?

Go online to complete the Social Studies Explanation.

Check for Understanding:

Did Radical Republicans' legislative reforms "change the whole fabric of Southern society"? Provide evidence to support your position.

Discovery SOCIAL STUDIES
EDUCATION | **TECHBOOK**

How did the Civil War and Reconstruction affect life for future generations of Americans?

10.3 An Era Ends

photo: Getty Images

LESSON OVERVIEW

Introduction

In this concept, you will learn why federal troops left the South and why Reconstruction ended. You will also analyze how that change affected Americans, especially African Americans in the South.

Essential Question

How did the Civil War and Reconstruction affect life for future generations of Americans?

Lesson Objectives

By the end of this lesson, you should be able to:

- Summarize events leading to the conclusion of military Reconstruction.

- Evaluate the short- and long-term effects of Reconstruction on various groups.

Key Vocabulary
Which terms do you already know?

- ☐ amnesty
- ☐ Compromise of 1877
- ☐ electoral college
- ☐ Fifteenth Amendment
- ☐ Fourteenth Amendment
- ☐ Jim Crow laws
- ☐ Ku Klux Klan
- ☐ literacy test
- ☐ *Plessy v. Ferguson*
- ☐ poll tax
- ☐ Radical Republicans
- ☐ Reconstruction
- ☐ Redeemers
- ☐ Rutherford B. Hayes
- ☐ "separate but equal"
- ☐ Thirteenth Amendment

ENGAGE

**How did life change when the troops left the South?
Visit Engage to learn more.**

Essential Question

How did the Civil War and Reconstruction affect life for future generations of Americans?

EXPLORE

The Election of 1876

What effect did the election of 1876 have on Reconstruction?

Enthusiasm for Reconstruction Fades

By 1870, many people in both the North and the South were becoming weary of battling Reconstruction. Many Northerners were tired of struggling to change the South. They did not want to continue to send troops to the South to protect African Americans. They wanted the federal government to move on and focus on economic growth and other issues.

For their part, many white Southern Democrats felt that the federal government had overstepped its bounds by placing the Southern states under military rule. They also believed that the majority of Republican government officials were corrupt and were able to stay in power only because of backing from the federal government. In addition, Democrats opposed the expensive social programs that Republican leadership had put in place and then paid for with tax dollars.

Southerners called Redeemers wanted to *redeem* their government, which means to restore to a favorable position. What they really wanted was to regain their lost power from Radical Republicans and African Americans.

Redeemers used any tactics they could, both legal and illegal, to prevent African Americans from voting. Because the Fourteenth Amendment guaranteed equal protection of the law, they could not pass laws that explicitly discriminated against African Americans. Instead, they took away African Americans' rights in other ways. One example was a poll tax, which is a tax that one has to pay before voting. Because many African Americans could not afford to pay the tax, they could not vote.

Discovery | SOCIAL STUDIES
EDUCATION | **TECHBOOK**

How did the Civil War and Reconstruction affect life for future generations of Americans?

In 1872, Republican president Ulysses S. Grant was reelected. That same year, Congress passed the General Amnesty Act, which allowed many former Confederates to run for public office. Intimidation and violence kept many African Americans and Republicans away from the polls.

In 1873, a financial crisis swept the nation, causing many businesses to fail and millions of people to lose their jobs. Many Americans blamed Grant for the downturn and began to lose faith in Republican leadership. Northerners' focus shifted away from Reconstruction and rights for African Americans back to their own finances and the economic problems affecting the nation.

The Compromise of 1877

The presidential election of 1876 provided an opportunity to end military rule in the South. That year, Rutherford B. Hayes, a Republican, ran for president against Samuel J. Tilden, a Democrat. Tilden won a majority of popular votes, but the results of the electoral vote were unclear. Three states, South Carolina, Florida, and Louisiana, had each submitted two sets of electoral ballots. According to one set, Tilden was the winner. According to the other set, Hayes had won. Congress created a special Electoral Commission to settle the dispute. But the commission stalemated: It was made up of both Republicans and Democrats, and members of each party supported their own candidate.

photo: Library of Congress
The 1877 Electoral Commission.

In early 1877, the members of the commission reached a compromise. The Democrats agreed to accept the ballots that made Hayes the winner in exchange for the Republicans agreeing to withdraw the federal troops from the South. This agreement became known as the Compromise of 1877, and Hayes was declared the winner of the presidential election.

photo: Library of Congress
The Electoral Commission of 1877 declared Rutherford B. Hayes president.

Achievements of Reconstruction

What were the long-lasting achievements of Reconstruction?

Although federal troops left the South in 1877, Reconstruction had important, long-lasting effects. It brought the two parts of the nation back together and established the federal government's authority over the states. Although people still debate whether certain powers should belong to the federal government or the states, the supremacy of the federal government was solidified by the Civil War and Reconstruction.

Another important result was the granting of amnesty, or forgiveness, to most Southerners who had fought for the Confederacy. Amnesty meant that former Confederates could keep their property and take part in the political process. In some countries of the world, people who have participated in a civil war are punished much more severely; they are sometimes prohibited from participating in government. After the Civil War, tensions still existed between the North and the South, but granting amnesty showed, in the words of Abraham Lincoln, "charity for all."

Other lasting achievements of Reconstruction were the end of slavery and the federal government's recognition of African Americans as citizens of the United States. By passing the Thirteenth Amendment, Congress ended slavery in North America forever. The Fourteenth Amendment annulled the *Dred Scott* decision, in which the U.S. Supreme Court ruled that African Americans were not and could never be citizens and had no rights. The Fourteenth Amendment declared the freed African Americans citizens, and it guaranteed all citizens equal treatment under the law. Finally, the Fifteenth Amendment extended voting rights to African American men.

photo: Library of Congress

These students are shown at the law library of Howard University, which was founded in Washington in 1867 and named for the director of the Freedmen's Bureau.

These amendments did not initially succeed in protecting the rights of African Americans in the South and beyond. During the late 1800s and the first half of the 1900s, people in both the North and the South found ways to discriminate against African Americans. But the Civil War amendments did create a constitutional basis for many of the civil rights that African Americans would gain in the 1950s and 1960s. Additionally, the equal protection promised by the Fourteenth Amendment was eventually extended to other groups of Americans, including women, people with disabilities, and people in poverty.

Education for African Americans was another long-lasting effect of Reconstruction. The Freedmen's Bureau built more than 1,000 schools for African Americans. After the bureau closed, African Americans worked to keep many of these schools open.

The bureau also funded many colleges and universities for African Americans, some of which, such as Howard University and Morehouse College, are still open today. In addition, postwar state constitutions began to guarantee public education for all. Although many schools were segregated, state commitment to universal public education was an important milestone in American history.

The Limits of Reconstruction

In what ways did Reconstruction fail to achieve its goals?

Although Reconstruction had long-lasting achievements, it did not succeed in protecting African Americans' rights. Even while federal troops remained in the South, groups such as the underground Ku Klux Klan harassed and terrorized people to maintain white power and privilege.

After 1877, these organizations played less of a role because their goal of white supremacy was achieved through legal methods. Laws such as poll taxes and literacy tests severely limited African Americans' right to vote. Jim Crow laws enforced segregation in public places such as restaurants, railroad cars, and schools. African Americans and whites attended separate schools. Some restaurants refused to serve African Americans, while others seated them in a distinct area. On trains, individual cars were designated "White" or "Colored."

In 1896, segregation by law was challenged in a Supreme Court case called *Plessy v. Ferguson*. Homer Plessy, an African American, was arrested for trying to ride in a "whites only" railroad car in Louisiana. Plessy believed that the equal protection clause of the Fourteenth Amendment prohibited racial segregation laws.

But the Supreme Court did not agree. It announced the "separate but equal" doctrine, holding that segregating public facilities by race did not violate equal protection as long as the facilities for African Americans and whites, though separate, were equivalent.

Partially as a result of the *Plessy* ruling, segregation laws remained in place in the South until the middle of the 1900s.

photo: Library of Congress

Some African Americans left the South and moved to the West in search of equal treatment and better opportunities.

During and after Reconstruction, many African Americans simply gave up hope of seeing an end to discrimination and poverty in the South and moved out of the region. For example, Benjamin "Pap" Singleton, who had once been enslaved, started a community for African Americans in Kansas. He encouraged African Americans in the South to move there or to other western communities. By 1879, about 50,000 African Americans had left the South for Kansas, Missouri, Indiana, and Illinois.

In the early 1900s, many more African Americans moved from the South to northern cities in search of jobs and equal treatment; this movement came to be known as the "Great Migration." Although the situations African Americans found in the North were often no better than those they had left, the Great Migration helped increase the role of African American culture in the broader American society.

Political Legacies

What were the political effects of Reconstruction?

During Reconstruction, African Americans' political gains were significant. Two African American senators and 19 congressmen served in the U.S. Congress, including Robert Smalls, who served from 1875 to 1879 and 1881 to 1887. Hundreds more were elected to state offices around the South.

But the lasting political effect of Reconstruction was to forgive African American disenfranchisement. After Reconstruction ended, poll taxes, literacy tests, and intimidation prevented many African Americans from voting, and few were elected to public office. From 1878 to 1955, there were no African Americans elected to the Senate and never more than two African Americans in the House.

DISCOVERY | SOCIAL STUDIES
EDUCATION | **TECHBOOK**

How did the Civil War and Reconstruction affect life for future generations of Americans?

The "Solid South"

Reconstruction also had long-term effects on the two major political parties. Northern Republicans had been the party in Congress that supported African American rights during Reconstruction. But once redemption occurred, many Southerners who now controlled politics in their states did not forgive the Republicans. A strong majority of white Southerners voted Democratic for nearly a century. Politically, the region became known as the "Solid South." Although many African Americans might have voted Republican, white Southerners denied them their voting rights, so Democrats won most elections in the South until the late 1960s.

Explore this investigation and take a position on whether Reconstruction was a success.

Another legacy of Reconstruction was Southern distrust of the federal government. The Civil War had begun partially over the issue of states' rights. The Union victory meant that the federal government was supreme. Yet, when the federal government forced new political structures on the South, many Southerners thought it was taking powers that should belong to the states. During the civil rights movement of the 1950s and 1960s, Southerners cited states' rights when they opposed federal laws and policies forcing them to desegregate.

Consider the Essential Question:

How did the Civil War and Reconstruction affect life for future generations of Americans?

Go online to complete the Social Studies Explanation.

Check for Understanding:

Describe the most important outcome of Reconstruction. What made this outcome so significant?

photo: Library of Congress

10.4 African American Life After Reconstruction

LESSON OVERVIEW

Introduction

In this concept, you will examine the practices and policies that were used to deny African Americans their basic rights. You will also learn how African Americans responded to this denial of their rights.

Essential Question

After Reconstruction, how did African Americans respond to racial discrimination?

Lesson Objectives

By the end of this lesson, you should be able to:

- Evaluate practices and policies used to deny African Americans' civil rights.

- Examine African American responses to economic challenges and the denial of civil rights.

Key Vocabulary

Which terms do you already know?

- ☐ Booker T. Washington
- ☐ Fourteenth Amendment
- ☐ grandfather clause
- ☐ Ida B. Wells
- ☐ Jim Crow laws
- ☐ literacy test
- ☐ lobbyists
- ☐ lynching
- ☐ National Association for the Advancement of Colored People (NAACP)
- ☐ *Plessy v. Ferguson*
- ☐ poll tax
- ☐ segregation
- ☐ W. E. B. Du Bois

 SOCIAL STUDIES TECHBOOK

After Reconstruction, how did African Americans respond to racial discrimination?

ENGAGE

How did Ida B. Wells stand up to injustice? Visit Engage to learn more.

> ## Essential Question
>
> After Reconstruction, how did African Americans respond to racial discrimination?

EXPLORE

Jim Crow Laws and Voting Barriers

How did state and local governments promote racial segregation?

After the Union defeated the Confederacy in the American Civil War, the U.S. government attempted to rebuild the nation. The period known as Reconstruction lasted from the end of the Civil War until 1877, when federal troops were withdrawn from the states of the former Confederacy. During Reconstruction, the federal government stepped in to protect the newly freed African Americans. The Fourteenth Amendment made African Americans U.S. citizens and the Fifteenth Amendment protected African American men's right to vote. Federal troops occupied the South to help protect these rights. In 1865, Congress created the Freedmen's Bureau to build new schools and other infrastructure and help African Americans find work. For the first time, African Americans were even elected to state governments and Congress.

Legal Segregation

Many white Southerners resented Reconstruction policies and the freedom that African Americans now had. Before the Civil War, enslaved African Americans had been their property. White Americans had benefited greatly from their "free" labor and from feeling superior to those they commanded. When Reconstruction ended in 1877, white Southerners returned to leadership roles. They worked to reverse the rights and power that had been given to free African Americans and return them to their former status. However, Southerners could not change the Constitution; instead, they tried to bypass it with policies known as Jim Crow laws.

Jim Crow laws required racial segregation, or separation, of most public accommodations. Jim Crow laws affected nearly all public facilities across the Southern states. For example, in North Carolina, African Americans were not permitted to use the same library facilities as whites. In Virginia, African Americans were fined for sitting near whites in theaters, public halls, or other places of entertainment. In Alabama, it was illegal for restaurants to serve both African Americans and whites unless a wall separated the African American dining area; prisoners were assigned to racially segregated cells; and white nurses could not treat African American patients. These laws from specific states are mere examples of the different types of Jim Crow laws passed. Similar laws were instituted across all Southern states.

By 1885, most Southern states had legally required segregation throughout public life. However, these types of laws were not just in the South. States in the western areas of the country, such as Arizona and Wyoming, also had such laws. States that had not done so before wrote laws to prevent marriage between African Americans and whites. Approved in 1910, Oklahoma's law against interracial marriage stated the "marriage of any person of African descent . . . to any person not of African descent, or the marriage of any person not of African descent to any person of African descent, shall be unlawful and is hereby prohibited within this State."

Voting Restrictions

In addition to passing Jim Crow laws, state and local governments also implemented a variety of policies to keep African Americans from voting. Voting restrictions in Southern states, such as the grandfather clause, virtually eliminated African Americans' ability to influence the political process. The grandfather clause allowed anyone who had been a qualified voter before the Civil War to automatically register to vote; this also extended voting rights to people whose ancestors were allowed to vote. As African Americans did not have the right to vote until 1870, this essentially nullified the Fifteenth Amendment. However, the clause enabled many illiterate or impoverished whites to vote because they were not excluded under the voting restrictions. The clause was adopted by seven states between 1895 and 1910. It was not until the court case of *Guinn v. United States* in 1915 that the Supreme Court found all state grandfather clauses to be unconstitutional.

photo: Library of Congress

Segregated facilities lasted well into the 20th century. This man drinks from a "colored" water cooler in 1939.

In 1890, Mississippi became the first state to implement a poll tax. Citizens who wanted to vote had to pay the tax before voting. As many African Americans did not have enough money to pay, they could not vote. Soon, 11 more states followed suit. Another voting barrier was the literacy test. In Alabama and other Southern states, voters were required to read and explain a section of the state constitution to the county clerk.

Discovery SOCIAL STUDIES
EDUCATION TECHBOOK

After Reconstruction, how did African Americans respond
to racial discrimination?

Clerks typically chose difficult passages for African Americans and simple sentences for white voters. This practice weeded out not only the African Americans who could not read, but also virtually anyone the clerks wanted to exclude.

In most Southern states during Reconstruction, more than 90 percent of voting-age African American men were registered to vote. By 1892, voting restrictions reduced that figure to approximately 6 percent in Mississippi. African American voter registration in Louisiana fell from 95.6 percent in 1896 to 1.1 percent in 1904.

"Separate but Equal"

How did Plessy v. Ferguson *solidify segregation policies?*

In 1890, Louisiana passed the Separate Car Act, a Jim Crow law that segregated the state's railcars. The law required all railroads in the state to provide "equal but separate accommodations" for white and African American passengers. The law also prohibited passengers from entering railcars not assigned to their own race. However, many African American professionals in New Orleans felt that this law was unconstitutional.

Breaking the Law on Purpose

On June 7, 1892, a passenger on the East Louisiana Railroad named Homer Plessy sat in a "whites only" train car. Plessy was Creole—a person of mixed European (primarily French and Spanish) and African descent. Even though Plessy's skin was light colored and he was mostly European in ancestry, Louisiana's segregation laws considered him to be black. Because of that, sitting in the "whites only" car got him arrested, but it was no accident that Homer Plessy sat in the "whites only" car and refused to move.

Plessy was part of a civil rights organization, a group of people fighting for equal rights for African Americans. The organization was called the Citizens' Committee to Test the Constitutionality of the Separate Car Law. His organization wanted to go to court to challenge Louisiana's 1890 Separate Car Act by violating the law on purpose in order to establish a test case. Plessy hoped his arrest would begin a legal fight that would result in the end of all Jim Crow laws. Sure enough, the case of *Plessy v. Ferguson* made it all the way up to the Supreme Court of the United States.

The Supreme Court's Decision

Plessy's lawyer argued that the Separate Car Act was unconstitutional. He said the law violated the Thirteenth and Fourteenth Amendments of the Constitution, which had outlawed slavery and made African Americans citizens of the United States. The Supreme Court heard the *Plessy v. Ferguson* case on April 13, 1896, and handed down its decision on May 18. In a 7–1 vote, the Court ruled that state laws such as the Separate Car Act do not force people into slavery and, therefore, do not violate the Thirteenth Amendment.

SUPREME COURT OF THE UNITED STATES.

photo: Library of Congress

The Supreme Court in 1894.

The ruling also concluded that most segregation laws did not violate the Fourteenth Amendment as long as separate facilities were "equal." The majority of the court stated that segregation laws, by nature, did not violate the equal protection clause of the amendment. As long as the facilities provided the same accommodations, they could remain separate. The majority opinion, authored by Justice Henry Billings Brown, recognized that the Fourteenth Amendment was intended to create absolute racial equality before the law. However, the ruling also stated that the amendment was not intended to end all legal distinctions based on race, or to enforce social equality in the United States. In short, the judges concluded that segregation is a legal form of discrimination.

This Supreme Court's decision in *Plessy v. Ferguson* reinforced the precedent that segregation was an acceptable practice. It supported the idea that separating people by the color of their skin was not unconstitutional, as long as the facilities provided to both groups were equal. As a result, the Supreme Court's decision permitted the passage of many Jim Crow laws throughout the South. After *Plessy v. Ferguson*, legal segregation would last well into the 1960s. During this time, the meaning of "equal" was stretched and debated many times over.

Explore this resource to interpret a Supreme Court Justice's objection to the *Plessy* ruling.

White Supremacy

How was racial discrimination practiced by private citizens after Reconstruction?

Many Americans who supported segregation justified racial discrimination by claiming that white people of European ancestry were superior to people from other racial and ethnic backgrounds. They believed that nonwhites should not have a voice in American politics and society, and that African American society should remain separate from mainstream white culture.

Around the beginning of the 1900s, many whites in the South and in other regions of the country began to romanticize the days of the Confederacy. Crude stereotypes of African Americans were common in popular culture. For example, D. W. Griffith's *Birth of a Nation* was one of the first motion pictures to achieve commercial success.

Discovery SOCIAL STUDIES
EDUCATION TECHBOOK

After Reconstruction, how did African Americans respond to racial discrimination?

Griffith's film portrayed the Ku Klux Klan as a band of heroes that liberated Southern society from corrupt African American rule. In 1915, the Klan reemerged in the United States and its membership surpassed three million during the 1920s. During this time, the Klan was a largely political organization that supported candidates who opposed immigration and civil rights for African Americans.

After Reconstruction, societal norms and customs in the South and beyond were established to maintain a system of white supremacy. Racial discrimination was enforced not only by the government, but also by private citizens and institutions, including businesses and churches. Private citizens and institutions used a variety of techniques to preserve white supremacy. For example,

photo: Library of Congress

People crowd the streets of Waco, Texas, to witness the lynching of Jesse Washington. Several men in the tree appear to be securing chain or rope.

African Americans were expected to speak deferentially, or with respect, even to younger whites by calling them "sir" or "ma'am."

White supremacists in the South and elsewhere also used acts of violence and intimidation to enforce white supremacy. Groups of citizens often publicly punished African Americans who were thought to have violated racial norms. Because of this, African Americans lived with the threat of personal harm or even death for failing to show sufficient respect for whites. Lynching, an often public act of murder committed by a group of citizens as punishment for a perceived crime, was commonplace.

The National Association for the Advancement of Colored People (NAACP), a civil rights organization, created an Anti-Lynching Committee in 1916 to establish a public awareness campaign about this horrific act. In 1919, the committee published a study called *Thirty Years of Lynching in the United States, 1889–1918*. The committee found that more than 3,200 African Americans were lynched during this period.

In the South, political leaders openly supported policies designed to maintain white supremacy. For example, Benjamin R. Tillman, governor of South Carolina from 1890–1894 and later a U.S. senator, was a known white supremacist. Tillman was a strong supporter of lynching as an appropriate law-enforcement policy. With leaders, such as Tillman, creating policies that kept African Americans in a cycle of poverty and limited civil rights, African Americans found it difficult to improve their living conditions.

Finding Hope in the Church

How did churches help African Americans cope with segregation?

Living in a society dominated by white supremacy posed numerous dangers and obstacles for African Americans. Coming together as a community to support one another helped them survive and sometimes prosper. The emergence of African American churches, colleges, and newspapers helped the African American community cope with challenging social and economic circumstances.

African American Churches

By the end of the 1800s, going to church had long been part of African American life. In the early 1800s, many free African Americans living in the North had joined white Baptist and Methodist churches. However, as their numbers in a congregation grew, white churchgoers often left to form new churches separate from African Americans. In this way, American churches became increasingly separated along racial lines. In 1787, opposed to the restrictions that limited the number of African Americans who were allowed to attend church services, a former slave named Reverend Richard Allen started his own church in Philadelphia: the Bethel African Methodist Episcopal Church. Other African Americans followed suit. The African Methodist Episcopal Church soon spread to African American communities in the North and South. At the same time, the African American Baptist community also was growing. The first African Baptist church began in the South around 1750.

photo: Library of Congress

Several African American families gather outside a church in Georgia.

After the Civil War, African American missionaries traveled to the South to help open African American churches there. In 1870, Southern African Americans established the Colored Methodist Episcopal Church (now called the Christian Methodist Episcopal Church). Then, in 1894, Southern African American Baptists created the National Baptist Convention. To this day, it is the largest African American religious organization in the country. Organized activities, such as church socials, picnics, and Bible study, provided a sense of community and helped African Americans find hope and inspiration while living with the challenges of segregation and discrimination.

The church was a place of worship, but it was also a place of information, education, and social and political connection. Church leaders and prominent church members were also often influential business owners and public figures in their local African American communities. African American businesses catered to African American citizens, providing barbershops, banks, insurance companies, and other services.

Discovery | SOCIAL STUDIES
EDUCATION | **TECHBOOK**

After Reconstruction, how did African Americans respond to racial discrimination?

As African American churches grew in numbers, they raised money and organized efforts to help build schools and teach African Americans to read and write. As a result, literacy among African American Southerners increased to nearly 60 percent by 1900. The efforts to educate African Americans led to the establishment of black colleges.

A College Education

How did African Americans use education to increase their opportunities?

During the mid-1800s, many historically black colleges and universities (HBCUs) emerged around the country. Many of today's important HBCUs were founded in the decade or so after the Civil War and emancipation. Some of these schools were primarily religious and sought to train ministers. Others emphasized public service, science, or general education. All of these schools aimed to educate people who would lead the new African American citizens to prosperity in a reconstructed, slavery-free nation.

The ICY

Cheyney University of Pennsylvania is the oldest institution of higher learning for African Americans. This university began in 1837, before the Civil War, as the African Institute. It was later renamed the Institute for Colored Youth (ICY). The idea and the money for the school came from a West Indies immigrant named Richard Humphreys. Humphreys believed that if education was the key to improving life for former enslaved people, African Americans needed to be trained as teachers. In his will, Humphreys gave $10,000 to a group of 13 Quakers. He charged them to create a school "to

photo: Library of Congress

The baseball team from Morris Brown College in Atlanta, Georgia, was composed entirely of African American students.

instruct the descendants of the African Race in school learning, in the various branches of the mechanic Arts, trades and Agriculture, in order to prepare and fit and qualify them to act as teachers." In the school's early years, it provided training for young African Americans to be teachers or tradesmen through a classical education.

Support of Freedmen's Bureau

Several historically black colleges and universities were founded in the South after the Civil War and the abolition of slavery. Institutions such as Howard University (established in 1867) and Morehouse College (established 1867; originally the Augusta Theological Institute) offered a liberal arts education.

These HBCUs were supported by the Freedmen's Bureau. This Reconstruction-era organization helped former enslaved people adjust to freedom in many ways, and one important way was through education. Colleges and universities such as these trained students to be teachers and to serve as religious leaders. Other Southern schools focused on preparing students for jobs in industrial or agricultural fields.

Land-Grant Colleges

Prominent African American professors and scholars debated about what the focus of education should be for African Americans. Some desired a classical education based on the study of literature and history, while others promoted vocational training in a specific agricultural or industrial field. The Morrill Land-Grant Act of 1862 provided federal land for the establishment and funding of educational institutions "to teach such branches of learning as are related to agriculture and the mechanic arts."

Tuskegee University in Alabama, originally founded as the Tuskegee Institute in 1881 by Booker T. Washington, is a prime example of a "land-grant college" created through these funds to serve African American students. Tuskegee established an example for several HBCUs that were later organized under a second Morrill Act in 1890, an amendment to the first act, which promoted creating land-grant colleges for African American students. However, despite the opportunities granted by these institutions, racial segregation in the South and beyond made it difficult for African American students to study in schools other than the HBCUs. Until the desegregation efforts of the mid-1900s, African American students were constrained in the educational opportunities available to them.

Spreading the News

How did African Americans use newspapers to give themselves a voice in society?

Freedom's Journal was the first African American-owned and operated newspaper in the country. Published in New York for two years (1827–1829), it was joined by numerous other African American newspapers in the years following the Civil War. For example, *The Chicago Defender*, founded in 1905 by African American Robert Abbott, was a weekly newspaper for primarily African American readers. Other papers such as *The Afro-American* in Baltimore, Maryland, and *The Louisiana Weekly* published stories about local African American communities. They also provided information pertinent to African American society that was generally shunned by the white newspapers, such as ads for African American businesses. In a similar way to colleges and churches, newspapers contributed to African American public life and helped create communities that had been repressed for 150 years.

Discovery EDUCATION | SOCIAL STUDIES TECHBOOK

After Reconstruction, how did African Americans respond to racial discrimination?

One important journalist who covered these types of topics was Ida B. Wells. Wells was born into slavery in Mississippi in 1862. Her parents were highly involved in the Republican Party during Reconstruction, and her father attended Shaw University, a school for newly freed slaves founded in 1870, but dropped out to help his family. After her parents died, Wells moved to Memphis, Tennessee, and began teaching there. Because education was important to her family, Wells also attended summer classes at Fisk University, an African American college in Nashville. While teaching in the Memphis schools, she also wrote articles for *The Evening Star*, a black-owned newspaper, about the inequalities she saw during her experience with the Chesapeake and Ohio Railroad company and in the segregated schools. As a result, she was fired from the teaching job and began working for the newspaper full-time.

photo: Library of Congress

A newsboy sells copies of the Chicago Defender, *a daily newspaper for African Americans.*

In 1889, Wells was offered a position equal to editor at the Memphis newspaper *The Memphis Free Speech and Headlight*. Eventually, she became co-owner. Using a pen name to hide her identity, Wells wrote editorials about violence and injustice against African Americans. She openly opposed segregation in the schools. When her friend and neighbor Tom Moss and two others were lynched in 1892 after defending Moss's store against a mob, she spoke out. Angry readers destroyed her newspaper office, but that did not stop her. Wells continued her crusade to investigate and stop lynchings for the rest of her career.

Booker T. Washington

How did African American leaders promote equality and social justice?

The late 1800s and early 1900s saw the emergence of two leaders—Booker T. Washington and W. E. B. Du Bois—who had contrasting backgrounds and different philosophies regarding how African Americans could achieve social, political, and economic equality.

The Great Accommodator

photo: Library of Congress

Booker T. Washington was a leading advocate for practical and industrial education as a way to advance in society.

Booker T. Washington was one of the most visible reformers and educators of his time. Born into slavery in 1856, he moved with his family to Malden, West Virginia, after emancipation. He began working at age nine in a salt furnace, and he later worked as a domestic servant for a prominent white family in the town. Washington was determined to get an education. In 1872, he enrolled at the Hampton Normal and Agricultural Institute in Virginia. After graduation, he returned home to teach. He also sought further studies and later taught at Hampton as well. His experience as a professor helped him emerge as a leader of the African American community.

Washington's beliefs centered on acceptance and accommodation by African Americans. Rather than trying to change white people and white society, Washington believed African Americans should concentrate on bettering themselves. Rather than demanding respect, he thought African Americans should earn it.

According to Washington, African Americans would succeed by gaining education in practical skills. He did not believe protests would lead to racial equality and mutual respect. He thought that African Americans should learn industrial trades, such as farming, and practical, manual labor skills. By showing that they were hardworking, patient, and enterprising, Washington believed African Americans would gain the support and respect of white Americans. Following this path would lead to a complete integration of society. The Tuskegee Normal and Industrial Institute in Alabama—which began as a one-room college—was founded in 1881 on these principles. Washington was named its first teacher.

W. E. B. Du Bois

How did Booker T. Washington and W. E. B. Du Bois differ in their philosophies?

W. E. B. Du Bois was a Harvard University-trained scholar and political thinker. Born in Massachusetts in 1868, Du Bois graduated from Fisk University at the age of 20. In 1895, Du Bois received a PhD from Harvard for his dissertation, *The Suppression of the African Slave-Trade to the United States of America, 1638–1870.* Although his degree was in history, Du Bois was trained in the social sciences and was highly interested in the social conditions of African Americans.

Discovery | SOCIAL STUDIES
EDUCATION | **TECHBOOK**

After Reconstruction, how did African Americans respond
to racial discrimination?

Du Bois believed that Washington's practical approach
to ending discrimination would create lasting
oppression and permanent segregation. According
to Du Bois, African American accommodation to
second-class status would only strengthen racial
prejudice and discrimination. Instead, Du Bois called
for political action and a strong civil rights movement.

Du Bois wanted African Americans to fully educate
themselves and gain a wide intellectual base. His plan
of action was to first promote a small group of
college-educated African Americans, also known as
"The Talented Tenth." He wanted the world to see that
African Americans could be intelligent, articulate, and
cultured. Du Bois thought African Americans should
demand the respect and rights that belonged to them
as equal human beings.

photo: Library of Congress

*W. E. B. Du Bois believed in education and
activism as a way to gain equal rights.*

**Explore this investigation
to learn more about the
differences between
Washington and DuBois.**

As time passed, Du Bois's strategies of
outright protest gained wider popularity.
In 1905, he led an organization called
the Niagara Movement. The 29 African
American members of the Niagara
Movement called for "every right that
belongs to a free-born American—political,
civil, and social." Although the group made little headway, it endured and eventually
blended into the modern civil rights movement.

Forming National Civil Rights Organizations

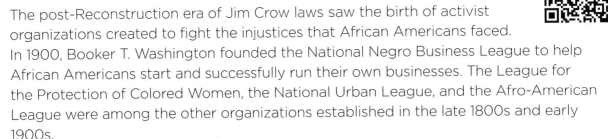

What is the NAACP? Why were organizations like this established?

The post-Reconstruction era of Jim Crow laws saw the birth of activist
organizations created to fight the injustices that African Americans faced.
In 1900, Booker T. Washington founded the National Negro Business League to help
African Americans start and successfully run their own businesses. The League for
the Protection of Colored Women, the National Urban League, and the Afro-American
League were among the other organizations established in the late 1800s and early
1900s.

African American social justice groups advocated for the economic, political, and social
advancement and legal equality of African Americans. One of the most prominent of
these organizations was the National Association for the Advancement of Colored
People, or the NAACP. Today, the NAACP is still the largest civil rights organization in
the United States.

photo: Getty Images

Membership in the NAACP extended to the youth of the nation.

The NAACP was founded in February 1909, partially in response to a major race riot that occurred in Springfield, Illinois, in August 1908. Six people were killed, many were injured, and thousands fled their homes as a result of the riot. This and similar events made it clear to many African Americans and whites that things needed to change, and soon. People of both races came together for a meeting and established the NAACP. The response to the NAACP was overwhelming: In its first 10 years, ranks swelled from 60 to more than 50,000 members. By 1919, there were 220 local branches across the nation.

The goals of the NAACP were simple: end discrimination and segregation in all areas of life. Early on, the group unsuccessfully lobbied Congress to pass a law against lynching. To lobby Congress is to try to convince lawmakers to support and pass certain legislation. Over time, the NAACP won several major court cases against the federal government, such as winning the right of African Americans to serve as officers in World War I and the desegregation of schools in 1954.

Even though it fought for African American rights, white leadership initially controlled the NAACP. In 1920, James Weldon Johnson was appointed as its first African American executive secretary. Since Johnson's appointment, only African Americans have held this influential post. Over the years, the organization has evolved to encompass all races. Its modern mission is now to "ensure the political, educational, social, and economic equality of rights of all persons and to eliminate race-based discrimination."

Making the Move

Where did many African Americans move after Reconstruction?

The end of Reconstruction marked the beginning of a nearly century-long migration trend for African Americans away from the South. Although the "Great Migration," the movement of millions of African Americans out of the South, did not begin until the early 1900s, a smaller version of this relocation started during the late 1800s.

Moving West

After the Civil War and emancipation, many African Americans lived by moving from place to place within the South in search of work. However, the threat of racial violence, as well as the daily oppression of Jim Crow laws, convinced many in the African American community to leave the South altogether.

Discovery | SOCIAL STUDIES EDUCATION | TECHBOOK

After Reconstruction, how did African Americans respond to racial discrimination?

Moving west had some of the same attractions for African Americans as for whites. The work was hard, but the land was cheap. A settler could escape his or her past and start over. African Americans who migrated west named themselves Exodusters, after the Book of Exodus in the Bible. A former slave named Benjamin "Pap" Singleton convinced many African American families to move to Kansas and establish settlements.

During the late 1860s, Singleton and his supporters had urged African Americans to purchase farmland in Tennessee. However, Singleton turned his attention to Kansas when whites in Tennessee refused to sell him quality land. At one point, a rumor spread that the U.S. government had reserved land in Kansas for former enslaved people, but this rumor later turned out to be false. Through the support of his Edgefield Real Estate and Homestead Association, between 1877 and 1879 Singleton helped more than 20,000 African Americans migrate to Kansas.

Moving North

Starting around the 1890s, larger numbers of Southern African Americans began moving to Northern cities. They settled in places such as Chicago, New York, Detroit, and Philadelphia. However, they continued to face racial discrimination and prejudice. Although racial segregation was not legally enforced in the North, it was largely accepted and privately enforced by white society. Many restaurants, hotels, retail stores, and other private businesses would not serve African Americans. Many European Americans saw African Americans as inferior and different. Some were angry at the possibility of losing their jobs to African Americans. African Americans often had to live in crowded, substandard housing. Even in the 2000s, Northern cities still have large areas that are racially segregated.

photo: Library of Congress

In February 1880, more than 900 black families from Mississippi reached St. Louis, Missouri.

Discrimination and hostility often led to violence and mob rioting. Between 1900 and 1908, violent race riots occurred in large cities such as New York City, and smaller urban areas such as Greensburg, Indiana. It seemed that no matter where they called home, African Americans could not escape discrimination and injustice in the United States.

Influential African Americans

Who were some prominent African Americans of the late 1800s and early 1900s?

In spite of racial discrimination and segregation, many African American scholars, innovators, and business leaders distinguished themselves during the late 1800s and early 1900s.

photo: Library of Congress

George Washington Carver stands in a field, holding a piece of soil.

George Washington Carver, Scientist

Among other talents, George Washington Carver is remembered as one of the nation's most important plant scientists. Carver was born into an enslaved family in Missouri during the Civil War. When he was young, Carver taught himself to read and write using an old primer. Carver was an excellent student with a wide variety of interests and talents who went on to study art, music, and botany in college.

In 1896, Booker T. Washington hired Carver to run the agricultural program at the Tuskegee Institute, a traditionally African American college in Alabama. At Tuskegee, Carver spent most of his adult life teaching and conducting groundbreaking research and experiments. He invented hundreds of uses for peanuts, sweet potatoes, and other crops. His inventions included paints, plastics, and a type of gasoline. Carver worked with African American farmers to help them grow better crops. He convinced people to rotate their crops to keep the soil healthy. He helped revolutionize farming in the South by providing alternative crops to cotton, which strained the soil. Cotton crops were also affected by the boll weevil, a beetle that could eat and destroy large cotton crops. Carver's experiments on the uses of peanuts and sweet potatoes helped create a market for these products. Thanks to Carver, peanuts became a staple crop in the United States.

Garrett Morgan, Inventor

Unlike Carver, Garrett Morgan had little formal schooling. However, practical experiences helped him to become an accomplished inventor. Morgan was born in Kentucky in 1877. As a young man, he moved to Ohio and worked in sewing machine factories. With this job, he learned all there was to know about these machines. He used his knowledge to invent an improved sewing machine that could stitch in a zigzag pattern. His machine and the repair business he started were both a success. In the early 1900s, Morgan experimented with chemical solutions to help fix sewing issues.

His experiments led Morgan to design a new hair cream for African Americans. Morgan's other inventions included a gas mask and a mechanical traffic signal. His financial success allowed him to help support civil rights organizations such as the NAACP. He also started a newspaper, the *Cleveland Call*.

Madam C. J. Walker, Entrepreneur

Born on a plantation in Louisiana in 1867, Madam C. J. Walker was one of the most successful African American entrepreneurs of the early 1900s. After beginning to lose her hair in the 1890s, she started experimenting with store-bought hair products.

Discovery SOCIAL STUDIES
EDUCATION TECHBOOK

After Reconstruction, how did African Americans respond to racial discrimination?

Then, according to Walker, the answer to her prayers appeared to her in a dream. Walker developed her own hair and scalp formula from a formula she says she came up with in her sleep. Saving money to invest in her business, Walker sold her products door-to-door in Denver.

In 1908, Walker moved her successful company to Pittsburgh. She opened a school, Leila College, where she trained others to sell her products. Two years later, she opened a factory, beauty salon, and second training school in Indianapolis. She later moved to New York and invested in real estate there. By the time she died in 1919, Walker was one of the wealthiest African Americans in New York. By many estimates, she had earned at least a million dollars.

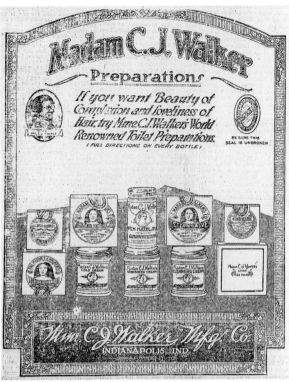

photo: Library of Congress

This advertisement pitches Walker's products for hair and skin complexion.

Like Morgan and other successful African Americans, Walker used her money to help the African American community. She donated funds to help African American students attend college in the South and donated to causes, including the National Conference on Lynching.

New educational opportunities and a growing sense of community established by both schools and churches gave hope to many African Americans after Reconstruction. These advances paved the way for influential leaders and financially successful inventors and business owners, such as Booker T. Washington, Ida B. Wells, Garrett A. Morgan, and Madam C. J. Walker.

Despite these advances, African Americans in all parts of the country continued to face racial segregation and limited civil rights. This legacy of slavery would continue to haunt American society for many years to come.

Consider the Essential Question:

After Reconstruction, how did African Americans respond to racial discrimination?

Go online to complete the Social Studies Explanation.

Check for Understanding:

Why was the U.S. Supreme Court's decision in *Plessy v. Ferguson* important?

11.1 Invention and Mechanization

photo: Library of Congress

LESSON OVERVIEW

Introduction

In this concept, you will explore technological developments that transformed life in the United States after the Civil War. You will analyze changes in areas such as industry, agriculture, communications, and transportation.

Key Vocabulary
Which terms do you already know?

☐ Alexander Graham Bell
☐ assembly line
☐ corporation
☐ horizontal integration
☐ Industrial Revolution

☐ scientific management
☐ Thomas Edison
☐ transcontinental railroad
☐ vertical integration

Essential Question

How did the development of new technologies change life in the United States?

Lesson Objectives

By the end of this lesson, you should be able to:

•   Explain how industrialization changed the production of goods and services and transformed American society.

•   Identify and explain the most important causes of industrialization.

•   Describe and explain the impact of new technologies and innovations in various areas of American life.

Discovery EDUCATION | SOCIAL STUDIES TECHBOOK

How did the development of new technologies change life in the United States?

ENGAGE

Was the telegraph America's first Internet? Visit Engage to learn more.

Essential Question

How did the development of new technologies change life in the United States?

EXPLORE

Industrialization in the United States

How did industrialization in the United States contribute to rapid change?

A major trend in the history of the United States, industrialization was the process by which everyday goods changed from being crafted by the hands of artisans to being mass-produced in factories by machines. The process of industrialization fundamentally transformed the American economy. New inventions and advanced machinery made it possible for businesses to efficiently mass-produce goods that were demanded by many people. As a result, products became affordable to larger segments of the population. In addition, industrialization led to changes in the way American businesses were organized and operated. Both of these developments had positive and negative consequences.

The industrialization of the United States had its origins in the Industrial Revolution, which began in England during the 1700s. During this period, producers began to use machines such as the steam engine to make textiles, or cloth products.

By the early 1800s, industrialization spread to other countries, including the United States, where textile factories in towns such as Lowell, Massachusetts, began to emerge. After the Civil War, America's industrialization accelerated as a result of new inventions that incorporated steam-engine technology. Steam-powered shovels were used for mining and steam-driven turbine generators produced electricity, which then was used to power even larger factories. As technology improved production methods, factories in major cities in the North and West began to mass-produce goods. The country's industrial transformation soon spread to productive enterprises beyond textiles, such as steel and oil.

Impact on Society

As a result of industrialization, the United States became a more urban nation. In the early 1800s, most Americans lived in the country's rural areas and small towns, but industrialization changed the population distribution of the United States. Because most new factories were located in cities, many people migrated from rural areas to urban areas for work. As a result, urban populations soared. Philadelphia's population increased from about 120,000 in 1850 to about 845,000 in 1880. In 1850, Chicago had only about 30,000 residents. Twenty years later, its population was more than 500,000. Industrialization also changed the physical size and appearance of American cities. City centers that were once small enough to be navigated by foot were replaced by metropolitan areas with public transportation systems. Cities that once were filled with buildings no more than a few stories tall were now dominated by skyscrapers and suspension bridges.

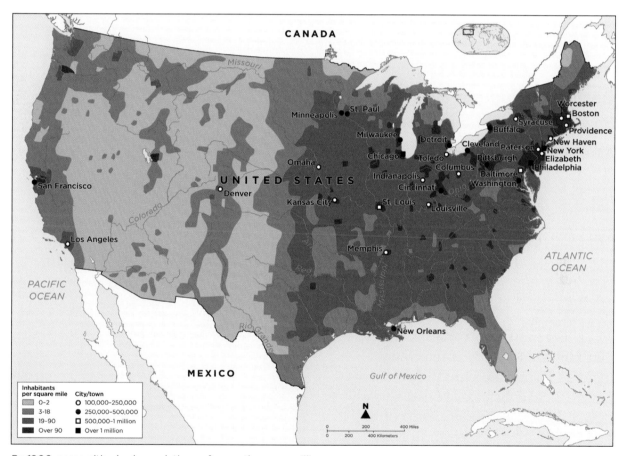

By 1900, some cities had populations of more than one million.

The country's industrial transformation and urbanization also contributed to its increasing diversity. Hoping to find better lives and steady work in American factories, millions of immigrants arrived in the United States in the late 1800s and early 1900s. Many came from eastern and southern European and Asian countries that, in the past, had rarely been sources of American immigration. The arrival of these "new immigrants" created cultural and economic tensions over the meaning of American citizenship.

Discovery | SOCIAL STUDIES
EDUCATION | **TECHBOOK**

How did the development of new technologies change life in the United States?

Explore this interactive to learn more about how industrialization changed society.

Industrialization also affected the class structure of the United States and contributed to income inequality. As the industrial companies grew larger and more powerful, a wealthy upper class of business leaders began to dominate American society and politics. A few industrial giants, such as Andrew Carnegie and John D. Rockefeller, attained levels of wealth that at one time seemed unimaginable. Larger businesses also hired managers and other office workers to perform administrative tasks. These white-collar jobs paid more than factory and farmwork, and contributed to the emergence of an American middle class. However, unskilled workers, often immigrants, who toiled in factories and in mines often lived in poverty and faced very difficult and often unsafe conditions both at home and at work.

Many factors led to the United States becoming a more industrial nation after the Civil War, including improved methods of getting raw materials and making products.

Better Production Methods

How were production methods mechanized?

Assembling Raw Materials

As the production of goods expanded, the demand for more raw materials to make those products also increased. Raw materials are resources that can be manufactured, processed, or combined to create a new and useful product, such as the wood that is made into a chair. To meet the demand for raw materials, business leaders supported the extensive search for underground resources such as iron ore, coal, and petroleum. During the late 1800s, vast deposits of iron ore were mined under the land around Lake Superior. As a result, the total amount of iron ore mined in the United States increased from 7 million tons in 1880 to more than 27 million tons by 1900.

Mechanized methods of removing minerals from underground also drove progress. Scientists developed an early power tool called the longwall cutter to cut coal out of the earth. This tool greatly increased how much coal a single worker could extract, or pull out, at a time. People soon discovered that vast oil deposits lay deep beneath the earth. Before this time, people thought that oil only existed near the surface of the ground. Soon, workers drilled wells that reached the deep oil deposits.

photo: Library of Congress

Early oil wells in Texas.

The oil gushed out of the wells at an alarming rate, which made drilling for oil simpler. Extensive pumping to get the oil to the surface was not needed. These oil wells came to be called gushers.

Before the Civil War, making large amounts of steel was a long, expensive process. However, in the 1850s, a British inventor named Henry Bessemer developed an inexpensive way to make large quantities of steel. This method came to be called the Bessemer process. It involved pouring molten iron into a large container and then blasting the iron with air. This process removed impurities and changed the iron to steel. In 1864, U.S. steel companies began to use the Bessemer process, and by 1880, nearly all steel companies used it.

During the early 1900s, a new steel-making technique, the open-hearth process, would replace the Bessemer process. The open-hearth process had the advantage of being able to make steel from scrap metal. This process also allowed for control over the quality of the steel's chemical composition. However, in the mid-1900s, the open-hearth process was replaced by the basic oxygen process, which is an enhanced, updated form of the Bessemer process.

Producing Products

After the Civil War, production methods were also improved by using a highly organized and methodical approach. In factories, companies hired thousands of workers and gave each worker a specific task. For example, consider a company that makes chairs. One group of workers would make the legs, another group would make the backs, and a third group would make the cushions. This method of organizing workers was called division of labor.

Then, in the early 1900s, an automobile manufacturer named Henry Ford began using division of labor with the assembly line. This process often involved workstations along a moving conveyor belt. The product would move along the belt, and at each station, a worker would add something to the product. Each worker repeated the same function over and over. By the end of the assembly line, the workers had completed making the product, in this case, an automobile.

Another innovation that became popular during this time was scientific management. Scientific management was a way of improving workers' efficiency by eliminating unnecessary actions or tasks. The idea was pioneered by Fred W. Taylor, who studied how long it took factory workers to complete their tasks and determined which actions took too long or required unnecessary motions.

photo: Library of Congress
How does this milk bottling plant illustrate characteristics of industrialization?

Scientific management streamlined the production process by making sure each worker, tool, and task was absolutely necessary for the job.

Over time, companies that used steam-powered machines for production and manufacturing replaced them with gasoline-fueled machines and later, electrically powered machines. As a result, the U.S. factory system became more efficient and powerful. The retrieval of raw materials and the production of goods increased and improved. The movement from steam power to fuel power and electricity also strongly affected transportation.

The Driving Force of Transportation

What inventions helped to expand the railroad system?

As companies gathered more raw materials and produced more products, they needed better transportation networks to move raw materials to factories and to move products from factories to stores. Railroads solved this problem.

In 1829, George Stephenson, an English engineer, developed the first public railroad, which used a steam locomotive for power. A steam locomotive pulls the weight of the train cars using the power generated by a water boiler and a system of exhausting the steam to create a draft in its firebox. The firebox is the area of the engine where fuel, such as wood or coal, is burned, producing heat to boil the water and create steam. The draft mechanism draws huge amounts of air through the firebox, allowing fuel to be

photo: Paul Fuqua

Steam locomotives were used to power trains across North America from the mid-1800s to the mid-1900s.

burned rapidly. Stephenson also developed a standard gauge for all railroads—4 feet, 8.5 inches. The gauge is the width between the inside sections of running railroad tracks. The cost of constructing and operating a rail line depends on the gauge size, and numerous gauges were used in early rail systems to save money or improve stability. Soon, railroads throughout Europe and the United States adopted Stephenson's gauge as the standard size.

A number of technological changes helped railways provide safer and more efficient transportation. In 1869, a U.S. inventor, George Westinghouse, developed an air brake that could automatically stop a train. Before air brakes, the early brake system on trains required that an operator, or brakeman, physically apply a hand brake in each car, signaled by the train engineer. Air brakes significantly enhanced the safety of speeding locomotives. In addition, by the 1870s, railroad companies began to use steel for rails, which were much more durable than iron rails. Steel rails broke less often and could carry heavier loads of cargo. The development of the refrigerated railroad car enabled companies to transport fresh meat to markets far away. The demand for fresh meat in these markets was high, and meatpacking became a profitable industry.

As these new developments helped expand the railroad industry, several companies rushed to build and complete rail lines after the Civil War, which created competition in the railroad industry. The competition between these businesses helped keep fare costs lower for riders. No single company could charge too much because customers were able to find a competing railway line with less expensive fares.

Soon, railroads expanded into a nationwide network. The Union Pacific and Central Pacific railroads completed a transcontinental railroad in 1869. The success of new rail lines in the West was partially due to the consolidation, or combination, of older railroad companies in the East during the late 1800s. Through the consolidation of several networks, passengers were able to travel on many of one company's lines at a low cost. Now, many more raw materials, goods, and people could be transported from coast to coast in a week instead of months. Before long, other railroad lines crossed the country. In addition to goods, the railcars brought people in search of new opportunities.

A New Workforce

How did the workforce expand in the United States?

As the number of mines, steel mills, factories, railroads, and other businesses grew, companies needed more workers. New sources of labor from both inside and outside of the United States contributed to the nation's industrial transformation. Between 1870 and 1920, the population of the United States increased from about 40 million to more than 100 million residents. This boom, which was fed primarily by immigration, provided the workforce that was needed to maintain industrialization.

During the mid-1800s, growing companies often recruited people to move to the United States by offering incentives, or special offers, such as reduced fares on ships. People in Europe responded positively to these pull factors. Other events and push factors, such as political and religious persecution and the Irish Potato Famine (1845–1852), forced many immigrants to leave their homelands and move to the United States. About 7.5 million immigrants, mostly from northwestern Europe, entered the United States from 1820 to 1870. The railroads employed these immigrants to construct the railroad tracks, and the factories recruited them as laborers at low wages.

From 1881 to 1920, the number of immigrants increased even more. During this period of "new immigration," about 23 million immigrants flooded into the United States. These new immigrants came more frequently from southern and eastern European countries such as Italy, Russia, and Poland, instead of northern and western European countries. Scores of immigrants also arrived from China and Japan, primarily to work in the West.

Industrial jobs were also filled by native-born Americans. In rural areas, farms and businesses could not provide enough jobs for the increasing population, particularly as machines gradually replaced human laborers. The need for additional hired hands on farms greatly decreased. As a result, many people living in the rural areas moved to cities to work in factories. In addition, many African Americans moved away from Southern rural areas after the Civil War, seeking better economic opportunities than sharecropping and new lives away from racial discrimination.

photo: Library of Congress

Five immigrant women wait to be registered at Ellis Island in the early 1900s.

The arrival of immigrant and native-born unskilled laborers in American cities created a situation where there were more available workers than available jobs. As a result, factories found workers easy to replace. This labor surplus kept wages low and gave employers little incentive, or reason, to provide workers with safe and pleasant working conditions. As the workforce expanded, new business models would emerge as the nation continued to industrialize.

A Corporate World

What new business methods shaped industrialization?

As a result of industrialization, businesses had to reconsider how they were organized and funded. Large companies needed new business models to support the rapid growth of industry across the United States. They needed to find ways to make operations more efficient.

Integration

Some businesses began to combine into very large companies that sometimes dominated entire industries. These businesses formed around an innovative economic theory called vertical integration. In this system, one company controls all stages in the production of one product. For instance, consider the automobile industry. One company could control the making of parts for the vehicle, the assembly of the vehicle, and the selling of vehicle. In the early 1900s, Henry Ford formed an automobile company that used vertical integration. Other companies also used this business structure because it ensured that all stages of production—from the refining of raw materials to the sale of a finished product—were controlled by the same large company. Smaller companies faced difficulties getting access to raw materials or competing with the prices set by larger, integrated companies. Many companies still use vertical integration.

Business leaders in the late 1800s and early 1900s also used horizontal integration to combine businesses from the same industry into single entities. For example, a large oil company would acquire all of the oil refineries in a single region, forcing all oil for the region to be refined at one of its refineries. This strategy drove out competition and allowed the integrated company to set prices.

Investment: Stocks and Bonds

As American businesses grew, they needed massive amounts of capital, or money, to maintain production levels. Large numbers of workers needed to be paid. Raw materials needed to be obtained. Machines needed to be purchased and maintained. As a result, the industrial era saw the arrival of innovative practices for funding business operations. Financial institutions that specialized in making large loans to corporations emerged. Bankers, such as J. P. Morgan, became a driving force behind the growing economy because they were able to provide significant loans.

Businesses also raised capital by organizing into corporations. A corporation is a business that issues shares of company ownership, called stock, in order to raise capital. Corporations had the added benefit of helping to make sure business owners would not be financially ruined by business failure. Stockholders were only responsible for the shares of stock they agreed to purchase. In addition, stockholders could sell shares of stock they had purchased at any time. They could also purchase shares of stock of other companies if they desired. Corporations also issued loan certificates, called bonds, to raise money for expansion. Investors who purchased bonds agreed to provide businesses with funds on the condition that they would be paid back, with interest, at a later date.

Selling stocks and bonds was important to corporations because it provided them with much-needed capital. Stocks and bonds also contributed to the rise of an investment culture in the United States. Some investors who could afford to purchase many shares could become incredibly wealthy. In addition, by buying and selling stocks and bonds, individual Americans citizens were given opportunities to benefit financially from the country's industrial expansion. However, these practices also brought risks to investors who did not act wisely.

Bureaucracy

As some American businesses became very large, they began to organize their workers in new and innovative ways. Used in businesses and governments, a bureaucracy is an organizational structure that divides work into categories. For example, a large retail store might establish separate departments for merchandising, sales, marketing, and administration. This division of labor created a type of work called management. A manager is responsible for directing and controlling the work in a department.

Discovery SOCIAL STUDIES
EDUCATION **TECHBOOK**

How did the development of new technologies change life in the United States?

Bureaucracies often form a hierarchy. The people higher in the hierarchy have more responsibility for the business and almost always receive more pay. Usually, fewer people work in the highest positions. As a result, companies with bureaucracies form a type of pyramid structure, as shown in the diagram.

During the industrial era, management positions began to require more professional training. As result, a new form of social class emerged called

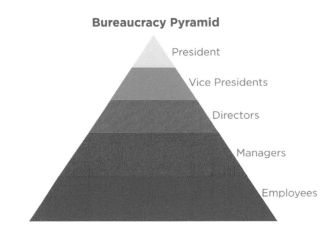

Bureaucracy Pyramid

President
Vice Presidents
Directors
Managers
Employees

This pyramid diagram shows a structure often used for bureaucracies in businesses.

white-collar workers because they typically worked in clean, white dress shirts. These workers usually had a college education and received high pay. White-collar workers included managers and other trained professionals such as doctors and lawyers. In contrast, people who did manual labor in factories and other companies often had less education and received less pay. These people came to be called *blue-collar* workers because they were known for working in blue denim shirts.

photo: Library of Congress
These men sit in open railroad cars on their way to work in the mines. How does their clothing compare with the clothing of white-collar workers?

photo: Library of Congress
White-collar workers at the White House business office.

Advertising and Sales

How were people lured into purchasing new goods?

Innovative marketing and advertising techniques for products also contributed to the nation's industrial growth by expanding the market for manufactured goods. As demand from businesses increased, an industry devoted to marketing and advertising emerged. During the 1870s, advertising agencies helped companies to increase the sale of their goods. N. W. Ayer & Son in Philadelphia, one of the first agencies, emphasized the services that it could provide, such as writing advertisements and drawing images for ads. Soon, many other agencies followed. By the 1920s, agencies were creating advertising campaigns for many types of businesses.

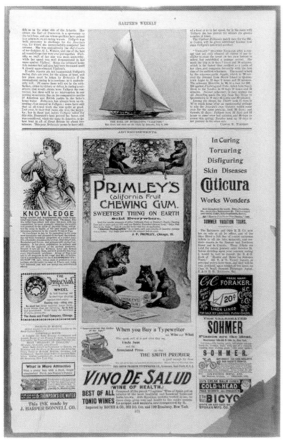

This page from Harper's Weekly *magazine (1894) shows 15 advertisements.*

photo: Library of Congress

Department Stores

Some merchants also formed large department stores, such as Marshall Field & Company of Chicago and R. H. Macy of New York. These department stores offered a wide variety of merchandise, such as clothing and accessories for adults and children, kitchen appliances, furniture, and often food. In addition, store owners began to tell their salesclerks to promote brand-name goods. The demand for everyday items, as well as luxury products from recognizable brands, contributed to industrialization by driving the increased production of manufactured goods.

Mail-Order Catalogs

In 1872, Montgomery Ward & Company of Chicago formed the first mail-order business to sell a diverse assortment of goods. Soon, this company began to produce catalogs that described products, complete with illustrations and prices. Added to this, the company offered a money-back guarantee if the customer was not satisfied with the product.

Before long, Sears, Roebuck and Company and other companies also started a mail-order business. Ordering by catalog became very convenient for people living in rural areas far away from towns or cities. The expansion of the railroads and the establishment of the parcel-post system further enhanced this method of sales.

During the late 1800s and early 1900s, the sale of goods using mail-order catalogs soared. For example, in 1888, Montgomery Ward sold $1 million worth of goods, but by 1913, this company sold $40 million worth of goods. The innovative mail-order approach greatly expanded the market for manufactured goods by allowing American consumers to purchase items from around the country and have them delivered to their doorsteps.

Inventions for the Field

What inventions helped to improve agriculture?

The modernization of agriculture industrialized farm production and reduced the need for human labor on farms. The innovations produced a surplus of food, which the growing U.S. population required, but they shifted the American lifestyle away from its roots in agriculture.

Discovery EDUCATION | SOCIAL STUDIES TECHBOOK

How did the development of new technologies change life in the United States?

Mechanical Reaper

For centuries, farmers used hand tools such as sickles and scythes to harvest grain. Using these tools involved long hours of backbreaking work. In the 1830s, though, Cyrus McCormick developed a machine that could harvest large amounts of grain faster and with fewer workers than previous methods. The machine is called a reaper. Pulled by a horse, reapers worked best on flat farmland and, as a result, sold well in the Midwest. During the 1920s, farmers began to use tractors to pull mechanical reapers. Farmwork became easier, and agricultural production in the United States expanded rapidly.

Steel Plow

In 1836, a manufacturer named John Deere invented the first steel plow. Before this time, farmers used iron plows. However, the thick prairie sod often stuck to these plows, which frustrated many farmers. Realizing this, Deere constructed a plow made out of a steel saw. As he had hoped, when he used the plow, the soil did not stick to the plow blade. Soon, Deere began to manufacture thousands of steel plows. They made farming more efficient and significantly increased the crop yields, or the amount of food produced in one growing season. The growing U.S. population depended on these large yields, and companies that manufactured steel plows, such as Deere & Company, became prosperous.

Combine

During the 1920s, farmers started to replace their reapers with a machine called a combine. A combine could cut grain, separate it from the main plant, and clean it all in one operation. Reapers could only cut grain. During the 1880s, companies constructed combines powered by steam engines and later replaced these engines with internal-combustion engines, which are fueled by diesel or gasoline. Because the combine could accomplish both cutting and threshing the grain, even fewer workers were required on the farm to gather the edible parts of the grain.

Steam-Powered Machines

After the Civil War, some farmers began to use steam-powered machines to work the fields. These machines, such as tractors, often replaced the heavy pulling work of mules, horses, and oxen. Although the machines were much more powerful than animals, they were also more expensive and difficult to maintain. As a result, many people who had small farms continued to use animals. However, by the early 1920s, gasoline-powered machines became available. These machines were lighter and easier to use than the steam-powered ones and, as a result, more farmers used them. However, many farmers went into substantial debt by purchasing the expensive machinery required for them to compete with larger landholders.

Everybody's Talking

How did communication methods improve due to American inventions?

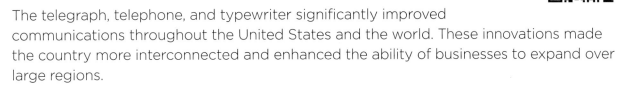

The telegraph, telephone, and typewriter significantly improved communications throughout the United States and the world. These innovations made the country more interconnected and enhanced the ability of businesses to expand over large regions.

The Telegraph

In 1837, the American inventor Samuel F. B. Morse invented the first telegraph that had practical use. Six years later, the U.S. government built a telegraph line from Washington, DC, to Baltimore, Maryland. Soon, many New York City newspapers began to use the telegraph to send news.

Why did the telegraph gain such quick popularity? Before the development of the telegraph, people sent long-distance messages written by hand through mail. Usually, mail was carried by horse-drawn wagons. Letters sent overseas had to be transported on ships. It could take weeks and sometimes months to send long-distance messages. However, the telegraph sent messages along a wire by using electric currents. Telegraph operators sent messages using Morse code, which involved a series of dots and dashes. A specific combination of dots and dashes represented each letter in the alphabet.

By using the telegraph, companies and individuals could send long-distance messages in a matter of seconds instead of weeks or months. Workers at the stock market on Wall Street used a type of telegraph called a stock ticker to quickly and easily send information about stocks and the price of investments to companies. This quick communication of information enabled citizens all over the country to buy stocks and bonds from one another. It also contributed to the emergence of an investment culture in the United States.

At first, numerous telegraph companies existed, which sometimes made service confusing and inefficient. Some companies built poor telegraph lines and had poor maintenance. However, during the 1850s, the Western Union Telegraph Company gained control of many of its competitors and greatly improved telegraph service. Telegraph lines connected most of the major cities in the United States by the 1860s, which included transcontinental lines. However, by the late 1890s, a new invention caused telegraph service to gradually decline.

The Telephone

In 1876, Alexander Graham Bell invented the first telephone. He sent the first message from one room to another—a distance of a few feet. However, he quickly improved this device. By August 1876, he received a one-way, long-distance call that covered eight miles. By October of that same year, he conducted a two-way long-distance call.

The following year, Bell connected telephone lines to a switchboard. A switchboard allowed the interconnection of telephone circuits to establish telephone calls, which greatly reduced the number of lines needed to connect people within an area.

By 1900, the United States had about 600,000 phones. At first, only the wealthy could afford this service, but as prices gradually came down, telephone service spread throughout the country. One of Bell's companies, the American Telephone and Telegraph Company (AT&T), installed a transcontinental telephone service by 1915. Five years later, about a third of U.S. households used the telephone.

The telephone had many advantages over the telegraph. First of all, people could send instantaneous verbal messages. They could not do this with the telegraph. Most people could use a telephone, but telegraphs required trained operators to send messages. In addition, telephone messages could be longer and more detailed than telegraph messages. For these reasons, telegraph services in the United States gradually declined following the invention of the telephone.

The Typewriter

Although many people attempted to build a typewriter in the 1700s and early 1800s, Christopher Latham Sholes developed the first practical typewriter around 1868. E. Remington and Sons began to sell this machine by 1874. By the early 1900s, companies began to construct portable typewriters, which made their use widespread. Typewriters greatly improved communications for businesses by making messages more readable. People no longer had the problem of deciphering the scribbles of someone's handwriting. A skilled typist also could type correspondence much faster than a person could write it by hand. Today, computers have mostly replaced typewriters. However, typewriters have had a significant effect on digital communications. The QWERTY keyboard used on computers and some cell phones is based on the typewriter keyboard developed by E. Remington and Sons after the typewriter was purchased from Sholes.

The Wizard of Menlo Park

How did electricity transform American society?

Thomas Alva Edison (1847–1931) pioneered early forms of communication technology, as well as electricity-related inventions. Edison patented many inventions during his lifetime. To patent an invention means to obtain the sole legal rights to it. Edison was an active amateur scientist who conducted many experiments in his spare time. For instance, his first significant invention was an electric vote recorder in 1869. However, many politicians of the time rejected this invention, so Edison focused his efforts on inventions for which there was a strong public demand. Major success came later that year when Edison patented the Universal Stock Ticker, a system for communicating stock prices over a long distance using telegraphic wire.

With the funds from selling an invention, the quadruplex telegraph that could send up to four messages over the same wire at the same time, Edison became a full-time inventor. In 1876, he opened a workshop in Menlo Park, New Jersey, staffed by a team of researchers. Edison's work at Menlo Park was a team effort. In 1877, Edison and his assistants invented the phonograph, a device for recording and reproducing sound. The light bulb followed in 1879.

photo: Library of Congress

Edison, shown here as a young man, sits next to his second phonograph in Washington, April 1878.

Edison also opened one of the world's first electric power plants in New York City in 1882. The plant used direct current (DC) electricity to deliver power to the homes and offices in a small localized area. Meanwhile, George Westinghouse (the air brake inventor) and Nikola Tesla (1856–1943) made additional discoveries in the use of electricity during the late 1800s. They developed a device, the transformer, which could transmit high-voltage alternating current (AC) electricity over long distances. AC electricity expanded the widespread use of electricity in urban households and businesses, as power could now reach establishments further away from the power plant.

By end of the 1800s, electric lights had begun to replace gaslights. The availability of electric power also caused a shift away from horse-drawn vehicles to electric streetcars. Edison and the innovations he developed revolutionized the use of electricity in the nation. His inventions continued to influence American life and technology well beyond his lifetime.

Complete this activity to describe your favorite invention from the industrial age.

Polluting the Environment

How did industrialization impact the environment and society?

The surge in industrialization after the Civil War had a major impact on the natural environment. As the number of factories increased, cities soon became overcrowded with workers. Many of the people in cities used coal to heat homes and other buildings. Burning coal filled the air with smoke and soot. The growing number of power plants, steel mills, and factories also spewed smoke and soot into the atmosphere.

Discovery | SOCIAL STUDIES
EDUCATION | **TECHBOOK**

How did the development of new technologies change life in the United States?

By the early 1900s, air pollution became so heavy in industrial cities that people needed streetlights to see during the day. Cities often had poor sanitation and, as a result, sewage entered the water supply. The polluted water caused typhoid fever and other diseases. Efforts to control pollution did not gain momentum until the 1960s.

Explore this investigation to take a position on the impact of industrialization.

The removal of minerals from underground also had caused extensive environmental damage. For example, coal mining produces chemicals such as iron sulfates that enter streams and kill plants and animals living in the area. Before the 1970s, there were few laws that controlled the damage caused by coal mining.

The acquisition of natural resources through mining, logging, and farming also cleared away large portions of forests through a process known as deforestation. This process threatened other untouched natural areas, such as pure water springs, waterfalls, and swamps. The rapid and unrestricted destruction of the environment set the stage for federal land management and the creation of national parks, which came about during the Progressive Era.

Consider the Essential Question:

How did the development of new technologies change life in the United States?

Go online to complete the Social Studies Explanation.

Check for Understanding:

Did the benefits of industrialization outweigh the costs?

photo: Library of Congress

11.2 The Growing West

LESSON OVERVIEW

Introduction

In this concept, you will examine the westward expansion in the United States after the Civil War. You will also analyze how this expansion changed the country, who benefited from this change, and who was harmed by it.

Essential Question

Who benefited from the second wave of westward expansion in the United States?

Lesson Objectives

By the end of this lesson, you should be able to:

*   Explain factors that led to westward expansion after the Civil War.

*   Evaluate consequences and impacts of westward expansion.

*   Evaluate the impact of westward expansion on Native Americans.

*   Describe the experiences of women, immigrants, African Americans, and other minority groups in the West.

Key Vocabulary
Which terms do you already know?

- [ ] assimilation
- [ ] Californios
- [ ] Cesar Chavez
- [ ] Chief Joseph
- [ ] Dawes Severalty Act of 1887
- [ ] Geronimo
- [ ] Homestead Act of 1862
- [ ] Plains Indians
- [ ] reservation
- [ ] Sand Creek Massacre
- [ ] Sikhism
- [ ] Sitting Bull
- [ ] transcontinental railroad
- [ ] Wounded Knee

Discovery | SOCIAL STUDIES
EDUCATION | TECHBOOK

Who benefited from the second wave of westward expansion in the United States?

ENGAGE

Who won the race for land? Visit Engage to learn more.

Essential Question

Who benefited from the second wave of westward expansion in the United States?

EXPLORE

The Transcontinental Railroad

How did railroads expand across the continent?

After the Civil War, the United States continued its course of industrialization. This process involved replacing products made by hand—often at home—with products made by machines in factories. The growth of industrialization required improved methods to transport raw materials and finished goods. Before long, the railroad system in the United States would expand significantly and connect distant parts of the nation.

Explore this interactive to learn more about key places in the growing West.

The railroads would not have become the country's transportation backbone without massive government support and subsidy, or financial assistance. Congress enacted the Pacific Railroad Act in 1862, which gave two companies—Union Pacific Railroad and Central Pacific Railroad—the assignment of building a transcontinental railroad. When completed, this rail line would cross the continent, connecting the East Coast with the West Coast. The federal government paid the railroad companies $16,000 per mile, and sometimes more, to plan and build the track.

Additionally, the government purchased or traded for the land needed to build the rail line. The government granted this land to the railroads, along with additional neighboring lands. The land grants were not so valuable at the time, but once the railroad was completed, land values would skyrocket. A railroad already existed from the East Coast to Chicago. Soon, workers extended this track westward to Omaha, Nebraska.

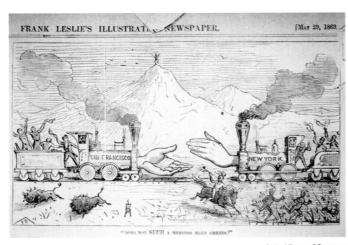

FRANK LESLIE'S ILLUSTRATED NEWSPAPER. [MAY 29, 1869.

"DOES NOT SUCH A MEETING MAKE AMENDS?"

photo: Library of Congress

In 1869, Leland Stanford, the president of Central Pacific Railroad, drove in the last spike to connect the transcontinental railroad.

The Union Pacific Railroad began to build track heading west from Omaha. The Central Pacific Railroad started to build track moving east from Sacramento, California. To work on these rail lines, the companies hired thousands of European and Chinese immigrants and former Civil War soldiers. The workers faced many difficulties, such as crossing rugged mountains and dealing with fierce storms.

On May 10, 1869, the two rail lines connected at Promontory Summit, Utah Territory. The nation's first transcontinental railroad was complete.

With the completion of this railroad system, plenty of resources, goods, and passengers could travel coast to coast in 8 to 10 days. By the end of the 1900s, the United States had constructed four more transcontinental railroads. The population of cities along the railroads, such as Santa Fe, New Mexico, and Kansas City, Missouri, soared. The railroads encouraged immigration and spurred the development of mining, farming, and cattle ranching in the West.

Mining and Logging Industries

How did the natural resources of the West feed industrialization?

Mining

Manufacturing industries needed resources to power their machines and raw materials from which to make goods. People soon realized that vast amounts of wood, coal, iron ore, copper, silver, and gold lay untapped in the West. Mines sprang up throughout the West, especially in certain mountainous areas that held large mineral deposits. In areas where someone discovered some gold or silver, mining towns would quickly form. Prospectors, or people looking for mineral resources, would move in, causing a population boom. These settlements came to be called boomtowns. However, if the gold or silver in the area became depleted, as it usually did, people abandoned these towns, and the settlements often became "ghost towns."

Prospectors used various methods to hunt for gold and silver, including panning. One approach involved dipping a pan into a river or streambed. When the prospector brought the pan out of the water, it contained sand, gravel, and possibly gold. Metals such as gold and silver are much heavier than sand. The prospector would swirl the pan around, causing the sand to wash away with the water; and with luck, a small quantity of the precious metal would remain at the bottom.

Some mining sites contained gold and silver deposits, or lodes, deep underground. Because retrieving these metals required heavy equipment, companies, instead of individuals, mined these lodes. In areas that had company mines, boomtowns often had more stability.

Logging

Because people needed wood to build factories, houses, and various businesses, the demand

photo: Library of Congress

Tunnels beneath mines provided ventilation, water drainage, and a rail system for transporting ore.

for lumber soared. Before the Civil War, the states of Maine, New York, and Pennsylvania provided most of the lumber for the United States. After the war, as the forests were depleted, logging gradually shifted to the West. By the early 1900s, the West provided most of the lumber for the United States, which is still true today.

The life of a logger was in many ways different from the life of a miner. Miners often worked their claims for months. A logger, also known as a lumberjack, worked at a site for a few weeks and then moved on to another camp. Why do you think this was? Miners would also usually work for themselves, but loggers worked for a company. Loggers lived in large camps that would include a bunkhouse, a cookhouse, and a dining hall.

Both logging and mining took a toll on the environment in the West. Loggers and pioneers often cut down vast areas of forest, leaving the land barren. These acts of deforestation, or the clearing of forests, reduced the natural habitat of native species and contributed to erosion. Without tree roots to hold the soil in place, a large rainstorm would result in muddy conditions and possibly even a landslide. In addition, miners often lost large amounts of minerals by using careless mining practices. These minerals

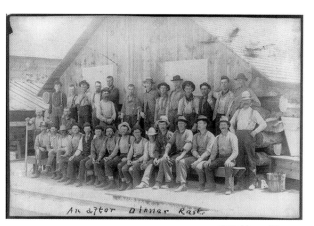

photo: Library of Congress

A group of lumberjacks pose outside a building after eating dinner at a logging camp.

would build up and clog water channels, decreasing a stream's water-carrying capacity and possibly leading to flooding. The minerals sometimes seeped into the drinking water, and if too much accumulated, the water could become contaminated and unsafe for drinking.

Cattle Drives

How did ranching develop in the West?

During the Civil War, many ranchers in Texas left their land and served in the military. After the war, they returned to their ranches and found that their cattle had become much more numerous. Many ranchers had thousands of head of cattle wandering across the range. This oversupply presented a problem. The price of beef in their region was low. To make a profit, the ranchers had to find a way to transport their cattle to eastern markets, where consumers were willing to pay higher prices for beef.

photo: Library of Congress

Cowboys eat near a chuck wagon. This type of wagon carried food and cooking supplies for cattle drives.

The Kansas Pacific railroad reached Abilene, Kansas, in 1867. If the ranchers could reach Abilene with their cattle, then the cattle could be shipped east on the railroad. To achieve this goal, ambitious cattlemen began to lead cattle drives north 700 miles or more from Texas to Abilene. This drive came to be called the Chisholm Trail.

Other cattle drives developed from Texas to the west, such as the Goodnight-Loving Trail to New Mexico and Colorado, and many ranchers made huge profits. The prosperity of cattle towns soared as well. For example, in 1867, 35,000 cattle entered Abilene. Four years later, 600,000 cattle arrived in the town. Before long, cattle ranching spread north from Texas across much of the West, including states such as Colorado, Wyoming, and Montana.

The increased number of cattle created new environmental risks, however. When ranchers allowed their livestock to overgraze, or eat all of the vegetation in an area, the topsoil often could not support new grass. As a result, there was more erosion, and dust storms became more severe.

Homesteaders

How did the U.S. government support the development of farming in the West?

Supported by laws such as the Homestead Act in 1862, huge numbers of farmers moved west after the Civil War. This act provided would-be farmers with 160 acres of land for five years at no cost. After five years, if a person or family lived on the land and made improvements, such as building a house and a fence, then the land was theirs permanently. Because so many farmers moved west to take advantage of this act, they came to be called homesteaders.

Discovery SOCIAL STUDIES
EDUCATION **TECHBOOK**

Who benefited from the second wave of westward expansion in the
United States?

Supporters of westward expansion in
Congress hoped settlement would
encourage business growth throughout
the nation's economy. Meat and grain
from western farms would meet the
needs of a growing population and also
could be exported abroad. New
transportation networks would connect
diverse regions and support industrial
growth. During the last half of the
1800s, the government enacted laws to
support settlement and effective use of

photo: Library of Congress
People stand in front of a log cabin at the Daniel Freeman homestead near Beatrice, Nebraska.

natural resources in the West. For example, the Morrill Act of 1862 granted each state
30,000 acres of federal land for each representative or senator the state had in the U.S.
Congress. The states were required to sell the land and use the money to form and
maintain colleges that taught mechanical arts and agriculture. Many of the country's
major public universities—including the University of California at Berkeley, Texas A&M,
Purdue, and Penn State—were founded as land-grant colleges and universities. Between
1865 and 1900, the number of farms in the United States more than doubled, and farm
exports increased exponentially.

In addition, the government devised a plan to open Native American reservations in the
Oklahoma Territory for settlement. The Dawes Severalty Act of 1887 took land that once
had belonged to Native American nations and made it available to settlers. On April
22, 1889, thousands of people lined up on the border of the territory. When the starting
gun was fired at noon, they rushed to stake a claim. The first land run had begun. In one
day, cities such as Oklahoma City, Norman, and Stillwater were founded. According to
one report, the city of Guthrie went from nonexistent to a population of 10,000 that
afternoon.

Because of the mass movement of farmers and other settlers to the West, the
population of the United States west of the Mississippi River soared from almost
7 million in 1870 to almost 17 million in 1890.

Life on Farms

How did families on farms in the West survive?

The main cash crop grown on Western farms was wheat, especially in the
Dakotas, Kansas, Nebraska, and Oklahoma. Other cash crops included
potatoes, barley, corn, and oats. Farmers reserved as much land as they could for
growing cash crops to sell, but they also had to be self-sufficient. Sometimes, the
nearest town was hundreds of miles away. As a result, farmers had to provide their own
food, shelter, and clothing using the materials available to them.

Farm families survived by eating foods they grew or raised. Common foods included corn muffins, wheat bread, pork, chicken, and mutton. Many farms had at least one cow that supplied the milk and cream necessary to make several dairy products, including butter and cheese.

Many farmers made their first shelter by digging holes into hillsides. On the prairie, they used sod cut from the ground as building material for houses. These sod houses used little wood, which was scarce on the prairie, and kept cool during the summer and warm during the winter. However, they were naturally extremely dirty. If farmers earned enough money from selling crops, they could have lumber shipped in to build a larger house.

photo: Library of Congress

This family poses in front of their sod house near Codburg, Nebraska, in 1887.

Clothes during this period were often made out of wool or cotton. Wool, spun from the fleece of a sheep, kept farmers warm during the freezing winters. Denim was a sturdy cotton fabric that men wore for manual labor. Farm women usually wore calico dresses, along with sunbonnets to protect their eyes from the bright sunlight of the Great Plains. The fabric for this attire was also made from cotton. Like denim, calico cloth was produced in the textile mills in the East, and then shipped to towns along the railroad.

In addition, farm families often faced severe weather conditions, including thunderstorms, tornadoes, and dust storms.

As farms grew, farmers cut down more natural vegetation. Also, many farmers grew wheat, which did not adequately protect the soil. For these reasons, dust storms became more severe. During the Dust Bowl of the 1930s, these storms devastated many farms in the West.

Looking North

What role did physical geography play in the settlement of Alaska during the Klondike Gold Rush?

Although the families living on farms in the West faced difficult living conditions, life in the extreme northwest corner of North America brought challenges that were even more extreme. The large area that now makes up the state of Alaska has a subarctic climate, with summers that are brief and cool and winters that are unbearably harsh at times. A chain of more than 300 volcanic islands stretches to the southwest, nearly 1,200 miles into the Pacific Ocean, while much of the interior region is a snowy and mountainous wilderness. Yet in spite of its extreme physical geography, Alaska became part of the nation's Manifest Destiny after the Civil War.

Discovery SOCIAL STUDIES
EDUCATION **TECHBOOK**

Who benefited from the second wave of westward expansion in the
United States?

On March 30, 1867, the United States purchased from Russia the large peninsula and islands of what was then the Alaskan territory. U.S. Secretary of State William Seward negotiated the $7.2 million land purchase after having spent years convincing Congress and others that Alaska was essential to the nation's development. Seward's conviction was based on the idea that the people of the United States had the Manifest Destiny to expand across North America from shore to shore. Critics, however, denounced the purchase of Alaska as "Seward's Folly" and "Seward's Icebox." They argued that it was foolish for the United States to spend so much money on territory thousands of miles from centers of commerce in the East. On the other hand, supporters of Seward's purchase argued that the land deal ended the possibility of Russian control in North America, created access to the northern Pacific Ocean, and increased the size of the nation by almost 20 percent. When Seward was later asked to recall his greatest professional achievement, he replied, "The purchase of Alaska, but it will take the people a generation to find it out."

Early Settlement

For several decades after its purchase, Alaska seemed of little importance. Some trappers and traders settled on the territory's Arctic shore. They traveled to the former Russian outpost at Sitka or trading posts such as Wrangell, Kodiak, and Kenai. Military personnel were sent to build and staff army bases, but these proved expensive to maintain in such remote territory. By 1870, all trading outposts except for Sitka had closed. Only around 100 soldiers remained in Alaska.

Early U.S. settlement in Alaska consisted primarily of government employees scattered throughout the frontier posts and a small population of rugged civilians who made a living off of fur, whaling, hunting, and the trade of other natural resources. At the time of the first U.S. census of Alaska in 1880, only 430 people out of 33,426 were categorized as "white settlers." The vast majority of Alaskan residents were Alaskan natives, and 1,756 people were categorized as "Creole," which meant they were native to Alaska but born of Russian descent. The discovery of gold, however, changed everything.

The Klondike Gold Rush

After small discoveries of gold in and around Sitka, the first Alaskan mining district was established in May 1879. The following year, prospectors found gold nuggets in a creek east of Sitka. The big strike brought people north from San Francisco and Portland. This led to the development of Juneau, Alaska's current state capital. As more prospectors arrived, settlement patterns began to change. Census figures report that in 1890, Juneau had 1,253 residents, and more than 400 people lived across the channel in the new mining town of Douglas. However, mining was not the only flourishing industry in the Alaska territory. With more than 3,000 rivers and almost 100 lakes, as well as access to the Pacific Ocean, Arctic Ocean, Bering Sea, and Chukchi Sea, the fishing and canning industries also grew to employ approximately 2,000 people.

In August 1896, a group of prospectors found gold just across the border from Alaska, in the remote Yukon region of Canada. The Klondike Gold Rush was on! It took about a year for news of the gold strike to reach the lower United States, and during this time, people claimed all of the gold stakes in the newly named Bonanza Creek. However, the "stampeders," or newly arriving prospectors, were unaware. Between 1890 and 1900, the Alaskan population nearly doubled, as an estimated 70,000 or so adventurers migrated to the Klondike.

photo: Library of Congress

Women prospectors on their way to the Klondike in 1898.

Many of the fortune seekers attempted the most direct routes to the Klondike across the Chilkoot and White Passes. Both trail crossings involved harrowing treks through mountainous terrain. The Chilkoot Pass required a 3,000-foot climb, and the White Pass trail was nicknamed Dead Horse Trail because so many horses were lost on the narrow, rock-strewn path. Travelers on these routes often endured blinding snowstorms, avalanches, fierce winds, and temperatures that fell to –50°F. Many were forced to walk and use pack animals to carry their belongings.

In addition to heading for the Klondike, the gold rush also saw prospectors fanning out across Alaska in hopes of finding riches. By 1890, for example, the northern boomtown of Nome on the Seward Peninsula had nearly 13,000 residents, and the city of Skagway had nearly 3,200. Then, in 1902, gold was found in Tanana Hills, which led to the founding of the central city of Fairbanks. Although the area was rich in this particular mineral, prospectors needed to dig 200 feet below the hard permafrost to retrieve anything.

Economic and Demographic Changes

How did the growing West impact U.S. investment and population trends?

Financial Boom or Bust

The growth of the West made fortunes for many people who invested in railroads, mines, logging, and cattle. However, this growth also caused many people to lose large amounts of money. For example, when cattle ranching increased during the 1870s, many people from the East invested in the cattle industry with the hope of making easy profits. However, the harsh winter of 1886–1887 killed many cattle. The devastation ended the cattle boom and caused some investors to go bankrupt.

Discovery | SOCIAL STUDIES
EDUCATION | **TECHBOOK**

Who benefited from the second wave of westward expansion in the United States?

Some speculators also invested in mining companies, hoping to get rich quick. Few succeeded—mostly because only a few mines struck truly rich mineral deposits. Those that did, such as the Comstock Lode in Nevada, generated huge profits for investors.

Population Movement and Growth

The movement westward caused a shift in the U.S. population. From 1880 to 1900, the portion of the people in the United States living west of the Mississippi increased from about 22 to 27 percent. Some territories gained enough population and economic activity to become states. Between the years 1876 and 1896, Colorado, North Dakota, South Dakota, Montana, Washington, Idaho, Wyoming, and Utah all became states.

Not only did the U.S. population shift westward, but it also moved more to cities. In 1880, 28 percent of the population lived in cities; 20 years later, that number had increased to 40 percent.

Some cities grew to national importance, including Chicago, Kansas City, and St. Louis. Chicago became a center for railroads, the grain trade, and the stockyards. By 1870, its population had reached almost 300,000. Kansas City, located on the transcontinental railroad, grew from less than 4,000 in 1865 to 163,000 in 1900. St. Louis developed as a manufacturing and railroad center and reached a population of about 310,000 in 1870.

Because of the gold rush, San Francisco had developed into a major city before the Civil War. After the war, the rapid growth of this city continued; it reached a population of 342,000 in 1900.

photo: Library of Congress

The Great Union Stock Yards of Chicago, 1878.

In 1896, the Utah territory, which was home to a large Mormon population, achieved statehood. Early Mormon settlers had wanted statehood for many years, and church leaders had mounted several campaigns to end their territorial status. However, members of Congress objected to many of the Mormons' strict religious beliefs. Statehood became possible only after the Church of Latter-day Saints officially renounced the practice of polygamy during Utah's sixth attempt to encourage Congress to rally behind their efforts. Statehood expanded the political rights of Mormon voters, giving them a stronger voice in both state and national politics.

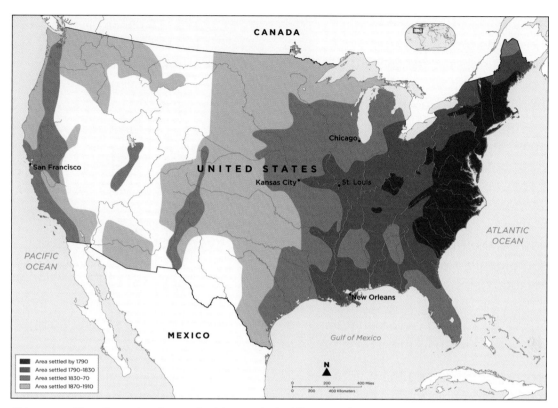

This map outlines the major stages of settlement in the West over time.

Native Americans in the West

How did the U.S. government respond to Native American populations in the West?

Before the Civil War, the U.S. government reserved large areas of land in the West for the exclusive use of Native American nations. The government had pushed some of these nations westward from their native lands in the East. These tracts of land were called reservations because the land was reserved for the exclusive use of the nations. However, with the westward expansion of railroads, mines, farms, and ranches, many Euro-Americans demanded more land west of the Mississippi for their use.

In response to this pressure, the U.S. government began to redraw reservation boundaries. This policy not only decreased the size of the reservations, but also carved out the best land for settlement and left the least-desirable land for Native Americans. This left Native Americans with inadequate wild game for hunting and, as a result, led to widespread poverty among many of the nations.

Dawes Severalty Act

Some reformers believed that the living conditions for Native Americans would improve if they used land for farming. With this idea in mind, the U.S. government passed the Dawes Severalty Act in 1887, also known as the General Allotment Act. At that time, Native American nations owned reservation land as a group.

Discovery | SOCIAL STUDIES
EDUCATION | **TECHBOOK**

Who benefited from the second wave of westward expansion in the United States?

However, the Dawes Act divided up the land on the reservations by male-headed households, giving each household its own land to use for farming. Non-Native Americans who wanted more land for settlement supported the Dawes Act. For them, the key aspect of this law was severalty, or separateness. Supporters realized that if large pieces of Native American lands traditionally used for hunting and collecting food were divided up into smaller family farms, then the rest of the land on the reservations would become available for settlement by outsiders. Persuading Native Americans to take up farming became government policy.

photo: Library of Congress

In this physical education class, evidence of assimilation can be seen in the Native American boys' uniforms and haircuts.

The process of increasing the number of Native Americans who individually owned land for farming came to be called allotment, meaning sharing out. Eventually, the government redistributed the land on 118 reservations in this manner. The Dawes Act did not affect some reservations in remote areas that white settlers found undesirable.

Native American Schools

Allotment disrupted Native American cultural practices and their nomadic lifestyle. In fact, one of the main goals of the policy was to assimilate Native Americans into white culture. *Assimilation* is the process of one distinct culture taking on the cultural traits of another. Another form of assimilation involved boarding schools. In an attempt to make Native Americans conform to white culture, the U.S. government began a program that involved sending Native American children to boarding schools. This policy forced Native American families apart.

At these schools, teachers used various methods to make Native American children give up their cultural practices and take on the practices of white culture. For example, school leaders made native children get haircuts in a style that was the same as Euro-American haircuts. If children practiced their Native American culture, such as speaking their native language or practicing their native religion, they were punished harshly. Students typically spent half the day in the classroom and half on work assignments. Although Native American cultures had diverse roles for men and women—and many cultures even recognized alternative "two spirit" genders—the clothing requirements, behavior expectations, and work assignments at these schools were given according to traditional white gender roles. Young women cleaned, sewed, cooked, did laundry, and completed housework. Male students learned trades such as carpentry or blacksmithing and chopped firewood. Finally, the schools often had poor living conditions and, as a result, children frequently suffered from disease and malnutrition.

Assimilation

There were two contrasting ideas behind these assimilation policies. Some people were genuinely concerned about Native Americans' welfare. They thought assimilation would enable Native Americans to prosper economically and share in the American Dream. Others were simply looking for a humane way to eliminate Native American land claims. Thus, whatever the motives, assimilation policy assumed that Native American culture was inferior.

In response to the redrawing of reservation boundaries and the allotment and assimilation policies, many Native American nations decided to fight back.

Native Americans Fight Back

How did Native Americans come into conflict with the U.S. military?

Because the U.S. government took away much of the land promised to Native Americans, many Native nations decided to fight to defend it. The Nez Percé, led by Chief Joseph, fought against the U.S. Army in the Pacific Northwest. The Sioux, Comanche, Cheyenne, and other Plains Indians took up arms to resist being forced to move to cramped reservations. The Apache, led by Geronimo, fought against the military force of the United States in defense of their homelands in the Southwest. The mistrust and broken promises resulted in a series of fierce wars between Native Americans and the U.S. military in the late 1800s. Eventually, the U.S. military suppressed these rebellions.

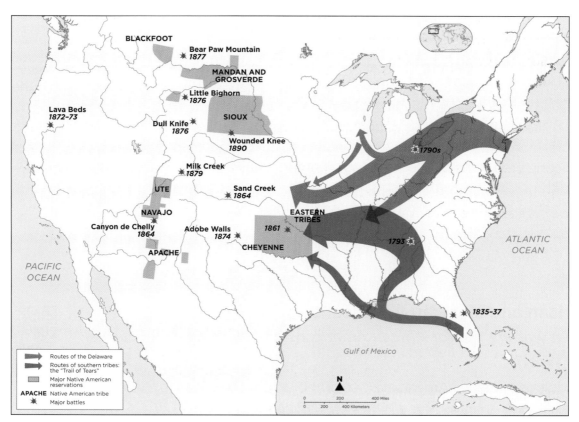

This map shows Native American resettlement routes, reservations, and significant battles.

Who benefited from the second wave of westward expansion in the United States?

Sand Creek Massacre

In 1864, the U.S. military told a group of Cheyenne and Arapahoe peoples that they could settle at Sand Creek in Colorado and promised to protect them from attack. However, on November 29, U.S. soldiers surrounded the Sand Creek camp, which consisted mostly of women and children. Most of the camp's men were on a hunting expedition. John Smith, a local Indian agent who witnessed the event, estimated the soldiers numbered 800 to 1,000. Some of the officers told the officer in command, Colonel John Chivington, that the Native Americans had been promised protection. Even so, Chivington ordered his soldiers to open fire, killing between 150 and 500 Native Americans. Congress investigated the slaughter at the Sand Creek Massacre and reprimanded Chivington, but he was never punished.

Battle of the Little Bighorn

In 1874, after the discovery of gold in the Black Hills of South Dakota, thousands of miners settled in this region. However, this land belonged to the Sioux nation. In fact, they viewed this land as sacred territory and also used it for hunting. Soon, the Sioux nation started a war against the United States, which included a huge victory for the Native Americans, led by the Sioux chief Sitting Bull. In June 1876, a combined force of Sioux and Cheyenne surrounded and attacked 250 U.S. soldiers led by Lieutenant Colonel George A. Custer. The Native Americans killed all the soldiers. The Battle of the Little Bighorn is also known as Custer's Last Stand. However, despite this victory, the U.S. government succeeded in forcing the Sioux to give up their land in the Black Hills.

Wounded Knee Massacre

In 1890, a group of about 350 Lakota Sioux surrendered to the U.S. military at Wounded Knee in South Dakota. At that time, the Lakota practiced the Ghost Dance, which they believed would restore their lifestyle to the way it was before the Europeans arrived. The military feared that this dance would cause the Native Americans to revolt. Because of this, many soldiers were on edge when the Lakota gave up their weapons. Then, someone fired a shot. No one knows whether it was a soldier or a Native American who fired the shot. However, in response, the soldiers fired on the Lakota and killed about 300 native people, including women and children.

The massacre at Wounded Knee marked the end of open warfare between Plains Indian nations and the United States.

African and Mexican Americans in the West

What was life like for African Americans and Mexican Americans in the West?

In addition to Native Americans, two of the largest minorities in the West were African Americans and Mexican Americans.

African Americans

To escape discrimination in the South after the Civil War, thousands of African Americans migrated to the West. These migrants named themselves Exodusters, which derived from the Book of Exodus in the Bible. A former enslaved man named Benjamin "Pap" Singleton convinced many African American families to move to Kansas and establish settlements to start a new life there. In fact, a rumor spread that the U.S. government had reserved land in Kansas for former slaves, but this rumor later turned out to be false. Singleton, through the support of his associates at the Edgefield Real Estate and Homestead Association, helped more than 20,000 African Americans migrate to Kansas between 1877 and 1879. There, they set up farms, shops, hotels, and schools.

Many other African Americans became cowboys. In fact, scholars estimate that African Americans made up about 25 percent of all the cowboys in the early West. Some African American cowboys had been enslaved on ranches before the Civil War and, after the war, became cowboys on these ranches. Others, such as Nat Love and Bose Ikard, had been enslaved in the South; they moved to the West after the Civil War hoping to be free of discrimination, as the Exodusters did.

photo: Library of Congress

African American settlers gather in Nicodemus, Kansas.

However, both the Exodusters and African American cowboys dealt with discrimination in the West. White cowboys and ranch owners often treated black cowboys as inferior. Also, many Exodusters ended up working as laborers or house servants for white farmers and ranchers.

After the Civil War, the U.S. government created six regiments of African American troops to be stationed in the West. Nicknamed "buffalo soldiers" by Native Americans, thousands of African Americans found opportunity serving in the army. Here, they patrolled areas of Kansas, Texas, and Oklahoma, helping keep the peace.

Mexican Americans

From the 1600s to the early 1800s, Spain owned the region that is now Texas, New Mexico, Arizona, Nevada, Utah, California, and western Colorado. During this time, Spanish colonists from Mexico formed many settlements in this region, especially along the coast of California and in southeastern Texas. When Mexico won independence from Spain in 1821, Mexico gained control of this vast region.

Discovery SOCIAL STUDIES
EDUCATION TECHBOOK

Who benefited from the second wave of westward expansion in the United States?

The idea of Manifest Destiny encouraged Americans to covet this land. Manifest Destiny is a phrase used to describe, explain, or justify the nation's pioneering spirit to expand across the continent from the Atlantic to Pacific Ocean. In 1846, the Mexican-American War broke out as many Americans hoped to secure lands from Texas to California. When the United States defeated Mexico, the two countries signed the Treaty of Guadalupe Hidalgo (1848). The treaty transferred this large Western region to the United States. It also stated that the Mexican Americans who had settled land in this region could keep their land.

photo: Library of Congress

Mexican farm worker, San Joaquin Valley, California, 1936.

Despite this agreement, during the next decades many Mexican Americans lost land to white Americans. The white settlers used many methods to seize this land, including force and fraud as well as legal means. For example, the U.S. government often used the allotment method with land that was owned by Mexican American groups. The government told these groups that their land must be divided up into plots that were owned by individuals. Many Mexican Americans could not afford to maintain individual plots and had to sell their land, mostly to white ranchers.

For decades after the Mexican-American War, Mexican citizens living in areas annexed by the Treaty of Guadalupe Hidalgo left the region for Mexico. Few Mexican citizens immigrated to the United States during this period. However, beginning in the 1890s, industries connected with westward expansion attracted Mexicans to the United States to work on farms, in mines, or on railroads. The Mexican Revolution, which lasted from 1910 until 1920, created instability in the country and increased the flow of immigrants to the United States. Between the 1910s and the 1920s, the number of Mexican immigrants to the United States increased from about 20,000 to between 50,000 and 100,000 per year.

Mexican Farmworkers in California

In the early 1900s, a large share of Mexican immigrants traveled to California to work on farms. Around this time, irrigation and other farming improvements increased agricultural production in California's central valleys. As a result, the need for workers in these areas increased. American-owned farm companies hired recruiters to find workers, help them make the border crossing into the United States, and locate places to work. Many of these recruiters relied on dishonest tactics, and working conditions for farmworkers in California and beyond were often poor.

Initially, most Mexicans who arrived in California for work intended to return to Mexico during the agricultural off-season. At that time, it was easy for people to make border crossings, and a circular migration pattern developed. In 1917, Congress passed the Immigration Act. This law imposed restrictions on crossborder travel. For example, Mexicans were required to take literacy tests and physical examinations at each crossing. This law disrupted the circular migration pattern and convinced many to stay in California permanently. By 1920, Mexicans made up the largest single ethnic group in California's San Joaquin Valley. Across the Southwest, Mexican Americans grew up in migrant farm families that faced low wages, long working hours, and difficult conditions. Many who were born and came of age during this time period, including Dolores Huerta and Cesar Chavez, would later begin a mass movement for farmworkers' rights.

Over time, Mexican culture influenced much of American culture in the Southwest, including the region's food, architecture, and clothing. For example, Mexican Americans first cultivated the crops that grew in the region, especially corn, which has become a staple in tacos, burritos, enchiladas, and other Mexican American foods. Pueblo houses (Spanish for "village") were constructed of stone or adobe, similar to the dwellings of the native Pueblo peoples of the Southwest. Cowboys in the Southwest also wore sombreros and ponchos to keep themselves warm and dry during the rain.

Immigrants in the West

Why did immigrants come to the West?

Immigrants from Europe

As the United States industrialized after the Civil War, railroads and other businesses needed more workers. The casualties of the war also contributed to a severe shortage of laborers. To ease this situation, railroad companies sent agents to European countries to recruit workers. They even offered reduced steamship fare for people willing to come to the United States and work for the railroad. Improved transportation provided by steamships and trains made the trip to the western United States much easier.

photo: Library of Congress

A Chinese family in California, 1898.

The situation of farming in Europe increased the incentive to emigrate. For one, many European farmers were going bankrupt. They could not sell their wheat because they could not match the lower price of wheat produced in Minnesota and the Dakotas. Many of these farmers poured into the United States. Other Europeans who wanted to become farmers went to America because farmland in Europe was scarce and expensive.

For these reasons, thousands of Europeans immigrated to the United States after the Civil War. From 1865 to 1900, yearly immigration to the United States averaged more than 375,000. Many of the newcomers went to work on railroads in the West and in mines and established farms. Most of these immigrants came from northwestern Europe, including Ireland, Germany, Denmark, Norway, and Sweden.

Immigrants from East Asia: China, Japan, the Philippines, and Korea

In the 1850s, a wave of Chinese immigrants joined scores of other fortune seekers in California to mine for gold. After the Civil War, the Central Pacific Railroad recruited thousands more Chinese to come to the United States to work on the Transcontinental Railroad. By 1880, about 105,000 Chinese lived in the United States—mostly in California. Many Chinese immigrants established small businesses such as laundries and lived in ethnic enclave cities such as San Francisco. However, at that time, an economic depression hit the United States, and many Euro-Americans feared that the Chinese immigrants undercut wages and took away jobs from them. In fact, Chinese workers on the Central Pacific Railroad were paid $27 a month, compared with the $35 a month that the railroad paid Irish workers for the same work. Nonetheless, several riots broke out and many Euro-Americans called for immigration restrictions. In response, the U.S. government passed the Chinese Exclusion Act in 1882, which halted the immigration of Chinese people into the United States for 10 years. Congress made the law permanent in 1902, but repealed it in 1943.

The Chinese Exclusion Act created a labor shortage on West Coast farms, orchards, mines, canneries, and railroads. As a result, many Japanese workers immigrated and at first served as migratory laborers. Some eventually purchased their own farms and businesses selling fruits and vegetables. Japanese farmers often settled in areas others avoided because of poor growing conditions. Employing innovative and efficient agricultural methods, they were often successful and in many cases earned higher wages and profits than other farmers. Some perceived that Japanese workers were taking away their opportunities. In 1907, the federal government reached a "Gentlemen's Agreement" with Japan to limit Japanese immigration to the United States. Later, in 1924, Congress passed an Immigration Act that prohibited the immigration of all Asian workers.

Immigration restrictions against Chinese and Japanese laborers created labor shortages on farms and other businesses in the western United States. In 1899, the United States annexed the Philippines. Because Filipinos were now U.S. nationals, many came to the West during the early decades of the 1900s. Most Filipino immigrants worked on sugar plantations in Hawaii and on farms in California. Filipino migration to the country slowed in the 1930s, after Congress agreed to grant the Philippines independence and placed a cap on Filipino immigration.

The early 1900s also saw the first wave of Korean immigration to the United States. Between 1903 and 1905, more than 7,000 Korean laborers moved to Hawaii. There, they worked on the islands' sugar plantations.

More than 1,000 of these immigrants moved to the continental United States, most to California. Korean immigration was also disrupted by the 1924 Immigration Act. It did not resume until the second half of the 1900s.

The Arrival of Indian Immigrants in the West

In 1903, immigrants from India began arriving in the United States. Most were Sikhs from the Punjab region of northern India. Many worked on northern California's Western Pacific Railway, and others constructed roadways, bridges, and tunnels. Some 2,000 Sikhs helped construct a road that stretched 700 miles from Oakland to Salt Lake City. After 1907, when immigrants from India began arriving in the United States through the port of San Francisco, many Punjabis settled in the valleys of central California. Although most practiced Sikhism, others were Muslims. In the Central Valley, they labored on farms, and eventually many purchased their own land. In 1912, the first gurdwara, or Sikh house of worship, was established in the United States by agricultural workers in Stockton, California.

Indian immigrants encountered resistance and even violence. In 1907, Sikh mill workers in Washington State were attacked by a mob of white lumberjacks. Many moved to Canada in response. In 1913, California passed a law that barred persons not eligible for U.S. citizenship from owning land in the state. Many Sikh farmers in the Central Valley were forced to give up their property. In 1917, Congress passed immigration legislation that halted the arrival of Indian immigrants in the United States for the next three decades.

Women in the West

What was life like for women in the West?

photo: Getty Images

Martha Canary, also known as Calamity Jane, was a frontierswoman of the West.

Much of the work in the growing West was considered "man's work." Women were strongly and actively discouraged from living on their own and working as miners, loggers, cowhands, and laborers. Their status, compared with men, was not much different than it was in the East.

Many women who were wives of farmers and ranchers led what seemed like fairly traditional lives. However, the Homestead Act allowed single women to claim their own land, and many of them did. As a result, some women owned farms or ranches. Homestead women often focused on domestic chores, such as making clothes, cooking food, and taking care of children.

Of course, raising a family, keeping house, managing a farm, living separated by a full day's ride or more from the nearest "neighbor," all with no telephone, electricity, running water, or sewage system, was hard work.

Discovery SOCIAL STUDIES
EDUCATION **TECHBOOK**

Who benefited from the second wave of westward expansion in the United States?

Life for women outside a family could be harsh. Discrimination discouraged or excluded them from many forms of work and from living independently. Single women could work as schoolteachers, but they were often forced out of their job if they married because married women were not allowed to teach.

Thousands of women did go to mining towns, where they worked as waitresses, boardinghouse managers, laundresses, and dance-hall entertainers. Martha Canary was about eight years old when her parents moved with her to mine for gold in Montana. Within a few years, her parents were dead, and Martha was on her own. At various times, she worked as a scout, camp cook, server, dancer, and bullwhacker (the driver of an ox wagon) hauling goods from town to nearby mining camps. We know of Martha today because she was made famous under her nickname, Calamity Jane, as the heroine in the *Deadeye Dick* series of dime novels.

Explore this resource and create a museum exhibit devoted to one group's experiences in the West.

In an attempt to attract more women to the West, the legislatures of Western territories and states often passed laws that granted women more rights, such as equal pay, child custody, and divorce laws. All of the states that gave women the right to vote before 1900 were located in the West—Wyoming, Utah, Colorado, and Idaho. In 1916, Jeanette Rankin of Montana was the first woman elected to the U.S. House of Representatives.

Consider the Essential Question:

Who benefited from the second wave of westward expansion in the United States?

Go online to complete the Social Studies Explanation.

Check for Understanding:

What caused the migration of many Americans west of the Mississippi River at the end of the 1800s? What were the effects of this migration?

photo: Library of Congress

11.3 Coming to America

LESSON OVERVIEW

Introduction

In this concept, you will explore the causes of increased immigration during the late 1800s and early 1900s. You also will examine the government policies and public responses to this wave of immigration.

Key Vocabulary
Which terms do you already know?

- ☐ anarchism
- ☐ Angel Island
- ☐ Chinese Exclusion Act
- ☐ Ellis Island
- ☐ ethnic enclave
- ☐ nativism
- ☐ nativist
- ☐ pull factor
- ☐ push factor

Essential Question

In what ways did the American Dream become a reality for immigrants to the United States?

Lesson Objectives

By the end of this lesson, you should be able to:

- Describe trends of and explain factors leading to increased immigration during the late 1800s and early 1900s.

- Evaluate governmental and public responses to the "new" immigration of the late 1800s and early 1900s.

Discovery | SOCIAL STUDIES
EDUCATION | **TECHBOOK**

In what ways did the American Dream become a reality for immigrants to the United States?

ENGAGE

What was it like to pass through Ellis Island? Visit Engage to learn more.

Essential Question

In what ways did the American Dream become a reality for immigrants to the United States?

EXPLORE

Waves of Immigration

Why did immigrants come to the United States?

By the mid-1800s, the Industrial Revolution had created major changes in the United States. Cities and urban centers grew as more people moved from the rural United States, mainly in search of work. In 1870, 52 percent of Americans worked on farms. By 1890, this number had dropped to 43 percent, and by 1920 it had plummeted to 29 percent.

The changes that were occurring were not just a result of people moving from the countryside. People from other countries were also flocking to American cities. This trend was evident in New York City. In 1890, New York City's population was 1.5 million. By 1920, the city's population had reached more than 5.6 million. The promise of jobs and a better life combined with push factors at home—such as poverty, famine, religious persecution, and political upheaval—fueled massive waves of immigration to the country beginning in the middle of the 1800s. This first wave of immigrants came mostly from England, Ireland, and Germany.

Immigration from other parts of Europe increased in the 1880s and after. By 1900, immigrants from Italy, Russia, and southern and eastern Europe were arriving to the United States in record numbers. When Russian ruler Czar Alexander II was killed in 1881, some non-Jewish Russian citizens blamed the czar's assassination on the Jewish population in the region. In response, a series of violent anti-Jewish riots, called *pogroms*, swept across the Russian Empire between 1881 and 1884. As a result, some 200,000 Russian and Eastern European Jews came to the United States to escape religious persecution by 1890. Even more would come in later decades.

At the same time, Italians seeking economic opportunities also moved to the United States. Earlier, Italian immigrants had primarily been northern Italian business owners and tradespeople looking for new markets for their products and services. However, these later immigrants were commonly poor farmers and peasants from southern Italy and the island of Sicily.

Italian emigration rose in 1861 after Italian unification brought stability to the country and improvements in medicine and hygiene spurred population growth. However, this success was not matched by Italy's economy and food supply; industrialization was far too slow to support Italy's growing population. People had to choose between leaving and starving. Often, the young and middle-aged men left first—if they were fortunate enough to afford a transatlantic ticket. Once in the United States, they hoped to earn and save enough money to buy passage for the rest of the family.

photo: Paul Fuqua

Immigrants from many countries and backgrounds lived in New York's Lower East Side.

During this time period, many Slavs also emigrated from eastern and central Europe. In the first decade of the 1900s, more than two million people came to the United States fleeing ethnic discrimination and political repression in the Austro-Hungarian Empire. Many other immigrants came from Europe as well—notably from Greece, Romania, Germany, United Kingdom, Portugal, and Scandinavia. Between 1900 and 1920 alone, some 14.5 million immigrants arrived on the shores of the United States.

Chinese immigrants traveled to California in search of wealth after word of the Gold Rush spread. By 1851, 25,000 Chinese had made the long journey only to find hard work and little gold. Competition between Americans, Chinese, and Europeans made the Chinese look for employment elsewhere, including on the railroads and in the service industry. Many eventually settled in San Francisco, where they provided domestic services to white families, opened restaurants, and manufactured leather goods.

Explore this interactive to learn more about historical trends in American immigration.

Getting Along

How did immigrant groups adapt to life in the United States?

Jobs drew immigrants to industrialized cities such as New York, Boston, Pittsburgh, Chicago, and San Francisco. Facing social and cultural barriers, including language and religion, immigrants often settled in tight-knit neighborhoods composed of members of their own ethnicities.

Discovery EDUCATION | SOCIAL STUDIES TECHBOOK

In what ways did the American Dream become a reality for immigrants to the United States?

These communities were typically called enclaves. An enclave is an area, often in a city, in which a culturally distinct group of people lives separately from people of other groups. The Jewish and Italian *enclaves* in Boston's North End area, Little Italy in New York City, Jewish neighborhoods on the Lower East Side of Manhattan or Chicago's West Side, and Chinese neighborhoods in San Francisco are examples of these types of communities. These ethnic enclaves served important needs of newly arrived immigrants, who rarely spoke or understood any English.

Residents of such ethnic enclaves not only lived together, but also often worked together. For example, in 1890, about 90 percent of the workers constructing canals and other infrastructure for the New York City Public Works Department were Italian immigrants. Similarly, in Chicago, virtually all the city's road workers were Italian. The Lower East Side of Manhattan was dotted with sweatshop factories where many Jewish immigrants worked in the garment industry manufacturing clothing. By 1880, San Francisco was home to more than 7,500 Chinese-run commercial laundries.

photo: Library of Congress

Why do you think these immigrant boys in Boston are attending school at night?

Just as newly freed African Americans built a sense of community by forming churches, founding schools, and creating newspapers for their people, immigrants worked to build their own support systems. As immigrants settled in ethnic communities, the residents established their own institutions such as newspapers and churches. They also formed mutual aid societies such as Chicago's Italian "Società di Unione e Fratellanza," the Society of Unity and Brotherhood, founded in 1866. In San Francisco, aid societies called *huiguans* helped new Chinese immigrants find employment and provided public services such as fire safety and sanitation. Mutual aid societies served to share advice and friendship, help newcomers get settled, and help one another survive difficult times. Immigrants established banks, grocery stores, libraries, religious centers, and other institutions in their ethnic neighborhoods.

Immigrant groups did not always settle in ethnic enclaves. In the late 1800s, the settlement house movement, which started in England to provide aid and education to the working poor, moved to the United States. Many immigrants who arrived in the United States were poor and did not have the means to pay for adequate housing. In response to this growing poor immigrant population, reformers founded settlement houses in U.S. cities. In 1886, the first settlement house was founded in New York City. Hull House, founded in Chicago by Jane Addams, a pioneering social worker, in 1889, was one of the most well-known settlement houses in the country. By the late 1800s, there were nearly 400 settlement houses in the country with almost half of them in large industrial cities.

photo: Library of Congress

Chinese laborers in California carry sacks of minerals from a mine.

While settlement houses provided shelter for immigrant populations, they also set out to assimilate immigrants to the United States. Assimilation is the process by which immigrants or other minority groups take on the characteristics of the dominant culture. To help them become "Americanized" and enter the labor force, the immigrants, working class, and poor who lived in settlement houses received education in subjects such as history, literature, and art, and were taught middle-class American values. Childcare and other social services, such as public kitchens and baths, helped lessen some of the harsh conditions of living in poverty.

Difficult Living and Working Conditions

What were living conditions like for immigrants?

Although newer immigrants may have felt at home in their ethnic enclaves among neighbors from the "old country," living and working conditions were typically difficult, particularly for unskilled laborers. Many immigrants arrived with little or no money, and salaries in the United States in the late 1800s were not enough to support a family. Social worker Robert Hunter, in his 1904 study of poverty, concluded that nearly 13 percent of the U.S. population lived in poverty and were "much of the time underfed, poorly clothed, and improperly housed."

photo: Library of Congress

Jacob Riis's photograph of a tenement fire escape shows that it was used as an extension of the apartment.

Improper housing included crowded apartment buildings, or tenements. Tenements were squeezed together, typically with less than a foot of space between buildings. Most lacked running water, toilets, or adequate fresh air and lighting. Privacy was virtually nonexistent. By 1900, some 80,000 tenements had been constructed in New York City.

There were no regulations preventing landlords or residents from cramming as many people as possible into these unsanitary and unsafe spaces. The Jewish Lower East Side was one of the most crowded neighborhoods in the world. In 1900, there were around 700 residents per acre in the Lower East Side. Modern city blocks in New York are about five square acres. Today, there are about 42 New York residents per acre.

An investigative journalist named Jacob Riis took photographs documenting tenement living conditions. Riis sometimes found up to 12 or 14 people sleeping in one small room. In his 1890 book *How the Other Half Lives*, Riis's striking photographs drew attention to the problems of tenements.

With such conditions, the tenements were a breeding ground for disease. In the mid-1800s, epidemic outbreaks of typhoid fever, smallpox, and cholera were common in urban areas. By 1900, these diseases had been largely contained because of improved sanitation. However, by that time, poor air quality in clustered tall buildings had brought a new killer. New York City experienced more than 8,000 deaths each year from tuberculosis.

Immigrants at Work

What working conditions did immigrants face?

If living conditions were crowded and unsafe for immigrants, working conditions were not much better. In 1900, the United States was the most dangerous country in the world for industrial workers. Without government regulation, factories were often poorly lit and unsanitary, and machinery was not regularly serviced. Factory workers performed the same repetitive task for 10 hours or more a day, six days a week.

Immigrant women and children made up a large percentage of factory workers in places like the Lower East Side. They were paid less than men and worked similar long hours, sometimes with heavy machinery and equipment. By 1900, nearly 1.7 million children were employed in factories.

In the textile mills, children helped keep the cotton looms running through the night. If they appeared sleepy, cold water might be thrown in their faces to keep them awake. The long hours in difficult conditions also meant more injuries and even deaths for women and children alike.

Workplace safety in the factories was often overlooked. Employers were usually not held responsible for on-the-job injuries. Until worker's compensation insurance became common in the 1910s, it was cheaper for factory owners not to make safety improvements.

photo: Library of Congress

A trade parade was held to honor the victims of the fire. The Triangle Shirtwaist Factory fire spurred calls for workplace safety laws and led to a rise in support for labor unions.

Perhaps the most shocking workplace tragedy in the United States occurred at a garment factory in New York. In less than 20 minutes, 146 people died in the Triangle Shirtwaist Factory fire in 1911. Some of the workers were only 14 years old. The fire broke out on the eighth floor, and the people on the ninth floor were trapped.

The fire escape had not been regularly maintained or inspected, and it collapsed under the weight of people trying to make their way to safety. The doors to the stairwells had been locked to prevent the workers from stealing. The ninth-floor windows opened, but when the fire department sent up their ladders, they only reached to about the sixth floor. The fire hoses also did not have enough pressure to get water to the ninth floor.

The devastation of the Triangle Shirtwaist Factory fire increased the public's awareness of the harsh working conditions in American factories. The fire showed both leaders and citizens that more needed to be done to protect American workers. Reformers lobbied government officials to pass laws to make workplaces safer. The New York legislature created the Factory Investigating Commission. As a result of the commission's findings and recommendations, more than 30 laws were passed to protect workers. These laws included stricter fire codes, such as adding more exits and building firewalls, improved ventilation and sanitation, and restrictions on child labor.

Attitudes Toward Immigrants

How were immigrants treated?

The First Wave

From the 1830s to the Civil War, the first massive wave of European immigration had brought people from northern and western Europe to the American shores. In the 1840s, a potato famine caused widespread starvation in Ireland, pushing many Irish to the United States. Many other immigrants during this time came from Germany and Great Britain. In the western United States, the addition of lands after the Mexican-American War and the annexation of Texas added around 80,000 Mexicans who had been living in those regions to the U.S. population. The treaty ending the Mexican-American War made these Mexicans citizens of the United States. The Gold Rush in California in 1849 also attracted immigrants, many from China.

Immigrants leave a ferry.

photo: Library of Congress

These immigrants faced a mixed welcome. Many of the European immigrants quickly found jobs working in the growing industrial cities or took advantage of government programs to distribute lands in the western territories to farmers. In New York City, Irish immigrants gained power and influence inside the Democratic Party and the police force. Pennsylvania allowed its public schools to provide classes taught in German to accommodate new immigrant children.

Discovery EDUCATION | SOCIAL STUDIES TECHBOOK

In what ways did the American Dream become a reality for immigrants to the United States?

Many German immigrants in particular were skilled workers who brought their trades with them from their homelands. Germans such as Henry Lomb, who found success creating eyeglasses and the eye care company known today as Bausch & Lomb, and Levi Strauss, who founded Levi's jeans and other products, represented the achievement of the American dream.

These early immigrants also faced opposition. Most of the immigrants from Ireland were Catholic, which some native-born Americans saw as a threat to the majority Protestant religion in the United States. Many immigrants faced discrimination in jobs. In the 1850s, an anti-immigrant political party called the American Party, or the Know-Nothing Party, quickly gained popularity and won several seats in the U.S. Congress. In the 1860s, California passed laws placing special taxes on businesses that hired Chinese workers.

After the Civil War

By the 1870s and 1880s, the immigration patterns had shifted. Many new immigrants were coming from eastern and southern Europe. Very few of these immigrants spoke English, as the earlier Irish immigrants had, and most were Catholic, Orthodox, or Jewish. Many came from countries that faced violent political turmoil. They practiced chain migration, which involves recruiting friends and family members from the same town or region of their countries of origin.

Again, many native-born Americans worried that these new arrivals threatened American culture. Anti-immigrant political groups, workplace discrimination, and social discrimination were common. Cartoons in newspapers and stories in magazines promoted stereotypes of new immigrants as uneducated, uncivilized, and dangerous. Chain migration and discrimination contributed to the development of ethnic enclaves and segregated, or separated residential neighborhoods.

Some of this discrimination came from "older" immigrants whose families had arrived in the United States less than 50 years earlier. For example, despite the religious connection, many German Jews who had arrived 20 to 40 years before sought to distinguish themselves from the Russian and Polish Jews. They saw these newcomers as an inferior group of immigrants. They claimed that these people were ill suited to the American way of life because they were uneducated and unaccustomed to republican institutions such as elected legislatures.

Despite this opposition, millions of immigrants came to the United States looking for a better life, and many found what they sought. Like the earlier waves of immigrants, many immigrants from the 1880s to the 1920s found jobs, homes, and bright futures for their families in the United States.

Closing the Doors on Immigration

How did nativists seek to restrict immigration in the late 1800s?

Although factory owners may have liked cheap workers, and landlords liked the never-ending source of renters, not all residents wanted immigrants on American soil. In the 1840s, nativists had organized to try to keep immigrants from gaining political, social, and economic power. When the second surge of immigration began in the 1880s, nativists again fought against the influx of immigrants. Immigrants were blamed for the overcrowding, sanitation, and crime issues plaguing American cities. Nativists also disliked immigrants because of their Roman Catholic or Orthodox Christian religion. They believed that new immigrants would change the culture of the United States.

photo: Library of Congress

This 1882 newspaper cartoon criticized the Chinese Exclusion Act.

Before the 1880s, immigration was not heavily regulated, but pressure from nativists helped change that. In 1882, Congress passed the Chinese Exclusion Act, barring Chinese immigrants from settling in the United States. Chinese Americans were accused of taking "real" Americans' jobs. They were also blamed for keeping all workers' wages low because Chinese immigrants were often willing to work for lower wages than other people would accept. That same year, an immigration act set a 50-cent immigration tax for everyone entering the country. It also prohibited immigration of convicts, "lunatics," or those dependent on the state for basic needs.

Additional legislation was proposed that would have restricted immigration through literacy tests. The Immigration Restriction League, which was founded in 1894 by three Harvard College graduates, was a strong supporter of literacy tests. Members of the League believed that the United States was not capable of assimilating immigrants into the American culture. They believed that the "new" immigrants of the late 1800s, who were primarily from Italy and Eastern Europe, were not able to learn American values. As a result, the League proposed establishing literacy tests to further limit immigration. With this plan, an adult would have to be able to read a minimum of 40 words in any language to be permitted to stay in the United States. Another proposal would have established quotas, setting limits on the number of immigrants from specific places.

In what ways did the American Dream become a reality for immigrants to the United States?

With the passage of the Chinese Exclusion Act and the 1882 Immigration Act, the United States government needed to set up new offices to oversee the immigration process. In 1891, the federal government established the Office of the Superintendent of Immigration. Part of the Treasury Department, this office was responsible for inspecting new immigrants at every port of entry.

Welcome to the United States!

How did the immigration process work?

On January 1, 1892, the federal government opened its first and most famous immigration station, Ellis Island. Located near the Statue of Liberty in New York Harbor, it processed more than 17 million immigrant arrivals between 1892 and 1954. In addition to inspection facilities and detention rooms for immigrants, the station housed cafeterias, a hospital, railroad ticket booths, and even representative offices for immigrant aid services. Soon, more stations were built in Boston, Philadelphia, and other traditional ports of immigrant entry. Known as "Ellis Island of the West," Angel Island opened in San Francisco Bay in 1910. This station was similar to Ellis Island, except that most of the immigrants processed here were from Asian countries rather than Europe.

Some 450,000 people were processed through Ellis Island in its first year of operations. Immigrant processing was a multistep procedure. First, immigration officers collected passenger manifests, or lists, from arriving ships. Then, they questioned and examined all arriving immigrants to determine if they should be allowed in the country.

The inspection process took anywhere between three to seven hours. Doctors checked each hopeful arrival for 60 different signs of illness—anything from wheezing to limping. If diseases such as tuberculosis or cholera or signs of mental illness were detected, the person was detained. People who were believed to be sick were assigned to the hospital for observation and medical care, or they were deported to their place of origin at their own expense or at the expense of the ship that brought them.

After passing their medical exam, immigrants were questioned by legal inspectors. These inspectors asked about personal information, including their names and ages and whether they had family in the United States or a place to stay. Beginning in 1917, people older than 16 also had to pass a reading test. If they got through all this, newcomers were shown where to get railroad or ferry tickets and sent on their way. If not, they could be detained for further evaluation or deported.

Whether a person was admitted to the United States did not depend only on their health or responses to legal questions. The process could be influenced by any number of factors, including stereotypes or an inspector's mood or personal feelings. Inspectors might reject immigrants because they had no money. Or, they might be rejected because they had no friends, family, or plan and seemed likely to become a public ward, or someone the state would have to take care of.

photo: Library of Congress

Immigrants wait their turn to be inspected in corralled lines on Ellis Island.

In the western part of the country, in particular, numerous immigrants from China, Japan, Russia, and South Asia were detained on Angel Island. Some 175,000 Chinese landed there between 1910 and 1940. The Chinese Exclusion Act greatly reduced the number of Chinese people entering the country. However, those Chinese people who had been born in the United States or were legal spouses or children of Chinese Americans were still allowed to enter the country. Immigrants entering the country had to present relatives or witnesses, people who spoke to authorities to provide evidence explaining why the immigrant should enter the country. If their relatives and witnesses lived on the East Coast, or if the authorities took issue with their appeals, they could wait in detention for weeks, months, or even years to be allowed in the country. The Chinese Exclusion Act remained in effect until its repeal in 1943.

Becoming Citizens

How did the government increase regulation of immigration?

When immigrants to the United States become citizens today, they must declare an oath of allegiance to the United States. The exact wording of the Oath of Allegiance has changed over the years. However, an oath has been in existence since 1778.

Since the late 1700s, there have been naturalization laws in the United States. Naturalization is the process used to grant U.S. citizenship to a foreign citizen after certain requirements are met. In the 1700s and 1800s, the naturalization process was not very organized. Federal law gave any court of record, from a local court to a state court to a federal court, the jurisdiction to grant citizenship to applicants. The court that granted citizenship kept a record of the naturalization process. There was not one central place where naturalization records were kept. In addition, there was little guidance from a higher court or federal organization on how to administer the naturalization laws.

As a result of the lack of guidance, President Theodore Roosevelt ordered a commission to study the U.S. nationalization process in 1905. The study confirmed the lack of uniformity among naturalization courts in the United States.

By 1906, the Basic Naturalization Act of 1906 was established. This act created the Bureau of Immigration and Naturalization, which was put in charge of regulating the naturalization process. The act also created the procedure for naturalizing citizens that was used between 1906 and 1952. This very lengthy process required prospective citizens to proclaim loyalty to the United States and petition a state court for citizenship.

photo: Library of Congress

Drawing of Jewish immigrant children repeating the oath of allegiance to the United States, New York City, 1906.

To be considered, the applicant had to be a resident of the country for five years and "of good moral character." After a period of investigation and court proceeding, a judge would decide whether the candidate qualified to become a citizen. If accepted, the candidate took an Oath of Allegiance to the U.S. Constitution.

Complete this activity to analyze "The New Colossus," the poem on the Statue of Liberty.

While the naturalization laws regulated the citizenship process, the path to becoming a citizen could often be long and difficult for immigrants. In addition to regulating the process, the laws were also geared toward naturalizing citizens who were deemed the easiest to assimilate.

Leaders, in the late 1800s, often recalled arguments of the "Know-Nothings" political party members of the 1840s and 1850s who declared that immigrants of different races and religions or from countries with tyrannical governments could not understand the principles of the U.S. government and should not be made citizens. As a result, nativists pushed for these stricter restrictions on immigration and naturalization for immigrants to the country. Despite the difficult path immigrants had to travel to become citizens, millions of immigrants passed through U.S. ports in the early 1900s in hopes of achieving their dreams of success in the United States.

Consider the Essential Question:

In what ways did the American Dream become a reality for immigrants to the United States?

Go online to complete the Social Studies Explanation.

Check for Understanding:

Define *nativism*. How did nativist movements affect the lives of immigrants living in the United States?

11.4 City Life

LESSON OVERVIEW

Introduction

In this concept, you will learn about the urbanization that the United States experienced during the late 1800s and early 1900s. As industrialization created more jobs in cities, cities drew immigrants from other countries and from the U.S. countryside. What would it have been like to live in a city such as New York, Chicago, or San Francisco during this time?

Key Vocabulary

Which terms do you already know?

- ☐ Chester Arthur
- ☐ Grover Cleveland
- ☐ James Garfield
- ☐ lobbyists
- ☐ political machine
- ☐ spoils system
- ☐ suburb
- ☐ Tammany Hall
- ☐ tenement

Essential Question

How did industrialization drive American urbanization in the late 1800s and 1900s?

Lesson Objectives

By the end of this lesson, you should be able to:

- Describe trends and explain factors leading to urbanization of the United States during the late 1800s and early 1900s.

- Describe how American cities and American society as a whole changed as a result of industrialization.

- Describe the influence of urbanization on American politics.

 | SOCIAL STUDIES TECHBOOK

How did industrialization drive American urbanization in the late 1800s and 1900s?

ENGAGE

What words would you use to describe cities? Visit Engage to learn more.

Essential Question

How did industrialization drive American urbanization in the late 1800s and 1900s?

EXPLORE

The Rise of Cities

Why did U.S. cities grow?

In 1870, the urban population of the United States was 9,902,361. Compare the urban population figure to the 28,656,010 people living in rural areas. About 80 percent of all people in the United States lived on farms in 1870. However, by 1920, the trend had clearly shifted in the opposite direction. More than half of all U.S. citizens lived in urban areas in 1920. The United States was clearly experiencing a period of urbanization, meaning that the number of cities and the number of people living in those cities increased dramatically. Why were so many people leaving life on the farms and moving to U.S. cities?

Industrialization, Urbanization, and Immigration

Throughout the late 1800s and early 1900s, three important trends worked together to dramatically reshape the United States:

- industrialization

- urbanization

- immigration

The process of industrialization fueled the country's urban growth. Cities were often built around mines, factories, ports, and railroads. As factories developed near water sources or where iron and coal deposits were uncovered, these industries began to grow. As a result, workers began flocking to these areas to work in those industries. The growing population in cities was fueled not only by U.S. citizens moving from farms to the cities, but also by immigration. As immigrants moved from Europe and Asia to escape religious persecution, famine, and other hardships, they often ended up in American cities in search of opportunities to work in factories or in trades.

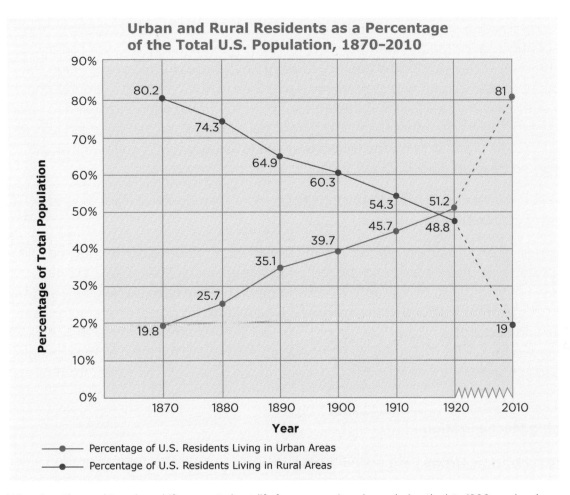

Urban and Rural Residents as a Percentage of the Total U.S. Population, 1870–2010

What does the rural-to-urban shift suggest about life for average Americans during the late 1800s and early 1900s?

The growth of the country's urban population created an expanding market for goods made in factories. This large population provided a demand for factory-made products. To meet this demand, factories grew and began making more and more products. As a result, still more workers were drawn to cities to work in factories. In summary, industrialization and urbanization fueled each other in a continuous cycle.

Industrialization and urbanization also contributed to the emergence of new industries that drew even more workers to urban areas. The cities were centers of manufacturing. They also were places where goods were bought, sold, and marketed. As a result, America's urban areas were home to most of the nation's wholesale and retail commerce.

Discovery | SOCIAL STUDIES
EDUCATION | TECHBOOK.

How did industrialization drive American urbanization in the late 1800s and 1900s?

While these trends were the main driving forces behind the growth of cities, other factors, such as improved transportation, technological advances, and racial discrimination, also influenced urbanization.

New Technology and Social Issues Fuel Urban Growth
What other factors contributed to urbanization?

Growth of the Railroads

Railroads developed rapidly through the mid- to late 1800s. The completion of the transcontinental railroad in 1869 gave the railroads a major boost. Goods could now be transported across the country faster than ever before. However, when the transcontinental railroad was started, railroad construction practices were not consistent from one company to another. For example, when the transcontinental railroad was completed, there were more than 20 different gauges, or distances between rails on a track, in use. Standardizing the tracks over the 1870s and 1880s enabled a single network to develop, linking towns and cities all across the country.

From 1880 to 1900, U.S. railroad track mileage more than doubled from around 90,000 to nearly 200,000 miles.

Industrialization and urbanization grew in tandem with the development of the railroads. That is because the railroads and the factories helped each other grow. On one hand, factories forged the steel rails and spikes and made the railroad ties, engines, and train cars. On the other hand, railroads distributed manufactured goods from factories to stores and customers all over the country. As factories expanded, so did the cities where factory workers lived. The growing city populations needed food for all their people. The railroads provided it by transporting agricultural products such as wheat from farms to the cities.

Farming Mechanization

Industrialization created both push and pull factors for rural-to-urban migration. Factory jobs and the possibilities of city life attracted young men and women who were raised in rural areas. In 1890, the average annual wages for farm labor in the United States were $233 while the average for manufacturing workers was $439. In addition, machinery radically reduced the need for farm labor. McCormick's reaper began to mechanize harvesting in the 1840s. In 1902, an even more revolutionary invention appeared: the tractor. Earlier tractors with enormous steam engines had been failures. The engine in Hart and Parr's 1902 tractor was a gasoline-fueled internal combustion engine, roughly the same as the engines in most of today's cars. Gas-powered tractors hauled reapers and eased the work of clearing, plowing, and planting. As technological advances took over the work that most farmworkers used to do by hand, farms needed fewer laborers to operate the machinery. Farmworkers found themselves out of work. Industrializing cities offered job opportunities for these workers.

photo: Library of Congress

A photograph from 1898 shows African American men working in an Illinois factory to produce parts for a naval ship.

Racial Discrimination

After Reconstruction ended, Jim Crow laws and racial discrimination prevented African Americans in the rural South from buying land and from obtaining high-paying jobs. Over time, increasing numbers of African Americans looked to the country's growing cities for economic opportunities and social advancement.

This trend began slowly. In 1910, nearly 80 percent of African Americans living in southern U.S. states remained in rural areas. However, the lure of jobs in northern factories drew many to the North on a small scale. This contributed to the country's urban growth. Starting around 1915, African American migration from the rural South to the industrial North would increase more dramatically.

Widespread Urbanization

Where did urbanization occur?

The country's largest cities were found in the Northeast. However, cities in the Midwest and the West grew rapidly as well. For example, in 1900, St. Louis, Missouri, had a population of 575,238 and San Francisco, California, boasted a population of 342,782. Although the largest city, in terms of population, was New York City in 1900, Chicago, Illinois, proved to be one of the fastest growing urban centers during this period. What contributed to rapid urbanization in Chicago?

Chicago Grows Its Big Shoulders

In a 1916 poem, Illinois-born writer Carl Sandburg recorded his observations of city life in his famous poem called "Chicago." In the poem, Sandburg described Chicago as:

> Hog Butcher for the World,
>
> Tool Maker, Stacker of Wheat,
>
> Player with Railroads and the Nation's Freight Handler;
>
> Stormy, husky, brawling,
>
> City of the Big Shoulders.

DISCOVERY | SOCIAL STUDIES
EDUCATION | **TECHBOOK**

How did industrialization drive American urbanization in the late 1800s and 1900s?

photo: Library of Congress

CHICAGO IN 1820.

What geographic features shown in this image most contributed to Chicago's future growth?

photo: Library of Congress

THE GREAT UNION STOCK YARDS OF CHICAGO.

Chicago's Union Stock Yards held hundreds of cattle in pens before they were shipped for production.

Sandburg's rich description of the city painted an accurate portrait of Chicago in the early 1900s. Chicago was a city where train lines from the east met train lines from the west. Moreover, Chicago had access to the Great Lakes and the Mississippi River. Chicago's rail yards became the center of the railroad shipping industry. Chicago was home to the Pullman Palace Car Company, the leading manufacturer of railroad passenger cars. Chicago was the center of the meatpacking industry with companies such as Swift and Armour. Cyrus McCormick located his factory there, and the city became the leading manufacturer of agricultural machinery. It was also home to the retail catalog sales giants Sears, Roebuck and Company as well as Montgomery Ward.

Because of its location as a transportation and agricultural center, Chicago developed the first futures market for grains in the United States. Today, this market, known as the Chicago Board of Trade, is the largest market for agricultural products in the world. Similar to a stock exchange, the "commodities exchange" buys and sells future corn, wheat, soybean, and cattle products.

Explore this investigation to learn more about invention and mechanization.

Workers flocked to Chicago in order to find jobs at the many factories, warehouses, and businesses that sprung up there. Chicago's African American population grew from about 4,000 in 1870 to about 15,000 in 1890. This was largely a result of migration from the South. From 1850 to 1890, Chicago grew by a factor of more than 30—from a population of just about 30,000 to more than one million.

Urban Economic Hubs

What economic activities flourished in U.S. cities?

For many people, the lure of the city was a job in a factory. Factories employed men, women, and even children. There were many opportunities for unskilled or poorly educated workers. Cities also served as shipping hubs and offered jobs for laborers on railroads, in docks, or in warehouses.

With more people working in factories, there was a greater need for stores selling food, clothing, housewares, tools, and other manufactured items. Most retail outlets needed stock workers and delivery drivers, and all but the smallest operations needed sales assistants. There was construction work on housing, office buildings, and roads and bridges. There were hotels and restaurants and entertainment venues. People sold personal services such as barbering and shoe-polishing.

Rowland H. Macy and Marshall Field changed retailing with the department store. For years, R. H. Macy in New York was the largest single store in the country. However, Macy's was later surpassed by Marshall Field's store in downtown Chicago. Field's offered 73 acres of shopping, including the first in-store restaurant for shoppers. These giant, elegant stores offered attentive customer service and tried to make shopping a glamorous activity.

An urban middle class also began to appear. Educated workers found jobs as bank tellers, schoolteachers, and office workers. Newspapers hired reporters, typesetters, and printers and purchased paper, ink, typesetting machines, and printing presses.

Cities as Centers of Finance

Industries tied to finance also grew in U.S. cities. The finance industry includes businesses and organizations that manage and lend money. Banks, credit companies, insurance companies, and stock brokerages are all part of the finance industry. Finance made U.S. industrialization possible. Manufacturing industries needed capital, or money, to run and to grow. They often obtained loans or sold stock in their companies to raise this capital. As a result, banks and other financial institutions were built in city centers.

Large cities such as New York, Chicago, and San Francisco boasted stock, bond, and commodities exchanges. Many stock exchanges, such as the New York Stock Exchange, were established before the widespread growth of industry in the late 1800s. The New York Stock Exchange was founded in 1792. However, as manufacturing industries grew in the late 1800s, investments in corporations increased. The industrial success of the period created growing numbers of middle- and upper-class citizens. Those who wanted to share in the profits of successful businesses invested money in the new technologies of the time. The increase in investments provided businesses the money they needed to expand their business operations.

Discovery EDUCATION | **SOCIAL STUDIES TECHBOOK**

How did industrialization drive American urbanization in the late 1800s and 1900s?

Like the stock exchange, banking was an important industry in U.S. cities. Banks provided a place for working people to save and withdraw their money when it was needed. Banks loaned, or invested, the money people deposited to an entrepreneur seeking to start new businesses or to an existing business seeking to expand. In the early 1890s, bank loans in the United States were valued at more than $4 billion, a $3 billion increase from 1870. As business owners became successful, they repaid the loans and stored their profits in the bank. This circulation of money from the bank to business owners, and back to the bank, gave banks the capital they needed to operate successfully. However, money lending could be risky. What might happen to the banking system if the loans are not repaid?

photo: National Archives

The Irish-born Cudahy brothers founded the meatpacking company shown here in 1890.

Still, every downtown had its own bank. Branch banking was rare before the 1920s, and interstate branch banking, or banking in multiple states, was illegal. Every bank had private security guards to protect against robberies. The bank building itself was elegantly designed, with Greek columns and high ceilings. The detailed architecture of the buildings and the emphasis placed on bank security illustrated that banks and financial centers were viewed as important places in the urban landscape.

Upscale Suburbs and Working-Class Tenements
How did the lives of well-off and poor city dwellers differ?

Urbanization coincided with a time of growing economic and social inequality among Americans. Cities, therefore, became home to people with very different lifestyles. Cities began to develop the first public transportation systems during the late 1800s. San Francisco, Chicago, Kansas City, Los Angeles, and Washington, DC, all built cable car systems that carried passengers around the city. In 1889, Boston installed the nation's first electrified streetcar system.

New York's subway system opened in 1904. Public transportation allowed residents to live in one part of the city and work elsewhere. This was a tremendous help to married couples who were no longer restricted to jobs in the same neighborhood.

photo: Library of Congress

Cable cars share the road with automobiles in Washington, DC.

Mass transit also increased social divisions in cities. People who had enough money moved to neighborhoods away from the noise and smell of heavy industry. They could isolate themselves from the cities' problems. As mass transit lines grew outward, planned communities followed, creating the first streetcar suburbs. These communities offered more space, fresh air, and privacy.

Meanwhile, many immigrants and rural transplants who could not afford to settle in suburbs, including African American arrivals from the South, lived near their factory jobs in the city. These urban residential districts were dirty, noisy, and crowded. Swelling populations added pressure to these neighborhoods. Residents of these neighborhoods typically lived in dark, cramped apartment buildings known as tenements. One common design, the dumbbell tenement, organized four apartments on a floor with two shared toilets and one narrow air shaft to let in light. Large families sometimes shared apartments or even rooms.

Urban Living Leads to Problems

What problems arose in U.S. cities?

Tenements were dangerous and unsanitary. These living areas were often poorly ventilated, lacking indoor plumbing, and crawling with pests such as rats and mice, which are known to spread disease.

Tenement Living Leads to Unsafe Conditions

The high population densities of cities caused health and environmental difficulties. For example, in 1890, the immigrant neighborhood of the Lower East Side in New York housed more than 700 people per acre. Rapidly growing populations walked unpaved streets littered with garbage, horse droppings, and food waste. Meatpacking plants dumped animal carcasses and chemicals into the same lakes and rivers that supplied drinking water. Steel mills produced slag, or waste from metal processing, and other waste products containing hazardous chemicals. Households dumped their used wash water in the streets. Crews of pigs ran wild in New York, and rats ran wild everywhere. Trash and waste in the streets led to water and land pollution, which was potentially dangerous for the people living in cities.

Increase in Diseases

Before the work of scientists such as
Louis Pasteur and Robert Koch, people
remained unaware of the causes of
sickness. Death from old age and heart
failure was much less common than
today. Nationwide, in 1900, 30 percent of
all deaths were children under age five.
One-third of deaths were from infectious
diseases such as pneumonia, tuberculosis,
intestinal ailments, and diphtheria.

photo: Library of Congress
Entrance to tenement, Providence, Rhode Island, 1912.

New York City suffered repeated
epidemics throughout the 1800s. Cholera struck in 1832, 1849, 1854, and 1866. More than
1,800 people died from smallpox in 1872. Diphtheria killed nearly 4,900 in 1881 and more
than 4,500 in 1887.

Crime

In addition to pollution and disease, crime was a growing problem in U.S. cities. In 1875,
composer Theo Rosenstein wrote a song called "Three Cheers for our City's Defenders"
in honor of law enforcement officers in cities at the time. In one verse, Rosenstein wrote:

"Tho' danger the City has bounded With robbers and villains, a host, Let signal to duty
be sounded; You'll find ev'ry man at his post."

**Explore this resource and
then write your own
investigative report
about city life during
industrialization.**

During the late 1800s, police departments
were controlled by the city or local
governments, not the central government.
In cities, police officers were pulled
from the local population, which meant
that police officers had a good working
knowledge of the city and people they
served. However, local control over the
police departments posed some problems. For example, a police officer's authority
often was restricted to the area in which he or she was assigned to cover. If a crime
occurred in an area outside their sphere of authority, then the police officers could not
take action. Although the presence of police officers did deter criminals, some police
officers were corrupt and inefficient, which helped to spread crime in urban areas.

City Government

How did cities respond to the problems of growth?

Communities had long relied on volunteers to respond to fires. Existing
volunteer police and fire services were inadequate to deal with the needs
of expanding urban populations. City dwellers did not know most of their neighbors.

By the end of the 1800s, professional police officers and firefighters had begun to patrol cities. Cincinnati established the first municipal professional fire department in 1853. Chicago established a professional fire department in 1858, but it was not enough. In 1871, the Great Chicago Fire destroyed three and a half square miles of the city, including one-third of the city's homes.

Cleaning Up U.S. Cities

The health problems of cities also were clearly bigger than people could handle on their own. People turned to their government for help. States and cities took steps to address health as a public issue by gathering groups of educated people and instructing them to solve common problems. Starting in the early 1800s, cities created boards, commissions, and departments to improve public health, to ensure a supply of clean water, and to dispose of human and factory waste. In 1869, Massachusetts created the first state board of health. By 1900, 40 out of 45 states had state boards of health.

They did not know the causes of scarlet fever, typhus, yellow fever, diphtheria, smallpox, dysentery, or the other diseases that regularly killed thousands of people. However, they had a general idea that living in crowded conditions with raw sewage, bad air, questionable water, dirt, and animals had something to do with it.

The New York City Board of Health was created in 1805 to address a yellow fever epidemic plaguing New Yorkers. The board was instrumental in dealing with disease epidemics that arose during the 1800s. However, in the late 1850s, many citizens argued that the board was led by corrupt politicians. In 1866, fear of a cholera epidemic convinced the state to take action and create a new independent health department that was not run by a political party. One major change was that the board would include trained physicians. Instead of waiting for outbreaks of disease and then reacting, the new board would try to prevent disease. These changes were soon tested and proved successful. New York's 1866 cholera epidemic killed one-tenth the number of people killed by the preceding epidemic in 1849.

After 1881, a common sight in New York was the street sweeper. These were men in white uniforms who carried a shovel or broom and wheeled a cart for waste. A large portion of their work was picking up horse droppings.

In 1855, Chicago developed the first completely underground sewer system. Construction started at the river's edge. There, trenches for pipes were dug into the ground. The sewers were to operate by gravity, so they had to slope down toward the river. As construction progressed further from the river, the lines got higher and higher. Most of the system was built above what used to be ground level. The sewer lines were covered up and new streets were built on top. Downtown Chicago still has two levels today.

Discovery SOCIAL STUDIES
EDUCATION | **TECHBOOK**

How did industrialization drive American urbanization in the late 1800s and 1900s?

Barriers to Public Health

There were also strong forces fighting against public health efforts. New York City's Board of Health faced opposition from William Magear "Boss" Tweed's political machine. A political machine is a group that controls the actions of a political party. Tweed's organization, Tammany Hall, operated through graft. Graft means that a politician uses his or her political authority for personal gain. Tammany Hall did not want public agencies to have power unless Tammany Hall controlled them. Tweed pushed through a new city charter that returned health control to the city. Corrupt politicians scuttled, or eliminated, many proposals to clean up the streets, inspect drinking water supplies, and inspect milk and other foods.

Chicago was the first city to require milk pasteurization, the process of boiling milk to kill bacteria. However, the Chicago Health Department was unable to enforce its rules. The city's milk came from 12,000 dairies in four different states. Lobbyists fought for dairy interests at the state level, and the states found various ways of disempowering the city and obstructing its attempts to protect public health. This was typical. Oscar Coleman De Wolf served as Chicago's commissioner of health in the late 1870s and 1880s. He took bold steps such as instituting workplace

photo: National Archives
Street cleaners worked to remove garbage from the roads in an attempt to clean up the city and reduce health issues among citizens.

health and safety inspections and attempting to move the slaughterhouses to the city's edge. These moves upset the city's business leaders, and they pushed De Wolf out of his job.

The New Leisure

How did urbanization lead to new cultural and leisure activities?

Just as cities were hubs for economic activities, they also became centers of arts and entertainment. Unlike farmworkers, middle-class urban workers had time and money to dedicate to leisure.

Arts and Culture

Cities became centers of learning, culture, and entertainment. Although most young people did not attend high school or college, they did go to grammar school, which went through grade 8. Literacy rates increased steadily following the Civil War. In 1870, about 20 percent of all Americans could not read or write in any language; by 1920, just 6 percent lacked those skills. Urban immigrants created foreign-language newspapers in Polish, Italian, Yiddish, and other languages to serve members of their groups. As many as 160 foreign-language newspapers were in print in 1914.

photo: Library of Congress

After his death, much of Samuel J. Tilden's estate was used to fund a public library in New York. This photograph shows the main reading room of the library around 1910.

African Americans also published newspapers with stories of particular interest to their community. One of these was the *Christian Recorder* of Philadelphia, "Published by the African Methodist Episcopal Church in the United States, for the Dissemination of Religion, Morality, Literature and Science." The *Recorder* was in print from 1861 to 1902.

Cities also opened or expanded public libraries to serve citizens. Detroit's first public library opened in 1865 with a collection of 5,000 books. Just 12 years later, Detroit opened a new library building with some 34,000 volumes.

In the years after the Metropolitan Museum of Art opened in New York in 1870, art museums appeared throughout the United States. Chicago's Field Museum of Natural History, named for retail giant Marshall Field, opened in 1893. This museum was originally built for the Columbian World Exposition, held in Chicago as a demonstration of that city's world significance. The Field Museum displayed artifacts relating to science, archaeology, art, and natural history. During this same time period, symphony orchestras formed in cities such as St. Louis, Cincinnati, and Minneapolis.

Sports and Amusement

What sports and amusement activities arose in urban areas?

Urban residents sometimes sought an escape from the challenges of daily life, and as American cities grew, new businesses and civic projects gave people places to go. Families, who would be at separate jobs and schools much of the day, could go on outings to spend time together. Young men and women could find time to mingle, away from their families or crowded group homes, on "dates" that were much less formal than traditional "courtship." Young men, who were paid more than young women, were expected to arrange and pay for these dates.

Amusement parks such as New York's Coney Island offered visitors the chance to ride roller coasters and play games. Resorts such as Atlantic City, New Jersey, developed along train lines to attract people from nearby cities. Closer to home, city planners built public parks in urban neighborhoods. These parks gave residents the opportunity to enjoy nature and allowed cities to keep certain districts from becoming too densely developed. On July 1, 1874, 3,000 Philadelphians visited the nation's first zoo for its opening day.

Discovery | SOCIAL STUDIES
EDUCATION | TECHBOOK.

How did industrialization drive American urbanization in the late 1800s and 1900s?

Spectator sports also grew in popularity. The Cincinnati Red Stockings organized as the nation's first professional baseball team in 1869. Seven years later, the National League formed with teams from Cincinnati, Boston, Chicago, New York, Philadelphia, St. Louis, Louisville, and Hartford, Connecticut. Football, boxing, and horse racing were a few other popular spectator sports of the day. In 1875, the first Kentucky Derby was run before a crowd of more than 10,000 spectators.

Not all urban residents were free to participate in and enjoy these activities. For example, African American baseball players were prohibited from playing major league baseball, while African American spectators were required to sit in designated sections of inferior seats at baseball games.

photo: Library of Congress

Crowds of people gather to observe the bear pits in a Memphis zoo.

photo: Library of Congress

Fans outside Ebbets Field purchase hot dogs before a Brooklyn Dodgers baseball game in 1920.

The late 1800s and early 1900s also marked the beginning of new popular forms of entertainment. Vaudeville shows featured a wide variety of singing, dancing, and comedy acts. Around the early 1900s, new technology brought audiences motion pictures, or movies—pictures that move. The first cinemas were dubbed nickelodeons because tickets cost a nickel.

The Sky's the Limit

How did city landscapes change?

Industrialization and technological progress enabled the use of new building materials such as steel-framed concrete. Combined with the growth of cities, these technologies helped create a building boom like none that had come before it.

Perhaps the most visible sign of this progress was the skyscraper. Numerous technological developments helped make the skyscraper—a term originally used to describe any building with about 10 stories or more—possible. During the late 1850s, inventors designed the elevator, removing the major obstacle to building taller buildings.

The key accomplishment in developing the elevator was not getting it to go up but getting it to go down slowly and to stop smoothly. With Elisha Otis's development of an emergency braking system, the elevator presented a much safer way to be lowered from great heights. Otis demonstrated his invention at the 1853–1854 World's Fair in New York's Crystal Palace. He would ride up several stories high on a platform hoisted by a rope. When he neared the ceiling, an assistant would cut the rope. Observers were amazed when he did not plummet to the ground.

Architects responded to these innovations by designing taller buildings supported by thick walls and cast-iron frames. The frame was meant to bear the building's weight, and the concrete held it steady against twisting and swaying. However, cast iron was simply not strong enough to bear the weight of a 10-story building. After the introduction of the Bessemer Process for producing strong steel, the construction of extremely tall skyscrapers became possible. The first all-steel-frame building was built for Rand-McNally in Chicago in 1889.

photo: Library of Congress
Early skyscrapers in Pittsburgh, between 1910 and 1920.

Over the next few decades, skyscrapers came to dominate large cities all around the United States. Land in the business district of a city was scarce and very expensive. Skyscrapers provided needed office space for cities' growing economies. They also gave cities a visual identity and a source of pride. Architects such as Louis Sullivan and Daniel H. Burnham designed many early skyscrapers in cities such as New York, Chicago, St. Louis, and Buffalo. Architect John Parkinson designed the 12-story Braly Block in Los Angeles, completed in 1902.

Not everyone, however, appreciated skyscraper architecture. Some cities, including Los Angeles, Boston, and Philadelphia, passed laws limiting the height of buildings in order to protect the sunlight and fresh air in their business districts.

City Parks

Cities also created parks as places of quiet and relaxation and to preserve nature. Park designer and conservationist Frederick Law Olmsted created a new profession— landscape architecture—and changed city life. Olmsted designed and brought to life Boston's Emerald Necklace, New York's Central Park, Prospect Park in Brooklyn, and the U.S. Capitol Grounds. Olmsted's other parks included the Southern Parkway in Louisville; Washington Park, Jackson Park, and the Midway Plaisance in Chicago; and Belle Isle Park in Detroit. The cities that did not hire Olmsted used his ideas. Olmsted invented the term landscape architecture, along with the concepts of the multiuse large urban park, the parkway, and the residential suburb.

Discovery SOCIAL STUDIES
EDUCATION TECHBOOK

How did industrialization drive American urbanization in the late 1800s and 1900s?

The Rise of the Political Machine

How did the social changes of urbanization lead to a transformation of city governments?

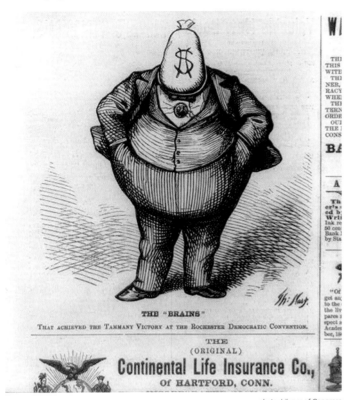

THE "BRAINS"

THAT ACHIEVED THE TAMMANY VICTORY AT THE ROCHESTER DEMOCRATIC CONVENTION.

THE
(ORIGINAL)
Continental Life Insurance Co.,
OF HARTFORD, CONN.

photo: Library of Congress

Political leaders such as William "Boss" Tweed gained considerable political power thanks to the support of immigrants and other new urban residents.

As the growth of industry and urbanization created social problems in cities, city governments found themselves ill prepared to provide services to the city residents. Because of the lack of organization in government, political machines emerged and began to take control of city governments. Political machines were organizations that informally exchanged political favors for promises of votes. Machines ruled Chicago, St. Louis, New Orleans, Minneapolis, Pittsburgh, and many other cities and towns. The most notorious of these political machines was born in New York City. The Democratic Party machine called itself the Tammany Society and was housed in Tammany Hall. For decades, Tammany politicians, led by William Magear "Boss" Tweed, exerted a great deal of influence over the city. They took kickbacks, or payments, in exchange for awarding government contracts or jobs. Party bosses accepted bribes in exchange for favors. These corrupt organizations handled millions of dollars in graft.

Leaders of political machines used the people of newly formed urban areas to their advantage. Immigrant groups made up nearly half of the population in most cities. Party bosses often catered to immigrant groups by providing them with jobs or a place to live in exchange for votes in elections. Having the large population of immigrants on their side often gave the party bosses the votes needed to keep their party in power.

Although the main function of political machines was to keep control of the government in their hands, political machines also had some positive influences in their communities. Governments controlled by political machines could make decisions to improve a city's infrastructure without opposition from government officials from another party. As a result, political machines were responsible for constructing streets and docks and running fire and police departments. Many immigrants relied on political machines for social services and job referrals. In exchange for these benefits, these immigrants were willing to pay bribes, give votes, and go along with the political machine. Thus, although a spirit of reform marked the era, many immigrants opposed political changes. Removing political machines from power would have cost them important benefits.

Nativism and Cultural Conflict

How did urbanization and immigration shape politics at the local and national levels?

The tendency of immigrant populations to side with party bosses sometimes led to tensions between native-born and immigrant Americans. The sheer volume of immigrants to new cities also contributed to this tension. Feelings of nativism ran high and influenced a number of social issues, including education and the use of alcohol. Nativism is the idea that the needs of native-born citizens should be favored over those of immigrant populations.

Nativists in the late 1800s worried about the patriotism of immigrants and about their competence as voters. They supported discriminatory policies that segregated, or isolated, African Americans, Jews, Catholics, Latinos, and Asians. These groups were excluded from living in mostly white neighborhoods, from working many desirable jobs, and from enjoying public accommodations such as parks and swimming pools. As a result, many immigrants lived in ethnic enclaves and created their own institutions. Non-nativist educational leaders, as well as the general public, worried about literacy. People from all these groups debated whether public schools in ethnic neighborhoods should offer classes only in English to force immigrants to assimilate.

Distrust of Roman Catholics among nativists was also strong, and the majority of immigrants from Ireland and Italy were Catholic. Debates regarding the proper role of public schools and the influence of the Church in education were common.

Many public school leaders tried to remain religiously neutral. Men such as Horace Mann wanted to teach literacy and citizenship for secular reasons and to avoid religious controversy. However, many Catholics saw public schools' neutrality as an attempt to force their children to become Protestant. To escape the public schools, the Catholic Church started many private schools.

Because Catholic schools did teach literacy and citizenship, some Catholics thought their schools should be publicly funded. Nativists strongly objected to providing public funds to schools operated by the Catholic Church. Liberals, or people who were open to nontraditional viewpoints and ideas, argued that the First Amendment's Establishment Clause created a "wall of separation," prohibiting public support of religious institutions.

Temperance and Party Alignment

The push for temperance, or prohibition of alcohol, also pitted nativists and Protestants against immigrants and Catholics. The temperance movement was led by Protestants who viewed alcohol as sinful. They said it caused social ills such as laziness, poverty, and insanity. From the 1850s onward, the temperance movement focused much of its efforts on Irish and German Catholics. These immigrant groups spent their Sundays enjoying a day off of work. They gathered with family for outings and social events. Many Irish and German immigrants resented being told how they may or may not use their leisure time or being criticized for the practice of drinking wine when taking Communion, a religious ritual.

Discovery EDUCATION | SOCIAL STUDIES TECHBOOK

How did industrialization drive American urbanization in the late 1800s and 1900s?

Across the nation, voters came to follow certain patterns. Immigrants and Catholics tended to support Democratic Party candidates. Southerners also strongly supported the Democratic Party regardless of whether they lived in cities or the countryside. Native-born Northerners and Protestants tended to vote for Republicans. These patterns reflected the divisions between North and South, urban and rural, and immigrant and native-born that existed throughout this era.

photo: Library of Congress

This political cartoon, created in 1902, illustrates the contrasting views on temperance during the early 1900s.

Political Divisions

What competing political viewpoints emerged during the late 1800s?

During the late 1800s, two competing viewpoints dominated U.S. politics. On one side were the traditional political machine politicians, and on the other side were the reform-minded leaders.

Throughout much of the late 1800s, political machine politics dominated local and national governments. By the 1870s, corruption was widespread throughout much of the nation's government. The spoils system, in practice since 1812 but intensified with Andrew Jackson's presidency, dominated federal politics. Under this system, the heads of government agencies had the power to make hiring decisions. They hired people loyal to them—those who voted the party line or campaigned for them and their party. Qualifications were often irrelevant.

Political machines, such as Tammany Hall, took advantage of the spoils system. They rewarded their supporters with jobs. Immigrants and other city dwellers who often needed public assistance received aid from political machines. In turn, these immigrant groups and other members of the urban population supported the machine's politics.

Tammany Hall was originally created to oppose what was seen as an elitist Federalist Party. As a result, Tammany Hall often catered to minority and immigrant groups and impoverished white citizens.

DEMOCRATIC REFORMERS IN SEARCH OF A HEAD.

photo: Library of Congress

This 1876 political cartoon parodies the divides within the Democratic Party. The group on the left, identifiable by their heavy work shoes, fight a faction on the right, identifiable by their formal dress shoes. The group on the left represents Tammany Democrats.

In the late 1800s, elitist, reform-minded leaders began to oppose the spoils system and the institutionalized corruption. For example, New York politician Samuel Tilden, who lost the presidency to Rutherford B. Hayes through the Compromise of 1877, dedicated years of his career to opposing Tammany Hall. These leaders rejected machine politics and supported "good government" campaigns. A group called the mugwumps led the push for government reform. The mugwumps were a group of long-time Republican supporters who included well-known cynics such as author Mark Twain and cartoonist Thomas Nast.

Efforts to Reform Government

How did civil service reform take place?

One goal of most political reformers was the replacement of the spoils system with the civil service system. Under a civil service system, candidates for government jobs have to meet specific, job-relevant qualifications. Often, there is a competitive examination. Appointees can be fired for incompetence but not for their politics. They could keep their jobs regardless of the wishes of the administration. Not all politicians supported civil service reform. A faction within the Republican Party, known as the stalwarts, disagreed strongly.

OUR MARTYRED PRESIDENTS.

photo: Library of Congress

What do you think was the artist's purpose for creating this image?

This issue turned from political debate to national tragedy in 1881. A compromise Republican ticket of presidential candidate James Garfield, a reformer, and vice-presidential candidate Chester A. Arthur, a stalwart, had won the election. A few months after taking office, Garfield was assassinated. His killer, Charles J. Guiteau, was a disgruntled Republican supporter. He believed he deserved a job under the spoils system, but he did not get one. Guiteau explained his decision to shoot Garfield by stating that it made the stalwart Arthur the new president.

An appalled nation called for civil service reform. In 1883, Arthur signed the Pendleton Civil Service Act. This instituted the nation's first civil service system. This law covered only a small portion of all government jobs. It was expanded over time to include most positions. This act led to the creation of a civil service exam. People who wanted to work for the government had to take the exam.

If the candidate performed well, he or she would be considered for the job. If not, the candidate would not be considered.

Getting the job had nothing to do with one's political dealings. As a result, the political machines that emerged to correct the social ills industrialization and urbanization caused began to lose importance.

Reform was decisive in the presidential election of 1884. The mugwumps abandoned the Republican Party after it nominated U.S. Senator James G. Blaine for the presidency. Blaine was widely known to be corrupt but had never been charged or convicted. The mugwumps threw their support behind Democratic candidate Grover Cleveland. Cleveland narrowly won the election, thanks, perhaps, to the influence of the mugwumps in a close, pivotal election in New York State.

Urbanization led to both positive changes, such as improved transit systems, the growth of suburbs, and new forms of entertainment, and negative changes, such as inferior housing, sanitation issues, crime, and government corruption. In short, urbanization brought about new challenges for its citizens and governments. While citizens recognized the problems urbanization caused, they were often ill equipped to make widespread changes for the better.

Over time, however, citizens would step up their efforts to reform the social and political issues plaguing the country.

Consider the Essential Question:

How did industrialization drive American urbanization in the late 1800s and 1900s?

Go online to complete the Social Studies Explanation.

Check for Understanding:

In what ways did the rural and urban populations of the United States change between 1860 and 1920? Did these changes improve life in cities?

12.1 Rise of the Millionaires

photo: Library of Congress

LESSON OVERVIEW

Introduction

In this concept, you will analyze how continued industrialization in the United States contributed to the rise of large businesses and powerful business leaders. Many Americans debated the impact of this development and how the country's economic system addressed the fundamental questions of economics.

Essential Question

Were America's great industrial giants champions of free enterprise?

Key Vocabulary

Which terms do you already know?

- ☐ Andrew Carnegie
- ☐ capitalism
- ☐ command economy
- ☐ Cornelius Vanderbilt
- ☐ economy
- ☐ entrepreneur
- ☐ Gilded Age
- ☐ Interstate Commerce Act of 1887
- ☐ John D. Rockefeller
- ☐ laissez-faire
- ☐ market economy
- ☐ mixed economy
- ☐ monopoly
- ☐ private enterprise
- ☐ robber barons
- ☐ scarcity
- ☐ Social Darwinism
- ☐ supply and demand
- ☐ trust

SOCIAL STUDIES TECHBOOK

Were America's great industrial giants champions of free enterprise?

Lesson Objectives

By the end of this lesson, you should be able to:

- Define basic economic concepts and explain the role of economic systems in addressing the fundamental questions of economics.
- Explain how industrialization changed American business practices and organization.
- Evaluate governmental responses to economic problems created by industrialization and the emergence of big business.

ENGAGE

In what ways did Alexander Graham Bell change America? Visit Engage to learn more.

Essential Question

Were America's great industrial giants champions of free enterprise?

EXPLORE

Fundamental Economic Questions

How does scarcity relate to economic production?

According to the U.S. Department of Labor, the average American household spends about $2,500 a year on entertainment. However, spending (or not spending) money on entertainment is a choice. Some households spend more than the average, some spend less, and not every household spends its entertainment budget in the same way. One family might choose to spend money on movies. Another family might attend concerts or sporting events.

Families are forced to make decisions about how to spend their entertainment dollars because of a problem known as scarcity. Scarcity means there are not enough resources to satisfy all human wants for goods and services. Because household incomes are limited, families may not have enough money to attend as many movies, concerts, or ball games as they would like. Even if they do have enough money, there are only so many hours of free time each day, and movie theaters, concert venues, and stadiums only have a limited number of seats.

As you can see from this example, the problem of scarcity forces people and groups to make choices about spending money and investing time. Economics is the study of how individuals and groups allocate, or distribute, resources to meet unlimited human wants with limited resources. Because of scarcity, there are three questions that societies must constantly address. These questions are sometimes called the fundamental questions of economics:

- *What* goods and services will be produced?

- *How* should the goods and services be produced?

- *Who* will benefit from goods and services that are produced?

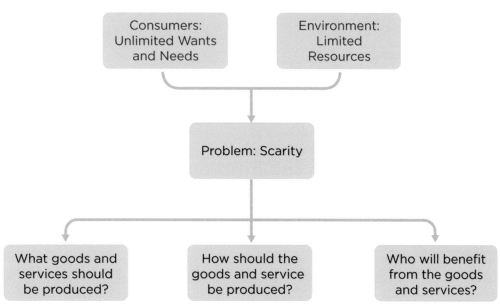

Unlimited needs and limited resources contribute to the problem of scarcity.

Discovery Education | SOCIAL STUDIES TECHBOOK

Were America's great industrial giants champions of free enterprise?

Types of Economic Systems

What systems do people establish to address the issue of scarcity?

All over the world, societies address the fundamental questions of economics in different ways. An ***economic system*** is a framework of formal and informal rules a society establishes for deciding what to produce, how to produce, and how to distribute goods and services. Economic systems are often categorized as traditional, command, or market-based.

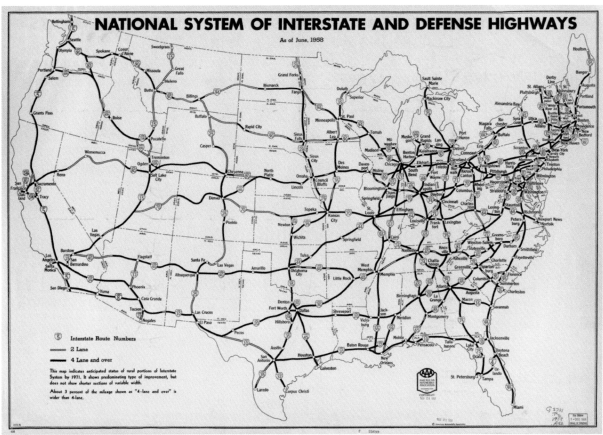

NATIONAL SYSTEM OF INTERSTATE AND DEFENSE HIGHWAYS

As of June, 1958

photo: Library of Congress

How are interstate highways evidence of the United States' mixed-market economic system?

It is important to note that all societies have mixed economies, meaning that they contain elements of all three types. For example, even though the United States has a primarily market-based economy, practices associated with traditional and command economies are also found there. For this reason, the economy of the United States is sometimes called a mixed-market system.

Traditional Economic Systems

In a traditional economy, customs and habits from the past are commonly relied upon to resolve issues of economic production and distribution. Activities such as hunting, gathering, and subsistence farming often form the backbone of a traditional economy.

Examples of traditional economies today include the Inuit in the Arctic region, the Aboriginal peoples of Australia, and the Maasai of East Africa. In these societies, property rules are embedded in customs and habits. For instance, there is often a custom of sharing among the community members.

Although the word *traditional* may suggest that modern societies do not follow this system, traditional elements can be found even in fully developed societies, such as the United States. For example, many artisans in the United States continue to produce and sell clothing, furniture, and artwork made by hand, rather than relying on more efficient means and machinery. In addition, American families commonly distribute wealth from generation to generation through inheritance.

Command-Oriented Economic Systems

In a command-oriented economy, the main authority, usually the central government, determines how a society addresses the three fundamental economic questions. In such a system, economic decisions are often intended to serve the public interest. Infrastructure and productive machinery may be publicly or privately owned, but the government decides how they are used. In command-oriented systems, the government also often sets the prices for all of these products and services, and individual economic choices are limited.

Cuba's economic system is an example of a command-oriented economy. There, the government controls the production and distribution of most food, beverages, and medicine in the country. The national government owns the telephone service provider and banking system, and it also controls access to Internet service providers.

The economy of the United States, although market-based, contains many command-oriented elements. For example, the country's local, state, and national governments all collect taxes for the purpose of building roads, bridges, schools, and other public goods. In addition,

Complete this activity to demonstrate your understanding of economic systems.

different levels of government in the United States enforce regulations designed to protect workers, consumers, and the environment.

Free Enterprise

How do market-based economies address the fundamental questions of economics?

The United States has a market-based, or free enterprise, economic system. In a market-based economy, interactions between self-interested consumers and producers determine how the society decides what, how, and for whom to produce goods and services.

In a market-based system, the decisions that businesses make are driven by a desire to make money, which is known as profit motive. Because of profit motive, businesses produce goods and services that are demanded by consumers in the marketplace, and they refrain from producing goods and services that they are unable to sell. In a market economy, the fundamental question of "what to produce" is driven by consumers. When consumers purchase vanilla ice cream instead of rocky road, for example, they are in effect "voting" for businesses to produce even more vanilla.

photo: Library of Congress

How does the free enterprise system promote innovations such as the assembly line?

Because of profit motive, businesses address the fundamental question of "how" to produce goods and services by attempting to find the most efficient and least costly production methods possible. Businesses constantly invest money to develop technologies that control production costs and increase profits.

Production innovations of the late 1800s and early 1900s, such as the assembly line, the combine, and the use of electricity in factories, were all the result of businesses seeking to make their production processes more efficient and less costly. As production becomes more and more efficient, as it did during industrialization in the United States, businesses are able to offer goods and services to more consumers.

Finally, market-based economies address the fundamental question of "who" by distributing goods and services to consumers who are willing and able to pay for them. Because individuals and businesses act out of self-interest, fewer consumers are willing to pay for goods and services as the prices increase. However, businesses want to sell at the highest possible price. When consumers and businesses come together in the marketplace to exchange goods and services, they determine which prices will satisfy both sides.

An important component of any market-based economic system is competition between businesses. Producers compete with one another to attract customers to purchase their products. As a result, competition motivates businesses to keep prices low and product quality high. It also encourages innovations in production. Businesses that find ways to efficiently produce goods will have an advantage over their competitors because they will be able to charge consumers less in the marketplace. Businesses that make inferior products or that produce goods inefficiently will be forced to improve production or leave the marketplace.

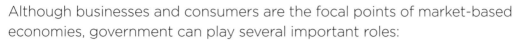
Governing a Free Enterprise Economy

What is the role of government in a market-based system?

Although businesses and consumers are the focal points of market-based economies, government can play several important roles:

- Government serves as a kind of "referee" in the marketplace to make sure that businesses and consumers honor their agreements with one another.

- Governments redistribute wealth. Sometimes, the market-based system distributes wealth in a manner that is not considered desirable by society as a whole. In these cases, the government uses taxation and spending to redistribute wealth from one segment of society to another.

- Governments attempt to correct market failures. In a market-based economy, there are times when the marketplace either contributes to, or is unable to prevent, undesirable outcomes. To prevent such situations, governments enact policies called *regulations*, or ground rules for businesses to follow, when producing and selling goods and services.

- Governments provide societies with public goods. There are some items, known as public goods, to which all citizens need access but that the marketplace cannot always provide. These public goods include roads, schools, and libraries. A key role of government in a market-based economy is to provide society with these public goods.

Roles the Government Can Play	
Role	**Examples**
Government ensures that businesses and consumers honor their agreements with one another.	• A housepainter who completes work for a contract, but goes unpaid, can take her customer to court • Homeowners can bring a company to court if they have a contract to do home improvements, for instance, and they never do • Union workers demanding an increase in minimum wage can take their company to court if negotiations are refused
Government can redistribute wealth.	• Low-income housing and assistance for the poor • Federal student loans for college tuition • Social Security payments to the retired and disabled
Government can attempt to correct market failures.	• Food product and workplace safety laws • Anti-pollution and environmental safety regulations • Assisting major companies that go into bankruptcy, such as banks and the automotive industry
Government can provide society with public goods.	• Police and fire departments • Construction of roads and utility lines • Public schools

In market-based economic systems, governments often play four different roles.

Throughout the nation's history, particularly since industrialization in the 1800s, Americans have debated the extent of the government's authority within each of these four roles. Some believe that government's role in the economy should be minimal. They reason that market-based economies work best when consumers are free to make as many of their own economic decisions as possible. The idea that government's role in the economy should be limited is known as *laissez-faire*, which in French means "leave it alone." Others argue that strong government regulation and oversight are necessary to ensure that all citizens are given a fair chance to succeed in a market-based economy.

During the late 1800s, as the United States continued to transform into an industrial nation, the philosophy of laissez-faire ruled the day. However, the United States also began to experience the consequences of industrialization. These consequences included a wider income gap between the rich and poor and deteriorating workplace conditions. Many Americans began to demand that government take a more prominent role in addressing the everyday problems that confronted the nation.

Creating the Corporate Model
How did the organization of business change in the 1800s?

The decades following the Civil War saw immense industrial growth in the United States. During this era, the railroads expanded into new territories, steel and petroleum production increased, and electrical power became more commonplace. The country became more interconnected by extending its transportation and communication networks. More Americans had access to innovative home appliances and technologies, such as the telephone and the radio. The U.S. population continued to grow in the cities. More immigrants entered the country, and the process of urbanization created difficult living conditions for those with little money. Class distinctions between the wealthy and the poor also became more pronounced, particularly between skilled and unskilled employees.

Industrial growth had additional impacts. The sweeping technological advances changed the way businesses were organized. It also led to the creation of a new class of business tycoons. In their climb to the top, these entrepreneurs profoundly changed the American economy and society. The methods of organizing businesses that these industrial giants used included corporations, trusts, and holding companies.

Corporations

In the early years of industrialization, most businesses were owned by just one or a few people. Owners invested their own money or took small loans to run their companies. They typically managed their businesses themselves or had a small administrative staff. Often, a family member or close friend served as a manager.

Over time, the technological advances of industrialization required that businesses invest more money in machines, buildings, and distribution methods than ever before. A successful business needed large factories filled with expensive machinery.

The increased need to raise huge amounts of cash to finance, or pay for, rapid improvements changed the way businesses were organized.

To raise the money they needed, businesses began to form corporations. A corporation is a company that is jointly owned by different people who purchase shares of stock, or ownership, in the business. By selling shares of stock and forming corporations, businesses raise large sums of money they can use for operations and growth. By purchasing shares of stock, individuals can benefit from the growth of companies.

They do not need to run or manage these companies on a daily basis. Stockholders are also freed from legal responsibility for the corporation's failures or wrongdoings. Finally, the owners of a corporation enjoy limited liability. This means that they are not responsible for the company's debts beyond what they invested. The first corporation, the Boston Manufacturing Company, was established in 1813. Industrialization contributed to the formation of many more corporate-based companies after the Civil War.

Trusts

In addition to forming corporations, large businesses took steps to attempt to free themselves from competition from other businesses in the same industry. By eliminating competition, firms could increase profits by raising prices without worrying about consumers choosing to purchase goods from other firms. The attempt by businesses to combine several different firms from the same industry is known as horizontal integration.

photo: Library of Congress

This political cartoon, inspired by Ida Tarbell's exposé of the insidious extent of the political and economic influence of Standard Oil, shows the company as a many-tentacled octopus winding around the steel, copper, and shipping industries, and around a state house, the Capitol, and reaching for the White House.

One prominent example of horizontal integration is called a trust. A trust is a combination of separately owned businesses controlled by a single person, known as a trustee. Technically, the trustee does not own controlling shares in the individual companies that have joined together; the members of the trust trade stock for trust certificates. Trusts were organized similarly to today's professional sports leagues. In professional sports, separately owned teams join together to create single leagues that are managed by commissioners. All of the companies in the trust agree to abide by similar guidelines.

Trusts were able to have complete control over entire industries without technically having a single owner. This enabled them to avoid the laws designed to prevent the formation of monopolies. In 1882, the first major trust was assembled when Standard Oil Company combined with several smaller oil producers and refineries.

Discovery EDUCATION | SOCIAL STUDIES TECHBOOK.

Were America's great industrial giants champions of free enterprise?

At the peak of its power, the Standard Oil Trust owned 14 different companies and was the majority shareholder in at least 12 more. This gave Standard Oil dominant control in the oil business. It controlled petroleum production, transportation, oil refinement, and the marketing of oil to consumers and business. The trust's dominance in the marketplace meant that it owned the pipelines, set the shipping rates, and decided the prices for oil. Consumers and smaller businesses had little influence over these prices and could hardly compete with Standard Oil. This trust held what is known as an oligopoly. In an oligopoly, a few businesses dominate the entire market. Oligopolies limit competition just as monopolies do.

Holding Companies

When lawmakers began writing laws to limit the power of trusts, business leaders organized a different type of combination known as a holding company. A holding company is a parent corporation that owns stock or assets in other companies. A holding company does not conduct any business activities on its own, such as producing and selling goods and services. Its purpose is simply to own substantial parts of other companies through buying and selling shares of stock. One early example of a holding company is the Cities Service Company. American entrepreneur Henry Doherty formed this holding company in 1910. Cities Service Company owned oil, electricity, and natural gas companies. This company stood the test of time. In 1965, Cities Service Company became CITGO. Another major holding company, General Motors, was founded in 1908. At the time, General Motors owned only one automobile manufacturing company. Over the next few decades, it purchased more than 20 others.

Consequences of Monopolies

What were the consequences of how corporations, trusts, and holding companies were organized?

The emergence of corporations, trusts, and holding companies helped a handful of entrepreneurs, or risk-taking business creators, to grow powerful and earn unprecedented wealth. Some of these industrialists became wealthy by leading businesses that produced and sold actual goods. However, another source of income for entrepreneurs was the ownership and trade of stocks in public corporations. Jay Gould, for instance, began buying railroad bonds in the 1850s and soon became a wealthy stockbroker in New York City. Through stock manipulation, he and his partners gained control of several railroad lines. By 1890, Gould owned more than 13,000 miles of railroad.

Instead of calling it a "Golden Age," Mark Twain referred to this time period, in which large businesses began dominating American society, as the "Gilded Age." Twain used the term *gilded* to criticize what he and many others saw as corruption and greed that was beneath the surface of immense economic growth and innovation.

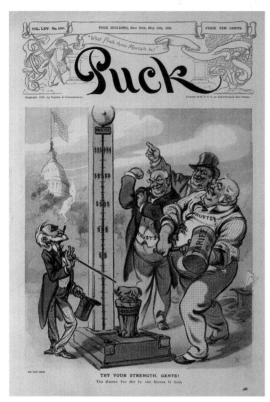

photo: Library of Congress

How does the representation of trusts in this cartoon reflect the American consumer's opinion of them?

Critics of the changes that came about during the Gilded Age were concerned that business combinations undermined competition. Critics believed that this was a threat to the country's free-market economy. They argued that while eliminating competition might have been beneficial to large businesses, it was harmful to ordinary consumers and workers. In the absence of a competitive marketplace, businesses had little incentive to offer their customers high-quality goods or affordable prices. They also argued that businesses had little reason to offer their workers competitive wages or safe and healthy working conditions.

Despite many Americans' concerns about the power wielded by large new business structures and the rise of millionaires during the Gilded Age, the federal government was initially reluctant to pass and enforce regulations to limit the power of large business combinations. While many Americans struggled to make ends meet, a few businessmen earned unprecedented wealth.

Barons and Philanthropists: Vanderbilt and Rockefeller

How did Cornelius Vanderbilt and John D. Rockefeller rise to prominence?

Cornelius Vanderbilt

Cornelius Vanderbilt built most of his fortune in shipping and railroads. Born into a poor Dutch family in New York in 1794, Vanderbilt worked on the Staten Island Ferry service as a young man. With $100, he bought a boat and began a small ferry business of his own. Vanderbilt's ferry service became known for its low prices, and his business grew. He eventually bought more boats and then sold them all to purchase steamships.

By the 1840s, Vanderbilt had more than 100 steamships and had earned the nickname of "robber baron" because his critics claimed he stole business from competitors by offering cheaper prices and using unfair business practices to control transportation. In the 1860s, Vanderbilt also began investing in railroad lines. By consistently offering lower prices than competitors, Vanderbilt reportedly made nearly $25 million in his first five years in the railroad business. In 1869, he established a railroad monopoly in the Northeast by consolidating the Hudson River Railroad and New York Central Railroad.

Discovery | SOCIAL STUDIES
EDUCATION | **TECHBOOK**

Were America's great industrial giants champions of free enterprise?

Although many considered his cost-slashing methods to be ruthless, the result of Vanderbilt's efforts was an efficient, well-constructed, and well-run railway system that served much of the East. In New York City, Vanderbilt arranged the construction of the Grand Central Terminal, which gave jobs to thousands of unemployed workers after an economic crisis known as the Panic of 1873. Although Vanderbilt was not initially known for donating his wealth to charitable causes, the fortune he earned financed the establishment of Vanderbilt University in Nashville, Tennessee.

John D. Rockefeller

John D. Rockefeller was another industrial leader of the 1800s. A native New Yorker, Rockefeller moved to Cleveland with his family when he was in high school. After finishing school, he got a job as a bookkeeper. Rockefeller always excelled in math and business. In 1859, he formed his first partnership by brokering grain, meat, and agricultural goods. The business was very profitable, and Rockefeller used his earnings to invest in a small oil refining company in 1863. Oil refining is the process of turning crude oil, which is extracted from the ground as petroleum, into useful products such as gasoline and heating oil.

photo: Library of Congress

John Davis Rockefeller (1839–1937) transformed the oil industry by organizing it into a monopoly.

Two years later, Rockefeller moved into the oil business. He recognized the potential profits due to technological improvements in the oil refinement process. In 1870, he organized the Standard Oil Company. By the next decade, Rockefeller was worth approximately $18 million. By the mid-1890s, Rockefeller's companies controlled almost all of the oil refining in the United States.

John D. Rockefeller's control over the marketplace helped make gasoline affordable for many Americans, which helped support the coming age of the automobile. Rockefeller also used a substantial portion of his wealth for the overall benefit of society. He contributed great amounts of money to establish what became Spelman College, the Rockefeller University, and the University of Chicago. He also founded the General Education Board in 1903, which later became the Rockefeller Foundation, to help improve high schools in the South. His donations created a sanitary commission that was responsible for nearly eradicating hookworm in 11 Southern states. Throughout his life, Rockefeller's overall charitable donations amounted to nearly $525 million.

Barons and Philanthropists: Carnegie and Morgan

How did Andrew Carnegie and J. P. Morgan rise to prominence?

Andrew Carnegie

photo: Library of Congress

Andrew Carnegie (center, front row) donated money to the Tuskegee Institute to help educate African Americans.

Born in 1835, Andrew Carnegie was a poor Scottish immigrant who came to the United States when he was 13 years old. Carnegie's father, a handloom weaver, lost work after the invention of the power loom. The family made the journey to the United States in search of better economic opportunities. As a young man, Carnegie was hired as a personal assistant to a Pennsylvania Railroad superintendent. He worked his way up the ladder and eventually became a superintendent himself.

When the Civil War ended, Carnegie quit his job at Pennsylvania Railroad and started a business called Keystone Bridge Company, which built steel and wrought iron bridges for railways and roads. He made that business extremely successful. In 1873, Carnegie organized the first of his steel manufacturing companies. He immersed himself in learning all the details of steel production. He cut time and labor from processes wherever he could, even when it resulted in increased worker injuries or deaths.

Some Americans thought Carnegie was a controversial business tycoon, or a robber baron. Influential businesspeople were sometimes called "robber barons" because they grew successful by paying low wages, taking advantage of gaps in the laws, and sometimes ignoring the laws completely. As an industry leader, Carnegie was famous for breaking strikes and labor unions, lowering wages and labor costs, and demanding 12-hour workdays. One employee described how the men "work twelve hours, and sleep and eat out ten more. You can see a man don't have time for anything else. You can't see your friends or do anything but work."

However, the industrialists of the 1800s were also philanthropists, or wealthy people who donate to charities for the overall good of society. Carnegie gave more than $350 million to charity. His money built public libraries and funded scientific research and college scholarships. Carnegie also founded an institution to provide technical training to the working-class youth in Pittsburgh. Carnegie's training institute later became Carnegie Mellon University. The parents of many of these students worked in the factories Carnegie owned.

Discovery SOCIAL STUDIES
EDUCATION TECHBOOK

Were America's great industrial giants champions of free enterprise?

In addition to spending huge sums as a philanthropist, Carnegie also invested money to modernize his industry. He replaced old equipment with the newest and most efficient products available. As a business owner, Carnegie used vertical integration to organize his steel company. Vertical integration is an organization system in which a company controls all stages of a good's production. Carnegie's corporation controlled iron ore deposits, coal mines, ship fleets to transport resources, and factories to manufacture the finished products. By 1901, the Carnegie Steel Company was worth more than $400 million. By the time Carnegie retired in that same year, he was the world's wealthiest person.

J. P. Morgan

J. P. (John Pierpont) Morgan bought Carnegie's steel company in 1901. He also founded one of the world's leading financial companies. J. P. Morgan made his money by investing in the railroads and the steel industry. Born in Connecticut in 1873, Morgan was the son of a successful German financier. Morgan himself completed college and started his career in an investment company in New York City. In 1895, he took over his father's firm and renamed it J. P. Morgan & Company.

Explore this interactive and take a position on the impact of industrialists during the Gilded Age.

Morgan's innovative corporate restructuring and banking practices made it possible to turn the company's debts into profits. Morgan became a member of the boards of directors of several railroad companies, gaining influence over their business decisions. After the Panic of 1893, the railroad companies needed his investments to restore financial stability. He opposed the disorderly competition between many railways in the East, so he gained control of them and reorganized them by purchasing large quantities of stock. By 1902, he was one of the world's most powerful railroad tycoons, owning about 5,000 miles of U.S. railroad lines.

Morgan was also a great collector of important works of art and books. Morgan's philanthropy included donating much of the artwork from his collection to New York's Metropolitan Museum of Art. Morgan's contributions to the museum made it one of the leading art collections in the world. In 1924, the building that housed his book collection became a public library.

In spite of this philanthropy, J. P. Morgan and his banking firm were controversial. For many, Morgan wielded too much control over the country's electric, steel, and railroad industries. After the crisis known as the Panic of 1907, Morgan's company stepped in to assist the nation's failing banking system. The bank acquisitions that Morgan made during this crisis gave him major control over the nation's leading financial institutions. Although he was distrusted by many government officials, reformers, and some ordinary citizens, Morgan remained a symbol of American laissez-faire economics until he died in 1913.

Supporting a Hands-Off Approach

How did Americans justify their support of a laissez-faire government?

Although the upper class was growing in the late 1800s, it was still small in comparison to the total population. Some 18 million immigrants, most of them poor, came to the United States between 1880 and 1910. They worked long hours and often lived in poverty, and there were few laws regulating living and working conditions in the United States.

Many industrialists argued against government interference in the economy in support of a laissez-faire approach. They said that social and economic change should occur naturally. They argued that a free-enterprise economy is best supported when consumers and producers can engage in whatever business they want, with whomever they want, without any restriction or controls. However, it was not only the powerful robber barons who kept the government from interfering. Many Americans of all classes believed in the predominant ideas of the day—individualism and laissez-faire economics—which contributed to resistance to government intervention in business issues. Several popular concepts, based on both science and religion, helped people justify these beliefs. These included the cultural influence of author Horatio Alger, Social Darwinism, and the Gospel of Wealth.

Individualism

The predominant philosophy of this time emphasized individualism, or the idea that each person was responsible for his or her own successes or failures in business and in life. People's hard work would allow them to improve their circumstances in life. This idea was reinforced and made popular through stories at the time. During the mid-1800s, American author Horatio Alger (1832–1899) wrote books promoting the "American Dream." His dime novels centered on poor street boys living in an urban city. In each book, the main character overcame great hardship to become extremely wealthy and successful. Horatio Alger's stories promoted the idea that a combination of hard work and determination was the true secret to success. Alger sold more than 20 million copies of his novels. Along with his novels, Alger helped sell and popularize the idea that anyone could become successful in America without the help of the government.

Social Darwinism and Eugenics

Social Darwinism was a social theory based on naturalist Charles Darwin's biological theory of natural selection. In his scientific studies, Darwin noted that some plant and animal species were better adapted to their environments than others. Those that were better adapted were the most likely to survive, reproduce, and perpetuate themselves. Herbert Spencer, a British scientist, called Darwinian evolution in the human population "survival of the fittest."

Discovery | SOCIAL STUDIES | **TECHBOOK**

Were America's great industrial giants champions of free enterprise?

Social Darwinists believed that the people with the most skills, intelligence, and talents would rise to the top and succeed. Those without these traits would not. For Social Darwinists, financial success was a sign of superiority. Social Darwinists argued that over time, the human species would improve and become more talented, and the weaker members of society would fail to thrive and reproduce. Any government interference would ruin this scientific evolutionary process.

Some used the theory of Social Darwinism to justify their belief in Anglo-Saxon racial superiority. Social Darwinists argued that human history was a struggle between races, and that natural selection created the wealth and power of Americans of northern or western European heritage. A related belief called eugenics argued that a society could improve its population with selective breeding. Eugenics supporters wanted to remove from the population persons who were thought to be inferior. This included immigrants from southern Europe and Asia, but also extended to the poor, mentally ill, and many people with disabilities. Beginning in the 1890s, states such as Connecticut and Indiana passed laws designed to prevent some citizens from marrying and having children. Eugenics advocates also supported laws that limited immigration from targeted regions of the world. Colleges and universities established admissions quotas limiting the enrollment of Jews and other minorities.

Gospel of Wealth

Some powerful Americans did not agree with Social Darwinism. Andrew Carnegie agreed with the notion that certain people were born with more talents or skills. He believed that God chose who got these traits and thus decided who would be successful. Carnegie also believed successful, wealthy people had a moral duty to help those less fortunate than themselves. He expressed these ideas in an 1889 essay "The Gospel of Wealth." Carnegie's philanthropy worked against the ideas of Horatio Alger's individualism and survival of the fittest in Social Darwinism. It promoted a moral obligation to improve the standard of living for everyone in society.

photo: Library of Congress

How does this book cover demonstrate the independence and self-reliance of American individualism?

The Federal Government Responds

What were some early attempts to address monopolistic business practices?

As big business gained power, cases involving economic regulation and economic freedoms came before the Supreme Court. In decisions made during the late 1800s and early 1900s, the Supreme Court supported the government's traditional laissez-faire approach to the economy, posing a barrier to the regulation of big businesses. Between 1902 and 1917, the Supreme Court struck down 10 federal laws that Congress had passed to regulate business and increase fair competition. These rulings endorsed the idea that dealings between private businesses and employees were outside the scope of government powers.

In 1886, the federal courts took their protections of big business even further. In deciding the case *Santa Clara County v. Southern Pacific Railroad Company*, the Supreme Court determined that corporations are legal people and have the same rights as actual living people. As a result, many state regulations of corporations were tested in federal courts to verify whether they violated the corporation's constitutional rights. Because corporations had the same rights to property, contracts, and other freedoms, they could work around the laws to conduct their business. For instance, because the Fourth Amendment gave the right to freedom from random searches, it became difficult to inspect corporate businesses and uphold health and safety laws.

photo: Library of Congress

The Interstate Commerce Commission, 1905.

Interstate Commerce Commission (ICC)

The federal government took a laissez-faire approach to the economy through most of the 1800s. However, as politicians and the public watched corporate power grow, eventually Congress decided to take legislative action. Congress's first strike at the trusts took aim at the railroads. In the decades after the Civil War, the railroad industry had grown immensely. Railroads were privately owned and completely unregulated. Powerful railroad barons had bought up smaller railroads and created monopolies. These companies used their market control to charge extremely high prices.

In particular, railroads started charging high rates for shipping agricultural products to cities. Farmers needed the railroads to transport their grain. The only alternative to rail transportation was horse and cart, but horses were too slow. The food would spoil in transit. Farmers in the Midwest came together to protest the high costs and demand something be done.

Discovery SOCIAL STUDIES
EDUCATION **TECHBOOK**

Were America's great industrial giants champions of free enterprise?

In response, Congress passed its first serious attempt to regulate industry in 1887. Congress used its constitutional authority "to regulate commerce . . . among the several states" and passed the Interstate Commerce Act. The Interstate Commerce Act banned numerous practices used by the railroads. These included making private and secret agreements on special rates and charging higher rates for short trips. The law also established the Interstate Commerce Commission, or ICC. The ICC was a five-member enforcement board that monitored prices and competition within the railroad industry. The law also required that railroad companies submit reports documenting their business.

Although the Interstate Commerce Act was a step in the direction of regulation, it did not prove to be effective in the long run. The ICC had difficulty determining fair rates for all railroad travel. It also struggled to remain neutral in making its decisions. The law applied only to railroads that crossed state lines. Travel within a state remained unhindered by regulations.

Sherman Antitrust Act

Three years later, Congress attempted to control the corporate trusts. In 1890, the Sherman Antitrust Act prohibited many business practices that resulted in the creation of monopolies. Under the Sherman Antitrust Act, one corporation would not be able to control prices or regulate quantity in a particular industry.

The language of the Sherman Antitrust Act may seem powerful and simple. In practice, the law was ineffective. First, because of the influence of business leaders, the federal government rarely used the law to break up business combinations. Even when the law was put before the court, federal court decisions weakened its authority. For example, in 1895, a Supreme Court decision's narrow interpretation of the words trade and commerce reduced the law's effectiveness. The case involved the American Sugar Refining Company, which controlled 98 percent of the country's sugar manufacturing. The Supreme Court ruled that the company's monopoly did not violate the Sherman Act because manufacturing was not "trade" and, therefore, it was not covered by the law.

Despite Congress's apparent intent to restrict monopolies, one significant effect of the Sherman Antitrust Act was to break up trade unions. Trade unions are organizations of workers in the same trade, such as plumbers or steelworkers. Workers formed trade unions to gain power in labor negotiations with their employers, which often were trusts. In 1893, for example, a federal court used the Sherman Act to rule that a trade union of striking dockworkers in New Orleans was an illegal business organization. Because the dockworkers had prevented the boarding and loading of ships, the court reasoned that the trade union had illegally restrained interstate and foreign commerce.

Although early regulatory measures such as the Sherman Act were ineffective, they marked the beginnings of a change in the U.S. government's laissez-faire policy.

SOCIAL STUDIES
TECHBOOK

The Business of Politics

How did American politics change after Reconstruction?

Corruption

Before the Civil War, the politics of the nation were divided by region: North versus South. Slavery was a dominant issue. Northerners were concerned with transportation infrastructure, while Southerners wanted to repeal high tariffs, or taxes on imported goods. After Reconstruction, however, American politics were dominated by industrialization, as well as corruption.

Political corruption resulted from the attempts of big businesses to influence government policy making. For instance, in the late 1800s, there was a major attempt to cut back on government spending to resolve the post–Civil War debts. Government officials, particularly in the South, experienced salary cuts. At the same time, industrialists bribed politicians for government favors. John D. Rockefeller gave one senator more than $44,000. At least two state treasurers were accused of stealing hundreds of thousands of dollars from state reserves.

For decades, politicians had used the spoils system as a way to raise campaign money. In exchange for contributions, they would give their loyal patrons political jobs after their election. The Pendleton Civil Service Reform Act (1883) had started to reform this system. However, in the 1890s, only around 10 percent of the 132,000 civilian government jobs were actually controlled by the federal government. The rest were in the hands of the politicians and political parties. Payoffs and bribery were still common practice.

photo: Library of Congress

What does this political cartoon suggest about the relationship between legislatures, big business, and the common people?

Discovery EDUCATION | SOCIAL STUDIES TECHBOOK.

Were America's great industrial giants champions of free enterprise?

Tariffs Again

Throughout the 1800s, the federal government collected tariffs, which are taxes placed specifically on imported goods. Tariffs supported trade between the North and the South and gave American manufacturers a competitive advantage. Tariffs made foreign goods more expensive, making consumers more likely to buy products that were manufactured in the United States. High protective tariffs also helped support industrialization in the United States because the tariffs decreased competition between domestic and imported goods. This prompted companies to invest more money in building factories and hiring workers in the United States. During the Civil War, protective tariffs had climbed higher as a way to help pay for the war. After the Civil War, Northern Republicans held power. They kept a high protective tariff in place to support the big businesses that were growing in the Northeast.

The tariff issue became a major issue in the 1888 presidential campaign. Running for reelection, President Grover Cleveland denounced the high tariffs. He said they created an inefficient economy and protected only the wealthy. Republican candidate Benjamin Harrison defended the protectionist measures. He backed his party's argument that the tariffs were good for industrialization by increasing wages and protecting workers against low-wage competition from other nations.

After Harrison won, his administration fulfilled its promise to protect big business. In 1890, Congress passed the McKinley Tariff, the highest tariff the nation had ever implemented. The tariff bill was sponsored in Congress by Representative William McKinley of Ohio, who would go on to be elected president in 1896. Although this legislation somewhat increased revenue to the federal government and helped the development of domestic markets, the 1890 tariff also contributed to high prices for consumers. This sparked widespread dissatisfaction among Americans. As a result, Grover Cleveland defeated Harrison in the 1892 presidential election, and Democrats introduced legislation to lower tariffs across the board.

Consider the Essential Question:

Were America's great industrial giants champions of free enterprise?

Go online to complete the Social Studies Explanation.

Check for Understanding:

How did industrialization contribute to political corruption during the Gilded Age?

12.2 Labor and Populism

LESSON OVERVIEW

Introduction

In this concept, you will investigate the economic and social problems industrialization created and evaluate how the early labor and farmers' movements responded to these problems.

Essential Question

How were the early labor and farmers' movements alike? How were they different?

Lesson Objectives

By the end of this lesson, you should be able to:

- Explain the impact of industrialization and laissez-faire policies on American workers.

- Evaluate the early labor movement in addressing economic and social problems created by industrialization.

- Explain the impact of industrialization and laissez-faire policies on American farmers.

- Evaluate the effectiveness of the Populist Party and other political movements in addressing economic and social problems created by industrialization.

Key Vocabulary

Which terms do you already know?

- [ ] American Federation of Labor
- [ ] collective bargaining
- [ ] deflation
- [ ] Eugene Debs
- [ ] Farmers' Alliance
- [ ] gold standard
- [ ] Haymarket Riot
- [ ] Homestead Strike
- [ ] inflation
- [ ] International Workers of the World
- [ ] Knights of Labor
- [ ] labor union
- [ ] laissez-faire
- [ ] Populist Party
- [ ] Pullman Strike
- [ ] Samuel Gompers
- [ ] socialism
- [ ] strike
- [ ] The Grange
- [ ] William Jennings Bryan

Discovery SOCIAL STUDIES
EDUCATION TECHBOOK

How were the early labor and farmers' movements alike?
How were they different?

ENGAGE

Did farmers and miners have common interests? Visit Engage to learn more.

| **Essential Question** |
| How were the early labor and farmers' movements alike? How were they different? |

EXPLORE

An Industrialized America

How did industrialization affect employees of U.S. businesses?

As a result of industrial growth in the United States, the American workplace in urban areas became increasingly impersonal. With the improvements in production methods, small shops were replaced by large factories equipped with machines. Many factory jobs required little or no training. Artisans, who trained for many years at their craft and formed personal relationships with apprentices and coworkers, were replaced by unskilled workers. Many of these workers were immigrants. Small business became big business, and American companies began to produce goods and materials in much larger quantities and a much greater pace than in the past. Over time, the value of goods manufactured in the United States increased from about $3 billion in 1896 to around $13 billion in 1910.

Despite the dramatic rise in production, factory workers did not receive much of the profit, and many working-class families lived in poverty. Immigration to cities and migration away from rural areas meant that competition for factory jobs was high. This had the effect of keeping wages low. In fact, most unskilled workers were interchangeable. A steel worker in Pittsburgh did the same job with the same equipment as his counterpart in Cleveland or Buffalo or anywhere else.

photo: Library of Congress

Immigrant workers gather in the courtyard of a New York City tenement.

Although the U.S. economy was expanding in general, several economic downturns occurred around the late 1800s and early 1900s. During these times, unskilled workers were hit the hardest, and wage cuts and high unemployment rates were common.

Sharp Class Distinctions

The sharp class distinctions between the wealthy and the poor that developed during the Gilded Age, as a result of industrialization, also shaped the workplace. During the late 1800s, big businesses gradually took over smaller companies. The owners of large businesses were stockholders who often lived far away. They did not develop personal relationships with their employees. As companies began to have hundreds or thousands of employees in dozens of locations, it became less likely for owners to know anything about their employees at all, even their names.

With little government interference, large corporations' laissez-faire policies allowed them to operate freely with little responsibility for the employees' well-being. Stockholders invested in public companies, hoping they would earn profits. To increase their business profits, the stockholders often demanded that companies cut costs. These demands often contributed to low wages, layoffs of many unskilled workers, and avoiding expensive safety measures. In short, labor was viewed more and more in economic terms—as a commodity rather than as actual people performing work.

Individualism

The prevailing philosophy of the day emphasized individualism, which reinforced the idea that each worker was completely responsible for his or her own success or failure. People's hard work would allow them to improve their circumstances in life. The individual worker should be allowed to succeed or fail without any outside interference or help from the government. This idea was reinforced and made popular through stories at the time. Horatio Alger (1832–1899) wrote a series of fiction books that popularized the rags-to-riches story of the self-made individual. In books such as *Ragged Dick, Luck and Pluck,* and *Tattered Tom*, Alger portrayed underprivileged youths who win fame and wealth through hard work, diligence, and perseverance.

photo: Library of Congress

The children of immigrants also worked to support their families as unskilled laborers, picking vegetables in the fields.

Despite the idea that each person should be able to succeed with enough hard work, many workers were powerless to change their individual situation under the new authority of big businesses. To increase their effectiveness, groups of workers began to unite and form labor unions. Together, they negotiated with their employers to improve wages and work hours through a method known as collective bargaining.

Explore this interactive to learn more about how industrialization affected different groups of Americans.

However, employers and some Americans objected to the idea of collective bargaining by labor unions. Many believed organized labor threatened popular ideas about individualism and free enterprise. Some saw labor unions as un-American. Those who objected to collective bargaining believed that individual workers should be responsible for advancing their own careers through hard work. They also felt that workers' wages should be established by the free market and not through collective bargaining between workers and their employers. As a result, the American public did not always sympathize with workers during labor confrontations.

The Plight of the Working Class

What was life in the United States like for working-class families?

Free to Be Poor

In 1900, the average U.S. worker earned $438 a year—not enough to support a family. Women and children also worked to support their families but were paid less to perform the same or similar duties as adult men. Urban industrial laborers worked six days a week with no vacations, holidays, or pay for sick days. There were no health plans, retirement plans, or benefits of any kind. For example, the working class did not receive medical or injury benefits, and pregnant workers were often fired. Families could not afford to save money for emergencies. These conditions were widespread. Looking for a new job would not necessarily solve a working family's problem.

Worker Health and Safety

Before 1900, the U.S. government did not regulate working conditions, and because there was so much competition for unskilled jobs from the large supply of available workers, companies had little incentive to take better care of their employees. The working conditions in mines, factories, and sweatshops were difficult and dangerous. In these places of business, a workday could last anywhere from 10 to 12 hours, and the pace of work was fast. Because the government did not assess whether or not machines operated safely, factory machinery sometimes posed physical dangers, such as lost fingers and limbs. Young girls faced the danger of getting their hair caught in spinning machines. In the mines, workers faced the threat of cave-ins and explosions, as well as health complications from breathing in toxic dust all day. During the early 1900s, American workers faced a high possibility of dying on the job. For instance, the National Safety Council estimated that between 18,000 and 21,000 workers died from work-related injuries in 1912 alone.

Child Labor

In the 1880s, most of the states with school attendance laws did not require children to attend school after the age of 14. Many states had policies to allow children who worked to quit school earlier. Economic circumstances kept many poor children from attending school, and instead, they worked to support their families. Factory companies hired children to work in unskilled jobs because their small hands could easily handle miniature tools and parts, and the companies could pay them lower wages than adults. The children who did not work in factories sold newspapers or shined shoes on street corners. Some children worked as messengers or street peddlers. Between 1890 and 1910, the number of working children in the United States jumped from 1.5 million to 2 million. Children under 16 years of age might work 12 or more hours per day for a dollar. Most parents of these working boys and girls required them to hand over all or almost all of their earnings.

ROLL OF HONOR.

photo: Library of Congress

Young boys who sold newspapers were known as newsboys and wore a similar style of hat.

Younger children who did not work for wages also contributed to their family's survival. Children begged on the streets, sometimes stealing food for their starving families. Other children scavenged along the railroad tracks for coal that had fallen from the locomotives. Their families would use the coal to heat their stoves for cooking and for heat during the winter.

Children also faced malnutrition and poor health. Quality food or health care was often inaccessible and expensive. For the urban poor population, living and working in the cities decreased their overall quality of life.

Company Towns

What were company towns?

The American worker's economic dependence on their employer was particularly apparent in company towns. Company towns were owned and operated by a single business. These towns typically posed significant challenges for workers and their families. For example, the town of Pullman, Illinois, was founded by the owner of Pullman Palace Car Company, George Pullman. Pullman located his factory near transportation where land was cheap. The Pullman Company owned the land and all of the property in the town. There was no local government except the town manager who was a Pullman employee. The town manager decided which stores were permitted to open. The library stocked books that the town manager approved.

Discovery | SOCIAL STUDIES
EDUCATION | **TECHBOOK**

How were the early labor and farmers' movements alike?
How were they different?

There was even a live theater that produced plays approved by the town manager. By the beginning of the 1900s, company towns such as Pullman were becoming more and more common, particularly in the mining industry.

Because the company owned all the stores, homes, and businesses in these towns, they could control the prices of the goods workers would need and the rent for worker housing. Workers often had to purchase items on credit at the company store because their wages were not high enough to cover the price of basic survival. In company towns such as Pullman, rent was high compared with other locations in Illinois. For example, after paying the groceries and utilities, workers had to pay about $29 to rent

photo: Denver Public Library

Sometimes, company towns were built near coal mining mountains, such as this town for the Rocky Mountain Fuel Company in Colorado.

a Pullman cottage. The same dwelling in Chicago cost about $18 to $20 to rent. Hiring preference was given to workers who actually lived in Pullman, so most workers paid the higher rent costs to have a job.

As a result of the high prices in company towns, workers often ended up owing money for their rent or for goods purchased on credit. They had to continue to work to attempt to pay their debts, but each month, their debts grew. The monthly expenses and accumulated debt increased the workers' dependence on their employers, placing them in a position with very few alternatives to escape the harsh conditions. Workers endured these conditions because they needed to earn a living and support their families.

The Labor Movement

How did workers respond to difficult conditions?

Through the late 1800s, difficult living and working conditions caused many workers in several different industries to question individualism. They banded together to demand better working conditions and economic security, including higher pay, better hours, and safer conditions. They often used confrontational tactics such as organizing strikes. A strike takes place when a group of laborers stops all work to force an employer to comply with demands for improvements. Between 1881 and 1905, labor strikes increased in frequency. Nearly 37,000 labor strikes took place during this period, involving seven million workers.

In response to poor conditions, workers also began to join labor unions in greater numbers. Although unions had started in the early part of the 1800s, some organizations, such as the National Trades' Union, faced declining membership after the financial depression of 1837. Toward the latter part of the century, however, many workers returned to these organizations in order to negotiate new labor policies with large corporations.

Early labor unions were craft unions, also known as trade unions. These organizations focused on improving working conditions for skilled workers from a single craft or occupation. Specialized iron and steel workers, skilled meatpacking industry workers, and garment workers formed their own craft unions. Because craft unions did not include unskilled workers, who were commonly immigrants and women, their membership was often composed only of white men.

The Great Railroad Strike

In July 1877, railroad workers across the country took part in a major strike that would significantly impact the labor movement. They were protesting the cutting of wages and demanded increased responsibility from the railroad companies for work-related injuries. Although the Great Railroad Strike began in West Virginia, it quickly spread to nine other states, including Maryland, Pennsylvania, Illinois, and Missouri. Strikes occurred in major industrial cities, including Baltimore and Chicago, as well as Pittsburgh and Reading in Pennsylvania. The angry protests lasted throughout the month of July and often became violent.

photo: Library of Congress

Scene from the great railway strike, East St. Louis, Illinois, 1886.

The purpose of the strikes was to halt commerce in the country by preventing goods from moving along the railroads. Losing so much profit, the railroad owners would be forced to listen to the workers' grievances.

Governors brought in state militias to end the strikes, but when the soldiers refused to force the strikers back to work, federal troops were brought in. By the end of the strike, approximately 100 people across the country were dead.

Although the strike lasted only a few weeks, union organizers had a renewed sense of power against big businesses. The strikes had shown the ability of workers to unite and challenge accepted business practices. The disruption and violence associated with the strikes prompted politicians and business leaders to enact policies to prevent widespread chaos from reoccurring. New state militia units were formed, and many cities constructed National Guard armories in case a violent strike would occur. The Great Railroad Strike demonstrated the power of unified labor, but it also showed that big business and the government would use force to maintain business as usual.

How were the early labor and farmers' movements alike?
How were they different?

National Labor Organizations

How did the national labor movement make progress for workers?

While groups of workers sometimes had different goals and preferred different strategies, as the workers became more active in demanding better conditions, it became clear that there were some changes that would benefit most workers. As a result, the labor movement that began during the early formation of trade unions gradually transformed into a national labor movement. Two large-scale assemblies of workers led the fight for better working conditions: the Knights of Labor and the American Federation of Labor (AFL). While both of these groups represented the interests of working people, each had its own set of goals and its own preferred strategies for achieving those goals.

Knights of Labor

The Knights of Labor was founded in 1869 in Philadelphia, Pennsylvania, as a small organization of local tailors. Unlike a craft union, the Knights of Labor welcomed workers of any occupation, skilled and unskilled, including machinists, cutters, shopkeepers, and farmers. At its height in the mid-1880s, the group had more than 700,000 members across the nation. This was in part due to the leadership of Terence Powderly. A lawyer from Scranton, Pennsylvania, Powderly was elected to chair the Knights of Labor in 1879. Under Powderly's leadership, the Knights developed its goal of a "cooperative commonwealth" of workers from all industries and skills. The organization sought to include everyone in the development of its goals, regardless of gender, race, job skills, or social status.

The Knights of Labor's causes included an eight-hour workday, safer work conditions, payment for work injuries, and an end to child labor. To achieve these goals, the union's leadership emphasized reform, cooperation, and compromise with company leaders, rather than strikes and boycotts. The Knights wanted industrial workshops and stores to be collectively owned by members of the union, meaning that rather than profits being paid to shareholders, they would be divided among the workers. To unite workers across the nation, the Knights of Labor held the first Labor Day celebration in 1882.

Many goals of the Knights of Labor were ambitious and considered by some to be unrealistic. Powderly wanted to present a united front of laborers demanding extensive reforms. However, dissent among members about the organization's goals and priorities reduced the size and influence of the organization across the nation. Skilled and unskilled workers, for instance, had different needs and wants. Similarly, the tensions among ethnic groups of immigrants and nativists proved too difficult to overcome.

However, the organization met with some success, such as leading a national strike against Jay Gould's railroad system. This strike resulted in an agreement that promised striking workers would be rehired, paid their previous wages, would receive notification of pay reductions, and would be compensated for overtime.

Despite some initial triumphs, membership in the Knights of Labor declined rapidly after several people were killed during a violent confrontation known as the Haymarket Riot. The Knights of Labor was gradually replaced by a collection of trade unions for skilled workers known as the American Federation of Labor.

American Federation of Labor

The American Federation of Labor (AFL) was established in 1886 with Samuel Gompers as president. This group was a collection of trade unions. Gompers did not want to strive for major societal reforms as the Knights of Labor had. Gompers's disagreement with the Knights' approach and goals was so strong that he refused to join an alliance with them. Instead of supporting national societal change, Gompers wanted unions to focus on day-to-day problems in their specific industries, which he called "bread-and-butter" issues.

photo: Library of Congress

The Knights of Labor accepted members from among the working women in America.

The AFL expected each trade union to come to its own agreements about work hours, wages, and ways to handle complaints between workers and bosses. These individual groups would then stand up in support of one another in making demands. For instance, if the electricians needed to strike, the plumbers, carpenters, and others also would strike. The AFL was successful because it pushed for reforms that specific unions demanded rather than broad national change. Despite this concentrated focus, the AFL also had success on the national level through the Clayton Antitrust Act in 1914, which allowed union activities against practices that harmed consumers, such as trusts and monopolies.

Because the AFL leaders believed that skilled workers had more power to cause change, the AFL excluded from its membership all unskilled workers. Many of these workers were European immigrants or African Americans. These populations provided a steady stream of unskilled workers, and, in response, racism and nativism prevented unity among all workers in many cases. Despite these barriers, the AFL was the leading national labor organization until the late 1920s and the Great Depression.

Discovery | SOCIAL STUDIES
EDUCATION | **TECHBOOK**

How were the early labor and farmers' movements alike?
How were they different?

Backlash Against Labor
How did incidents of violence affect the labor movement?

The Haymarket Riot

Beginning on May 1, 1886, members of several local Knights of Labor branches went on strike in Chicago, demanding an eight-hour workday for all. Approximately, 80,000 workers marched together peacefully in downtown Chicago, carrying their union banners. However, as the strike continued on May 3, violent confrontations between workers and the police occurred, leaving one person dead and several injured. The next day, between two and three thousand workers met at Chicago's Haymarket Square to protest the violence and to continue the call for a shorter workday. Initially, the gathering was peaceful. After most demonstrators had already left, some 200 police officers moved in to make sure the crowd dispersed. At that point, an unknown person threw a bomb. The police responded with gunfire. At least seven police officers and four laborers died, and there were more than 100 injuries.

Although it was not clear who had thrown the bomb, the media, business leaders, and the government all blamed the protesters. Today, the event is referred to as the Haymarket Riot, the Haymarket Affair, the Haymarket Incident, or the Haymarket Massacre, depending on one's perspective. Because authorities and most news sources blamed the Knights of Labor, the event led to a backlash against organized labor. People began to see unions as violent agitators. The loss of public trust in unions hindered any possibility of progress on major workplace reforms such as a shortened workday. Knights' leader Terence Powderly condemned the violence. Nonetheless, many workers gave up their membership in the Knights after the incidents on Haymarket Square. Many switched their allegiance to Gompers and the AFL.

The Homestead Strike

Another major setback to the labor movement occurred as a result of the Homestead Strike in 1892. Homestead, Pennsylvania, was the headquarters of the Carnegie Steel Company. Homestead employed about 3,800 workers at the time. With steel prices dropping and the union at Homestead growing in strength, negotiations over wages between the union workers and the company broke down in early June.

Henry Frick, chairman of the company, locked out the union workers by building a gated fence with barbed wire around the mill. Both Frick and his boss Andrew Carnegie believed the workers would abandon their union to keep their jobs. Frick hired temporary unskilled workers, known as scabs, to replace the workers and keep the factory productive in an attempt to break the union. Union workers protested outside of the mill. Frick responded by hiring 300 guards from the Pinkerton Detective Agency. The guards were to protect the scabs from the protesting union workers.

photo: Library of Congress

This drawing depicts the violent riot that ensued between the Pinkerton security guards and the striking workers in Homestead, Pennsylvania.

The Pinkerton guards arrived in early July, and a crowd of workers met them at the river. A fierce gun battle ensued. By the end of the day, the guards had surrendered, and at least 10 people were dead. Many more were injured. The governor sent in thousands of state troops to prevent further violence. A few weeks later, Frick was gravely injured in an assassination attempt. Authorities were successful in putting the blame on the strikers. Several influential union leaders were blacklisted, unable to work in their skilled trade again. Many other skilled workers who went on strike were permanently replaced. The event also left a lasting impression on workers. The steel industry would remain without strong union representation until the 1930s.

The Pullman Strike

The Pullman Strike in 1894 and its violent conclusion were another major setback to the national labor movement that added to the public's negative perception of labor unions. In 1893, the country was in an economic depression. The Pullman Palace Car Company, the leading manufacturer of railroad sleeping cars, needed to maintain profits by lowering labor costs. The company slashed wages by about 25 percent and laid off about 2,000 workers. However, rents and prices for goods in the company town of Pullman remained high, despite the slash in workers' salaries.

In May 1894, the Pullman workers went on strike. President of the American Railway Union (ARU) Eugene Debs called for railroads to stop running trains with Pullman cars attached. Soon, around 250,000 other railroad employees had joined the Pullman workers' protest against the company. Local labor unions held sympathy strikes in more than two dozen states and territories around the nation from Ohio to California. The ARU told railroads they could operate without Pullman cars. However, most railroad companies had contracts requiring them to pull the sleeper cars. Passenger train activity was severely disrupted, particularly around Chicago, which was the largest railroad center in the Midwest.

The strike had a nationwide impact because the trains also carried mail and freight containing meat and grains. The Illinois governor sympathized with the laborers, but the issue went to federal court. Federal judges ruled the strike disrupted a government service (the U.S. Mail) and interstate commerce. They said the strikers violated the Sherman Antitrust Act. Federal troops were sent to Chicago to end the strike and order the strikers back to work. Until the troops arrived, the strike had been relatively peaceful.

Discovery SOCIAL STUDIES
EDUCATION | **TECHBOOK**

How were the early labor and farmers' movements alike?
How were they different?

However, in Chicago, the soldiers opened fire into a crowd of nearly 10,000 people. Many were killed or injured before the ARU ended its boycott. Union leader Debs and hundreds of others went to jail. The Pullman workers continued their strike for a short time to no avail. By the time the strike ended, it was clear that federal power would be used against organized labor.

Labor and Politics

What was the connection between socialism and the early labor movements?

Late in the 1800s, the idea of socialism increasingly appealed to the working class. Socialism calls for common ownership and control of the fundamental means of production, such as farms and factories. It also seeks to equalize a society's distribution of wealth. For instance, socialism emphasizes the nationalization of monopolized branches of industry and trade. This means that in a socialist economy, the national government would own the banks, railroads, utility companies, and communication networks. Pricing for these goods and services would be determined by efficiency and access for all rather than by how much profit shareholders could earn.

Socialists also advocate for the government ownership of corporations so that all workers can share profits. Opposed to individualism and capitalist laissez-fair policies, socialism promotes a collective system that shares a company's profits among the workers, reducing inequalities of wealth. Socialist activists work toward this goal through advocating more political and workplace equality, better workplace protection, and wider opportunities for growth.

The first labor-oriented U.S. political party, the Workingmen's Party, was formed in 1828. Party members, known as "Workies," were mainly craftsmen and skilled workers. They wanted educational opportunities, shorter workdays, and more economic protections. One party member, George Henry Evans, established the first labor-oriented newspaper, the *Working Man's Advocate*, in 1829. While this party had some success in electing members to municipal governments, the party split in the 1830s. Some members joined the Democratic Party, while others formed the short-term Equal Rights Party in 1833.

After the Workingmen's Party disbanded, other groups formed around labor-based social reforms. The American Socialist Party was founded in 1901. By 1912, the party's membership had increased to more than 100,000. Some 1,200 public officials, including the mayor of Milwaukee, Wisconsin, were members of this party. Public interest in socialist ideas extended beyond just members of the Socialist Party. During this time, there were more than 300 different socialist-leaning newspapers in circulation, with one newspaper called *Appeal to Reason* selling more than 700,000 copies a week.

American Socialism

Eugene Debs is sometimes called the "Father of American Socialism." Debs was born in Indiana in 1855 to a poor immigrant family. As a young man, Debs worked as a railroad worker. By the 1890s, he was president of the American Railway Union. He helped found the Socialist Party of America and served as the party's presidential candidate in five separate elections.

photo: Library of Congress

Having come from a working-class immigrant family, Eugene Debs wanted adequate pay and dignity for workers in America.

Debs proposed radical reforms for the United States. He believed the government should own all industries and divide the profits among skilled and unskilled workers alike. Although this would decrease the wealth of business owners and managers, Debs argued that it would ultimately help the United States as a whole. By controlling industry and elevating the wealth of the workers, the national government could enhance the country's industrial growth. However, Debs's version of "American Socialism" was not as radical as other socialists. Others pushed for the complete abolition of the capitalist system and of private profit. By taking a more moderate approach to socialism, Debs could appeal to a wide range of American workers who had varying political beliefs.

To spread the word to workers, Debs led strikes, gave speeches, and wrote articles for socialist papers. Early on, Debs became a vocal proponent of First Amendment rights as well as labor protections. He was arrested and jailed for his involvement in the 1894 Pullman Strike. In 1918, he was arrested again for making a speech favoring peace instead of participation in World War I. He garnered nearly one million votes in the presidential election of 1920, even though he was in jail.

In addition to his work with the Socialist Party, Debs was also active in the early years of another, more radical organization. This was the Industrial Workers of the World, or IWW, founded in 1905. The IWW was led by mining union activist William Haywood, known as Big Bill, and other prominent trade union leaders. The Industrial Workers of the World wanted to create a single group in support of all workers much like the Knights of Labor.

Discovery EDUCATION | SOCIAL STUDIES TECHBOOK

How were the early labor and farmers' movements alike?
How were they different?

Unlike the Knights, the IWW did not believe in any compromise with big business. The IWW called for revolution. Its leaders and organizers wanted to do away with the elite "ruling class" and the wage system entirely. The group encouraged its members, nicknamed "Wobblies," to take direct action in fighting the corporate system. To accomplish this goal, they led hundreds of strikes all over the country. Although the success of the IWW was limited, its radical tactics often resulted in numerous arrests and a lot of publicity.

The Plight of Farmers

What issues were affecting farmers in the late 1800s?

Farmers faced their own issues in the 1800s. Much of a farmer's livelihood depends on factors that a person cannot control, such as weather, plant pests, and crop diseases. For example, prolonged droughts in the Great Plains during the 1890s had severe economic and social impacts on the region. Droughts are periods of extremely little precipitation. Agriculture and related industries, such as food processing, depend on the water supply from precipitation. The droughts also caused infestations of insects and plant diseases. In the dry climate, wildfires became frequent, placing people, their livestock, and the wildlife around them in danger. As a result of crop losses and a decrease in livestock, farmers lost much of their income. The overall reduced income for farmers left many small-town businesses without customers.

Changes in farming methods also caused unforeseen problems for farmers in the late 1800s. The technological boom of the 1800s made farming more mechanized and more efficient. Capitalist business owners organized large-scale wheat fields in California, and gang-plows operated by migrant workers harvested massive amounts of crops from commercial farms. These highly productive and efficient machines made large-scale farming easier than it had ever been before. As farms around the world became more efficient, worldwide grain output increased. The increased supply led to lower prices. For instance, the average price of a bushel of wheat dropped all the way from $1.25 in 1871 to 62 cents by 1900. This was good for the consumers who purchased the wheat but not for farmers whose income depended on this crop. This decrease in the overall level of prices for goods is known as deflation, which is an economic trend that farmers tried to avoid.

Agriculture had rarely made people wealthy, but many farmers were suddenly facing poverty and bankruptcy during the late 1800s. It was common practice for farmers to take out a loan in the spring to purchase seeds and supplies and then repay the loan in the fall after harvesting. Farmers also borrowed money to purchase the expensive mechanical equipment they needed to compete with other farmers.

photo: Harper's Weekly
During the 1870s, waves of grasshoppers moving across the Great Plains devoured everything in their path.

However, as the prices for farmed goods fell, it became more difficult each year for farmers to repay their loans from the spring or even the mortgages on their homes.

As deflation continued, the cost of transporting goods to market created an additional burden on farmers' wallets. Railroad rates varied greatly in the latter part of the century. Many farmers only shipped their agricultural produce short distances. However, railroads charged higher rates for "short hauls" than they did for long-distance travel. Farmers thought that railroads unfairly charged them higher storage and shipping rates than other industries. They called for government regulations of railroad rates and fees. As a solution to their financial burdens, they also called for government reform of the nation's monetary policies.

Free Silver Versus the Gold Standard

Why did farmers push for monetary reform?

Farmers looked to monetary policy to address their financial problems. Many supported policies that would increase the money supply in the United States. If there was more money in circulation, many farmers argued that banks would compete with one another as lenders. They believed lower interest rates on loans would attract more business. This, in turn, would help farmers who borrowed money each spring. Also, if more money was available, it would indirectly drive both wages and agricultural prices up. This would increase farmers' earnings and, thus, help them pay their debts.

photo: Library of Congress

What does this political cartoon reveal about the opposing sides between free silver farmers and the sound money doctrine?

Free Silver

One proposal to increase the amount of money in circulation was the unlimited coinage of silver dollars, or "free silver." Free silver was an inflationary policy, meaning that it would decrease the value of money, because the amount of silver metal used to make a silver dollar was worth less than a dollar. Farmers were borrowers, so they favored inflation. If there is inflation, then money borrowed in the spring has more purchasing power than the same amount of money they would use to repay it in the fall.

Discovery EDUCATION | SOCIAL STUDIES TECHBOOK.

How were the early labor and farmers' movements alike?
How were they different?

Gold Standard

Farmers and others looking to increase the supply of money were opposed by advocates of a so-called sound money policy. Sound money advocates favored a gold standard. They believed that currency backed by gold would provide stability for the national economy. They believed that the price of gold would remain steady. The farmers, however, thought that a gold standard favored lenders rather than debtors. They said the gold standard would only benefit bankers and large companies. Along with the farmers' growing concerns about railroads and agricultural debt, the debate over money led to organized political movements.

Protecting Agricultural Interests

What early organizations represented the interests of farmers?

Similar to the industrial workers in urban areas, farmers began to see the need to organize collectively to address the economic problems they encountered. The Grange, the Farmers' Alliance, and the Populist Party all worked for better working conditions and greater economic stability for farmers.

The Grange

The first organization to fight for agricultural interests was the Order of Patrons of Husbandry. Also known as the Grange, or the Granger Movement, this organization was established in 1867 by employees of the U.S. Department of Agriculture.

The Grange was initially a social organization. Its purpose was to bring isolated farm families together for social gatherings. However, it soon became more of a political and economic organization. By 1875, the Grange had around 800,000 members. The Grange movement fought for restrictions on railroad and grain-storage fees. Local chapters set up their own cooperative processing factories. Some also created joint marketing systems. Some states passed "Granger laws" to help with these efforts. The Grange was different than other organizations of this time because it permitted women to join.

photo: Library of Congress

How do these scenes of farm life portray the spirit of teamwork among farmers?

By the late 1870s, the Grange was in decline. Many local chapters had spent too much money on their cooperative machinery and supplies. Membership had dwindled to around 100,000 by 1880. As the Grange fell out of favor, a new network of farming interest organizations replaced it—the Farmers' Alliance.

The Farmers' Alliance

The first Farmers' Alliance chapters began in 1875 in Texas. By 1890, there were Farmers' Alliance organizations across the country. At the same time, a Colored National Farmers' Alliance also had around one million African American members. These alliances both worked to promote economic policies that favored the farmer.

The groups advocated for inflationary monetary policies, a graduated income tax, government control or national ownership of railroads, and low-interest loans for agriculture. With things looking bleak for agrarian, or farming, interests, the Farmers' Alliances moved into politics by forming their own political party—the Populist Party.

The Populist Party

Who supported the Populist Party? Who opposed it?

Initially, the Farmers' Alliance tried to cooperate with the two major political parties—the Democrats and Republicans—to bring about political change, but neither party had fully supported its agenda. The Farmers' Alliance had successfully backed some state legislative and gubernatorial candidates. It also helped elect three senators and about 50 congressmen in the 1900 elections. These successes provided some hope, but farmers demanded much more.

Pushing for more political power in 1892, the network of Farmers' Alliances formed the Populist Party, also known as the People's Party. The Populist Party wanted political changes in addition to economic policy changes. Members of the party wanted to shift power from big business owners and financiers to the common people. Some of the main elements of the Populist platform were:

- unlimited silver coinage

- direct election of federal senators

- public ownership of the railroads

- federal warehouses for farmers to store crops and the ability to borrow money based on the current market price

- a graduated income tax

DISCOVERY EDUCATION | SOCIAL STUDIES TECHBOOK

How were the early labor and farmers' movements alike? How were they different?

Although the party was popular in the Midwest, many white farmers in the South did not join with the Populists. Some were afraid that if they voted against the Democratic Party, neither the Populists nor the Democrats would win. Southern farmers would be stuck with the hated Republican representatives.

For a time, the Populist Party in the South welcomed the support of African American as well as white voters. Thomas E. Watson, a leader of the Georgia Populists, noticed that nationally the white vote was split between the major political parties. As a result, he argued the Populists could succeed by "making it in the interest of both races to act together." But Southern Democrats appealed to white voters' racial resentments. They put Populists on the defensive for including African Americans. Soon, Watson and most Southern Populists backed away from supporting racial equality.

Why do you think the cartoonist thought the Populists might "swallow" the Democratic Party?

Explore this investigation and take a position on whether the struggles of laborers and farmers formed a single movement.

The Populist Party presidential candidate James Weaver gained less than 10 percent of the vote in the 1892 elections. However, populism was not dead and continued to have influence. By 1896, the Democratic Party had adopted some of the Populist Party's core policies, including silver money. The Democrats also acquired the support of Populist leader William Jennings Bryan and chose him to run as their presidential candidate. Although the Populist movement died out by the late 1890s, Populist ideas were carried on by the social and political reformers of the Progressive Era, which was about to begin.

Consider the Essential Question:

How were the early labor and farmers' movements alike? How were they different?

Go online to complete the Social Studies Explanation.

Check for Understanding:

Should efforts to create better conditions for farmers and laborers should be seen as a single movement?

12.3 The Progressive Reformers

photo: Library of Congress

LESSON OVERVIEW

Introduction

In this concept, you will explore the Progressive Era, the period during the late 1800s and early 1900s when a spirit of reform swept across the country. Supporters of the Progressive movement sought to address problems present in nearly all areas of American life. Many of the changes made during this time continue to affect Americans' lives today.

Essential Question

How well did the Progressive movement address the consequences of industrialization?

Key Vocabulary
Which terms do you already know?

- [ ] initiative
- [ ] Jane Addams
- [ ] muckraker
- [ ] National American Woman Suffrage Association
- [ ] Nineteenth Amendment
- [ ] nominating conventions
- [ ] primary election
- [ ] Progressive movement
- [ ] Prohibition
- [ ] recall
- [ ] referendum
- [ ] Robert La Follette
- [ ] scientific management
- [ ] settlement house
- [ ] Social Gospel movement
- [ ] suffrage
- [ ] temperance
- [ ] Upton Sinclair

Discovery SOCIAL STUDIES
EDUCATION **TECHBOOK**

How well did the Progressive movement address the consequences of industrialization?

Lesson Objectives

By the end of this lesson, you should be able to:

- Describe the Progressive movement and explain factors leading to its emergence.
- Evaluate the Progressive Era's responses to political corruption.
- Evaluate the Progressive Era's responses to economic and social problems created by industrialization.
- Evaluate the Progressive Era's impact on women, immigrants, and African Americans.

ENGAGE

Why was reform needed? Visit Engage to learn more.

Essential Question

How well did the Progressive movement address the consequences of industrialization?

EXPLORE

The Rise of the Progressive Movement

How did the Progressive movement form?

Supporters of the Progressive movement hoped to confront the consequences of rapid changes that swept the nation after the Civil War. Progressive reformers came from a wide variety of backgrounds. They were Republicans and Democrats, African American and white, women and men, wealthy and middle class. To achieve their goals, they worked at the local, state, and national levels.

Despite the broad nature of the Progressive movement, most Progressives shared common ideals and goals. Progressives believed that industrialization and urbanization had caused significant problems in U.S. society. They believed citizens and the government should work together to correct these problems.

Recall, for example, the corrupt political machines and party bosses that had gained control of many large cities' municipal governments. Progressives opposed these political machines. They wanted to install governments that were less corrupt and more responsive to citizens' needs. Progressives and officials, they believed, could address the filthy tenements and dangerous working conditions faced by the urban poor. They could develop modern and efficient methods of managing government. They could even promote democracy and equality.

photo: Getty Images

Walter Rauschenbusch was a leader of the Social Gospel movement who challenged the ideas of laissez-faire and the Gospel of Wealth.

Unlike many Americans of the Gilded Age, Progressives rejected the idea of laissez-faire, which stated government should remain outside of direct economic and social action. Instead, Progressives believed that government should take an active role in U.S. society. Local governments should create and run efficient city services. State governments should pass laws and develop social welfare programs. The national government should flex its muscle by challenging corporations, passing new laws, and otherwise reshaping society.

The Progressive movement shared some ideals and similarities with other important social movements of the 1800s. The Social Gospel movement, for example, emerged during the 1870s as Protestant religious leaders called for increased rights for workers and the urban poor. By the late 1890s, Walter Rauschenbusch, a New York Baptist pastor sometimes called the "Father of the Social Gospel," had begun arguing that Christians must seek to correct sins against humanity, such as hunger and poverty, to fulfill their religious duties. Rauschenbusch's book *Christianity and the Social Crisis* encouraged Christians to work for social justice. Progressives built on Social Gospel goals and shared the movement's opposition to greed and corruption.

Although Progressives shared many beliefs, a great deal of variation existed within the movement. Progressive reform movements had different particular goals or areas of focus. Many Progressive leaders were middle-class Americans who sought to change the way working-class Americans lived. Sometimes, these changes were ones that working-class Americans did not want. Progressives had varying beliefs about whether immigrants and African Americans should enjoy equal rights and opportunities with white Americans. White and African American reformers often worked separately. White Progressives often ignored the problems of African American life.

Discovery EDUCATION | SOCIAL STUDIES TECHBOOK

How well did the Progressive movement address the consequences of industrialization?

A Nation of Reformers

Who were the Progressives?

The Progressive movement gathered Americans who believed in the need for sweeping reform. Women played key roles in developing the Progressive movement, and reporters and intellectuals helped call attention to the need for change. Reforming politicians also enacted changes that reshaped how Americans lived, voted, and worked. Who were some of these Progressives?

Women

Women played a significant part in the Progressive movement. For decades, Americans had seen women as vital to protecting the morals and strength of U.S. families. Many middle-class white women, therefore, believed they had a duty to call for reforms that helped families and home life. The number of women's colleges, and the number of women attending college, had expanded greatly after the Civil War. For example, by 1898, more than 61,000 women attended college. This figure included 1,800 African American women. While the majority of colleges served both male and female students, most female students attended women's colleges. There were about 119 women's colleges in 1901. This gave the growing body of middle-class women better access to educational opportunities. Reform-minded, educated young women could find jobs as social workers, nurses, or teachers. U.S. society discouraged married middle-class women from holding jobs outside the home. However, these women had the time, energy, and intellect to volunteer on reform committees.

photo: Library of Congress

What does this political cartoon suggest about women's roles in U.S. society during the Progressive Era?

Middle-class women formed clubs to work for social improvement. Called "clubwomen," some raised money to fund libraries or other services. Others organized campaigns asking politicians to create child labor laws. Working-class women, in contrast, lacked the education and influence to organize these types of social welfare clubs. Many toiled long hours at factories for low pay. In time, however, middle-class and working women came together to form organizations such as the Women's Trade Union League. These unions sought better wages and working conditions for women.

Middle-class urban African American women faced discrimination from their white counterparts, however. White women's clubs typically excluded black members, and most white reformers had little interest in issues that affected African Americans such as lynching or segregation. African American women formed their own clubs to work for reform along the same lines as had white women. The Neighborhood Union, for example, organized African American women all across Atlanta, Georgia. This club established day cares and kindergartens, organized shelters for local homeless families, provided classes to teach young wives and mothers needed household skills, and campaigned to improve educational opportunities for African American youth.

Politicians

Progressive politicians helped bring the reforms supported by women, intellectuals, and others to life. Progressive leader and future president Theodore Roosevelt, for example, strengthened labor laws and barred racial segregation in New York's public schools when he was the state's governor. Arkansas Governor George Washington Donaghey contributed to the formation of six state universities and enacted political reforms to encourage direct democracy.

The best-known Progressive governor was Robert La Follette of Wisconsin. Elected in 1900, La Follette transformed Wisconsin into a national leader of the Progressive movement known as a "laboratory of democracy." La Follette created a government partnership with scholars from the University of Wisconsin to develop Progressive programs. Among his successes were enactments of state laws raising taxes on railroads, safeguarding workers' rights, and encouraging direct democracy. In 1906, La Follette became a U.S. senator and used this platform to call for nationwide Progressive reforms.

Muckrakers

How did journalists strengthen the Progressive movement?

Muckrakers, or journalists who exposed governmental corruption and abuses of big business, played vital roles in the Progressive movement. Muckrakers such as *McClure's Magazine* editor Lincoln Steffens, photographer Jacob Riis, and writer Ida M. Tarbell created works that drew public attention to the problems of society. Steffens' *The Shame of the Cities*, for example, explored the problems caused by political corruption in local government. Corruption, he suggested, meant the party bosses and local officials benefited from bribes while allowing businesses to overcharge residents or provide shoddy, or inferior, services.

Riis's *How the Other Half Lives* collected photographs of tenement life that shocked middle-class Americans. Tarbell's *The History of the Standard Oil Company* attacked the business practices of the oil monopoly and inflamed the call for government regulation.

Discovery SOCIAL STUDIES
EDUCATION | TECHBOOK

How well did the Progressive movement address the consequences
of industrialization?

Among the best-known of the muckrakers was Upton Sinclair. Sinclair spent several months investigating the working conditions of the Chicago, Illinois, meatpacking industry, which employed thousands of poorly paid workers, many of whom were immigrants. His findings became the basis of his 1906 serialized novel *The Jungle*. This book gave a fictionalized account of the lives of meatpacking workers with blunt descriptions of the unsanitary and often dangerous conditions that they faced. The public outcry that followed the publication of *The Jungle* contributed to the passage of two new federal laws: the Meat Inspection Act and the Pure Food and Drug Act.

photo: Library of Congress

Upton Sinclair's writing exposed unsanitary conditions at facilities such as this Chicago meatpacking plant.

Rise of Realism

How did the Progressive movement lead to the rise of realism?

The spirit of the Progressive Era inspired the works of other writers and artists. A greater emphasis on showing life as it really was, known as realism, appeared throughout the arts. Jacob Riis, for example, sought to tell stories about the struggles of everyday life in urban ethnic neighborhoods through his photographs. Novelist Theodore Dreiser drew on the real-life experiences of people he knew to write novels such as *Sister Carrie* and *An American Tragedy*, which attacked greed and other societal consequences of industrialization. In *An American Tragedy*, the real tragedy is not that a character murders his girlfriend. The tragedy is that U.S. society created a man who could do such a thing.

Some notable literature from the early decades of the 1900s described perspectives of immigrants. *Bread Givers*, a 1925 novel by Anzia Yezierska, tells the story of the youngest daughter of a Jewish immigrant family in New York City. The story demonstrates conflicts of immigrant life, including the struggle between cultural assimilation and tradition.

photo: Getty Images

One of Frank Lloyd Wright's most famous designs was Fallingwater, a home in Pennsylvania.

In visual arts, architect Frank Lloyd Wright turned away from the highly decorated, historically influenced building styles of the late 1800s. Wright designed structures that he believed were in harmony with their inhabitants and the surrounding natural environment. Wright's buildings were not designed merely to be seen by the outside world. They were also designed to inspire and promote efficiency among the people who would live and work in them

Educational philosopher John Dewey drew on the ideas of realism to argue that the best democratic society rested on the involvement of a well-informed public. He believed schools could best embody democratic ideals by teaching

Complete this activity to learn more about realism during the Progressive Era.

children to reason critically and to actively participate in society. Dewey believed that knowledgeable, thinking citizens would be most likely to choose the best politicians and to then hold them responsible for their actions. This connected to Progressives' efforts to increase direct political involvement and reduce corruption from political machines and party bosses.

Progressive Political Reform

How did Progressives work to end the power of political machines?

Progressive reformers believed that individual citizens had the right and the duty to take part in government. They found existing governments and political systems to be inefficient and corrupt. One main goal of Progressivism was to apply to U.S. society the principles of logic and efficiency that made up scientific management. This theory used an approach borrowed from manufacturing and aimed to achieve the greatest output through standardization of methods and the smart use of resources. Progressives believed these ideals could also reshape government for the better.

New Forms of City Government

Cities and other municipalities provided a laboratory for Progressive political reforms. In 1900, a major hurricane devastated Galveston, Texas. Citizens there temporarily installed a five-person commission to manage the city government after its existing government, headed by a mayor, did not respond quickly enough.

Galveston Disaster, Public school 25th st. and Ave P.

photo: Library of Congress

Hurricane damage to a public school in Galveston, Texas, 1900.

Discovery SOCIAL STUDIES | EDUCATION | TECHBOOK

How well did the Progressive movement address the consequences of industrialization?

Residents decided that the city commission style of government was so efficient that they kept it even after the hurricane was cleaned up. Progressives adopted the city commission system in other cities around the United States. The city of Dayton, Ohio, popularized a blended government with a city commission headed by a city manager. City commissions were often less corrupt and more efficient than more traditional forms of government with a single elected leader.

Election Reforms

After the Civil War, many Americans objected to the Constitution's original process for selecting U.S. senators. As the Constitution was written, state legislatures were responsible for selecting members of the senate, while American voters directly elected members of the House of Representatives. Under this system, Senate seats could remain vacant for long periods of time if state legislatures were not controlled by a single political party. In addition, Progressives believed that members of state legislatures were more responsive to the demands of big business than they were to the needs of their constituents. In 1913, Progressive reformers won the passage and ratification of the Seventeenth Amendment. This put the election of senators directly in the hands of the people.

Progressives also wanted to make other elections less corrupt. At the national level, reformers supported the passage of a series of campaign finance reform laws. The Tillman Act of 1907 barred direct contributions to federal election campaigns by corporations. The Publicity Act, passed in 1910, later required Congressional candidates to publicly reveal information about their campaign finances.

Progressives aimed to lessen outside influences at the state level, as well. In Wisconsin, Governor La Follette instituted the direct primary election, which allowed voters, rather than party leaders, to choose candidates for office. Direct primaries spread quickly across the nation. By 1917, all but four states had adopted some form of direct primary.

Progressives also sought to expand democracy by adopting the secret ballot in elections and increasing time periods for voter registration. Before the early 1900s, voting was public. In the first U.S. elections, eligible voters simply stated the name of the candidate to cast a vote. Paper ballots emerged in the 1800s. However, the ballots were often color-coded according to the political party. A voter would take his or her paper ballot and place it in a glass bowl to cast a vote. Because the bowl was glass, it was obvious who the person voted for based on the color of the ballot.

Supporters of political machines such as Tammany Hall would employ people to monitor how people voted. Those who voted for the "wrong" party in the eyes of the political machine would be threatened with violence. The idea of the secret ballot, which was first practiced in Australia, was born to prevent voter intimidation and make the voting practices fair. In addition to voter intimidation, political machines often doctored voter lists to include ineligible voters, such as children or deceased people. Members of the political machine would cast illegal votes on behalf of those ineligible voters to guarantee a win for their candidate. Stricter voter registration laws were passed to prevent this practice.

Increased Reforms and Limitations

How did Progressive reforms serve to both advance and limit the rights of citizens?

Initiative, Referendum, and Recall

Progressive reformers sought to give voters more say over the workings of their states' politics in other ways. Progressives supported three major new political practices. The first of these was the initiative. This practice gave voters the right to propose a new law and put it up for vote by collecting citizens' signatures in support of the proposition. In contrast, the referendum allowed voters to approve or reject a law proposed by their state's legislature. Finally, Progressives called successfully for the adoption of the recall in several states to allow voters to remove a poorly performing political leader from office.

The required number of voter signatures for the initiative process varied by state. Although several states already allowed municipal, or local, initiatives, South Dakota became the first state in 1898 to accept a statewide initiative process. Utah, Oregon, and other states soon followed suit. Early laws that were passed from initiatives by citizens provided funding for permanent road improvement in Oregon and free textbooks in Arkansas. Several states also passed their own liquor laws based on the initiative process.

Together, the initiative and referendum processes have come to be known as "direct legislation" because they allow citizens to propose new laws and undo legislation.

photo: Library of Congress
Robert La Follette of Wisconsin became a national leader of efforts to reform the political process.

Most states passed laws allowing for referenda at the same time as they allowed for initiatives. In 1910, Maine voters rejected legislation to set a regulation on alcohol limits. Four years later, Montana voters defeated a legislative measure to establish an athletic commission. In 1922, California voters exercised their right to say "no" by denying new rules for governing tenement housing in a separate referendum.

The recall process was based on the idea that elected leaders must adequately represent the direct will of the people. In 1908, Oregon became the first state to apply the recall statewide rather than to just local officials. Although opponents rallied against the recall, stating it would lead to political instability, many states, particularly in the West, created statewide recall processes. In 1921, North Dakota Governor Lynn Frazier became the first U.S. governor removed from office via recall.

Discovery EDUCATION | SOCIAL STUDIES **TECHBOOK**

How well did the Progressive movement address the consequences of industrialization?

While many see initiatives, referenda, and recalls as tools for improving citizen engagement and increasing direct democracy, these processes are not without their critics. Recall elections might make it difficult for government officials to tackle difficult or unpopular decisions. Initiatives and referenda often require citizens to perform significant levels of research to make an informed decision. Referenda and initiatives can also be affected by advertising campaigns and special interests.

Limitations of Progressive Reforms

Sometimes, Progressive reforms failed to expand the democratic process to everyone. Some Progressive governments developed policies that effectively kept African Americans from voting. Virginia's Progressive-Era state constitution, for example, limited the right to vote. Only veterans of the Civil War and their descendants, people who paid a certain level of property taxes, and people who could explain the new constitution could vote. Soon after, the state added poll taxes and literacy tests to further limit voting. North Carolina added a poll tax and literacy test to its state constitution in 1899. Other Progressive governments limited the voting rights of immigrants. Prior to this time, many states had allowed people who were not citizens to vote. During the Progressive Era, however, states including Alabama, Colorado, Wisconsin, and Oregon all restricted voting to citizens only.

Progressive Social Reform
How did Progressives seek to reform U.S. society and morals?

Along with political reform, Progressives saw considerable room for improvement in the country's social and economic systems. One set of Progressive reformers mostly hoped to help the urban poor, for example. Poverty was especially widespread among the ethnic communities that had swelled as immigrants flocked to the United States seeking industrial jobs. Many people in these neighborhoods lived in cramped, airless, and unsanitary tenement apartments with little access to health care or other services.

In 1889, Jane Addams, a Progressive reformer in Chicago, decided to try to help some members of the city's immigrant community by opening a settlement house. A settlement house is a neighborhood center that provides services and activities for the economically disadvantaged. It is designed to build the strengths of individuals, families, and the community. Reformers in London, England, had begun social settlements earlier that decade. This movement tried to counteract the problems caused by urbanization and industrialization. Well-educated, middle-class, native-born citizens "settled" at sites in poor urban neighborhoods. There, they developed programs and services to help their neighbors. Addams and fellow reformer Ellen Gates Starr were inspired by the settlements they saw on a trip to London. Back in Chicago, the two opened one of the first U.S. settlement houses, Hull House. It became the inspiration for dozens of other settlement houses around the country.

When Hull House opened, it was surrounded by a bustling immigrant population mostly from southern and eastern Europe. In time, the neighborhood also grew to include Mexican and African American residents. Addams, who lived at Hull House, and her fellow social workers provided numerous services for the community. They taught classes in English and citizenship to help new immigrants adjust to the United States. They provided day care and kindergarten for children while parents worked. They organized clubs and ran a library. Hull House residents opened the city's first public playground and campaigned for increased city services. On a broader level, residents supported a variety of Progressive causes, such as women's suffrage and labor reform.

The Temperance Movement

While Addams and Hull House's residents focused largely on the needs of immigrant communities, other Progressives connected these same people to some of the country's gravest problems. Immigrants from Germany, Ireland, Italy, and elsewhere brought cultural practices of alcohol brewing and drinking with them. However, many Progressives, especially middle-class women, came to support more conservative policies such as temperance. Temperance activists called for Americans to drink less intoxicating liquor. Often, the activists wanted to enact prohibition to end the sale and consumption of alcohol altogether.

RESULT OF LAZINESS AND INDULGENCE IN DRINKING.
THE SHERIFF LEVIES ON THE HOUSEHOLD FURNITURE — CONSOLATION. — THE BOTTLE

photo: Library of Congress

This poster, created in the 1880s, shows the harmful effects of alcohol on the family.

U.S. support for temperance had begun in the early 1800s in some Protestant churches. In 1874, the Women's Christian Temperance Union (WCTU) organized in Cleveland, Ohio, and soon gained nationwide support. Members of the WCTU pointed to alcohol as the cause of many problems, including crime, domestic violence, and poverty. Restricting or barring alcohol, they argued, would improve the plight of those affected by these evils. By the end of the 1800s, the WCTU had added another cause to its mission. This new cause was gaining the vote for women. Women, the organization believed, could be trusted to support temperance at the ballot box—if only they had the ballot.

Votes for Women

How did Progressives work to gain the vote for women?

The women's movement had first emerged in the United States before the Civil War. Women's rights supporters sought social and political equality for women, but many believed that abolition was a more important national goal. After the Civil War, women's rights advocates began to focus more squarely on the right to vote, or suffrage. However, suffragists did not agree on the best way to achieve this goal.

Two separate women's suffrage organizations formed in 1869. One, the National Women Suffrage Association, declared its intent of winning the vote through a constitutional amendment. The other, the American Woman Suffrage Association, worked to secure the vote at a state-by-state level.

photo: Library of Congress

Suffragists in a parade.

In 1890, the women's suffrage movement gained new life. Wyoming entered the United States as the first state to guarantee women's suffrage in its state constitution. The two women's suffrage associations overcame their differences to unite as the National American Women's Suffrage Association (NAWSA). Elizabeth Cady Stanton was named the first NAWSA president. This new organization campaigned heavily for women's suffrage over the next few decades.

Activists gave several practical arguments for this right. Women, according to activist Alice Stone Blackwell for NAWSA, were required to pay taxes and follow the laws so they should have a voice in making them. Women could more easily support measures that were important to women. Women were increasingly educated and had shown their commitment to social reform. In short, activists claimed, women's suffrage would cleanse the political system of corruption, support efforts for better education and government services, and improve workplace conditions. However, not everyone supported women's suffrage. Alcohol brewers and distillers, political machines, men who ran big businesses, and many Southerners opposed extending the right to vote because they expected women voters to oppose their interests.

By the early 1910s, the suffrage movement had become a national topic of discussion. The Progressive Party headed by Theodore Roosevelt became the first national political party to include women's suffrage in its campaign platform in 1912. Suffragists, led by former NAWSA president Alice Paul, formed a more radical organization, called the Congressional Union, to draw attention to the cause. Paul and her supporters went on hunger strikes, held parades, and generally engaged in more extreme actions than had NAWSA. On March 3, 1913—the day before incoming President Woodrow Wilson's inauguration—the Congressional Union organized a massive suffrage parade in Washington, DC. Tensions between suffrage marchers and opponents gained national attention.

Three years later, NAWSA president Carrie Chapman Catt proposed a more moderate plan for winning the vote. She relied on coordinated efforts from local and state suffrage associations across the country to gain support for the cause. The movement generated enough backing for several states, including New York, Michigan, and South Dakota, to grant women at least some voting rights. Catt also tirelessly promoted the passage of a national Constitutional amendment securing women's suffrage.

In 1919, Congress passed the Nineteenth Amendment guaranteeing women the right to vote. The amendment then went to the states for ratification. It took only a little more than one year for enough states to approve the amendment to guarantee its addition to the U.S. Constitution, ending women's decades-long struggle for voting rights.

Socialism and Radicalism

Why did socialism gain support during the Progressive Era?

During the Progressive Era, some liberal reformers were drawn to the growing socialist movement. Socialism calls for the government or citizen groups to control property and resources rather than private individuals. Farmers and laborers struggling during the late 1800s had found aspects of socialism appealing. The continued rise of the labor movement and interest in government-sponsored social, economic, and political reforms meant that socialist ideals seemed in line with contemporary thinking. Progressive intellectuals such as Upton Sinclair and John Dewey identified with socialist ideals. Popular American heroes including Helen Keller also campaigned for socialist causes.

photo: Library of Congress

This 1894 cartoon from Harper's Weekly *criticizes Eugene Debs's power in the railroad industry. Debs was president of the American Railway Union.*

During the late 1800s, several Socialists, including Victor Berger and Eugene V. Debs, founded the Social Democratic Party. In 1901, that party became the Socialist Party. These Socialists sought to support the needs of the working class and encourage social welfare programs through collective action. The party's 1912 platform, for example, called for the creation of government programs to reduce unemployment. It also supported laws requiring that workers receive at least one-and-one-half-days off each week. The party supported women's suffrage and called for direct election of the U.S. president.

Socialism gained enough support that some Socialist politicians won major political offices. Berger won election to the U.S. Congress from Wisconsin in 1910. That same year, the city of Milwaukee, Wisconsin, elected the nation's first Socialist mayor. Debs ran unsuccessfully for president five times, receiving more than 900,000 votes in 1920.

Discovery EDUCATION | SOCIAL STUDIES TECHBOOK.

How well did the Progressive movement address the consequences of industrialization?

Progressivism and African Americans

How did African Americans seek change during the Progressive Era?

 Although the Progressive movement threw its weight behind reforms in various parts of society, many Progressives had little interest in reforming race relations. However, African American leaders and white supporters, nevertheless, hoped to channel some of the reforming spirit of the time to improve the situation for African Americans.

A prominent African American leader of the Progressive Era was W. E. B. Du Bois. A native of Massachusetts, Du Bois was a highly educated sociologist who focused on ways to address discrimination. In 1905, Du Bois and other African American intellectuals formed the Niagara Movement to campaign for civil rights. The Niagara Movement spread slowly across the country but failed to attract much mainstream support.

photo: Library of Congress
A sharecropper and farmworkers in a cotton field, 1908.

Meanwhile, race relations in the United States were very poor. Laws required racial segregation in parts of the country, especially the South, but even in the North, discrimination and tensions existed.

In 1908, a mob in Springfield, Illinois, violently attacked the African American community after a local African American man was accused of a crime. After two days, the Illinois militia ended the riot. However, the violence and destruction shocked some white Americans.

White supporters joined with members of the Niagara Movement to found the National Association for the Advancement of Colored People (NAACP) in 1909. The NAACP became the leading African American civil rights organization in the country. Among its early goals were the passage of an anti-lynching law and the expansion of voting rights for African Americans.

A year after the foundation of the NAACP, the National Urban League formed. Like the NAACP, the National Urban League had both white and African American members. The organization mostly sought to help African Americans moving to cities from the rural South. At first, the National Urban League focused primarily on New York City, but over time, it expanded to include other major U.S. cities. It assisted migrants in finding jobs and homes and in settling into their new environment.

Progressivism and Immigration
How did immigrants respond to the Progressive movement?

Progressives also had a sometimes uneasy relationship with immigrants. Many Progressives sought to improve the lives of the urban poor, including immigrants. However, some of these same Progressives believed that immigrants must change or rethink their cultural traditions. For example, supporters of the temperance movement disagreed with the Catholic practice of drinking wine for Communion. Many Progressive reformers viewed themselves as more "American" than the immigrants and pushed immigrants to adopt what they considered American cultural traditions and behaviors. As a result, immigrants often opposed Progressive reforms.

The Progressive Era was also a time of growing opposition to the waves of "new" immigrants who came to America from regions—such as southern Europe, eastern Europe, and Asia—that had not traditionally provided settlers to the United States. Federal laws limited immigration from Asia, including the Chinese Exclusion Act of 1882 and the Immigration Act of 1924.

Even as Progressives were not always welcoming to immigrants, immigrants sometimes resisted Progressive reforms. Southern and eastern Europeans who had religious or cultural ties to alcohol opposed temperance policies. Others resented Progressive suggestions that their home cultures were less advanced than U.S. culture.

New York, Ellis Island. reg. No. 3163 E

photo: Library of Congress

Immigrants walking across pier from bridge at Ellis Island.

Immigrants who benefited from the Democratic political machines of the cities disliked Progressive election reforms. Democratic machine leaders helped immigrants obtain jobs, navigate the complex legal system, and access city services. Election reforms weakened the power of machines and made it more difficult for immigrant voters to influence politics.

Progressive Era shifts of voting day from Saturday to Tuesday, for example, made it hard for immigrant laborers to get to their polling places. The adoption of new municipal commission forms of government also weakened the power of political machines and party bosses. Immigrants who benefited from these systems disliked the newer systems, which they felt were less interested in serving working-class interests.

Complete this interactive to decide which reforms you would have prioritized as a big city mayor.

The Progressive Movement's Impact

The Progressive movement had a lasting impact on both the political and social systems of the United States. Progressive leaders targeted social ills and made strides in correcting government corruption, increasing voting rights for citizens, and improving living and working conditions for industrial workers. As with any movement, there were clear winners and losers who emerged from the Progressive Era. The Progressive movement inspired future generations to challenge unfair systems and continue to fight for civil rights.

Consider the Essential Question:

How well did the Progressive movement address the consequences of industrialization?

Go online to complete the Social Studies Explanation.

Check for Understanding:

Were Progressive activists successful in achieving their goals? Take and defend a position on this question.

12.4 Progressivism in the White House

photo: Library of Congress

LESSON OVERVIEW

Introduction

In this concept, you will learn about the major Progressive Era policies enacted by the federal government. You will also analyze government efforts to conserve and protect the environment and natural resources.

Essential Question

How did the Progressive Era change the role of the federal government?

Lesson Objectives

By the end of this lesson, you should be able to:

- Evaluate major Progressive Era policies enacted on a national scale by the federal government.

- Analyze the emergence of governmental efforts to conserve and protect the environment.

Key Vocabulary

Which terms do you already know?

- [ ] Benjamin Harrison
- [ ] Eighteenth Amendment
- [ ] Federal Reserve System
- [ ] Federal Trade Commission
- [ ] National Park Service
- [ ] Seventeenth Amendment
- [ ] Sixteenth Amendment
- [ ] Square Deal
- [ ] Theodore Roosevelt
- [ ] William Howard Taft
- [ ] William McKinley
- [ ] Woodrow Wilson

ENGAGE

What's it like to go camping with the president? Visit Engage to learn more.

Essential Question

How did the Progressive Era change the role of the federal government?

EXPLORE

Steward of the People

How did Americans perceive Theodore Roosevelt?

In 1900, William McKinley was elected to a second term as the president of the United States. However, a short time into his presidency, on September 6, 1901, an anarchist assassin named Leon Czolgosz shot the president. Eight days later, McKinley died from his injuries. McKinley's vice president, Theodore Roosevelt, then became president. Roosevelt was only 42 years old when he took office, making him, at the time, the youngest person to serve in this office.

Roosevelt enjoyed widespread popularity, partially because of his military leadership during the Spanish-American War. When war was declared, he recruited a volunteer cavalry that nicknamed itself the "Rough Riders." During the war, the efforts of the Rough Riders helped U.S. forces capture important ridges above Cuba's capital city Santiago. From this position, the American military forced the Spanish to flee and surrender the city. Although many Rough Riders were killed in the battle, Roosevelt became a national hero.

photo: Library of Congress

Theodore Roosevelt, leader of the Rough Riders, during the Spanish-American War.

Because of his success in the war, Americans developed a strong affection for Roosevelt. They called him either Teddy or T. R. Shortly after his nomination for vice president in 1900, Roosevelt described himself to colleague (and sometimes political rival) Mark Hanna as follows: "I am as strong as a bull moose and you can use me to the limit."

"Bull Moose" also became a popular nickname for Roosevelt. It summed up his reputation for strength and vigor. Later, the Progressive Party would informally adopt the nickname and call itself the Bull Moose Party. The party nominated Roosevelt for a third term in 1912. The party platform reflected Roosevelt's principles. Among these were diminishing the influence of big business in politics. Other Progressive ideas that Roosevelt supported were women's suffrage, social insurance for the unemployed, and a federal income tax.

Anti-Big Business

When he was governor of New York, Roosevelt had supported state government reforms for stricter control of business. His refusal to obey the bosses of the political machines had angered some rich industrialists. Now, Roosevelt claimed he would continue McKinley's policies, which tended to favor big business. As president, Roosevelt kept McKinley's cabinet members to establish continuity. However, many business leaders feared that Roosevelt would push for more control of industry by the federal government. Soon, these business leaders discovered their fears were justified.

Theodore Roosevelt's Reforms: First Term

What reforms did Roosevelt implement during his first term?

Trust Buster

In 1890, Congress passed the Sherman Antitrust Act, and President Benjamin Harrison signed the act into law. The goal of the Sherman Antitrust Act was to prohibit powerful combinations of businesses that might restrict trade or interfere with competition between companies. However, the legislation was seldom used in the first decade after passage. Many businesses continued to form trusts to monopolize, or dominate, entire industries. Because trusts reduced competition among businesses, the prices of many products increased significantly.

Trusts were especially strong in the railroad industry. In 1901, business leaders J. P. Morgan, John D. Rockefeller, James Hill, and E. H. Harriman formed a trust known as the Northern Securities Company. This huge trust controlled almost all the railroads in the West. After President Roosevelt claimed that the Northern Securities Company had been created for the purpose of reducing competition between railroads, the federal government used the Sherman Antitrust Act to file a lawsuit to break up the trust. In 1904, the Supreme Court supported the government's lawsuit and dissolved the Northern Securities Company into separate businesses.

Discovery EDUCATION | SOCIAL STUDIES TECHBOOK.

How did the Progressive Era change the role of the federal government?

During his two terms in office, Roosevelt approved federal government lawsuits against 43 other companies that held monopolies in different industries. Government actions dissolved the oil trust of John D. Rockefeller and the tobacco trust of James B. Duke. Because of Roosevelt's efforts to use the federal government to break up monopolies, he gained another nickname, the "trust buster."

The Square Deal

During the late 1800s, the federal government often became involved in disputes between labor unions and corporate management. The government usually settled the dispute in support of the management. Roosevelt, in contrast, believed that the government should treat labor unions more fairly. In the spring of 1902, about 150,000 coal miners went on strike in Pennsylvania for better pay and working conditions. These strikers were members of a labor union called the United Mine Workers. Although many people supported the coal miners, they also became worried that the ongoing strike would affect coal supplies. As the strike continued in the fall, many schools and hospitals in eastern cities claimed that they would have no fuel for the winter if the strike was not settled.

Roosevelt could not legally control the strike. Instead, he requested that the mine owners and union leaders meet formally to end the dispute through arbitration, or settlement by outside observers. The mine owners refused. Upon learning this, Roosevelt claimed that if arbitration did not happen soon, he would have the army take control of the mines and operate them. He also asked J. P. Morgan to help settle this strike. Morgan, one of the wealthiest men in the United States, controlled railroads, which needed coal. Settlement of the strike was in his interest. Morgan succeeded in negotiating a compromise between the miners and the mine owners, which included a pay raise for the miners.

When asked about his involvement with the strike, Roosevelt stated that he wanted to give the miners a "square deal." In a speech, Roosevelt used the term this way: "We must treat each man on his worth and merits as a man. We must see that each is given a square deal, because he is entitled to no more and should receive no less."

THE LION-TAMER

photo: Harper's Weekly

In this political cartoon, Roosevelt "tames" trusts, which have been depicted as lions.

The phrase "square deal" came to define Roosevelt's policies with labor unions, and Roosevelt used it during his reelection campaign of 1904 to describe other reform policies he supported. Roosevelt won the election by about 2.5 million votes—the largest margin of any president up to that time.

Theodore Roosevelt's Reforms: Second Term
What reforms did Roosevelt implement during his second term?

Shipping Rates

After Roosevelt was reelected, he became more aggressive with many of his reforms. For example, during the late 1800s and early 1900s, railroads often favored certain large-volume freight shippers by offering them rebates, or money back for shipping goods with a railway. Railroads also could increase rates whenever they wanted without government control. This system favored large shippers and interstate railroads. Small businesses and local railroads could not compete. As a result, small shippers, including farmers who shipped goods by rail, had difficulty staying profitable. They could not afford high shipping rates, and railways did not offer small shippers high enough rebates to offset their costs.

Roosevelt firmly opposed these practices and argued with Congress to pass a law that applied limits on the railroad industry. Eventually, Roosevelt achieved part of his goal. In 1906, Congress passed the Hepburn Act. This law prohibited railroad companies from raising rates without government approval. However, the act did not completely eliminate rebates.

Food Safety

During the late 1800s, meatpacking developed into a huge industry with highly unsanitary conditions. Grotesque scenes and gory details of a meat-packing plant were described in Upton Sinclair's novel *The Jungle*, which was published in 1906. Roosevelt read this novel and was shocked. Soon, he ordered an investigation of the meatpacking industry, which confirmed the unsafe conditions described in the novel.

Roosevelt told Congress that he would publish the investigation's report if the unsanitary conditions were not soon corrected. Congress quickly passed two acts of legislation in 1906. The Federal Meat Inspection Act required a federal agency to inspect all meat shipped across state lines. The Pure Food and Drug Act required accurate labels and prohibited the manufacture or sale of food and medicine with dangerous ingredients or contaminants. It also required that all food and medicine containers have ingredient labels. These laws were meant to improve sanitary conditions and to protect consumers from unsafe products. Opponents of the bill worried that it would create a large bureaucracy of government food inspectors.

Discovery EDUCATION | SOCIAL STUDIES TECHBOOK.

How did the Progressive Era change the role of the federal government?

"New Nationalism"

In 1907, major firms in the stock market declared bankruptcy, leading to an event called the Panic of 1907. This caused a recession, or a decline in spending and employment. Many business leaders blamed this financial crisis on the Progressive reforms of Roosevelt. The economy recovered by 1909, casting some doubt on these previous accusations. However, Roosevelt lost the nomination for a third term and left the presidency in 1909. William Howard Taft, Roosevelt's successor, became the next president, but he angered many progressive Republicans by not being firm enough in controlling big business. As a result, a progressive faction, or offshoot, formed in the Republican Party. This development created tension between progressives and conservatives in the party.

Roosevelt gave a speech in 1910 that attempted to lessen the tension. In this speech, Roosevelt explained a policy called New Nationalism, which involved the president acting as a caretaker of the public welfare. The ideas of New Nationalism summarized Roosevelt's political approach, which emphasized social and economic reforms for the benefit of the less fortunate. However, Roosevelt could not heal the division between progressives and conservatives.

During the next election in 1912, Roosevelt responded by forming the Progressive Party, or Bull Moose Party, to run for a third term as president. By doing this, Roosevelt weakened the Republican Party, since many Republicans voted for Roosevelt instead of the Republican candidate, President Taft. As a result, the Democratic candidate, Woodrow Wilson, won the election for the presidency.

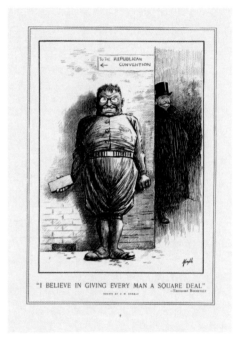

photo: Harper's Weekly

This political cartoon lampooned the rivalry between Theodore Roosevelt and William Howard Taft.

Woodrow Wilson's Reforms

What reforms did Wilson implement during his presidency?

A former president of Princeton University, Woodrow Wilson was a scholarly statesman and a staunch Progressive. Compared with Roosevelt's ideas of New Nationalism, Wilson seemed conservative when he presented a program of policies called New Freedom. Roosevelt saw the federal government as a force for ensuring economic and social justice. Wilson did not advocate for social justice as many Progressives wished. He also believed that once government had controlled economic abuses, it should fade into the background of American life. As president, Wilson focused on preventing monopolies and creating economic opportunities for small businessmen through drastic reduction on tariffs—taxes on imported goods—as well as banking reform, fair trade, and antitrust laws.

photo: Library of Congress

Woodrow Wilson (1856–1924) was the 28th president of the United States.

Tariffs

A tariff is a tax that is placed on imported goods when they enter a country. Tariffs are usually collected to help domestic industries and to raise money for the government. President Wilson believed that tariff rates needed to be reformed. Previous tariffs set by Congress were meant to protect U.S. farm crops and manufactured products. High rates meant that imported products cost more than American products. However, tariff rates failed to slow the downward trend of food prices because of an oversupply of crops. At the same time, the cost of many items purchased by farmers, such as manufactured equipment, continued to increase.

Wilson urged Congress to pass a law that lowered tariffs. In response, Congress passed the Underwood Tariff Act in 1913. This act lowered the average rates of tariffs from 40 percent to 25 percent. The law also removed tariffs entirely from certain goods such as sugar, wool, iron ore, and steel. This allowed the prices of those imported goods to compete with similar products of American producers, which benefited American consumers.

Banking

Wilson also argued for an extensive reform of banking and currency laws. He thought that the banking system needed to run more efficiently to enhance businesses. To accomplish this, Wilson supported the establishment of a nationwide centralized banking system. He also believed that a new federal currency was needed to assist the flow of money.

Six months later, Congress passed the Federal Reserve Act of 1913, which formed a national banking and currency system similar to the one Wilson supported. Twelve Federal Reserve Banks were created with the authority to issue Federal Bank Notes, the official U.S. currency, to nationally chartered private banks. Those banks were able to borrow the money at a fixed interest rate. The rate did not rise during the period when the loan was repaid. This kept the banking system stable.

Business

President Wilson supported many Progressive reforms to the federal government's regulation of business. Wilson thought the United States needed an independent government agency to ensure fair trade practices. Congress agreed and established the Federal Trade Commission in 1914. This agency became responsible for maintaining free and fair competition between businesses and protecting consumers from unfair business practices.

Discovery | SOCIAL STUDIES
EDUCATION | TECHBOOK

How did the Progressive Era change the role of the federal government?

Even though Theodore Roosevelt succeeded in breaking up many trusts, several big businesses continued to set up arrangements that used unfair business practices. The main reason for this was the Sherman Antitrust Act. This act used unclear wording, which allowed some businesses to find loopholes in the law and create economic restrictions that limited the ability of other businesses to compete with them.

For example, businesses created holding companies to continue their dominance over entire industries. A holding company is an organization that controls one or more other companies by owning controlling shares of their stocks and bonds. Some holding companies were able to create monopolies by owning enough stock to control several companies from the same industry. Because of this, Wilson wanted to strengthen the Sherman Act's rules against monopolies.

Explore this investigation and take a position on which president best embodied the spirit of the Progressive movement.

In 1914, Congress passed the Clayton Antitrust Act, which used more specific language than the Sherman Antitrust Act. The Clayton Act not only declared that monopolies were illegal, but also stated that any business practices that could easily lead to the formation of monopolies or practices that resulted from monopolies were also illegal.

Progressivism and the Constitution

How did Progressivism change the U.S. Constitution?

From 1913 to 1920, the momentum of Progressivism on a national level strongly influenced the formation of several amendments to the Constitution.

Sixteenth Amendment

Before 1913, each state imposed an income tax on the people living in the state. However, Congress did not have the power to tax U.S. citizens. This situation greatly limited the ability of the federal government to financially support various policies and programs. To correct this, Congress proposed the Sixteenth Amendment, which empowered Congress to impose a federal income tax. Soon, the states ratified the amendment, and it became part of the Constitution, increasing the power of the federal government to collect money from its citizens.

One of the significant impacts of this amendment was that it eliminated a need to rely on tariffs to raise money. This change would come in handy a few years later, when the government needed to finance World War I. Revenue from income taxes also provided money for the construction and maintenance of roads, bridges, and schools.

Seventeenth Amendment

According to the original U.S. Constitution, the legislature of each state appointed the U.S. senators to represent the state. The people of each state, therefore, did not directly vote for their U.S. senators. Many people complained about the corruption of this process when wealthy men bought votes among state legislators to become senators. The Seventeenth Amendment to the Constitution was created to change this process, in response to the complaints. The amendment establishes that two U.S. senators will represent each state, and the voters of each state will directly elect these senators.

To this day, not everyone is pleased with the Seventeenth Amendment. Critics of the amendment say that it has had a negative impact on the Constitution by giving state power to the federal government because state officials are no longer in charge of choosing senators. Conservative politicians have even proposed repealing the amendment. Supporters argue that the Seventeenth Amendment solved the problem of corruption in the legislative branch and gave citizens more direct power to decide which legislators represent their state.

photo: Library of Congress

In 1922, federal agents seize a still, a device that separates alcohol from corn or other mashed products.

Eighteenth Amendment

During the late 1800s and early 1900s, many reformers supported national prohibition. Prohibition is the banning of the selling and consumption of alcoholic beverages. These reformers supported prohibition mainly to eliminate the problems alcoholism, or addiction to alcohol, was causing in the country. Reformers believed that establishing prohibition would significantly lessen problems such as family abuse, crime, and absenteeism. Influenced by large reform groups, such as the Women's Christian Temperance Union, the states, in 1919, ratified the Eighteenth Amendment, which imposed the national prohibition of alcohol.

The Eighteenth Amendment has the distinction of being the only amendment in U.S. history to be repealed. Enforcing prohibition proved virtually impossible. Instead of having a positive impact on social problems, the amendment contributed to an increase in organized crime that supplied illegal liquor. Overall, prohibition did not decrease the level of alcohol consumption or crime during the 1920s. By 1925, at least six states had passed laws that prevented local police from investigating prohibition violations. The federal ban also had very little support in most municipalities of the Northeast and Midwest. In December 1933, the great experiment with social reform officially ended with the passage of the Twenty-First Amendment to repeal prohibition.

Discovery | SOCIAL STUDIES
EDUCATION | **TECHBOOK**.

How did the Progressive Era change the role of the federal government?

Nineteenth Amendment

The Progressive Party headed by Theodore Roosevelt became the first national political party to include women's suffrage in its campaign platform in 1912. The National American Women's Suffrage Association (NAWSA) successfully campaigned for women's voting rights in several states in the 1910s. In 1919, Congress passed the Nineteenth Amendment to guarantee women the right to vote. The amendment then went to the states for ratification. In a little more than 12 months, enough states voted to ratify this amendment.

The Nineteenth Amendment had a long-lasting legacy on American politics by changing the face of the electorate. By guaranteeing that women have a voice in the government, it helped further the cause of equal rights for all. The amendment also paved the way for women to take on a more public role in society and the government. Since the passage of this amendment, women have advocated for continued equality in society and the workplace.

Protecting the Environment
How did conservation begin in the United States?

After the Civil War, many hunters killed millions of buffalo in the West. Often, railroad owners who considered the buffalo an obstacle to railroad construction paid these hunters. While some killed buffalo for commercial reasons, others just did it for sport. As a result, by 1890 only about 500 buffalo existed in the United States. This wasteful slaughter outraged many people, including Progressive reformers.

The slaughter of the buffalo symbolized the attitude of many Americans toward natural resources in the United States at the time. To counteract that view, reformers pushed for conservation. Conservation is the preservation, care, and management of the environment and natural resources. As a first step toward conservation, the U.S. government, in 1872, established the world's first national park— Yellowstone National Park.

Naturalists, such as John Muir, sought to have the government establish more national parks. However, Muir was more than a conservationist. He was also a preservationist.

photo: Library of Congress
Theodore Roosevelt and John Muir at Glacier Point, Yosemite, around 1909.

While conservationists sought to responsibly use resources, preservationists sought to completely protect natural areas from use. Muir traveled through many wilderness areas in the United States and lived for years in Yosemite Valley. He was the first person to explain how glaciers formed the valley millions of years ago.

In 1890, Muir helped convince Congress to form Yosemite National Park and Sequoia National Park. Two years later, he established a conservation group called the Sierra Club, which remains a leading conservation organization today.

Muir and other naturalists, such as George Perkins Marsh, spread the word about preservation by writing books about the subject. Then, the conservation movement received a huge boost when Theodore Roosevelt became the U.S. president.

Conservation Movement Expands

How did Theodore Roosevelt support the conservation movement?

Theodore Roosevelt was an avid outdoorsman. He rode horses, hunted game, hiked in wilderness areas, and ranched in the Dakota Territory. Not surprisingly, he felt sympathy for the conservation movement. When Roosevelt became president, John Muir suggested to him to increase the amount of forest reserves in the United States. Roosevelt responded by setting aside 194 million acres of forest as national preserves. In addition, he formed 51 federal bird reserves and several national game preserves. He also established several new national parks, including Crater Lake, Mesa Verde, and Wind Cave.

Roosevelt also wanted to make sure the government strictly regulated the use of land and water resources to avoid the overuse of these resources. To help achieve this, he supported the Reclamation Act of 1902, which established regulations for the federal use of land in the West for irrigation and hydroelectric development.

President William McKinley appointed a committed conservationist, Gifford Pinchot, as the secretary of interior. When Roosevelt became president, he made Pinchot the head of the Forest Service and later, the chairman of the National Conservation Commission. As chairman, Pinchot organized the first inventory of the natural resources in the United States. Today, the government continues to conduct this inventory periodically. By cataloging how people use land and water resources, scientists can determine how this use changes the environment.

In addition, Pinchot convinced the government not to sell sites for hydroelectric plants to private developers. He urged that these sites be kept under federal control. Pinchot wrote the following excerpt, which reveals his views about the use of water power:

"It is of the first importance to prevent our water powers from passing into private ownership as they have been doing, because . . . it is the only great unfailing source of power. Our rivers, if the forests on the watersheds are properly handled, will never cease to deliver power."

Discovery | SOCIAL STUDIES
EDUCATION | **TECHBOOK**

How did the Progressive Era change the role of the federal government?

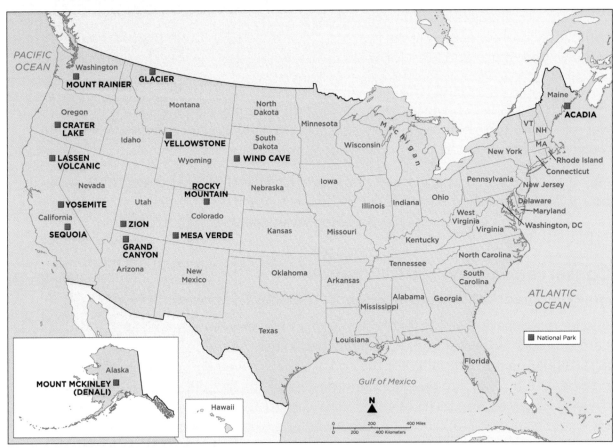

This map shows the national parks established in the United States by 1920.

The conservation movement was influenced by the ideas of Progressivism. It sought to use the powers of the federal government and the presidency to protect the natural environment. In 1906, the federal Antiquities Act authorized the president to protect "objects of historic or scientific interest." Presidents of the Progressive Era used this authority to protect a number of areas that were later made national parks. These include Grand Canyon, Olympic Forest, Zion Canyon, and Acadia.

President Wilson greatly disappointed environmentalists when he signed the controversial bill to dam the Hetch Hetchy River near Yosemite. However, Wilson also signed the bill creating the National Park Service, based on an idea proposed by then-President Taft in 1912. In addition, Wilson signed the bill that promoted Grand Canyon from a national monument to a national park.

Explore this interactive to learn more about the early conservation movement and the creation of national parks.

Over time, the active involvement of the federal government and the White House with social reforms, especially during Wilson's presidency, shaped the strong centralized character of the nation during the years of international conflict to come.

Consider the Essential Question:

How did the Progressive Era change the role of the federal government?

Go online to complete the Social Studies Explanation.

Check for Understanding:

Compare and contrast the reforms of Presidents Theodore Roosevelt and Woodrow Wilson during the Progressive Era.

Discovery | SOCIAL STUDIES
EDUCATION | **TECHBOOK**

What were the costs and benefits of the United States becoming a global power?

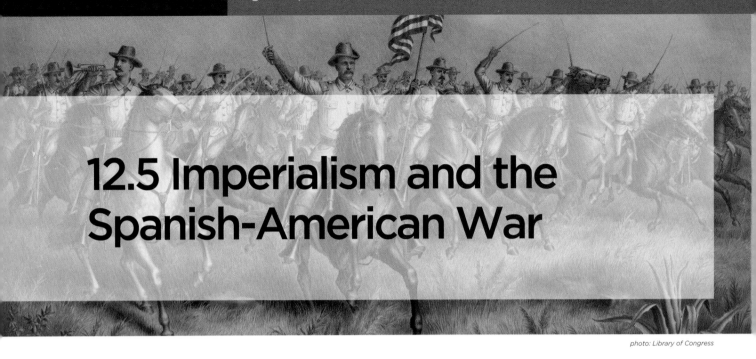

12.5 Imperialism and the Spanish-American War

photo: Library of Congress

LESSON OVERVIEW

Introduction

In this concept, you will explore how and why the United States shifted from an isolated country to a powerful player on the global stage.

Key Vocabulary
Which terms do you already know?

☐ American Anti-Imperialist League
☐ annex
☐ colony
☐ Dollar Diplomacy
☐ imperialism
☐ isolationism
☐ isthmus
☐ jingoism
☐ Monroe Doctrine

☐ neutrality
☐ Open Door Policy
☐ Panama Canal
☐ Queen Liliuokalani
☐ Roosevelt Corollary
☐ Spanish-American War
☐ yellow journalism

Essential Question

What were the costs and benefits of the United States becoming a global power?

Lesson Objectives

By the end of this lesson, you should be able to:

* Describe and explain factors that contributed to imperialism during the late 1800s and early 1900s.

* Assess the impact of the Spanish-American War on the United States and on U.S. foreign policy.

* Analyze the arguments of a variety of Americans who opposed imperialism.

* Evaluate U.S. policies in a variety of world regions during the era of imperialism.

ENGAGE

What are the greatest burdens of global leadership? Visit Engage to learn more.

Essential Question

What were the costs and benefits of the United States becoming a global power?

EXPLORE

Roots of Imperialism

What is imperialism?

In the mid-1800s, the idea of Manifest Destiny drove U.S. territorial expansion. This was the idea that the United States was "destined" to control the North American continent and spread its culture, economy, and values. As the United States industrialized during the late 1800s and early 1900s, an idea similar to Manifest Destiny emerged. Only this time, there was a new sphere of influence in mind—the entire world.

The late 1800s and early 1900s came to be known as the "Age of Imperialism." *Imperialism* is when a strong nation has authority over a smaller or weaker territory through economic, political, or military power. During this period, the United States extended its influence internationally. It was not the only country to do so. European countries, such as the United Kingdom, France, Germany, and Portugal, and the East Asian country of Japan were also attempting to expand their influence and territory.

One of the primary motives for European countries and Japan to expand their territory was economic in nature. Industries in Europe and Japan needed raw materials, such as cotton, tin, and rubber. Japan and most of Europe had to seek these necessary raw materials for their industries outside their borders.

European nations established colonies in Africa, India, Indonesia, and other locations in Asia to obtain the raw materials needed for expansion. European countries extracted these materials from their colonies and transported them back home for processing in factories. In addition to providing raw materials, the new colonies also supplied a large labor force. European countries set up plantations in their colonies, and the citizens of the colonies then provided the labor to run those plantations.

Discovery | SOCIAL STUDIES
EDUCATION | **TECHBOOK**

What were the costs and benefits of the United States becoming a global power?

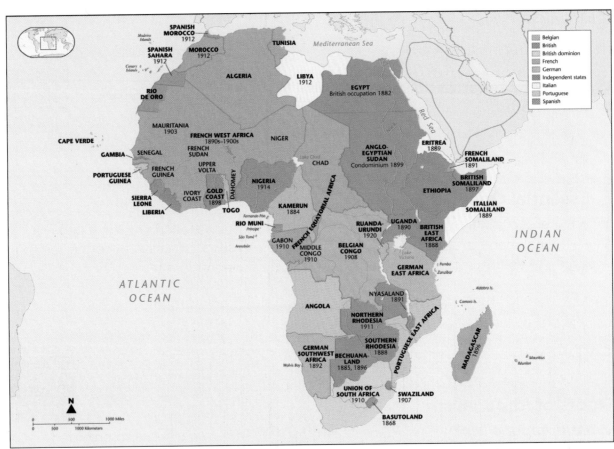

At the Berlin Conference of 1884–1885, European powers established terms for the colonization of Africa.

Competition between European countries for new colonies was intense in some areas of the world, and there was no set of international guidelines to help countries avoid conflict in the face of competing colonial claims. To avoid conflicting colonial claims in Central Africa, major European powers gathered for a series of discussions at the Berlin Conference from November 1884 to February 1885. These meetings set the rules for how European powers would colonize Africa. By the early 1900s, these powers had seized control of most of the African continent, with the exception of Liberia and Ethiopia. These colonies gave European countries access to an abundance of raw materials, inexpensive land and labor, and new markets in which to sell their goods.

The Age of Imperialism Begins

Why did the United States look to extend its influence abroad during the Age of Imperialism?

The European and Japanese rush for new territories helped encourage imperialism in the United States. Like the European and Japanese imperialists, U.S. imperialists cited economic reasons to justify the country's expansion, as well as moral, nationalistic, and militaristic motives.

Economic Motives

The U.S. economy was growing increasingly dependent on international trade. In the early 1800s, the United States had played a minor role in international trade. Over the course of the century, U.S. trade with other nations grew, especially exports, which grew from only 3 percent of the world's exports in 1800 to 15 percent in 1900. By the 1890s, about one-fourth of U.S. farm products and half of its petroleum resources were being sold abroad.

U.S. politicians, bankers, manufacturers, and others believed the young nation must expand its markets and its influence. They thought that if the country failed to compete in the international free market, it would lose out to the European powers. This quest for international markets and other raw materials, such as sugar, spices, and coffee, led to attempts to establish political and economic control over foreign territories.

photo: Library of Congress

A group of Protestant missionaries gathers in Fuzhou, China, around 1890.

Religious Motives

Motives for U.S. expansion went beyond economics. Some felt that imperialism was a religious duty. The Social Gospel movement, which called for reforms to uplift the poor in American cities, also provided an argument for U.S. imperialism. The religious sentiments behind the Social Gospel movement motivated missionaries to work abroad. U.S. clergy such as Josiah Strong wrote that the United States must expand its global influence in order to convert non-Christians around the world. Strong said it was the duty of Americans to promote Christian beliefs everywhere. He believed non-Christians were uncivilized and in need of protection. U.S. missionaries traveled to Africa and Asia. By 1890, some 500 missions had been founded in China alone.

The Frontier Thesis

In his essay "The Significance of the Frontier in American History," historian Frederick Jackson Turner explored the relationship between westward expansion and the American spirit. After the superintendent of the 1890 U.S. Census declared that the frontier was "closed," because the western portion of the country was mostly settled, Turner's "frontier thesis" became immensely popular among intellectuals and the public as a justification for U.S. expansion abroad. Turner's public-speaking skills captivated audiences in Chicago, Illinois, and elsewhere, and his lectures were published nationwide.

Discovery EDUCATION | SOCIAL STUDIES **TECHBOOK**

What were the costs and benefits of the United States becoming a global power?

Turner believed the open frontier had been the most important force in American history. It had brought new opportunities to rugged entrepreneurs. It had enabled people to start over and prosper or fail on their individual strengths alone. Now, after the settlement of the West, Turner said, expansion was finished. He posed the question: How would the United States continue to flourish and grow without the strength, individualism, and freedom instilled by expansionism? Expansion into foreign territories beyond the continental United States would provide a new frontier for the American spirit of democracy and free-market capitalism.

National Superiority and Social Darwinism

Another argument for expansion was one of national pride. Many U.S. politicians and businesspeople wanted to prove the nation's military strength and superiority to the rest of the world. Many held an attitude that came to be known as jingoism. A jingoist is an extreme nationalist, a person who strongly identifies with a country or nation and believes his or her country or nation is superior to all others. The American jingoists favored war and foreign conquest as a means to bring glory to the nation. They called for an aggressive foreign policy to compete for colonies with the United Kingdom, Germany, and other international powers of the time.

Many supporters of imperialism also used Social Darwinism to justify their beliefs. According to some Social Darwinists, the United States and other western nations were entitled to expand elsewhere because they were naturally superior to people living in targeted areas. However, some Social Darwinists opposed imperialism because they feared expansion could lead to an influx of U.S. immigrants from regions they considered to be inferior.

A Need for a Strong Military

To expand its land holdings around the world, the United States would need to be both economically and militarily strong. Imperialists such as Alfred T. Mahan, a captain in the U.S. Navy, argued that the United States must have a strong military, specifically a strong navy, to expand and protect territories in foreign countries. In his 1890 book, *The Influence of Sea Power Upon History*, Mahan called on leaders to build the country's naval power and establish global naval bases where U.S. fleets could refuel and rest. In the early 1890s, congressional funding allowed the U.S. Navy to construct more battleships to add to a fleet containing nearly 700 ships. The addition of these battleships gave the U.S. Navy the strength it needed to compete with European navies.

Explore this interactive to learn more about the United States' increasing global influence.

A combination of militaristic, economic, religious, and political motives drove U.S. imperialism in the late 1800s and early 1900s. The theories of American expansion, including Turner's frontier thesis and Mahan's naval supremacy, would come into play in the coming Spanish-American War.

Going to War with Spain

What led to the Spanish-American War?

Before the country's industrial expansion, U.S. foreign policy was primarily isolationist. The Monroe Doctrine of 1823 stated that the United States would stay out of European affairs. It acknowledged and accepted existing European control of territories in the Americas. However, it also declared the Americas closed to further European colonization. The Monroe Doctrine also stated that any attempt by Europeans to forcibly expand their control in the Americas would be taken as a direct threat to the United States.

Control of the Americas

Over time, American politicians began to use the Monroe Doctrine as a justification to involve the United States in Latin American affairs. For example, in 1862, French Emperor Napoleon III tried to gain control of Mexico. After the American Civil War ended, the United States used its diplomatic power, based on the Monroe Doctrine, to urge French withdrawal from Mexico. Encouraging intense Mexican resistance against French rule, the United States was able to help prevent a major European country from colonizing another one of its neighbors.

By the end of the 1800s, Cuba and Puerto Rico were the only places in Latin America remaining under Spanish rule. For many years, Cubans had been attempting to overthrow the Spanish. The United States became involved in these conflicts in the 1890s. Several U.S. businesses had a vested interest in Cuba. Some 90 percent of the sugar produced in Cuba was sold to the U.S. market. Americans had also invested money, machinery, and employees in the Cuban sugar industry. By 1894, only 20 percent of all Cuban sugar mills were still owned by Cubans.

Spain was a threat to the economic relationship between Cuba and the United States. For example, a trade agreement that reduced tariffs for many Cuban exports, such as sugar and coffee, ended in 1894. During the agreement between Spain and the United States, Cuba was free to import from and export to the United States. However, Spain then introduced more taxes and trade restrictions in Cuba. As a result of such economic interferences, Cubans began fighting against Spanish control in February 1895. Cubans' fight for independence, which in many ways mirrored the American colonists' struggle for independence, was strongly supported by Americans who wanted to protect business interests in Cuba and promote democracy around the world.

Yellow Journalism

Journalists helped fuel Americans' support of Cuban independence during the late 1800s. William Randolph Hearst's *New York Journal* and Joseph Pulitzer's *New York World* began printing highly dramatized stories about the conflict in Cuba. To win readers, these publishers competed to produce the most sensational headlines, which sometimes had little to do with the truth.

Discovery SOCIAL STUDIES
EDUCATION | **TECHBOOK**

What were the costs and benefits of the United States becoming a global power?

False but dramatic stories of starving women and children or the execution of brave revolutionaries were produced to make Americans want to read more. This exaggerated reporting became known as yellow journalism. This term comes from a popular cartoon character called the Yellow Kid. After Hearst's paper hired the cartoon's original artist away from Pulitzer's *New York World*, Pulitzer responded by hiring a new artist to create the same character in his paper. The rivalry between the two Yellow Kid cartoons symbolized the newspapers' willingness to go to great lengths to lure readers away from the competition.

Hearst's publication of correspondence between two Spanish diplomats pushed the United States and Spain closer to war. A note written by Don Enrique Dupuy de Lôme, Spain's U.S. ambassador, was published in the *New York Journal* on February 9, 1898. The letter was addressed to the Spanish foreign minister, but, somehow, Cuban rebels intercepted the letter and passed it through their channels to the U.S. secretary of state. In the letter, de Lôme insulted U.S. President William McKinley and his Cuban policies. Many Americans were furious.

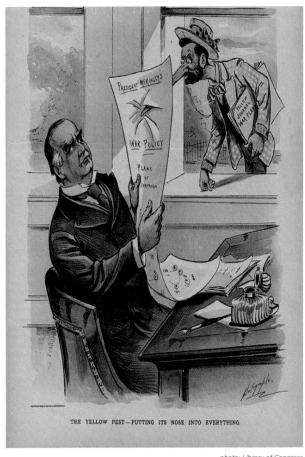

THE YELLOW PEST—PUTTING ITS NOSE INTO EVERYTHING.

photo: Library of Congress

What does this cartoon suggest about the role of yellow journalists?

Sinking of the USS *Maine*

Less than one week later, on February 15, 1898, the warship USS *Maine* exploded, and the war became a reality. The *Maine* had been stationed in Havana Harbor since January 25, 1898. It was there to protect U.S. citizens and business interests in Cuba. On the night of February 15, a terrible explosion rocked the boat. Spanish officials and civilians rushed to aid the survivors. Several of the *Maine*'s officers survived, but 266 U.S. sailors lost their lives.

An inconclusive investigation identified a mine that detonated under the ship as the cause of the explosion. However, yellow journalism helped convince the public that the Spanish had set a bomb. Outraged citizens wanted to avenge the deaths of their fellow Americans. Three days after the explosion, Hearst's *New York Journal* became the first American paper to sell more than one million copies. Pushed to the brink of war, Congress agreed to intervene in April 1898. The Spanish-American War had begun.

Spoils of War

What was the outcome of the Spanish-American War?

The Spanish-American War, which was a continuation of the Cuban War of Independence, officially began on April 25, 1898. By the time the United States entered the war, the Cuban rebels had already been fighting against the Spanish army. The rebels now controlled the countryside. The Spanish had been pushed into urban areas, where they were easier targets for the U.S. military. The war ended fairly soon with a ceasefire on August 12.

photo: Library of Congress
American troops boarding a transport steamer.

Cuba was granted independence from Spain in December 1898. Only 385 U.S. soldiers were killed in battle, and about 1,600 were wounded. With the relatively few battle casualties, U.S. Secretary of State John Hay dubbed the swift and decisive victory a "splendid little war." Although U.S. casualties were low, nearly 2,000 soldiers died from yellow fever and another 1,500 from typhoid fever.

Theodore Roosevelt

The war also saw the emergence of a new national hero and later U.S. president, Theodore Roosevelt. A native of New York City, Theodore Roosevelt served as assistant secretary of the U.S. Navy. In May 1898, he resigned his post to help prepare for the upcoming war. Roosevelt organized the First Volunteer Cavalry by bringing together a group of men from all different walks of life. The group, nicknamed the "Rough Riders," consisted of cowboys, miners, Native Americans, college athletes, and musicians, among others. After training in San Antonio, Texas, Roosevelt's unit left for Cuba in June.

The Rough Riders participated in a few different battles but are best remembered for leading the charge on July 1, 1898, in the Battle of San Juan Hill. Roosevelt's offensive enabled the United States to capture San Juan Hill, which overlooked the Spanish fort at Santiago de Cuba. The Spanish fleet was soon forced out of Santiago's harbor and defeated by the U.S. Navy.

Roosevelt was hailed as a hero and went on to become governor of New York in 1899, and later became vice president when President William McKinley won reelection in 1900. McKinley and Roosevelt's easy victory in the election showed that the American public supported imperialist policies. The victory in the Spanish-American War and reelection of McKinley illustrated a clear shift in U.S. foreign policy. The majority of Americans now supported imperialism over isolationism.

Treaty of Paris

The Spanish-American War led to the Treaty of Paris, an 1898 peace agreement between Spain and the United States. The United States paid Spain $20 million to acquire the Philippines. Spain surrendered its claim to Cuba and the Cuban debt of $400 million that the United States would have to repay. The Teller Amendment, an amendment passed in April 1898 when the United States declared war on Spain, stated that the United States would not take control of Cuba at the end of the war.

The Treaty of Paris also gave the western Pacific island of Guam and the Caribbean island of Puerto Rico to the United States. In 1900, Puerto Ricans were granted limited self-government. The U.S. government passed the Foraker Act, which created a legislative body of 35 elected representatives. The same act gave the U.S. president the right to appoint the Puerto Rican governor, judges, and all cabinet ministers.

Taking the Philippines

Why did anti-imperialists question annexation of the Philippines?

During the Spanish-American War, U.S. forces had traveled to Hong Kong and the Philippines. A U.S. fleet, led by then-Commodore George Dewey, destroyed the Spanish fleet at the Battle of Manila Bay on May 1, 1898. President McKinley then ordered U.S. troops that were stationed in nearby Hong Kong to engage the Spanish army in the Philippines. They arrived in August, forced the Spanish army to surrender, and occupied the capital city of Manila. Meanwhile, in June, after Dewey's victory, Filipinos proclaimed their independence.

After the Spanish-American War, Spain agreed to give up the Philippines for $20 million. The United States paid this sum in December 1898, and President McKinley found himself in a difficult situation. The U.S. Army and Navy were protecting the Philippines. McKinley was concerned that, if the United States left the Philippines, another global power would come in and take over, erasing any economic, religious, or military gains the United States had accomplished there.

Annexation

Instead of simply leaving the Philippines, McKinley sought to annex the territory. This would mean that, instead of keeping their newly declared freedom, Filipinos would be subjects of the foreign U.S. government. Their land would be U.S. property. At the time, McKinley said that continuing U.S. occupation was "necessary" to "uplift" the Filipinos and bring Christianity to the area. Like many Americans, McKinley was oblivious to the fact that most of the country was already Roman Catholic.

Aside from the religious motivation, the annexation of the Philippines was also motivated by a need to answer the problems raised by Turner's "frontier thesis." If the United States could successfully expand into the Pacific and East Asia, then, in fact, the U.S. frontier was not closed. Americans could continue to mine the new opportunities provided by new lands beyond the Pacific on the Asian mainland. This expansion would also boost the national superiority of the United States and lead to demands for an increase in its naval power.

LIBERTY TRACTS. No. 1.

THE

CHICAGO LIBERTY MEETING

HELD AT

CENTRAL MUSIC HALL

APRIL 30. 1899

"No man is good enough to govern another man without that other's consent. When the white man governs himself, that is self-government; but when he governs himself and also governs another man, that is more than self-government—that is despotism."—*Abraham Lincoln, Speech of October 16, 1854.*

"Our reliance is in the love of liberty which God has planted in us. Our defense is in the spirit which prizes liberty as the heritage of all men in all lands, everywhere. Those who deny freedom to others, deserve it not for themselves, and under a just God cannot long retain it."—*Abraham Lincoln, Letter to H. L. Pierce, April 6, 1859.*

"IF THIS BE TREASON, MAKE THE MOST OF IT."—*Patrick Henry.*

PUBLISHED BY
CENTRAL ANTI-IMPERIALIST LEAGUE
TACOMA BUILDING, CHICAGO
1899

photo: Library of Congress

Among the members of the American Anti-Imperialist League were notable figures such as Andrew Carnegie, Mark Twain, and Samuel Gompers.

Anti-Imperialist Response

Some Americans objected to the proposal to annex the Philippines and were growing more critical of U.S. imperialism. In 1898, a group of powerful politicians and business leaders who disagreed with expansion created the American Anti-Imperialist League.

The American Anti-Imperialists condemned the annexation of the Philippines, declaring it "hostile to liberty," immoral, and unjust. Group members, including steel magnate Andrew Carnegie, said that annexation squashed the rights of the free men of the Philippines and violated the American ideals of limited government and self-determination. They thought imperialism was contrary to democracy.

Another voice of opposition to annexation stemmed from racism. In the view of some, Filipinos were nonwhite and inferior.

Many anti-imperialists feared annexation would lead to a major influx of nonwhite immigrants. They feared immigrants would burden the U.S. labor system, taking jobs from white citizens and depressing wages. Some feared that Asians and Pacific Islanders were not intelligent enough to operate factory machinery or be productive members of U.S. society.

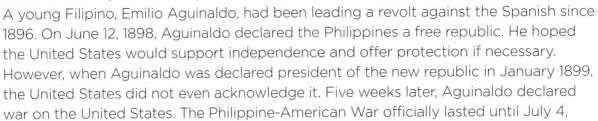

Discovery EDUCATION | SOCIAL STUDIES TECHBOOK.

What were the costs and benefits of the United States becoming a global power?

War in the Philippines

How did Filipinos respond to the annexation of the Philippines?

Anti-imperialists ultimately lost the argument regarding the Philippines. Like the anti-imperialists, Filipinos strongly objected to U.S. annexation. A young Filipino, Emilio Aguinaldo, had been leading a revolt against the Spanish since 1896. On June 12, 1898, Aguinaldo declared the Philippines a free republic. He hoped the United States would support independence and offer protection if necessary. However, when Aguinaldo was declared president of the new republic in January 1899, the United States did not even acknowledge it. Five weeks later, Aguinaldo declared war on the United States. The Philippine-American War officially lasted until July 4, 1902, but fighting continued for many years after that as some Filipino troops continued to resist American rule.

Some 4,000 U.S. soldiers and about 20,000 Filipino rebels died during the Philippine-American War. Additionally, around 200,000 Filipino civilians died as a result of starvation, disease, and war-related violence. Because the war was so controversial among the American public, it was often called an "insurrection." U.S.

photo: Library of Congress

U.S. soldiers and Filipino prisoners at Manila, 1899.

leaders wanted to avoid the idea that Filipinos were fighting to rid their land of a foreign enemy, and that the United States was that enemy.

Throughout the war, the U.S. government looked for a way to escape the conflict while still maintaining a political foothold in the region. This was important if the United States wanted to continue its imperialist activities in Asia. In 1900, President McKinley had appointed General William Howard Taft (later the 27th president of the United States) as governor of the Philippines. Taft began a campaign to pacify elite Filipinos and those who did not agree with Aguinaldo's tactics of guerrilla warfare. This method was dubbed the "policy of attraction." Taft intended to prepare the Filipinos for independence by gradually increasing self-government in the Philippines. Under Taft, the United States also sponsored economic-development projects.

In 1916, Congress passed the Jones Act, which was also known as the Philippine Autonomy Act. The Jones Act declared that the United States would "withdraw their sovereignty over the Philippine Islands as soon as a stable government can be established therein." The Jones Act established a Philippine legislature made up of Filipino men elected to the post. By 1921, Filipinos had taken over control of the internal government. Despite this increased power, the Philippines did not achieve independence until 1946, when the U.S. and Filipino governments signed a Treaty of General Relations. This treaty recognized the Republic of the Philippines as a self-governing nation.

Keeping the Door Open

How did the United States maintain its economic interests in China?

The United States had been formally and informally conducting trade with China since the late 1700s under a free-trade system. In the late 1800s, U.S. leaders grew increasingly more concerned about other foreign nations that were acquiring influence in China. They worried that a weakened China could be divided up into separate colonies controlled by specific European powers—similar to what had happened in Africa. U.S. Secretary of State John Hay set out to protect the interests of the United States in China.

The Open Door Policy

Hay proposed a formal agreement among Germany, the United Kingdom, and other European powers to "keep the door open" for one another in China—hence the term Open Door Policy. Hay's proposal created a free, open market in China. International commerce would be equally open to all, regardless of nationality.

9003—Company of Boxers, Tien-Tsin, China.

photo: Library of Congress

A company of Boxers, Tien-Tsin, China.

As part of the plan, Hay suggested a flat tariff for everyone doing business in China. He asked that the Chinese collect this money themselves. This clause would dissolve economic advantages and level the playing field for all foreign countries.

The Open Door Policy was set in motion in September 1899. However, in the spring and summer of 1900, an event in China known as the Boxer Rebellion threatened to destroy the entire policy.

The Boxer Rebellion was a rural uprising among Chinese peasants who blamed foreign interests for the country's problems. The "Boxers" got their name from a secret martial-arts society. They wanted to drive all foreign citizens out of China and reclaim the country for nationals only.

The Boxers traveled the countryside around Beijing in packs. They attacked Christian missionaries, burned foreign-owned properties, and trapped foreign citizens in their diplomatic headquarters. They killed Chinese people who had converted to Western religions. In June 1900, the Qing emperor of China, in support of the Boxers, declared that all people from foreign countries should be killed. For two months, the Boxers made war on foreign citizens and Chinese Christians in Beijing.

Discovery | SOCIAL STUDIES
EDUCATION | **TECHBOOK**

What were the costs and benefits of the United States becoming a global power?

Responses to the Boxer Rebellion

As the violence escalated, foreign governments sent armies to help free their nationals from Beijing. The increase in foreign military presence concerned the United States. As European troops moved through China, they sometimes secured and occupied specific areas of the country. Hay worried the foreign powers would use this moment as an excuse to carve up and divide China, like they did to Africa in 1884.

In July 1900, Hay revised his Open Door Policy notes. He reminded European powers of the importance of respecting Chinese territory and government. At the same time, the United States contributed more than 2,000 soldiers to the multinational effort to help end the Boxer attacks in Beijing. This large U.S. force was able to enforce the Open Door Policy.

The Boxer Rebellion ended on August 14, and the Chinese Christians and foreign citizens held hostage in Beijing's diplomatic district were freed. On February 1, 1901, the Chinese government disbanded the Boxer society. In September of that same year, the Chinese signed a multinational treaty, which included the United States, ending the Boxer Rebellion.

Aloha, Hawaii

How did the United States gain the Hawaiian Islands?

The Spanish-American War resulted in the United States exerting its imperial will internationally. At the same time, U.S. imperialism began to focus on the islands of Hawaii. Located about 2,500 miles off of the West Coast of the United States, the islands of Hawaii had for centuries been a sovereign nation. However, in 1898, the same year as the Spanish-American War, the United States annexed Hawaii. This acquisition came after a long political struggle between U.S. business interests and the native Hawaiians.

One of the earliest formal interactions between Hawaii and the United States was the Reciprocity Treaty of 1875. This agreement allowed Hawaii to sell its sugar to the United States. In return, the United States received special economic privileges in Hawaii. With the renewal of the treaty in 1887, the United States was also granted rights to use Hawaiian land that would later become the Naval Station Pearl Harbor. In 1891, a new queen came to the throne in Hawaii. Queen Lydia Kamakaeha Liliuokalani wanted to restore the power of the Hawaiian monarchy.

Spurred by the possibility of a new tariff on foreign goods, including sugar from Hawaii, a group of U.S. sugar and pineapple growers organized a coup d'état, or revolution, to overthrow Queen Liliuokalani in 1893. Under the leadership of Sanford Dole, these businesspeople conspired for the U.S. government to annex the Hawaiian Islands, which would eliminate the tariffs, open new markets, and increase their profits. The queen stepped down to avoid bloodshed and called on the U.S. government to help her regain the monarchy. However, President Benjamin Harrison supported the coup. He authorized U.S. troops and U.S. Minister to Hawaii John L. Stevens to aid the businessmen.

Queen Liliuokalani of Hawaii, 1898.

photo: Getty Images

The next U.S. president, Grover Cleveland, initially opposed the idea of annexing Hawaii. He even went so far as to call the coup an act of war and referred to the assistance provided by the United States as an "armed invasion." He petitioned Congress to reinstate the queen, but the petition was rejected.

The Spanish-American War stoked the flames of imperialistic zeal. Even though it was unrelated to the situation in the Philippines, U.S. political leaders similarly feared the Hawaiian Islands would be annexed by another power. At the urging of President McKinley, the United States annexed Hawaii on July 7, 1898. The citizens of Hawaii were declared citizens of the United States, and the former sovereign nation was put on track to become a U.S. state. Sanford Dole, the leader of the 1893 coup, became the territory's first governor in 1900.

Even before the United States formally gained control of Hawaii, American-owned food businesses that operated there recruited immigrants to work on sugar and pineapple plantations. Starting around 1880, workers arrived from Japan, China, the Philippines, Korea, and Portugal. African Americans from the United States also moved to the islands. These immigrants dramatically changed Hawaii's population. In the middle of the 1800s, indigenous, or native, people accounted for more than 95 percent of Hawaii's population. By the 1920s, fewer than 20 percent of the islands' residents were indigenous Hawaiians.

With the annexation of Hawaii, the United States gained control of the deep-water naval port at Pearl Harbor, on the island of Oahu. This was a significant gain for the U.S. Navy and for the United States as a military power. The addition of wealth from natural resources in Hawaii, including sugar plantations and fruit groves, greatly boosted the U.S. economy.

Cuba After Platt

What was the significance of the Platt Amendment?

While the Pacific region was ripe for U.S. imperial ambitions, the Caribbean was also important to the plans of the United States for expansion, primarily due to its closeness to the U.S. mainland.

Discovery SOCIAL STUDIES
EDUCATION | **TECHBOOK**

What were the costs and benefits of the United States becoming a global power?

After the Spanish-American War ended, U.S. troops remained in Cuba for several years. Under military guidance, new schools were set up, the economy was reorganized, and health measures were taken against diseases such as yellow fever. In late 1900, delegates gathered to write a new constitution for Cuba.

As the group worked, the U.S. Congress established a set of conditions to be met before military occupation would end. The list of terms was known as the Platt Amendment, after U.S. Senator Orville Platt of Connecticut. Although Cubans were unhappy with how much power the Platt Amendment gave the United States, they approved it on June 12, 1901.

Terms of the Platt Amendment

The Platt Amendment placed strict limits on Cuba's sovereignty. It also provided the United States with

photo: Library of Congress

In this cartoon, Cuba, depicted as a woman, is presented with two choices.

a legal solution for maintaining its influence in Cuba, in spite of the Teller Amendment's earlier statement that the United States would not control the country. According to the Platt Amendment, the United States assumed the right to interfere in Cuban affairs to help preserve the country's independence. It also received the right to buy or lease lands for naval bases. In addition, Cuba agreed to not enter into treaties that would compromise the freedom of the country or allow other nations to use its land for military purposes. The new Cuban government included the terms of the Platt Amendment in its constitution. The Platt conditions would be repealed in 1934, following rising nationalism in Cuba and escalating criticism in the United States.

Policing the Western Hemisphere
How did the Roosevelt Corollary change U.S. foreign policy?

In the 1890s, the United States took the Monroe Doctrine to mean that the country should interfere in Latin America when necessary. President Theodore Roosevelt took a more assertive approach, viewing the Monroe Doctrine as a tool to keep European powers from colonizing the Americas. Roosevelt wanted the United States to take a more aggressive stance as a police force in the Americas to keep European nations out of the region. His ideas were later labeled the "Big Stick" approach.

For instance, Roosevelt demonstrated a stronger foreign policy during the Venezuela Crisis of 1902. Venezuela was deeply in debt to European powers, and it refused to pay back the money. To force payment, British, Italian, and German fleets formed a blockade of Venezuelan ports. An all-out war seemed imminent.

Concerned about an invasion that would threaten the Monroe Doctrine, Roosevelt sent U.S. Navy warships near the Venezuelan coast to conduct "exercises," which were intended to show off U.S. naval power without actually engaging in battle. There was no use of force and no direct threat or challenge to the British and German blockade. Still, this tactic convinced the Europeans that the United States would be willing to engage in war to enforce the Monroe Doctrine. The United Kingdom and Germany decided to end their blockade and allowed the United States to arrange a financial solution.

photo: Getty Images

This cartoon portrays the United States as a rooster and European countries as cooped-up hens.

Roosevelt Corollary

In 1904, Roosevelt's aggressive foreign policy led to an addition to the Monroe Doctrine known as the Roosevelt Corollary. A corollary is a claim or idea that follows directly from another. The Roosevelt Corollary was presented as an extension of the Monroe Doctrine.

Announced in December 1904, the Roosevelt Corollary promised that the United States would intervene in Latin American affairs if necessary. If a Latin American country did not fulfill its financial obligations, or if it behaved in a way that invited "foreign aggression," then the United States would intervene to protect American interests.

Acting on this promise, in 1905, the United States intervened in the financial affairs of the Dominican Republic, which was then called Santo Domingo. As with the Venezuela affair, the United States stepped in to make sure Santo Domingo repaid its debts to European countries, while being protected from blockages and other methods that might harm its economy. In the following decade, the United States used the corollary to justify intervening in Cuba, Nicaragua, Haiti, and Mexico. The Roosevelt Corollary was also used to justify overseeing the construction and management of the Panama Canal.

Building the Panama Canal

Why did the United States take sides in the Panamanian revolt against Colombia?

In 1881, France began constructing a canal that would join the Atlantic and Pacific Oceans so that ships could avoid the long sea journey around the southern tip of South America. This was an enormous and expensive undertaking. The canal was to extend about 40 miles through mountains and swamps. The annual rainfall of up to 140 inches created flooding and landslides that would wash away the excavation work.

Discovery | SOCIAL STUDIES
EDUCATION | **TECHBOOK**

What were the costs and benefits of the United States becoming a global power?

Between 16,000 and 22,000 workers died of disease, snakebites, and accidents. The growing costs, the increasing risk due to the civil war between Panama and Colombia, and the seemingly impossible task finally defeated the project. The French engineer in charge of the project, Ferdinand de Lesseps, ran out of funds and was charged with mismanagement. He died in 1894, long before the canal was completed.

photo: Library of Congress

Railroad cars helped bring supplies and men in and out of the canal while it was under construction.

Following the Spanish-American War, the idea of a canal in Central America became more important to the United States. During the war, U.S. ships were forced to sail around South America to get from the Atlantic Ocean to the Pacific Ocean, which was costly and inefficient. It was a 13,000-mile journey that hindered U.S. ability to maintain order in the Americas. When President Roosevelt came to power in 1901, completion of a canal became a priority.

A major obstacle to completing a canal was that the planned canal crossed Colombian territory, of which Panama was then a part. Colombia had already rejected the U.S. proposal to construct a canal there. U.S. interests supported Panamanian rebels in their effort to break from Colombia and establish a self-governing nation. In exchange for support, once the Panamanian rebels got power, they would give the United States the land it needed for the canal. Roosevelt approved the idea, and the conspirators went ahead with their plans.

At the beginning of November 1903, the first U.S. Navy warship sailed into the area to support the Panamanian rebels. U.S.-administered railroads also stopped running trains from Colón, Colombia. This left Colombian soldiers stranded and away from the struggle.

Panama announced its independence on November 3. On November 6, the United States formally recognized Panama as a new nation. On November 18, the Hay-Bunau-Varilla Treaty was signed. This treaty gave the United States the right to build its canal in exchange for $10 million up front and $250,000 a year starting in 1912. Panama gave up control of a 10-mile-wide strip extending from coast-to-coast and dividing the country in two. After a decade planning and building, the canal opened for maritime use in August 1914. Today, the American Society of Civil Engineers lists the Panama Canal as one of the Seven Wonders of the Modern World.

© Discovery Education | www.DiscoveryEducation.com

Preserving and Promoting U.S. Interests

How did Roosevelt and Taft preserve and promote U.S. interests abroad?

As president, Theodore Roosevelt helped enlarge the sphere of influence for the United States. In addition to strengthening the Monroe Doctrine and constructing the Panama Canal, Roosevelt was also the first U.S. citizen to receive a Nobel Peace Prize. The Nobel Committee gave him the prize for negotiating a peace deal between Japan and Russia, successfully ending the Russo-Japanese War of 1904–1905.

Since the end of the 1800s, Russia had controlled Port Arthur, a warm-water port in Manchuria, on the Yellow Sea. The port was a great commercial and strategic holding in East Asia. In 1904, the Japanese attacked the Russian fleet there, determined to regain control of the area. Battle after battle ensued. Although the Japanese won several significant victories, the monetary cost and loss of life was high.

A year later, both sides were ready for the war to end. The Japanese enlisted Roosevelt to help broker peace. In September 1905, the Treaty of Portsmouth was signed. The treaty gave Japan three important areas: Port Arthur, the southern portion of Sakhalin Island, and Korea. Russia kept the northern part of Sakhalin Island and was not forced to purchase this land from the Japanese.

photo: Library of Congress

A political cartoon of Uncle Sam seated at a table with a Chinese official while three men representing Great Britain, Mexico, and Japan look on.

Throughout the peace negotiations, Roosevelt's primary concern was preserving U.S. interests. He wanted to make sure Japan and Russia each maintained some control in the area. He felt it would be in the best interest of the United States if there was a balance of power rather than a single controlling power.

William Howard Taft succeeded Roosevelt as president in 1909. Taft implemented a foreign policy known as "Dollar Diplomacy." Taft's primary foreign policy concern was to preserve and expand trade. His idea of diplomacy was to promote U.S. business interests abroad.

DISCOVERY EDUCATION | SOCIAL STUDIES TECHBOOK

What were the costs and benefits of the United States becoming a global power?

Taft appointed Philander Knox as secretary of state. Knox was not a diplomat. He was a corporate lawyer who helped consolidate U.S. Steel. Taft worked for international stability and peace because he believed peace would improve financial opportunities for Americans. He used offers of investments and loans to persuade other countries to agree to U.S. plans. Taft took credit for helping prevent wars between Peru and Ecuador and between Haiti and the Dominican Republic. He also took credit for preserving order in China and Honduras. However, Dollar Diplomacy failed to prevent revolutions in Mexico, the Dominican Republic, and Nicaragua.

Explore this investigation and take a position on whether the benefits of imperialism outweighed the costs.

Although Roosevelt and Taft differed in their approaches, they continued McKinley's imperialistic efforts. Together, they helped make the United States a global power.

Consider the Essential Question:

What were the costs and benefits of the United States becoming a global power?

Go online to complete the Social Studies Explanation.

Check for Understanding:

What role did economic interests play in the Spanish-American War, the Open Door Policy, and the annexation of Hawaii? What were the economic impacts of these actions?